MATTERING PRESS

Mattering Press is an academic-led Open Access publisher that operates on a not-for-profit basis as a UK registered charity. It is committed to developing new publishing models that can widen the constituency of academic knowledge and provide authors with significant levels of support and feedback. All books are available to download for free or to purchase as hard copies. More at matteringpress.org.

The Press' work has been supported by: Centre for Invention and Social Process (Goldsmiths, University of London), European Association for the Study of Science and Technology, Hybrid Publishing Lab, infostreams, Institute for Social Futures (Lancaster University), OpenAIRE, Open Humanities Press, and Tetragon, as well as many other institutions and individuals that have supported individual book projects, both financially and in kind.

MAKING THIS BOOK

Mattering Press is keen to render more visible the unseen processes that go into the production of books. We would like to thank Endre Dányi, who acted as the Press' coordinating editor for this book, Joe Deville for editing and his work on the book production, Julien McHardy for editing and design, the two reviewers Geof Bowker and Claire Waterton, Steven Lovatt for the copy editing, Alex Billington and Tetragon for the typesetting, and Will Roscoe, Ed Akerboom, and infostreams for their contributions to the html versions of this book.

BOXES

A Field Guide

EDITED BY

**SUSANNE BAUER,
MARTINA SCHLÜNDER
AND MARIA RENTETZI**

MATTERING PRESS

ISBN: 978–1-912729–01–2 (pbk)
ISBN: 978–1-912729–02–9 (pdf)
ISBN: 978–1-912729–03–6 (epub)
ISBN: 978–1-912729–04–3 (html)

Mattering Press has made every effort to contact copyright holders and will be glad to rectify, in future editions, any errors or omissions brought to our notice.

CONTENTS

List of figures   9

Contributors   16

Boxing Practices   25

Preface and Acknowledgements   26

INTRODUCTIONS

1   The Generative Possibilities of the Wrong Box
    Martina Schlünder   29

2   The Epistemology of the Familiar: A Hymn to Pandora
    Maria Rentetzi   37

3   Navigation Tools for Studying Boxes: A User's Manual
    Susanne Bauer   45

I · TRAP

4   Inscribing the Soul: Cerebral Ventricles as Symbolic and Material Boxes
    Jameson Kısmet Bell   55

5   Better Shelter
    Emily Brownell   73

6   Slide Box: How to Stock Some Thousand Cancer Cases
    Ulrich Mechler   93

7   System Box (Tray) with Wasp
    Tahani Nadim   109

II · JUKE

8   Thinking Inside the Box: The Construction of Knowledge in a Miniature Seventeenth-Century Cabinet
    Stephanie Bowry   127

9   Musical Instrument Boxes. Hidden Information: Cases for Musical
     Instruments and Their Functions
     Beatrix Darmstädter   145

10   Boxing Crickets: A Taxonomy of Containers for Singing and Fighting
     Ensifera
     Martina Siebert   157

III · TIME

11   Contesting the Box: Museums and Repatriation
     Stewart Allen   169

12   Archaeology and Cigarettes: 'Ekphora' and 'Periphora' of the
     Archaeological Identity through Cigarette Packs
     Styliana Galiniki and Eleftheria Akrivopoulou   187

13   More than a Toy Box: *Dandanah* and the Sea of Stories
     Artemis Yagou   203

IV · CARGO

14   The *Ur*-Box: Multispecies Take-off from Noah's Ark to Animal Air
     Cargo
     Nils Güttler, Martina Schlünder, Susanne Bauer   215

15   Parcels Render Neglected People Visible
     Tanja Hammel   231

16   Boxes, Infrastructure and the Materiality of Moral Relations: Aid and
     Respect after Cyclone Pam
     Alexandra Widmer   241

V · BLACK

17   'As Modern As Tomorrow': The Medicine Cabinet
     Deanna Day   255

18   The Green Minna: Transporting Police Detainees in Imperial
     Berlin
     Eric J. Engstrom   271

19   Scaling Up from the Bench: Fermentation Tank
     Victoria Lee   289

20 Deep Time History: The Lure of the Black Box
Dagmar Schäfer   307

VI · TEXT

21 Panels and Frames: Toward a New Relationship between Text and
Image in Academic Writing
Pit Arens and Martina Schlünder   327
22 Analogue Privacy: The Paper Shredder as a Technology for
Knowledge Destruction
Sarah Blacker   365

VII · ICE

23 Biobank Boxes: Technologies of Population
Susanne Bauer   381
24 The Magic of Dropbox, its Virtuality and Materiality
Shih-Pei Chen   397

VIII · ANXIETY

25 Domestic Reservoirs: Managing Drinking Water in Taiwanese
Households
Yi-Ping Cheng   409
26 Keep Calm and Carry One: The Civilian Gas Mask Case and its
Containment of British Emotions
Mats Fridlund   425
27 Cardboard Box: The Politics of Materiality
Maria Rentetzi   443

IX · COUNT

28 Petri dish (boîte de Petri, Petrischale)
Mathias Grote   459
29 Prussian Census Box: Moving and Freezing Data
Christine von Oertzen   473
30 Black-Boxing Knowledge: Glass Dosimeters and Governmental Control
Maria Rentetzi   481

X · MIRROR

31 The Mirror Trap
Etienne S. Benson   493

32 Shifting Medical Bottles: In Between Medical and Indigenous Worlds
Johanna Gonçalves Martín   505

33 Guarding the Memory: Photographic Glass Plates Negatives' Boxes
Mirka Palioura, Spyridoula Pyrpili, Myrto Vouleli   525

34 Lousy Research: The History of Typhus Vaccine Production, 1915–1945
Martina Schlünder   539

XI · TOOL

35 The Mechanic's Toolbox and Tool Chest: A Nexus of the Personal and the Social
Don Duprez   559

36 Surgeons' Chests from the Mary Rose
Hanako Endo   571

37 Ruminations on an Electrotherapeutic Box
Jan Eric Olsén   583

38 Reliquary: A Box for a Relic
Lucy Razzall   597

39 The Research Box
Bonnie Mak and Julia Pollack   607

LIST OF FIGURES

FIG. 1.1   Linné's classification of the animal kingdom, 1735 (excerpt)   28

FIG. 2.1   Clay pyxis, 410–400 BC no. 13676 *a*, National
Archaeological Museum, Athens, Hellenic Ministry of
Culture and Sports/Archaeological Receipts Fund   36

FIG. 3.1   Retired overseas containers, reused to house workshops
and storage in Kyrgyzstan   44

FIG. 4.1   Berengario da Carpi, *Tractatus de fractura calve sive cranei a
Carpo editus* (1518)   54

FIG. 4.2   Berengario da Carpi, *Isagoge breves* (1523)   59

FIG. 4.3   Joannes de Ketham *Fasciculus medicine* (1495)   65

FIG. 5.1   'Better Shelter' refugee housing unit   72

FIG. 5.2   Interior image of a Better Shelter prototype   75

FIG. 5.3   Paul Lester Wiener's design for portable and modular
temporary housing   79

FIG. 5.4   Earthquake tents from after the San Francisco earthquake
of 1906   80

FIG. 5.5   Earthquake cottages provided for some victims of the
1906 earthquake in San Francisco   81

FIG. 5.6   Earthquake cottage being moved by horses   81

FIG. 5.7   Dadaab Refugee Camp, Kenya   85

FIG. 6.1   Microscopic slide box from the collection of German
pathologist Karl Lennert   92

FIG. 6.2   Same slide box as above, detail   97

FIG. 6.3   Filing cards, Lennert Collection   103

FIG. 7.1   Box   108

FIG. 7.2   Boxes waiting in factory   111

FIG. 7.3   Boxes waiting in museum   112

FIG. 7.4   Our wasp in a box   114
FIG. 7.5   Bugs in boxes   117
FIG. 7.6   Wasps in a box   117
FIG. 8.1   The Augsburg Art Cabinet, Museum Gustavianum,
              Uppsala, Sweden   126
FIG. 8.2   Gilded and ebony-veneered cabinet demonstrated by the
              master carpenter (left) to his client (right), UUK31   132
FIG. 8.3   The front side of the cabinet   135
FIG. 8.4   Miniature book, UUK 212   137
FIG. 9.1   Tartölten in their case, SAM 208 – SAM 212   144
FIG. 9.2   The case for the violin made of tortoise shell, SAM 638   149
FIG. 9.3   The spinettino in its box, SAM 121   149
FIG. 9.4   The case for four recorders signed with '!!' SAM 171   152
FIG. 10.1 Disposable straw cage (without cricket)   156
FIG. 10.2 Force-grown gourd container with wooden lid   160
FIG. 10.3 Round box cricket container made from grey clay, with lid   161
FIG. 11.1 The Marischal College and Marischal Museum, Aberdeen   168
FIG. 11.2 Poster for 'Going Home' exhibition in Marischal Museum
              2003–2004   177
FIG. 11.3 Photograph of repatriation ceremony in Marischal
              Museum, 2003   179
FIG. 12.1 Cigarette packs used for storage in the Archaeological
              Museum of Thessaloniki   186
FIG. 13.1 *Dandanah*, The Fairy Palace   202
FIG. 14.1 *Ur*-Box   214
FIG. 14.2 Kircher's ark, floor plan   217
FIG. 14.3 Model of a cargo plane in the entrance to Frankfurt
              Airport's Animal Lounge   220
FIGS. 14.4A, 14.4B Salvation of swallows in 'Aktion Südflug'   221
FIG. 14.5 Animal Lounge, Frankfurt Airport   223
FIG. 14.6 Transportation of a killer whale   226
FIG. 14.7 Container requirement 55, for dolphin and whale species   226
FIG. 15.1 A wooden box from the Natural History Museum –
              Archives of Life, Basel, Switzerland   230

FIG. 15.2 A cardboard box filled with wooden boxes at the Natural
History Museum – Archives of Life, Basel, Switzerland   236

FIG. 15.3 Menus for 'After Hours Summer Edition, Chillen im
Museum', 11 September 2014   237

FIG. 16.1 'Aid is seen on-board an Australian RAAF C-17 Globemaster in transit on March 16, 2015 to Port Vila, Vanuatu'   240

FIG. 16.2 'Plane arrives in Port Vila with aid packages'   243

FIG. 17.1 First prize medicine cabinet designed by S. C. Carpenter
in Cleveland, Ohio   254

FIG. 17.2 Third prize medicine cabinet designed by John W.
Knobel in Ozone Park, New York. Fourth prize medicine
cabinet designed by Marvin J. Neivert in Lawrence,
New York   261

FIG. 18.1 The Green Minna in front of a police station   270

FIG. 18.2 Unloading the Green Minna in the courtyard of the
Central Police Station   274

FIG. 18.3 In need of a box   281

FIG. 19.1 50kl stirred aerated fermenter   288

FIG. 19.2A Rotary drum fermenter   295

FIG. 19.2B Laboratory-scale fermentation apparatus   295

FIG. 19.2C Large-scale fermentation apparatus   296

FIG. 19.3A Aerating system of the perforated tube type for a huge
propagating tub   296

FIG. 19.3B Early forms of perforated tube systems: a) inverted T, b)
perforated ring, c) spiral sparger   297

FIG. 19.3C Network of perforated tubes   297

FIG. 19.3D Different kinds of spargers: a) single nozzle sparger, b)
ring sparger, and c) micro sparger   297

FIG. 19.4 Agitator wing designs   298

FIG. 19.5 Scaling up: (1) shake flasks (small-scale), (2) jar
fermenter (small to medium-scale), (3) pilot plant
(medium-scale), (4) tank (large-scale)   299

FIG. 20.1 元末明初的黑漆书箱 Black shellac lacquer book-box
from the late Yuan/early Ming Dynasty   306

FIG. 20.2 'Circuits in a Box' 312

FIG. 20.3 'Transfer between Boxes' 312

FIG. 20.4 'Boxed-up Ghosts' 318

FIG. 20.5 'Scenes in "the Black"' 320

FIG. 22.1 *Haberling Sicherheitsbehälter* at the Max Planck Institute for the History of Science 364

FIG. 22.2 Paper shredder at the Max Planck Institute for the History of Science 364

FIG. 22.3 Hama paper shredder (designed for home use) 366

FIG. 22.4 The paper shredder's metal 'teeth', spinning shaft, and paper fragments produced 367

FIG. 22.5 Abbot Augustus Low's illustrations of his 'waste-paper receptacle' invention for his 1909 patent application 370

FIG. 22.6 Adolf Ehinger's 'diagrammatic top-plan view of a shredder' 371

FIG. 22.7 Ron Hildebrand sweeping shredded paper fragments into a 'compactor' to produce 'paper bales' 375

FIG. 22.8 Shredded paper fragments in the process of being reconstructed by the 'Stasi-Schnipselmaschine' 376

FIG. 22.9 Larger, hand-torn paper fragments in the process of being reconstructed by the 'Stasi-Schnipselmaschine' 377

FIG. 23.1 Freezer tanks at -160°C. Biobank sample storage for a study on nutrition and health in Denmark 380

FIG. 23.2 Biobank tanks in their habitat 387

FIG. 23.3 Epidemiological box-apparatus: the 2 x 2 contingency table 389

FIG. 23.4 A hydraulic model of population 390

FIGS. 23.5A, 23.5B Left: Hospital box, Herlev Hospital, opened 1976; Right: Biobank elevators inside Herlev Hospital 392

FIG. 24.1 The Dropbox icon 396

FIG. 24.2 What a data centre looks like 404

FIGS. 25.1, 25.1B Mirror perspective. Pictures and details of water dispensers 408

FIG. 25.2 Flow chart: material paths of drinking water in Taiwanese households 412

FIG. 25.3 Flow chart: material path and appliances of 'warm' drinking water in Taiwanese households 417

FIG. 25.4A Jio's water dispenser 418

FIG. 25.4B Wu's water dispenser 418

FIG. 26.1 General civilian anti-gas respirator carrying case with British civilian gas mask 424

FIG. 26.2 Civilians walking on the streets of London with gas mask cases after the outbreak of the Second World War 427

FIG. 26.3 The British civilian gas mask and officially issued cardboard gas mask case, with cord for carrying 429

FIG. 26.4 Carry one everywhere 430

FIGS. 26.5A, 26.5B Gendering the fear of gas 433

FIG. 26.6 Gas mask box counts in London by Mass Observation 434

FIG. 27.1 A homeless man sleeps inside a cardboard box on Ermou street in central Athens in the early hours of Sunday, 28 June 2015 442

FIG. 27.2 Albert Jones's patent for the improvement in paper for packing, 1871 448

FIG. 27.3 American singer Wyoma Winters was named Miss Folding Paper Box 1952 at the annual Folding Paper Box Association of America 452

FIG. 27.4 An elderly homeless African-American woman pushes a pram with a large cardboard box on top 453

FIG. 28.1 Petri dish 458

FIG. 29.1 Prussian census box as used for the 1871 census, reconstructed to size by Norbert Massuthe, Berlin (2016) 472

FIG. 29.2 Prussian Counting Card, 210x210 mm (1871) 475

FIG. 30.1 An open glass DT-60 personnel dosimeter 480

FIG. 30.2 A set of ten original DT-60 dosimeters packaged with instructions and specifications 484

FIG. 30.3 Children in Fukushima with their radiation dosimeters called 'glass badges' 485

FIG. 31.1 'Mirror trap set, showing trigger mechanism, mirror, and rubber bands, fastened to bottom of door' 492

FIG. 31.2 A modified design of the mirror trap   497

FIG. 32.1 Drawing of a variety of medicine bottles, made by a
Yanomami health agent   504

FIG. 32.2 Pharmacy of a health post containing an assortment of
medicines and other medical equipment   508

FIG. 32.3 Doctor's case for carrying injectable medicines during a
visit to the villages   509

FIG. 32.4 A Yanomami health agent looks for medicines carried to a
village in a special backpack, and also within a Yanomami
basket   509

FIG. 32.5 Drawing of a mother holding a child, with a diversity of
containers for diarrhoea medicine   515

FIG. 32.6 Area of the roof above the hearth   515

FIG. 33.1 Box by Agfa, Germany   524

FIG. 33.2 Box by Lastre M. Cappelli, Italy   531

FIG. 33.3 Box by J. Jougla, France   532

FIG. 33.4 Box by Grieshaber Frères & Cie, France   532

FIG. 33.5 Box by Richard Jahr, Germany   533

FIG. 33.6 Box by Gevaert, Belgium   535

FIG. 33.7 Box by Gevaert, Belgium   535

FIGS. 34.1A, 34.1B The box and the imprinting of its content:
During and after feeding the lice   538

FIG. 34.2 A set of Sikora boxes and its kin species   541

FIGS. 34.3A, 34.3B Empty boxes (healthy lice) and full boxes (filled
with Rickettsia prowazeki)   544

FIGS. 34.4A, 34.4B A sanitary train during the Serbian typhus
epidemic of 1915, and men leaving the train after having
been de-loused in the steam bath   547

FIGS. 34.5A, 34.5B Dissecting units at the Behring Institute, Lwów
around 1942   549

FIG. 34.6 Louse feeders at the Behring Institute, Lwów ca. 1942   551

FIG. 34.7 Jews-Lice-Typhus, Nazi propaganda poster, 1941   552

FIG. 35.1 Highboy Tool Chest   558

FIG. 35.2 A wheeled, steel chest with a wooden top   558

FIG. 36.1 The surgeon's chest from the surgeon's cabin in the Mary
Rose, the Mary Rose Museum, Portsmouth   570

FIG. 36.2 Another surgeon's chest from the Mary Rose   573

FIG. 37.1 Open electrotherapy box   582

FIG. 37.2 Closed electrotherapy box   584

FIG. 37.3 George Adams's prototype; 1785 essay on electricity or a
later edition   588

FIG. 38.1 Reliquary with scenes from the martyrdom of St Thomas
Becket, c.1173–1180   596

FIG. 39.1 Research Box, on display   606

FIG. 39.2 Research Box, in closed form   606

FIG. 39.3 Research Box prefers human companionship   608

FIG. 39.4 Research Box, detail of performance   609

FIG. 39.5 Research Box, field marks   610

FIG. 39.6 Research Box, in Kavala   611

FIG. 39.7 Research Box, on display in the Kavala Municipal Tobacco
Warehouse   612

FIG. 39.8 Research Box, at the Copenhagen Business School   614

FIG. 39.9 Human interlocutors at the Copenhagen Business School,
building enquiry machines; meanwhile, Research Box
reconfigures itself as an enquiry machine   614

FIG. 39.10 Enquiry machines in Copenhagen   615

FIG. 39.11 Research Box, transformed into enquiry machine   615

FIG. 39.12 Research Box, performing the digitisation of a text   617

FIG. 39.13 Research Box, drawing attention to the varying sizes of
digitised texts and images   618

FIG. 39.14 Research Box, performing as a publication in the
humanities   621

CONTRIBUTORS

ELEFTHERIA AKRIVOPOULOU studied Archaeology & Museology at University of Athens. She is a PhD candidate at the Faculty of History, Archaeology & Social Anthropology of the University of Thessaly. She works as an museologist at the Archaeological Museum of Thessaloniki. She has dealt with excavation work and museological research at many museums as well as at the Greek Ministry of Culture. Her research has been published in conference proceedings and periodicals.

STEWART ALLEN completed his PhD in social anthropology at the University of Edinburgh in 2014. He pursued a postdoctoral fellowship at the Max Plank Institute for the History of Science between 2014 and 2016 and has previously written on knowledge production, skill, and how narratives of social good are produced and circulated. He is the author of the book *An Ethnography of NGO Practice in India: Utopias of Development* published by Manchester University Press.

PIT ARENS graduated from the Akademie der Bildenden Künste (Academy of Fine Arts) in Munich and the Académie des Beaux-Arts in Paris. His interdisciplinary work moves between science and art, craft and sculpture, theory and practice, text and image. He works in different media: sculpture, installation, film, drawing and ceramics.

SUSANNE BAUER is professor in Science and Technologies Studies (STS) at the Centre for Technology, Innovation and Culture, University of Oslo. Trained as environmental scientist and epidemiologist, her work in the social studies of science has unpacked calculative infrastructures and data politics in the health sciences. Her current research interests range from the conditions of intensified data recombination and the making and circulation of regulatory knowledges, to airports as multiple borderlands, and logistics as technoscience.

ETIENNE BENSON is an associate professor in the Department of History and Sociology of Science at the University of Pennsylvania. He studies animal history, the history of ecology, and the history of environmentalism, with a focus on the nineteenth- and twentieth-century United States. He is the author of *Wired Wilderness: Technologies of Tracking and the Making of Modern Wildlife* (2010).

SARAH BLACKER is a lecturer and postdoctoral researcher at the Munich Center for Technology in Society at the Technical University of Munich. Her research examines the production and circulation of scientific knowledge about the relation between environmental contamination, racialization, and health inequalities in the era of financialization.

STEPHANIE BOWRY is a historian specialising in the cultural performance of museums during the sixteenth and seventeenth centuries. She completed her PhD on the visual representation of the world in early modern curiosity cabinets and its reflection in contemporary art practice in 2015. Her most recent research project, funded by the Leverhulme Trust and hosted by the School of Museum Studies, University of Leicester, examined the relationships between gardens and art galleries from 1500 – 1750.

EMILY BROWNELL is a lecturer in Environmental History at the University of Edinburgh. Her book, *Gone to Ground: An Environmental History of Dar es Salaam, Tanzania*, was published in 2020 by the University of Pittsburgh Press. Her work focuses on environmental, infrastructural, and planning histories in East Africa.

SHIH-PEI CHEN is a digital humanities researcher at Max Planck Institute for the History of Science, where she researches and develops digital methodologies for studying the history of science, technology, and medicine. She specializes in conducting text analyses, text/data mining, data visualization, and geospatial analyses to answer historical research questions. Her current project develops tools to explore thousands of Chinese local gazetteers in unprecedented ways.

YI-PING CHENG obtained her PhD from the department of Sociology, Lancaster University in the UK in 2013. Her PhD thesis discussed the domestic consumption in Taiwan, and her research foci mainly relate to home consumption, material culture and sociology. Starting from 2014, she works as an assistant professor in the department of Public Affairs and Civic Education, in National Changhua University of Education, Taiwan.

BEATRIX DARMSTÄDTER graduated from Saxophone Classic, Musicology (PhD 1998), Philosophy, and 'Education and Cultural Communication Management' with honors. Since 2001, she works as the curator of the collection of historic musical instruments (SAM) of the *Kunsthistorisches Museum* Vienna (KHM). Her main organological research topic is the application of 3D-CT (non-contact) measurement of historical woodwind instruments. In addition, she focuses on biographical research on Austrian instrument makers, and on performing practice.

DEANNA DAY is a writer and historian. Her writing about science and culture, humans and cyborgs, and women and data has appeared in Lady Science, Model View Culture, Cabinet, Slate, and elsewhere around the internet. She lives in Los Angeles. http://deannaday.net

DON DUPREZ received his PhD in Social Anthropology from the University of Edinburgh. His current research explores reproduction, religious hybridization and efficacy among Hmong communities in the United States. Duprez has also conducted research among Japanese transnationals, Chinese Americans, and Chinese Han and ethnic minority populations. His research interests include health and religion, ethics, epistemological and ontological issues, time and memory, feminism, gender, transnational and communities in diaspora. He is currently based in Denver, Colorado.

HANAKO ENDO is a lecturer at Japanese Red Cross College of Nursing. Her research interest is mainly in Shakespeare from the perspective of the history of medicine. Her articles include 'Illyria as the Carnivalesque State: *Twelfth Night* and the Consumption of Alcohol' (2016) and 'Bloodletting and the Control of Passion in Shakespeare's *Julius Caesar*' (2018). She is now working on a book on Shakespeare and Medicine.

ERIC J. ENGSTROM is a historian of psychiatry and research associate in the Department of History at the Humboldt University in Berlin. He received his BA from Lewis and Clark College in Portland, OR, his MA from the Ludwig-Maximilians-Universität in Munich, and his PhD from the University of North Carolina Chapel Hill. He has published widely in the history of psychiatry. He is currently researching the history of forensic politics in Berlin, 1887–1914.

MATS FRIDLUND is a historian of science and technology at the Max Planck Institute for the History of Science in Berlin and the University of Gothenburg and has previously held positions at universities in Finland, Denmark, England and the USA. He studies the cultural and political history of technology and materiality where his current research program interrogates the role of science and technology in the emergence and globalization of terrorisms since the 19th century.

STYLIANA GALINIKI is an archaeologist at the Archaeological Museum of Thessaloniki and holds a PhD from the National Technical University of Athens (School of Architecture). Her research focuses on the use of antiquity in the construction of social identity and the public performances of collective memory. She is also a published novelist.

JOHANNA GONÇALVES MARTÍN is an anthropologist, medical doctor and epide-miologist, who has worked for several years with the Yanomami in Venezuela, and is currently a post-doctoral researcher at the Institute for Area and Global Studies (EPFL). She is interested in the anthropology of health and wellbeing among Amazonian peoples, including life protecting practices, bodies and ter-ritories, gender and fertility, and the relationships between indigenous peoples and a diversity of outsiders, including doctors.

MATHIAS GROTE is a historian, philosopher and ex-practitioner of the life sciences. He is interested especially in recent developments of microbiology as well as in molecular biologies beyond genetics (Membranes to Molecular Machines. Active Matter and the Remaking of Life, Chicago 2019). In another project, he pursues the question of how the 20th century sciences have managed to canonize knowledge through media such as the handbook (https:// historyofknowledge.net/lbtb/). He is assistant professor at Humboldt University of Berlin.

NILS GÜTTLER is a historian of science and technology. He received his doctorate in the history of science from Humboldt University, Berlin. His dissertation appeared as *Das Kosmoskop. Karten und ihre Benutzer in der Pflanzengeographie des 19. Jahrhunderts* (2014). Currently he is a postdoctoral fellow at the chair for science studies at the ETH, Zurich. His ongoing research focuses on the environmental history of the Frankfurt-am-Main airport.

TANJA HAMMEL is a postdoctoral research fellow at the History Department at the University of Basel and teaches at the History Department at the University of Zurich. She is a member of the interdisciplinary research project "African Contributions to Global Health: Circulation Knowledge and Innovations" wwww.globalhealthafrica.ch. Her areas of interest are in the history of science and knowledge, new colonial history, visual history, South African history, biographical studies as well as museum and critical heritage studies.

JAMESON KISMET BELL is an assistant professor in the Department of Western Languages and Literatures at Boğaziçi University in Istanbul, Turkey. His research interests include literature and medicine, the body and knowledge, as well as performance and media studies. His recent book, *Performing the Sixteenth-Century Brain: Beyond Word and Image Inscriptions* (Berlin: Lit Verlag, 2018), bridges literary criticism and history to offer close readings of the first visually accurate representations of the body and brain.

VICTORIA LEE is assistant professor in the Department of History at Ohio University, where she teaches and writes about modern science and technology.

She is currently writing a book about Japanese society's engagement with microbes in science, industry, and environmental management. She has published in *Historical Studies in the Natural Sciences, New Perspectives on the History of Life Sciences and Agriculture* (ed. Denise Phillips and Sharon Kingsland), and *Osiris*.

BONNIE MAK is an associate professor at the University of Illinois, jointly appointed in the School of Information Sciences, History, and the Program in Medieval Studies. Her first book, *How the Page Matters* (2011), examines the interface of the page as it is developed across time, geographies, and technologies.

ULRICH MECHLER is a researcher at the Museum of Medical and Pharmaceutical History of Kiel University. His research interests include collection and object-based studies in the history of science and medicine. In his dissertation he investigated transformations of disease research in postwar medicine using the case collection of the German pathologist Karl Lennert. Currently he works as Postdoc Fellow on a collection of female pelvic bones about clinical birth medicine in the 19th century.

TAHANI NADIM is a sociologist of science and Junior Professor in the Institute for European Ethnology at the Humboldt-Universität zu Berlin in a joint appointment with the Museum für Naturkunde Berlin. She is a member of the Centre for Anthropological Research on Museums and Heritage (CARMAH). Her research focuses on the datafication of natures and its consequences. She heads the department 'Humanities of nature' at the Museum für Naturkunde Berlin.

CHRISTINE VON OERTZEN is a senior research scholar at the Max Planck Institute for the History of Science in Berlin, Germany. She explores the material culture of data processing since the nineteenth century. She is co-editor of the 2017 Osiris volume on *Data Histories* (with Elena Aronova and David Sepkoski) and of *Working With Paper: Gendered Practices in the History of Knowledge* (with Carla Bittel and Elaine Leong), published by the University of Pittsburgh Press in 2019.

JAN ERIC OLSÉN is an independent scholar living in Malmö, Sweden. He has written widely on the history of medicine and is currently completing a book on the material heritage of blindness and the complex relation between vision and touch in Western culture.

MIRKA PALIOURA studied French Letters and Art History (BA, PhD Athens University, MA Université Paris I Panthéon-Sorbonne). She has edited two books and presented several conference papers on nineteenth-century Greek art. She has taught at the Athens School of Fine Arts and the Hellenic Open University. She has also worked in the Greek Ministry of Culture. She is a Member of the Hellenic Association of Art Historians and is currently working in the Finopoulos Collection – Benaki Museum.

JULIA POLLACK is creative program manager at the Carl R. Woese Institute for Genomic Biology at the University of Illinois. She previously worked as a librarian at Bronx Community College in New York, and a user experience (UX) designer at a technical consulting agency in Urbana.

SPYRIDOULA PYRPYLI (BA in Greek philology and MA in museology) holds a PhD in museology and has been working in Greek museums and galleries. She is now teaching ancient Greek, modern Greek literature and history in Greek high schools, art history and museology in Ioannina University (Greece). Her research interests focus on the social role the museum, the digital museum, the relation between museums and public history.

LUCY RAZZALL is a teaching fellow in Shakespeare and Renaissance Literature at University College London. Her research focuses on the relationships between early modern literature and materiality. She has published on, amongst other things, emblem books, relics, and early modern print, and she is currently finishing her first book, *Boxes and Books in Early Modern England*.

MARIA RENTETZI is professor at the Technical University Berlin. She has published widely on the history of nuclear sciences with an emphasis on gender, material culture, and science diplomacy. A physicist by training, Rentetzi currently leads an ERC Consolidator Grant that studies the history of radiation protection and the role the International Atomic Energy Agency has played as a diplomatic and political international institution in shaping radiation policies and nuclear diplomacies.

DAGMAR SCHÄFER is a historian of science, technology and China, currently directing Dept. III Artefacts, Action, Knowledge at the Max Planck Institute for the History of Science. She has published widely on the Premodern history of China; technology, materiality, and the processes and structures that lead to varying knowledge systems; and the changing role of artefacts—texts, objects, and spaces—in the creation, diffusion, and use of scientific and technological knowledge.

MARTINA SCHLÜNDER is a research fellow at the Max Planck Institute for the History of Science in Berlin. As a scholar in feminist science studies she explores and analyses the politics of technoscience in reproductive technologies, their broader implications in the history of eugenics, biopolitics and feminisms.

MARTINA SIEBERT works as area specialist for China at the Staatsbibliothek zu Berlin and as independent scholar. She researches and publishes on Chinese exploration into nature and technology through history with a focus on the styles and agendas of presenting and organizing that knowledge in writing, including how scholars approached the realm of the inexplicable.

MYRTO VOULELI is a conservator (paper, photography) at the Historical Archives of National Bank of Greece. She holds degrees from the Institute for Conservation of Arts, Athens and London-Camberwell college of arts. Her work experiences range from the Byzantine Museum of Athens, Benaki Museum in Athens to Guildhall Library in London and Bibliotheca Alexandrina in Egypt.

ALEXANDRA WIDMER is assistant professor in the Anthropology Department at York University. Her research program examines the social and political lives of biomedicine and science in colonial and postcolonial contexts. She has published on demography's implications in state attempts at the management of populations, the medical education of Pacific Island men and women to work in colonial contexts and Pacific Island women's reproductive health, especially indigenous women's caregiving practices at birth.

ARTEMIS YAGOU is a historian of design and technology. She is research associate at the Research Institute for the History of Science and Technology of the Deutsches Museum (Munich), currently working on 'How they Played: Children and Construction Toys (ca. 1840–1940)', funded by the German Research Foundation (DFG). Additionally, she is preparing a monograph on luxury in early modern southeastern Europe. She has published extensively, including *Fragile Innovation: Episodes in Greek Design History* (2011).

BOXING PRACTICES

containing, diagnosing, treating, categorising, classifying, imagining, dreaming, injuring, remembering, erasing history, sheltering, collecting, storing, ordering, entertaining, concealing, performing, scaling, uniting, re-ordering, facilitating, enhancing, appropriating, abducting, educating, instructing, smoking, surprising, contradicting, confining, locking up, moving, shipping, sexing, pairing, combining, juxtaposing, compressing, interlacing, assembling, policing, jailing, culturing, converting, consuming, controlling, governing, unveiling, storytelling, sequencing, fragmenting, separating, destroying, freezing, carrying, distributing, purifying, transforming, comforting, frightening, awaiting, simulating, seducing, huddling, isolating, obstructing, black-boxing, measuring, captivating, encompassing, encasing, recording, creating, surviving, revealing, enshrining, sanctifying, waiting, taxonomising, individualising, dissecting, inscribing, meditating, visualising, archiving, miniaturising, representing, monumentalising, protecting, transporting, caging, handling, recombining, extending, attracting, displaying, mobilising, conserving, repatriating, saving, nurturing, caring, safeguarding, circulating, re-using, networking, recycling, rendering, disrespecting, disordering, making, hiding, organising, fighting, booking, relating, fermenting, growing, producing, maintaining, operating, industrialising, liberating, reducing, associating, connecting, building, hybridising, matching, keeping, incriminating, defreezing, transferring, sharing, backing up, preparing, threatening, signalling, awakening, practising, training, persuading, commercialising, modernising, housing, displacing, enclosing, portioning, signifying, disappearing, monitoring, preserving, managing, recognising, misrecognising, holding, dosing, healing, encapsulating, covering, wrapping, packaging, enveloping, reconfiguring, informing, identifying, fixing, behaving, reflecting, personalising, excavating, voyaging, powering, electrifying, ruminating, framing, occluding, killing

PREFACE AND ACKNOWLEDGEMENTS

This book opens a new field – box studies – and serves as its first field guide. It does this in a performative way: in mobilising elements of natural history like taxonomies and identification keys, this book makes space for a generative critique of western epistemologies and their orderings. As an open-ended experiment with an impossible 'natural history' of boxes, this field guide invites a change in our habits of valuing and observing, and of how we are involved and connected to our environment. Setting off with a multivocal introductory section, we organized the book into 11 sections, which is but one of possible orderings. Indeed, this book calls for perpetual reassembling and provides a range of tools to do so, for example in the keywords featuring box practices and the taxonomies that precede each essay.

The boxes in this book have gathered contributors across disciplines, from art history to technology studies, from archaeology to musicology, from computer science to history of medicine – providing tools for unlearning academia´s disciplinary 'boxings'. We thank all the participants in the conference 'Knowledge in a Box' held in Kavala in August 2012. Discussions at the Kavala conference inspired us to stay with box studies, a project that has since turned to the study of box *practices*.

The editors wish to thank Timo Roßmann for his dedicated proofreading and formatting of every essay in this book before submission. We thank OPO-Foundation Zurich and Collegium Helveticum at ETH Zurich as well as Goethe University Frankfurt am Main for funding and support. At Mattering Press, we thank our editors, Endre Dányi, Julien McHardy and Joe Deville, and our copy editor Steven Lovatt. Many thanks to the two non-anonymous reviewers Geof Bowker and Claire Waterton, as well as to Sandra Widmer, Helen Verran, Berti Schulte and Liz Martin for their support at various stages of this project. Last but not least, we thank all authors who responded to our call for box studies and for the enthusiasm and commitment they brought to this project.

INTRODUCTIONS

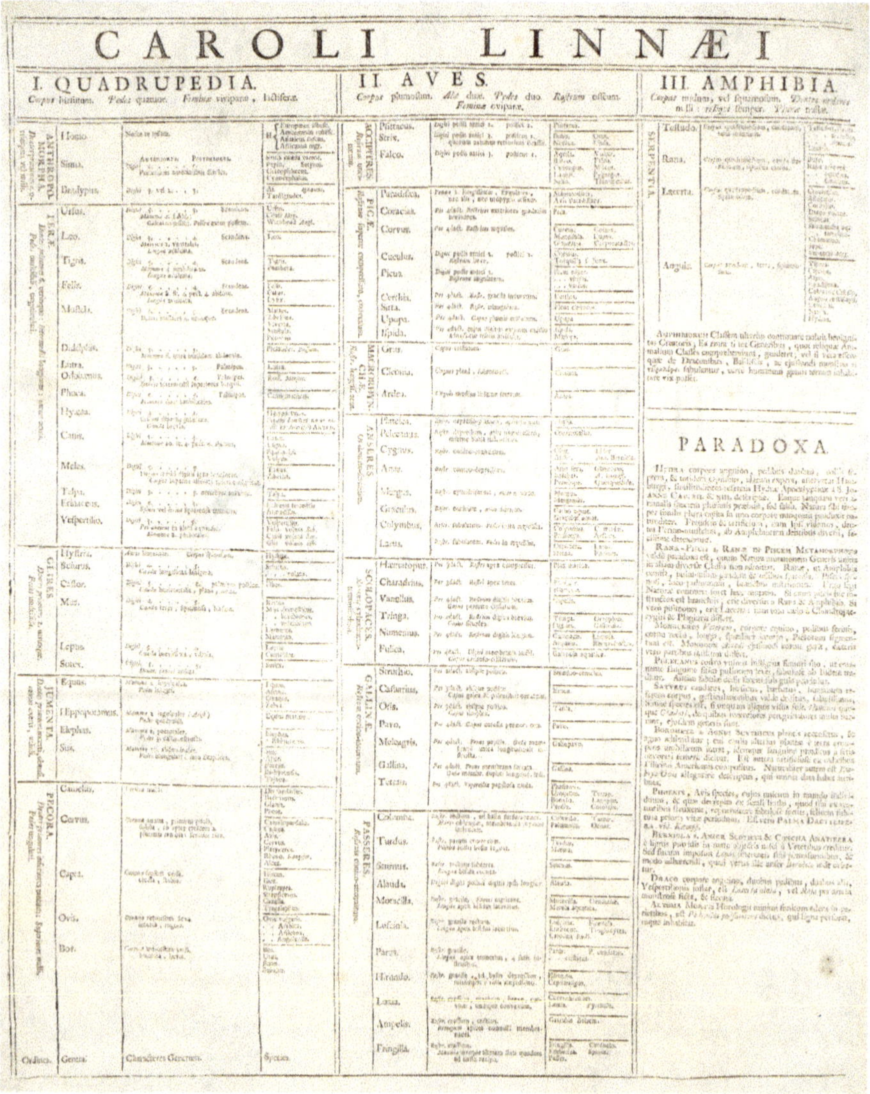

CAROLI LINNÆI

I. QUADRUPEDIA.
Corpus hirsutum. Pedes quatuor. Femina vivipara, lactifera.

II. AVES.
Corpus plumosum. Alæ duæ. Pedes duo. Rostrum osseum. Femina ovipara.

III. AMPHIBIA
Corpus nudum, vel squamosum. Dentes molares nulli: reliqui semper. Pinnæ nullæ.

PARADOXA

FIG. 1.1 Excerpt of Linné's classification of the animal kingdom, 1735 (source: Carl Linné: Systema naturae 1735, Internet Archive, https://archive.org/details/mobot31753002972252/page/n11/mode/2up)

I

THE GENERATIVE POSSIBILITIES OF THE WRONG BOX

Martina Schlünder

IN THEIR DARKLY COMIC NOVEL *THE WRONG BOX* (1889), ROBERT LOUIS Stevenson and his step son Lloyd Osbourne tell of the itinerary of a wandering corpse. Hidden by different people in varying containers (a barrel, a piano) the always less than honourable intention to get rid of the body by secreting the box or sending it to uninvolved parties triggers a potentially endless plot revolving around the wanderlust of a body that is always in the wrong box, at the wrong place, or delivered in the right box but to a wrong recipient. Stevenson and Osbourne, who shortly after the novel's publication moved from London to Samoa, where they entangled themselves in colonial politics (Colley 2004), paint a pitiless portrait of an imperial, colonising society that cannot contain its systematic, endemic greed, and instead unsuccessfully tries to hide it. *The Wrong Box* enacts a scheme of complex, systematically failing relations between the practices and materialities of doing dead bodies. Never do container, content, owner, sender, or recipient of the container match. It is this tension that keeps the story going.

In a similar vein this book investigates the (non-matching) relations box practices produce. It enacts a new field of analysis – box studies – and serves as its first field guide. By studying the relation of practice and materiality, the book explores the impact of boxes as epistemic tools in ordering, containing, and classifying the worldly mess. The book goes about this in a performative way: as naturalists of the eighteenth century tried to order, contain, and control the abundance and overflow of nature, this book explores a cornucopia of boxes and box practices by mobilising elements of natural history like the interplay of images, taxonomies, and identification keys. In contrast to naturalists of the past, however, the goal is *not* to establish an encyclopaedic order. Whereas taxonomies are based on detailed descriptions of isolated items, our intention is to explore boxes, not as singular objects, but rather as emerging material that is enacted in specific practices. Thus we are not interested in a taxonomy of boxes; we are striving for classification, working typologies of box practices.

In the Pandora myth, the opening of the box is the moment when all evil spreads over the world and mankind. In contrast, this book identifies the *closure* of knowledge production into the boxes and dogmata of western epistemology as the true evil, as a true epistemic crime. In following Pandora's gesture of opening a forbidden box, this book begins to lift the lid on the box of western epistemic infrastructures. The 'god's trick' (Haraway 1988, 583), the 'modernist settlement' (Latour 1999,14) managed to pacify the violence of the religious wars over the one truth (god) that had raged over Europe in the seventeenth century (Shapin/Schaffer 1985). Our disclosure recognises the high price others paid when this violence was exported to the colonial projects of European countries. The hard-won epistemic unity unleashed unprecedented violence in the encounters with non-Christians and non-white people, who were devalued as nomads, barbarians, and savages. And such devaluing continues, alas, too close for comfort. This is a book that delights in odd juxtapositions; it is not a book which comforts.

Our focus here is not the black box so beloved of STS scholars. Opening the lid on the box of western epistemic infrastructures is not the same as open-ing the black box of the scientific method, as so many science studies scholars have done before. Neither does the new field of analysis we articulate here seek to add another layer to the academic in-fights setting constructivism against positivism. Nor does it want to add and release new things into the box, or suggest how a black box could be used in a different way. Following Stevenson and Osbourne, this book is about the ins and outs of a complex system, the practices of hiding, excluding, and hierarchising knowledge in systematic ways. It follows those who want to intervene in the fabric, the very grid of modernity and its ordering tools. How to detach, uncouple, and dissociate classifica-tions from the modern constitution, its universal claims and its colonial pasts and presents? How to bring taxonomies and boxes into a different terrain? How to cross the shallows of the modern settlement and make an impossible natural history of boxes possible? If we understand the sealing of the box of knowledge production as the epistemic crime of the modern settlement, what kind of epistemic wrongdoing, misdeeds, delinquencies, and transgressions do we need in order to open the box, to change the grid, to render different cosmopolitics possible?

Western epistemology hides its rules, its limits and exclusions in its infra-structures of thinking, in the ways that things and thoughts, materials and con-cepts are ordered or boxed-in; by boxing-in and formatting *not* being part of a critical epistemic discourse; by formats and narratives being taken for granted, like infrastructure's transparency (Star and Ruhleder 1996). I am thinking here of the order of an academic paper, the hierarchisation of concepts and theories over materials and methods, and the unanimity of an introduction even in multi-authored and edited books and papers.

This book does not argue through new theories and concepts. Rather it intervenes in a performative way. Its interventions are on the level of formats and methods. It pushes the limits and the hidden rules of western epistemology: what counts as object or subject, as living or inorganic, as nature or culture. In doing so it also serves as a user's guide to committing epistemic counter-crimes: by breaking epistemic rules, by contesting the boundary between the content and the container, between nature and culture, and by subjecting the ordering device – the infrastructure of ordering – to the same rules that usually only apply to the content and the contained.

Our book commits minor crimes: it has opened, after all, by comparing a mordant British novel – later made into an entertaining film comedy – to a serious academic epistemic challenge, and it goes on to offer three introductions that contest and connect with each other. And there are also more major transgres-sions: we try to do a natural history of things that the modern constitution has declared as non-nature, as inorganic, and as non-living and abstract.

The slapstick of our little and not-so-little epistemic crimes helps us avoid an iconoclastic critique. We do not mean to purge all classifications and taxonomies just because they have been part of an imperial, still hegemonic epistemology. Instead, we seek a generative critique (Verran 2001) that implies keeping present, i.e. *not* purging, the tensions that have emerged as result of historically contaminated classifications. Keeping the tensions between container and content, keeping the boxes open, allows 'generative disputes'.

Instead of critiquing wrong boxes in a way that often reproduces the epistemic tools, methods, and infrastructures it wants to critique, we strive for a metabolic account that starts to digest and decompose epistemic infrastructures through the generative critique. The metaphor of metabolism contains the practices of generative critique we pursue with this field guide. It connects the practices of decomposing (Verran 2001, Kenney 2015) with those of the 'Cannibal' movement in Brazil in the 1920s (Járaugui 2015). Digesting colonial stereotypes instead of purging modernity from its colonial remainders generates the unexpected. How to decompose and digest, for instance, a contaminated theory of civilisation that praises the box as an icon of civilisation in contrast to the cultures of so-called nomads, barbarians, and savages? How to compost a reactionary cultural theory that has been used to justify racism, colonialism, even genocides for centuries, making sure that all the seeds from which life might spring anew are well and truly cooked in the process? How to metabolise the antifeminism that the Pandora myth epitomises, accumulated over centuries, and still effective? How to develop the epistemic dissensus embedded in the here and now of a multiple introduction? How is the epistemic potential of a multiple introduction operationalised in ways that do not silence and purge, but make epistemic tensions visible and tangible?

This book does not provide finished solutions, but rather wants to cut a path. The taxonomies of box practices that open each paper are not ironic, since they do not want to ridicule western epistemology. They do not want to add a little bit of playfulness and imagination to the iron rules of reason. Instead, the taxonomies move epistemology to a terrain where it finds its plural. Western epistemology still uses its alleged singularity to make objects comparable. In traditional field guides, for instance, this is done by taking the concept of species for granted, hiding the complex histories and structures of this concept in its infrastructure of thinking.

By committing epistemic counter-crimes, by pushing against Western epistemic rules and norms, the book wants to transform epistemology into a field that thinks of itself as one box among others (a box species, if you will), that makes its infrastructures available for comparison in a true comparative epistemology (Fleck 1935/1979). By exploring the box more generally as the epitome of relations, and as a form that might contain other forms and other possibilities of relation, this field guide might help us to reveal new box practices containing new relations that we still do not know, even though we are in urgent need of them.

We want to study boxes as 'snap-shots' of specific encounters in the field. Thus a field guide seems to be an appropriate companion. Florence Merriam (1863–1948) is credited with writing the first of its kind. Merriam's interest in birds was not only fed by academic curiosity; it was rather her activism against the bird feather trade and the fashion industry that sparked her passion for bird watching (Dunlap 2011). Historically, field guides have been situated between activism and academy, amateurs and experts, modernity and its others. Field guides are heavily imbued with the values of modernity. They transfer scientific knowledge into the hands of amateurs, who again feed their knowledge of the field back to experts, taxonomists, biologists, and geologists. Imbued with modern scientific knowledge (its classifications and taxonomies), they also evoke non-modern ideas of nature. They do not follow, for instance, the boundaries of biology, since they also study the inorganic parts of nature like minerals.

What do field guides usually do? They help the novice cut a path into the undergrowth and into the ubiquity of the ordinary, where everything seems to look and behave in undifferentiated ways. They help to rethink and freshly perceive formerly unremarkable objects and actions. Their use demands a change in habits of valuing, observing, and in modes of involvement and connection to our environment.

A field guide is not made for a coffee table or a study. It is a portable book that you can take with you into the field. But the guide also projects the field into your hands (or into your pocket). The book is also part of the field, as it helps to establish it. Its main task is to help to identify a specific element in the field, to gain certainty of an object under scrutiny. Traditional field guides work through abstractions and categorisations. They apply taxonomies and biological systems that were created in studies and natural history museums, where researchers had time to study dead objects in detail. Observation and comparison are key methods of identifying species. In the field, however, looking for a match, (back and forth between the bird in the wild and those in the guide) has to happen quickly, since the bird under scrutiny might fly away at any moment. The interplay between image and text, and especially captions, are crucial for the moments when birders actually compare and try to identify specific kinds of bird. In field guides, taxonomies provide the pattern for recognition, but identification in the field relies on directed attention, experience, and trained intuition: it all happens at a glance. Field guides are part of an assemblage, a complex practice of simultaneously looking, observing, perceiving, listening, writing, and sometimes drawing. This assemblage includes different tools like binoculars, books, paper, pencils, and all of the senses.

To consider boxes as part of modern classifications is to look at the nature of containers, and to offer a way of unpacking the boundaries between nature and culture that boxes help to contain as part of the modern constitution. We like field guides' focus on practice, how they are made for lively 'outside' encounters (i.e. in the field and beyond disciplines) in which those outside are not mere observers but rather involved participants whose attention is crucial for making such encounters possible. We also appreciate the pragmatic use of different ways of knowing incorporated by the field guide genre, the awareness of time constrains, and the worldliness in which encounters may happen.

But we also have to modify specific features so that implicit orders become more visible. We want to avoid, for instance, the typical strategies of traditional field guides that use social analogies and cultural stereotypes in their descriptions of nature (Schaffner 2008: 408–09). Law and Lynch (1988: 277–78) describe the field guide's common denominator as a commitment to naturalistic assumptions. Their epistemology relies on references to a universal taxonomy as authoritative power, reliance on a representational image theory, strategic use of text and interplay between captions, stylised pictures, and nature 'out there'. These elements are the ingredients of modernity that this book wants to challenge. In fact, this book is an exploration of the legacy and the future of wrong boxes.

REFERENCES

Colley, A., *Robert Louis Stevenson and the Colonial Imagination* (London: Routledge, 2004).

Dunlap, T., *In the Field, among the Feathered: A History of Birders and Their Guides* (New York: Oxford University Press, 2011).

Fleck, L., *Genesis and Development of a Scientific Fact* (Chicago: Chicago University Press, 1979; translated from the German original *Entstehung und Entwickung einer wissenschaftlichen Tatsache. Einführung in die Lehre vom Denkstil und Denkkollektiv*, Basel: Schwabe, 1935).

Haraway, D., 'Situated Knowledges: The Science Question in Feminism and the Privilege of Partial Perspective', *Feminist Studies*, 14.3 (1988): 575–99.

Jáuregui, C., 'Oswaldo Costa, Antropofagia, and the *Cannibal Critique* of Colonial Modernity', *Culture & History Digital Journal*, 4.2 (2015): e017 (doi: <http://dx.doi.org/10.3989/chdj.2015.017>).

Kenney, M., 'Counting, Accounting, and Accountability: Helen Verran's Relational Empiricism', *Social Studies of Science*, 45.5 (2015): 749–71.

Latour, B., *Pandora's Hope: Essays on the Reality of Science Studies* (Cambridge: Harvard University Press 1999).

Law, J., and M. Lynch, 'Lists, Field Guides, and the Descriptive Organization of Seeing: Birdwatching as an Exemplary Observational Activity', *Human Studies*, 11.2–3 (1988): 271–303.

Merriam, F., *Birds Through an Opera-Glass* (New York: Chautauqua Press, 1889).

Schaffner, S., 'A Response to Ursula Heise', *American Literary History*, 20.1–2 (2008): 405–09.

Shapin, S., and S. Schaffer, *Leviathan and the Air Pump: Hobbes, Boyle, and the Experimental Life*, (Princeton: Princeton University Press 1985).

Star, S. L., and K. Ruhleder, 'Steps Toward an Ecology of Infrastructure: Design and Access for Large Information Spaces', *Information Systems Research*, 7.1 (1996): 111–34.

Verran, H., *Science and an African Logic* (Chicago: Chicago University Press, 2001).

FIG. 2.1 The National Archaeological Museum of Athens hosts two unique *pyxides*, red-figured vessels with lids that, surprisingly, have survived together with their content: white lead powder (lead carbonate hydroxide, *psymithio* in ancient Greek), used to beautify the face. The Figure shows a clay pyxis, 410–400 BC no. 13676 *a*, National Archaeological Museum, Athens, Hellenic Ministry of Culture and Sports/ Archaeological Receipts Fund (photographer: Maria Kontaki)

2

THE EPISTEMOLOGY OF THE FAMILIAR: A HYMN TO PANDORA

Maria Rentetzi

IN A PRELIMINARY FASHION, HERE I OUGHT TO PAY ATTENTION TO THE etymological origins of the box. To start with, the meaning of 'box' comes from the Latin *buxus,* which is a transliteration of the Greek *pyxis* (πυξίς, plural *pyxides*). Initially this was a cylindrical box with a separate lid, made of fine wood from the tree *pyksos* (known in Latin as *Buxus sempervirens,* a flowering tree native to southern Europe and ideal for crafting delicate wooden objects, especially boxes) (Rutherfurd Roberts 1978).

In the Classical world, *pyxis* was associated with cosmetic and jewellery boxes. The *pyxides* often contained make-up powder, hair accessories, and ornaments, and were used almost exclusively by women. Surviving *pyxides,* mostly Greek pottery, lead us to 400 BC, to ancient Athens, where women used them to enhance their femininity, covering blemishes and imperfections with their content: *psymithio* – that is, lead carbonate hydroxide. As a symbol of femininity and a sign of domesticity, the ancient box reveals its content through its imagery: its decorative images depict scenes that take place in *gynaikonitis,* women's quarters, where women are getting dressed and doing their hair and make-up, or appear in wedding scenes (Oikonomou 2015).

With such a status, *pyxis,* as the myth demands, names the most precious holding: Pandora's box. In Hesiod's *Theogonia,* Pandora is described as the first female human, moulded out of earth and water by the Greek god Hephaestus at Zeus's command. Zeus's additional gift to her was a large *pyxis,* yet she was specifically instructed not to open it. Curious, impatient, and certainly disobedient to the gods, Pandora soon opened the *pyxis.* Regretting it too late, she 'contrived baneful cares for men' (Fraser 2011: 22). Filled with a myriad of evils, the open box released them all; besides one, hope (Fraser 2011: 22). Hence, a proverbial reference by now, Pandora's box denotes a source of extensive troubles.

Mythology, and more specifically Pandora's myth, provides a glimpse of what I call the *epistemology of the familiar*: the attempt to show how mundane objects that occupy our everyday lives are linked to the emergence of new structures of knowledge, new concepts, and new research directions. In short, an epistemology of the familiar is the study of the ordinary, the ephemeral, and the often unnoticed, such as a box. But how could such a humble form of materiality as a box be epistemologically important? The box, to remind you, names at once the container and its content, a double meaning that connects two principles at the same time. On the one hand, stands the principle of materiality that sees the container as a physical storage system, and the content as the material within it. On the other hand, I recall Jacque Derrida's nomological principle, the principle according to the law where the box as a container orders and at the same time is ordered by the content (Derrida 1995). At first glance, the container seems to follow its content, be conditioned, defined, and prescribed by it. It comes second, as a result, and in an orderly, hierarchical way. The principle of materiality appears to condition the nomological, to be distinct and dominant. Content and container are seen through a sequential lens, enforcing the claim of the former to condition the latter. In a common sense, boxes – meaning the container – preserve and protect their content, are used for storage or to transport precious things, and frequently work as simple aesthetic artefacts. What is valuable, then, is the content – that which remains within, precious and privileged. The container, meanwhile, plays a simple functional role existing only for, and because of, its content. Building up a hierarchical sequence, the *content* comes first and the box – the *container* – exists in its favour, for it, because of it.

This perspective strips materiality from its nomological sense, leaves it naked, and allows the physical to pretend that it is not socially ordered. Instead, I argue that the box institutes the nomological principle through which order is given: Pandora's *pyxis* does not exist without its relation to the evils it contains – hope included – and, thus, the contradictions and ambiguities these entail (Fraser 2011). Content and container are inextricably connected to form a material object from which the principle of order and rules of reason are given. Obviously, the *pyxis* is a physical object, which plays a central epistemological role in human lives. It signifies aspects of ancient femininity, questions the hierarchy between gods and humans, and exists only in relation to – *not* subordinate to – its content: the evils, hope, or *psymithio*. More importantly, the *pyxis* works as a metaphor. Thanks to her curiosity, Pandora's box bestows upon mankind not only all evils and troubles but also the gift of knowledge. Releasing the evils into the world marks the end of human innocence, the beginning of knowledge, the pain of defining the human condition. The world is finally balanced. Fire is not the only privileged gift that Prometheus provided to humans. Pandora's box brought into life an array of pains, leaving hope in an ambiguous status having provided knowledge to humans.

At this point it is relevant to mention that the ancient Greek *pyxis* acquired an additional meaning in modern Greek: it denotes the compass, the instrument that allows us to navigate. It is thus knowledge and navigation that mark the passage from the material to the nomological. This does not mean that the physical is absorbed by order, but that both remain in an always negotiable relation. Let me remind you that, historically, objects were the ones that enforced the fabrication of specific boxes. Having the need to pack up easily and move, nomadic tribes used to carry their light holdings in rawhide envelopes, while box-like containers appeared in civilisations that were settled and well-established in firm dwellings. The box embodies this memory of settlement, a condition of civilisation. In a similar manner, the sarcophagus in Ancient Egypt, a box-like stone coffin, followed the shape of the corpse, often a royal mummy, which it was destined to protect. In Ancient China a series of nested boxes, a set of caskets of graduated size that each fitted inside the next largest box, were designed to host and protect Buddha's precious relics, his genuine finger bones, each conditioned by the size of the respective fingers. Moving to the modern period, throughout the eighteenth century the need to protect and transport precious Parisian porcelain led to the construction of elaborate wooden or metal boxes (Rentetzi 2011). Meanwhile, the value of diamonds, rubies, and emeralds was enhanced by storing them in boxes decorated with gold.

But, contrary to the impression one might have, the box is more than a shelter for its content. It is an artefact, an object made by a human being, one of cultural and historical importance that ascribes meaning to, shapes, and is shaped by its content. The box is therefore an object of epistemic interest: it conveys the accumulated knowledge of a historical period and stands as the concrete evidence of medical history (Endo, this volume); it works as source of lost knowledge (Darmstädter, this volume); it becomes a repository of strong arguments in scientific meetings (Mechler, this volume), a performative thinking tool (Schaefer, this volume), a regulatory device constitutive of concepts of public health and safety (Rentetzi, 'Black-boxing Knowledge', this volume). Thus, the box is necessarily the relation between the container and the content. It cannot be understood outside it, without it. The box is at once an object and a relation, a material and a metaphor, a physical entity and a significant association of the nomological principle and that of materiality.

I like to think of some favourable examples. In the early 1900s Pierre Curie carried radium in his pocket, and scientists touched it with their bare hands; meanwhile, radioactive materials arrived from the Bohemian mines to the Vienna Radium Institute in glass bottles sealed merely with corks. Well into the 1920s, containers for radium needles and tubes were made of lead or iron, signifying the beginning of the era of radiation protection. These developments in the ways radium products were historically packaged, transferred, and shipped – the boxes of radium products – reveal changes in assumptions about safety issues connected to the element (Rentetzi 2011).

Moving to the later twentieth century, the container transport system becomes an instantiation of how the material orders the globalised world. According to Alexander Klose, this instantiation signals a change in the fundamental order of thinking and things – a reification into single principle called the container principle (Klose 2009). The cross section of physicality and ordering, the relation of the container to its global standardisation, is linked to an array of other issues: microeconomics, labour provisions, international economic diplomacy, national and international agreements on tariffs, the development of technologies, but also the reestablishment of human settlements. Boxes – containers, in this case – function as primary epistemic objects that define our own way of thinking and practising.

Philosopher Mark Johnson has argued for the important role of the container schema in defining our understanding of 'in' and 'out'. Our experience is structured in a significant way prior to any concepts, and even independent of them

(Johnson 1990). Thus, basic experiential structures are present regardless of any imposition of concepts. The container schema – one that consists of a boundary which distinguishes an interior from an exterior – is a powerful image that structures our daily experiences. As Johnson describes the start of an ordinary day, 'you reach into the medicine cabinet, take out the toothpaste, squeeze out some toothpaste, put the toothpaste into your mouth, brush your teeth, and rinse out your mouth'. Indeed, the container schema is integral to many of the orientational feats that we all perform constantly in our daily lives: as extensions of our selves (Duprez, this volume); containers of fears and anxieties (Fridlund; Rentetzi 'Cardboard Box', both in this volume); even as an understanding of our own bodies as containers (Day, this volume).

Contemporary material scientists take this metaphor one step further, and scale it down (Uchida et al. 2007). Designing synthetic materials, material scientists mimic macromolecular structures and biological processes. At the intersection of biology and material science, what seem to have significant value are container-like protein architectures that allow the introduction of multifunctionality in a single cage. Viruses serve as an illustrative example. Their structural analysis reveals that all viruses are partially constituted by a protein shell architecture comprising a limited number of subunits that contain and protect the viral genome. This structure allows them a great deal of synthetic flexibility, and stands as a model for the controlled assembly of functional architectures in cases of synthetic materials. In short, the container schema stands as a powerful epistemic tool, opening up new experimental practices, and even producing new kinds of materials.

This field guide stands as an instance – more accurately as numerous instances – of how the physical is at the same time nomological, of how mundane things – boxes, in this case – shelter within themselves both order and materiality, thereby producing our knowledge about the world. Last but not least, beyond playing with metaphors, a book is a box. Let us take this collection of articles as a box in itself, as a container and as a thing in containers. Literarily and figuratively, this field guide puts in practice the epistemology of the familiar and, at the same time, it guides surprising openings of forbidden boxes.

REFERENCES

Darmstädter, B., 'Musical Instrument Boxes: Hidden Information – Cases for Musical Instruments and Their Functions', this volume.

Day, D., '"As Modern as Tomorrow"': The Medicine Cabinet', this volume.

Derrida, J., 'Archive Fever: A Freudian Impression', *Diacritics*, 25.2 (Summer, 1995): 9–63.

Duprez, D., 'The Mechanic's Toolbox and Tool Chest: A Nexus of the Personal and the Social', this volume.

Fraser, L. G., 'A Woman of Consequence: Pandora in Hesiod's *Works and Days*', *The Cambridge Classical Journal*, 57 (2011), 9–28.

Fridlund, M., 'Keep Calm and Carry One: The Civilian Gas Mask Case and its Containment of British Emotions', this volume.

Johnson, M., *The Body in the Mind: The Bodily Basis of Meaning, Imagination, and Reason.* (Chicago: University of Chicago Press, 1990).

Klose, A., *The Container Principle: How a Box Changes the Way We Think* (Cambridge, MA: MIT Press, 2016).

Mechler, U., 'Slide Box: How to Stock Some Thousand Cancer Cases', this volume.

Oikonomou, E., 'Gynaikon Technasmata', *National Archeological Museum*, 2015, <http://www.namuseum.gr/object-month/2015/feb/feb15-gr.html> [accessed 9 February 2017].

Rentetzi, M., 'Black-boxing Knowledge: Glass Dosimeters and Governmental Control', this volume.

——, 'Cardboard Box: the Politics of Materiality', this volume.

——, 'Packaging Radium, Selling Science: Boxes, Bottles, and Other Mundane Things in the World of Science', *Annals of Science*, 68,3 (2011): 375–99.

Rutherford Roberts, S., *The Attic Pyxis* (Chicago: Ares Publishers, 1978).

Schäfer, D., 'Deep Time History: The Lure of the Black Box', this volume.

Uchida, M., et al., 'Biological Containers: Protein Cages as Multifunctional Nanoplatforms', *Advanced Materials*, 19 (2007): 1025–42.

FIG. 3.1 Retired overseas containers, reused to house workshops and storage in Kyrgyzstan (photograph by Susanne Bauer, 2018)

3

NAVIGATION TOOLS FOR STUDYING BOXES: A USER'S MANUAL

Susanne Bauer

THIS FIELD GUIDE TO BOX PRACTICES EXPLORES BOXES IN THEIR WIDEST sense and scope – from test tubes and storage containers to cases and chests, from toolboxes to entire buildings, or even digital boxes that are distributed, rather than contained. Boxes do lots of things: they open and close, fold and unfold, hold still or speed up. Boxes work as sorting devices, they categorise and draw boundaries, they shut out, they enclose. They hide, store, silence, or expose, and bring about alignment, separation, filtering, or enhancement. Sometimes boxes are firmly moored and bound to a place, but often they are in motion, and mobilise what they contain. Whether as an ark or a Trojan horse, boxes can be cunning devices: they can harbour stowaways or smuggle things. Boxes can be shipped as cargo, with a destination in mind or just floating around. Unlike free-floating signifiers, they materially hit the road and produce friction (Tsing 2004). Even when they are on the move, boxes encounter responsive and resistant matter; they are active participants in 'worlding' and re-worldings (Haraway 2016, 50).

Boxes and box practices have been key to scientific knowledge production, from cabinets of curiosity in Renaissance Europe and colonial expansions of natural history, to twenty-first-century biobank storage. Today's Euro-American knowledge was formed around objects amassed from colonies and stored in imperial collections. The epistemic infrastructures of such collections continue to enact Eurocentric orderings, for instance by categorising differences into hierarchies of progress and development, divisions and exclusions of others as 'non-civilised'. Their material infrastructures and supply chains, epistemic and economic, are thereby tainted with violence.

If there were a science of boxes today, it would be logistics, a field continually on the rise with capitalism's inescapable logics of the circulation of goods. Indeed, logistics has become world-making (Dommann 2011, Cowen 2014, Klose 2016); its devices include standardised containers, but also box management tools like tracking systems, performance indicators that optimise workflows. Performance indicators have entered nearly all sectors – science and everyday life, corporate worlds, public services and academia. Logistics devices such as databases, checklists, and standards combine with earlier forms of bureaucracy to order and infrastructure social worlds (Star 1999). Indeed, logistics seems the twenty-first-century actualisation of 'the project of a general science of order' described by Foucault (1994) in his user guide to *The Order of Things*.

However, classifications and ordering devices can become 'entrapments', as much a physical as an epistemic snare (Squire 2015, Benson, this volume). Western divisions such as the nature/culture dichotomy are also examples of such entrapments that lock in our thinking (Haraway 1988, Latour 1993). Scientific practices have used boxes to enact analytic divisions, but at the same time, things keep falling between neatly designed categories and between the cracks of existing research infrastructures. Whatever classifications boxes craft to sort and neatly categorise things into discrete groups, another in-between space will pop up at the interstices between groups, and new boxes will claim the space in between. Each box or group of boxes stimulates this infinite process.

Interestingly, the terms 'box' and 'boxing' also have a nautical connotation: to 'box' a compass means to test and to calibrate an orientation device. Sailors have referred to 'boxing' as the rehearsing of the different points and compartments of a compass in a certain order (OED online 2017). The navigation technique used in seafaring consists of a needle, a compass and its grid of compartments, and observation of the stars. It plots one's orientation in the otherwise unstructured surface of the sea and its non-categorised, non-compartmentalised space. Techniques such as boxing the compass transform the 'smooth space' of the sea into a 'striated space' (Deleuze and Guattari 1987: 501), a space that is mapped, structured, and covered by coordinates. While these grids enable navigation, an overcoded space can revert to smooth space again. Boxings and the fixed techniques of orientation are relational as well – they are less stable than commonly assumed, and we need to understand, navigate, and engage in their performativity.

This book offers navigation tools for the study of boxes, modes of boxing, and emboxments (Engstrom, this volume). As a first navigation aid we make reference to – and recalibrate – a particular box that has been prominent in STS: the 'black box' (Latour and Woolgar 1986, MacKenzie 1993, Winner 1993). 'Opening the black box' of scientific knowledge production in STS was originally a constructivist move to render visible hidden assumptions and powerful mechanisms at the core of knowledge production. In studies of cybernetic models and beyond, STS analysed 'black-boxing' as a bracketing practice and exemplar of the naturalising and depoliticising work in the modern sciences. Yet, in Michel Serres's account of the black box, we also find a different cue: Serres (2008: 110) relates the black box to a space of resonance and transmission, shifting our attention to listening instead of seeing and (visual) representation, to thresholds, mixtures, transductions, passageways, and sensations, as well as to the social boxes we inhabit. This redirects attention from the cybernetic black box to the myriad ways boxes populate and animate relational spaces.

Thus, rather than aiming to uncover what is hidden inside black boxes, or identifying and categorising this 'content', this book invites an exploration of relational ontologies infrastructured through box practices. Addressing but also going beyond the box practices of categorising, comparing, abstracting, and deducting, box studies help de-centre standard infrastructures of knowledge-making (Law & Ruppert 2016, Deville et al. 2016). By means of assembling a much broader array of box thinking, this field guide aims to foreground the complex work that material box practices do in infrastructuring things and relations, as well as the enduringly violent orderings and exclusions that boxes may also afford.

Our second navigation tool is the abducted field guide that we use in a performative mode in order to make space for generative critique (Verran 2001). Experimenting with a natural history of boxes through the format of a field guide invites readers to think about boxes and box practices differently. It helps examine tensions between orienting, ordering, and organising, and contrary moments of disruption and multiplication. We do not aim to construct a fixed taxonomy of boxes to identify species with a documented reference specimen, but rather expose the field guide format to recalibrate our thinking about box practices and their infrastructuring work. Hence the book performatively turns the field guide method inside out, exposing the ways it works and fostering perpetual recalibration of our approaches in the study of orderings. In organising these box stories, we have resisted imposing the assumed logic of any single classification, chronological or geographic schema, or predefined genealogy. Instead, playing on Borges' fantastic bestiary (Foucault 1994), we invite readers to delve into a range (but not a totality) of box materialities, which can sensitise us to the resonances and frictions at work in box practices. Our attention to materiality is less about material culture or a grammar of things than about materialisation-in-practice. Thus we are interested in the range of material relations that boxes afford, enact and compel.

Our third navigation tool works with identification keys and their modes of relating and layering. In botanical and zoological field guides, identification keys are used to taxonomise and identify species within their manifold diversity, for example based on their morphology, behaviour, or habitat. Such guides thus function as multi-layered aids to decision. Our field guide to box practices abducts these cross-cutting identification devices. Each box essay begins with an image, a box 'taxonomy', and keywords related to box practices. The identification keys that precede each box chapter work in a bottom-up mode, in that they derive from but exceed the scope of the box essays. As bottom-up taxonomies, the abducted identification keys challenge assumed epistemological classifications: they generate many possible entry points and performatively work towards de-centring taxonomic grids. Instead of a chronological or alphabetical order, we introduced another transversal set of productive identifiers or taxa – trap, juke, time, cargo, black, text, ice, anxiety, count, mirror, tool – to organise this book. We chose a prime number – eleven – for these identifiers, which also resists neat subgrouping. Rather than defining and enclosing groups, these keys open up and generate new connections and resonances. These impossible taxa give rise to more imaginative engagements that help crack open and de-centre academic orderings and their formats (Arens and Schlünder, this volume).

The box essays in this volume include a broad range of boxes: mundane household containers (Cheng), scaled-up bioreactors (Lee), precious early modern knowledge artefacts (Razzall), and basic refugee housing kits (Brownell). They range from toy boxes (Yagou), gas mask boxes as routinised preparedness during the First World War (Fridlund), emboxments of crickets for pleasure (Siebert), and emboxments of detainees (Engstrom). Box arrangements render objects available in an organised way: toolboxes make tools handy (Duprez), medical cabinets confine the private (Day), and the librarian's media box configures her heuristics (Mak and Pollack).

Systems of knowledge in particular are replete with box practices, including the 'boxing of ideas' (Parker 2013). But they also literally rest on the circulation, boxing, and categorising of things, and their mobilisation as objects in natural history (Hammel, Nadim), modern life sciences (Grote, Mechler, Schlünder), and population counts (von Oertzen, Bauer). Boxes assemble things and enact orderings into container and contained – in transportation but also measurement processes (Rentetzi). Putting layers of boxes and packages around content contributes to creating its value (Darmstädter, Olsén). Some boxes are just abandoned remainders, mere packaging of contents that are discarded as waste (Blacker), or else reused and inhabited by others who are confronted with austerity regimes (Rentetzi). Boxes are present when we store, categorise, and transport things such as tools, specimens, office materials, or files on the screen. They make up the scaffolding of our understanding and thinking in medicine – even the brain is a body box (Kısmet Bell). Moreover, digital tools and storage are, as much as material archives, also replete with box practices (Chen).

Boxes can teleport, release, or spill the things they carry. Boxes come attached to influential imaginaries like the *Wunderkammer*, the ark, or the *ur*-box (Güttler et al.). Boxing biological material and artefacts, as in colonial science, raises issues of ownership and restitution (Allen). Archive boxes, treasure chests, and miniature cabinets work as framing devices that render things into knowledge objects and, by carefully enclosing them, enact them as objects of epistemic value (Bowry, Schäfer). Entire institutions are set up to present fragments of the past (Endo, Razzal, Palioura et al.). The museum itself is a box and a time machine, with intersecting, folded temporalities and unintended teleportation – like cigarette boxes used to store archaeological finds (Galiniki and Akrivopoulou). While logistics, map-making, and orientation devices are entangled in a history of colonialism, with their imposition of boundaries between Occident and Orient, Global North and Global South, here, close attention to box practices and their transductions invites more daringly speculative modes of box studies. Following the aid boxes (Widmer) and attending to practices of enveloping (Gonçalves) can help us de-centre fixed, hegemonic orderings and make space for the multiplicity of box practices.

This field guide to box practices is a call for further box studies. As enquiry into taxonomies, this book is not about taming boxes somehow located 'in the wild', by means of an inventory. Rather it invites us to stay with the tensions between identification keys and the world. The field guide exposes techniques of ordering and identifying to testing and calibration – its website invites perpetual boxing as a means of understanding, speculating, and intervening in the orderings that go with box practices. To this end, a compass – and reference maps as we know them – won't do. Or, to say the least, they are in urgent need of recalibration.

REFERENCES

Cowen, D., *The Deadly Life of Logistics: Mapping Violence in Global Trade* (Minneapolis: University of Minnesota Press, 2014).

Dommann, M., 'Handling, Flowcharts, Logistik: Zur Wissensgeschichte und Materialkultur von Warenflüssen', in P. Sarasin and A. Kilcher, eds, *Zirkulationen*. Zurich: diaphanes 2011, pp. 75–103.

Deleuze, G., and F. Guattari, *A Thousand Plateaus* (Minneapolis: University of Minnesota Press, 1987).

Deville, J., M. Guggenheim, and Z. Hrdličková, *Practising Comparison: Logics, Relations, Collaborations* (Manchester: Mattering Press, 2016).

Foucault, M., *The Order of Things: An Archaeology of the Human Sciences* (New York: Vintage Books, 1994; English translation of *Les Mots et les Choses*).

Haraway, D., 'Situated Knowledges: The Science Question in Feminism and the Privilege of Partial Perspective', *Feminist Studies*, 14.3 (1988): 575–99.

——, *Staying with the Trouble: Making Kin in the Chthulucene* (Durham: Duke University Press, 2016).

Klose, A., *The Container Principle: How a Box Changes the Way We Think* (Cambridge MA: MIT Press, 2016).

Latour, B., and S. Woolgar, *Laboratory Life: The Construction of Scientific Facts* (Princeton NJ: Princeton University, 1986).

Law, J., and E. Ruppert, *Modes of Knowing: Resources from the Baroque* (Manchester: Mattering Press, 2016).

OED online, 'box, v.4', Oxford University Press, 2017, <https://en.oxforddictionaries. com/definition/box> [accessed 6 March 2017].

MacKenzie, D., *Inventing Accuracy: A Historical Sociology of Nuclear Missile Guidance* (Cambridge, MA: The MIT Press 1999).

Parker, M., 'Containerization: Moving Things and Boxing Ideas', *Mobilities*, 8.3 (2013): 368–87.

Serres, M., *The Five Senses: A Philosophy of Mingled Bodies* (London: Bloomsbury, 2008).

Squire, R., 'Immobilising and Containing: Entrapment in the Container Economy', in T. Birtchnell, S. Savitzky, and J. Urry, eds, *Cargomobilities: Moving Materials in a Global Age* (New York: Routledge, 2015), pp. 106–24.

Star, S. L., 'Ethnography of Infrastructure', *American Behavioral Scientist*, 43.3 (1999): 377–91.

Tsing, A. L., *Frictions. Anthropology of Global Connection* (Princeton, NJ: Princeton University Press, 2004).

Verran, H., *Science and an African Logic* (Chicago: Chicago University Press, 2001).

Winner, L., 'Upon Opening the Black Box and Finding it Empty: Social Constructivism and the Philosophy of Technology', *Science, Technology, & Human Values*, 18.3 (1993): 362–78.

I

TRAP

FIG. 4.1 Berengario da Carpi, *Tractatus de fractura calve sive cranei a Carpo editus* (1518) (source: Wellcome Library, London)

4

INSCRIBING THE SOUL: CEREBRAL VENTRICLES AS SYMBOLIC AND MATERIAL BOXES

Jameson Kısmet Bell

Terminology: cerebral ventricles, cerebral cellulae, and containers or chambers of the soul. **Location**: centre of the brain. **Material**: cluster of four interconnected cavities surrounded by brain matter. **Function**: from the fourteenth to sixteenth centuries, believed to contain human rational faculties of common sense, imagination, reason, and memory; uncertain function between the sixteenth and eighteenth centuries; after eighteenth century, demonstrated to be responsible for the production and circulation of cerebral-spinal fluid. **Morphology**: continuous spherical containers until the sixteenth century. Dissection demonstrated each ventricle to follow the contours of the brain and brain stem. Two lateral ventricles are symmetrically 'C' or 'new moon' shaped; middle ventricle connects lateral ventricles to the fourth ventricle and each shape varies with cerebral development. **Volume**: adaptable capacity for imagination, reason, and memory; approximately 25–35 ml of fluid. **Access**: imagined through contemplation; visible through cerebral dissection; visible through medical imaging techniques. **Record**: recorded in speech, writing, gestures of dissection, and medical imaging techniques.

Keywords: containing, diagnosing, dissecting, imagining, injuring, inscribing, meditating, remembering, treating, visualising

DREAM OF CONTINUITY

THIS ESSAY WILL GUIDE THE READER THROUGH THE DEFINITION, TREATMENT, performance, and access to a particular set of medieval and renaissance boxes that were located in the centre of the brain, namely, the cerebral ventricles, or cells. A *ventricle* was an anatomical space or cavity whose purpose was to contain. The stomach, heart, bowels, bladder, chest, and uterus were all defined as ventricles or 'little bellies', where ventricle was the diminutive of the Latin *venter* or belly. A second term was also commonly applied to these important mental spaces, namely *cellula*, the diminutive of *cella*, or 'small store-room, chamber or cabinet' (Whitaker 2007: 48). Until the mid-sixteenth century, three cavities in the brain were thought to contain the faculties of the soul: imagination, reason, and memory (Green 2003: 131). These anatomical spaces were defined by their metonymic quality of 'continuity' and 'containment', becoming secure little boxes for the soul. In the sixteenth century, however, through a shift in the medium of communication—namely from oral signifiers to graphic and typographic signifiers—the power of the body to be 'continuous' and 'contained' was ruptured by two related inscription practices. Cutting the body and inscribing the results on paper effectively transferred the soul from inside the head to the surface of the printed page.

In this theory that located the soul in the cerebral ventricles, not only were these cavities passive containers that enclosed the faculties of imagination, reason, and memory, but they also actively transferred animal spirits between them, allowing for proper mental functioning (Kemp 1990: 53–71). The galenic concept of animal spirits, or *pneuma*, united anatomy, physiology, and psychology so that blood could be rarefied into its subtlest part. These animal spirits, in turn, could be consciously controlled as they passed between ventricles. An example of proper and improper use of these containers can be seen in the following sixteenth-century treatment of a head wound, as well as a doctor's method of diagnosis. In the year 1518, the Duke of Urbino, Lorenzo de' Medici, fell off his horse and injured his head in a riding accident. Shortly thereafter, Berengario da Carpi, professor of anatomy and surgery at the University of Bologna, was called to his aid. Da Carpi treated the Duke of Urbino for a break in 'continuity' of the skull, which he diagnosed as a fractured occipital bone.

The treatment relied upon a surgical classification that sought to determine the 'genus' of the injury in order to recognise the specific patient's 'species'. Da Carpi wrote that a surgeon must initially recognise if a patient's symptoms could be classified as either 1) an internal break related to mental functioning in the cerebral ventricles, or 2) an external break, which was isolated to the skull. Diagnosis required expert training in recognising symptoms such as a perceptible break in the skull, a patient's reported vision impairment, vertigo, fever, vomiting, or disordered speech (da Carpi 1518: 1–7). The signs could then be compared with a patient's complexion (hot, cold, wet, or dry), temperament (sanguine, choleric, phlegmatic, or melancholy), dominant element (earth, air, fire, or water), and season of injury (winter, spring, summer, or autumn). Once de' Medici's injury was properly diagnosed as an external break where the membranes, brain, and ventricles remained undamaged, prognostication (treatment) should follow the standard medieval surgical method of removing bone fragments or relieving pressure with surgical instruments (trepanation), applying plasters, and finally offering the patient potions in the correct proportion to his or her complexion, temperament, elements, and season. Following Plato's *Timeaus*, which emphasised the spherical shape of the skull as the most protected and immortal part of the human body, a continuous skull contained the brain, which in turn contained the soul. A discontinuous skull could not enclose the soul efficiently, allowing for the soul to potentially leak out of any open wounds (Kısmet Bell 2018: 59–60). Remarkably, the Duke of Urbino recovered from this risky procedure, and within two months Professor da Carpi published the first book on treating cranial fractures, *Tractatus de Fractura Calve Sive Cranei a Carpo Editus* (On Fracture of the Skull or Cranium). Initially hesitant to publish his treatment methods, da Carpi recounts a dream that convinced him of the necessity of sharing a detailed account of diagnosing and treating head injuries:

> There appeared to me in my dream a certain person whose hat was topped by a rooster's crest, decked out with winged sandals of gold and bearing a golden wand in his hand around which a serpent was coiled. He was quite recognizable to me in that form as Mercury. I know that a rooster, his crest, winged sandals, a golden wand, and a serpent are the attributes of a physician,

for antiquity regards a man of such form to be a consummate physician (da Carpi 1518: 15).

From the dream vision's accessories—a hat with a rooster's crest, winged sandals, and a caduceus of gold—da Carpi recognised Mercury, one of the deities of medicine, who then instructed the doctor to write a book on head injuries 'for the good of mankind' (da Carpi 1518: 15). After this blessing from his medical muse, da Carpi wrote his text that provides the reader with a definition of the anatomy of the head and its potential injuries, the information being drawn from both personal witness and ancient authority. The treatise first establishes a method for recognising the diverse symptoms of various wounds, and then moves on to the difficult challenge of prescribing treatment.

The title page of *On Fracture of the Skull or Cranium* includes an image of the lateral view of a man's head on which three circles are superimposed (see **FIGURE 4.1**). These circles represent the containers in which the inner senses of a human's intellectual soul reside, knowledge of which was considered essential for proper treatment of head injuries. Reading the image from left to right, the first circle symbolises the location of the organs of *common sense* and *imagination* (phantasy) in the front of the head, while *judgment* and *reason* reside in the centre circle, and *reminiscence* and *memory* in the posterior circle in the back of the head. The circular lines themselves demarcate the border between body and soul, and the continuity of each faculty. They signify the resemblance of a circle to the shape of the head, which also appears as the ideal form of the sphere.

Not only da Carpi, but doctors and surgeons across Europe utilised the metaphors of 'continuity' and 'container' to diagnose illnesses of the intellectual soul, treat head injuries, and prescribe natural and artificial treatments to enhance normal intellectual performance. Pain or injury to the front of the head signified an injury to the first ventricle, in which resided common sense or imagination. Such injuries tended to be associated with the patient seeing strange images or combinations of image fragments. Damage to the central ventricle was thought to cause aphasia, or an inability for the rational faculty to judge or understand the meaning of sensible impressions. These were diagnosed by incoherent speech. Injury to the rear of the head and the posterior ventricle caused memory loss. This theory that located the inner senses in the ventricles

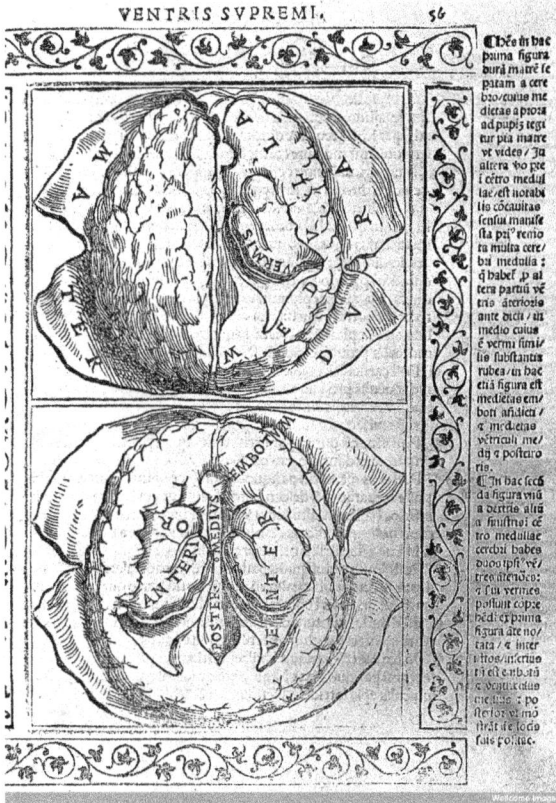

FIG. 4.2 Berengario da Carpi, *Isagoge breves* (1523) (source: Wellcome Library, London)

of the brain dominated epistemological discussion for much of the medieval period, from the fourth to the sixteenth century.

However, as we will soon see, this theory was challenged when sixteenth-century anatomists began to dissect the body through post-mortem division of the body's parts; the body they inscribed in text and image no longer possessed a neat line demarcating an inside and outside. As professor of surgery at the University of Bologna, da Carpi would have been present at annual mandatory public anatomies (dissections), though many more than those on official record were probably preformed. An altered relationship between continuity, containment, dissection, and inscription arose from this change in knowledge presentation, which in turn emptied the ventricles of their container capacity.

Yet da Carpi's first book *On Fracture of the Skull or Cranium* presented a body that was both continuous and discontinuous, the reason for which can be partially explained by the very performance of the inner senses. This proper performance of the inner senses returns us to his dream.

Aside from its conformity to the rhetorical convention of presenting a medical book as blessed by the god of medicine—the dream da Carpi recounted was included in the dedication to the very same Lorenzo de' Medici, in hopes of future patronage—, da Carpi's dream can also be interpreted through this theory of the inner senses that were located in a specific space in the head. The dream of Mercury appeared initially as fragmented images from da Carpi's faculty of memory: human form, golden colour, a rooster's crest, winged sandals, and the caduceus. Once visualised in the chambers of the soul, the allegorical fragments were judged and assembled into a coherent whole by his rational faculty—it is worthwhile to note that da Carpi translates the visible qualities of the hat and staff into intellectual judgment of 'the form to be a consummate physician'—in order to arrive at knowledge or recognition of the allegorical figure.

After their initial acquaintance, Mercury continues the dialogue with the following words of encouragement to the author to publish his findings: 'Begin then and first meditate alone in silence and hide your meditations in the chambers of your memory. Examine your purpose from all sides thoroughly. Then proceed slowly to take up your pen without resort to authority or witness' (da Carpi 1518: 1–2). What we see in both the title page image and da Carpi's retelling of his dream is a shift in the form of knowledge of the human body, head, and brain. The dream vision and printed image of the inner senses (see **FIGURE 4.1**) give specific examples of the brain as a container in which words and images are stored, assembled, and judged. Paradoxically, however, we also see the dream vision's instruction to 'take up your pen without resort to authority or witness'. This form of externalisation of knowledge – taking up the pen and inscribing one's thoughts on paper – brought with it extreme epistemological consequences, both for the usefulness of the description of the head and brain as a container and also for a doctor's reliance on knowledge gained from past masters of anatomy.

By writing and subsequently printing his text, da Carpi's focus shifted from his teachers at the University of Bologna – most notably Alessandro Achillini

(1463–1512) and Gabriele Zerbi (1445–1505) – to himself. Da Carpi had a strained relationship with these two professors of medicine and philosophy, who as key members of what is historically called the 'Pre-Vesalian Period' in the history of surgery and anatomy, often criticised each other's treatments in competition for patrons, patients, and students (De Santo 1999: 205–08). Da Carpi combined anatomical and surgical knowledge from the medieval masters of anatomy, in particular the fourteenth-century Italian Mondino de' Luzzi's *Anathomia,* a text that had been canonical for university education in surgical knowledge since it was first written. Mondino compiled treatments from the eleventh-century Persian philosopher Ibn Sina (Avicenna), and even the ancients Galen of Pergamum, Hippocrates, Aristotle, and Plato. By utilising the newly discovered technology of print, as well as his own anatomical observations, da Carpi moved his knowledge outside the containers of his brain and onto the printed page. The continuity of these containers had been broken, not in the material sense of a head injury, but in a formal sense in that they no longer contained knowledge that was visible outside the body.

CONTAINING THE SOUL

The system of thought that defined the brain and body as containers had survived a long history by the time it reached da Carpi. Not only did it guide the framework in which the soul was discussed in da Carpi's surgical text, but it was also popular in philosophical and theological writings as well. By analysing the metaphors of continuity and containment, one sees that as the usefulness of these descriptions abated, the very contours of the soul and body changed.

The theory that the soul is divided into parts and resides in three ventricles in the head first appeared in the fourth century CE as a mixture of Aristotle's definition of the human intellectual faculties taken from *de Anima,* Neo-Platonism's emphasis on a hierarchical ontology found in Plato's *Timaeus* – which located the intellectual soul in the head because it was the most perfect, sphere-like organ – and Galen of Pergamum's humoral and pneumatic physiology (Bell 2009: 1–9). This mixture of natural philosophy and anatomy provided a plausible anatomical structure to show where and how the mind functioned. The theory of the inner senses remained incomplete until the fourth century when Syrian bishop Nemesius wrote a passage that unified anatomy, physiology, and natural philosophy (see below). Once one has sensed an object with the five external senses (sight, sound, touch, taste, and smell), common sense or phantasy then assembles that object into an image in the first cell or ventricle. Thereafter, sense data is passed from container to container in an increasingly rarefied form:

> The faculty of imagination hands on things imagined to the faculty of thought, while thought or reasoning, when it has received and judged them, passes them on to the faculty of memory. The organ of memory too, is in the posterior cell of the brain (Nemesius 2008: 1).

In addition to the tactile metaphor of 'passing', many additional medical and everyday comparisons described how the inner senses functioned within their little cells. In his recent book, *Metaphors of Memory*, Douwe Draaisma offers a wonderful walk through the history of the metaphors of memory, and explains several useful descriptions of the mind's activities such as 'knife and whetting stone', 'wax seal' and 'digestion'. Each of these ancient and medieval metaphors offered a vague but useful explanation of how the mind engages the world through sense data (Draaisma 2000: 22–44). As a knife, the active soul sharpened itself by carving away the nonessential sense data from common sense and imagination to arrive at the truth in the rational and memory faculties. As a wax seal, the mind passively received sensible data from the external world that pressed itself into the soul. As digestion, the mind concocted the sensible data, cooking away the waste in the 'little bellies' as it utilised only the most important information gained from sight, sound, touch, taste, and smell.

The function of the head as 'container' is common to all these metaphors of the mind. The inner senses contained the substance of the soul, and whether the mind was active or passive, the ethereal substance was cut, pressed upon, or digested within these containers (Olshewesky 1976: 391–94). The head, like the body, functioned as a series of containers in which one could imagine the contents of the soul becoming increasingly refined. As mentioned in the introduction to this paper, the womb, bowels, bladder, stomach, chest, and head were all understood as containers, and diverse properties could be analogically transferred between anatomical regions. Just as the stomach 'concocted' its contents (food) through digestion, the brain also 'concocted' its contents through thought in its 'little bellies'. The remaining, unused elements of digestion were expelled from the stomach through the bowels while, analogically, the brain 'expelled' its foul contents from the mouth through inappropriate language, or through the nose and ears as fluids. The physiology of another container, the womb, was also metaphorically transferred to the head and the intellectual soul. Like a child who develops in the womb, thought was also 'conceived' in the head, developed until it was mature, and 'birthed' into the world through speech, writing, or the arts. Da Carpi's dream, which commands him to 'first meditate alone in silence and hide your meditations in the cloisters of your memory', was a directive to not give birth prematurely. Such a mishap could possibly result in a disfigured text or disordered speech, these being signs of a potential break in his mental faculties.

The combination of these psychological, anatomical, and physiological descriptions provided a very detailed as well as complex set of concepts by which to understand both the mind and the body. Imagining the brain as a container also allowed one to imagine various sizes of containers, the most important of which were large architectural structures, or memory theatres. Commonplace mnemonic images were stored within these contained spaces, allowing an individual to walk around within imagined buildings in search of stored memories. Francis Yates's *The Art of Memory* traces the history of the diverse mnemonic techniques as they appeared in sixteenth- and seventeenth-century writings on rhetoric, logic, and natural philosophy. One was either born with a naturally good memory, or one could use artificial commonplaces to improve one's memory (2000: 1–5). Da Carpi's dream of Mercury was one such commonplace. Allegorical images such as the rooster's crest, winged sandals, and the caduceus allowed da Carpi to remember and judge these images to be the god of medicine as well as to utilise their rhetorical force to persuade a patron.

In this memory culture, that which one was to remember – a manuscript, an oration, or even a medical technique for treating head wounds – was committed to memory with exacting precision. Yates argues that, from the ancient world to the Renaissance, the art of memory was like a form of 'inner writing' (2000: 6). If one wanted to remember more than one topic, one imagined interconnected spaces in which one inscribed and stored the treasures of memory. An imaginative walk through these chambers, the discovery of commonplace images that stood for items, and the order in which these items were to be remembered, allowed one to recall texts, speeches, and techniques in their entirety.

The shift in the form of knowledge – from allegorical words and images stored in the chambers of memory to visual images and text inscribed on the printed page – transformed the containers of the soul into benign ventricles of the brain. It should be acknowledged here that 'inscription' is borrowed from Latour's sociological theory of 'science in action' in which modern scientists live by a strange form of 'mania of inscription' and the proliferation of 'files, documents, and dictionaries' (1986: 48). Alongside the visible image, the written and printed word also became 'inscription devices', transforming pieces of matter into documents (1986: 51). Unlike modern inscriptions that are written to be seen, renaissance textual inscriptions were written to be heard, spoken, and visualised in one's imagination, reason, or memory faculties that were contained in the ventricles of the brain.

DISSECTING AND INSCRIBING: OPEN ACCESS TO THE SOUL

Five years after da Carpi published his *On Fracture of the Skull or Cranium*, he published *Isagoge Breves* (*Brief Introduction to Anatomy*, 1523), a summary of anatomical knowledge based on Mondino's fourteenth-century anatomy text, *Anathomia corporis humani*. The *Isagoge Breves* was itself a compendium to a larger text da Carpi had written as a commentary to Mondino in the first decade of the sixteenth century and reprinted in 1522. In the *Isagoge*, da Carpi includes a series of anatomical images, thereby shifting knowledge from inside the containers of the brain to the visible markings on the printed page. Though still based on the authority of Mondino's *Anathomia*, it departs from this text in several key ways. One of the anatomical images can be seen as the first visibly accurate representation of the cerebral ventricles – the anatomical structures in which the inner senses were thought to be located (see **FIGURE 4.2**). Compared with the symbolic image of the three circular containers of the soul (see **FIGURE 4.1**), this naturalistic representation demonstrates a problem many sixteenth-century anatomists encountered when treating both mental and physical ailments: what happens to knowledge when it is inscribed outside the body?

FIG. 4.3 Joannes de Ketham *Fasciculus medicine* (1495) (source: Wellcome Library, London)

One answer to this question can be found in da Carpi's initial fear of publishing his text, a fear that was rooted in a loss of authority. Inscribing information outside the body reduces the control one has over it. If he shared his knowledge, it would no longer be his own personal possession, stored and guarded in his memory, only to be accessed when and if he deemed necessary. University and municipality authorities took strict measures to define who, when, and where medical knowledge could be accessed and shared, which in turn sanctioned a social hierarchy of licensed and unlicensed doctors and surgeons (Siraisi 1990: 16–24).

After one has taken a pen and inscribed knowledge in words and images, to be infinitely multiplied by the newly invented printing press, the signs are now stored in the pages of a book, equally accessible by anyone. The oral tradition, by which guild knowledge was passed from master to apprentice, guarded in storehouses of the elect's memory, slowly came to an end. The manuscript culture, by which a single hand-written text was guarded by the masters of a guild and stored in the learned gestures of the doctor or surgeon's body, was no more. Information that can be mechanically inscribed by the printing press revealed a new form of 'open access' knowledge.

'Open access' has another meaning too: through the practice of dissecting and opening bodies for the sake of knowledge, the once continuous body with its series of containers is now open. The inside of the box is revealed to the world. In Italy in the fifteenth century and in Northern Europe in the early sixteenth century, university student attendance during annual public dissections was required, though students often procured more bodies, creating an illegal black market for cadavers and clandestine dissections. What is written about the anatomy of these bodies, however, like the allegories of the inner senses, seems quite strange to modern readers. The goal of the annual dissections, rituals rigorously controlled by the university and city authorities, was not so much knowledge of the body but an assurance that the dissected body matched the words of the ancient masters. Anatomy in the early sixteenth century – cutting the body into its parts for the sake of knowledge – was less a discovery of new features than a proof of the manuscript's veracity, which in turn demonstrated the power of the ancient master's speech.

The traditional form of these early public dissections was a comparison of the visible structures of the dissected body with the spoken word of the anatomist who read from Mondino's *Anathomia* (Carlino 1999: 1–20). Joannes de Ketham's *Fasciculus medicine* (1495) offers a view into a public dissection scene (see **FIGURE 4.3**). At the top of this figure, an academically trained doctor reads from Mondino's *Anathomia*. In the foreground, a barber surgeon cuts the body based on the authority of the spoken text. Students to the left and right of the body listen to the text while glancing at the broken contours of the body.

The body visualised in imagination and compared with allegorical images of the body in memory held more epistemological weight than the visible body itself. In cases of discrepancy, the manuscript prevailed. Da Carpi and his teacher, Gabriele Zerbi, had heated debates – debates that would rage throughout the sixteenth and seventeenth centuries as humanist and classicist authors questioned medieval manuscripts and thus, vicariously, ancient knowledge – about the structure of the brain and its functioning, most notably about an imaginary cerebral organ called the *rete mirabile* ('wonderful' or 'miracle' net).

Here, the form of da Carpi's epistemic practices is also important, a form that allowed him to disprove the existence of the *rete mirabile*. The *rete mirabile* was supposed to be an anatomical structure at the base of the cerebral ventricles of ungulates; it was transferred to human anatomy by Galen of Pergamum. It was thought to bridge body and soul by converting body humours into *animal spirits*, or the elusive substance of the soul. These animal spirits were the contents of the inner senses, or that which moved back and forth between the ventricles, allowing both body and soul to remain continuous and contained. A brief look to the future shows that these animal spirits would become the key intermediary component of Rene Descartes' (1596–1650) seventeenth-century idealist natural philosophy that divided mind and the body and yet retained their continuity. The animal spirits, which Descartes described in his *L'Homme* (*Treatise on Man*, 1662) as 'a very fine wind, or rather a very lively and pure flame', provided the substance by which the body interacted with the intellectual soul (Vol. XI: 129).

Da Carpi, however, had not yet made a formal leap to a materialist philosophy where a mind could exist as logically separate from the body. His focus was on an imaginary organ, the *rete mirabile*. After apparently participating in more than one hundred dissections without once observing this *rete mirabile*, da Carpi claimed in his *Isagoge Breves* that Zerbi and his ancient authorities were wrong and the *rete mirabile* must not exist (da Carpi 1523: xv). Rather than move from the external sense of sight to the internal narrative of Mondino's *Anathomia*, visualising the body in imagination and reason, and finally remembering an allegorical organ situated in memory, da Carpi's new grammar of knowledge moved between text and dissected body, and concluded that the evidence of the body possessed greater authority. As with the rhetorical emphasis of his dream, da Carpi's hyperbolic claim to have attended 'more than one hundred dissections' should not detract from the shift in form. The same modification in form that caused an imaginary organ to disappear, allowed a visible organ, the ventricles of the brain, to materialise before his eyes.

The shift from the brain as a series of containers for the soul to a functioning organ with its own sets of rules was not a quick or sudden one. Nor was the shift in knowledge from the inner senses to knowledge that was external, stored in the printed book, a quick transition. It would not be until the eighteenth century that the relationship between the ventricles and the production and circulation of cerebrospinal fluid would be hypothesised. From Italy to England, Germany, France, and Spain, these dual images of symbolic circles (see **FIGURE 4.1**) and detailed anatomical representations of the head and brain (see **FIGURE 4.2**) appeared side by side throughout the sixteenth and early seventeenth centuries. However, the difference between intellectual knowledge accessed and represented as symbols and commonplaces that guided the thinker through the labyrinths of memory, on the one hand, and sensible knowledge inscribed on the printed page, on the other, is a useful marker to delineate the temporal difference from the Middle Ages to the Renaissance. This difference marks a formal change in knowledge, and one index of this change is that da Carpi produced two very different images of the ventricles of the brain.

In **FIGURE 4.1**, da Carpi presents the brain symbolically. The minimal sensible data – three circles – function as a memory device for the doctor or surgeon to remember the anatomy of the head that he had memorised from Mondino. Like the dream of Mercury and the symbol of the caduceus, these circles function as mnemonic tools to meditate on the purpose of the body stored in the chambers of memory. The lack of naturalistic detail in the image forces the viewer back into the chambers of the soul, repeating the axioms and aphorisms memorised from the manuscripts of Mondino, Hippocrates, Avicenna, and others. The symbolic image provides a means for meditation on the contents of a doctor's memory gained through years of training and practice, without which a misdiagnosis could occur.

The second image, however, reaching a broader audience by way of a series of transfers – from dissection to sight, from sight to pen, from pen to paper, from paper to woodblock, and finally from woodblock to the printing press – circumvents the meditative movement of the inner senses. Knowledge is no longer introspective, based on a comparison of what is seen with images stored in the containers of the soul. In its place, knowledge is externalised, and the dissected body is now compared with increasingly naturalistic images and commentary stored on the printed page. This change in the form of knowledge brought with it a change in the form of the brain, head, and body, effectively emptying the containers of their contents and spreading one's soul onto the printed page.

Yet the containers were not completely empty. Dissection rituals based on Mondino's *Anathomia* emphasised the intellectual form of the body rather than its visible structure. The body that cut – the dissector with the knife – followed the traditional form of knowledge even as the product of that knowledge was changing. In his commentary on Mondino, da Carpi describes the methodological movements of sawing through the cranium, cutting the external cerebral membranes, the brain matter, and finally arriving at these containers of the soul:

> Then cut lightly through the middle until you reach the greater anterior [lateral] ventricle. Before you reach the depth of the lacuna [infundibulum] note that the ventricle is divided into right and left...Phantasy, which retains the appearance of the particular senses, is located in the anterior angle. Imagination, which apprehends those appearances received by phantasy, is in the posterior angle; it apprehends them by composing and dividing, not by perceiving that this thing is this (da Carpi 1521: 157).

In this passage, da Capri describes the two lateral ventricles, which are the foremost in the theory of the inner senses and often described as one chamber. The role of a cerebral dissection, even when compared with a cadaver and a detailed anatomical image (see **FIGURE 4.2**), was to demonstrate the ideal form of the head as a container for the soul. The image of these ventricles, as well as the gestures of dissection, was still based on the assumption that the head is a container for the soul. After this passage, da Carpi's commentary on Mondino continues to describe the visible structure of ventricles as well as the *vermis* (little worm) by which the animal spirits pass between the ventricles. Knowledge of this physiological process allowed the doctor to differentiate illnesses of the inner senses caused by blockages of the passageways, which could be caused by an imbalance of humours or a fracture of the skull.

Altering a form of knowledge is an *awkward* practice, in the sixteenth-century sense of the term where 'awk' means to turn 'back or behind'. Problems of assimilating new techniques into established procedures create not a linear movement forward, but backward glances, stops and turns. For da Carpi and other sixteenth-century doctors who followed this labyrinthine epistemic path as it twisted inside and outside the body, the contours of the soul were inconclusive. Internally, the soul was adaptable to imagined spaces of the chambers of memory, both continuous and contained. Externally, however, the soul was limited not by the small narrow passages called the cerebral ventricles, but by the details of the body inscribed with a knife, pen, and paper. As the form of knowledge shifted from memory and speech to vision and inscription, the contours of the body memorised in allegorical images adapted to the contours of the body recorded in ink on paper. Likewise, the soul transferred from boxes of imagined spaces to a series of visible traces.

REFERENCES

Bell, J., 'The Brain as Material and/or Idea? Metaphor and Representation in Early Modern Cell Doctrine', *Historia Medicinae*, 1 (2009): 1–9.

Carlino, A., *Books on the Body: Anatomical Ritual and Renaissance Learning*, trans. by Anne C. Tadeschi (Chicago: University of Chicago, 1999).

da Carpi, J. B., *On Fracture of the Skull or Cranium* (1518), trans. by L. R. Lind (Philadelphia: The American Philosophical Society, 1990).

——, 'Berengario da Carpi (1470–1530). Commentary on Mundinus (1521)', in *Studies in Pre-Vesalian Anatomy. Biography, Translations, Documents*, trans. by L. R. Lind (Philadelphia: The American Philosophical Society, vol. 104), pp. 157–65.

——, *A short introduction to anatomy (Isagogae Breves)* (1523), trans. by L. R. Lind (Chicago: University of Chicago Press, 1959).

De Santo, N. G. et al., 'Berengario da Capri', *American Journal of Nephrology*, 19 (1999): 199–212.

Descartes, R., *Oeuvres de Descartes*, 13 vols., ed. by Charles Adam and Paul Tannery (Paris: Vrin/CNRS, 1964–1974).

Draaisma, D., *Metaphors of Memory: a History of Ideas about the Mind*, trans. by Paul Vincent (Cambridge: Cambridge University Press, 2000).

Green, C., 'Where did the Ventricular Localization of Mental Faculties Come From?', *Journal of History of the Behavioral Sciences* 39 (2003): 131–42.

Kemp, S., *Medieval Psychology* (New York: Greenwood, 1990).

Kısmet Bell, J., *Performing the Sixteenth-Century Brain: Beyond Word and Image Inscriptions* (Berlin: LIT Verlag, 2018).

Latour, B., and S. Woolgar, *Laboratory Life: The Construction of Scientific Facts* (New Haven: Princeton, 1986).

Nemesius, *On the Nature of Man*, trans. by Robert Sharples and Philip Van Der Eijk (Liverpool: Liverpool University Press, 2008).

Olshewesky, T., 'On the Relations of the Soul and Body in Plato and Aristotle', *Journal of the History of Philosophy* 14 (1976): 391–404.

Simpson, J. A., and E. S. C. Weiner, eds., *The Oxford English Dictionary*, 2nd ed. (Oxford: Clarendon Press, 1989).

Siraisi, N., *Medieval and Early Renaissance Medicine: An Introduction to Knowledge and Practice* (Chicago: University of Chicago Press, 1990).

Whitaker, H., 'Was Medieval Cell Doctrine More Modern Than We Thought?', in Henri Cohen and Brigitte Stemmer, eds, *Consciousness and Cognition: Fragments of Mind and Brain* (Amsterdam: Elsevier, 2007), pp. 45–51.

Yates, F., *The Art of Memory* (Chicago: University of Chicago Press, 2000).

FIG. 5.1 'Better Shelter' refugee housing unit, shown constructed alongside the flat pack boxes in which it is shipped (source: courtesy of Better Shelter, www. bettershelter.org)

5

BETTER SHELTER

Emily Brownell

Dimensions: 5.14 m × 3.15 m × 2.74 m, Area: 17.5 m², **Height**: 3.14 m.
Packing Weight: 98 kg. **Packing Volume**: 1.5 m³. **Materials**: constructed out
of 71 metal pipes and 36 plastic panels. Also includes solar panel and shade net.
Assembly: to assemble a 'Better Shelter' unit you will need between 4 and 8
hours. And it requires four people to lift the two boxes into place for assembly.
Assemble following manual. **Origin**: originated under the guidance of the
'social enterprise' company called Better Shelter, owned by the Housing for All
Foundation, established by the Ikea Foundation. **Behaviour**: once constructed,
serves as a shelter for displaced people for up to three years. Recommended for
five people or fewer. **Habitat**: most likely to be found in areas after a natural or
manmade disaster where refugees are living until they can be moved elsewhere.
Also found on display in exhibits for temporary shelter and modular design,
such as Design Miami/Basel. **Distribution**: scope of distribution yet unknown.
Some can be seen in Greece and Macedonia or at the Falkenbergs Museum
in Sweden. The United Nations High Commission for Refugees has ordered
10,000 as of May 2015. **Migration**: not yet clear what the migratory patterns
of these boxes will be. Depends on the durability of units and opportunities
for reuse. **Cost**: one shelter, plus shipping, assembly and preparation of site,
costs US$1755.

Keywords: sheltering, mutability, permanence, humanitarianism, innovation

THE BOXES OUTSIDE THE BOX

THE 'BETTER SHELTER' IS A BOX DELIVERED IN FOUR BOXES. YOU'LL DESTROY the outside ones and then construct the inside one. The outside ones are for shipping. They seek to be as small and flat and lightweight as possible, while the inside one, when constructed, seeks to be as durable and spacious as possible. This is an important, confounding, and aggravating conundrum that has in many ways driven knowledge production of the Better Shelter unit. These outside boxes are cardboard boxes from Ikea. On the long end of each, there is a sticker with a barcode, arrows to indicate which side should be placed up, and an indication of its weight: nearly 100 kg total. In small isotypes the sticker shows that inside is a panel kit, which, when put together, will be one 'refugee housing unit'. Next to this there is an isotype of a family: one mother and one father, with two children holding their hands. Not a home or even a house, but a unit of housing, for refugees. No other type of housing I can think of explicitly specifies what type of human will live inside it. But this is temporary housing for what is a temporary human type. At least that is the theory.

Many of us have wrestled with these outer boxes on our living room floors, constructing the contents only to be extracting tiny Allen wrenches and jettisoned screws out of thick carpet pile weeks later. The technical term for this box is a flat pack, invented by Gillis Lundgren at Ikea in the 1950s. In Ikea's origin story, the idea of selling furniture in flat cardboard boxes was hatched when Lundgren took the legs off of a table so it would fit in his car.[1] The notion was to sell furniture in parts at cheaper prices, leaving the customer at the mercy of inscrutable assembly diagrams. This saved on labour and shipping costs, and it soon became the iconic innovation of the company.

These flat pack boxes, once sealed at the factory, will then be loaded into an even bigger box, a shipping container. One of the most salient selling features of the Better Shelters is that forty-eight of them can fit into a 40-foot high cube sea container. That forty-eight Better Shelters can fit in one shipping container is essential. By UNHCR estimates in 2015, 59.5 million people are now refugees, and in the previous year an average of 42,500 people daily became refugees, asylum seekers, or internally displaced people (UNHCR 2015). The average number of inhabitants in a refugee camp is 11,400 (UNHCR 2012). This means that 60 shipping containers of Better Shelters will be needed to construct the average refugee camp, assuming the nuclear family of four drawn on the side of each box. The shipping container thus becomes the modern verdict on good design, considering the logistics of humanitarian aid. With containerisation, the logic of the world is the logic of the box (Klose 2015; Levinson 2008).

THE INSIDE BOX

FIG. 5.2 Interior image of a Better Shelter prototype (source: courtesy of Better Shelter, www.bettershelter.org)

Do not yet discard the outside box. Just flatten it and set it aside for a moment. We'll return to it later. Inside you'll find metal poles, connectors, wires, bolts and screws, and insulated lightweight panels. The shelter is to be constructed by first putting together a frame with the poles and connectors to make the skeletal form of a 188-square-foot rectangle. Then the roof and sides of the shelter are hung on to the frame. The entirety can be assembled in about four hours. Lastly, a shade fabric, designed to keep the unit cool during the day and warm at night, is fastened over the roof and sides. There is a solar panel for an interior light and a USB outlet in the unit. As of now, each unit of refugee housing comes at the steep cost of $1755 per unit.

This box is making headlines as 'innovative', introducing a modular approach to shelter.[2] It is the product of a partnership between Ikea and the UNHCR, in part because of the company's history with the exterior flat pack box and as part of a broader trend of 'corporate social responsibility' (Rajak 2011). The partnership was motivated by the design dilemma of how to create a lightweight, durable, and easily assembled shelter that can also endure in harsh climates. Ikea is certainly not the only one 'innovating' the tent, however (Mallonee 2014).[3] Nor, despite the use of this signifying term, 'innovation', is there much new about this effort to re-think refugee housing. A quick search of the US patent database for 'temporary shelter' brings back over 500 results. And in fact, almost forty years ago, Fred Cuny, an expert on post-disaster shelter, wrote, 'Let me emphasise this fact: new housing types are not needed. Every relief agency has a file cabinet full of bright ideas submitted by graduate students, industrial designers, and architects, which offer the ultimate solution to the world's housing problems' (Prizeman 2003: 58). And yet tents remain the most ubiquitous form of refugee shelter, due to both their material and design. As we know, refugees can remain in camps for years, and in some cases decades, so tents, which last about six months on average, do not offer adequate longevity as structures. They are also relatively porous and poorly insulated from extreme weather. But tents can easily be purchased online for a few hundred dollars, and cheaper if bought in bulk. They also go up quickly and come down quickly. It is nearly impossible to beat the thrift of a refugee tent. Going back at least as far as the San Francisco earthquake of 1906, the tent has been the iconic shelter of the refugee. It is inexpensive, easy to ship and lightweight; hundreds will fit into a shipping container unit. Made mostly out of polycotton, the average refugee tent can be widely (and often locally) sourced (Zhang 2015). It does not require special parts if it breaks, and it is quintessentially temporary, even if it is inhabited for years on end; that is, if a refugee tent is used long past its expected lifetime, it still never *appears* stubbornly permanent; in its very abjectness and mutability it signals waiting and transition.

THE HOUSE AND THE BOX

With its own set of challenges and constraints, many would point out that temporary housing exists in a separate category than permanent housing, but here I argue that all considerations of temporary shelter are underpinned by enduring ethical and stylistic questions of how similar a home can be to a box, and how close a refugee shelter can be to a home. To consider the implications of these questions, we return first to the exterior flat pack box. Cardboard is indeed one of the most elemental and alarming materials of modern human shelter. It constitutes the iconic material of the homeless in America. When kept in the shape of a box, it provides temporary cover from the elements, while flatted it offers protection from the ground. The image of someone living in a cardboard box frequently accompanies the argument for housing as a fundamental human right: the cardboard box signifies the anti-home.

But beyond the collective agreement about the cardboard box as impoverished material, the idea of a box as shelter becomes complicated as ethical, cultural, and material wires converge and cross. Architects in the International Style movement beginning in the interwar period adopted the box as muse, building almost entirely in squared-off angles and lines. Internationalists eschewed the sentimentality and referential kitsch they saw in the backwards glance of other architectural movements. The house as box was emancipation from the past, unencumbered, shorn of decor. The box rendered the house a riddle of how to maximise functional space and streamline production, while ninety-degree angles conveyed precision, technology, and modernity. As Le Corbusier famously put it, a house should be a machine for living. This new boxy house also transcended geographical space. Through the promise of factory-produced modularity and simple materials such as reinforced concrete, International Style would live up to its name by transcending the local, provincial, and parochial in substance as well as form. And yet following the Second World War, some architects felt they must return to building a different world. Building was not just about reconstruction, but it offered an opportunity for rethinking how the architect should mediate between man and technology. In 1946, Ralph Walker, later president of the American Institute of Architects, expressed concern about these very issues:

> I believe this concept of shelter as a machine, of an architecture of functional utility, and of one in which material values are stressed to the omission of all else, must bear its burden of question as to whether it too has not contributed largely to the brutality of modern man, a brutality so evident in this War (Walker 1946: 230).

Walker's critique took aim at the architect as the eraser of the past, but also at the new technical obsession with materiality. He was sceptical and cautious about approaching shelter as only a sum of its parts, and imagined a role for post-war architects in reclaiming a humanity lost in the war. Yet certainly the era of the technocratic, mass solution had not run its course. As the suburb began to sprawl its way out across the American landscape in little Levittowns (Marshall 2015; Jackson 1987), the replicable house had drastically parted ways with high modernist sensibility, and found mainstream application. By the 1960s, the house as box signalled white middle class flight from American cities. The folk singer Malvina Reynolds, on her way from San Francisco to Daly City one day in 1961, looked out on the mushrooming suburbs and penned her famous song, 'Little Boxes', an anthem mocking the sameness and soullessness of the new American future.

In this same post-war world but in a different landscape, Europe was reeling from the destruction of its housing stock. International organisations and national governments began for the first time to provide shelter other than tents to foreign nations (Prizeman 2003; Davis 1978).[4] One foray into this new form of assistance was a joint collaboration between the United States War Production Board and The New School for Social Research. Under the leadership of the architect Paul Lester Wiener, the mission of this collaboration was to 'devise and design basic universal parts [for shelter] suitable for quantity manufacture, capable of production in sufficient quantities to supply both American and overseas war needs for all the agencies of the government concerned herewith'.[5] The final product described in a 1945 *New York Times* article bears a striking resemblance to Ikea's design and ambitions seventy years later (**FIGURE 5.3**). Wiener's design sought universal applicability through a 'departure from conventional methods':

Instead of being erected from the floor up, the buildings are assembled "from the roof down". In the place of the usual load-bearing exterior walls and partitions, there are "curtain" walls in the form of panels that are "hung" inside the uprights or posts that support the roof, thus leaving virtually all interior space free of encumbrances (Cooper 1945: 1).

FIG. 5.3 Paul Lester Wiener's design for portable and modular temporary housing (source: University of Oregon, Special Collections and University Archives)

The two-bedroom house created by Wiener – one of a few patented designs in the programme – shipped at approximately 0.9 cubic feet per square foot of floor surface, compared to the 'conventional panelized prefab house, which required two cubic feet of shipping per square foot of floor surface'.[6] Space and weight, as ever, were at a premium.

As far as I can tell, Wiener's housing never went into mass-production under his collaboration with the War Production Board. The project and partnership was terminated in 1944, and Phillip Youtz, Wiener's partner in the endeavour, wrote that the collaboration was ultimately 'a continuous struggle against interference in government by commercial monopolies and cartels, but I feel that it was a very worthwhile piece of war work'.[7] Youtz's comment offers a clue into what stalled the project, which clearly wasn't a failure of design. The obstacles were part of the political and economic landscape onto which their temporary housing units were to be constructed.

In short, temporary housing represented relief to those displaced and an impediment to others. Consider these three photographs, taken four decades before the war in the aftermath of the 1906 earthquake in San Francisco. The first (**FIGURE 5.4**) is an image of Golden Gate Park dotted with the white peaks of army relief tents.

FIG. 5.4 Earthquake tents from after the San Francisco earthquake of 1906 (source: Wikimediacommons[8])

The second photograph (**FIGURE 5.5**) shows two rows of small cottages. Over 5000 of these temporary houses, known as 'earthquake cottages' were constructed throughout the city after the war. Inhabitants paid $2 rent per month until they had paid off the 10 by 14 foot buildings for $50 (Rafkin 2012).

The third photograph (**FIGURE 5.6**) is an image of four sturdy horses tied to a carriage, towing a cottage through the streets of San Francisco to the site where it would become part of a refugee's permanent new home.

FIG. 5.5 Earthquake cottages provided for some victims of the 1906 earthquake in San Francisco (source: National Park Service, Golden Gate NRA)

FIG. 5.6 Earthquake cottage being moved by horses (source: San Francisco History Center, San Francisco Public Library)

While tents can be folded up and put away until the next disaster, boxes (houses?) can have an altogether different second life. San Francisco's earthquake shacks were carted all across the Bay Area and some of them still exist, over a hundred years later (Landes 2014). Since the San Francisco earthquake, through the long years of the Great Depression, through the New Deal and the Tennessee Valley Authority's experimentation[9] with a 'truckable house' and prefabrication, the permanence of impermanent housing always posed a threat to urban planners and the construction industry (Bruce and Sandbank 1943: 13). While the design problem facing Wiener and others after the war may have felt new to the architect, its context was already fraught territory. The challenge of the box was seemingly to create shelter that was not *too* durable to disturb market forces.

The box's potential for re-use and transformation is at the heart of the question of whether temporary housing makes it into the hands of displaced peoples. Tasked with good design, Wiener and other architects purposefully imagined their structures to serve multiple uses. But conversely, the more re-useable a structure was, the more it posed the threat of living too long, becoming a 'slum' and harming the post-war housing industry. It was a question of whether, in the terms of the day, relief and rehabilitation were two separate entities, or if one was a continuation of the other. The United Nations Relief and Rehabilitation Administration (UNRRA), the organisation spearheading the international relief efforts in both Europe and Asia following the war, at one point expressed interest in Wiener's design, but it was also wary of investing in temporary shelter. In a meeting with Wiener the head of the Industrial Rehabilitation Division made clear that the 'UNRRA's functions in liberated territories did not extend beyond a period of six months after liberation, and that all shelter functions [...] would be confined to actual minimum shelter during this six months' period'.[10] The politics of local economics could clearly also play out across continents: temporary shelter was not to disturb local building industries.

The UNRRA's reluctance to use Wiener's shelter reflected a general disconnect amongst architects, aid providers, and local building industries. There was no consensus about what defined a refugee shelter in terms of materials, economies, and temporalities: one man's box could be another man's house. In

Britain for example, between 1944 and 1949 over 150,000 temporary prefabs were built to help with housing scarcities. Cloaking class anxieties in calls for good design and building, people reportedly feared the proliferation of 'jerry-building, tumbledown shacks, caravans, shoddy work, ribbon development, draughts and leaks and everything that's bad in building'. And indeed, by 1964 only 29 percent of the original prefabs had been vacated in England and Wales (Vale 1995: 1–21).

Meanwhile the United States had its own housing emergency as thousands were relocated for wartime factory production. With the Lanham Act of 1940 the government allocated 150 million dollars for building housing and other facilities for those working in the mushrooming wartime defence industry. By 1943, that amount had risen to 1.3 billion dollars and the dwellings designed under the act cost an average of $3,000 (Reed 1995: 12). Rather than create what was perceived as an urban slum problem with temporary structures, wartime housing often moved people outside cities, requiring them to leave when the factory was no longer needed. The Lanham Act also stipulated that, after the war was over, all temporary buildings must be destroyed within two years (or packed up and sent overseas) to protect and promote the private building industry and to prevent 'the creation of "ghost" towns' (New York Times 1945). Perhaps the 'commercial monopolies and cartels' that Youtz complained about were those invested in assuring the post-war need for housing expertise, labour, and materials. These temporary boxes threatened the development and expansion of the new 'little boxes' of post-war American suburbia.

Following the war, as Ralph Walker introspected about the future of his field, the architectural profession was busy becoming a split self. One half relished small-scale design solutions, while the other half took on the mantle of the master city planner. Wiener himself after the war went on to partner with the architect José Luis Sert to create city plans for Bogotá, Colombia; Chimbote, Peru; and Havana, Cuba (Bastlund 1967: 27). The city planner resolutely sought to purge the temporary. One of the loudest critics of temporary shelter was the New York Post columnist Charles Abrams, who at the time was a legal advisor to the New York Housing Authority. In one Post article regarding wartime housing, Abrams warns:

> Temporary housing has always proved costly and permanent. The "tempo-
> rary" hovels built after the San Francisco Earthquake and the Galveston flood
> hung on for decades after the emergency had passed. The recent wartime
> temporary homes built by the federal government have produced more last-
> ing slums in America than we have cleared through all our federally aided
> slum clearance programs (Abrams 1961).

By the time of his death in 1970, Abrams was regarded worldwide as a housing expert, and had been sent on planning missions by the United Nations to
Pakistan, Ghana, India, the Philippines, and Bolivia, among other places (Illson
1970: 26). The post-war architect's split self revealed the danger of professional
and historical compartmentalisation. When a project merely existed as a design
challenge, the larger cognitive dissonance could be quieted but not overcome
in the long run.

THE BOX TODAY

Where would a container unit with 48 Better Shelters be unloaded if it were
shipped tomorrow? Maybe in Jordan or Turkey to house Syrian refugees
(McClelland 2014), or at the Dadaab refugee camp in Kenya, the largest in the
world, where over 300,000 Somalis have lived since 1991. Dadaab today is a
mix of tents and structures made of other materials such as corrugated tin, tree
branches, blue plastic tarps, and cloth.

Maybe the container unit would go to Haiti to compensate for the Red
Cross, which has recently come under fire for having built only six permanent
houses rather than the 130,000 promised following the 500 million dollars
it raised in donations after the 2010 earthquake (Elliott and Sullivan 2015).
Without deeply examining the case of Haiti and the Red Cross, this statistic
suggests that even when money is ostensibly not an issue, shelter is never
as simple as finding a way to put a larger lightweight box inside a smaller
one and loading it in a shipping container. Assembling the Better Shelter on
site – unfolding the map and accounting for the nuts and bolts and figuring
out how everything fits together – mirrors the larger logistical assemblage of
refugee housing. It is surely not easy to decide what and how to get where,

FIG. 5.7 Dadaab Refugee Camp, Kenya (source: Wikimediacommons)[11]

and to whom. And yet too often 'logistics' become a convenient scapegoat of deeper questions around humanitarian aid, expatriate expertise, global capitalism, and local realities. Alternatives to the refugee tent have largely spent their lives on paper, not as three-dimensional objects. And yet ironically their design challenge is proposed as distinctly material: a chance to practically design in the real world.

Mid-century European refugees posed a threat to the building industry because they were not leaving: improving their temporary shelter might thus – in the eyes of builders and urban planners – create structures and environments that would slip into a permanent state of decrepitude. Today, both the temporal and the spatial dimensions of being a refugee are more fraught. The 'average' displaced person today is waiting to go elsewhere. No one wants to believe that refugee camps are a permanent destination for those displaced from their homes, and yet many spend major portions of their lives in them. And thus perhaps waiting to be relocated perversely *also* reinforces the logic of the tent. Not just because it is cheap but because it signifies – almost promises to all involved – an end to being a refugee. This is not to argue that anyone would rather live in a tent, but that its materiality may also tell a story and compel action. The tent can equally function as a cloak of impermanence that conveniently allows persistent inaction: *You see, look. They won't be here for long.*

Will states see these Better Shelters as a threat to the promise of temporary aid and assistance? Should it be a corporation (despite its humanitarian commitments) that benefits from the move to utilise more permanent and secure structures? Why deploy finished shelters and not materials for self-building? Will Better Shelters attract more people to the refugee camps or signal resignation to the permanent status 'refugee' has taken on in the twenty-first century? What if Better Shelter is better than the shelter found in local communities? While design might not always matter as much as designers would like to think, materiality certainly does. And designers and aid organisations are not the only ones who can claim and manipulate materials. As Nasser Abourahme writes in his essay on cement in a Palestinian refugee camp:

> buildings and structures, infrastructural networks, things like electrical wiring, sewage pipework and so on, but also the materials that go into the processes of their assemblage as a camp – cement, concrete blocks, plastic tubing, corrugated tin or zinc sheets (*zinco* in vernacular Arabic) – do not just play an enabling or intermediary role, they mediate action and practice in contingent and often unexpected ways (Abourahme 2015: 203).

Simply changing the materials used to construct shelter, whether this is undertaken in protest by those who seek more permanence or by aid organisations to provide better shelter, will alter more than just the environment of the camp: it will also transform and reshape the politics of being a refugee in localised and contingent ways. Many critiques of refugee housing design focus on the need for context-specific shelter due to differences between climates, cultures and environments, but refugees and their own manipulation of materials also claim ownership to shape their environments.

Since I first drafted this essay in the early summer of 2015, there has been an immense and dramatic surge of refugees across the globe, and indeed the current set of political questions gaining traction as a result is not for the most part regarding how to stop creating refugees but how and where they will now live. To look back at the post-war experience is not to suggest that history is repeating itself. But it is in part to note that the currently proposed 'innovative' solutions look strikingly similar to their predecessors. The problem still presents itself as the challenge of designing a larger box that can fit inside a smaller box, and making it as cheap and shippable as possible. For the designer this also remains a deeply humane enterprise: how can we offer people displaced from their homes a better and safer shelter? But this is not a problem caused by the paucity of technical solutions or logistical plans. Perhaps the most important continuity to note from the mid-century experience is simply that the box will never offer a solution of its own accord. The design impulse is to think of refugee housing as something utterly separate from a home, a neighbourhood, and even a life more generally. Yet one must consider all the things beyond the flat pack. There is no consensus among or between states, communities, institutions, and markets on what is temporary, nor any agreement about how close a box can be to a house. Even in the course of one's life, these things can be wildly recalibrated.

NOTES

1   http://www.ikea.com/ms/en_GB/about_ikea/the_ikea_way/history/1940_1950.html

2   https://www.youtube.com/watch?t=88&v=Ect-FwtK-84

3   See also: http://www.borgenmagazine.com/eight-designs-refugee-shelters/ and NK (2015), available at: http://inhabitat.com/prefab-friday-shrimp-housing/

4   Davis (1978) writes, 'The whole phenomenon of "donor" provision of shelter is comparatively recent and I have found no evidence of emergency housing (other than tents) being given by one country to another prior to World War II. Therefore, the provision of shelter can be seen as coinciding with the development of aid, rapid transportation, and the growing spirit of internationalism mentioned earlier, and also the continual increases in disaster casualties'.

5   Article 1, Copy of Contract between WPB and the New School for Social Research Box 6 PLW papers.

6   Memo Daves to Wiener, Re: Structures (1946), Box 7 PLW Papers.

7   Youtz to Wiener (5 August 1944), Box 14 PLW Papers.

8   Available at: https://upload.wikimedia.org/wikipedia/commons/d/d6/Camp_in_Golden_Gate_Park_Under_Military_Control_After_the_1906_San_Francisco_Earthquake.jpg

9 The Truckable house was the predecessor to the mobile home. The Tennessee Valley Authority project, created under the New Deal, was originally formed to build eighteen dams along the Tennessee River to prevent the river from flooding and in turn flooding the Mississippi. For the construction of these dams, temporary communities had to be set up. Because the workers often changed location, 'the TVA project is remembered in particular for the contribution that it made to the relationship between factory production and demountability and portability' (Vale 1995: 54).

10 Memorandum on meeting with officials of OPRD and UNRRA (23 May 1944) Box 7 PLW Papers.

11 Available at: https://commons.wikimedia.org/wiki/Category:Dadaab#/media/ File:Refugee_shelters_in_the_Dadaab_camp,_northern_Kenya,_July_2011_ (5961213058).jpg

REFERENCES

Abourhame, N., 'Assembling and Spilling-Over: Towards an "Ethnography of Cement" in a Palestinian Refugee Camp', *International Journal of Urban and Regional Research*, 39.2 (March 2015): 200–17.

Abrams, C., '"Temporary" Housing is Tomorrow's Slums', *New York Post* article reproduced in *Housing: A National Security Resource, Conference and Exhibition Pamphlet* (Cambridge: Albert Farwell, Bemis Foundation, 1961).

Bastlund, K., *José Luis Sert: Architecture, City Planning, Urban Design* (Zurich: Les Editions d'Architecture Zurich, 1967).

Bruce, A., and H. Sandbank, *A History of Prefabrication* (New York: John B Pierce Foundation, 1943).

Cooper, L. E., 'Design for Prefabricated Houses for War-Torn Areas is Perfected', *New York Times*, 16 March 1945, p. 1.

Davis, I., *Shelter After Disaster* (Oxford: Polytechnic Press, 1978).

Elliott, J., and L. Sullivan, 'How the Red Cross Raised Half a Billion Dollars for Haiti and Built Six Homes', *Propublica*, 3 June 2015, <https://www.propublica.org/ article/how-the-red-cross-raised-half-a-billion-dollars-for-haiti-and-built-6-homes> [accessed 10 October 2015].

Illson, M., 'Charles Abrams, Worldwide Housing Expert, Dies', *New York Times*, 23 February 1970.

Ikea,'About Ikea', <http://www.ikea.com/ms/en_GB/about_ikea/the_ikea_way/ history/1940_1950.html> [accessed 27 November 2015].

Ikea Foundation, 'Designing a better home for refugee children', <https://www. youtube.com/watch?t=88&v=Ect-FwtK-84> [accessed 27 November 2015].

Jackson, K., *Crabgrass Frontier: The Suburbanization of the United States*, 1st edn (New York: Oxford University Press, 1987).

Klose, A., *The Container Principle: How a Box Changes the Way We Think*, trans. by Charles Marcrum II (Cambridge, Massachusetts: The MIT Press, 2015).

Levinson, M., *The Box: How the Shipping Container Made the World Smaller and the World Economy Bigger* (Princeton, NJ: Princeton University Press, 2008).

Prizeman, M., 'Emergency Dwelling', *Architectural Design*, 73.4 (July/August 2003): 57–63.

Mallonee, L.C., 'Homes for Refugees: Eight New Designs for Conflict Housing', 1 August 2014, <http://www.theguardian.com/sustainable-business/2014/jul/30/refugee-shelters-new-designs-ikea-fema-military-haiti-jordan-syria-iraq> [accessed 15 September 2015].

Marshall, C., 'Levittown, the Prototypical American Suburb', *The Guardian*, 28 April 2015, <http://www.theguardian.com/cities/2015/apr/28/levittown-america-prototypical-suburb-history-cities> [accessed 15 September 2015].

McClelland, M., 'How to Build a Perfect Refugee Camp', *New York Times Magazine*, 13 February 2014, <http://www.nytimes.com/2014/02/16/magazine/how-to-build-a-perfect-refugee-camp.html?_r=1> [accessed 10 October 2015].

NK, 'Prefab Friday: S.H.R.I.M.P. Housing', *Inhabitat*, <http://inhabitat.com/prefab-friday-shrimp-housing/> [accessed 2 November 2015].

Rafkin, L., 'Earthquake Refugee Cottages', *New York Times*, 4 February 2012.

'Use of Temporary War Housing By Returned Veterans Urged', *New York Times* (1 June 1945), p. 17.

Rajak, D., *In Good Company: An Anatomy of Corporate Social Responsibility* (Stanford: Stanford University Press, 2011).

Reed, P. S., 'Enlisting Modernism', in Donald Albrecht, ed., *World War II and the American Dream: How Wartime Building Changed a Nation* (Cambridge: MIT Press, 1995).

Roth, M., '8 Designs for Refugee Housing', *Borgen Magazine*, 19 August 2014. <http://www.borgenmagazine.com/eight-designs-refugee-shelters/> [accessed 15 September 2015].

UNHCR, 'Displacement: The New Global Challenge', UNHCR Global Trends, 2012. <http://unhcr.org/globaltrendsjune2013/UNHCR%20GLOBAL%20TRENDS%202012_V05.pdf> [accessed 1 July 2015].

——, 'Worldwide Displacement Hit All-Time High as War and Persecution Increase', UNHCR News Stories, 18 June 2015, <http://www.unhcr.org/558193896.html> [accessed 15 October 2015].

Vale, B., *Prefabs: A History of the UK Temporary Housing Programme* (London: E & FN SPON, 1995).

Walker, R., 'The Architect and the Post-War World', *Journal of the A.I.A.*, May 1946.

Zhang, S., 'Helping Refugees Isn't Just about Designing Better Shelters', 2 November 15,<http://www.wired.com/2015/11/helping-refugees-is-not-about-designing-better-shelters/#slide-x> [accessed 2 November 2015].

ARCHIVAL MATERIAL

PLW Papers (Paul Lester Wiener Papers, University of Oregon)

Article 1, Copy of Contract between WPB and the New School for Social Research Box 6 PLW papers

Memo Daves to Wiener, Re: Structures (1946), Box 7 PLW Papers

Memorandum on meeting with officials of OPRD and UNRRA (23 May 1944) Box 7 PLW Papers

Youtz to Wiener (5 August 1944), Box 14 PLW Papers

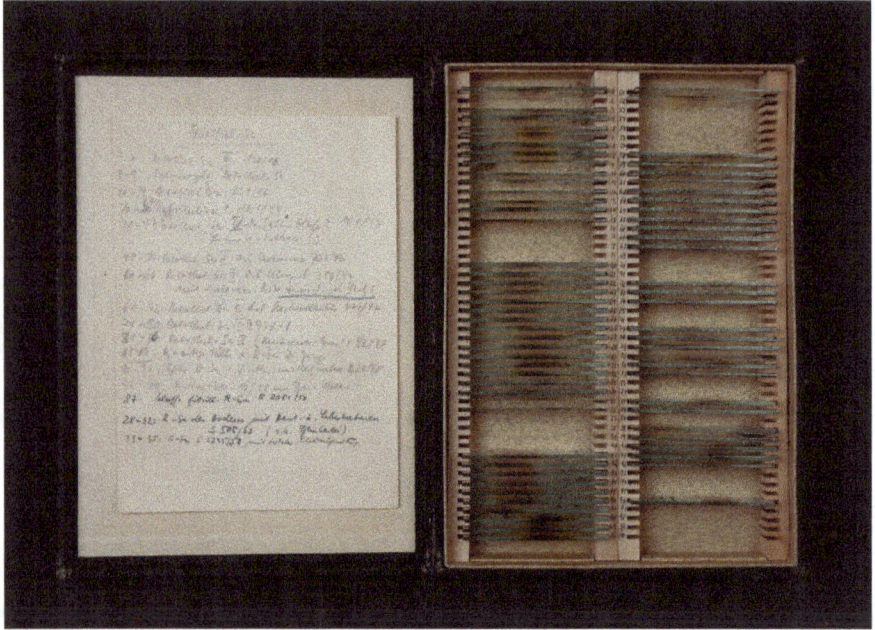

FIG. 6.1 Microscopic slide box from the collection of German pathologist Karl Lennert

6

SLIDE BOX: HOW TO STOCK SOME THOUSAND CANCER CASES

Ulrich Mechler

Box: slide box. **Appearance**: functional, mostly unadorned; if old, often worn out. **Size**: different sizes, but usually (like this one) about 19.5 x 27.5 x 3.5 cm. **Habitat**: not far from microscopes, life sciences research institutes, medical facilities (particularly pathology), archives, sometimes museums. **Origin**: nineteenth century, probably England or Germany. **Migration**: spreading from botany over the entire field of life sciences. **Status**: still widespread.

Keywords: collecting, archiving, ordering, classifying

OUR BOX DATES BACK TO THE 1940S AND IS DESIGNED AND MANUFACTURED for a single specific purpose. It is a storage container for microscopic – more specifically, histological – specimens, briefly called *slides*. Our box contains 124 of them. Histologic slides are the ubiquitous working tools of pathologists when working with a microscope, which is what most of them do most of their time. Histologic slides preserve human tissue samples, either taken post-mortem and examined in the context of an autopsy of deceased patients, or, more commonly nowadays, taken intravitally during the diagnostic examination of patients. Removed during a surgical procedure, the tissue sample undergoes elaborate laboratory processing in which it is artificially changed and preserved. After the tissue has been dehydrated, it is embedded in paraffin. Next, a so-called microtome is used to cut 4-micrometer-thick tissue sections which are then mounted on a glass microscope slide, usually measuring 26 x 76 mm. The section is then stained and sealed with a cover slip. Under the microscope, pathologists examine the slide and search for minute anomalies in the tissue pattern that they can correlate with a disease entity. Particularly in the case of malignant tumour-forming diseases, the histological examination is a central component of the diagnosis; a given tumour can be specified (by a process called 'typing'), and in many cases, to the patient's relief, a true malignant process can be excluded.

Histopathology, the science of pathologically altered tissues, developed in the last third of the nineteenth century. It changed our knowledge of diseases fundamentally. In the twentieth century it became an important branch of diagnostics, with greatly increasing significance for patients. This development continues today: histopathology strives for a theoretical understanding of diseases, their causal pathophysiological mechanisms, and their manifestations and effects on the organs, tissues, and cells. In pursuing this goal, histopathology is always dependent on the examination of specific individual cases of illness. Theoretical disease research and practical application in diagnostics are thus intertwined, and it is from this epistemic tension that our box has emerged. Tracing the emergence of this specific type of box in the nineteenth century opens an insight into the material culture of a specific 'thinking collective' (Fleck 1935). Exploring the history of our individual box deepens this insight through the example of a particularly intricate chapter of disease research in the twentieth century. The practice of knowledge production in histopathology is substantially shaped by the medial qualities of its mundane objects, including slides.

Our slide box belongs to the extensive collection of microscopic slides amassed by the German pathologist Karl Lennert (1921–2012) over the course of his entire professional life. Karl Lennert is considered one of the most outstanding scientists of German post-war medicine. His special research interest was the diseases of the blood-forming organs: bone marrow, spleen, and especially the lymph nodes. Lennert gained international recognition in the 1970s for developing a classification of the so-called non-Hodgkin lymphomas, a subgroup of the malignant lymphomas, the tumours of the lymph nodes. The diagnosis of these diseases has always been considered particularly complicated, while corresponding problems also shaped their theoretical and systematic understanding. For many decades, the question of how to classify lymphomas was a particular problem in tumour pathology. Emblematic of this situation is the laconic and oft-cited comment of the Australian pathologist Rupert Allen Willis that 'Nowhere in pathology has a chaos of names so clouded clear concepts as in the subject of lymphoid tumors' (1948: 760).

Karl Lennert's collection contains around 10,000 cases of diseases that show lymph node infections, mostly malignant lymph node diseases. Each case is a material-semiotic ensemble, containing strictly selected and highly compressed clinical information and, of course, some slides (usually four, sometimes up to thirty). The oldest cases date back to the 1940s, when Karl Lennert was a student. He added the latest in the 1990s, years after he retired. Lennert's collection reflects half a century of history of pathology. Considered together, the cases bear witness to rapidly evolving laboratory techniques and a gradually deepening biological understanding of lymphoma disease. This is reflected in changing disease names that resulted from new knowledge, definitions, boundaries, and concepts of disease. During this period of post-war medicine, not only the diagnosis of lymphoma changed, along with all its methodological and epistemological conditions, but also disease research itself, its infrastructure, and its socio-technical and institutional conditions. With his lifelong passion for meticulous collecting, Karl Lennert appears more like a scholarly type of the nineteenth century; nevertheless, he was a forerunner of modern biomedical disease research in Germany.

Lennert's collection also reflects his biography as a scientist. It starts with an aesthetic fascination that was developed into a profound expertise and finally flowed into a research programme pursued for decades. Lennert's collection was the central tool of his entire work. And the principle of success of this work was his detailed familiarity with the histological morphology of the disease, its variants, stages, and varieties. This knowledge, in turn, was based on his meticulous and dogged collection of cases that he considered notable. Again and again, Lennert revised these cases, compared them with others, and related them to current research results. The manner in which the collection is organised is therefore by no means uniform; indeed, the collection can be considered an adjustable research instrument, whose functionalities were adapted to meet changing conditions and objectives.

One such adaptation of the collection to new requirements will be outlined in our focus on a single box, which will show how Lennert aligned his research interests to the demands of modern postwar pathology and its strictly clinical and therapeutic orientation. In the early years of his research, Lennert used flat wooden boxes for storing the cases, like the one shown here. The 124 slides archived in our box belong to sixteen different patients, or cases, from the years 1946 to 1952. All of the patients were suffering from a disease that was known at the time as 'retothel sarcoma'. This diagnostic term is no longer in use today, because it refers to a group of diseases that are nowadays differentiated – although all of them show a similar course in that they are aggressive, rapidly progressing types of malignant lymphoma. They are similar, then, without being identical. Classifying diseases histologically means searching for hardly detectable patterns and cutting demarcations into an ocean of possible variations of appearance. Sorting slides in a box can be a subtle and quite complex epistemic endeavour.

THE EMERGENCE OF THE MICROSCOPIC VIEW AND ITS MATERIAL ENVIRONMENT

Although microscopes had been available since the seventeenth century, they did not begin to play a role in medical research until the middle of the nineteenth century. Various reasons are cited for this delay: the insufficient quality of early microscopes, the lack of experience of the early microscopists, and the lack of

FIG. 6.2 Same slide box as above, detail

a theory that would provide a sound paradigm to substantiate the new visual experiences. An important reason probably lay, however, in a fundamental methodological deficiency and its far-reaching consequences. The French anatomist Xavier Bichat (1771–1802) is considered the founder of histology at the beginning of the nineteenth century. He of all people mistrusted the microscope, and opined that '[…] physiology and anatomy, do not seem to me, besides ever to have derived any great assistance [from microscopic instruments], because when we view in an object obscurely, every one sees in his own way, and according as he is affected' (Bichat 1813: 42). Bichat speaks here of a lack of trans-subjective evidence, and thus of something that is considered essential today for scientific knowledge, namely reproducibility. Once removed, organic tissues undergo rapid decay processes; without fixation, their analysis is a one-time event that cannot be repeated. This deficiency cannot be compensated for in speech or drawings, because what the observer saw always remains subjective – 'every one sees in [their] own way, and according as [they are] affected'. In short, microscopic specimens of organic tissues, and what they revealed to the eye, were unstable and, consequently, immobile.

The microscopic slide as we know it today was not developed until the middle of the nineteenth century. Beginning in the 1830s, Canada balsam was used as an embedding medium; from 1849 glycerine was the favoured substance; ten years later it was gelatine. At the same time, techniques were developed for dehydrating the tissue with alcohol and turpentine, and for embedding tissues in wax, stearin, or gum arabic (Smith 1915: 86 ff). In 1869, the German medical scientist Edwin Klebs published his paraffin-embedding method, the method of embedding tissue that is still the dominant technique in histological lab routine today (Klebs 1869). As Hans-Jörg Rheinberger stresses, only then did the most important condition for a broad application of microscopic methods and their lasting epistemological impact exist: permanence (2005: 71). Klebs's microscopic slide guaranteed that that which was seen became permanent, making it possible to revise an object, if necessary to re-evaluate what was seen, and to compare the object with older or more recent objects. With a permanent slide, the phenomenon we are looking at is separated from any accidental occurrences when or where it appeared. And this gives it discursive authority.

The microscopists of the time were definitely aware of the significance of this innovation. In 1856, the German anatomist Hermann Welcker stressed the 'estimable, conclusive' advantages of permanent slides, and the possibility they provided to 'be able to show a specific object at any moment' (1856: 5). Welcker even devoted an entire book to a problem that automatically arose: the 'storage of microscopic objects' (1856). A permanent slide that can be archived generates a need for practical and appropriate storage technology. A standard work on scientific microscopy dating to 1860 mentions a commercial producer of slide boxes. Included is an illustration and a description of a slide box exactly resembling ours. In addition to the boxes, the author describes smaller 'card boxes for holding 24 slides' or 'cabinets' of varying sizes and qualities (Balfour 1860: 36). The announcement by the resourceful salesman is an indication that a microscopic slide culture was rapidly taking root. Microscopic collections proliferated, a development that had other constraints and side effects. The industrial production of glass led to a massive availability of cheaper glass slides. With this, the older variants of specimen holders made of wood or ivory disappeared. Also, standard formats became established. Out of a multiplicity of dimensions, the so-called 'English format' of 76 x 26 mm, or 3 x 1 inch, became the standard in Germany. The above-mentioned slide boxes and cabinets of 1860 were already made for this format.

Slide box and slide cabinet, however, also point to different types and contexts of collection. Slide collections grew in large institutions, such as departments of pathology, in the form of teaching collections or case archives. The furniture offered for these collections – 'a cabinet of Honduras mahogany, capable of holding [...] 2000 slides, eleven pounds' (Balfour 1860: 36) – was recommended for its suitability, durability, and large capacity – and came at a concomitantly formidable price. In contrast to such a centralised, immobile accumulation of slides, to which the actors must go, a handy slide box hints at small collections of individual researchers or ambitious laypersons and their informal get-togethers. The Microscopical Society of London, founded in 1839, was primarily a platform for contact and the exchange of ideas, techniques, and specimens. Above all it was a forum in which the participants took turns to examine a spot on a slide through a microscope (Smith 1915: 88).

The slide box resulted from new technical attributes of microscopic specimens: permanence and archivability. But the slide box is also an indication of a fundamental property of the slide itself, namely that it can be readily mobilised. Bruno Latour (2006) has pointed out the important role of mobile and invariable representations for the distribution of knowledge. *Immutable mobiles* are crucial parameters when it comes to winning allies and resources. To be sure, slides are not inscriptions on paper in the sense meant by Latour. Slides show the tissue itself – a complex morphological visibility that eludes the abstraction and reduction involved when we write things down. It is this surplus of significance that cannot be expressed exhaustively that makes up the potential of the slide. And it is precisely this that made necessary a universally standardised format for the newly permanent specimens. The slide can be circulated and fitted into various contexts and uses. It is compatible with the infrastructure of the most varied actors. In short, the slide box is the representative of this universal mobility.

SLIDE BOXES IN KARL LENNERT'S COLLECTION

Our slide box is only a tiny piece of the puzzle of Karl Lennert's collection. It belongs to a set totalling 110 slide boxes, known by Lennert as the 'autopsy archive', which again is only a part of the total collection. The autopsy archive with its 110 boxes is historically the oldest part of the entire collection. How is it organised? How did Lennert work with it?

Two types of collection have already been mentioned: the teaching collection and the case archive. These types pursue different strategies, but we can still find both in modern pathology departments. Regardless of the fact that the teaching programme is dominated by high-quality photographic reproductions in textbooks, atlases, and Internet platforms, we still have so-called slide series for microscopy courses for students. These are sets of slide boxes, each of which contains a set of identical cases, i.e. slides that were prepared from a single block of tissue. Residents in pathology also train their eyes with the help of small, carefully selected sets of cases in slide boxes that are at the disposal of all pathologists in the department. In addition to these highly selective compilations, every pathology department has an archive. Already, for legal reasons, all analysed cases are archived for at least ten years. For a long time, and to some extent even today, these archives were also used as a reservoir from which suitable cases for a specific research project could be selected as needed.

In Lennert's collection, both strategies exist in equal measure. Nineteen of the 110 boxes comprise a teaching collection. Each of the nineteen boxes is allocated to an organ system. They contain slides of the most important diseases that can affect the organ. Lennert created this collection for autodidactic purposes. Here we can see that, before specialising, he wanted to master the universal, i.e. the entire scope of histopathology. This includes not only knowledge of the basic types of tissue and their specific pathological deviations, but also knowledge of the optical effect of different staining techniques that highlight the various structures of the tissue. Lennert prepared all of the slides himself; he also wanted to master the histological laboratory technology himself.

The nineteen boxes are numbered, and of course the flat containers were stacked so as to save space. The small sides of the boxes are also labelled, so that they can be read from the side, making the stacked box identifiable. Therefore, only a few steps are required to find a box and a specific slide. The nineteen slide boxes are a kind of compendium of histopathology. With these cases, Lennert learned histomorphological seeing, and on the basis of these teaching files he could calibrate his eyes repeatedly. We do not know how long he used this training tool, although presumably it was only for a few years. At any rate, he was not content with a textbook or with a local departmental collection. He wanted to have his own transportable collection that contained his initial study subjects. This resource accompanied him for his entire professional life. The great majority of Lennert's boxes, however, are organised in a different way: they contain chronologically filed cases. Our box with the sixteen cases of 'retothel sarcomas' is among these. It is one of the oldest; its first case dates to 1946. At this time, there were three boxes and thus three disease categories, one each for myeloid and lymphoid leukemias, and one for lymphomas, all of which were catalogued as reticular sarcomas. Each time a box was filled, a new one was started. The boxes were numbered consecutively. Our box is accordingly designated as 'ReSa 1'. Thus, the classification of the boxes follows a very simple formula that reflects the nosology and systematic understanding of the late 1940s.

In this case archive, Lennert collected all available cases of the special subject he had chosen: the malignant diseases of the hematopoietic system. The case archive fulfilled two functions, the first of which was that it captured the phenomenal breadth of the subject and therefore formed the material basis for the outstanding expertise in malignant lymph node diseases that the young scientist Karl Lennert had already acquired in the mid-1950s. At the same time, with this stock he created a pool of cases that could be used for the processing of his own research questions. We find individual cases from the collection in Karl Lennert's publications, and decades later entire case series from the autopsy archive were drawn upon for analyses of aspects of diseases. Here, the epistemological productivity of permanent specimens and their revision becomes evident. An investigation of a slide can always only be based on the historical state of knowledge at a given time. Therefore, a slide always remains subject to general revision, because there are always elements that are not yet foreseeable and not yet recognisable. That is its potential. Diseases, understood as entities – i.e., as clearly defined self-contained and discrete objects – are not natural unchangeable quantities. New laboratory methods, new theoretical insights, and new therapeutic procedures repeatedly challenge an entity. The cases of rare diseases meticulously compiled by Karl Lennert were a reservoir for investigating newly generated questions on the basis of available cases. The slide box is a container of future unanticipated questions, and possibly their answers.

In both parts of the collection (the teaching collection and the case archive) the slide appears as a boundary object that leads from one epistemological context to another. Autopsies, from which all of these cases are derived, are used in the final assessment of a case. The point is to clarify what happened in the body of a patient – and possibly was not recognised during his lifetime. Transferred to the collection, however, the cases served other interests. Here it was no longer a matter of the final clarification of a specific case, but of the disease itself.

The two parts of the collection point to two different strategies for comprehending a disease. Teaching collections represent the entire field of relevant phenomena. Their intelligible reference point is the prototype of a disease; their actual material objects are carefully selected examples of a category that show prototypical qualities (Daston and Galison 2007). Typically enough, the slides in Lennert's teaching collection no longer have registration numbers. Hence all references to the patient, his or her case history and its documentation are cut off. In these cases the slide is merely a signifier. It shows *a* sarcoma, *a* metastasis, etc. Antetypes don't have a history. The case archive, in contrast, is a complete chronological registration of all relevant incoming cases. This strategy comprehends the disease as a spectrum of infinitely different variants, forms and stages. The two strategies, to identify the prototypic and to comprehend the variance, complement each other and are mutually dependent in the definition of an entity.

The consecutive registration of all relevant cases also has another effect, however. It virtually provokes disturbances, borderline cases that do not fit into the categories, ones that lie crosswise to their boundaries and thus undermine the organised structure. The established order of diseases represented by antetypes in the teaching collection and by the categorical structure of boxes in the archive are here undermined. The scruples and doubts of classification in the daily routine of diagnosis become evident, generating new questions and research projects. Precisely here, the limits of the box are evident. In the autopsy archive the slide boxes demonstrated their advantages. As a standard tool in pathology, they were inexpensive and available. They were also mobile – both spatially-logistically and epistemologically – because as a classification in material form they can be adapted to the most varied contexts. It is only when we try to relate filed cases to each other in a new manner that the slide box proves inflexible.

SLIDES AND FILING CARDS

The 110 boxes of the part of the collection entitled 'autopsy archive' are, as I have mentioned, the oldest part of Lennert's collection. In his first years in pathology, Lennert mainly examined material from autopsies. A few years later, he moved to a different department and there he took on a new main responsibility: the diagnosis of biopsy specimens of hematological diseases. These examinations concerned living patients from whom a tissue sample was taken in order to obtain insights into the disease from which they were suffering. Here too, he collected interesting cases, but the slides were no longer deposited in classical slide boxes. Now he deposited the slides in small paper pouches that consisted of a filing card folded and fastened with three paper clips. This technique created a pocket into which he placed the slides. On the front side there was room for notes.

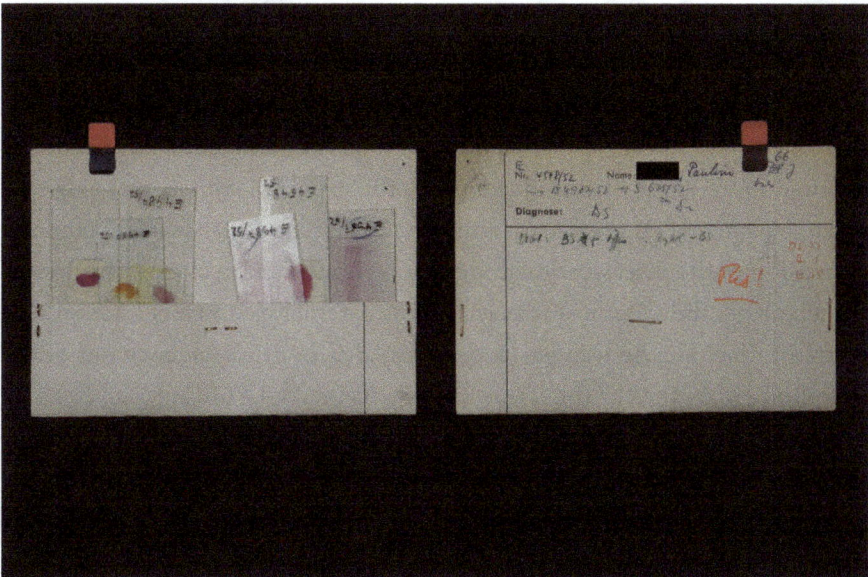

FIG. 6.3 Filing cards, one of 5,400 bioptic (intravital) cases from the Lennert Collection.

Why this change of filing technique? For a long time, the histological examination of biopsy specimens was a very uncertain undertaking. Misdiagnoses were frequent, particularly in the case of malignant lymphomas. While in an autopsy we are dealing with the end stage of a disease visible in a fully open body, in biopsy specimens it is an early or even initial stage in a tiny piece of tissue. The histological condition is consequently less specific and much more difficult to assess. Not least because of these problems, several biopsies were often carried out at different times. Thus, the revision of an older case was no longer merely an option, but was highly likely to become a necessity. Each time that new tissue from a case arrived, the older slides and the original diagnoses were reassessed. For this, newly prepared slides had to be added to old cases. On the other hand, the revision often resulted in a new diagnosis and thus a change in category. The case changed its place in the structure of the collection.

The central question in Lennert's professional life became how to improve lymphoma diagnosis, and hence he pursued an issue that began to gain urgency in the 1950s. At that time, the treatment of tumours with x-rays developed into a serious therapeutic option. It became evident that different tumours are differently sensitive to radiation. The more aggressive the progress of the disease, the more sensitive are the cells when exposed to radiation. Moreover, the first cytostatic drugs (in the form of nitrogen mustard and urethane) had become available in the late 1940s. Although the therapeutic results were modest at first, there were now various therapy options. Of course, differentiated treatments required more differentiated diagnoses – the expected course of the disease had to be anticipated prior to planning the treatment. Prognosis is a temporal dimension of the disease, something that is strange to the static snapshots of the histologic slide. But it was exactly these external parameters Lennert that wanted to include; he wanted to assess the degree of malignancy out of the morphologic picture of the tissue sample. To make headway here, Lennert began to follow up on the further clinical course of cases that had previously been examined, and to contextualise them with all relevant data (blood count, treatment, survival time). A filing card provides room for such notices; a box doesn't. For each slide there is only a single line for notes on the inside of the lid of the box. Only the underlying disease and the case number were included as information.

As lymphomas were systematically investigated, more and more categories were distinguished in the structure of the collection. Lennert separated out new entities and differentiated subtypes. The diseases that are combined under the term 'Retothel-Sarkom' in our box already comprise three entities in the so-called Kiel classification of 1974, behind which Lennert was the driving force (Bennett et al. 1974). Today, dozens of types and subtypes are distinguished. The slide box cannot cope with these changing needs and practices. The arrangement in the boxes is fixed. The cases are added consecutively according to an inalterable system. It is just as impossible to prioritise individual cases by means of subcategories as it is to add slides with newly prepared stains. For this, the slides have to be painstakingly taken out of the slots in the boxes and re-sorted.

By contrast, the cardboard pouches arranged in a filing cabinet form a highly mobile experimental system. The cases can be removed and re-sorted, in batches or individually. With a technique employing filing cards, things can be moved around. Gaps can be closed. Room can be made as needed. Moreover, new slides prepared from the likewise-archived tissue blocks using new laboratory methods can be accommodated with the individual cases. The new information gained in the process can be added to the previous notes. In fact, the cases were repeatedly revised over long periods of time, placed in flexible new categories, and related to the newest state of research. The key structural element of the collection now lay in the mobility of all elements and categories, which embodied an open mind for unanticipated things. The filing card pouches form the infrastructure of a research process from which a new classification system emerged. In 1974, the so-called Kiel classification was published. Its categories are clearly recognisable in the collection.

And the box? The box has a quality that the filing card pouches do not have. It is robust and stable; it protects the fragile slides reliably from careless handling. This feature made it indispensable for Karl Lennert throughout his professional life. Lennert's letters, and the notes on the filing cards, show how, as his scientific reputation grew, he operated in a constantly growing network of scientists and medical practitioners. Whereas all of the cases in the autopsy archive come from the hospital where Lennert was employed, many of the biopsy cases in the filing card pouches came from a great number of German hospitals or from other countries. The slide, as immutable and mobile, is easily compatible with an inexpensive resource that is available everywhere: the post office. As a well-known expert on the diagnosis of lymph nodes, Lennert was often consulted in difficult cases. Colleagues with whom he was acquainted sent him rare or unusual cases. Karl Lennert's correspondence reveals a lively exchange within the scientific community. Slides were circulated. For transporting these delicate slides by post, miniature slide boxes were used.

But classical slide boxes like ours were also still used. They accompanied Karl Lennert in his luggage when he travelled. There are several such slide boxes with selected slide sets in the collection. They are labelled with the names of large cities and dates – the dates and places of important conferences, workshops or tutorials. Despite the high-quality microphotographs and useful practical projection techniques that were readily available in the 1960s and 1970s and were employed in presentations, the original slides were always at hand. For these scientists, every meeting was an opportunity to discuss findings together under a microscope. The slide was always the most immediate and strongest argument.

And today? Using ultra-high resolution scanners, complete slides can be digitalised. This offers considerable advantages, and some technological enthusiasts assume that in the foreseeable future servers will take the place of the old slide archives. Many pathologists are sceptical, however. They point out that no reproduction technique can transport the optical brilliance, the radiance, and the rich details that an impeccable slide reveals to the eyes under a good microscope. One could say that this may change in time. However, the argument seems rather to confirm that microscope and slide continue to comprise the core elements of the identity of the thinking collective of pathologists. These instruments shape not only their daily work, but also their self-conception, and therefore appear indispensable. The slide box will probably still be around for some time.

ACKNOWLEDGEMENTS

The ideas and context of this essay are the results of an interdisciplinary research project on the biopsy collection of Karl Lennert, a collaboration between the Medical and Pharmaceutical Collections of the University of Kiel and the Kiel Lymph Node Registry. The project was funded by the Volkswagen Foundation.

REFERENCES

Balfour, J., *The Botanist's Companion: Or Directions for the Use of the Microscope and for the Collection and Preservation of Plants* (Edinburgh: Adam and Charles Black, 1860).

Bennett, M., et al., 'Classification of Non-Hodgkin's Lymphoma', *Lancet*, 304.7877 (1974): 405–08.

Bichat, X., *A Treatise on the Membranes in General: And on Different Membranes in Particular* (Boston: Cummings and Hilliard, 1813).

Daston, L., and P. Galison, *Objektivität* (Frankfurt a. M.: Suhrkamp, 2007).

Fleck, L., *Entstehung und Entwicklung einer wissenschaftlichen Tatsache* [1935] (Frankfurt a. M.: Suhrkamp, 1980).

Klebs, E., 'Die Einschmelzungs-Methode, ein Beitrag zur mikroskopischen Technik, *Archiv für mikroskopische Anatomie*, 5.1 (1869): 164–66.

Latour, B., 'Drawing Things Together: Die Macht der unveränderlich mobilen Elemente', in A. Belliger and D. J. Krieger, eds, *ANThology, Ein einführendes Handbuch zur Akteur-Netzwerk-Theorie* (Bielefeld: transcript, 2006), pp. 259–308.

Rheinberger, H. J., 'Epistemologica: Präparate', in: A. te Heesen and P. Lutz, eds, *Dingwelten. Das Museum als Erkenntnisort* (Köln, Weimar, Wien: Böhlau, 2005), pp. 65–75.

Smith, G. M., 'The Development of Botanical Microtechnique', *Transactions of the American Microscopical Society*, 34.2 (1915): 71–129.

Welcker, H., *Ueber Aufbewahrung mikroskopischer Objecte nebst Mittheilungen über das Mikroskop und dessen Zubehör* (Giessen: Ricker, 1856).

Willis, R. A., *Pathology of Tumours* (London: Butterworth & Co., 1948).

FIG. 7.1 Box

7

SYSTEM BOX (TRAY) WITH WASP

Tahani Nadim

Colour: white. **Size**: 115 x 90 x 40 mm. **Material**: recycled cardboard. **Weight**: 60 g. **Cover**: Chromolux paper, 80 gsm, glossy, embossed. **Producer**: Fapack. **Inlet**: plastazote, polyethylene foam sheet glued to bottom of the box. **Contents**: whole insects, insect parts, pins, labels, nightmares. **Habitat**: insect collection, Museum für Naturkunde Berlin. **Population trend**: increasing as it replaces old or outdated storage. **Mode of being**: excessive but orderly. **Likes**: the smell of naphthalene. **Dislikes**: water.

Keywords: waiting, taxonomising, individualising

DIAGNOSIS

THIS RECTANGULAR BOX COMMONLY APPEARS WITHOUT A LID. IT IS TO BE found in the insect collection of the Museum für Naturkunde Berlin, mostly in the company of similar boxes. It typically rests in so-called insect drawers, but it can also be observed on its own near the work stations of entomological researchers, as well as stacked with other boxes in the open supply shelves of the entomological collection. While in the latter case the box is devoid of content, in the former two cases it contains small insects, often in conjunction with labels, mounted on stainless steel pins. The box is made of recycled cardboard, which unlike plastic prevents the built up of electrostatic charge that could damage sensitive anatomical parts like hair, antennas, wings, or legs. It is distinguished by a) its relatively tall sides, precluding any contact between the top of the pin and any items which might cover the box, and b) its wrapping, which consists of white, glossy Chromolux paper, embossed with a faux leather pattern. The box has been folded using creasing, where (in contrast to mere grooving) a steel rule presses the cardboard into a steel channel, allowing neat folding without cracking. Accordingly, the folded edges are crisp and smooth, with an approx. 3 mm crease plane along its ventral edges. Its corners are held together by small glue tabs (not staples), which are dimly visible beneath the wrapping. Unlike the cigar and odd chocolate boxes that can still be found in some parts of the collection, this box is decidedly *professional*, that is, its sole purpose is to contain museum specimens. As such it is also properly 'non-reactive'. This means that no chemical or material residue from its components detracts from or interferes with the properties of the object contained. The box is lined with a 0.7 mm polyethylene foam base – a lightweight, odourless, and buoyant foam, into which the pins are sunk and secured.

HABITUS

Boxes are reared by hand in the south of Berlin (Neukölln, Firma Fapack), where they reach maturity within two days before migrating to the Museum für Naturkunde in the north of Berlin. They begin their lives as sheets of recycled cardboard (usually 120 x 80 cm or 90 x 70 cm) before being cut to size, creased, notched, folded, glued, and covered with acid-free paper. This process involves seven machines and four workers. Upon arrival at the museum, boxes are stored on supply shelves in various locations within the entomological collection, their distribution and allocation managed by the insect preparator.

FIG. 7.2 Boxes waiting in factory

BEHAVIOUR

Boxes are waiting. Waiting to be filled, waiting to be moved, waiting to be stored, waiting to be nestled into an insect drawer with fellow boxes. They are patient. They will have to endure a lot of transport and traffic before they can slide into the mostly calm order of cabinets. But even then, their respite is prone to disturbances. If, for example, they are chosen to house a type specimen or the only specimen of a rare variation, they will most likely experience further perturbations. Also, they are liable to rearrangements in the wake of taxonomic revisions, admittedly not a frequent threat to their stillness, but a constant one nonetheless.[1] Gazing at their solemn and unhurried presence in the various cabinets and shelves, it is difficult not to succumb to a notion of natural history as an essentially timeless pursuit. A steadfast circle of collecting, classifying, ordering. On closer inspection, though, it becomes evident that the box is definitely of a particular time. The glossy paper and its rather tacky faux leather embossing strike even the box's manufacturer as 'traditional'.[2] Indeed, the Museum für Naturkunde is the only customer still requesting this sort of paper. The production specifications for the box were inherited from the Kartonagenfabrik Reich after the fall of the Berlin Wall (the museum is located in what used to be East Berlin). Instructions from the museum only specify that system boxes need to stay the same as they 'have always been'.

Yet while the design of the box makes it a relic of the 1980s, its placement in some of the historical cabinets and insect drawers transforms it into a harbinger of the advanced order of a modern science. There the crisp, white, standardised box stands out in sharp contrast to the dusty, ornamental, wooden labyrinth of the insect collection, where different styles clash and disparate biographies have left their traces in records and routines. The box is thus perched atop a precarious assemblage which combines the practices of natural history with the demands of modern biology, two realities that have commonly been narrated on

FIG. 7.3 Boxes waiting in museum

the basis of their irreconcilability. Rather than solving or settling anachronisms, daily activities within the museum continuously parley with obsolescence: QR codes are stuck onto nineteenth-century drawers, and a state of the art SatScan collection scanner is nestled amid a digitisation suite built with left-over furniture spanning more than a decade of styles.

IN USE

The digger wasps arrived from Thailand. I did not witness their landing but I am most certain that they were transported in a box not unlike the system box. It was probably lined with additional supporting pins along the inner edge, and might have contained a cotton ball that would capture any head or leg or other body part falling off during shipping. Collected in the course of the Thailand Inventory Group for Entomological Research survey (2006–2009) – led by the University of Kentucky – they have been sent to Berlin for identification. Most are pinned, using minutien pins, fine stainless steel needles (0.2 mm). Some wasps, too small to be pinned, are glued to tiny triangular cardboard strips, so called card points. They all carry uniform labels noting the location of their capture, including GPS coordinates. The labels are yellow, following the colour codes first introduced by Martin Lichtenstein (1780–1857) to denote the geographic origin of specimens. The initial coding went as follows: yellow indicates *Orientalis,* white *Palaearctic,* light green *Neoarctic,* blue *Aethiopos,* dark green *Neotropis* and violet Australian region (Damaschun 2010). In preparation for our taxonomic examination, we grab fresh system boxes and group the wasps: the larger black ones with the blue metallic sheen go in one box, the two-tone ones (black head and thorax, rusty red abdomen) move into another, the tiny glued ones into another still. Carefully we pin each specimen into the plastazote that lines the base of the box, making sure that we do not bend the pins, and that the wasps are aligned evenly, facing the same direction, mirroring the neat rectilinear framing provided by the box.

In facilitating this first division of specimens, the box already proves its centrality to the taxonomic enterprise which, crudely put, is an attempt to find the right kind of box for the wasps. In more scientific terms, taxonomy seeks to identify and describe species according to more or less strict conventions

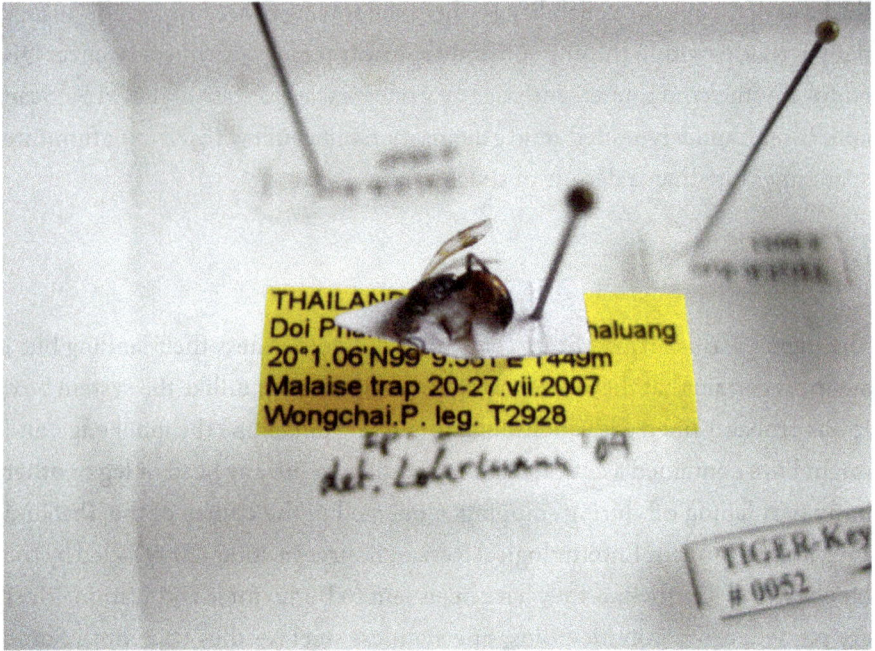

FIG. 7.4 Our wasp in a box

and endow them with a name, more specifically, a Latin name consisting of a name identifying the genus and a second one identifying the species. Unlike the description, this naming follows an extremely strict nomenclature. Once the name is published, it sticks, and the wasps will move into the genus- and species-appropriate box, drawer, and cabinet. The box is part of the tailoring that things have to submit themselves to in order to fit the purposes of natural history. By entering the box, the wasp transforms into an 'epistemic object', suspended between the material and the conceptual and distinguished by its potential 'to unfold indefinitely' (Knorr-Cetina 2001: 190). The box aims to facilitate the gradual unravelling of this waspish object: its inspection, probing, and comparing, so that it will come (temporarily) to settle conceptually in the taxonomic lineage of digger wasps, and materially, in the appropriate cabinet in the museum collection.

There, boxes are arranged and nestled in glass-topped insect drawers, a composition which is referred to as the 'tray system'. Using boxes and drawers, this system divides specimens order by order, family by family within the order, and genus and species within each family. This 'tray system' was most likely first developed by geologists, who used small open boxes, grouped in drawers according to location of extraction, to store and organise their minerals and rocks (Smith 1922). According to Smith, the tray system was adopted for zoological specimens by the United States National Museum in its hymenoptera (wasps, bees, ants, and sawflies) collection around 1910. The museum 'tried a number of different sizes [of boxes], not only in the width (...) but also in the length, and after trying out all of them (...)' it settled on what it considered 'by far the most satisfactory way of housing the collection' (S. A. Rower, cited in Smith 1922: 77). The tray system replaced the Comstock box and Schmitt box systems, which consisted of small wooden boxes with a solid lid attached on hinges.

In preparation for the wasps' ultimate boxing, the box provides a provisional holding cell along which we shall construe differences, kinship, and identity. Formally, as part of a wider grid, it upholds the promise of order in natural history which Foucault (2007) associated with the figure of the 'table'; like the list and the catalogue, the table constitutes a promissory genre of knowledge which allows us to pretend that the world is made up of parts that can be delineated, named, enumerated, and boxed. Like the standardised box holding so many different creatures, the table too allows for equivalence in the wilderness, allowing us to apprehend diversity even if this is only on a spreadsheet. That the box is standardised helps amid the sheer infinite variation contained within the cabinets. Boxing the wasp is the first step towards scientifically knowing the wasp, because only in combination with the box does the wasp become legible to the taxonomic apparatus which can now bear down on the tiny creature.

In order to identify the wasps, we need to craft elaborate descriptions of their bodies and compare them to descriptions and bodies of similar wasps, that is, wasps of the same genus collected in what is called the Indo-Burma biodiversity hotspot. We order similar wasps from other museum collections, and collate taxonomic descriptions from the entomological library. More boxes containing digger wasps arrive: a wooden one from Linz, Austria, one from the Smithsonian, two large square cardboard boxes with lids from the American Museum of Natural History, and a system box carrying only two specimens from Naturalis in Leiden. Boxes are thus essential not only for containing but also for mobilising specimens, pointing to the importance of *exchange* in the making of taxonomy (Ellis and Waterton 2005). While the epistemic import of the cabinet has been elaborated by te Heesen and Michels as a 'scientific apparatus' (2007), the box too serves this purpose, albeit in less sturdy, faithful fashion. Unlike the cabinet, the box moves easily, and although it more often than not ends up in a cabinet, its traffic is less predictable. So far it has circulated around the spaces of the entomological collection, but it has also ventured into the exhibition area and it might, once the wasps have been identified and their descriptions published, be placed in another box and shipped back to Thailand.[3]

The box gives the individual its coherence, shielding it from the intrusion of other specimens that are not of its genus. The spatial arrangement of the box thus mirrors the spatialisation that Foucault identified as being so crucial to natural history as it developed into a more systematic practice. With the foundation of botanic gardens and zoological collections, we witness, according to Foucault, a change of 'space in which it was possible to see them [animals and plants] and from which it was possible to describe them' (2007: 143). The locus of natural history, he continues, 'is a non-temporal rectangle', or, we might say, a box (ibid.). The rectangle of the box and the table are engaged in a process of purification, by which Foucault meant the purging of certain kinds of knowledge and apprehensions from the practice of natural history. But the box also indicates a spatial purification which came upon natural history museums in the nineteenth century when they began structuring their collections along two distinct activities: taxonomic research and public display. As an integral part of the museum's collection, the system box is exclusively to be found backstage, that is in what is called the research or study collection, in contrast to the display or show collection (*Schausammlung*) that is presented to the public. No longer the sole purview of amateur enthusiasts, museum collections became structured according to scientific rigour and, importantly, had to satisfy the demands of the new taxonomic regime, such as the collection of large series (to evidence natural variation). Kohler (2006) describes how this led to the professionalisation of museum staff and the extension of the remit of curators' work, no longer only caring for specimens indoors, but going out into the field to actively collect. The disarticulation of study collection and display collection is recounted as having been particularly acrimonious in the case of the Berlin museum where the newly opened building (1889, on Invalidenstrasse), while designed for a

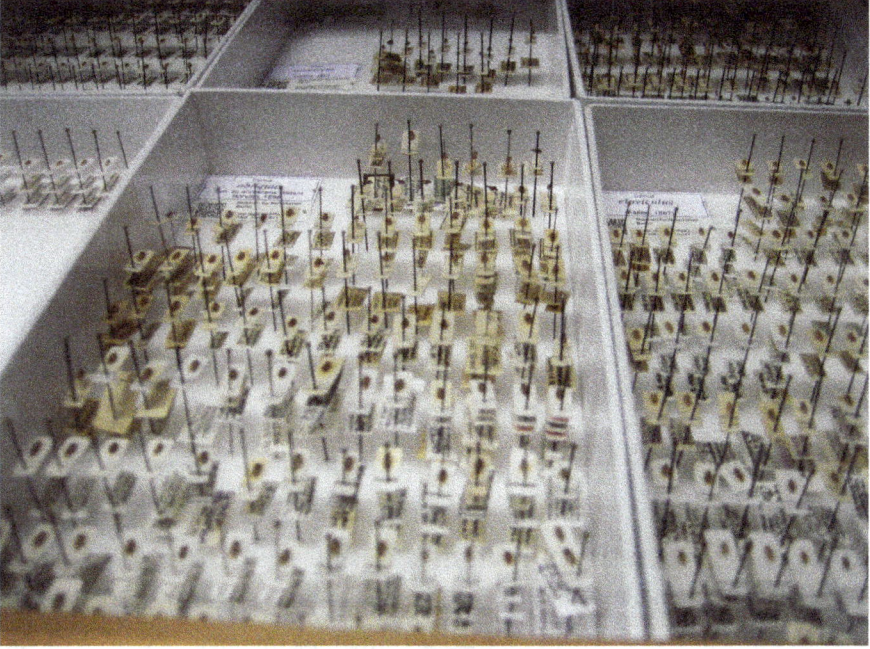

FIG. 7.5 Bugs in boxes

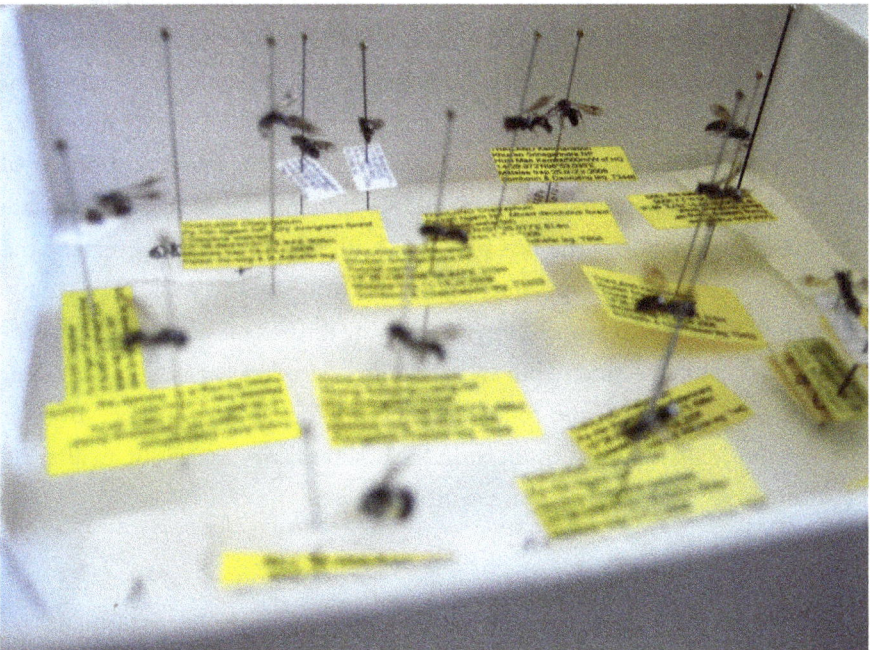

FIG. 7.6 Wasps in a box

holistic collection open to researchers and public alike, was divided into scientific (research) and public (display) collections. This division, instituted by museum director Karl August Möbius (1825–1908), had already been in place at Harvard's Museum of Comparative Zoology and London's Museum of Natural History, and was to become the model for all other European natural history museums. It was the effect of a novel 'scientific rationality in which a search for laws as revealed by recurrences at the level of the average or commonplace came to prevail over the fascination with nature's singular wonders' (Bennett 1995: 41). Despite its focus on the normal, the division meant that boxes such as ours were hidden from public view.

ON SHOW

In his paean to the tray system, Smith makes mention of the boxes' penchant for spectacle: no longer do we have to remove each specimen for closer examination, but we can now place the entire box containing the specimen beneath the microscope. This reduces environmental interference and minimises the need for handling the specimens. And so I move the box containing the smallest of the wasps, the ones glued to the card points, underneath a Leica stereomicroscope. I adjust the two bendy arms of the additional light source so that their rays point inside the box, whose white insides reflect the light and brilliantly illuminate the specimens. It is a dazzling spectacle as the light and the magnification reveal the grooves, hair, veins, tarsal parts, mandibles, antennal segments, and intricate sculpturing of the body. The box becomes both a systematic tool serving the taxonomic cataloguing of specimens, and the setting for the 'analytical staging' of specimens (Kretschmann 2006: 80). Moving the box underneath the microscope's lens, and directing lights and attention, detaches the wasps from their mundane surroundings, and renders them individual representatives of their species. But it also disjoins them from the stolid masses eking out an afterlife in the crepuscular ambience of museum cabinets:

> [I]n the [...] boxes, everywhere almost, the white deities who inhabited those sombre abodes had flown for shelter against their shadowy walls and remained invisible. Gradually, however, as the performance went on, their

vaguely human forms detached themselves, one by one, from the shades of night which they patterned, and, raising themselves towards the light, allowed their semi-nude bodies to emerge, and rose, and stopped at the limit of their course, at the luminous, shaded surface on which their brilliant faces appeared behind the gaily breaking foam of the feather fans they unfurled and lightly waved, beneath their hyacinthine locks begemmed with pearls, which the flow of the tide seemed to have caught and drawn with it; this side of them, began the orchestra stalls, abode of mortals for ever separated from the transparent, shadowy realm to which, at points here and there, served as boundaries, on its brimming surface, the limpid, mirroring eyes of the water-nymphs. (Proust 2006: 885)

Sitting in the stalls of the Opéra in Paris, young Marcel Proust observes the boxes which have become the stage for the real drama, the Duchesse de Guermantes and her entourage. Like the wasps, they too are emplaced on the basis of name and family. The box here serves as a protective container that is essential for the maintenance of social order, but also as a scenic setting, a veritable diorama that allows the young Proust to craft his ingenious associations. The specimens in his box transcend their initial (human) form, become entangled with feathers, flowers, and minerals, and rise into an entirely new class of creatures, suspended in the semi-height of the *bel étage* but utterly other and unreachable. Proust was a keen reader of the works of naturalists like Henri Fabre, and his descriptions of Parisian society are tinged with the kinds of observational mannerisms one can find in the ethological accounts of modern biology.[4]

Proust's *tableau vivante* found its match in the habitat diorama, a form of display where specially prepared specimens would be arranged 'lifelike' in front of painted backdrops that depicted their natural environment. While Foucault aligned the development of natural history to a succession of forms of knowledge (from show to table to series), the diorama combines these forms (2007: 286). Its invention – like the tray system, it originated in the American Museum of Natural History – is most often discussed as a response to the emergence of modern biology, which pitched systematicists against zoologists and museums against laboratories and other research institutions (Nyhart 1996, 2004). With respect to natural history museums, which were so adept at and, more importantly, adapted to the classificatory enterprise, modern biology posed a challenge as expertise (and legitimacy) moved to laboratories, field stations, and university departments. Karl August Möbius took over the Berlin museum in 1887, and not only separated the collection but strived for the display to go beyond a mere extension of the systematic catalogue of the scientific collection. Instead, he wanted the display to show the relationship between specimens, make associations across times and places, and generally imbue the display with sense and meaning for the benefit of a wider public (*Sinn stiften*) (Kretschmann 2006: 79). Foucault saw the shift initiated by Cuvier and, later, Darwin as a movement from classifying to a causal system – and morphology to functionality. It was with the recognition of evolutionary change that nature stopped being 'a homogenous space of orderable identities and differences'; instead, an all-encompassing, continuous idea of life emerged that was, as Gary Gutting put it, no longer of time but in time (1989).

Inspecting the different specimens we had ordered, I remove all those collected in Thailand, China, Laos, Vietnam, India, and Burma, and combine them in a new system box.[5] They will now serve as comparative variables in determining the identity of our wasps. It is an odd menagerie for creatures that are usually solitary. Much as the diorama offers a spectacularly theatrical scene, the system box too provides a specific perceptibility that, while certainly more sober than the diorama, can still contain drama. But the blandness of the box does its best to bracket off the imagination. According to Foucault, the removal of distractions, the exclusion of histories and general emptying out of context (the 'purification') was crucial to natural history (2007: 142). This convention of a purifying space carried into the stylisation of the laboratory environment, and indeed there is something to the box's whiteness that signals a laboratory state. Suspended in between the white walls of the box, the wasp is no longer critter, nightmarish crawler, but specimen, ready to come apart under the surgical gaze of the entomologist. Fixed on the needle, and hovering under the spotlight, it shines, its strangeness both exaggerated and domesticated. The white arena of the box, emptied of its six-legged contents, exudes stillness. I am reminded of Jenny Diski's 'wish for whiteout', the desire for 'a place of safety, a white oblivion' (in pursuit of which she sets sail for Antarctica) (2008: 2). Foucault noted oblivion, along with drama and alienation, as part of the resources that come with '[t]he flow of development' and modern biology (2007: 286). Here visibility is no longer attained through 'the grid of natural history' (ibid.: 287). Instead, the box structures a perceptibility that, akin to a whitewash, erases reference points, horizons and shadows to find purchase in objectivity (distance, a plane removed from environment).

The oblivion of the whiteout was institutionalised in the space of the 'white cube', the quintessential exhibition space for modernist art. Pioneered by New York's Museum of Modern Art and its founding director Alfred H. Barr (1902–1981), the white cube's distinct feature is the apparent lack of any distinctive features. Like Diski's imagined Antarctica, the sanatorium and the laboratory, the white cube is characterised by its emptiness and minimalism. Walls whitewashed, floors plain, all fixtures hidden away from sight, the white cube is stripped of all visual distraction and forces the viewer's gaze solely upon the works of art which are hung at respectable distances from each other; sculptural works are placed in the centre of the room.[6] What seemingly disappears in the white cube is context – any indication of a situation in time and social space. Unencumbered by politics and life, the art works can thus unfold their aura. For Brian O'Doherty, the white cube produces not only a specific aesthetic experience but works upon the art works themselves, which respond to the spatial conditions afforded by it (1999). This is then the ambivalence of the space: at once claiming neutrality to give art works their utmost autonomy, while also determining the production of a very specific kind of art work that was conceived in relation to the space.

The white cube is a disciplining space that manifests a clear distinction between the inside and the outside, so crucial to the conceptual and minimalist art of the time that was riding on the fantasy of interiority as autonomy. As Duncan put it, 'what matters is their [the art works'] power to demonstrate the art-ness of art and to transcend the meaning of those other beer and soup cans that are *not* in the art museum' (2005: 5). The system box, too, adjudicates between an inside and an outside, its border serving on occasion as a material and conceptual partition; maintaining the taxonomic order is a sort of border patrol. An additional advantage is that the box, once set into the insect drawer with other similar boxes, obstructs the spread of museum pests, bugs, and moths that consume their fellow insects. But therein also lies its impossibility. Because insects are countless. The boxes are wimpy safeguards for 'what we all already know: that insects are without number and without end, that in comparison we are no more than dust, and that this is not the worst of it. There is the nightmare of fecundity and the nightmare of multitude. There is the nightmare of uncontrolled bodies and the nightmare of inside our bodies and all over our bodies. There is the nightmare of unguarded orifices and the nightmare of vulnerable places. There is the nightmare of foreign bodies in our bloodstream and the nightmare of foreign bodies in our ears and our eyes and under the surface of our skin' (Raffles 2010: 201–02).

NOTES

1 The journal *Zookeys* lists fifteen revisions for arthropods in 2015. The leading journal *Zootaxa*, published daily (!), lists four revisions in its August 2015 issues alone.

2 Interview, Firma Fapack, 30 July 2015.

3 The box containing the wasp was shown as part of the exhibition '*Tote Wespen fliegen länger*' [Dead wasps fly further], Museum für Naturkunde Berlin, 3 March – 4 May 2015.

4 Incidentally, towards the end of his life, ailing and bedridden, Proust compared himself to a digger wasp as he 'bestowed the digger wasp's peculiar kind of care' upon all the books he knew he would not be able to read. In a letter to his editor, Gallimard, quoted by Anita Albus: 'Exiled from myself, so to speak, I seek refuge in the volumes that I caress as I am no longer able to read them, and I grant them the foresight of the digger wasp [...]' (2011: 127, my translation). Digger wasps show interesting parental care as they paralyse their prey (such as grasshoppers) and drag it into the nest for their offspring to eat once they hatch.

5 All belong to the genus *Alysson*, which had been identified by the Museum's digger wasp expert as the appropriate primary assignation.

6 O'Doherty characterises the removal of fixtures: 'the firehose in a modern museum looks not like a firehose but an esthetic conundrum' (1999: 15).

REFERENCES

Albus, A., *Im Licht Der Finsternis: Über Proust* (Frankfurt am Main: S. Fischer, 2011).

Bennett, T., *The Birth of the Museum: History, Theory, Politics, Culture: Policies and Politics* (London; New York: Routledge, 1995).

Damaschun, F., ed., *Klasse, Ordnung, Art: 200 Jahre Museum Für Naturkunde* (Rangsdorf: Basilisken-Presse, 2010).

Diski, J., *Skating to Antarctica* (London: Virago, 2008).

Duncan, C., *Civilizing Rituals: Inside Public Art Museums* (London; New York: Routledge, 2005).

Ellis, R., and C. Waterton, 'Caught between the Cartographic and the Ethnographic Imagination: The Whereabouts of Amateurs, Professionals, and Nature in Knowing Biodiversity', *Environment and Planning D: Society and Space*, 23. 5 (2005): 673–93.

Foucault, M., *The Order of Things: An Archaeology of the Human Sciences* (London: Routledge, 2007).

Gutting, G., *Michel Foucault's Archaeology of Scientific Reason: Science and the History of Reason* (Cambridge: Cambridge University Press, 1989).

te Heesen, A., and A. Michels, 'Der Schrank als wissenschaftlicher Apparat', in A. te Heesen and A. Michels, eds., *auf/zu. Der Schrank in den Wissenschaften* (Berlin: Akademie Verlag, 2007), pp. 8–15.

Knorr-Cetina, K., 'Objectual Practice', in T. R. Schatzki, K. Knorr-Cetina and E. von Savigny, eds, *The Practice Turn in Contemporary Theory* (London; New York: Routledge, 2001), pp. 184–97.

Kohler, R., *All Creatures: Naturalists, Collectors, and Biodiversity, 1850–1950* (Princeton, NJ: Princeton University Press, 2006).

Kretschmann, C., *Räume öffnen sich: Naturhistorische Museen im Deutschland des 19. Jahrhunderts* (Berlin: Walter de Gruyter, 2006).

Nyhart, L., 'Natural History and the New Biology', in N. Jardine, J. A. Secord and E. C. Spary, eds, *Cultures of Natural History* (Cambridge: Cambridge University Press, 1996), pp. 426–44.

——, 'Science, Art, and Authenticity in Natural History Displays', in S. de Chadarevian and N. Hopwood, eds, *Models: The Third Dimension of Science, Writing Science* (Stanford, CA: Stanford University Press, 2004), pp. 307–35.

O'Doherty, B., *Inside the White Cube: The Ideology of the Gallery Space* (Berkeley: University of California Press, 1999).

Proust, M., *Remembrance of Things Past, Volume I*, trans. by C. K. S. Moncrieff (Ware: Wordsworth Editions, 2006).

Raffles, H., *Insectopedia* (New York: Pantheon Books, 2010).

Smith, R. C., 'The Tray System for Insect Collections', *Transactions of the Kansas Academy of Science*, 31 (1922): 77–81a.

JUKE

FIG. 8.1 The Augsburg Art Cabinet, Museum Gustavianum, Uppsala, Sweden (photograph by kind permission of and copyright University of Uppsala Art Collections)

8

THINKING INSIDE THE BOX: THE CONSTRUCTION OF KNOWLEDGE IN A MINIATURE SEVENTEENTH-CENTURY CABINET

Stephanie Bowry

Box: the Augsburg Art Cabinet. Other names: Uppsala Art Cabinet, Gustavus Adolphus's *Kunstschrank* (art cupboard), *Schreibtisch* (writing desk). **Type**: miniature curiosity cabinet or *Kunstschrank*. **Origin**: Augsburg, Germany, 1625–1631. **Family**: one of six *Kunstschränke* which were designed by the Augsburg merchant and collector Philipp Hainhofer (1578–1647) between 1610 and 1635. **Size and shape**: the cabinet measures ca. 240 cm (height) by 120 cm (width) and has the appearance of a three-tiered box comprising pedestal, *corpus*, and crown. **Behaviour**: the cabinet's sumptuous materials and diverse contents were designed to engage both the mind and senses. The main body of the cabinet may be rotated 360° on its axis, and all four sides may be opened and explored. It also contains a number of hidden drawers and compartments. **Voice**: seldom heard, but contains a virginal which may be programmed to play three melodies at particular times of day when connected to a clock in the crown. **Habitat**: Museum Gustavianum, Uppsala University, Uppsala, Sweden. **Migration**: Augsburg, Germany, to Svartsjö Castle, Uppland, Sweden (1633), to Uppsala Castle, Sweden (early 1650s), to Library Hall, Gustavianum, Uppsala University (now Museum Gustavianum) (1694), to University Hall, Uppsala University (1887), restored to former Library Hall, Museum Gustavianum (1997) (Cederlund and Norrby 2003: 4–5) in storage (2019). **Status**: largely intact, some damaged and missing parts and objects, and some later additions to its collection.

Keywords: performing, entertaining, containing, juxtaposing, compressing, miniaturising, concealing, revealing, ordering, categorising, representing, monumentalising

THIS PHOTOGRAPH OF THE FRONT OF A SEVENTEENTH-CENTURY CABINET (**FIGURE 8.1**) reveals a complex, hybrid structure. Constructed from a rich variety of materials, including wood, metal, ivory, glass, marble, shell, and coral, its intricately carved and painted surfaces showcase a diverse range of media presented through a variety of techniques. Yet despite its visually spectacular appearance and wealth of ornament, it is essentially an elaborate wooden box, tripartite in structure and comprising from bottom to top, pedestal, *corpus,* and crown. In this photograph, two sets of doors open outwards to reveal a virginal in the upper section of the cabinet, and a series of miniature paintings and sculptures in the lower section. Yet arguably this box does not function solely as a protective container for objects and artworks: rather, the cabinet and its contents enjoy a symbiotic relationship, together constituting a single object and work of art in its own right. Furthermore, the Augsburg Art Cabinet, as it is now known, was not merely a piece of decorative furniture, static and silent, but a miniature 'curiosity cabinet' whose purpose was to reflect the representation of the world performed in the great universal collections of the early modern age.

This paper explores how the Augsburg Art Cabinet was deployed as a means of constructing knowledge of the world for its seventeenth-century audience through its visual, spatial and representational practices. In particular, I examine the use of physical framing devices, including architecture, iconography, and miniature objects, and how these were both experienced and understood to relate to concepts of knowledge-building during the seventeenth century. The paper offers some reflections upon the contemporary display methods used for the cabinet and how this early modern object is undergoing a slow metamorphosis which has stimulated the creation of new objects. I argue that the practices this miniature cabinet employed are still relevant today and should give museum professionals cause to reconsider our own position with regard to knowledge production and its interpretation. I shall begin by outlining a brief definition of the term 'curiosity cabinet', before considering the importance of boxes as both physical structures and as rhetorical framing devices during the early modern era. I then introduce the Augsburg Art Cabinet as a specialised form of cabinet.

DEFINING THE CURIOSITY CABINET

Cabinets of curiosity may be broadly defined as privately-owned collections of 'extraordinary' objects – typically those perceived as rare, beautiful, ingenious, or strange – which flourished in Europe from the late fifteenth to the early eighteenth centuries. Nevertheless, the history and etymology of the term 'cabinet of curiosity' are problematic (Olmi 2004 [1985]: 129). While in use throughout the early modern period (MacGregor 2007: 11), the term may refer to a physical cabinet, to the space in which the collection was housed and displayed, to the collection itself, or to related spaces such as libraries and gardens. Moreover, there pre- and co-existed many alternative terms, each of which possessed its own shades of meaning, evoking the distinguishable but subtle differences in the many types of collection which existed at this time, such as the *scrittoi*, a small, wood-panelled study which might contain both real and painted objects (MacGregor 2007: 12–13), and the *Kunstkammer*, or 'art chamber', which denoted a collection dedicated to the products of art and artifice. Likewise, the term 'curiosity' describes a shifting, nebulous concept during the early modern period, which had many different meanings and could be applied in a variety of contexts, of which intellectual endeavour was but one. Barbara Benedict defines it as 'the ambitious penetration of the unknown and the astute penetration of the untrue' (2001: 29). This version of curiosity was the driving force behind a thirst for knowledge which had yet to acquire the naïve and credulous overtones it increasingly accrued during the late seventeenth and early eighteenth centuries (Preston 2006: 91).

Then, as now, the 'cabinet', like the word 'museum', described many different types of collecting activity (Findlen 2004 [1989]: 160), whose practitioners were drawn not only from royalty and the nobility, but also from professional and mercantile backgrounds (Meadow 2002: 184), and included women as well as men. By the early seventeenth century these collections were prolific, and while some were more specialised, they often remained diverse in their scope (MacGregor 2007: 30). Some, such as the collection founded in London by father-and-son gardeners the John Tradescants, comprised art, antiquities, natural historical specimens, weaponry, coins, tools and instruments, and ethnographic items (Tradescant 1656: fols. 13^v–14^r). The purpose of assembling such a collection, as the English philosopher and courtier Francis Bacon (1521–1626) contended, was to furnish, 'in small compass a model of universal nature made private' (Bacon 1688: 55). Moreover, by collecting both natural and artificial objects, collectors hoped to investigate 'the various modes of Natures admirable workes, and the curious Imitators thereof' (Tradescant 1565: 6ᵛ). The cabinet was thus perceived to function as the mirror and microcosm of the natural world.

A SPECIALISED FORM OF CABINET

The *Kunstschrank* – literally, 'art cupboard' – was a particular feature of seventeenth-century collecting practice (Baarsen 2000: 4), and was designed to function as a miniature version of the *Kunstkammer*, although this designation did not preclude the inclusion of items from the natural world. These cabinets typically consisted of a collection of mostly artificial objects housed within a single, ornate and complex piece of furniture, and might perform a dual role as both a stand-alone collection and as the centrepiece to a larger repository (Hooper-Greenhill 1992: 120). If the cabinet aimed to reflect the world in a room, the *Kunstschrank* aimed to do so in a box, illustrating how, as Susan Stewart (1993: 43) contends, 'A reduction in dimensions does not produce a corresponding reduction in significance […]'. The *Kunstschrank* was also symptomatic of the early modern fascination with boxes and containers, and their symbolic properties.

CONTAINING THE WORLD IN THE SIXTEENTH AND SEVENTEENTH CENTURIES

Boxes and containers were integral to the construction and organisation of knowledge in early modern collecting practice. Writing in 1565, the Flemish physician, librarian, and custodian of collections Samuel Quiccheberg (1529–1567) described an ideal collection of objects. This collection would constitute nothing less than a 'theatre of the world', and would contain five categories of objects – objects relating to the collector and his or her realm, artificial objects, natural objects, tools and instruments, and objects relating to the representation and documentation of history (Bowry 2015: 97–117). Interestingly, both furniture and boxes in the form of 'little cabinets, chests, boxes, cases, small wicker-baskets, [...] little towers, pyramids themselves imitating chests' were listed as subcategories of collectible objects in their own right, not only for their aesthetic merit, historical interest, or exotic provenance, but for their role in 'recovering or revealing individual things in themselves' (Quiccheberg 1565, trans. Leonardis 2013: 22). Boxes in curiosity cabinets therefore served a symbolic purpose in which an object or image was identified by and through its receptacle, while the acts of concealment, containment, and revelation were perceived to uncover or heighten an object's significance and relationship to other objects within the collection.

THE CONSTRUCTION OF THE AUGSBURG ART CABINET

The Augsburg Art Cabinet represents an especially large and lavish example of a *Kunstschrank*. It was constructed between 1625 and 1631 in Augsburg, Southern Germany, renowned from the mid-sixteenth century as one of the chief exporters of richly-decorated furniture (Baarsen 2000: 3). The cabinet itself was probably the work of Ulrich Baumgartner (1580–1652), but approximately thirty specialist artisans worked on its decoration. When new, it housed a collection estimated at a thousand objects, many of which survive today (Cederlund and Norrby 2003: 3 and 13; Josefsson 2014: 56). These include such diverse items as a miniature human skull carved from bone, a pair of beard-curling tongs, a monkey's claw, a strap of human skin, a pair of mechanical dolls, a chess set, and a relic of the true cross. Woven into the fabric of the cabinet are many more objects, including semi-precious stones such as lapis lazuli, and miniature paintings.

The Augsburg cabinet was one of six designed by the merchant, diplomat, and collector Philipp Hainhofer, of which three now survive. Hainhofer had cabinets made to order for wealthy clients, but others, such as this one, were constructed without a specific buyer in mind, and filled with items from his own collection (Boström 2004 [1985]: 540). The cabinet was bought by the Augsburg Council and presented to King Gustavus Adolphus of Sweden as a diplomatic gift in 1632, on his entry to the city during the height of the Thirty Years' War. Hainhofer personally demonstrated the cabinet to the king and described how

After lunch his Maj[esty] looked at the third part of the writing desk and the summit with a coco d'India [Seychelles nut] (which I had to lift down) for one hour [...] and [I] was assured [that it] is a *magister omnium artium* [teacher of all the arts]. (Hainhofer cited in Koeppe 2008: 238)

It is evidence of the sheer intricacy of construction which seems to have defined the *Kunstschrank* that it required physical demonstration in order to be understood. As Barbara Kirshenblatt-Gimblett (2000: 129) has observed, '[i]t had literally to be performed to be known'. This necessity is further underscored by the Augsburg cabinet's inclusion of an image, in inlaid wood, of a smaller cabinet on a stand being demonstrated to a client in a workshop setting (**FIGURE 8.2**). As the cabinet also includes images of Augsburg, this could be interpreted as a piece of civic propaganda on the part of Hainhofer, advertising Augsburg

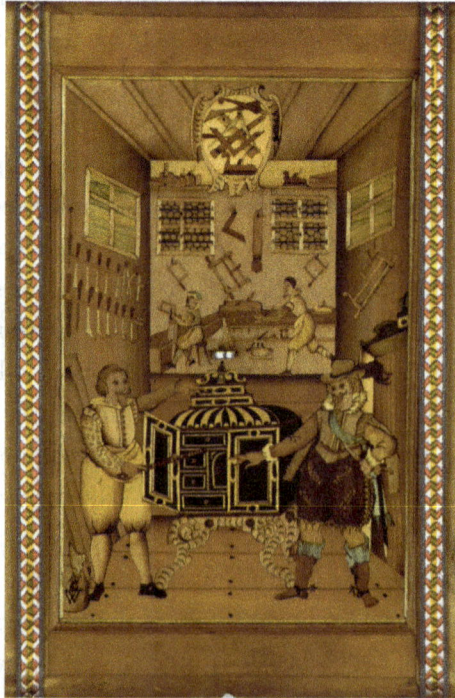

FIG. 8.2 In this image, a gilded and ebony-veneered cabinet is demonstrated by the master carpenter (left) to his client (right), UUK31. The reverse of this panel bears a second image of figures in a landscape outside the city of Augsburg (photograph by kind permission of and copyright University of Uppsala Art Collections)

as a centre of artisanal genius and luxury trade. However, it is also significant that this image not only effectively miniaturises and contains the image of a cabinet, or a technique associated with cabinets (intarsia), but also documents the cultural practice associated with cabinets: their manufacture, consumption, and clientele. The miniature, Stewart (1993: 66) argues, 'tends toward tableau rather than toward narrative, toward silence and spatial boundaries rather than toward expository closure'. The cabinet's attempt to encapsulate the world thus included the attempt to capture and contain the essence of itself within its self-imposed physical and conceptual boundaries.

Unfortunately for Gustavus Adolphus, he did not enjoy his cabinet for long – he was killed in the battle of Lützen just six months later, and the cabinet was disassembled and transported to the royal residence of Gustavus's widow, Queen Christina, at Svartsjö in Sweden.

THE ARCHITECTURE OF THE CABINET

I shall now examine each of the three elements of the cabinet in turn, in order to construct a fuller picture of their nature and relationship to each other.

The pedestal, upon which the upper body of the cabinet may be rotated 360 degrees, contains objects designed to help view the cabinet, including a collapsible table which may be removed and unfolded so that particular objects can be studied in detail and in comfort, and a drawer which converts into a step-ladder so that the top of the cabinet may be easily reached.

The *corpus*, or main body of the cabinet, is veneered in ebony – a costly, imported wood – but its heart is composed of oak and fir. It is here that the majority of objects were housed, within an intricate and layered arrangement of drawers, compartments, and removable panels. The Augsburg Art Cabinet demonstrably drew upon the structural elements of pre- and co-existing examples of material culture such as the writing desk, casket, polyptych, and shrine. Indeed, David Phillips suggests that the original meaning of the word *Kunstschrank* is 'art shrine' (Phillips 1997: 16). The cabinet's appearance is also comparable to a stepped tabernacle with architectural features such as swags and Corinthian columns, and reflects the argument that Baroque furniture pieces tended to be conceived as 'small monuments and were subject to the same architectural and aesthetic conventions as buildings' (Bussagli and Reiche 2009: 32). As a monumental structure (Argan 1989: 43), the cabinet sought to immortalise a particular mode of viewing and representing the world and time. Yet its theatricality of presentation was comparable to the Baroque *Bel Composto* or seamless integration of diverse media and themes, seen in seventeenth-century church interiors, which 'inspired devotion and conveyed a sense of mystery through illusion, surprise and sensual richness' (Bailey 2012: 158).

Finally, the cabinet is crowned by a mountain of *naturalia* – natural items from the earth and sea – including shells, coral, minerals, and crystals. On top of this sits half of a gilded Seychelles nut, or *coco de mer*, fashioned as a ewer balanced on the shoulders of Neptune, and in which sits a figure of Venus. The *coco de mer* was a highly-prized rarity in Renaissance Europe, and this element of the cabinet is designed partly as a piece of spectacle, but it also possesses strong symbolic connotations. The components of the mountain, while natural, have been assembled by human skill and ingenuity, therefore revealing the universal scope of the collection as a cabinet of art and the natural world, and the intersection, or joining, of these two categories. Moreover, the addition of Venus suggests a central theme of love, which arguably governs the symbolic and allegorical content of the cabinet (Boström 2004 [1985]: 548).

ICONOGRAPHY

The cabinet is richly decorated with miniature paintings, sculptures, plaques, and reliefs in which a large variety of artistic techniques are represented, from *pietra dura* to oil painting on alabaster. Even functional elements such as keyholes are festooned with Baroque imagery, and metamorphose into cherubim or the yawning mouths of grotesques. Images are often framed within individual cartouches, but when considered together they often tell a particular story or invite the beholder to reflect upon a certain theme. The inner doors at the front of the cabinet, for example, depict scenes from the Book of Genesis, portraying the creation of the creatures of the sea on the central panel on the left, and those of the land on the right (**FIGURE 8.3**). Smaller images representing allegories of the four elements and the four seasons appear on the silver plaques in the central section of the *corpus*, while the reverse of the cabinet contains images of

FIG. 8.3 The front side of the cabinet, displaying scenes from Genesis and an image of Christ crowned with thorns beneath the central door (oil on wood panel) (photograph by kind permission of and copyright University of Uppsala Art Collections)

the Last Judgement. The cabinet's iconography thus informs the beholder that the cabinet is designed to represent all of the world and all of time.

Beneath the double doors of the front side of the cabinet lie several more doors, compartments, and panels. An image of Christ crowned with thorns is located behind the first door, and beneath this lies another removable panel which offers a view of Augsburg. If this final panel is removed, one reaches the heart of the cabinet, which contains seventeen secret drawers each individually decorated with images of courtly love, forming a conceptual link with the 'Ship of Venus' at the top of the cabinet. Thus seamlessly combined within the same side of the cabinet are images relating to change and metamorphosis, the earthly and the sacred, and spiritual and temporal love, in which a multitude of interrelated meanings are possible.

Rather than view this object as the product of 'an obsessive *horror vacui*' (Rieder 1970), then, it is best to understand it as conveying a 'lost language of ornament' (Domeisen 2008), which functions as a framing device. As Domeisen argues,

> In picture frames and in the border of the illuminated manuscript, orna-
> ment negotiates between the real world outside and the fictional world
> of the text or painting. Ornament is containment. It is the home of meta-
> morphosis uniting and transforming conflicting worldly elements. It is an
> image of combination and a spectacle of transformation. Ornament is a
> method to subsume almost anything into the architectural idiom: human
> bodies, plants, militaria, geometric patterns, fantastical beasts – it is the
> realm of monsters and hybrids. Ornament is transgressive. (Domeisen
> 2008: 119)

Cabinets such as this one arguably employed certain fluid categories of things, such as *naturalia* and *artificialia* – natural objects and the products of craftsman-ship – in which objects might inhabit more than one category simultaneously. The Seychelles nut, for example, is a natural object manipulated by human artistry. Collectors delighted in objects which blurred the boundaries between the natural and the artificial, and Philipp Hainhofer actively sought out objects in which, as he put it, 'Art and Nature play with one another' (Boström 2004 [1985]: 551). The purpose of the cabinet was not to segregate things, although each object had its proper place, but rather to demonstrate the relationships between objects and ideas.

MINIATURE OBJECTS

Boxes and box forms are not only integral to the anatomy of the Augsburg cabinet; the cabinet also houses a large number of miniature boxes, containers or micro-encapsulations of a particular aspect of the cosmos.

If the notion of the box is extended to include miniature objects such as the tiny book (4 cm in height and 2.6 cm in width) produced in Munich in 1599 (**FIGURE 8.4**), it may be observed that this artefact was proof of human vir-tuosity and ingenuity, but it also reflects the fact that the *Kunstschrank* served to compress knowledge into as small a container as possible (Rieder 1970: 33).

The book contains two texts: the first, in Spanish, is a reflection on *conscientia*, or conscience, and the second, in Latin, comprises a litany, or prayer for the safeguarding of the Spanish realm. If the physical object was a repository of knowledge, the miniature object not only captured a form of situated knowledge but also drew attention to its representation within the allegorical sphere of knowledge that the cabinet enshrined. Knowledge of other worlds, both earthly and spiritual, might be held in the palm of the hand, and so through the conduit of the miniature, 'a narrow gate, opens up an entire world' (Bachelard 1994 [1958]: 155). Princely cabinets such as these thus physically demonstrated a temporal ruler's mastery or dominion over a geographical territory. Indeed, Quiccheberg recommended that his princely client install images and genealogical charts showing 'in exact order' the progression of significant persons 'in his universe' and his relationship to them all (Quiccheberg 1565, trans. Leonardis 2013: 3).

Furthermore, other box-like forms within the cabinet, such as the virginal, the miniature paintings, and the clock, are designed to contain supposedly uncontainable, intangible elements such as Music, Genius, and Time, and in this sense provide a microcosmic rendition of the *Kunstschrank* itself and a sense

FIG. 8.4 Miniature book, UUK 212. This tiny object measures 4 cm by 2.6 cm and boasts silver mounts and gold text (photograph by kind permission of and copyright University of Uppsala Art Collections)

of worlds within worlds. The miniature book, Stewart writes, 'speaks of infinite time, of the time of labor [...] and of the time of the world, collapsed within a minimum of physical space' (Stewart 1993: 39).

The cabinet in its miniature form can therefore be understood as a matter of complex and interwoven layers which gradually transport the beholder to smaller, larger, or different types of encapsulations of the world in its various aspects. It is in this sense more rightly a collection of lenses for looking at the world through material objects and their containers, in which the container, for perhaps the first time, enjoys a certain pre-eminence over the object.

CONTEMPORARY DISPLAY METHODS

Today, the Augsburg Art Cabinet is housed in the University of Uppsala's Museum Gustavianum, constructed with money donated by Gustavus Adolphus and situated opposite the cathedral in which the king lies buried. Until 29 September 2019, when the Museum closed for renovation, the cabinet formed the centrepiece of a gallery dedicated to the history of Uppsala University, and was displayed partially open but sealed within a cylindrical glass display case as an art object - and a curiosity - in its own right. In order that the objects it contains could be examined closely, many of them were removed from the cabinet and displayed thematically in a series of six wall and freestanding glass cabinets nearby. This method of display allowed the visitor to visually appreciate the cabinet and its contents from every angle. As a result, however, and despite its physical proximity to its seventeenth-century setting, the cabinet is in some sense alienated from its original context, which impacts upon its ability to function as a producer of knowledge. Thus, there has been what the artist and critic Paul Carter (2004: 24–5) calls a de-framing and a subsequent re-framing of the original seventeenth-century mode of display and interaction, in which touch was allied with vision. A digital interactive model mitigates this difficulty somewhat by enabling the viewer to rotate and disassemble the cabinet and explore some of its individual objects (Uppsala University 2008). Yet through this very different means of navigating the collection, and in the absence of a human demonstrator, 'Gone is the cloak of knowledge that once warmed the objects' (Kirshenblatt-Gimblett 1999: 132).

CONCLUSION

The Augsburg Art Cabinet provided a visual, tactile and powerfully theatrical performance of the key forms of knowledge production in the seventeenth century, in which the frame or means of containment surpassed the contained object(s) in importance. For historians of the museum such as Arthur MacGregor (2007: 17), the cabinet numbers 'among the most perfectly resolved expressions of the *Kunstkammer* ideal [...] in which every dimension of the standard curiosity collection was represented in miniature'. This cabinet not only comprises a complex 'family' of objects, but it also embodies a complex means of representing and understanding the world through specialised practices of collecting and display. Ultimately, it endures as a representation of the entanglement and manipulation of things, both material and conceptual, including systems of knowledge.

The cabinet's remit is to explore knowledge itself, but it is also to entertain, to be useful, to be a thing of beauty and an object of religious contemplation. The cabinet thus delights in what may seem to our taxonomic age incongruous juxtapositions. The intricacy of the Augsburg Cabinet, and its delight in not only encapsulating but also in subverting the world through objects neither wholly natural nor artificial, by blurring the boundaries between things, by hiding them from the gaze as well as overtly displaying them, also points to this. More importantly, it seeks to explore the limits of representation, and despite its sensuality and the manner of its operation – in which hidden things are slowly unveiled to the beholder – actually directs its audience to the possibility of worlds beyond the senses, and hence to worlds unknown. The existence of worlds invisible to human senses was of great interest to seventeenth-century philosophers, including Margaret Cavendish (1623–1673) who reflected that

> For many things our *Senses dull* may escape,
> For *Sense* is *grosse*, not every thing can *Shape*.
> So in this *World* another *World* may bee,
> That we do neither *touch, tast, smell, heare, see.*

> (Cavendish 1653: 43)

Moreover, the monumental quality of the cabinet offers, as Carlo Giulio Argan contends, 'a visible and plausible view of the world beyond the horizon of experience'. For, he argues,

> [...] to perceive something is not just to register it mentally, but to be solicited by it; the mind must create new systems of reference adapted to the perception of objects which are no longer "natural", but artificial products of man. (Argan 1989: 55)

The cabinet represents the fusion of different materials, techniques, cultures, geographies, ideologies, and themes. Its organic *naturalia* crown destabilises the rectilinear forms below, and makes the cabinet itself appear to be in the process of a mysterious transformation, hovering between the natural and the artificial, the temporal and the spiritual, the ancient and the modern worlds. The Augsburg Cabinet is thus also a persuasive rhetorical object which speaks of worlds beyond worlds as well as worlds within worlds.

There is also an element of poignancy in that this, the richest and most elaborate *Kunstschrank* to survive from the seventeenth century, now exists as a kind of time capsule for a particular way of looking at the world through material things. This should remind us all, in the best tradition of the *vanitas*, that it is not only material objects which disintegrate, it is also systems of knowledge, a phenomenon from which we ourselves, and our own knowledge paradigms and associated practices – museums, galleries, libraries, universities – are not immune. Doubtless in 380 years' time, our own systems and modes of knowledge construction will come under scrutiny and be consigned to a box.

Yet, paradoxically, this cabinet is far from a static relic of a past era: in fact, it has been continually translated and understood in new ways during its near-four-hundred-year history. Its collections served as teaching tools for university students as late as the nineteenth century (Josefsson 2014: 40), and in the early twenty-first century, the digital version of the cabinet located on the University of Uppsala's website allows visitors to view and manipulate a facsimile of this cabinet by turning it, removing panels, examining its components, or sorting objects into categories. Its music has also been digitally recorded, forming new objects of sound, including the sound of the virginal's mechanism being wound. To continue the natural metaphor, the cabinet has given birth to new versions of itself, which exhibit both reflections of and digressions from their parent. Far from being emptied of its secrets, this box possesses an undiminished power to beguile and to transgress boundaries. As its creator Philipp Hainhofer once observed, it remains 'a teacher of all the arts' (cited in Koeppe 2008: 238). It would be fascinating to explore these complex examples of cultural practice further, perhaps with a view to understanding their spiritual as well as temporal import, and how they were intended to concretise as well as to transcend time through the articulation of a space of 'intimate immensity' (Bachelard 1994 [1958]: 183).

ACKNOWLEDGEMENTS

With grateful thanks to Natasha Zedell-Wänn, Rebecca Flodin, and Anna Hamberg, University of Uppsala Art Collections, for their assistance in sourcing images for this paper.

REFERENCES

Argan, G. C., 'The Monument', in *The Baroque Age* (Geneva: Skira, 1989), pp. 41–51.
———, 'The Monumental', in *The Baroque Age* (Geneva: Skira, 1989), pp. 53–63.
Baarsen, R., 'An Augsburg Cabinet', *Bulletin van het Rijksmuseum*, 48.1 (2000): 135–37.
———, *17th-Century Cabinets* (Amsterdam: Waanders and Rijksmuseum, 2000).
Bachelard, G., trans. by Maria Jolas, *The Poetics of Space* (Boston, MA: Beacon Press, 1994 [1958]).
Bacon, F., 'A Device for the Gray's Inn Revels', in Brian Vickers, ed., *Francis Bacon: The Major Works* (Oxford and New York: Oxford University Press, 2002 [1688]), pp. 54–5.
Bailey, G. A., *Baroque and Rococo* (London and New York: Phaidon, 2012).
Benedict, B., *Curiosity: A Cultural History of Early Modern Inquiry* (Chicago and London: The University of Chicago Press, 2001).
Boström, H., 'Philipp Hainhofer and Gustavus Adolphus's *Kunstschrank*', in Donald Preziosi and Claire Farago, eds, *Grasping the World: The Idea of the Museum* (Aldershot: Ashgate, 2004 [1985]), pp. 537–59.

Bowry, S. J., *Re-thinking the Curiosity Cabinet: A Study of Visual Representation in Early and Post Modernity*, PhD Thesis, University of Leicester, 2015, <https://lra.le.ac.uk/handle/2381/32594> [accessed 5 November 2015].

Bussagli, M., and M. Reiche, trans. by P. McKeown, *Baroque and Rococo* (New York: Sterling, 2009).

Carter, P., *Material Thinking: The Theory and Practice of Creative Research* (Carlton, Victoria: Melbourne University Press, 2004).

Cavendish, M., '*Of many* Worlds *in this* World', in *Poems, and Fancies* (London: T.R. for J. Martin and J. Allestrye, 1653), pp. 44–5, Early English Books Online.

Cederlund, J., and M. Norrby, trans. by D. MacQueen, *The Augsburg Art Cabinet* (Uppsala: Uppsala University, 2003).

Domeisen, O., 'Beyond White Walls', *Architectural Design*, 78.6 (2008), 118–21, <http://onlinelibrary.wiley.com.ezproxy3.lib.le.ac.uk/doi/10.1002/ad.786/pdf> [accessed 21 November 2014].

Findlen, P., 'The Museum: Its Classical Etymology and Renaissance Genealogy', in Donald Preziosi and Claire Farago, eds, *Grasping the World: The Idea of the Museum* (Aldershot: Ashgate, 2004 [1989]), pp. 159–91.

Hooper-Greenhill, E., *Museums and the Shaping of Knowledge* (London: Routledge, 1992).

Josefsson, U., trans. by Annie Burman et al., *The Augsburg Art Cabinet* (Uppsala: Museum Gustavianum, Uppsala University, 2014).

Kirshenblatt-Gimblett, B., 'Performing Knowledge', in Pertti J. Anttonen, Anna-Leena Siikala, Stein R. Mathisen and Leif Magnusson, eds, *Folklore, Heritage Politics, and Ethnic Diversity: Festschrift for Barbro Klein* (Botkyrka: Mångkulturellt Centrum, 2000 [1999]), 125–39, <http://www.nyu.edu/classes/bkg/web/perf-know.PDF> [accessed 25 November 2014].

Koeppe, W., 'Collector's Cabinet of Gustavus Adolphus', in Wolfram Koeppe, ed., *Art of the Royal Court: Treasures in Pietre Dure from the Palaces of Europe* (New York: Metropolitan Museum of Art, 2008), pp. 238–41.

Law, J., 'Modes of Knowing: Resources from the Baroque', in J. Law and E. Ruppert, eds, *Modes of Knowing: Resources from the Baroque* (Manchester: Mattering Press, 2016), pp. 17–56.

MacGregor, A., *Curiosity and Enlightenment: Collectors and Collections from the Sixteenth to the Nineteenth Century* (New Haven and London: Yale University Press, 2007).

Meadow, M., 'Hans Jacob Fugger and the Origins of the Wunderkammer', in Pamela H. Smith and Paula Findlen, eds, *Merchants and Marvels: Commerce, Science, and Art in Early Modern Europe* (London and New York: Routledge, 2002), pp. 182–200.

Olmi, G., 'Science-Honour-Metaphor: Italian Cabinets of the Sixteenth and Seventeenth Centuries', in Donald Preziosi and Claire Farago, eds, *Grasping the World: The Idea of the Museum* (Aldershot: Ashgate, 2004 [1985]), pp. 129–43.

Phillips, D., 'The Cult of Saints and the Cult of Art', in *Exhibiting Authenticity* (Manchester and New York: Manchester University Press, 1997), pp. 5–27.

Pomian, K., 'The Collection: Between the Visible and the Invisible', in Susan Pearce, ed., *Interpreting Objects and Collections* (London and New York: Routledge, 1994 [1990]), pp. 160–74.

Preston, C., 'The Jocund Cabinet and the Melancholy Museum in Seventeenth-Century English Literature', in Robert Evans and Alexander Marr, eds, *Curiosity and Wonder from the Renaissance to the Enlightenment* (Aldershot: Ashgate, 2006), pp. 87–106.

Quiccheberg, S., trans. by A. Leonardis, *Inscriptiones Vel Titvli Theatri Amplissimi* (Munich: Monachii, 1565), Munich, Bavarian State Library, VD16 Q 63 (unpublished translation, 2013).

Rieder, W. P., 'An Eighteenth-Century Augsburg Cabinet', *The Burlington Magazine*, 112. 802 (1970): 32–7 <http://www.jstor.org.ezproxy3.lib.le.ac.uk/stable/876200> [accessed 21 November 2014].

Stafford, B. M., and F. Terpak, *Devices of Wonder: From the World in a Box to Images on a Screen* (Los Angeles: Getty Research Institute, 2001).

Stewart, S., 'The Miniature', in Susan Stewart, *On Longing: Narratives of the Miniature, the Gigantic, the Souvenir, the Collection* (Durham and London: Duke University Press, 1993), pp. 37–69.

Sundin, G., *A Cabinet of Play: A Study of Games and Pastimes in Philipp Hainhofer's Art Cabinet in Uppsala*. Bachelor's Thesis, Stockholm University, 2008, <http://www.gregersundin.se/download/a_cabinet_of_play.pdf> [accessed 24 November 2014].

The Virtual Art Cabinet, Uppsala University, 2008, <http://konstskapet.gustavianum.uu.se/webb/> [accessed 25 November 2014].

Uppsala University, 'Unique 17th-century Art Cabinet now on the Net' (press release, 19 January 2009) <http://www.uu.se/en/news/news-document/?id=462&area=2,3,6,16&typ=pm&lang=en> [accessed 5 November 2015].

Tradescant, J. [the Younger], *Musæum Tradescantianum: Or, A Collection of Rarities Preserved at South-Lambeth neer London* (London: John Grismond, 1656), Google ebook.

Weston, D. M., '"Worlds in Miniature": Some Reflections on Scale and the Microcosmic Meaning of Cabinets of Curiosities', *Architectural Research Quarterly*, 13.1 (2009), 37–48, <http://dx.doi.org/10.1017/S135913550999008X>.

FIG. 9.1 Tartölten in their case, SAM 208 – SAM 212 (photo copyright KHM)

9

MUSICAL INSTRUMENT BOXES. HIDDEN INFORMATION: CASES FOR MUSICAL INSTRUMENTS AND THEIR FUNCTIONS

Beatrix Darmstädter

Appearance: heterogeneous, pipe-shaped compartments. **Size**: dependent on outer forms of musical instruments and on their constructional parameters. **Habitat**: Europe; diverse social strata. **Origin**: case for *Tartölten*: Ambras (Austria), before 1578; case for the *spinettino*: Ambras (Austria), second half of the sixteenth century; case for four recorders: Catajo (Italy), sixteenth century, mark '!!'; case for a violin of tortoise shell: Imperial Treasury (Austria), made by Wenzel Kowansky, Vienna 1749. **Function (once)**: case for *Tartölten*: definition of a whole consort, storage; case for the *spinettino*: sound radiation, protection, adornment, musical use; case for four recorders: definition of a whole consort, transport, storage, frequent use; case for a violin of tortoise shell: work of art, showpiece, protection. **Function (today)**: case for *Tartölten*: object on display, definition of a whole consort; case for the *spinettino*: object on display, protection, adornment; case for four recorders: object on display, research specimen; case for a violin of tortoise shell: object on display, work of art.

Keywords: protecting, transporting, creating unities

IN MUSEUMS AND COLLECTIONS, CURATORS, RESTORERS, MUSICOLOGISTS, instrument makers, and musicians deliberate intensively upon the aesthetic identity of cases and etuis for musical instruments. The reflection process is orientated toward the evaluation of the historic values of the items and the assessment of mostly forgotten artisanal technologies, and it accounts for the artistic elements that characterise the object. Therefore boxes, cases, etuis, quivers, and sheaths rank among the most important semiophors – to use Krzysztof Pomian's term (1988: 81) – in collections of musical instruments, although in exhibitions they are mostly given an insignificant role as inconsiderable accessories far inferior to the renowned and artistically elaborated instruments. In fact, however, in the context of modern organology, these items – especially the cases of woodwind instruments – mutate from simple historical containers and useful transport aids into highly interesting objects of investigation that provide complex indications for musicology, modern instrument making, and performance practice.

Today's musicians need etuis that protect their instruments from environmental influences and from damage. The etuis should help them to transport their instruments securely and comfortably, and allow for quick handling in the course of putting the instrument into and taking it out of the case. Ideally there should be room for accessories in the etui, too. The high-tech material that is available for today's instrument cases is durable, light, and waterproof. The synthetic material of the interior lining has to be dust-binding and humidity-absorbing to create a certain climatic stability. The intended purpose of the case, and the expectations of the musicians, are known by the manufacturers, who produce commodities that fulfil the requirements of the musicians – this is consumer-oriented production. The design of instrument cases and etuis arises from concrete demands originating in the designated use. Thus it is clear that modern etuis and cases are merchandise, being – like all commodities – exchangeable and replaceable at any time. As far as contemporary items are concerned, clients, manufacturers, historians, and museologists agree that the function, which is the ontological criterion of such etuis, does not have any music-reference. The function is independent from the distinct instrument-model or instrument-type kept in the etui.

The instrument case produced according to modern requirements therefore qualifies as a commodity or consumer item, whereas the instrument case of the Renaissance and Early Baroque was usually crafted in accordance with criteria of the highest manual skills and craftsmanship *(techné)*. It can thus be referred to as an authentic, singular item created in the sense of Martin Heidegger's *'Werkschaffen'*, testifying to the mastery of highly qualified artisans, who occasionally signed their work (Heidegger 1960: 58). The material and form of the historic case comply with the requirements defined by the musical instruments.

We define three categories of instrument cases:

Cases of the first category and the instruments kept in them are in general interchangeable. These boxes serve as carriers to transport and protect the musical instrument. The empty case does not tell us much about the missing content.

The cases and etuis of the second category are similar to those of the first category but they form an inseparable aesthetic or functional unit with the instrument. The empty case tells us a lot about the conceptual details of the instrument. On the basis of its craftsmanship and artistic style, important information about the date of origin as well as about technological aspects of the instrument can be seen.

The objects possess the distinguishing marks of the antecedent categories, but in addition they may have a certain 'opus-character' because of marks or signatures. They inform us about musical and organological facts. This category includes in particular cases for woodwind instruments that indicate the length as well as the diameter of the instrument. Etuis of the third category are particularly interesting when their content is missing or has been separated from them. Although the instruments themselves – with their different pitches, that theoretically can be combined (sixths, fifths, fourths, thirds) – may be scattered worldwide, substantial rules for the formation or 'layering' of consorts can nevertheless be educed from these cases.

Due to the importance of instrument cases and etuis, it would be desirable to leave more room to them in exhibitions, and to give them proper consideration within educational museum events.

A short retrospective view of historic instrument cases and etuis shows that 'protection' and 'transport' is the purpose of the cases in the first category. Protection and transport have been relevant from the very beginning, and constitute the primal function of instrument cases. Whenever the forms and dimensions of the musical instruments do not change, a general exchangeability of the item exists. Contrary to the uniformity of musical instruments today, an immense variety of shapes can be seen within one and the same instrument class in the Renaissance and Early Baroque. So it is assumed that each instrument had its fitting case individually made by a box- or sieve-maker. The five *Tartölten*[1] from the inventory of the Ambras collection founded by Ferdinand II of Tyrol form, together with their instrument cases, a unique set of objects, in particular because these items are exclusively preserved in the collection of the *Kunsthistorisches Museum* Vienna and they are of exceptional artisanal and art-historical quality. The case as a semiophor is important in so far as it informs us about the togetherness of the existing *Tartölten*-consort, whose instruments were designed with matching concert pitches by an anonymous maker (see **FIGURE 9.1**). Regarding the compartments of the instrument case, no conclusion – neither about the exact pitch nor about the sort of instruments – can be drawn, because the division of the box does not mirror the outer form of the woodwind instruments or their sounding length. If posterity inherited merely the cases of these instruments without any *Tartölt*, it would be impossible to infer the sort, appearance, and workmanship of the instruments.

Instrument cases of the second category do not only serve as transport carriers and protection devices but they are also connected with the instrument as far as the aesthetics is concerned. This relationship is pointed out on the basis of the form, material, style, and ornaments of the case, or by the individual artisanal style of the maker. Diverging from category one, the original togetherness of the case and the instrument is given, and usually the instrument maker and the maker of the etui were one and the same person. The violin made of tortoise shell by Wenzel Kowansky (SAM 638, see **FIGURE 9.2**), who did not work as an instrument maker but who was a renowned box maker, is considered to be an art object. This object (acquired by the Habsburg Empress Maria Theresia in 1749), is, however, composite: the etui, the violin and the bow form a single aesthetic entity. One unique feature of this entity is the fine gold-wire bordure of the etui, that traces the exact contour of the individual instrument, and assigns the bow its proper place. Moreover, it was made to fit the rounded pegbox which is a very individual feature of Kowansky's instrument, and cannot be found

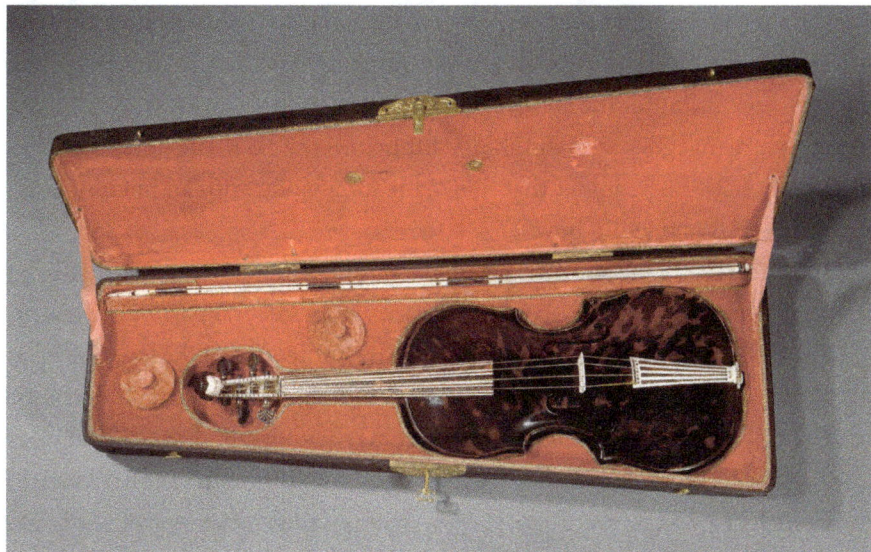

FIG. 9.2 The case for the violin made of tortoise shell, SAM 638 (photo copyright KHM)

FIG. 9.3 The spinettino in its box, SAM 121 (photo copyright KHM)

anywhere else. From the aesthetic point of view, the decorative elements of the instrument and the bow correlate with the ornamental details of the case – like the gold wire purling or the inlay of gold and ivory on the bow, as well as the gold wire bordure that goes with the golden fittings on the case. The opened etui by Kowansky tells the beholder that it is made for a violin with an uncommonly shaped pegbox and violin bow.

The outer box of the anonymous Italian *spinettino* (SAM 121, **FIGURE 9.3**) from the second half of the sixteenth century is an integral part of the instrument's aesthetic identity. Beyond improving the protection of the fragile corpus of cypress, it also enhances the sound radiation of this small instrument when it is open. This *spinettino* has a very special geometry, with individual angled sides intrinsically tied to the outer box. If the outer box of the *spinettino* and the case of the violin by Kowansky were passed down without their instruments, one could reconstruct most of the structural details of the instruments: The inner measurements of the outer box of the keyboard instrument provide information about the arrangement of the strings and their length, as well as about the approximate compass. By dint of the outer box, it is possible to identify the exact sort of instrument it was made to contain, and moreover the ornaments and aesthetic style help to date the instrument and to assign it to a certain region. The information given by cases of the second category is thus very dense and highly significant.

There is a third category of instrument case in the Renaissance and Early Baroque; into this category fall etuis that, in addition to their basic functions of protection and transport, have a very meaningful aesthetical component, showing an immanent reference between the musical instrument they unite and general musical parameters. These cases are of particular interest, and should be looked over closely, items of this category being inherently connected to the music itself. Martin Agricola leaves his readers – in the fourth edition of his *Musica instrumentalis deudsch* of 1545 – the following advice (1896: 158):

Cautela.
Wist auch meine lieben knaben
Wolt ihr gestimpte pfeiffen haben /
So keufft euch die jnn futtern fein
Dann die andern sind falsch gemein.

[Cautela. You know, my dear boys
If you like to have pipes in tune /
Buy them in nice cases
Because the others usually sound wrong.]

Woodwind instruments (*Pfeiffen*) that form a consort and therefore have the same pitch-standard (or at least pitches that match while playing together) are united in cases. Thus woodwind instruments that are not bought in etuis are single instruments with individual pitches. They are neither suitable for consort playing nor for making music with musicians who use different pitch levels. Standardised pitches did not exist from the medieval age to the classic. Instead, pitches developed on the basis of local predilections and regional traditions, and they varied by the musical genre, for which reason the free combination of woodwind instruments was largely impossible. Woodwind instruments in cases did not only stand out due to their compatible pitch, but they also formed an aesthetic – artisanal, visual and tonal – oneness. Agricola's statement is thus highly relevant for performance practice, as well as being trend-setting in terms of today's organological and museological work.

In the Collection of Historic Musical Instruments of the *Kunsthistorisches Museum*, Vienna, forty-three Renaissance recorders and four etuis are preserved, which equates to about one fifth of the worldwide existing items of this type. Of these recorders, all but ten are signed with marks. Among the cases for recorders, one object bears a mark. By dint of the mark and its variants, it is possible to define the origin of the items and to assign them to certain workshops. Although knowledge of this provenance does not reveal the togetherness of the instruments – which can only be defined by the pitch – artisanal, technological and aesthetic criteria may affirm the alliance of the instruments. The pitch is usually defined on the basis of geometric measurement, of impedance measurement, or by synthetic blowing using dry air and steady air pressure.[2]

The case for recorders (SAM 171, **FIGURE 9.4**) offers much hidden information about performance practice in the Renaissance (Darmstädter 2006: 264–65; Darmstädter and Lueders 2008: 95–105). This item is signed with one single silkworm moth ('!!') in the inside of the cap, which relates it to the workshop of the Bassanos in London (Lasocki and Prior 1995: 80).[3] The etui

FIG. 9.4 The case for four recorders signed with '!!' SAM 171 (photo copyright KHM)

belongs to the Este-collection and ranks among the original inventory of the museum. In historic documents this case is described as a single object, and it is not mentioned in connection with concrete instruments. Thus it was considered as an isolated object until 2008, when further analysis was carried out. The object was probably damaged in the course of the evacuation of the collection during the Second World War. In 1920 Julius Schlosser described the item as an entire case (Schlosser 1920: 80). There was lively interest among musicologists, instrument makers, and musicians to restore and reconstruct the case, because the variant of the stamp motive on the cap could be noticed on the sole of the foot of the alto-sized recorder 'SAM 135', too. For generations this particular instrument was said to be a 'typical solo flute' because of its bright and easy sound, its above-average compass, and many other conceptual details, like the progression of the inner bore, the elaboration of the foot-part, the dimension and position of the finger holes, the huge undercuttings, the shape of the window and labium, etc. All these features pointed to an exceptional, highly individual instrument, and led scientists to assume that this recorder never belonged to a consort, but was played in solo-music. Countless instrument makers copied this recorder and distributed it worldwide under the name of 'the Ganassi-recorder', because its playing properties corresponded largely with the characteristics of the recorder model 'B' in Silvestro Ganassi's *Opera Intitulata Fontegara* of 1535. In the middle of the 1990s, Maggie Lyndon-Jones cast doubt on this idea, and on the worldwide trend of using all these sketchy replicas of SAM 135 just for virtuoso solo music. She put forward the hypothesis that SAM 135 possibly belonged to a consort (Lyndon-Jones 1999: 262). Many instrument makers and musicians ignored her remark, but the reconstruction of the case SAM 171 provided the opportunity to analyse its historic material and artisanal know-how. Its cover was found to be of leather, in which the substances sulphur, chlorine, potassium, calcium, iron, and zinc were detected. The black colouration was done with iron gall ink. As aluminium, which is needed for white tanning, could not be found in the leather, a vegetal tanning was applied. Potassium and calcium were brought into the material in the course of liming. The parts of the case were fixed with animal glue, while the cover was possibly coated with a mixture of paste and glue to avoid gleaming blotches, and to secure water resistance (Thon 1856: 27; Darmstädter 2011: 103). Today scientists assume that cases for woodwind instruments with round shaped compartments were produced in a work-sharing process. In this process turners, tanners, bookbinders, and shoemakers may have participated. The inner lengths of the tubes are today 622.2 mm, 427.6 mm, 428.0 mm, and 287.0 mm. The etui comprises one tenor-sized recorder, two alto-sized recorders, and one descant-sized recorder. It is quite obvious that the proportions of the tubes with circa 2:3 suggest layers in fifths. The hypotheses that the alto recorder SAM 135 was kept in this etui may now be checked in practice: The instrument fits perfectly into the tubes of medium length.[4] The alto recorder SAM 135 has its pitch on g#[1] (at a[1] = 440 Hz). Finally we can state that the historic case united a consort in *mezzo punto*. Its missing descant should be tuned on d#[2] and the missing tenor recorder on c#[1]. Unfortunately no other fitting instrument that could complete this consort has appeared until now in the Viennese collection or anywhere else. So one has to assume that the recorders that originally belonged to the case SAM 171 did not survive. With the help of this etui, however, it has at least been possible to prove that the recorders with features described by Silvestro Ganassi were indeed combined in consorts and not (only) used as solo instruments. This fact is one of the most important conclusions in the field of performance practice within recent years, and it could never have been stated without the information given by the instrument case.

By translating the measurements and technological parameters of the recorder SAM 135 into the missing instrument sizes, and by using the information deduced from the etui, today's instrument makers are able to reconstruct the whole consort, and musicians can revive the sound of the lost instruments.

NOTES

1 *Tartölten* are double reed instruments with a slightly conical inner bore that runs helically through the interior of the whole corpus, on which equidistant finger holes enable the playing of precise tones.

2 In practice the applied method depends on the condition of the instrument and on the kind of sound production. The impedance measurement achieves good results for brass instruments (provided that the original mouthpiece is used), for recorders the implementation of organ blowing devices is advisable (on condition that the windway and the labium are intact), whereas for reed instruments the impedance measurement (single reed instruments) or acoustic calculation (all reed instruments) produce good results. The playing of the instruments by musicians is ineffectual because many subjective parameters (embouchure, air regulation, musical modulation, etc.) influence the sound, and all musicians compensate for the characteristics of their instrument, so that the musician always comes to the fore. Moreover, the playing of woodwind instruments by musicians is off-limits in museums – where the conservation and protection of the items is the central concern, humidity, heat and other negative influences are prohibited.

3 This sign symbolises the wings of the silkworm moth.

4 Due to the shrinkage of the wood, it seems that the diameters of the tubes decreased slightly. Originally there was enough space between the instrument(s) and the inner surface of the etui to wrap the recorders in a thin cloth to avoid unattractive scratches on the surface of the instrument(s).

REFERENCES

Agricola, M., 'Musica instrumentalis deudsch', 1st and 4th edn, Wittemberg 1528 and 1545, in *Publikation älterer praktischer und theoretischer Musik-Werke* (Leipzig: Gesellschaft für Musikforschung, 1896).

Darmstädter, B., 'Die Renaissanceblockflöten der Sammlung alter Musikinstrumente des Kunsthistorischen Museums', in *Sammlungskataloge des Kunsthistorischen*

Museums, vol. 3, ed., W. Seipel, with contributions by A. Brown (Vienna-Milano: Skira, 2006).

——, 'Die Zinken und der Serpent der Sammlung alter Musikinstrumente', in *Sammlungskataloge des Kunsthistorischen Museums*, vol. 7, ed., S. Haag, with contributions by B. Dickey and D. Salaberger (Vienna–Bergkirchen: Bochinsky, 2011).

Darmstädter, B., and W. Lueders, 'Über die Wiederherstellung eines bedeutsamen Blockflötenköchers', *Tibia Magazin für Holzbläser*, 33.2 (2008): 95-105.

Heidegger, M., *Der Ursprung des Kunstwerks* (Stuttgart: Reclam, 1960).

Lasocki, D., and R. Prior, *The Bassanos: Venetian Musicians and Instrument Makers in England, 1531–1665* (London: Scholar, 1995).

Lyndon-Jones, M., 'A Checklist of Woodwind Instruments marked!!', *The Galpin Society Journal*, 52 (April 1999): 243-80.

Pomian, K., 'Der Ursprung des Museums: Vom Sammeln', in *Kleine kulturwissenschaftliche Bibliothek*, vol. 9 (Berlin: Wagenbach, 1988).

Schlosser, J., *Die Sammlung alter Musikinstrumente. Beschreibendes Verzeichnis* (Vienna: Schroll, 1920).

Thon, Chr. Fr. G., *Die Kunst Bücher zu binden, oder die Buchbinderkunst auf ihrem neuesten Standpuncte*, 5th edn (Weimar: Voigt, 1856).

FIG. 10.1 Disposable straw cage (without cricket) (source: Bopuke 波普客 (Popcorn idea factory), 2015: 108)

10

BOXING CRICKETS: A TAXONOMY OF CONTAINERS FOR SINGING AND FIGHTING ENSIFERA

Martina Siebert

Box: caging, and facilitating handling (lightweight and with many holes); enhancing sound (while making the carrying pleasurable); controlling humidity and temperature to extend life (with time-honoured dignity in clay). **Size and shape**: spherical and 5 cm in diameter, or tube-shaped and about 5 cm in diameter and 18 cm in height, or a round box of 16 cm in diameter and 14 cm in height. **Colour**: according to the material, i.e. yellow (straw), white (bone or ivory), light to dark brown or middle grey (gourd, wood, clay). **Behaviour/ Activity**: hung on bedsides, used as decoration for garden parties, carried around in inside pockets, displayed on shelves, placed in the middle of an eagerly watching crowd. **Habitat**: sleeping rooms, scholars' studios, market places, gambling houses, museums. **Distribution**: Sinosphere, in the past also in Japan, but only for singing. **Migration**: from boxes with cricket residents to empty arts and craft objects in museums worldwide. **Status**: survived a period of endangerment in the 1960s and 1970s, but with this exception has been thriving in the Sinosphere since the eighth century; has experienced various changes and adaptations in material and shape.

Keywords: caging, facilitating handling, being disposable, emanating dignity, being collectible, enhancing sound, controlling humidity and temperature, extending life, attracting interest

TYPE I: MUSIC AND CARRYING BOX

<table>
<tr><td>In the seventh month, in the fields;</td><td>七月在野、</td></tr>
<tr><td>In the eighth month, under the eaves;</td><td>八月在宇、</td></tr>
<tr><td>In the ninth month, about the doors;</td><td>九月在戶。</td></tr>
<tr><td>In the tenth month, the cricket,</td><td>十月蟋蟀、入我牀下。</td></tr>
<tr><td>Enters under our beds.</td><td>('Seventh Month', in Book of Odes
詩經, trans. by James Legge)</td></tr>
</table>

<table>
<tr><td>The cricket is in the hall,</td><td>蟋蟀在堂、</td></tr>
<tr><td>And the year is drawing to a close.</td><td>歲聿其莫。</td></tr>
<tr><td>If we do not enjoy ourselves now,</td><td>今我不樂、日月其除。</td></tr>
<tr><td>The days and months will be leaving us.</td><td>('The Cricket', ibid.)</td></tr>
</table>

THESE TWO POEMS FROM THE CANONICAL *BOOK OF ODES* (SIXTH CENTURY BCE) lay out how crickets marked the passage of the seasons with their movement from their place of birth in the field into the warm houses of humans, undertaken in the hope of extending their lives for a while longer. Their chirping sound brought the end of a yearly cycle right under people's beds. This instinctive behaviour of the cricket was transformed into a courtly art and culture in China since at least the Tianbao era, i.e. 742 to 756, of the Tang dynasty. A collection of anecdotes about this era mentions how palace ladies hunted down crickets to put them in cages made from ivory sticks or gold wire, and placed them next to their pillows. While having a calming effect on their sleep, the 'autumn insect' (*qiuchong* 秋蟲), as the cricket is sometimes called, also reminded them of the passing of summer and the fading of their beauty, and maybe, as the *Book of Odes* encourages, to enjoy youth while it lasts. For the Chinese this is a strong and poetical image: palace beauties and insects, both caged, both doing time in an environment that feeds them and tries hard but will nevertheless not be able to eternally extend their singing lives or attractive beauty.

Nowadays, from late summer onward, small ball-shaped straw cages (**FIGURE 10.1**) are sold on Chinese city streets for a few pennies. The hand-woven cages have no exit and enclose one singing cricket, mostly coming from the biological family of *Tettigoniidae* crickets, and commonly named as katydid, bush cricket, or *guoguo* 蝈蝈. The cricket and its disposable cage are one, and are thrown away together after the insect has died and the object stopped working as a music box emanating chirping sounds. Food pieces are passed through the eyes of the lattice to 'wind up' the chirping; good care and a constant, warm temperature are repaid with chirping that lasts at least until late November, and sometimes even Chinese New Year, i.e. early February.

Japan most probably copied the custom of keeping singing insects in cages early on in the Heian period (794–1185) (Hammond 1983: 81). At the end of the nineteenth century the Irish-Greek writer Lafcadio Hearn (1850–1904), who had moved to Japan in 1890 to become a lecturer on English literature in Tokyo's Imperial University, wrote a full report on the different singing insects valued and on sale in Japan, with crickets being the most popular musicians (1898: 39–80). In Japan, we learn from him, beautiful cricket cages and the atmospheric sound they provide were used for decorating gardens during festivities. Their cages often mimicked bird cages, and it is said that the Japanese found as much difference between the singing of crickets and cicadas as Europeans find between larks and sparrows (Hammond 1983: 85).[11] Compared with the height of its commercialisation in the nineteenth century, the raising of singing crickets plays only a minor role in Japanese leisure today. Nevertheless, the insectarium of the Tama Zoo in Tokyo is reported to have yearly 'singing insect shows', and to sell electronic boxes emanating katydids' and other insects' (Pemberton 1994).

Chinese arts and crafts also invested creativity and expertise in providing collectible art objects to host crickets. The focus for these containers for singing crickets was on optics, touch, sound, and the transportability of the container in an inside pocket close to the cricket owner's body.

This is the habitat of Chinese force-grown gourd containers (**FIGURE 10.2**). The technology of these *fanpao* 范匏 or *mozi hulu* 模子葫芦, both meaning 'moulded gourd', was highly valued by the early Qing (1644–1912) emperors, but existed in its basic idea much earlier. A clay mould was put over the gourd flower, into which the gourd then grew, filling up the mould and reproducing in positive relief the shape and negative intaglio designs of the inside of the mould.[22] The covers of the gourd containers were carved from

FIG. 10.2 Force-grown gourd container with wooden lid (source: Ethnologisches Museum, Staatliche Museen zu Berlin, ID 39689; published courtesy of the museum; photo: Martina Siebert)

ivory, jade, or wood, and allowed air and sound to pass through them. The gourd containers thus not only had a pleasant, smooth touch and an elegantly decorated look, but their trumpet-like shape and permeable top functioned as a sound box for the chirping cricket. To enhance the volume of the sound, the serrated edges of the cricket's fore wings – used for stridulating – were sometimes even coated with wax (Laufer 1927: 16). When designed for sound and carrying, the containers mostly housed singing *Tettigoniidae*. But if an elite gambler was going to the teahouse or a tournament to boast about his possession, he might also put his fighting *Gryllidae* cricket into this kind of container, keeping it warm and listening, not to the beauty, but to the combativeness of the singing.

TYPE II: GAMBLING AND CARING BOX

From about the thirteenth century, another natural behaviour of the cricket was embedded into human culture: its ambition to fight till death for its territory. Although again based at the Chinese imperial court, the iconic proponents of cricket fights were this time not solitary court ladies, but one man in particular: the high minister Jia Sidao 賈似道 (1213–1275). The story goes that Jia could not stop gambling and look up from the tiny arena where two crickets fought for their lives, even when reports arrived about the Mongol invasion of China, which in the end brought about the fall of the Song dynasty in 1279.

Jia Sidao is, moreover, traditionally credited with being the author of the first monograph solely dedicated to crickets. The booklet elaborates on the evaluation of the shape and character of crickets for fighting, how they should be trained, fed, and cured when sick, and how to guide them through a tournament. While

FIG. 10.3 Round box cricket container made from grey clay, with lid (source: Ethnologisches Museum, Staatliche Museen zu Berlin, ID 39977; published courtesy of the museum; photo: Martina Siebert)

it is possible to identify about fifteen different titles on crickets in Chinese history before the early twentieth century, they cannot really count as independent texts, as they share numerous passages or even repeat older texts completely with very few additions (Siebert 2006: 165–67). This phenomenon is specific to monographs on crickets – and on quails, another animal kept by Chinese scholars for gambling. Titles on the cricket are thus like a 'box' of assorted knowledge which is handed from one author to the next, who might add pieces, or take superfluous or seemingly wrong ones out. This sharing of written knowledge about what makes a champion cricket continues until today, with the republishing of historical cricket books and the compiling of new guidebooks for professional and hobby cricket gamblers. But this knowledge also circulates freely within the cricket community, to Hugh Raffles 'in a spirit of democratic scholarship' (2011: 83).

When crickets of the family *Gryllidae* became precious fighters who could earn their masters money and prestige, new containers for the various purposes of raising, training, and fighting were developed to guarantee the crickets' health and strength. Constant temperature and humidity, darkness and no draught are crucial for the wellbeing of these insects, whose natural habitat is holes in the earth. Thus, cages are actually a difficult environment for them. From the thirteenth century, Chinese cricket lovers professionalised the culture of cricket fights and started to keep their pets in fairly spacious circular boxes made from the finest clay, with thick walls and a lid. Jia Sidao himself mentioned only containers in his book, and no cages (Meng 2004: 241–43). The interior of such boxes is normally furnished with a small, fan-shaped clay cubicle, open on one side for the insect to crawl in and sleep, but with a lid for the master to check on the insect, and with tiny porcelain bowls for water and food, filled daily with cucumber, rice, and sometimes cooked chestnuts. In the early twentieth century, Berthold Laufer reported that when a tournament was approaching, the cricket might even be fed a mosquito that had drunk its fill of the cricket's master's blood (1927: 16). Slightly larger clay containers without lids serve as training and fighting arenas. Here cricket and master learn to understand each other during the two to four weeks of training before the tournaments start at the autumnal equinox. The master 'talks' to the cricket by using a tickler made from rat or hare whiskers fixed to a handle, with which he brushes the sharp mandibles, head, and back of the insect to stir or control its aggression.

After a pause from the mid-twentieth century to the late 1980s, cricket fighting is back again, and accepted as an expression of Chinese high culture, despite the hard-to-suppress gambling that remains stubbornly connected with it. Hugh Raffles has reported on both of these cultural aspects, namely the Shanghai scene of back-room gambling on the one hand, and a cricket museum run by a scholar with a cultural mission on the other (2011: 74–115). In his ethnographic study, Yutaka Suga draws another distinction, namely that between cricket hunters, and buyers or fighting aficionados. Suga spotlights the difference in the knowledge systems that these differently motivated parties adhere to and work with. He shows how crickets are hunted down with professional knowledge about their habitats and habits, but are collected mainly for their size. When entering the Shanghai market, the insects are reevaluated and classified according to elaborate criteria that consider body colour, shape, and proportions as crucial (Suga 2006). Supporting Raffles's view that a 'taxonomy doesn't simply require judgment; it is itself a set of judgments', the evaluation classes of Chinese cricket aficionados stand on equal ground with scientific taxonomies (2011: 84).

Beginning with Jia Sidao, the literary tradition of cricket monographs also commonly included a chapter on 'collecting', not least because the specific location where a cricket was found was considered to have an influence on its prospects as a warrior. The Tang court ladies in the anecdote above considered catching the insect to be part of the fun. But artificial hatching of crickets and bush crickets is mentioned as long ago as the early seventeenth century by Liu Tong 劉侗 (1593–1636). Liu reports that in Hujia village 胡家村 near Beijing, crickets were hatched on warm oven beds to be sold for high prices as singers during winter, and for the Spring Festival in February. But, he adds, these artificially bred singers came with weaker voices then those hunted in the fields in autumn (Liu 1995–2002: 3, 51a). Today, many singing insects are still bred by humans, at least those in the lower price segment.[33] However, cricket-fight aficionados would never think this an appropriate pedigree for their champions.

A lot of money and prestige is involved in cricket fights today. Aficionados pay prices up to two thousand *yuan* (about $320), and sometimes even more for an insect; total stakes at gambling arenas can reach one million *yuan* (Raffles

2011: 91, 99). Cricket coaches equip themselves with ticklers kept in carved ivory tubes, and bury their champion crickets in small silver coffins (Hammond 1983: 83). The individualised evaluation applied throughout history to fighting crickets – and the connoisseurship and money it triggered – today seems to have spilled over to singing crickets. At Beijing markets, prices of up two hundred *yuan* per singing insect are paid.[44]

A TAXONOMY OF RELATIONALITY

Humans and crickets, crickets and boxes, and humans and boxes – these constitute the three main axes in the relationality that defines Chinese cricket culture. In the thirteenth century there was a move from cages to more bio-logically suitable closed clay containers, although cheaper singers remaining in cages – even straw cages that constituted a disposable composite with the enclosed insect. Artisanal masterpieces, such as force-grown gourd containers with elaborately carved lids, made cricket and box into, as Laufer has put it, 'inseparable companions' (1927: 15). The cricket was kept safe in the box, and the box was made complete by the singing of the cricket. While the shape of the gourd amplified the insect's chirping, and its size made it an ideal 'listen-while-you-walk' device, carrying it in an inside pocket kept the insect safe and warm. But the companionship of gourd container and cricket singer did not remain on equal terms as the relation and attraction between human and box became stronger over time. When the insect died and the box fell silent, the gourd container was just replenished with a new insect. Looked at in terms of the high prices these objects now achieve as collectibles, the insect has become an add-on, and is no longer the main purpose of these containers. The container has been emancipated from its original purpose; the singing insect inside the collectible is but an implement that makes the object work beyond its visual and haptic beauty. The gourd container thus moves between the functions and practices of carrying, touching, and listening, on the one hand, and on the other hand being a display object, collectible, and commodity.

Fighting crickets move through different containers in their life span of a few months. After being caught in a trap or net in the field, and carried in simple bamboo (or plastic) tubes to the market, they start their residence in the aficionado's home in a clay container that keeps them safe from late summer heat. Moved daily to a clay tray training ground using the fan-shaped cubicle, they finally find themselves in a fighting arena with an equally well-trained opponent. When the season gets colder, the fighting cricket might sometimes move to a gourd container close to the body of his master and, warmed by his body heat, accompanying him on his way to the teahouse. If they do their masters proud, they might move to their last box: a small silver coffin. Losers are thrown away – or set free, depending on how one looks at it.

Crickets define the boxes and containers in which they are kept, and different boxes make distinctions between species and usages. For example, when a gourd container houses a fighting *Gryllidae* cricket, its ground is plastered with a special kind of cement; when it houses a singing *Tettigoniidae* cricket, a wire spiral is placed inside to allow the insect an elevated perch. Depending on the desired usage, different cricket boxes may be designed for shelter, or else effective amplification and acoustics. And some boxes develop lives of their own. Gourd containers, as well as those made from clay, may be transformed into collectibles by their great age or the prestige of a specific kiln or shop. Although they are still identified as cricket containers, the boxes in this last category no longer need to host crickets to be of interest.

NOTES

1   A selection of Japanese cages is shown in Hammond 1983: 86.

2   Excavations at the old imperial summer palace of Yuanmingyuan unearthed thirty-seven fragments and four complete clay molds for force-growing gourds for cricket containers under the auspices of the imperial household department. See the report by the Beijing Municipal Cultural Relics Bureau in *Beijing wenwu yu kaogu* 北京文物與考古 = *Archaeology in Beijing*, 6 (2004): 79–89 ('简论含经堂遗址出土的葫芦器陶范' [Brief introduction to the clay models for gourd containers excavated at the historical site of the Jingtang hall]).

3   Lisa Gail Ryan has presented some photographs of such a contemporary breeding facility. See Ryan 1996: 29.

4   A popular daily documentary on Beijing television called *Shenghuo diaocha* 生活调查 (Enquiries into Daily Life) broadcast a twenty-minute report on the selling and buying of singing insects in Beijing. See *Shenghuo diaocha* '首都鸣虫专业委员会常务副会长兼秘书长赵伯'(The executive vice-chairman and secretary of the

capitals', Special Committee on Singing Insects Zhao Bo 赵伯), at <http://www.tudou.com/v/P01nOsFViRU> [accessed 12 November 2015].

REFERENCES

Beijing Municipal Cultural Relics Bureau (Beijing shi wenwusuo 北京市文物所), '简论含经堂遗址出土的葫芦器陶范' [Brief Introduction to the Clay Models for Gourd Containers Excavated at the Historical Site of the Jingtang hall]), in *Beijing wenwu yu kaogu* 北京文物與考古 = *Archaeology in Beijing,* 6 (2004), 79–89.

Bopuke 波普客 (Popcorn idea factory) (ed.), *Chinese Stuff,* 5th Edition (Beijing: Wuzhou chuanbo chubanshe, 2015).

Hammond, C., 'The Courtly Crickets', *Arts of Asia,* 13 (1983): 81–86.

Hearn, L., 'Insect musicians', *Exotics and Retrospectives* (Boston: Little, Brown and Company, 1898), pp. 39–80.

Laufer, B., *Insect-Musicians and Cricket Champions of China* (Anthropology Leaflet, Field Museum of Natural History, no. 22, 1927).

Liu, T., 劉侗 (Ming), *Dijing jingwu lue* 帝京景物略 [*Outline of Things and Scenic Sites of the Imperial Capital*], juan 3, 51a (Ming, Chongzhen 崇禎 edition, in *Xuxiu Sikuquanshu congshu,* Shanghai: Shanghai guji chubanshe, 1995–2002, vol. 729).

Meng, Z., 孟昭臉, *Zhongguo chong wenhua* 中國蟲文化 [Chinese Insect Culture] (Tianjin: Tianjin renmin chubanshe, 2004), pp. 241–43.

Pemberton, R. W., 'Singing Orthoptera in Japanese Culture', *Cultural Entomology Digest,* 3 (1994).

Raffles, H., 'Generosity (the Happy Times)', in Hugh Raffles, *Insectopedia* (New York: Vintage Books, 2011).

Ryan, L. G., *Insect Musicians and Cricket Champions – A Cultural History of Singing Insects in China and Japan* (San Francisco: China Books & Periodicals Inc., 1996).

Shenghuo diaocha 生活调查 (Enquiries into Daily Life), '首都鸣虫专业委员会常务副会长兼秘书长赵伯光' (The executive vice-chairman and secretary of the capitals Special Committee on Singing Insects Zhao Boguang 赵伯光), at <http://www.tudou.com/v/P01nOsFViRU/> [accessed 12 November 2015].

Siebert, M., *Pulu »Abhandlungen und Auflistungen« zu materieller Kultur und Naturkunde im traditionellen China* (Wiesbaden: Harrassowitz, 2006).

Suga, Y., 'Chinese Cricket-Fighting', *International Journal of Asian Studies,* 3.1 (2006): 77–93.

III

TIME

FIG. 11.1 The Marischal College and Marischal Museum, Aberdeen (source: Ikiwaner / Wikimedia Commons / Public Domain)

I I

CONTESTING THE BOX: MUSEUMS AND REPATRIATION

Stewart Allen

Box: the museum and the museum exhibition space. **Appearance**: buildings of diverse size and style housing different kinds of exhibition spaces and glass display cases showcasing varied artefacts and objects. **Size**: from small to large. **Habitat**: museums around the world. **Origin**: the first public museum is generally considered to be the Ashmolean museum in Oxford, England. Older private collections, however, are recorded in Ancient Greece and Mesopotamia.

Keywords: displaying, collecting, ordering, classifying, protecting, mobilising, performing, educating, conserving, appropriating, concealing, repatriating

Museum: 'A building or institution in which objects of historical, scientific, artistic, or cultural interest are preserved and exhibited. Also: the collection of objects held by such an institution' (OED)

THE MODERN PUBLIC MUSEUM IS KNOWN FOR ITS COLLECTING, SORTING, conserving, and exhibiting work; in this article, by framing the museum as a particular kind of box, I tell the story of how this box gradually relinquished these functions and came to be 'unboxed' in many ways.

I discuss the crisis of the museum box: the ways in which the function of the modern public museum shifted from a showcase and justification of Empire to one that could no longer translate nor encase its objects. A museum serves not only to contain and enclose particular objects but also to frame and tell stories or narratives with objects (see Appadurai 1988). This suggests that museum boxes are not simply given but rather emerge and are made by multiple practices, forces and actors, including political forces of colonialism and Imperialism and social forces of education and control. These forces are dynamic, not static; they are in a constant state of flux. Consequently, these same forces can also unmake a museum box or the objects it contains.

I tell the story of the museum box through the frame of the repatriation of a sacred headdress back to its originating community, and the exhibition that the headdress gave rise to. Along the way, I discuss how the museum box came to be opened and debated, how it relinquished its authority to define its objects, and in some cases relinquished the objects themselves. In the course of these processes, an altogether different kind of box was created, one based on newly developing notions of mutual respect, understanding, and increasing collaboration. The museum box, then, is no longer understood as a mere mute receptacle for the objects contained within it, but rather emerges in conjunction with its objects, each giving form to the other through their varied lines, traces, and trails (Ingold 2007).

A SACRED BUNDLE

In recent decades, an increasingly vocal debate has questioned the means and methods by which certain museum objects were acquired in the first place, the right of museums to display them, how they should be displayed and inter-preted, and whether certain objects (human remains, sacred objects, looted art, etc.) should be returned to their country of origin or former owners (or the descendants of these owners). The call for repatriation, for cultural treasures and ancestral remains to be removed from display or storage and returned to their communities of origin,[1] is one of the most pressing issues facing museums in the post-colonial era (Simpson 1996: 171). As this call grows ever louder, the debate has been brought firmly into the public and political arena, forcing professional institutions to address the issue. The debate has divided individuals who support such returns from those who are opposed to the loss of any part of their collections. So heated has the debate become that in 2002 the Declaration on the Importance and Value of Universal Museums was published, declaring the importance of objects for all of humanity, and not just the citizens of one nation. This document was signed by all the great museums of the world, includ-ing the British Museum, the Louvre Museum of Paris, and the Guggenheim and Metropolitan Museums of New York.

One of the most striking aspects of the declaration is its claim that as universal institutions 'museums serve not just the citizens of one nation but the people of every nation' (Declaration 2002). This statement suggests that the museum, unlike other institutions, offers a value- and ideology-free space through which objects may be displayed to the benefit of all people, rather than only the people of the nation in which a particular museum is to be found (Curtis 2006: 118). It further reflects, however, as Curtis (2006) notes, an essentialist or modernist view of the world; one that sees the modern Western museum, and by exten-sion Western thought, as depicting reality not only in a neutral way, but also in a *true* way over and above other ways of knowing (see also Hooper-Greenhill 2000). Such notions, however, as this article will illustrate, are increasingly being debated and challenged as museums and source communities wrestle with the complexities of this still emerging issue.

These contestations and dialogues are readily apparent in the current case, which centres on a sacred First Nation headdress which had lain in the storeroom of the Marischal Museum, University of Aberdeen, for over twenty years. In July 2003 it was repatriated to its original custodians, the Horn Society of the Kainai Nation/Blood Tribe of Alberta, Canada, and reintegrated back into important rituals and ceremonies. Neil Curtis, then senior curator of Marischal Museum, has written about the repatriation (Curtis 2006, 2008, 2010), describing how for many years the Kainai had been searching for a missing fourth headdress, part of a sacred bundle consisting of items used in ceremonies and rituals, which they believed was lost overseas. The headdress, a two-metre long red cloth with black and white eagle feather trailer, plays a crucial role in the Kainai Nation's annual sun dance. Mrs A. Bruce Miller of Aberdeen presented it to the museum in 1934 along with a number of other items from the Blackfoot Reservation in Montana, USA. It is thought likely that she visited the reservation in the 1920s and purchased the headdress along with a number of other items, including a decorated buckskin shirt and moccasins (Curtis 2008). Since no details were available on the origins of the headdress (e.g. tribal name), it had been cata-logued for many years as a 'war bonnet' (Curtis 2010). Some eighty years later, the Kainai learnt of the headdress in Aberdeen from a former volunteer of the Marischal Museum who was working with the Kainai Nation at the Pitt Rivers Museum, Oxford. In November 2002, a delegation from the Horn Society visited the museum where they were welcomed by the University Principal and museum staff. They conducted a 'smudging' ceremony before positively identifying the headdress as part of the missing sacred bundle.[2] A request for its repatriation was submitted soon after, and was considered by a special panel appointed by the University, including representatives from other museums in Scotland and a nominee suggested by the Horn Society. The panel agreed that the headdress was of fundamental spiritual significance to the Kainai Nation and should therefore be returned. Following approval by the University Court, a ceremony was held in July 2003 at the Marischal Museum where ownership of the headdress was transferred to the Kainai Nation's Mookaakin Cultural and Heritage Foundation. A memorandum of understanding between the Kainai and the University was also signed to help develop links between the two parties. In September 2003, the University's Marischal Museum opened an exhibition inspired by the story of the repatriation of the headdress, entitled 'Going Home: Museums and Repatriation' (Curtis 2008).

In *The Social Life of Things* (1986), Arjun Appadurai argued for a 'methodo-logical fetishism' in the analysis of objects as they circulate through space and time. That is, in order to understand the complex ways in which humans invest objects with different values, we must follow their 'careers', 'lives', and trajectories in motion as they are inscribed with different meanings and significances. From such a perspective, we can clearly distinguish the ways in which the headdress was bestowed with different meanings and uses as it circulated in and out of different social contexts. Prior to the 1920s, it existed not as an aestheticised object as such but rather as a sacred item central to religious ceremonies and cultural life. With its purchase by Mrs Miller, it was transformed not only into an object with economic value but also into an object that now *represented* a particular culture and way of life as an abstraction and as part of a private collection. This re-evaluation was further reified by the donation of the headdress to the University of Aberdeen in 1934, as it now became part of a publicly displayed collection that stood not only for a particular region and culture but also as part of a socially constructed hierarchy of value and classification. Finally, with its repatriation in 2003, it fades as a museum object and is reanimated once again as a ritual 'object' within a living culture.

MARISCHAL MUSEUM

Marischal Museum lies in Marischal College, in the centre of Aberdeen. A colossal building with a pinnacled, neo-Gothic façade, the College is said to be the second largest granite building in the world, after the Escorial in Madrid. Although its present form dates from 1906, it was originally founded in 1593 as the second university in Aberdeen following the foundation of King's College in 1495, giving rise to the boast that the city had as many universities as the whole of England! The two universities merged in 1860 as the University of Aberdeen.

Records indicate that a museum was established in 1786 with material that had been donated by generations of graduates, staff and friends of the University. The museum space was re-established in 1907 as the University's Anthropological Museum, incorporating the collections of the King's College Archaeological Museum, the Wilson Museum in Marischal College, and ethnographic and historical items from elsewhere in the University (Curtis 2012). As Southwood (2007) describes, the exhibitions and displays of the new anthropological museum were organised regionally around a theme of world ethnography. Tracing a route from Europe through North Africa, Asia, the

Americas, Oceania and Southern Africa, the exhibits were generally organised in the 'modernist' tradition, with culture and race rendered unproblematic structuring categories (see also Curtis 2012). It was in this exhibition that the headdress made its first and last appearance.

Eilean Hooper-Greenhill (2000), in a discussion of objects and their meanings, traces how the public museum developed in nineteenth-century Britain as an institution of power and legitimation for colonising other lands. She discusses how the museum idea, which she calls the 'modernist museum', shaped and constructed a certain view of other cultures for the ultimate aim of domination. The nineteenth-century public museum, she states, emerged in what became known as the modern period – the range of economic, political, and social transformations that took place following the Enlightenment, and the championing of reason as the source of progress in society (Hooper-Greenhill 2000). Drawing upon Benedict Anderson (1991) and his argument that three technologies of power characterise the modernist period (the map, the census, and the museum), Hooper-Greenhill notes how the modernist museum shares many of the underlying functions of the map. She notes how the modernist museum, like the map, depicts 'reality' in an apparently neutral way. Just as maps fix a name and a shape to a place, the modernist museum fits text to objects that signals how the object should be viewed (Hooper-Greenhill 2000). Museums and maps present a particular way of viewing the world, one that constructs relationships, defines territories, and proposes hierarchies of value depending on what is included or excluded. More importantly however, maps, like museums, are given the authority of the official; they are legitimated through the apparently neutral and inevitable medium of science.

Museums as public mediums of representation have the power to affect lives through the kinds of exhibits that they display. They shape attitudes and opinions towards the self and others, and as such are culturally generative, constructing frameworks for understanding (Hooper-Greenhill 2000: 19). Objects, depending on which are selected for display, how they are classified and how they are interpreted, construct meanings that have real effects on the world that is portrayed by them. This is why museum display is a political matter, and why today, in our multicultural societies, museums are such highly contested arenas.

The appointment of the University of Aberdeen's first professional curator in 1979 signalled a shift from the museum as a university research and teaching resource to one more in line with other public museums (Curtis 2012). Subsequently, new permanent exhibitions were inaugurated that not only took into account its consumption by a newly visiting public but also modernised the exhibits around more contemporary anthropological themes. From 1985 onwards, with the creation of a new permanent exhibition titled 'About Being Human' (1985–1994) that focused on cross-cultural themes such as gift-giving and attitudes to death, it was decided that the headdress should be placed in storage, since there were more appropriate artefacts to represent the themes of the exhibit (Curtis pers. comm.). This position continued, as Southwood (2007) notes, with the most recent permanent exhibition, titled 'Collecting the World' (from 1995), which focused on the collections and biographies of different benefactors and donors to the museum. This exhibition contrasted the 'exoticism' of the colonial era, through photographs and written extracts from the collectors, with reflections on the politics and ethics of colonial contact, contacts that resulted in the display of the objects on show. The displays therefore aimed to reveal the history of the museum and how museums classify collections (Curtis pers. comm.). 'Collecting the World' turned out to be the final exhibition at Marischal Museum, with the headdress remaining in storage until it was 'rediscovered' in 2002.

The shift from modernist museum display to a more reflective stance that questioned the power relations inherent to museum display arose from a broad trend within anthropology of questioning the power relations between academics and those whom they study. This attitude emerged from several related historical, intellectual, and political developments in the 1960s and 1970s, when anthropology's epistemological foundations and claims to ethnographic authority were shaken. Faye Ginsburg distinguishes these developments as the end of the colonial era with the assertions of self-determination by native peoples, the radicalisation of young scholars in the 1960s and the replacing of positivist models of knowledge with more interpretive and politically self-conscious approaches, and a reconceptualisation of 'the native voice' as one that should be in more direct dialogue with anthropological interpretation (1991: 95).

These developments led to what has been called a 'crisis of representation' within anthropology that can broadly be subsumed under the banner of postmodernism. Postmodernism constitutes a rejection of all claims to truth about cultures. It rejects modernist understandings, both grand theory within anthropology and the notion that ethnographic reality can ever be complete (Barnard 2000: 168). This new spirit led to a burst of literary critique in the 1980s that problematised the power relations between anthropologists and the people they have traditionally studied (see Clifford and Marcus 1986; Fabian 1983; Stocking 1985). This critique subsequently fed into museum contexts (e.g. Clifford 1988, 1991; Ames 1990, 1992; Karp and Lavine 1991), forming the basis of this emerging area of study.

As we can see, many different social, cultural, and political forces influence museum display, shaping how particular objects are made and 'unmade'. The public museum, particularly the public anthropological museum, reflects the deep social and political entanglements that academic anthropology underwent, and continues to undergo, affecting how objects are displayed and interpreted. The exhibitions of the Marischal Museum are indicative of this process, shifting from traditional accounts of objects and their relation to the people who produced them, to more reflective concerns with the role of the museum and the conditions under which its objects were collected.

THE EXHIBITION

The broad social and political developments discussed above influenced many aspects of the museum, including how objects were to be interpreted and displayed. Museums began to slowly change from bastions of truth, certainty, and authority to institutions that questioned and reflected upon their own foundations of being and knowing. Such transitions can be seen most forcefully in the exhibition that resulted from the repatriation of the headdress itself, which was centred on an *absence*, both of its principal object, and its meaning and use. Unable, or perhaps unwilling, to frame its objects in the traditional sense, the exhibition 'box', like the headdress itself, transitioned into something else. The exhibition became as much about a 'disappearing' object as about a disappearing museum.

During the time of the repatriation discussions, the University was in the process of withdrawing teaching from Marischal College and arranging for the principal part of the building to be leased out for redevelopment. Although the area occupied by the museum was not directly affected, long-term exhibition planning became impossible (Neil Curtis, pers. comm.). This is in contrast to most other museums, which have exhibition programmes that sometimes run years ahead. This state of affairs resulted in a very flexible policy with regard to proposed exhibitions, and provided the means whereby the museum could stage an exhibition on repatriation at short notice. The repatriation exhibit, 'Going Home: Museums and Repatriation', was an outcome of the experiences that the museum had encountered through the repatriation of the headdress, yet also, the particular constraints and uncertainties that the museum was subject to. The senior curator at the time, Neil Curtis, curated the exhibition and as he told me, he wanted to tell the story of the head-dress from the museum's side while also exploring the repatriation debate in a wider context.

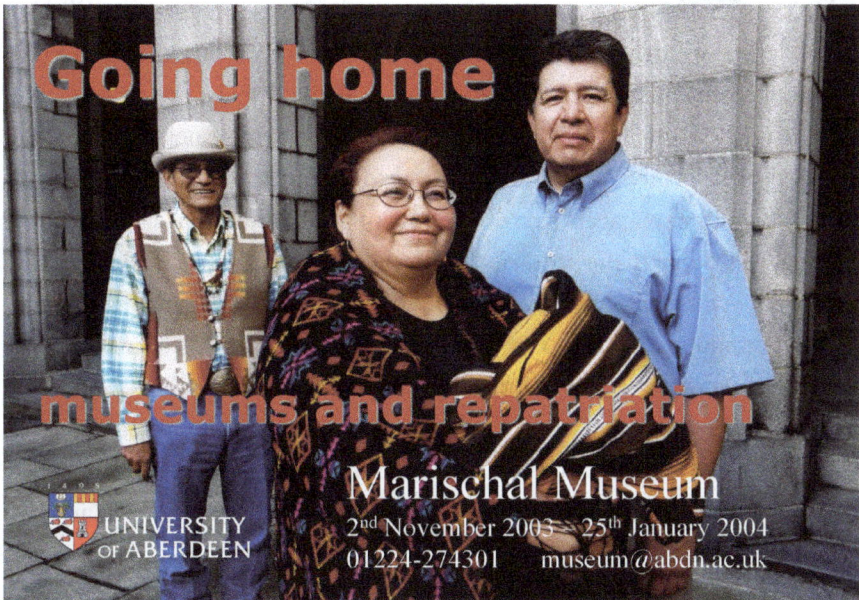

FIG. 11.2 Poster for 'Going Home' exhibition in Marischal Museum 2003–2004 (source: courtesy of the University of Aberdeen Museums, Scotland)

The exhibition itself was to fill the area used for temporary exhibitions – a small area at one end of the mezzanine level of the south gallery, consisting of three glass display cases and a partition that displayed the story of the headdress hand-over ceremony, the story of the repatriation as it was told in the national and international press, and a discussion board that invited visitors to have their say. The first case displayed various items such as moccasins and a beaded jacket that were also given to the museum by the same donor; the second case displayed a replica of the Lakota Ghost Dance Shirt,[3] loaned by Glasgow Museums to highlight other cases of repatriation; and the third case displayed other items held by the museum that further related to the issue of repatriation, such as a replica of part of the Parthenon Marbles.

The exhibition is a good example from which to consider the emergent nature of particular boxes, how they are made and materialised, and the uncertainties and absences that may engender knowledge production. Such uncertainties and absences occur at every level, from the disappearing Imperial project, to doubts over the role that an academic field science can serve, to ambiguities around the educational role of the public museum. As the following summary of the exhibition demonstrates, however, absences and uncertainties may actually help engender new understandings and insights rather than acting as a deleterious and unwelcome outcome.

The repatriation exhibit was shaped not only by wider social and political forces as outlined above, but further by the ideas and knowledge that emerged from the curator's engagement with members of the Kainai during the negotiations in the lead-up to the hand-over of the headdress. As Peers and Brown state, 'one of the most important elements of new relationships between museums and source communities is the extent to which they promote learning and growth for the museum profession' (2003: 10). Seeing artefacts that have previously been part of the museum's collection in their cultural contexts forces museum staff to become open to alternative ways of doing things. Museum members may become aware that these artefacts are part of living cultures and have ongoing meanings and uses for descendants of the source community. One example of how this was most viscerally experienced by museum staff was through their participation in the smudging ceremony[4] in the museum during the identification of the headdress by Kainai members. This gave museum staff an opportunity to appreciate what the headdress means to the Kainai today, enabling them to experience first-hand the appropriate care and respect accorded to a sacred bundle.

The smudging ceremony was the most visible form through which understanding and learning took place between museum staff and Kainai Nation members. However, learning and the creation of new knowledge and understandings was an ongoing process that began from the moment the two parties met. Neil Curtis has commented that from his experience of working with the Kainai he became further aware of his own preconceived ideas of Western rational superiority, since when he has become more sensitive to the issues of representation entailed in interpreting what the headdress means to other people and cultures (Curtis pers. comm.). This was reflected in the form that the exhibit took. That is, instead of arranging an exhibit about the headdress from an ethnographic perspective, Curtis focused on telling the story explicitly from the point of view of the museum rather than trying to represent Kainai beliefs. For this reason, the exhibit focused on the theme of repatriation and said very little about the

FIG. 11.3 Photograph of repatriation ceremony in Marischal Museum, 2003 (source: courtesy of the University of Aberdeen Museums, Scotland)

headdress itself. This also meant that he decided that the exhibition texts did not need to be approved by the Kainai first; an aspect that was also important given the short timescale of the exhibition's planning. Instead, the exhibition is the story of the repatriation from the Museum's point of view, and not a representation of another culture's cosmology. Thus, the traditional museum 'box' came to be undone. It stopped functioning either as an Imperial showcase or as a modernist tool of education and control. Rather, the Marischal Museum opened the lid to its particular box and laid bare its inner workings, and in the process initiated a whole new round of understanding, knowledge formation, and the creation of new relationships. Furthermore, learning and understanding continues through the curator's university teaching, as insights gained from the repatriation episode are communicated to other people – further highlighting the museum's reputation as somewhere that tries to reflect upon and challenge parts of its colonial past (Curtis pers. comm.).

Although formal collaboration was not involved in the creation of the exhibit, the exchange of ideas and the learning that took place between the two parties meant that the senior curator – the curator of the exhibit – was aware of, and sensitive to, many of the issues involved in representing another culture. This 'Other' was no longer embodied by an object frozen in time behind a glass partition, but was instead represented by the experience of knowing the living descendants of the original keepers of the headdress. This allowed for a much more acute cultural sensitivity, which was reflected in many related aspects of the repatriation exhibition. Foremost among these aspects was the University's agreement not to ask for a replica of the headdress. As Curtis (2008) describes, during panel negotiations, the Kainai explained that the headdress was a sacred item and that a replica of it would cause great offence, while the publication of photographs of it would also be disrespectful. It was therefore agreed that no replica would be requested and that photographs of the headdress would only be used within the University, despite this significantly limiting its ability to publicise the exhibition.

The repatriation of the headdress thus acted as a locus that allowed all kinds of new meanings and insights to develop, a locus predicated upon dialogue, respect, and understanding that ultimately led to the beginning of new links between Aberdeen and one of the First Nations of Canada.

OPENING THE MUSEUM BOX

Museums, for many years, were symbolic of unswerving knowledge-sets and steadfast understandings, reflected through their classical façades and resilient, authoritarian buildings. However, as Clifford has stated, they increasingly work the borderlands between different worlds, histories and cosmologies (1997a: 212). They are places of hybridity, exclusion, struggle and transit as different groups and people negotiate identities and collaborate over the meanings and representations of material artefacts. In this article, I have tried to show how one museum 'box' was opened and re-evaluated, and how a period of uncertainty and crisis was necessary for it to arrive at new roles and relationships. The experience of the Marischal Museum is also increasingly exemplary of a wider change in how museums see themselves and are seen by others. From being predominantly display cases of Empire, they now increasingly serve the people they once helped rule. Objects themselves, as Peers and Brown point out, and as I have demonstrated, can act as catalysts for these new relationships, both within and between different communities (2003: 5). Objects such as the headdress, which originated in communities often far away from the museum that appropriated them, are 'entangled' (Thomas 1991) within complex relations of colonial power. Their trajectories, the meanings placed upon them, and the uses to which they have been put, come to reflect the histories and ideologies of different societies. However, objects can also act as powerful driving forces for societal change, bringing people together, initiating dialogue and debate, understanding and respect. Objects in this sense are not just props to the centremost discussions of their human handlers, nor are they mere vehicles of symbolic meaning; rather, through their own particular material and phenomenological qualities – their 'emotive materiality', in Fontein's (2010) term – they exert real and tangible effects on the proceedings underway. The museum box, like the headdress, will continue to change and transmute, as new histories, experiences, and events are encountered and lived. Once a visual showcase of the artefacts of Empire and the latest classificatory schemas, the modern museum increasingly addresses the legacy of its colonial past through the entanglements of its objects with their original communities. History cannot be re-lived, but the choices that are made in the present moment, and the future, may at least help address past fractures and initiate new understandings.

In 2006, with teaching having been withdrawn from the building, most of Marischal College was leased to Aberdeen City Council for 175 years, to be restored and refurbished as its headquarters, with the newly restored building opening to the public in 2011. The University retained the east wing that includes the museum, Mitchell Hall and the former Anatomy Department. The museum has been closed to the public since July 2008 and now operates as a museum-collections centre, with conservation laboratory, research stores, offices and workshop, supporting the work of the University of Aberdeen's museums elsewhere. Once again, the museum and its collections are undergoing a new phase, shifting from a public museum back to a research centre, just as the headdress was transformed from a display piece back to a ceremonial artefact. Boxes, like life, are always on the move.

NOTES

1   Source communities (sometimes referred to as 'originating communities') are defined by Peers and Brown (2003) as both the communities from which material artefacts were collected, and also their living descendants today. The term most often refers to indigenous peoples in the Americas and Pacific, but also includes diasporas, immigrant groups, religious groups and settlers. It recognises that material artefacts play important roles in the identity of source communities and that such groups have legitimate moral and cultural stakes of ownership and control (Peers and Brown 2003: 2). In this new relationship, museums are conceived of as stewards of such material heritage, in contrast to their traditional role as authoritative interpreters of artefacts.

2   A smudging ceremony generally involves the burning of certain herbs (in this case 'sweet grass') to produce a cleansing smoke to purify people, sacred objects, and particular spaces, e.g. ceremonial grounds (Portman and Garrett 2006).

3   The Lakota Ghost Dance Shirt is a relic believed to have been worn by a Sioux warrior killed in the 1890 Wounded Knee Massacre. In 1891, the shirt was brought to Glasgow and sold to Kelvingrove Museum where it was displayed from 1892 to 1999. After a four-year campaign for its return led by Marcella Le Beau, secretary of The Wounded Knee Association and great-granddaughter of one of the survivors of Wounded Knee, it was repatriated back to the Lakota people.

4   A smudging ceremony generally involves the burning of certain herbs (in this case 'sweet grass') to produce a cleansing smoke to purify people, sacred objects, and particular spaces, e.g. ceremonial grounds (Portman and Garrett 2006).

REFERENCES

Ames, M. M., 'Cultural Empowerment and Museums: Opening up Anthropology through Collaboration', in S. Pearce, ed., *Objects of Knowledge* (London: The Athlone Press, 1990), pp. 158–73.

——, *Cannibal Tours and Glass Boxes: The Anthropology of Museums* (Vancouver: UBC Press, 1992).

Anderson, B., *Imagined Communities* (London and New York: Verso, 1991).

Appadurai, A., *The Social life of Things: Commodities in Cultural Perspective* (Cambridge: Cambridge University Press 1988).

Barnard, A., *History and Theory in Anthropology* (Cambridge, MA: Cambridge University Press, 2000).

Clifford, J., and G. E. Marcus, *Writing Culture: The Poetics and Politics of Ethnography* (Berkeley: University of California Press, 1986).

Clifford, J., 'Histories of the Tribal and the Modern', in J. Clifford, ed., *The Predicament of Culture: Twentieth Century Ethnography, Literature, and Art* (Cambridge, MA: Harvard University Press, 1988), pp. 189–214.

——, 'Museums as Contact Zones', in J. Clifford, ed., *Routes: Travel and Translation in the Late Twentieth Century* (Cambridge, MA: Harvard University Press, 1997a), pp. 188–219.

——, 'Paradise', in J. Clifford, ed., *Routes: Travel and Translation in the Late Twentieth Century* (Cambridge, MA: Harvard University Press, 1997b).

——, 'Four Northwest Coast Museums: Travel Reflections', In I. Karp and S. D. Lavine, eds, *Exhibiting Cultures: The Poetics and Politics of Museum Display* (Washington DC: Smithsonian Institution Press, 1991), pp. 212–54.

Curtis, N. G. W., 'Universal Museums, Museum Objects and Repatriation: The Tangled Stories of Things', *Museum Management and Curatorship*, 21.2 (2006): 117–27.

——, 'North America in Aberdeen: the Collections of Marischal Museum, University of Aberdeen', in A. K. Brown, ed., *Material Histories: Proceedings of a Workshop Held at Marischal Museum, University of Aberdeen, 26–27 April 2007* (Aberdeen: Marischal Museum, University of Aberdeen, 2008), pp. 69–75.

——, 'Repatriation from Scottish Museums: Learning from NAGPRA', *Museum Anthropology*, 33. 2 (2010): 234–48.

——, 'Public Engagement, Research and Teaching: The Shared Aims of the University of Aberdeen and its Museums', in S. S. Jandl and M. S. Gold, eds, *A Handbook for Academic Museums: Beyond Exhibitions and Education* (Edinburgh and Boston: MuseumsEtc, 2012), pp. 62–86.

Declaration on the Importance and Value of Universal Museums <https://committee

forculturalpolicy.org/wp-content/uploads/2013/06/CCP-WebLibrary-Museums-ICOM-Universal-Museums.pdf> [accessed 2 February 2017].

Fabian, J., *Time and the Other: How Anthropology makes its Object* (New York: Columbia University Press, 1983).

Fontein, J., 'Between Tortured Bodies and Resurfacing Bones: The Politics of the Dead in Zimbabwe', *Journal of Material Culture*, 15 (2010): 423–48.

Ginsburg, F., 'Indigenous Media: Faustian Contract or Global Village?', *Cultural Anthropology*, 6. 1 (1991): 92–112.

Hooper-Greenhill, E., *Museums and the Interpretation of Visual Culture* (London: Routledge, 2000).

Ingold, T., *Lines: A Brief History* (London: Routledge, 2007).

Karp, I., and S. D. Lavine, eds, *Exhibiting Cultures: The Poetics and Politics of Museum Display* (Washington and London: Smithsonian Institution Press, 1991).

Peers, L., and A. K. Brown, 'Introduction', in L. Peers and A. K. Brown, eds, *Museums and Source Communities: A Routledge Reader* (London: Routledge, 2003), pp. 1–17.

Portman, Tarrell A. A., and M. T. Garrett, 'Native American Healing Traditions', *International Journal of Disability, Development and Education*, 53.4 (2006): 453–69.

Simpson, M. G., *Making Representations: Museums in the Post-Colonial Era* (London: Routledge, 1996).

Southwood, H., 'Dust, History, and Politics: Assigning Meanings to Objects at Marischal Museum, 1980–2000', *Journal of Museum Ethnography*, 19 (2007): 121–34.

Stocking, G. W. Jr., ed., *Objects and Others: Essays on Museums and Material Culture*, History of Anthropology 3 (Madison: University of Wisconsin Press, 1985).

Thomas, N., *Entangled Objects: Exchange, Material Culture, and Colonialism in the Pacific* (Cambridge, MA and London: Harvard University Press, 1991).

FIG. 12.1 Cigarette packs used for storage in the Archaeological Museum of Thessaloniki

12

ARCHAEOLOGY AND CIGARETTES: 'EKPHORA' AND 'PERIPHORA' OF THE ARCHAEOLOGICAL IDENTITY THROUGH CIGARETTE PACKS

Styliana Galiniki and Eleftheria Akrivopoulou

Material: paper. **Size and shape**: about 5 x 7 cm, rectangular. **First use:** cigarette packs. **Last use:** archaeological 'diaries', storage packs of antiquities. **Decoration:** logos of tobacco companies. **Extra decoration:** hand-written notes. **Current environment:** Archaeological Museum of Thessaloniki. **Distribution:** from tobacco factory, to tobacco shops, to smokers, to excavation, to museum. **First content:** cigarettes. **Last content:** antiquities or their absence. **Non-material content:** memories, fantasies, gestures, mythologies, emotions. **Dipoles:** life-death, knowledge-ignorance, memory-oblivion, inclusion-exclusion. **Performances**: ekphora and periphora of loss.

Keywords: memory, identity, smoking, gender, materiality, emotional archaeology

Signs
Signs are lost
Signs disappeared
Turn invisible
Got no sign
Somebody got busted
Got a face of stone
And a ghostwritten biography

'Blind', Talking Heads

OLD CIGARETTE PACKS SEEM TO HINT AT THE MYTHOLOGY ATTACHED TO smoking in previous times, especially in our days, with the marginalisation of smoking and its ban – at least in public places. Such packs were subsequently used for the storage of archaeological finds, and are now kept in the storerooms or displayed in the exhibitions of the Archaeological Museum of Thessaloniki (AMTh), and of many other Greek museums. If the priority of archaeological museums is the rescue, study, and display of the material remains of antiquity, then for what reason do they retain, and sometimes even exhibit, modern industrial products, such as cigarette packs – that is, trivial objects which were meant to be discarded after their first use? Are these objects preserved simply because they belong to the past? To be sure, the institutional role of Greek archaeological museums is restricted to the preservation of ancient, not modern, objects. Could it then be that the preservation of the latter is being triggered by some other kind of valuation? And what is that? Does that valuation carry information about the past and/or meanings related to the present?

Being ourselves fanatical smokers, we felt the urge to investigate whether tobacco has imbued the past of the Archaeological Service, in order to remind ourselves of the role of smoking in the biography of archaeological practice – at least in Greece. Our desire was to give space to and recover a habit that is nowadays regarded as a disturbance, a problem, and not politically correct in a contemporary European country. And through this re-ordering of things and customs we also sought to assert our de-marginalisation as smokers, and our return in the public space.[1] First of all, though, the study of the lost value of smoking through the surviving cigarette packs in an official archaeological collection was a game of memory[2] – and, maybe, more than that.

At the heart of our quest was a sense of loss, the loss of the right to publicly perform an identity – the smoker's identity, now being banned. This retrieval was therefore pursued through the investigation of objects which, although connected with a lost habit, were themselves conserved, as if a now incriminated practice was transformed into a museum piece in need of storage and projection. The conservation of cigarette packs, on one side, and our study, on the other, were similar to the ritual and process of mourning. If the process of turning artefacts into museum exhibits parallels the process of mourning (Liakos 2004: 15–16), then the cigarette packs could be considered as a public expression and at the same time as a commission of mourning. This is what is meant by the ambiguous term *ekphora* in the title of our paper, which in the Greek tradition denotes the process of carrying the deceased to the place of burial, but also means the expression of an opinion through speech. In funeral ceremonies *ekphora* is succeeded by *periphora*, the ritual of public demonstration of the deceased among religious symbols. Therefore, we were faced with a simple question: why are smokers rejected when their waste is preserved? Does the study of garbage from adherents of a proscribed practice finally saying more about us than about those who in the meantime managed this garbage? Or does the preservation of these cigarette packs signify a choice regarding the museum's role as a guardian of the past and not as its excavator?

The oldest cigarette packs at the Archaeological Museum of Thessaloniki date from the early years of the presence of the Archaeological Service in Thessaloniki, which was first established exactly one century ago (Vokotopoulou 1986). Although the local Archaeological Service and the Museum did not acquire a permanent home until 1962, these packs survived for decades, following the fate of the archaeological finds that they contained, which were successively transferred to several exhibition and storage spaces. Moreover, in spite of a series of developments which were to occur in terms of administration, exhibition, and building conditions, the use of industrial boxes – and, thus, of cigarette packs – for the storage of finds never ceased, especially in emergency situations, such as a rescue excavation or in case of lack of funding for the purchase of modern packaging materials.[3]

What makes cigarette packs ideal for the storage of modest-sized or larger but fragmentarily preserved finds, is their hard material – paperboard or, more rarely, metal – along with the form of their opening, especially that of cases. The interior wrapping paper offers an additional protective material, while their surfaces are often convenient for taking cursory notes. Their archaeological contents, and the handwritten notes they may bear, connect them with specific excavations in the centre of the city, such as that of the Sarapis temple in the 1920s; with agonising attempts to rescue antiquities by storing them into crates, right before the outbreak of the Second World War, for instance; with excavations in the wider area, such as those in Derveni in the 1960s; and with particular individuals who worked at the Archaeological Service. They may further contain pieces of old newspapers that allude to the multicultural past of the city, while their own decoration and logos bear witness to the once flourishing Macedonian tobacco trade and its association with the ideological construct of 'hellenicity', after the incorporation of Macedonia into the Greek state (Charitatos and Giakoumaki 1998).

'If being collected means being valued and remembered institutionally, then being displayed means being incorporated into the extra-institutional memory of the museum visitors' (Crane 2000: 2). The Archaeological Museum of Thessaloniki has made use of cigarette packs on the occasion of three exhibitions, for the first time in 1998, at the exhibition on 'Prehistoric Thessaloniki'. In the introductory section of this exhibition, which was dedicated to the excavation of prehistoric sites in Macedonia during the early twentieth century, archaeological finds were complemented with 'objects typically used for their storage' such as 'packs of cigarettes and tobacco', included here in order to 'familiarize the public with the ambience of that era'. This was also the reason for the 're-use of some of the museum's old showcases' (Pappa 2001: 12–13).

With the re-exhibition of the museum's collections, it is again the section on Prehistoric Macedonia (Stefani 2009) that has incorporated cigarette packs and other products, 'which', according to the related label, 'were employed by those archaeologists who were the first to excavate prehistoric sites in Macedonia'. In this case, the exhibition is organised on the basis of the dipole 'archaeologists of the past-archaeologists of the present', inasmuch as the diametrically opposite side of the exhibition hall hosts a projection room where one can watch interviews with prominent modern prehistoric archaeologists. If this second space is dominated by the direct archaeological discourse, through the cinematographic representation of physical presence, then the first section, which throws light on the past of archaeological research, has incorporated physical presence through photographic representations and boxes. In this section, boxes function as talking objects (Tilley et al. 2006), substituting the voice of the first archaeologists, and taking over the role of human testimony; they intermediate the narration of archaeological action. All hints as to their original use, their relation to smoking and cigarettes, illness and medication, for instance, have been cast out of their biography. These objects are displayed purified of their original function, as parts of another biography or, better, of a hagiography. Human absence is thus represented as presence.

The cigarette packs are exhibited, along with other objects, in an old showcase placed near the entrance to the administrative spaces of the museum, and thus next to the Director's office. The label of this showcase reads: 'museum remains from the function of the Archaeological Museum of Thessaloniki in past eras'. This particular showcase does not belong to any exhibition and does not form part of any obvious museum narrative. It appears to be timeless, floating in a liminal space, at the threshold between the exhibition space and the 'inland' of the museum, as an introduction to a narrative in progress. This showcase was placed there at a time when the re-organisation of the museum's storerooms, and the discovery of accumulations of such later objects, led to the vision of an exhibition on the history of the museum. This was also the time when the digitisation of the museum's historical archive was begun.

The showcase in hand therefore marks the beginning of a process of re-contemplation on the part of the museum, as well as its choice of self-narration and self-exhibition. The museum is presented as a reliable guardian of the work of its predecessors (Pearce 1995: 27). The objects displayed in the showcase function as keepsakes of the archaeological community, so as to stress the continuity of its long life, to conceal its ruptures and discontinuities, and produce a romantic meaning-fullness (Pearce 1992: 197–98). The objects are removed from their historical context and, thus, frozen in timelessness, they are integrated into a mythology that inspires the sense of belonging to a glorious past. If every narrative has a beginning, then its starting point must always be defined. And the starting point chosen by the Archaeological Museum of Thessaloniki is not the time of the erection of its current building in 1962, but the time of the establishment of the Archaeological Service in 1912.

The storerooms of the pottery and metalwork collections of the Archaeological Museum of Thessaloniki house a number of industrial boxes, including packs of cigarettes. Although in most cases these no longer preserve their archaeological contents, they remain in the antiquities' storerooms. If we assume that these boxes were originally retained for want of other packaging material, then why were they not removed after the recent retrofit of the storage spaces, which formed part of a programme for the wider retrofit of the museum and the re-exhibition of its collections in 2006? When invited to answer this question, the curators in charge commented on the oldness of these objects, on their connection with the archaeologists who worked for the service in its early years, and, more vaguely, with unknown archaeologists of the past, on the suspicion of their association with excavations that were carried out a long time ago. Furthermore, the curators stressed the aesthetic value of these packs, and wondered whether the archaising scenes on some of them could have drawn upon ancient vase-paintings.

These 'poetics of the old' (Mavragani 1999: 183) were, in a way, further enhanced by us. During our research, we re-opened the packs, we admired and fully photographed them, we piled them up in chronological order but also according to their original price, which was inscribed on their side. We let the logos of the cigarette companies transfer us through space and time to Cairo, Alexandrea, Salonica. We further discovered, or perhaps re-discovered, the traditional – at least in Greece – habit of using cigarette packs as an accidental notebook for writing lists of things to do, rough accounts, even drawings and poems.[4] So we read and re-read the information that was scribbled on the cardboard of the packs: lists of numbers, administrative orders, dates, and place names. We also wondered who had designed the man's face that was hand-drawn on one of the packs: whose face was it, and why had the drawing remained unfinished? Was it really a man's face or was our approach gendered? Why were we thinking of 'him' and not of 'her'? The truth is that the majority of archaeologists in the past, and of smokers as well, were male (Kokkinidou 2012; Rudy 2005: 148–70) – although nowadays the balance has in both cases been reversed. So, the imagined official past has a gender, a male one, even in its very innermost unofficial aspects. In that sense our research could be considered a quest for a lost, 'old-fashioned', masculinity, or an attempt to redefine 'current' femininity – who knows?

Undoubtedly, the preservation of the packs to date is the accumulated result of a series of choices made in the past. The first of these is related to the excavator, who, instead of throwing the pack away – as one would normally do – decided to use it for the storage of archaeological finds.

The further preservation of the packs has resulted from an additional selection process, performed by several individuals, under various circumstances, and perhaps for various reasons during the following decades. Several times archaeologists chose to retain the boxes and repeat the choice of their predecessors not to discard them.

According to Susan Pearce, the selection process lies at the heart of collecting (Pearce 1992: 7). This process involves, on one hand, social perceptions of the value of objects within the frame of modernist narratives, and on the other hand, values that can be traced in the deeper levels of one's personality. If 'the transformation of an object from formally private to formally public' (Pearce 1992: 37) is an important aspect of collection-making, then hasn't the archaeologist, who once chose to use an object as private as a cigarette pack for the storage of antiquities, exposed a part of privacy to the public sphere? The cigarette pack functions, for each smoker, as a mark of his own identity. Once thrown away, it is immediately replaced, and so it is as if the same pack is always there in daily life, as an integral part of one's most private world. Could it be that the use of such an object, which is involved in the process of one's self-definition, for the storage of antiquities reflects a personal connection between the excavator and his finds, and his consideration of antiquities as part of his private world? Is it possible that this action does not denote the exposure of the private to the public, but the symbolical appropriation of the latter? Does the find belong, first of all, to me, who was the one to bring it to light? Could it be that this choice is, or at least was, indicative of the archaeologist's wider attitude towards the finds of the excavation he conducted? Is it, perhaps, precisely this relationship that is being acknowledged by those who eventually decide to preserve the cigarette pack?

As Maurice Rheims (1980) writes, 'the collector values the object for its associations, that it once belonged to and was handled by a man he can visualize as himself. The object bears witness: its possession is an introduction to history. One of a collector's most entrancing day dreams is the imaginary joy of uncovering the past in the guise of an archaeologist' (Rheims 1980: 51). Could we then assume that in the case of the packs retained at the museum, these roles are reversed, with the archaeologist disguised as a collector? The preservation of the packs was a choice, and not dictated by some institutional regulation. In a way, the groups of packs seem to form private collections that are 'safeguarded' within institutional public collections, such as those of archaeological museums. Interestingly enough, in the daily life of museums, it is not unusual even for objects belonging to official collections to be named after their excavator, and not their provenance. In this way, public cultural goods are assigned the character of objects of a private collection.

If the process that turns an object into a museum piece is one of selection, through which a certain value is assigned to it (Rheims 1980: 5), cigarette packs, in which antiquities are kept, enclose a content that has already been valuated as collectible. Nevertheless, it is not merely because of their content that they are deemed worthy of preservation; it is also because of their own rarity, since their production has now long ceased (Rheims 1980: 33). In a way, they are dead, relics of the past, and it is precisely this discontinuity that, according to David Lowenthal, focuses attention on them, particularly if scarcity or fragility threatens their imminent extinction (1985: 240). They are commemorative of an era not experienced by their contemporary users but carry the weight of the memories of individuals who have otherwise fallen into oblivion. Since *all* memories are necessarily related to oblivion (Hamilakis and Labanyi 2008: 12), cigarette packs are not only places of memory – 'lieux de mémoire', according to Pierre Nora (1989) – but also places of oblivion, places that denote loss and project absence (Meyer and Woodthorpe 2008).[5] They remain authentic evidence of the past, not just as industrial products, but also as carriers of traces of the lives of other individuals. All kinds of evidence attesting their use (notes, newspaper cuttings, etc.), are traces of a 'sensory memory' (Mavragani 1999: 177), that allows 'direct' contact with individuals of the past, and produces the sense of their surviving continuity.

The cigarette packs that no longer house archaeological content may be understood as 'cenotaphs',[6] empty tombs as monuments in honour of people whose remains are far from their native land. The empty boxes narrate how something that once existed is now gone. Could it be that, apart from the memory of the archaeologist, they are also related to the memory of the absent object? Isn't the ancient object thus humanised (Pearce 1992: 56–57)? A note found in an otherwise empty box, reading 'the box in which the two silver earrings, the silver ring, the silver Medusa/Gorgon mask and the fragments of a silver sheet were found' looks like a funeral inscription in honour of those objects, people, gestures, and habits which have been lost.

It appears that the continuing value attached to even those packs which are now empty is in some sense a residue of, or otherwise related to, the value that was, has been, or would be assigned to their 'most concealed body' – that is, their archaeological content. The outer part consecrates the content and, in its turn, the latter consecrates the pack. The act of opening a pack, exploring or simply glancing at its content, together with the expectation that the latter may be examined and offer valuable archaeological information, is a form of 'mnemonic excavation of this material, which brings into the present layered sympotic [i.e. relating to a symposium] meanings and stories' (Mavragani 1999: 183), as well as feelings.

Cigarette packs, within an environment that is devoted to the protection and display of the ancient past, form an Otherness. They are personal possessions, and even if their owner is anonymous, he may, by virtue of the cigarette packs, potentially be assigned an identity, somewhat vague but at the same time rather solid – that is, the identity of the archaeologist who performed his duties 'with a sense of mission', 'working with limited resources in difficult times' (Kotsakis 1998: 48). Consequently, being a lot more than mere artefacts, these packs are emblematic of a sacred figure, that of the archaeologist-missionary, who has become a reference point among the members of a specific community. Cigarette packs are covered with an historical dust, the dust of an ambiguous story, the length and narrative of which have not yet been conclusively determined. Whether they preserve their content or not, there is always a choice involved that incorporates them into a system, and this choice may be understood as a rite of initiation.

The one who chooses to preserve them is thereby initiated into this value system. In other words, the one who valuates them does so because he has been initiated into this particular value, which pertains to the association of packs either with archaeologists of the past or with an industrial production that has now ceased for good. If the act of collecting manifests itself as a sort of poetics that determines the process of one's self-definition, then the choice to preserve cigarette packs in museum storerooms as material evidence of archaeologists whose presence in the past retains great significance is an indirect statement of self-definition on behalf of the one who decides to preserve them: packs denote his or her own ability to recognise in them a certain value that echoes the value of the archaeologist who was the first to use them. Packs keep alive, among us, 'the first pioneers' (Kotsakis 1998: 89), and the recognition of this association turns them into powerful objects. Their preservation and possession constitute behaviours of power display (Pearce 1992: 45).

In addition, if the archaeological storeroom where the objects are kept forms the subsoil constructed by the museum itself *for* itself, as Umberto Eco suggests (1992: 38), then the preservation of packs further functions for the museum as a means of defining itself as an institution: the museum has a long history and is perfectly capable of preserving and narrating it.[7] Cigarette packs claim an 'anti-narrative' (Mavragani 1999: 178) amid the official museum narrative, attempting not to negate, but to appropriate the latter. The only way to assign a personal hue to the official museum narrative is by recognising in it the figures of the narrators. The only way for the individual to embrace collective memory is by recognising in it features of its own biography, by finding its own place within the 'symposium' (Mavragani 1999: 176) of the archaeological community.

Cigarette packs as museum objects take on a new familiarity. Their initial context is lifted and frozen in timelessness as they enter a mythology that acquires this new familiarity. In the words of Benedict Anderson (2003: 9, 10), the cenotaph-monument of the Unknown Soldier reflects 'an imagined community that visualizes itself as a political entity, as a nation'. In analogy to this, we may think of cigarette packs as monuments to the 'Unknown Archaeologist' that bring the imagined community of archaeologists together, as mnemonic places that bolster the ties among the members of this community. They thereby constitute sites of memory, 'lieux de mémoire' (Nora 1989) for the ritual contextualisation of archaeological identity, through its performance and refamiliarisation.

The museum is not a space restricted within its walls, but a place of utopia; it encloses an archaeological and social vision. By exhibiting traces of the work of the first archaeologists, it claims its place in the archetypal narrative of the nation and the archaeological community, in the Pantheon of the Eminent. In the end, the museum itself is a box that contains, apart from antiquities, archeologists, guards, and visitors, as well as an entire world of meanings, expectations, and ideas.

The acts of storing or exhibiting cigarette packs, of replacing them on or removing them from a shelf, cleaning, opening, and emptying them, involve the human body in the performance of memory. It is a ritual like the *ekphora* of mourning a lost world of meanings; and like the *periphora* through which carrying around and publicly displaying the alterity of the past is a way to appropriate it, to bring it to light as a matter for the present.

Our gestures further conjure up the performances of other individuals and their own gestures, from smoking to excavating, to the filling of the pack with archaeological material, and the making of notes. The preservation of the packs further embodies the performances of the users who were to follow, including ourselves. Besides, isn't this paper itself another performance? Our discourse becomes part of the packs' biographical discourse, our bodies and senses transform their narrative.

Still, our discourse has been far from detached. The way we approached the material, from the stage of looking for the packs to the stage of photographing them and piling them up according to their price, and even the fact that, on account of our obsession with seeking a mythology (or maybe more than one, if we take into account all our thoughts about gender and smoking) among all boxes we chose to focus on cigarette packs – doesn't all this strongly recall the archaeological practices of recording, stratifying, documenting, classifying, and selectively publishing those objects that are valuated as the most significant? Hasn't the study of these objects validated in a way the choices made by other individuals, along with their own place within the same imagined community? After all, isn't this study another form of valuation leading to their immortality? Through this, don't cigarette packs further claim a position within collective memory? Have we not also invested in them our deeper personal expectations and need to belong? And finally, have we not used these boxes in order to dispel our own fear of death and oblivion?

Coming to the end of this 'excavation', we feel that we have just tried to bring to light the invisible, non-material nature of emotions that are hidden in the material remains of the past, and in archaeological practice as well. We have noted that these emotions usually escape from the official scientific reports, like smoke from a humble cigarette. Perhaps the practice of an 'emotional archaeology' could reveal the multifaceted nature of people and objects, and their perpetual dialectics inside the memory box…

NOTES

1   As smoking is strongly connected with Greek identity, although the smoking ban was passed in 2012 and implemented by law to all public services and places, like coffee shops, it has never been accepted by smokers and coffee-shop owners. Furthermore, the enforcement of the ban during the recent and ongoing economic and social crisis in Greece was seen as an excuse for the government to divert public opinion from other serious problems. Since then, though the law is still in force, it has not been fully implemented. As Jarrett Rudy (2005) has shown, the 'freedom to smoke' is connected with liberalism and individuals' rights in the public space.

2   The study of material culture in the humanities has shifted towards the exploration of its role in the construction of individual and collective memory (Csikszentmihalyi and Rochberg-Halton 1981; Appadurai 1986; Tilley et al. 2006). Objects deemed to be of 'some intellectual, scientific, or psychological value' may also be housed at museums (Thompson 1979).

3   If objects, in general, contribute to the evocation of memory and its perpetuation, boxes in particular fall into a distinctive group, on account of their ability to contain, enclose, protect, and conceal other objects, which may as well function as mnemonic traces. According to the Dictionary of Symbols, 'the box, like all receptacles whose basic use is keeping or containing, is a feminine symbol which can refer both to the unconscious and to the maternal body itself' (Cirlot 1971: 31–32). From Pandora's Box to the black box of airplanes, the television set and the computer – all of them being boxes that enclose or reflect the world – the box is a space of accumulation of human experience. The act of opening and closing a box may well be associated with the dipoles life-death, knowledge-ignorance, external-internal world.

4   It is known that composers and lyricists of rebetiko song (a kind of Greek folk music) like Markos Vamvakaris, Eutychia Papagiannopoulou, Vasilis Tsitsanis, and poets like Nikephoros Vrettakos, Tassos Leivaditis, and Giannis Ritsos used to express their 'inspiration of the moment' by writing it down on cigarette packs. See Skabardonis 2008, Vrettakos 2008, Leivaditis 1978.

5   'Absence can be spatially located; second, that absence *can* have some kind of materiality (some kind of "stuff"); and, lastly, that absence can have agency [...] in a material environment such as a museum or a cemetery, *absence occupies a space*' (Meyer and Woodthorpe 2008).

6   We owe this metaphor to the museologist Marlen Mouliou (personal communication).

7   Ioulia Vokotopoulou's paper (1986) is fundamental as it incorporates local archaeological research into the narration of the city's past. This narration is a nostalgic one, being repeated again and again in different ways over the last few decades.

REFERENCES

Anderson, B., *Imagined Communities: Reflections on the Origin and Spread of Nationalism*, (London & New York: Verso, 2006).

Appadurai, A., *The Social Life of Things: Commodities in Cultural Perspective* (Cambridge: Cambridge University Press, 1986).

Crane, S., ed., *Museums and Memory* (Stanford: Stanford University Press, 2000).

Charitatos, M., and P. Giakoumaki, *Η ιστορία του ελληνικού τσιγάρου (History of Greek Tobacco)* (Αθήνα: ΕΛΙΑ, 1998).

Cirlot, E. G., *A Dictionary of Symbols* (London: Routledge, 1971).

Csikszentmihalyi, M., and E. Rochberg-Halton, *The Meaning of Things: Domestic Symbols and the Self* (Cambridge: Cambridge University Press, 1981).

Eco, U., *Πολιτιστικά κοιτάσματα. Προτάσεις για τη διατήρηση και τη διαχείριση της πολιτιστικής κληρονομιάς (Cultural fields. Propositions for the Preservation and Management of Cultural Heritage)* (Θεσσαλονίκη: Παρατηρητής, 1992).

Hamilakis, Y., and J. Labanyi, 'Introduction: Time, Materiality, and the Work of Memory', *History & Memory*, 20.2 (2008), 5–17.

Kokkinidou, D., *Οι γυναίκες στην Αρχαιολογία. Ιστορίες στο ημίφως (The Women in Archaeology. Stories in the Penumbra)* (Θεσσαλονίκη: Ζήτη, 2012).

Kotsakis, K., 'The Past is Ours: Images of Greek Macedonia', in L. Meskell, ed., *Archaeology Under Fire. Nationalism, Politics, and Heritage in the Eastern Mediterranean and the Middle East* (London: Routledge, 1998), pp. 44–67.

Leivaditis, T., 'Στίχοι γραμμένοι σε πακέτα τσιγάρα' (Verses Written on Cigarette Packs), in *Ποίηση*, τόμος 1 (Αθήνα: Κέδρος, 1978), 151–62.

Liakos, A., 'Τ' αγάλματα δεν είναι πια συντρίμμια. Τ' αγάλματα είναι στο μουσείο' (The

Statues are No Longer Fragments. The Statues are in the Museum), Τετράδια Μουσειολογίας, 1 (2004), 14–18.

Lowenthal, D., *The Past is a Foreign Country* (Cambridge: Cambridge University Press, 1985).

Mavragani, M., Ἀντικείμενα του παρελθόντος ή υλική μνήμη: Η κατανάλωση μιας ετερότητας' (Objects of the Past or the Materiality of Memory: The Consumption of an Otherness), in Μπενβενίστε, Ρ., Παραδέλλης, Θ., eds, Διαδρομές και Τόποι της Μνήμης. Ιστορικές και Ανθρωπολογικές Προσεγγίσεις (*Routes and Places of Memory. Historical and Anthropological Approaches*) (Αθήνα: Αλεξάνδρεια, 1999), 175–92.

Meyer, M., and K. Woodthorpe, 'The Material Presence of Absence: A Dialogue between Museums and Cemeteries', *Sociological Research Online*, 13.5 (2008), <http://www.socresonline.org.uk/13/5/1.html> [accessed 1 May 2012].

Nora, P., 'Between Memory and History: Les Lieux de Mémoire', *Representations*, 26 (1989), 7–25.

Pappa, M., Ἡροϊστορική Θεσσαλονίκη. Πρώιμες κοινότητες στην ενδοχώρα του Θερμαϊκού' (Prehistoric Thessaloniki. Early Communities in the Hinterland of the Thermaic Gulf), Θεσσαλονικέων Πόλις, 6 (2001), 11–26.

Pearce, S., *Museums, Objects and Collections: A Cultural Study* (Leicester: Leicester University Press, 1992).

——, *On Collecting: An Investigation into Collecting in the European Tradition* (London: Routledge, 1995).

Rudy, J., *Freedom to Smoke: Tobacco Consumption and Identity* (Montreal and Kingston: McGill-Queen's University Press, 2005).

Skabardonis, G., Ὅλα βαίνουν καλώς εναντίον μας (*Everything Goes Well Against Us*) (Αθήνα: Ελληνικά Γράμματα, 2008).

Stefani, L., 'Macédoine. La Préhistoire au musée de Thessalonique', *Archéologia*, 467 (2009), 60–68.

Thompson, M., *Rubbish Theory: The Creation and Destruction of Value* (Oxford: Oxford University Press, 1979).

Tilley, C. Y., W. Keane, S. Küchler, M. Rowlands, and P. Spyer, eds, *Handbook of Material Culture* (London: Sage, 2006).

Vokotopoulou, I., Ἰα πρώτα 50 χρόνια της Εφορείας Κλασσικών Αρχαιοτήτων Θεσσαλονίκης' (The first 50 years of the Ephorate of Classical Antiquities), Πρακτικά Συμποσίου Η Θεσσαλονίκη μετά το 1912, 1–3 Νοεμβρίου 1985 (Θεσσαλονίκη: Κέντρο Ιστορίας Θεσσαλονίκης, 1986), 1–65.

Vrettakos, N., Ἐξοδος με το άλογο (Ὕμνος στη χαρά). Σπαράγματα από στίχους που γράφτηκαν κατά τη συνήθεια του Νικηφόρου πάνω σε πακέτα τσιγάρων [Exit on the Horse (Hymn to Joy) Fragments of Verses Written by Nikephoros on Cigarette Packs, as was His Habit] (Αθήνα: Ποταμός, 2008).

FIG. 13.1 *Dandanah*, The Fairy Palace (photograph by Artemis Yagou)

13

MORE THAN A TOY BOX: *DANDANAH* AND THE SEA OF STORIES

Artemis Yagou

Name: *Dandanah*, The Fairy Palace – building blocks of solid glass. **Date of birth**: 1920. **Place of birth**: Germany. **Shape**: octagonal. **Size**: 278 x 277 x 40 mm. **Material**: wood, with a lithographed colour illustration on the lid. **Colour**: dark brown wood with multi-colour illustration. **Behaviour**: unpredictable and inspiring. **Habitat**: museum exhibitions, museum depots, private collections, auction houses. **Distribution**: eight in Germany, one in Canada, one in the United States. **Similar species:** Vitra re-edition (2003).

Keywords: containing, attracting, ordering, contradicting, surprising

THIS BOX IS A STRANGE SPECIMEN. IT IS AN OCTAGONAL WOODEN BOX with a sliding door, on which a multi-colour illustration is attached; it serves as the container for a set of children's building blocks made of glass. The box is elaborate, carefully designed, and has a complementary relationship with its fragile content. The colourful glass pieces are placed inside the container in a way specified by a 'packing plan' placed at the bottom of the box, facilitating their positioning and ordering. The box also contains six 'pattern sheets', showing possible designs to be made with the glass pieces (Yagou 2013). The geometric properties of the box and its contents are derived from the octagon and described in detail in the relevant patent (Deutsches Patentamt 1921). The patent text describes the object in question as a children's toy made of blocks of transparent material, especially coloured glass, whose forms are based on the regular octagon, a shape of both reflective and rotational symmetry. The patent text includes no reference to the box at all and is chiefly devoted to the geometrical attributes and relative dimensions of the blocks themselves. It claims that these octagon-derived shapes make it possible to create special and unique constructions, such as bridge-like structures, which were not feasible with previous types of building blocks – a claim which is rather presumptuous and quite unconvincing.

The set of building blocks was patented in the early 1920s by Paul and Blanche Mahlberg, an art historian and his wife, respectively. However, small inscriptions on the edge of the box lid state: 'Invented by Blanche Mahlberg' and 'Models and Designs by Bruno Taut' – and indeed, the object is usually attributed to renowned architect Bruno Taut. Although the box proposed by the Mahlbergs in the patent is a regular octagon (all sides being equal), the actual wooden box has sides of unequal lengths. This may be attributed to Taut's influence; it has been observed that the box has close geometrical affinities with Taut's *Monument des Eisens* of 1913, as well as with Indian temples. The India-inspired name and cover illustration, and the six pattern sheets, are also considered to result from Taut's input. Although there is a massive literature on Taut and his multifarious work, less is known about Paul and Blanche Mahlberg. According to one source, Paul Mahlberg was involved in the 1914 Werkbund exhibition in Cologne, where he also served as a member of the Jury (Speidel, Kegler and Ritterbach 2000). This was the exhibition where Taut presented one of his first major works, the famous *Glashaus;* Mahlberg was active as an architect and exhibition curator well into the post-war years (Speidel 2011). There is scant information about Blanche Mahlberg. However, she appears to be the translator of H. G. Wells's utopian novel of 1930, *The Open Conspiracy*.[1] In this book, Wells attempted to show how political, social, and religious differences could be reconciled, resulting in a more unified, inter-cooperating human race working towards a utopian society, and how everyone in the world could take part in an 'open conspiracy' which would 'adjust our dislocated world'.[2] Utopian themes such as those of Wells's book held a central significance in the conception and design of the *Dandanah*. Although the connection between Taut and the Mahlbergs remains unclear and undocumented, it may be inferred that they all belonged to progressive, intellectual circles of inter-war Berlin, and shared certain beliefs. It is reasonable to assume that the *Dandanah* is a synthesis between the Mahlberg patent and Taut's ideas.

The theme of utopia emerges in particular from the study of the illustration on the box lid. The geometric and ordered nature of the box's shape appears somehow at odds with the impressionistic and exotic character of the multi-colour illustration. The latter shows an imaginary building, a 'palace' made of glass pieces similar to those contained in the box. The image of this building occupies the larger part of the illustration; it is flanked by palm trees and appears to sparkle and radiate light, although, curiously, there are black rays to be seen against a dark blue background behind the building. Several individual glass pieces in green and blue are shown in the lower part of the image. The illustration includes a multitude of glass pieces, certainly many more than those contained in the box: it is obvious that the construction shown on the lid may not be made with the contents of the box. The spectacular illustration is a product of imagination, a vision conveying a fairy-tale impression further enhanced by the Indian-inspired name *Dandanah* and the subtitle 'The Fairy Palace – Building blocks of solid glass'. Although the toy was unnamed in the Mahlberg patent, the name *Dandanah – The Fairy Palace* (in English) is prominent on the box illustration and may be attributed to Taut. The use of the English language on the box cover is considered to be an indication that Taut wanted to promote the object internationally, possibly in the United States. *Dandanah* is an Indian word for a bundle of rods or pillars – in harmony with the box cover illustration of 'colourful palace designs reminiscent of India and exotic places' (Heckl 2010: 216; see also Speidel 1997; Speidel 2011). Apart from its Oriental connotations, *Dandanah* might also be a pun on Dada, the artistic and intellectual movement of the early twentieth century.[3] This appears likely given Taut's connections to and intellectual affinities with Dada (Boyd Whyte 2010: 178–98 and 138–141; Lodder 2006: 58; Benson 1993: 43–44). In any case, the impressive name and cover signify a clear move away from the attempted rationality of the patent descriptions and suggest a more complex picture; this paves the way for an exploration of the elaborate ideas and beliefs behind the toy.

The imaginary building on the box lid is a direct link to Taut's utopian schemes for architecture made of glass that had preceded the creation of the *Dandanah*. There is a great tradition of glass architecture, incorporating a mixture of influences including Oriental philosophies and mysticism. Architectural historian Haag Bletter is keen to emphasise the long history and thoroughgoing interest in literary and architectural conventions associated with glass and crystal, and points out that such iconographic themes stretch from King Solomon, Jewish and Arabic legends, medieval stories of the Holy Grail, through the mystical Rosicrucian and Symbolist tradition down to the twentieth-century avant-garde groups (Haag Bletter 1981: 20). Taut was deeply interested in Oriental cultures and saw a harmonious relationship between the sacred and the profane in the cultures of the Orient, especially India (Boyd Whyte 2010: 56). Critic Adolf Behne amplified this in his essay 'Wiedergeburt der Baukunst' that Taut included in his publication *Die Stadtkrone* of 1919: 'But isn't India even greater than the Gothic? At no time has Europe so nearly approached the Orient as during the Gothic age [...] Seen as a whole, however, the example of India stands high above all others as the purest oriental culture' (Taut 1919: 130–1). Taut included photographs of great Oriental temples in *Die Stadtkrone* and returned to this theme enthusiastically in *Ex Oriente Lux*, an article published at the beginning of 1919 (Boyd Whyte 2010: 56–57). During the 1930s, Taut went to Japan where he produced three influential book-length appraisals of Japanese culture and architecture, comparing the historical simplicity of Japanese architecture with modernist discipline (Speidel 2007).

Taut's attraction to the Orient may also be viewed in relation to the long-standing German fascination with an imagined East. It has been suggested that,

Germany being 'the middle country', 'a land in the middle', or 'the place that belonged to neither side completely', ideas and perceptions of the East have fascinated the German mind. The political fragmentation of the country, and the problems of unification, have underpinned the need to understand and delineate 'West' and 'East'. Additionally, Germany's obsession with modernisation and progress is often juxtaposed to centuries-old Eastern traditions and the perception of the East as a lost paradise. The complex and ambiguous process of Germany's adaptation to its own modernisation and nation-building has nourished the appeal and study of the distant Other, particularly in scholarly works of lyric and fantasy, and may be examined within the wider context of Orientalism (Roberts 2005).

Another significant dimension of the *Dandanah* box is technology-inspired. In the beginning of the twentieth century, not only was glass technology presented as a potential agent of change in engineering and architecture, but glass was also considered by Taut and others to be a metaphor for purity, innocence, and hope. Often, the call for light in buildings represented a symbolic dimension of a spiritualised, utopian architecture. Taut believed in architecture as a regenerative force in society at large, and that, through its power to dematerialise, glass lifted architecture above materialism, to a higher, spiritual level. In addition to the use of glass, many of the visionary architectural proposals of the early twentieth century emphasised the physical and plastic qualities of buildings through colour. Taut wrote that 'the glowing light of purity and transcendence shimmers over the carnival of unrefracted, radiant colours. [...] like a sea of colour, as proof of the happiness in the new life' (Taut 1919: 69). Commentators have also attempted to historicise and theorise the remarkable fascination with crystals found in contemporary art theory and practice. In aesthetics, science, and art production, the crystal embodies intimations of transparency, of vitalistic transformation, or of a purist stability; it powerfully articulates a line or gradation between the organic and inorganic (Cheetham 2010).

Although Taut intended to produce *Dandanah* commercially, this project did not materialise. Only a few copies were produced, which have become cherished museum objects and much sought collectors' items today. In the early 2000s, the Swiss company Vitra issued a reproduction of the *Dandanah*; the box lid was, however, only a simplified version of the original, as the Indian glass palace illustration was only shown on the cover of the enclosed leaflet.[4] The lid of the Vitra re-edition of the object was thus plain, compared to the original; the 'oriental' and mystical associations were removed from the exterior, turning the box into a sleek item compatible with a fashionable and perhaps more marketable modernism. One might argue that the Vitra re-edition expresses an attempt to control and modify the emotional content of the artefact and, in a sense, to rationalise it. Thus, the *Dandanah* becomes more appropriate to a clientele attracted by a minimalist, functionalist image of modernism, rather than by its more mystical aspects. The Vitra edition promotes a selective modernism, compatible with the company's wider strategy of reproducing and marketing modernist icons. The price-tag made the object inaccessible to all but a minority of consumers. What impression would the Vitra *Dandanah* give, when laid out on a contemporary living-room table? Arguably, it would suggest a lot about the owners' wealth, taste, and status. The re-edition is not meant to be a toy for children, but rather a decorative object or home accessory to be flaunted and appreciated by adults (Yagou 2013).

A further contradiction emerges in relation to the assumed users of the original object. Building blocks are supposed to be made for children, but they are designed by adults and express their preoccupations, concerns, and fantasies: these are projected onto children and suggest desired ways of behaving. In the case of the *Dandanah*, the illustration on the box's lid, the exotic name, even the unusual shape, generate great expectations; they fire the imagination and underpin a complex relation between the box's appearance and the content, the actual plaything. The highly geometric nature of the glass pieces, and the discipline required to use them safely (given the unusual and fragile nature of the material), somehow contradict the expectations created by the lid illustration. By hiding and selectively revealing, the box preoccupies the user and shapes to a great extent the object's identity. This is particularly significant if one thinks of the object as a product in the market, where the box or container becomes 'packaging' that often drives the purchasing act. In the case of playthings, the purchaser – for example, a parent – is more often than not different to the end-user – i.e. the child. Sometimes though, the adult purchaser also becomes a user by playing together with the child or children. In any case, the reality of play in everyday life is rarely documented; children do not normally leave records of their actions. Activities of daily life in domestic settings, and especially children as historical actors, usually remain in the shadow of adult activities. One wonders how children actually used this box and how they played with the glass pieces: how did the adult utopian fantasy, expressed so powerfully by the box lid illustration, influence the reality of children's play? Furthermore, the exuberant illustration is at odds with the highly ordered interior, which affords a limited number of solutions for packing the pieces, thus requiring disciplined action by the player after the play is over. Given the fragile and potentially dangerous nature of the glass pieces, it is assumed that proper positioning and safe packing of the pieces would be indispensable after playing. Despite the fancy cover illustration, there is a clear antithesis between the formalism of the austere octagon and the presumed spontaneity of free play activity.

Such thoughts emerge from the study of this unusual object and imply the fascination it generates as the focus of design discourse. Design discourse deals with artefacts, the meaning of which remains fluid and un-fixed, continuously arising in social interactions based on language. When objects of design are treated as language-like, interactive meanings and the practices they inform render materiality and technology subordinate to what people see. Unravelling such meanings may be achieved by, among other things, expanding design spaces through systematic reframing of existing artefacts. In this process, meanings emerge or disappear and thus new, unexpected and still unimagined meanings may be produced (Krippendorff 2006, 2011). Research along these lines generates a wealth of links to different as well as interconnected themes. In this vein, looking at the *Dandanah* from the perspective of its container may lead to alternative histories of the object. It could be the starting point to a 'sea of stories', a reference to a children's novel by Salman Rushdie, where the author speaks of

> [...] a thousand thousand thousand and one different currents, each one a different colour, weaving in and out of one another like a liquid tapestry of breathtaking complexity; [...] these were the Streams of Story, that each coloured strand represented and contained a single tale. Different parts of the Ocean contained different sorts of stories, and as all the stories that had ever been told and many that were still in the process of being invented could be found here, the Ocean of the Streams of Story was in fact the biggest library

in the universe. And because the stories were held here in fluid form, they retained the ability to change, to become new versions of themselves, to join up with other stories and so become yet other stories. (Rushdie 1993: 72)[5]

The *Dandanah*, almost a century old, is nowadays a rare and precious item. It resides quietly in museum exhibitions or museum depots, or lies as a treasured object in private collections and is sold for high prices at auctions. Formerly used by children as a toy – perhaps even mistreated, as the worn-out box and several damaged glass pieces indicate – it is now handled delicately and carefully preserved in museums or private collections. The box itself bears visible signs of wear, revealing traces of the people who have handled and used it over the years. Its material specificity in the present brings to the fore ideas, dreams, illusions, and actions of people long gone. Research on the *Dandanah* has illustrated the continuing allure of larger-than-life utopian themes; it has also pointed to the power of small things to challenge, inspire, and delight. The *Dandanah* box may be a small piece of material evidence, and no more than a detail in the history of design, but it is rich and replete with potential for different narratives. It is a mysterious and contradictory item, but also exciting and inspiring. This short essay has demonstrated that, by using the box of the *Dandanah* as a starting point, it is possible to discuss a variety of issues related to society and technology, to learn, reflect, and take pleasure in discovering aspects of human experience.

On a more general level, object-based museum research highlights the complex existence of objects by revealing their multiplicity and by demonstrating the ways in which they may act as pointers to a whole range of sociocultural issues. The development of object-based research could be of major importance in a culture that depends on being perpetually renewed, as this type of research adds value to the material repository and enables diverse stakeholders to reflect on society, ask new questions, formulate new answers, and in these ways contribute to shaping desirable futures. The richness of objects may be uncovered by historical research and may form the basis for a range of engaging museum activities. Exploring objects like the *Dandanah* may disclose a treasure of histories and potential meanings; the fascination of learning from mundane boxes is just one of these meanings.

NOTES

1   Published in Berlin by P. Zsolnay in 1928 under the German title *Die offene Verschwörung: Vorlage für eine Weltrevolution*, and republished as *Die offene Verschwörung: Aufruf zur Weltrevolution* in Frankfurt by Ullstein in 1986, as well as in Vienna by Zsolnay in 1983. *The Open Conspiracy* was published in English in 1928. A revised and expanded version followed in 1930, and a further revised edition in 1931, titled *What are we to do with our Lives?* A final version appeared in 1933 under its original title (Yagou 2013).

2   H.G.Wells, The Open Conspiracy, Chapter 2, gutenberg.net.au/ebooks13/1303661h.html#chap02 [accessed 21 November 2018]

3   Dada or Dadaism, a cultural movement that began in Zurich, Switzerland, during World War I and peaked between 1916 and 1922. Born out of negative reaction to the horrors of war, this international movement rejected reason and logic, prizing nonsense, irrationality, and intuition. The movement involved visual arts, literature, poetry, art manifestoes, art theory, theatre, and graphic design, and rejected the prevailing standards in art. Dada intended to ridicule the meaninglessness of the modern world as its participants saw it. <http://en.wikipedia.org/wiki/Dada> [accessed 2 October 2018]

4   A copy of the Vitra re-edition of the *Dandanah* is kept in the Badisches Landesmuseum, Karlsruhe.

5   Rushdie, Salman, *Haroun and the Sea of Stories*, Puffin, 1993. The title of this essay alludes to this book, a phantasmagorical story that begins in a city so old and ruinous that it has forgotten its name. *Haroun and the Sea of Stories* is a novel of magic realism, an allegory for several problems existing in society today, especially in the Indian subcontinent. The connection between this novel and the *Dandanah* is in a sense arbitrary, but also intriguing and perhaps intellectually fertile. <https://en.wikipedia.org/wiki/Haroun_and_the_Sea_of_Stories> [accessed 2 October 2018].

REFERENCES

Benson, T. O., 'Fantasy and Functionality', in Timothy O. Benson, ed., *Expressionist Utopias: Paradise, Metropolis, Fantasy* (Berkeley: University of California Press, 1993).

Boyd Whyte, I., *Bruno Taut and the Architecture of Activism* (Cambridge: Cambridge University Press, 2010).

Cheetham, M. A., 'The Crystal Interface in Contemporary Art: Metaphors of the Organic and Inorganic', *Leonardo*, 43.3 (2010): 250–56.

Deutsches Patentamt, *Patentschrift 340301*, 7 September 1921.

Haag Bletter, R., 'The Interpretation of the Glass Dream: Expressionist Architecture and the History of the Crystal Metaphor', *Journal of the Society of Architectural Historians*, 40.1 (1981): 20–43.

Heckl, W. M., ed., *Technology in a Changing World: The Collections of the Deutsches Museum* (Munich: Deutsches Museum, 2010), pp. 214–15.

Krippendorff, K., *The Semantic Turn: A New Foundation for Design* (Boca Raton: Taylor & Francis, 2006).

——, *Designing Design-Forsch-ung, not Re-search*, Keynote speech, Conference on Practice-Based Research in Art, Design & Media Art, Bauhaus-University Weimar, 1–3 December 2011

Lodder, C., 'Searching for Utopia', in C. Wilk, ed., *Modernism: Designing a New World 1914–1939* (London: V&A Publishing, 2006), pp. 22–40.

Roberts, L. M., ed., *Germany and the Imagined East* (Newcastle: Cambridge Scholars Press, 2005).

Rushdie, S., *Haroun and the Sea of Stories* (London: Puffin, 1993).

Said, E., *Orientalism* (New York: Vintage, 1979).

Speidel, M., 'Der Glasbaukasten von Bruno Taut', Unpublished manuscript (Munich: Deutsches Museum, 1997).

——, K. Kegler and P. Ritterbach, eds, *Wege zu einer neuen Baukunst, Bruno Taut 'Frühlicht'-Konzeptkritik Hefte 1–4, 1921–1922 und Rekonstruktion, Heft 5, 1922* (Berlin: Gebr. Mann Verlag, 2000).

——, ed., *Bruno Taut. Ex Oriente Lux: Die Wirklichkeit einer Idee* (Berlin: Gebr. Mann Verlag, 2007).

——, 'Stadtkrone und Märchenpalast. Zum Glasbauspiel von Bruno Taut', Unpublished manuscript (Karlsruhe: Badisches Landesmuseum, May 2011), reproduced in Yagou (2013).

Taut, B., *Die Stadtkrone* (Jena: Diederichs, 1919).

Yagou, A., 'Modernist Complexity on a Small Scale: The *Dandanah* Glass Building Blocks of 1920 from an Object-Based Research Perspective', *Deutsches Museum Preprint*, 6 (2013) <http://www.deutsches-museum.de/forschung/publikationen/preprint/> [accessed 2 October 2018].

IV

CARGO

FIG. 14.1 *Ur*-Box (source: Kircher, *Arca Noe* (1675))

14

THE *UR*-BOX: MULTISPECIES TAKE-OFF FROM NOAH'S ARK TO ANIMAL AIR CARGO

Nils Güttler, Martina Schlünder, Susanne Bauer

Species of box: aerial arks. **Other names**: box, chest, coffin, ark, bier, coffer, bottle, bucket, cage, can, car, case, cash box, casket, cell, container, crate, ferry, fund, jar, jug, money-box, motor, pall, sack, safe, small prison, strongbox, till, tin, trunk, urn, vessel, wealth, wheels. **Family**: shipping boxes. **Size and shape**: flexible, adaptable to various scales. **Habitat**: logistics buildings, cargo areas, aircraft. **Origin/first observed**: religious narratives, myths. **Distribution**: air cargo industry worldwide. **Behaviour**: migratory, restless, protective of its content. **Migration**: with air traffic, along supply chains worldwide. **Status**: in flux.

Keywords: protecting, saving, surviving, confining, locking up, transporting, moving, shipping, ordering, pairing, sexing, nurturing, caring, safeguarding

THE *UR*-BOX

IN THE SELFSAME DAY ENTERED NOAH, AND SHEM, AND HAM, AND JAPHETH, the sons of Noah, and Noah's wife, and the three wives of his sons with them, into the ark; They, and every beast after his kind, and all the cattle after their kind, and every creeping thing that creepeth upon the earth after his kind, and every fowl after his kind, every bird of every sort. And they went in unto Noah into the ark, two and two of all flesh, wherein is the breath of life. And they that went in, went in male and female of all flesh, as God had commanded him: and the Lord shut him in. (Genesis 7.13–16)

Like many survival stories, the narrative of the deluge is as much about salvation as it is about the foundation of a new world order. This manifests in some fundamental decisions that Noah has to make about ordering life: What is a kind? How many kinds are there? What is a pair? What is sex? The re-ordering is related to a complex logistical enterprise. One could call it one of the first multispecies take-off scenarios in human history. After shutting the doors, we read, God 'lifts' the ark 'up above the earth'. It would take more than a year before humans and non-humans were on terra firma again. Some accounts of the ark are very outspoken about the practical problems involved; the biblical text even mentions the challenge of ensuring an adequate food supply. Accordingly, the ark was made three hundred cubits in length, fifty cubits in breadth, and one hundred cubits in height – similar to the dimensions of today's ocean liner *Queen Elizabeth 2*.

Commentators have long discussed the verisimilitude of the biblical story of the ark. Athanasius Kircher, one of the most famous Jesuit scholars of the seventeenth century, dedicated a whole book to proving that the Noah myth matched recent observations in natural history (Kircher 1675). For instance, he pointed to the fact that the ark's ratio of 6/1 between length and height was still applied in shipbuilding. According to Kircher, it was also possible for Noah to have accommodated all animals known at the time. The Renaissance scholar even published several plans of the ark (**FIGURE 14.2**).

Kircher's ark looks like a gigantic box that has been divided into three storeys. Each floor is parcelled out into numerous compartments – rectangular boxes – that house the animal pairs (Browne 1983: 1–31). Humans and birds

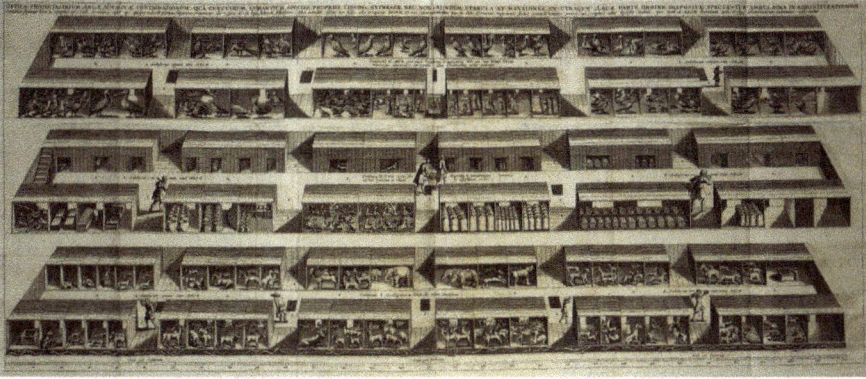

FIG. 14.2 Kircher's ark, floor plan (source: Kircher, *Arca Noe* (1675))

live together on the top level, and all the other animals are grouped at the bottom. The middle level serves as storage for equipment and supplies (Breidbach and Ghiselin 2006: 994).

In Kircher's pictures the ark evokes the concept of an *Ur*-Box, very similar to the *Urpflanze* that later inspired Johann Wolfgang Goethe's botanical studies. For Goethe, the *Urpflanze* was an ideal form or an ideal type that lay behind every individual plant, a dynamic force allowing organisms to come into being. What about thinking of the ark as the *Ur*-Box of all kinds of boxes? This association still seems to be present in the range of English translations of the Latin *arca*. It can be translated as box, chest, coffin, ark, bier, coffer, bottle, bucket, cage, can, car, case, cash box, casket, cell, container, crate, ferry, fund, jar, jug, money-box, motor, pall, sack, safe, small prison, strongbox, till, tin, trunk, urn, vessel, wealth, wheels. Looking into the *Ur*-Box through the lens of Ludwik Fleck's ([1935] 1979) temporal concept of '*Ur-Ideen*' (or 'pre-ideas' as the English translation has it), provides us with an even more historical understanding of the rhizomatic development of boxes from the ark. *Ur*-ideas are not designed as metahistorical concepts, but rather cross the temporal fabric of history like 'deep time'. Their movements are transversal, like heterogeneous geological formations sedimenting over time. As resources and pools for historical concepts, ideas, imaginaries, they allow specific actualisations. In a similar way, for us the ark both contains deep-time dimensions and enacts classification in terms of ideal types.

We are a group of historians and sociologists researching how life and nature are managed at airports. Our case study takes a closer look at Frankfurt airport, Germany's largest aviation hub. Boxes and containers figure large in this environment. Everything seems to be put into boxes, be it luggage, goods, cargo freight, non-human passengers, and even humans when you take planes as a kind of flying box. When we published our first article on the history of Frankfurt's animal terminal – the biggest of its kind in Europe – we were surprised to see that the illustrator of the science magazine associated our text with the biblical story of Noah's Ark.[11] As our research continued we realised that she was not the only one to draw this connection. Obviously, God and Noah were tackling problems similar to those that modern logistics in the era of global capital are facing now – at least when it comes to questions of survival, salvation, and security. So let us take a closer look at the most recent actualisation of the *Ur*-Box: what does a modern ark look like in animal air transportation; how should living goods and animal passengers be contained in practice; how can they be kept alive during the journey; what kind of boxes, books, or bibles are needed to bring even fish up into the air?

UP WITH THE ARK

'As the war brings aeronautics to its all-time high, to-day in terms of proved and practical aeronautics there are no more really isolated people, plants or animals anywhere on earth'. This statement, taken from the article 'The Great Crops Move', written by journalist Charles Morrow Wilson and published in Harper's magazine in 1943, pinpoints a crucial moment in the history of animal transportation by air: the Second World War. Whereas animals had quite rarely been transported by air in pre-war times, Wilson was astonished how busy the sky had become with 'seed flyers' only a few years later. American cargo airplanes seemed to be everywhere, not only supporting American troops in Europe and Japan, but also operating for economic purposes in South America and the Pacific. The new planes grew tremendously in size. Apart from all sorts of commercial goods, they carried a huge quantity of other non-human passengers: seeds and microorganisms, plants, and even livestock like ewes and rams, chickens, and insects. The dawning American Empire, as Wilson envisioned it, would be based on multispecies logistics.

The massive expansion of military air cargo during the war caused a late-modern revival of the imaginary of Noah's ark in the public domain. In 1953, for instance, the official newspapers of Frankfurt airport – the key airbase for American troops in Europe – termed the new cargo planes 'Noah's ark of the air'. Just a few years earlier, Frankfurt had served as a base for the Berlin airlift – an instantiation of the *Ur*-idea of salvation by (flying) arks, but also a crucial test case for Cold War logistics. The presence of a new class of non-human travellers, however, also encompassed civilian passenger aircraft. As it is still the case today, many such planes transported animals in their belly, mostly invisible to the human travellers. The ark has ever since become a widely used icon of animal transportation, and not only airborne transportation. We can find it in the advertisements of shipping agencies, and it also features in many ground facilities of animal transportation.

Border officials at London Heathrow refer to the room where the border control temporarily houses illegal or smuggled animals as 'Noah's Ark' (Morris 2014). JFK Airport, in turn, is currently building a new animal terminal that will be named 'The Ark' (ARK Development, LLC, 2012–2016). Frankfurt's animal terminal, called 'Animal Lounge', welcomes the visitor with a huge model of a Boeing 747. Parts of the cover are open, and inside we see several boxes containing horses – each box features the biblically correct number of one pair of each kind in the different modules (**FIGURE 14.3**).

During one of our site visits, we had the opportunity to enter a cargo plane that was parked in the area of the former airbase. Climbing into the empty aircraft before the boxes and modules were loaded, we were struck by the wide open space, which seems incredibly vast compared to a common passenger cabin. The space is geared to be compartmentalised through a system of preinstalled hooks and rails. In twenty-first century logistics, the belly of the aircraft – the interior of the 'ark' – is a highly managed space. As each cubic centimetre is utilised for storage, it is a space that economises as well as – in the case of animal air cargo – minimises the ecologies of its human and non-human travellers.

FIG. 14.3 Model of a cargo plane in the entrance to Frankfurt Airport's Animal Lounge (source: photograph by the authors)

THE HUMANITARIAN ARK

Autumn in Germany – the time when birds are heading south. On 18 October 1974, about 2000 swallows arrived at Genoa Airport from Frankfurt aboard nonstop Lufthansa flight LH306 (Gogné 1975). The swallows had travelled in cardboard boxes as airplane cargo, and even in the cabin – avian passengers as it were. Members of several nature conservation groups had collected them for the 'Flight South Campaign' ('*Aktion Südflug*') (FAZ 1974). Already in 1957, newspapers had reported that exhausted swallows had been rescued and brought to Cairo (FAZ 1957). Yet seventeen years later this had grown into a concerted campaign in Germany as well as in Switzerland and France; newspapers mentioned similar airlifts in which 100,000 birds were flown from Mulhouse to the French Riviera on one day. Volunteers had gathered the swallows, as they considered them too weak for their annual migration. Three major airlines and the German railways assisted the campaign. After placing the swallows in boxes, volunteers handed them in at local train stations. From here they were brought to Frankfurt Airport's freight terminal and flown south (**FIGURES 14.4A, 14.4B**).

FIGS. 14.4A, 14.4B Salvation of swallows in 'Aktion Südflug' (source: Ruge (1975: 5–8))

The airlift was one of the major species protection attempts in German history. It carried more than a million swallows to Northern Italy and Southern France. Whether the assisted take-off on behalf of nature conservation would help the survival of the swallow populations was controversial among ornithologists. The logistics of these airlifts were relatively low-tech: common household items were easily transformed into animal boxes. A conservation newsletter stated: 'For matters of transport, cases the size of a shoe box (or slightly bigger) have proved themselves in practice. Newspapers turn out to be the best underlay. Only avoid sawdust as it will suffocate the swallows' (Ruge 1975). West German environmental movements made the planes into temporary arks to rescue swallows. 'Helping nature' through technology resonates with Cold War understandings of development aid and modern logistics. It was a side usage of the still-new technological infrastructure, enacting a kind of surplus to technological progress. Moreover, aircraft helping out delayed avian travellers fitted smoothly into the marketing and charity campaigns of the airlines.

The widespread invocation of the ark in nature conservation and animal cargo is closely related to issues of security and safety, responding to the brutal practices that are usually associated with animal transportation on the ground. Compared to economy class, most animals fly quite comfortably, as airlines classified them as 'V.I.P.' cargo from the 1950s onwards. Yet still, in the first half of the 1970s nearly twenty per cent of all animals arrived at Frankfurt Airport as so-called 'D.O.A.s' (Dead on Arrival) (Anonymous 1976). Although this number has decreased to less than one per cent since the early 1990s, the aviation industry is still keen to avoid bad news, and to establish positive associations – for instance, a successful swallow airlift.

REGULATORY BIBLE

Do you remember your last take-off? Wasn't it a bit awkward? You wondered why the plane took off at such a flat angle. Why it took longer than usual to reach the cruising altitude. Why there was no news from the flight deck beyond the weather forecast. It was all business as usual. You didn't know, but probably there were a number of horses among your fellow travellers, deep down in the belly of the aircraft. They can't cope with a steep angle during take-off. The captain had to sign off a special load notification form beforehand. She knew. That's why she modified the angle. The NOTOC (special load notification to the captain) is part of the *LAR*, i.e. *Live Animals Regulations*. First published in 1969 by IATA, the trade association of all major world airlines, the *LAR* manual has developed over the last decades from a one-hundred-page black-and-white booklet into a volume of almost 500 pages, resembling a metropolis telephone book. IATA claims that *LAR* are the global standard and the essential guide to transporting animals by air in a safe, humane and cost-effective manner: '(…) a must for transporting animals humanely and in compliance with airline regulations and animal welfare standards' (IATA 2016b).

Live Animals Regulations (*LAR*) are concerned with practical problems. They provide in minute detail container requirements for the whole animal kingdom: stocking densities for specific species; tables with the acceptable ambient temperature ranges for animals; calculations of animal heat and moisture load during transport; a common description and size of adult animals; the colour, size, and exact placement of stickers on the containers. The regulations also specify incommensurabilities regarding aircraft loading. They state, for instance, where animals should not be loaded (for example, in the proximity of food or natural enemies). They also detail the minimum distance of separation from dangerous goods, and specify what kind of animals should never be accepted for transport: pregnant mammals, sick or injured animals, a nursing mother with young, an unweaned mammal (IATA 1994: ii–iv, 10; IATA 2011: iii–vi, 21). In contrast to Noah's mission, on which the future possibilities of life's generation and reproduction depended, the modern ark is more pragmatically attentive to mundane troubles.

LAR draw together all kinds of knowledge that is needed for a multispecies take-off and its logistics. In common with regulatory advice more generally, they come in the form of guidelines; in fact, they are an assemblage of lists, tables, graphs, enumerations, box sketches, numbers, and statistics. They are the core of animal air cargo operations, from the labelling of boxes to the specific handling of animals in and outside the boxes (**FIGURE 14.5**).

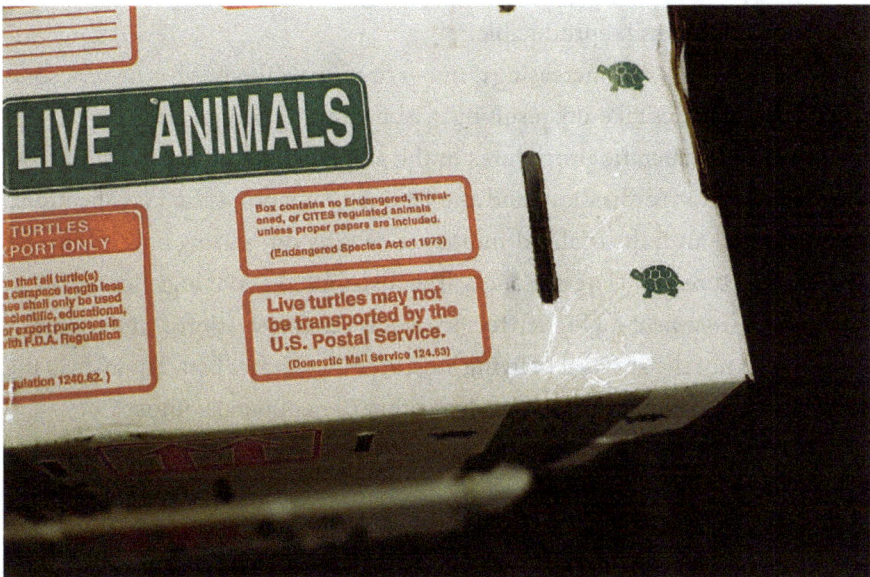

FIG. 14.5 Animal Lounge, Frankfurt Airport (source: photograph by Skúli Sigurdsson)

God provided Noah with some basic rules, and his ark was perfectly built for one long trip whose aim was to guarantee the survival of living creatures. *LAR*, in contrast, works as a regulatory bible that guarantees that the ark's modern version never comes to an end. The journeys of the 'logistical' ark are not designed as single or unique trips. They are 'units' in an endless loop of stops and take-offs. No longer just a material box, the logistical ark now consists of a sophisticated network of boxes and flows whose paths are by no means unknown but rather controlled and predictable. While Noah at the end of his journey sent out two birds in order to test whether it was safe to disembark, the economical version of the ark is imbued with a culture (a cult) of security. *LAR*, for instance, is updated after annual meetings of committees that assemble experts from fields as diverse as logistics and conservation biology.

The inventories and boxes needed for the handling of animal air cargo are largely box practices, both in terms of creating and applying categories to contain the animal world, and in the very mundane sense of packaging the animals for their journeys. Without lists and regulations like the *LAR*, large scale work such as the shipment of animal cargo would be impossible to coordinate. Lists and regulations help to accelerate the circulation of goods through global supply chains; they draw things together, establishing new connections, which in turn become traceable and reproducible.

Since the 1960s, the increasing number of animal take-offs has been accompanied by a logistics take-off, resulting in a burgeoning of regulation, documentation, and bureaucratic procedures in the animal air cargo business. In turn, the resultant standardisation, and the labour of adapting the classifications, has facilitated an industrialised multispecies take-off, setting and calling for an infrastructure of business models. The distributed ark of logistics is also an economic *agencement* – a French term for logistics corporations. Unlike Noah's mission it is not the survival of living creatures that comes first, but instead the survival of the company in the rough weather of neoliberal competition.

FISH CAN'T BREATHE

Fish have no use for the 'breath of life' provided by Noah's ark (Genesis 7, 15–16), but birds do need assistance when being conveyed by air. High altitude is a detrimental environment to all terrestrial and aquatic animals. At cruising altitude, with a stratospheric temperature of around minus sixty degrees Celsius, and low atmospheric pressure, even those species comfortably inhabiting the deeper layers of the atmosphere need technological assistance and managed cabin conditions. Catering for their needs requires maintaining miniature arks within the aircraft – as minimal ecologies in which they are able to survive for the duration of their transport. Animal air haulage also involves optimising the routes taken by travelling animals, to reduce travel time and the stress that results from these minimised ecologies. While maintaining minimal ecologies seems possible at a low-tech level (for small animals like most pets, smaller birds, or laboratory mice, for example), it becomes a challenge when dealing with large animals such as horses, many zoo animals, or large fish and sea mammals.

In terms of quantity, tropical fish are the largest freight of water animals shipped by air; they are traded globally and sold for private aquariums. But even dolphins, pelagic sharks, and whales have been transported in planes. Aquatic mammals and large fish cannot easily be transported in simulated habitats; some require assistance, such as being sprayed with water, or pro-vided with temperature-controlled water tanks or other special equipment to ensure their suspension in the water (**FIGURE 14.6**). Take the example of sharks as air passengers. Sharks were only first included in the *LAR* in 2011, which revision specified transportation requirements for pelagic sharks of forty to one hundred centimetres in length (**FIGURE 14.7**). For 'the shipment of larger fish or the bottom dwelling species, such as the pelagic sharks, that need to swim constantly [...] specially designed transport con-tainers' and equipment, as well as an accompanying attendant, are required (IATA 2011: 303). Air cargo operators already see markets for sharks with the development of large-scale public aquariums, especially in Asia and the Middle East. Current efforts in relation to IATA regulations are striving to expand their scope and to develop standards for the transportation of pelagic sharks in closed water tanks as well (Air Cargo News 2015; Air Cargo World 2013). Many such minimal ecologies are precarious rather than comfort zones; they are hardly habitat simulations but have been reduced to vital factors for bare survival.

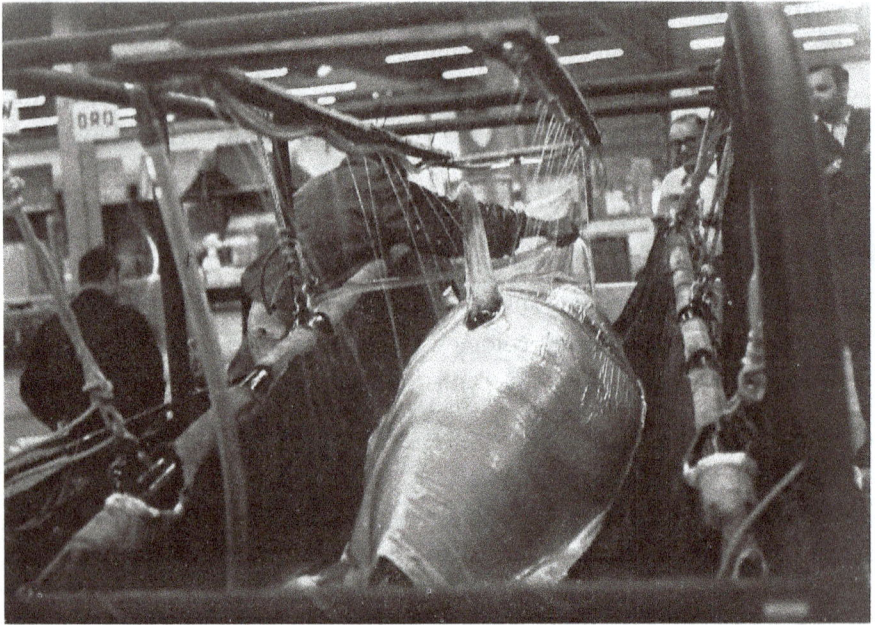

FIG. 14.6 Transportation of a killer whale (source: Anonymous 1975: 78)

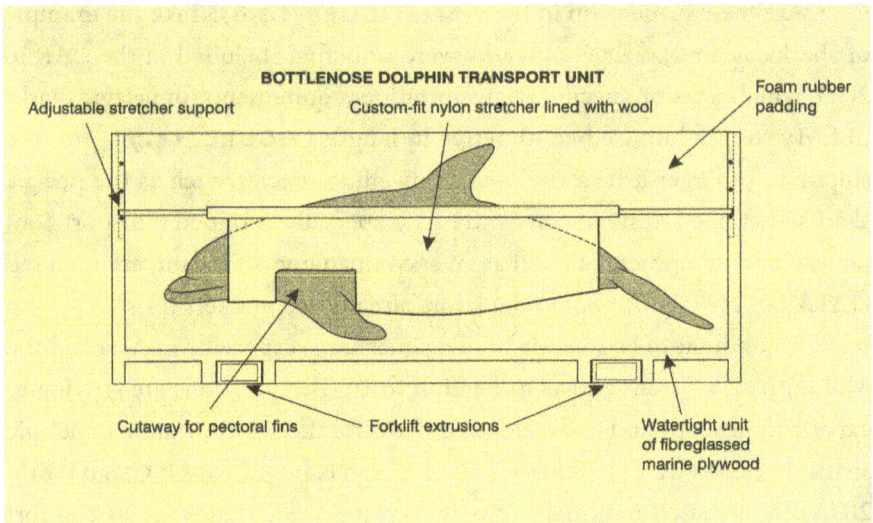

FIG. 14.7 Container requirement 55, for dolphin and whale species (source: *Live Animals Regulations, 37th Edition* (IATA 2011: 306))

Transporting animals – including humans – by air demands technological solutions to the problems posed by an inhospitable environment. Managed cabin conditions provide at the most an extended spacesuit for survival. Often providing only the most vital requirements to the animals, those minimal ecologies in the air also require time management, i.e. reduced flight time. Here, the *LAR* with its container requirements, not unlike Noah's ark (**FIGURE 14.2**) with its miniature cosmologies and container species for the entire animal kingdom, catches the cosmos by means of a box.

OUT OF THE BOX!

'Cat in the belly!' is an emergency call-code in the tightly scheduled and meticulously planned world of logistics. Something has happened; a box has broken, an item – in this case a living one – is out of control. No matter how many experts have been engaged in the construction of the apt and perfect box, and no matter how much effort has been put into securing the cat container correctly in the belly of a cargo-liner, be sure that there are always creatures who have but one idea: how to get out!

Replace the cat with any other animal that is brought up into the sky and then down to earth and you know why Frankfurt Airport maintains a special animal protection unit, located at one of the fire stations. First the belly has to be shut to keep the uncontrolled item in a more controlled space, confined from the airfield. There is always the next box waiting to be dispatched behind the one just stored away. Logistics work after the principle of the Russian doll or Chinese boxes. But the flow of boxes can be disrupted. It can take hours to catch a cat. In this case, everything has to be closed and shut down. No operation is possible. The ark cracks.

When it comes to questions of survival, salvation, and security, God and Noah were tackling similar problems to those faced by modern logistics in the era of global capital. The collaboration between God and Noah lifted species from the water currents. Yet twenty-first-century logistics align animal passengers with flows of goods and capital, and catches the animal kingdom within an all-encompassing regulation where the ark features in everyday life, self-descriptions, and material box practices. As much as through the freight terminals of our global airports, the *Ur*-idea of a box cuts transversally through history. The ark, as *Ur*-idea of the box, possesses a religious, military, humanitarian, beastly, economic or, in times of climate change, ecological function. What might be its future actualisations and proliferations? In what ways will it continue to confine, draw boundaries, include, exclude, or crack?

NOTES

I   See illustration by Lauren Weinstein, picture at the end of the text (Bauer, Blacker, Güttler, and Schlünder 2013).

REFERENCES

Air Cargo News, 'Sea vs Air: Even Sharks Prefer to Be Flown', *Air cargo News*, 24 November 2015 <http://www.aircargonews.net/news/single-view/news/sea-vs-air-even-sharks-prefer-to-be-flown.html> [accessed 19 November 2019].

Air Cargo World, 'Asian, Middle Eastern aquariums clamor for sharks', *Air Cargo World*, 17 October 2013 <http://aircargoworld.com/asian-middle-eastern-aquariums-clamor-for-sharks/> [accessed 19 November 2019].

Anonymous, 'Schwalben werden in den Süden geflogen', *Frankfurter Allgemeine Zeitung*, 11 October 1974.

——, 'Mittler zwischen Tier und Mensch', *Frankfurter Allgemeine Zeitung*, 16 August 1976.

——, 'Schwalben in den Süden', *Frankfurter Allgemeine Zeitung*, 11 October 1974, p. 9.

——, 'Schwalben per Flugzeug', *Frankfurter Allgemeine Zeitung*, 4 October 1957, p. 67.

ARK Development, LLC, 'The ARK at JFK', in ARK Development, LLC, 2012–2016. <http://www.arkjfk.com> [accessed 19 November 2019].

Bauer, S., S. Blacker, N. Güttler, and M. Schlünder, 'The Racehorse on the Runway', *Nautilus*, 26 December 2013 <http://nautil.us/issue/8/home/the-racehorse-on-the-runway> [accessed 19 November 2019].

Breidbach, O. and M. T. Ghiselin, 'Athanasius Kircher (1602–1680) on Noah's Ark: Baroque "Intelligent Design" Theory', *Proceedings of the California Academy of Sciences*, 4th series 57.36 (2006): 991–1002.

Browne, J., *The Secular Ark. Studies in the History of Biogeography* (New Haven/London: Yale University Press, 1983).

Fleck, L., *Genesis and Development of a Scientific Fact* [1935] (Chicago: University of Chicago Press, 1979).

Gogné, R. J. A., 'Ich flog mit den Schwalben', *Wir und die Vögel*, 1 (1975): 18 <https://www.nabu.de/tiere-und-pflanzen/voegel/artenschutz/schwalben/03542.html> [accessed 19 November 2019].

IATA, *Live Animals Regulations*, 21st edition (1994).

——, *Live Animals Regulations*, 23rd edition (1996).

——, *Live Animals Regulations*, 37th edition (2011).

——, 'Live Animals and Perishables Board (LAPB)', in IATA, 2016a <http://www.iata.org/whatwedo/workgroups/Pages/lapb.aspx> [accessed 19 November 2019].

——, 'Live Animals Regulations (LAR)', in IATA, 2016b <https://www.iata.org/whatwedo/cargo/live-animals/Pages/index.aspx> [accessed 19 November 2019].

——, 'Table of Contents', in IATA, *Live Animals Regulations*, 2016c <http://www.iata.org/publications/Documents/cargo-standards/ToC/TOC%20-%20LAR.pdf> [accessed 17 August 2016].

Kircher, A., *Arca Noe* (1675), in Linda Hall Library Digital Collections <http://lhldigital.lindahall.org/cdm/ref/collection/philsci/id/1227> [accessed 17 August 2016].

Kneerich, A., '"Ich glaub', mich laust der Affe!" Sonderbetreuung für lebende Luftfracht', *Flughafen Nachrichten / Frankfurt Rhein-Main Airport News*, 2 (1975): 76–80.

Morris, N., 'Stuck at Heathrow: The Live Animal Cargo Smuggled into Britain', *Independent*, 20 July 2014 <http://www.independent.co.uk/news/uk/crime/stuck-at-heathrow-the-live-animal-cargo-smuggled-into-britain-9617452.html> [accessed 19 November 2019].

NABU, 'Als die Schwalben per Lufthansa reisten. Die große Schwalben-Hilfsaktion 1974', in NABU <https://www.nabu.de/tiere-und-pflanzen/voegel/artenschutz/schwalben/03542.html> [accessed 19 November 2019].

Ruge, K., 'Die Schwalbenhilfe in Südwestdeutschland', *Wir und die Vögel*, 1 (1975): 5–8 <https://www.nabu.de/tiere-und-pflanzen/voegel/artenschutz/schwalben/03542.html> [accessed 19 November 2019].

Wilson, C. M., 'The Great Crops Move', *The Harpers Monthly*, June 1943, pp. 42–48.

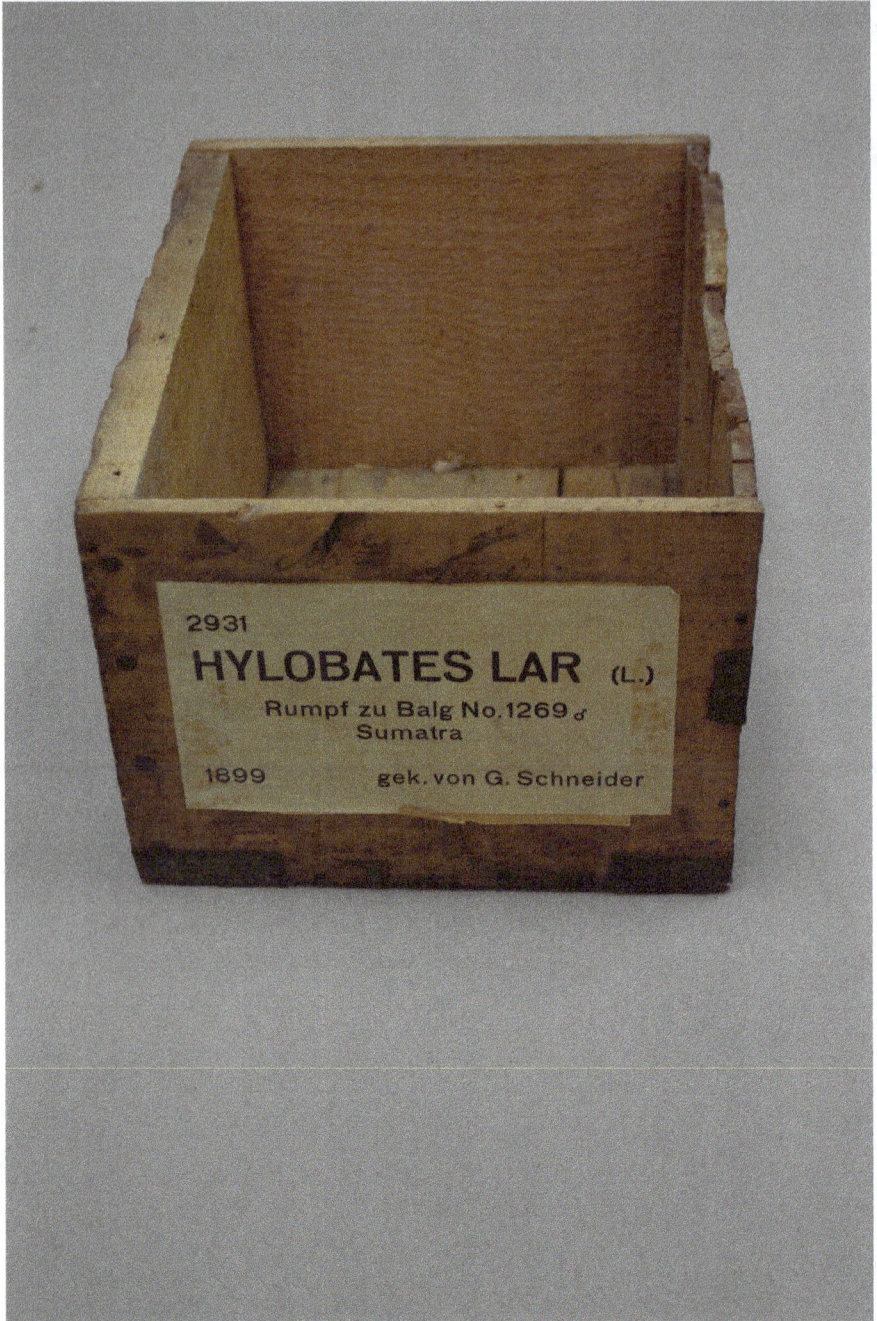

FIG. 15.1 A wooden box from the Natural History Museum – Archives of Life, Basel, Switzerland (source: photographed by Tanja Hammel, 10 September 2014)

PARCELS RENDER NEGLECTED PEOPLE VISIBLE

Tanja Hammel

Box: parcel in Natural History. **Material**: wood or cardboard. Wooden boards of different thickness, from different tree species, and from different points of time, in various colours depending on their materiality and the artefacts or biofacts they transported. Many of them are reused boxes that previously contained goods such as sugar, soap, cigarettes, photo glass plates, etc. **Size and shape**: one side is about 60 x 30 cm, of rectangular shape. **Behaviour**: they enveloped, safeguarded, and preserved their content on their journeys from the animals' natural habitat to the collection or laboratory where their content was researched or prepared for display. They connected sender and receiver over vast distances. **Habitat**: some endured and are still part of the storing infrastructure of natural history museums or private collections. Others, such as those at the Natural History Museum – Archives of Life, Basel, Switzerland, have been adapted for other purposes. **Migration**: the accessibility of the material allowed for its use by virtually everyone. On their way, parcels moved through the hands of numerous people, and were in contact with various vehicles – horse-drawn carriages, ox-wagons, and steamboats, for example – and animals – such as the various insect species that damaged them. **Collector**: Martin Schneider, Geosciences' Collection Manager at the Natural History Museum – Archives of Life, Basel, Switzerland. The museum was founded in 1821. Schneider and his predecessors have preserved a collection of boxes since the late nineteenth century and stored them in three large cardboard boxes. **Status**: largely intact, some damaged and missing parts; other parts remain but are differently used today. As they were often in use for transport until it became impossible, hardly any ephemeral cardboard parcel has been preserved. Where scraps remain, they can provide interesting information such as addresses, collectors' names, and the tags added later to store specimens.

Boxing principle: opening up, rendering visible, connecting, providing, enriching.

Keywords: containing, compressing, concealing, circulating, shipping, re-using, networking, recycling, abducting, assembling, combining, interlacing, rendering companion species visible

THIS PARCEL (**FIGURE 15.1**) WAS USED TO TRANSPORT PART OF A LAR-gibbon's skeleton from Sumatra to Basel. The content was part of German-born Gustav Schneider's (1834–1900) collection. Schneider was conservator of the natural history collection in Basel, Switzerland, from 1859 to 1875. At the same time, he traded specimens to make a living. He accumulated a rich collection that he sold to museums. Specimen dealing was much more lucrative than working at the museum, which is why he made this his main profession. He also acted as a taxidermist of the specimens he sold (see Schneider 1900).

Going through exhibitions at natural history museums such as those in Basel, visitors encounter white male Europeans as the sole actors in the field of natural history. But if curators attended to the routes by which the parcels arrived at the museums, and how the material on display was packed and transported, this narrative cannot persist. Focusing on parcels and their human companions, this article shows how parcels shed light on men and women collectors, both colonial and indigenous, who have hitherto been marginalised.

Due to the ephemeral nature of their material, we do not find many parcels from the eighteenth and nineteenth centuries in collections. Being part of everyday transport infrastructure, parcels as such were not considered note-worthy, and this is why there are hardly any illustrations depicting them. But parcels were nevertheless of vital importance in knowledge circulation. A scientist's or an institution's status increased with the number of parcels received. Parcels caused excitement among metropolitan naturalists, but also fear lest the contents be damaged or fail to reach the addressee. The boxes' content was, for metropolitan and, later, colonial urban naturalists, an intricate link between their laboratories and the 'field' in the wider world. This content provided metropolitan naturalists with evidence for taxonomy and theories, for example, for species' distribution and evolution by natural and sexual selection. Darwin's correspondence, for instance, is full of references to lost parcels, stolen manuscripts and specimens, and the resulting detailed, almost paranoid, enquiry about the whereabouts of parcels. In one hundred and fourteen letters to and from Darwin between 1828 and 1881, parcels are mentioned. Darwin always 'anxiously [...] hope[d] to hear that the parcel is safe', and was so concerned that he asked his correspondents to send parcels to his brother in London, not his home in the Kent countryside, where he feared it would get lost (Darwin to Japetus Steenstrup, 30 December 1849). He was 'much obliged for a single line to acknowledge' a parcel's 'receipt' (Darwin to J. F. W. Herschel, 7 May 1848), and when manuscripts were dispatched he asked his colleagues to inform him 'when [the] parcel is sent off' (Darwin to James Crichton-Browne, 31 January 1870). When a parcel's content was particularly valuable, he would send his servant in the tax-cart to pick it up (Darwin to J. D. Hooker, 19 July 1855, 30 December 1849; to Sowerby, 11 November 1850).

Parcels are *companions*, and have life forces. Let us extend Donna Haraway's concept of 'companion species' (Haraway 2003), which she particularly used for dogs, to inanimate beings such as parcels that may shape the scientific or professional person who comes into contact with them as much as the person shapes the parcel. Postcolonial and STS scholars have long debated whether there are different epistemologies or ontologies in different contexts. The main problem has been that for too long STS scholars have seen the world and science through Euro-American eyes. In this context, the nature/culture divide that distinguishes between animate and inanimate entities has determined how scholars think about actors in science. However, in Bantu society, for example, people do not differentiate between objects and persons, but see all animate and inanimate beings as forces of life in interaction (Connell 2007: 97–98). Seen from such a perspective, then, parcels may have 'life forces', like their human companions. One such force that is of particular importance here is the power they have to render visible their human companions who have hitherto been neglected because of their belonging to subordinate social groups – whether this subordination was based on ethnicity, gender, or social class.

Parcels render their less visible human companions visible when 'black-boxing' fails (see e.g. Endersby 2008: 65, 89–93, 97, 205–08; Musselman Green 2003: 367–92). Black-boxing, according to Bruno Latour, is the process through which aspects of science make themselves invisible when they are successful. When parcels arrive, as Darwin's letters show, they become opaque and obscure (Latour 1999). Looking for parcels in famous nineteenth-century naturalist's writings, such as Alfred Russell Wallace's accounts from the Malay Archipelago, we learn that locals filled parcels with their collected birds of paradise that Wallace then sent to England to become known (Wallace 1862). In Australia, botanists and botanical artists employed men aboriginal 'guides' and men and women collectors but did generally not acknowledge them by name. However, there are rare cases such as the herbarium sheets found at the National Herbarium of Victoria in Melbourne, from which we learn that parcels were packed by part-Aboriginal Australians Lucy and Thomas Webb, and Lucy Eades, who had also collected the plants that were career-making for German-born, Australia-based botanist Ferdinand Mueller (Maroske 2014: 74–75, 85). In Europe, volunteers and poorly-paid employees unpacked parcels. Parcels filled with botanical specimens, particularly from the Cape, were transported between Trinity College Dublin and 'the quay' on the donkey and cart of Jack Spain, an elderly disabled man (Fischer (ed.) 1869: 215).

Parcels allowed humans to negotiate power. Colonial collectors were aware of naturalists' dependence on them, and they voiced the need for tools and parcels. In the Cape, the colonial naturalist Mary Elizabeth Barber (1818–1899), for instance, stressed that boxes were 'not as "plentiful as black-berries" in the country' (Barber to Trimen, Highlands 15 April 1864); a striking analogy given the local rarity of blackberries. Scientists at urban or metropolitan institutions subsequently provided her with boxes. Metropolitan naturalists preferred colonial collectors who knew little about science and would content themselves with sending specimens. Botanist William Hooker, for instance, encouraged collectors to have their 'eyes open', but not to read books, since 'many of the best collections of plants' had 'been made without books' (1859: 419–20). Colonial collectors who were not content with this metropolitan attitude and aimed to show how important they were sometimes retained parcels to name specimens. George Bentham at Kew Gardens published seven volumes on Australian flora

(1863–1878) with the 'assistance' of Ferdinand Mueller, who had aimed to do it himself. The only possibility for Bentham to empower himself was to classify plants before sending them to the Royal Botanic Gardens at Kew (Lucas 2003: 255–81). Hooker's son and successor, Joseph Dalton, silenced his collectors in New Zealand, William Colenso and Ronald Gunn, in the same way as had his father before him (Endersby 2001: 343–58, Endersby 2009: 74–87). Ferdinand Mueller also silenced his women and autochthonous colleagues and collaborators, sometimes misspelling their names (Maroske, Vaughan 2014: 72–91, 91–172), in a sign that he wished to downplay their work in order to establish his own reputation as more than a collaborator of metropolitan scientists. Since the time of the Swedish naturalist Carl Linnaeus (1707–1778) it had been common practice among taxonomists not to acknowledge every individual collector in their studies. When Mueller was accused of 'plagiarism' against plant collectors, his Austrian colleague Joseph Armin Knapp defended him, arguing that it was 'downright absurd' to 'demand such a high degree of resignation and self-effacement' (1877: 597–617). To ensure mutual interchange between colonial and metropolitan naturalists and institutions, exchange societies were established that ensured the swap of specimens between collections worldwide. One example was the South African Botanical Exchange Society, founded in 1866, which aimed to ensure sufficient supply from a large number of amateur botanists. By 1868 approximately 9,000 duplicates had been sent abroad in parcels, and in return specimens from Europe, North America, and Australia entered South African herbaria (Gunn and Codd 1981: 183).

While recent studies have focused on the knowledge British scientists gained in the southern hemisphere, or the vital role autochthonous people's informal knowledge or collaboration played in the production of knowledge (see e.g. Jacobs 2006, McCalman 2009), parcels allow us to see further. The parcels retained by Australian botanical collections show how colonial naturalists exercised their power and emancipated themselves from British institutions at an earlier point in time than previously thought. The parcels demonstrate the impact people in the south had on the formation of new disciplines that have generally been believed to have emerged in the north. These mundane, ephemeral companion objects allow us to encounter women and men from different social and ethnic backgrounds, their access to parcels, and their impact

FIG. 15.2 A cardboard box filled with wooden boxes at the Natural History Museum – Archives of Life, Basel, Switzerland (source: photographed by Tanja Hammel, 10 September 2014)

on science. Museum exhibits would be many fewer, we would know much less about the world's flora and fauna, and some scientific disciplines may never have emerged without parcels.

The box in the photographs above remains hidden in the natural history museum's storeroom, enclosed in a cardboard box. Its lid, however, has recently been seen in the museum. The curators used it to decorate menu cards at special events (**FIGURE 15.3**).

Being used for this purpose, this new artefact raises awareness of the materiality and temporality of museum and science objects. It helps us to visualise the circulation of matter and being. The animal specimens, as well as the trees that the box and paper are made of, evolved over millennia and in distant parts of the world. This new artefact also reveals the museum's past practice or effect of 'cutting objects out of specific contexts' and 'therefore concealing the relations of power that produced the collection' (Clifford 1988: 220; Roque 2011: 5) and raises awareness of black-boxing. In fact, it works in the opposite way to

FIG. 15.3 Menus for 'After Hours Summer Edition, Chillen im Museum', 11 September 2014 (source: photographed by Tanja Hammel)

black-boxing and purification – scientists' de-contextualisation of specimens that arrived in parcels to construct 'pure' knowledge objects and separation between nature and culture (Latour 1993: 24, 44, 140). It is therefore a significant intervention that the museum now exhibits parts of the parcels and confronts visitors with their life stories. The boxes' histories had a vital impact on Western knowledge production and discipline building, so rendering them visible should be shortlisted on every (museum, university, archival) collection's agenda. This would allow us to reflect on the politics of knowledge production, and to take the history of science out of its black box.

ACKNOWLEDGEMENTS

Thanks are due to the workshop organisers, to the editors and participants, and to Balz Aschwanden, Melanie Boehi, Madeleine Gloor, Michael Schaffner and Christine Winter for their comments.

REFERENCES

Bentham, G., *Flora australiensis: A Description of the Plants of the Australian Territory*, assisted by Ferdinand Mueller, 7 vols (London: L. Reeve and Co., 1863–1878).

Clifford, J., *The Predicament of Culture: Twentieth-Century Ethnography, Literature, and Art* (Cambridge, MA: Harvard University Press, 1988).

Connell, R., *Southern Theory: The Global Dynamics of Knowledge in Social Science* (Cambridge/Malden, MA: Polity 2007).

Darwin, C., Darwin Correspondence Project (http://www.darwinproject.ac.uk), Darwin to J. J. S. Steenstrup, 30 December 1849, Letter 1281; Darwin to J. F. W. Herschel, 7 May 1848, Letter 1173; Darwin to J. D. Hooker, 19 July 1855, Letter 1722; 30 December 1849, Letter 1281; Darwin to J. C. Sowerby, 11 November 1850, Letter 1368; Darwin to James Crichton-Browne, 31 January 1870, Letter 7089

Endersby, J., '"From Having no Herbarium". Local Knowledge vs. Metropolitan Expertise: Joseph Hooker's Australasian Correspondence with William Colenso and Ronald Gunn', *Pacific Science*, 55.4 (2001): 343–58

——, *Imperial Nature: Joseph Hooker and the Practices of Victorian Science* (Chicago: Chicago University Press, 2008).

——, 'A Gunn and two Hookers. Friendships That Shaped Science', in: I. McCalman and N. Erskine, eds, *In the Wake of the Beagle. Science in the Southern Oceans from the Age of Darwin* (Sydney: University of New South Wales Press, 2009), pp. 74–87.

Fischer, L., ed., *Memoir of W. H. Harvey, Late Professor of Botany, Trinity College, Dublin: With Selections from His Journal and Correspondence* (London: Bell and Daldy, 1869).

Gunn, M., and L. E. Codd, *Botanical Exploration in Southern Africa* (Cape Town: A. A. Balkema, 1981).

Haraway, D., *The Companion Species Manifesto: Dogs, People, and Significant Otherness* (Chicago: Prickly Paradigm Press, 2003).

Hooker, W. J., *The Article Botany, extracted from the Admiralty Manual of Scientific Enquiry, 3rd edition, 1859: comprising Instruction for the Collection and Preservation of Specimens; together with Notes and Enquiries regarding Botanical and Pharmacological Desiderata* (London 1859).

Jacobs, N., 'The Intimate Politics of Ornithology in Colonial Africa', *Comparative Studies in Society and History*, 48.3 (2006): 564–603.

Knapp, J. A., 'Baron Ferdinand von Mueller: Eine biographische Skizze', *Z. Allg. Österr. Apotheker-Vereins*, 15.36 (1877): 597–617, trans. by D. Sinkora, 15 January 1977, p. 7, The Library of the Royal Botanic Gardens Melbourne.

Latour, B., *We Have Never Been Modern*, trans. by C. Porter (Cambridge, MA: Harvard University Press, 1993).

——, *Pandora's Hope: Essays on the Reality of Science Studies* (Cambridge, MA: Harvard University Press, 1999).

Lucas, A. M., 'Assistance at a Distance: George Bentham, Ferdinand von Mueller and the Production of *Flora australiensis*', *Archives of Natural History*, 30.2 (2003): 255–81.

Maroske, S., '"A Taste for Botanic Science": Ferdinand Mueller's Female Collectors and the History of Australian Botany', *Muelleria*, 32 (2014): 72–91.

Maroske, S., and A. Vaughan, 'Ferdinand Mueller's Female Plant Collectors: A Biographical Register', *Muelleria*, 32 (2014): 91–172.

McCalman, I., *Darwin's Armada. How Four Voyagers to Australasia Won the Battle for Evolution and Changed the World* (Sydney: Simon & Schuster Australia, 2009).

Musselman Green, E., 'Plant Knowledge at the Cape: A Study in African and European Collaboration', *International Journal of African Historical Studies*, 361 (2003): 367–92.

Roque, R., 'Stories, Skulls, and Colonial Collections', *Configurations*, 19.1 (2011): 1–23.

Schneider, G., jr, 'Gustav Schneider, 1834–1900', *Verhandlungen der Schweizerischen Naturforschenden Gesellschaft*, 83 (1900), lxxxiv–xciv.

Trimen Correspondence, Royal Entomological Society, St Albans, Naturalist Mary Elizabeth Barber to entomologist Roland Trimen (1840–1916), Box 17, Letter 37, Highlands, 15 April 1864.

Wallace, A. R., 'Narrative of Search After Birds of Paradise', *Proceedings of the Zoological Society of London* 1862, ed. by C. H. Smith, <http://people.wku.edu/chalres.smith/wallace/S067.htm> [15 September 2014].

FIG. 16.1 'Aid is seen on-board an Australian RAAF C-17 Globemaster in transit on March 16, 2015 to Port Vila, Vanuatu' (source: Getty Images, used with permission)

16

BOXES, INFRASTRUCTURE AND THE MATERIALITY OF MORAL RELATIONS: AID AND RESPECT AFTER CYCLONE PAM

Alexandra Widmer

Box variant: aid boxes. **Specific variant**: after Cyclone Pam, Vanuatu. March 2015. **Size and shape**: highly variable. Size often requires military plane or navy ship and significant knowledge and technical infrastructure. **Material**: cardboard, plastic, wood. **Colour**: variable. Often accompanied by white stickers indicating provenance, e.g. 'Australian Aid'. Stickers also indicate that contents should not be sold but distributed as aid. **Behaviour**: move through procedures that are seen as universal, but if local distribution networks are overrun, they are associated with feelings of disrespect. Also, movement makes those in control of networks into experts. **Habitat**: humanitarian crises. **Distribution and costs**: free (in short term) to recipient. In the case of Cyclone Pam, amounts promised: Australia, AUD 5 million; New Zealand, NZD 2.5 million, United Kingdom, GBP 2 million (Hayward-Jones 2015); China, CNY 30 million (Sim 2015). Local infrastructure maintained by local government. **Migration**: follows in wake of disasters caused by hurricanes, tsunamis. **Status**: urgent. This can justify disrespect of local authorities and forms of knowledge. **Contents**: 'The Necessities of life'. Tarpaulins, water, medicine, tents, rice, clothing. **Deliver**: consumables (see contents). **Perform**: expertise, aid, order. **Transport**: goods from one national economy to another. Also often transport goods between cultural frameworks that shape the meanings of objects, personhood, and exchange. **Provoke**: conflicts. **Reveal and/or heighten**: new or pre-existing struggles and unequal distribution. **Need**: local infrastructure, networks, and knowledge.

Keywords: transporting, disrespecting, dis/ordering, expert making

HURRICANES AND AID BOXES

THE SOUND ALONE OF THE WINDS FROM A CATEGORY-FIVE CYCLONE IS enough to terrorise the most steady of hearts. Sheltering with your family and your community on the floor of the strongest building in your village is an adventure at the beginning, when you're young, but the fun quickly turns to fear when the adults grow silent. Corrugated iron roofs are tossed around the village as easily as boats on seawater. Iron sheets, pitched around in 350-kilometre gusts, will damage anything that they hit. When palm trees are blown over, they do not go quietly. This one is different from the hurricanes people talk about, like Uma in 1987, or Ivy in 2004. You start to worry that this one may even be different than the one in 1950, when a wave swept over the island, and your village moved to the bigger island nearby. The one that older people still talk about.

In March 2015, the category-five cyclone Pam roared through Vanuatu, a nation of over eighty inhabited islands in the southwestern Pacific.[1] The cyclone crippled Vanuatu's infrastructure: an estimated ninety percent of the nation's buildings were impacted by the storm's effects; crops and livestock were damaged; telecommunications were paralysed, and water shortages became acute. An emotional President Baldwin Lonsdale, speaking from a conference on disaster preparedness he was attending in Japan, conveyed the urgency and scale of the damage to the international community, saying 'The humanitarian need is immediate, we need it right now' (BBC 2015).

Aid boxes began arriving shortly afterwards on New Zealand Hercules aircraft, Australian RAAF C-17s and Globemaster Australian C-17s, to the Bauerfield airport in Port Vila (**FIGURES 16.1, 16.2**). The airport and its runway, built to accommodate US military needs in World War Two, is large enough to accommodate such military planes, and was partially open by Sunday (Fox 2015), roughly forty-eight hours after the cyclone passed. A New Zealand navy ship anchored in the deep harbour, to be witnessed by all who ventured back to the seawall.

These boxes and their contents, once on the Australian military planes, on the runway, on the harbour wall, become 'aid' or 'aid and relief supplies'. In images of the aftermath of the cyclone, the boxes on planes or being loaded off planes appear solid and orderly amid the destruction of homes, crops, and

FIG. 16.2 'Plane arrives in Port Vila with aid packages' (photo credit: Evan Schuurman/ Save the Children from Barber 2015, used with permission)

infrastructure. They appear separate from the resilience and ingenuity of ni-Vanuatu (citizens of Vanuatu) cleaning up.

The boxes, generally referred to as 'aid', were accompanied by medical experts, search and rescue teams, and logistics experts from Australia and New Zealand. A UN team arrived from Europe. The boxes displayed 'Australian Aid' stickers that prominently labelled the provenance of the objects as well as the intended relationship between those receiving and those delivering.

The boxes, alongside the technical infrastructure, needed a knowledge network for experts to best distribute the contents. By early May, less than two months after the cyclone, a 'Post Disaster Needs Assessment [...] which will help in mobilizing additional resources for recovery and reconstruction' (Secretariat of the Pacific Regional Environment Programme 2015) was conducted by NGOs.

PAST BOXES

Boxes transporting manufactured objects have arrived from Australia, England, France, and China since Europeans took up long-term residence on the islands.

Virtually all manufactured goods in Vanuatu arrive there in boxes, as there is very limited factory manufacturing. At the end of World War II, military boxes with similar contents to that supplied after the cyclone – food, medicine, military equipment – were dumped into the sea by departing American troops, so that one of the remaining colonial powers (Britain) could not use them. This also meant that Islanders who had worked for Americans during the war could not consume the contents, which now form enormous reefs of cans, bottles, and scrap metal that are of interest to snorkelers and divers. This was aid precluded, the dumped boxes performing an attempt at severing relationship between the departing Americans and the British who remained, along with the French, as colonial powers until 1980.

Ships and planes have left Vanuatu with cargo as well. In the context of trade beyond the Pacific islands, sandalwood was harvested and shipped (1830s–1860s) to China, and copra (processed coconut) had some value on European markets. Beginning in the 1840s, people left, sometimes having been kidnapped, to work on plantations on other Pacific islands and in Australia. Now seasonal labourers, men and women, get short term contracts in Australia and New Zealand's agricultural industries.

THE ARRIVAL OF BOXES FORETOLD

Boxes of manufactured goods arriving on aircraft were prophesied and sought through the ritual efforts of groups of devotees in Papua New Guinea, Fiji, and Vanuatu from the 1930s. Such people – not the entire population of any of these countries – wondered about cargo boxes that arrived and contained objects that did not appear to require labour to be produced, or payment to be distributed. When Europeans arrived with such objects, their success, some members of these groups theorised, was a result of the success of their – the Europeans' – ancestors. It was then thought that boxes of desirable manufactured goods arriving in planes might also have been foretold by their own ancestors. These beliefs 'serve to reframe colonial experience into an intimately personal context. The desire to acquire cargo becomes a foil for re-establishing good relations with deceased relatives. Behind all of this, though, is a broader effort to reimagine a basic sense of self in relation to the local community' (Leavitt

2004: 183). Anthropologists have long observed that this cargo, as objects of desire (e.g. Lindstrom 1993), mediated relationships and power.

Too easily assigned the name 'cargo cult' in the past by colonial authorities and Western popular media, in Vanuatu such clusters of beliefs and ritual have been taken up by certain people anticipating the arrival of John Frum on the island of Tanna in the south of the country. The messianic figure first appeared in the late 1930s, saying that if people left the Presbyterian Church, and stopped following the colonial authorities and using currency, he would then return with wealth. During World War Two, the wealth that the American military displayed bolstered the belief that John Frum was American. Since then, John Frum has often been identified as a white American soldier who, if the rituals are performed correctly, will come to Tanna by plane to distribute goods. At one point, followers of John Frum even constructed a runway to facilitate his arrival (Fortune 2000).

The desires of those who await John Frum, and their fascination with objects, selfhood, and exchange, while not the most common instantiation – indeed, their numbers fell from 1000 in the 1960s to 300–400 in the 1980s (Fortune 2000) – do reflect the broad importance of objects for exchange and the production of personhood in the Pacific. This was first brought to the attention of anthropologists by Bronislaw Malinowksi (1922), and other renowned researchers like Marcel Mauss (1985, 1970), Marilyn Strathern (1988, 1999) and Annette Weiner (1992). Through this scholarship, Pacific Islanders have taught generations of anthropology students that participating in forms of exchange – this means giving *and* receiving in the right ways – can contribute to our moral personhood. Indeed, apprehending the centrality of exchange in human activity can show that personhood might not only be located in individual bodies, but also has the possibility of being socially and relationally constituted. It is culturally incumbent on all parties to make sure exchange, over time, is fair.

HURRICANES AND BOXES: ONE SIZE DOES NOT FIT ALL

Distributing the contents of the boxes after cyclone Pam was not easy. Vanuatu is a nation of over eighty inhabited islands, with terrain and waterways that have always posed complex and expensive logistical challenges for large scale (read colonial, capitalist, modern) transportation infrastructures. Furthermore, the infrastructure had been severely damaged in the cyclone. Answering the president's call, international NGOs arrived and implemented their standard procedures, but these did not go down well with ni-Vanuatu or international staff who were already working longer term in the country. Rebecca Barber, of Save the Children Australia, interviewed international NGO workers in Vanuatu about the first response. She writes:

> A number of staff interviewed during the course of this research said that failure on the part of newcomers to understand the Melanesian culture underlay much of the disharmony in the first weeks of the response. There were two parts to this issue: the first being a failure to show deference to figures of authority; the second being a pushing aside of national staff and international pre-cyclone staff, who between them had so much to bring to the response. (Barber 2015: 19)

She further quotes from email correspondence with an international humanitarian worker in May 2015:

> ...I walked into a room that was overflowing with white faces, the only Pacific person in the room apart from [the NDMO Director] was the Fijian SPC [Secretariat of the Pacific Community] representative ... the tension in the room was tangible and everything about it just felt "wrong" ... The NDMO Ni-Van staff (the people who should really have been in the EOC!) were all sitting in the office across the corridor. There is no way I wanted to sit and be based in that room. (Barber 2015: 19)

Many people working in Vanuatu reported similar experiences to Barber. Repeatedly, the goal of distributing boxes led those who had brought the boxes from abroad to sideline the knowledge and experiences of those living in the country as they attempted to implement standard protocols. Barber argues that in humanitarian disasters,

> the international community must show much greater readiness to move away from 'one-size-fits-all' systems and procedures, and understand its core

> role as providing surge capacity, technical advice and expertise to national actors to enable *them* to lead and coordinate disaster response in their own countries. (Barber 2015: 3)

This was published in her report to the Pacific Regional Consultation for the World Humanitarian Summit, submitted on behalf of the NGOs Save the Children Australia, World Vision Australia, Oxfam Australia, and CARE Australia.

The fact that Barber felt it necessary to make the point to international humanitarian groups that 'one size does not fit all', highlights that using infrastructure to transport boxes is not a neutral agenda. Boxes require networks and expertise, which are made of political relationships. Giving and receiving boxes brings people into new relationships and makes pre-existing political relationships visible.

FUTURES OF AID BOXES

Ni-Vanuatu, and the small numbers of people from other Pacific islands, and of Asian and European descent, in residence since the 1800s, have worked together to cope with cyclones for centuries, without boxes. There were strategies for burying water and food, or storing necessities in caves. Yet, as Chris Ballard pointed out in an op-ed piece in the *Sydney Morning Herald*, the fact that there have always been cyclones does not mean that Cyclone Pam is just another expected disaster to manage. That Port Vila is ranked the 'Disaster Capital of the World' by Natural Hazards Risk Atlas in their global risk analysis study also has to do with changes in the population and changes in land use, as well as global and regional climate change. Ballard writes,

> a real estate boom has seen vast swathes of the best agricultural land on islands such as Efate and Espiritu Santo converted from customary tenure into residential subdivisions, most of them acquired on long leases by Australian investors [...] There are sound reasons why so few traditional settlements were found along the coast of Efate in the 1840s [before the arrival of Europeans]. A healthy respect for cyclones and storm surges was foremost among them. (2015)

What is different this time is a concern on the donor's side that aid boxes do not come cheap. Ballard writes that the Australian government has already indicated that it will shift its efforts from disaster relief to more cost-effective disaster risk reduction. This will mean more planning for cyclones and other natural disasters (e.g. volcanic eruptions, earthquakes, and tsunamis) in the hope of forestalling widespread loss of life and damage to housing and infrastructure. This strategy will call upon webs of expertise that are accompanied by surveillance over land and coastlines.

What is also different this time, is that new international institutions and social movements are expanding the narratives about aid, islands, and climate change. Aid in the form of boxes of relief supplies is coming under critical scrutiny by those advocating climate justice and climate compensation (e.g. Friedman 2015). For example, an official from Dominica, a small island nation in the Caribbean, which was badly hit by torrential rains from Tropical Storm Erika, has argued that 'Rich countries' emergency relief was of no use to countries with economies flattened by weather disasters'. And, more trenchantly, 'They allow climate change to destroy you and then they provide you with tents and blankets' (Clark 2015). In June, three months after the cyclone, citizens in Vanuatu and neighbouring island nations drafted the 'People's Declaration for Climate Justice' (2015), demanding compensation from fossil fuel companies for destruction linked to climate change.

As very little factory manufacturing is undertaken in Vanuatu, engagements with boxes that arrive by ship and plane, and how their contents are distributed, has been a key dimension of the Islanders' experience of modernity. Longing and desire for manufactured goods, as well as processed foods, have been the affective cargo of boxes from ships and aircraft. The boxes are also accompanied by questions about who is best suited to distribute them, and who actually distributes them. Aid boxes are a material instantiation of a politics of distribution. What will it take for the boxes to perform and produce networks and relationships of compensation and equitable distribution? What knowledge, technology, and forms of affect will we need to transform relations of aid into relations of compensation and climate justice?

CODA

The hurricane winds die down. After you have spoken with your family on other islands, and heard how they fared (which you can do once cell phone towers are back up), and after you have seen your house and garden, you realise what is different this time is that with Cyclone Pam you wonder about climate change. You think about your garden land – if your family has managed to keep some from developers – up on the hill, and consider rebuilding your house there. You wonder how you will manage to get some of the water and food from the boxes at the airport. You know you and your children need these items now. You wonder about new and old kinds of reconciliations and relationships necessary to recover from the damage to the land, the climate, and humans.

NOTES

ı   This chapter was written in October 2015 and finalized in January 2017. Excellent ethnographic analysis of Cyclone Pam has since emerged that regretfully could not be included.

REFERENCES

Aulakh, R., 'Citizens of Tiny Island Nations Target Fossil Fuel Giants for Climate Change Compensation', *The Toronto Star*, 10 June 2010, <http://www.thestar.com/news/world/2015/06/10/tiny-island-nations-target-fossil-fuel-giants-for-climate-change-compensation.html> [accessed 15 October 2015].

BBC, 'Vanuatu Cyclone Pam: President appeals for 'immediate' help', *BBC World Service*, 16 March 2015, <http://www.bbc.com/news/world-asia-31866783> [accessed 1 October 2015].

Ballard, C., 'Port Vila: Disaster Capital of the World', *Sydney Morning Herald*, 21 March 2015,<http://www.smh.com.au/comment/port-vila-disaster-capital-of-the-world-20150320-1m3p32.html#ixzz3ml7s9fxC> [accessed 1 October 2015].

Barber, R., 'One Size Doesn't Fit All: Tailoring the International Response to the National Need Following Vanuatu's Cyclone Pam. A Contribution to the Pacific Regional Consultation for the World Humanitarian Summit', *ReliefWeb*, June 2015, <http://reliefweb.int/sites/reliefweb.int/files/resources/Reflections%20on%20Cyclone%20Pam_WHS%20Report.pdf > [accessed 1 October 2015].

Clark, P., 'Compensation Poses Sticking Point Ahead of Climate Change Talks', *Financial Times*, 4 September 2015, <http://www.ft.com/cms/s/0/54528a78–52e0–11e5-b029-b9d50a74fd14.html#axzz3nnOM6CoK> [accessed 1 October 2015].

Fortune, K., 'John Frum Movement', in B. Lal and K. Fortune, eds, *The Pacific Islands: An Encyclopedia* (Honolulu: University of Hawaii Press, 2000), p. 303.

Fox, L., 'Tropical Cyclone Pam: Aid from Australia and New Zealand Arrives in Vanuatu after Devastating Storm', *Australian Broadcasting Network/Reuters*, 15 March 2015, <http://www.abc.net.au/news/2015–03–15/cyclone-pam-aid-begins-to-arrive-storm-battered-vanuatu/6321280> [accessed 1 October 2015].

Friedman, L., 'How to Compensate Small Island Nations for Tropical Cyclone Damage', *Scientific American*, 17 March 2015, <http://www.scientificamerican.com/article/how-to-compensate-small-island-nations-for-tropical-cyclone-damage/> [accessed 1 October 2015].

Hayward-Jones, J. 'Post-Cyclone Aid to Vanuatu', *The Interpreter*, 18 March 2015, <https://www.lowyinstitute.org/the-interpreter/post-cyclone-aid-vanuatu> [accessed 26 January 2017].

Leavitt, S., 'From "Cult" to Religious Conviction: The Case for Making Cargo Personal', in H. Jebens, ed., *Cargo, Cult and Culture Critique* (Honolulu: University of Hawaii Press, 2004), pp. 170–87.

Lindstrom, L., *Cargo Cult: Strange Stories of Desire from Melanesia and Beyond* (Honolulu: University of Hawaii Press, 1993).

——, 'Cargo Cult at the Third Millennium', in H. Jebens, ed., *Cargo, Cult and Culture Critique* (Honolulu: University of Hawaii Press, 2004), pp. 15–35.

Malinowski, B., *Argonauts of the Western Pacific: An Account of Native Enterprise and Adventure in the Archipelagos of Melanesian New Guinea* (London: Routledge & Kegan Paul, 1922).

Mauss, M., *The Gift: Forms and Functions of Exchange in Archaic Societies* (London: Cohen & West, 1970).

——, 'A Category of the Human Mind: The Notion of Person, the Notion of Self', in M. Carrithers, S. Collins and S. Lukes, eds, *The Category of the Person: Anthropology, Philosophy, History* (Cambridge: Cambridge University Press, 1985), pp. 1–25.

People's Declaration for Climate Justice, 8 June 2015, <http://www.scribd.com/doc/268314902/People-s-Declaration-for-Climate-Justice> [accessed 1 October 2015].

Secretariat of the Pacific Regional Environment Programme, 'Severe Tropical Cyclone Pam – Post Disaster Needs Assessment', *ReliefWeb*, 6 May 2015, <http://reliefweb.int/report/vanuatu/severe-tropical-cyclone-pam-post-disaster-needs-assessment> [accessed 1 October 2015].

Sim, S., 'Vanuatu Cyclone Pam Aid: China Pledges $4.8 Million Worth Of Supplies, Ministry Says', *International Business Times*, 18 March 2015 <http://www.ibtimes.com/vanuatu-cyclone-pam-aid-china-pledges-48-million-worth-supplies-ministry-says-1850954> [accessed 26 January 2017].

Strathern, M., *The Gender of the Gift: Problems with Women and Problems with Society in Melanesia* (Berkeley: University of California Press, 1988).

——, *Property, Substance and Effect: Anthropological Essays on Persons and Things* (London: Athlone Press, 1999).

Weiner, A., *Inalienable Possessions: The Paradox of Keeping-while-Giving* (Berkeley: University of California Press, 1992).

v

BLACK

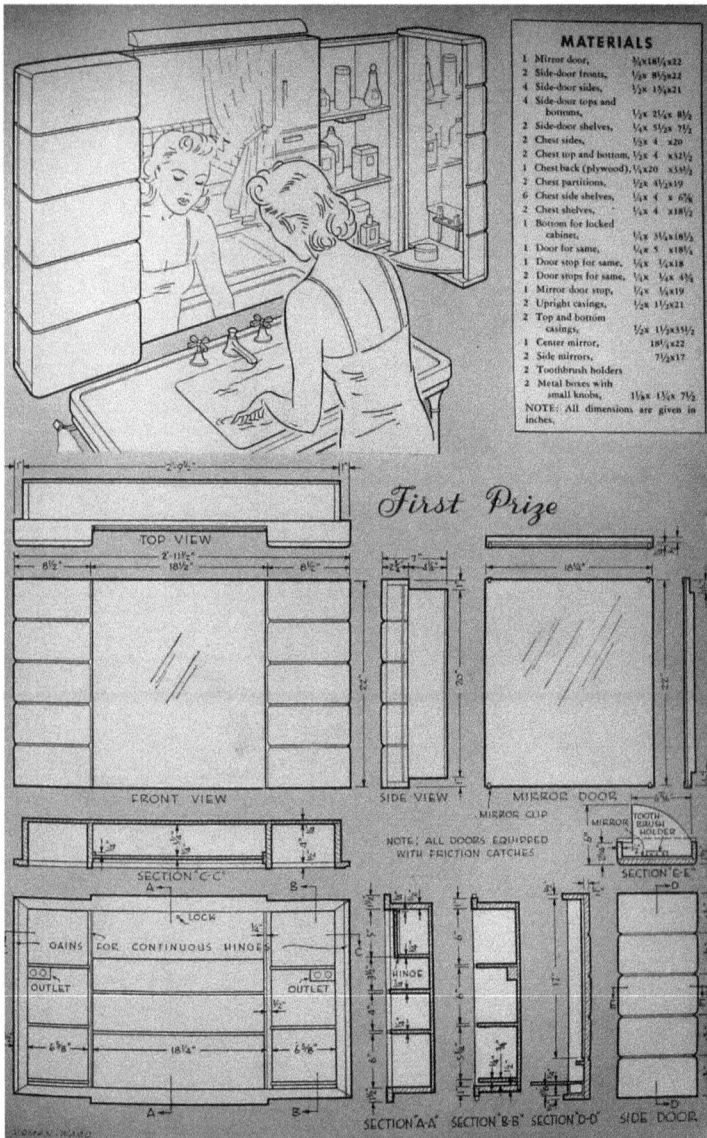

FIG. 17.1 First prize medicine cabinet designed by S. C. Carpenter in Cleveland, Ohio (source: 'Medicine Cabinet Contest Winners', *Popular Science Monthly* (Anonymous 1941: 147))

17

'AS MODERN AS TOMORROW': THE MEDICINE CABINET

Deanna Day

Box: medicine cabinet. **Shape**: rectangular. **Colour**: white and chrome. **Distribution**: every American home. **Habitat**: the bathroom. **Behaviour**: camouflaging, hoarding, and domesticating. **Special features**: illumination and mirrors. **Social relationships**: intimate and prescriptive.

Keywords: categorising, hiding, organising, instructing

IN THE EARLY 1930S, 10,000 NEW YORK CITY FAMILIES WERE PART OF A study conducted by the Office of the Commissioner of Accounts on the status of their home medicine cabinets. The report collected data about what kinds of drugs, devices, and other health care products the 'average' family kept on hand for 'first-aid treatment'. It came to a troubling conclusion: the average home medicine cabinet – the first line of defence in the protection of the family – was shockingly ill-stocked. It was full of outdated medicines and drugs that could cause terrible side effects. Furthermore, it was usually missing several items that the report considered to be absolutely necessary (Palmer 1936: 1–3).

In response, the Consumers' Project of the United States Department of Labor commissioned a bulletin to educate families about proper home health care. It began, 'The average medicine cabinet presents a formidable array of bottles, jars, and boxes. The crowded shelves may look like a miniature drug store, but still may not have on them those remedies which are best or most frequently needed for first-aid treatment in the home'. Especially problematic, the bulletin continued, was the fact that the contents of the average medicine cabinet were based on 'commonly held ideas' about best health care practices that were 'not based on sound medical facts'. The bulletin was meant to address this situation by providing families with a list of sixteen necessary items, which included drugs like pain relievers and burn applications, tools like hot water bottles and tooth brushes, and surgical devices like scissors and tweezers (Palmer 1936: 1–3).

In this instance, 'the home medicine cabinet' is two kinds of box. First, it is a literal box – the cabinet is the container that holds all of the consumer medical products and devices that the family needs. It keeps them close at hand, collected together, and easy to find, but it also appropriately hides them away, for reasons of both safety and propriety. But it is also another kind of box, for 'the medicine cabinet' is as much an ontological category as it is a physical reality. When the Consumers' Project made this list of the contents of their ideal cabinet, they were collecting and cataloguing a certain kind of health care object: small, intimate technologies of the body. In the process of doing so, they also attached a particular set of social meanings and expectations to these technologies.

In this chapter I argue that the physical reality of the medicine cabinet helped to both create and mirror Americans' ideas about health, hygiene, the body, and bodily maintenance during the course of the twentieth century. With a new set of objects – tools that belong in the medicine cabinet – there also came a new kind of person who was meant to be the steward and wielder of these tools. Casting 'the medicine cabinet' as an ontological category forces us to ask a new set of questions. Why was it created? Who uses it? Who benefits from it? What does it obscure? Answering these questions will help us to start piecing together a patient-oriented history of medicine at the turn of the century, with implications that continue to reverberate today.

MEDICINE CABINET AS MINIATURE DRUG STORE

The cultural narrative of the medicine cabinet is almost entirely one of medical consumerism, a consumerism that was also part of broader efforts to create a new kind of American citizen, both bodily and domestically (Leach 1994). The Consumers' Project report on the home medicine cabinet literally called the cabinet a 'miniature drug store'. Moreover, this consumerist impulse is often cast as technologically and scientifically determined. But it may be useful, and more nuanced, to think about the medicine cabinet not as just another set of shelves for household objects, but as something more akin (both literally and symbolically) to the doctor's black bag. This was the period in which physicians were professionalising and taking control of the practice of medicine. But although unacknowledged, twentieth- (and twenty-first-) century American patients have also been scientific medical workers, and the medicine cabinet has held their tools.

In the majority of the literature in the history of medicine, scholars have most often focused on professionals – physicians, surgeons, nurses, etc. – as they form communities, set standards for education and practices, and gatekeep to keep others out of their domain (Stevens 1999; Porter 1999; Starr 1984; Rosenberg 1995; Melosh 1982). Scholarship on patients, then, often focuses on patients' interactions with professionals: how they are compliant, or not; how their voices are heard or silenced; or how a patient's subjective experience of her body is at odds with the physicians' opinion. But patients also manage their health care *without* professional intervention: the times that they self-diagnose and self-treat, often relying on family members, friends, and other non-professional support networks. As a practical means, I argue this by focusing on the technology that they use, deploying a broad definition of technology that includes items like thermometers and blood pressure cuffs, but also pharmaceuticals, hot water bottles, bandages, toothbrushes.

The medicine cabinet, as both the place where these objects live and the ontological category from which they operate, does important, unexamined work in structuring this labour. What's more, the medicine cabinet is a crucial node in a sociotechnical network that often operates to obscure this labour in favour of a consumerist approach. The medicine cabinet materially reinforces the rhetorical and economic ways in which patients are cast as consumers, placing home-based medical care – and those who perform it – firmly within the realm of the private and the commodified. But if we can think outside of this narrative, and focus instead on the object in use, we can see the ways that patients work: how they create knowledge about their bodies, figuring out how they work, and what they should be.

MOVING THE MEDICAL BOX

Several scholars have examined a phenomenon related to the medicine cabinet, namely, the turn-of-the-century travelling medicine chest. Particularly present in the literature are the Tabloid brand medicine chests, manufactured by Burroughs Wellcome & Co. These portable chests were designed to be used in Britain's tropical colonies, in an explicit effort to bring modern, Western scientific medicine to areas of the world perceived to be in need of the benefits of white European culture. However, as Ryan Johnson has shown, these chests were often little more than a repackaging of centuries-old medicines, bandages, and tools. The modernity of Tabloid medicine chests was, in fact, largely about the chest itself and its categorical functions; as the box gathered certain items together, named and labelled them, and then stamped them with a trademarked brand, it stabilised and then standardised the particular medical practices and authority of its users. Whether or not the medicines inside were themselves modern hardly mattered – their organisation and their use was (Johnson 2008).

At the same time that the Tabloid medicine chest was making its way from Britain to her tropical colonies, domestic medicines were beginning to make a similar move from the kitchen cupboard to the bathroom cabinet. Like the

Tabloid chests, the early twentieth-century medicine cabinet collected and organised health care aids, but it also broadcast its own set of requirements and expectations. From its location to its size, the medicine cabinet dictated when, where, and how it should be used. As the medicine cabinet became a standard American household fixture, it was crucial in the process of solidifying cultural standards around home medical practice – standards of hygiene, morality, privacy, and gender (see, for example, Hoy 1996; Ogle 2000; Kline 2000; Cowan 1983; Moskowitz 2008).

Prior to the twentieth century, medicine chests, cupboards, and shelves of various kinds were quite common, but they little resembled the bathroom medicine cabinet we are familiar with today. For centuries, women were the primary providers of care for their families' health needs, and their medicinal products and tools were stored in the logical place, given the material constraints that were involved: the kitchen. The majority of medicinal remedies were mixed at home, using domestic recipe books that included remedies alongside recipes for meals and other household prescriptions. These recipes often utilised ingredients that would be found in the home kitchen and required the use of tools that would also be found there. Additionally, the location of domestic medicine in the family kitchen is consistent with pre-bacteriological ideas about health. When maintaining bodily harmony was part of an integrated system of care that also holistically included elements like diet, the logic of keeping medicines in the kitchen was obvious (Porter 1999; Vogel and Rosenberg 1979).

But at the turn of the century, medicine experienced a number of dramatic changes that were mirrored in the ways that lay individuals managed their health care at home. With the germ theory of disease, the professionalisation of medical care providers, and the invention of a score of new diagnostic medical technologies, the practice of medicine was becoming a more reductionist, standardised, and expert-driven affair (Bynum 1994; Warner 1997; Howell 1996). Furthermore, patients did not only experience these changes when they visited their physicians – they also experienced marked changes in the realm of at-home, non-expert care, where lay individuals began to perform increasingly scientific medical work themselves.

The move of the medicine chest from the kitchen to the bathroom wall occurred at the same time that individuals were expected to stop making remedies themselves and start using new antiseptics, professionally manufactured pain relievers, and scientific diagnostic tools like thermometers. Crucially, this change in use was predicated upon those users sharing a new scientific epistemology of the body. They had to believe a new idea in medicine at the turn of the century: that human bodies were standardised, and the same medicines would work equivalently on all. They had to believe, for example, that there was a shared normal body temperature, and that deviations from the norm meant ill health, not simple idiosyncrasy. This was a radical shift in understanding the body and using these kinds of medical technologies – the things found in the medicine cabinet – was one of the ways patients came to create this understanding for themselves. In other words, the new ontological category of the medicine cabinet was co-constituted with a new epistemology of the body that was itself created by the scientific labour of both domestic and professional users.

The location of this work was a key component in the construction of its meaning. At the turn of the century, Progressive Era reforms brought a scientific, rationalised, and professional approach to all kinds of endeavours, including indoor plumbing. One of the results was the modern bathroom: efficient and discrete. When new home plumbing systems were combined with late-nineteenth-century public health innovations like city sewage systems, the twentieth-century bathroom became the preeminent hygienic home health management space. While the standard late-nineteenth-century bathroom generally only housed a bathtub, sink, and toilet, twentieth-century bathrooms expanded to incorporate fixtures like foot baths, showers, towel racks, cup holders, and planned lighting fixtures – all in the name of improved sanitation, household management, and efficiency (Hoy 1996).

MEDICINE CABINET AS MOTHER'S TOOL KIT

These changes were part and parcel of another sweeping change occurring in the United States during the Progressive Era: a widespread consensus gathering around the notion of a national, consumerist standard of living. Historian Marina Moskowitz has described how during the early decades of the twentieth century new national distribution systems for manufactured goods combined with a new advertising and advocacy infrastructure to create a particular aspirational standard of living that embodied progressive ideals in consumer products (Moskowitz 2008).

But while Moskowitz's account develops in detail the ways that middle-class living spaces (including bathrooms) became part of the advertised iconography of the American home, what is missing are the ways that lay individuals actually utilised them; this is the crucial missing piece for understanding the domestic labour of American medicine. Patent applications and advertisements notwithstanding, historical evidence for daily practices inside the home is often difficult to find. However, I will now examine two evocative examples that suggest the contours of real-life medicine cabinet use, showing the ways that individuals maintained, used, and organised them: a short story by James Thurber, and reporting on medicine cabinets in the pages of the magazine *Popular Science Monthly*.

Thurber's short story, titled 'Nine Needles', was published in *The New Yorker* in 1936. After a brief introduction to set the scene, his narrator, who is shaving in the bathroom of his good friends' home, begins his diatribe about the medicine cabinet:

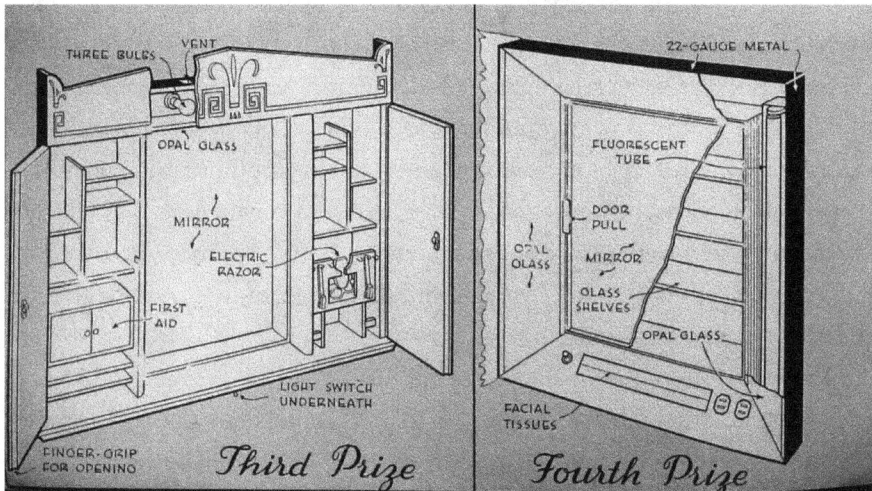

FIG. 17.2 Third prize medicine cabinet designed by John W. Knobel in Ozone Park, New York. Fourth prize medicine cabinet designed by Marvin J. Neivert in Lawrence, New York (source: 'Medicine Cabinet Contest Winners', *Popular Science Monthly* (Anonymous 1941: 148))

> I am sure that many a husband has wanted to wrench the family medicine
> cabinet off the wall and throw it out of the window, if only because the aver-
> age medicine cabinet is so filled with mysterious bottles and unidentifiable
> objects of all kinds that it is a source of constant bewilderment and exaspera-
> tion to the American male [...] It may be that the American habit of saving
> everything and never throwing anything away, even empty bottles, causes
> the domestic medicine cabinet to become as cluttered in its small way as
> the American attic becomes cluttered in a major way. I have encountered
> few medicine cabinets in this country which were not pack-jammed with
> something between a hundred and fifty and two hundred different items,
> from dental floss to boracic acid, from razor blades to sodium perborate,
> from adhesive tape to coconut oil. (Thurber 1936: 17)

The rest of the story is concerned with this protagonist's frustrations when, after opening the cabinet, nine sewing needles fall into the sink. He attempts to retrieve them using all kinds of objects that repeatedly hit him as they cascade out of the cabinet, including a toothbrush, iodine, and lipstick.

What is telling about this story is the way that the comedy would have depended utterly on the trope (still familiar to us today) of the ludicrously overstuffed medicine cabinet – the situation Thurber creates is acutely funny precisely because of its relatability. Yet despite the situational comedy, none of the items on their own would have seemed particularly out of place; the razors, the adhesive tape, the sewing needles, and the toothbrush are the small-scale equivalents of the household fixtures that Moskowitz describes. They fit comfortably within the class of consumer goods that embody the nebulous cultural values of health and hygiene, and they contribute in specific ways to the maintenance of proper modern bodies.

The story is also a compelling case because of the way it specifically paints the American man as the person frustrated by the medicine cabinet. The narra-tor/protagonist experiences this assemblage of goods as somehow more upset-ting or confusing than he imagines the American woman might be expected to. This framing is initially peculiar, in that the objects which fall out of the cabinet in the story (e.g. razors, bandages, toothbrushes, etc.) are generally not ones that have been culturally coded as specifically feminine. But what the narration makes clear is that what has been coded as female is the *category* of the medicine cabinet.

While scholars have long explored the domestic sphere as the palette for American women's consumerist expression, the private space of the medicine cabinet resists these characterisations. Its intimate position as a closed space within the already private space of the bathroom makes it a far less attractive canvas for displaying one's purchased goods. The role of the cabinet is clearer when we see it not as just a container for consumables, but as a place where work tools are categorised and housed, where the work in question is domestic medical stewardship. The woman of the house is presumably the one who gathers, organises, and is in charge of the tools of home body work. What Thurber's story illustrates is the extent to which the American medicine cabinet has demanded the attentive work of these female family members – one of the reasons why the overflowing medicine cabinet trope has proliferated so widely is precisely that we know it needs careful maintenance in order to work properly. Consequently, it is the women of the house who are blamed when it does not.

In the Consumers' Project Report discussed earlier, there is another example of the trope of the poorly stocked medicine cabinet, but in this case the narrative is a much more serious and cautionary one. The story begins with the tale of a small boy running into the family home with a badly scratched knee. When he arrives inside for help there is no antiseptic to be found in the medicine cabinet. There is, however, a two-year-old bottle of cough medicine readily (and uselessly) at hand (Palmer 1936).

The boy's mother knew that maintaining the family medicine cabinet was a crucial responsibility, but it was also a complicated and time consuming one. The report makes it clear that the mothers of America were felt to be in need of expert instruction on the subject.

Although the explicit purpose of the report is concerned with consumption – it is literally a guide of things to buy and have on hand – practically it reads far more like a training manual, communicating to the non-expert the practical knowledge of professionals about what kinds of medicines to use, and how. It not only contains explicit details about products and brands, but also step-by-step instructions on when and how to use them in order to be the most capable and responsible parent possible. Being proficient in the use of the medicine cabinet was considered to be a crucial step in the moulding of a healthy family.

According to Moskowitz, engineering the family home – or, more exactly, the house – was a further, and explicit, way in which this virtuous ideal was perpetuated. She writes

> At the heart of the organization of middle-class spaces, whether domestic or public, was a belief in environmental determinism, that the material world not only reflected the status of those who lived in it, but could in fact help shape that status. [...] Objects and spaces were freighted with, and thus carried, significant values of middle-class life, such as the importance of etiquette and social codes, privacy and interiority, investment, and careful management. (Moskowitz 2008: 18)

Or, as one advertisement for Kohler put it, 'There is one room in every home which is the key to the real standards of living of that household [...] [the bathroom] reflects your sense of refinement, your ideals of hygiene and sanitation'. It is, the ad goes on, a matter of pride.

This sentiment also seems to go beyond mere consumerism, even an American consumerism that has been inextricably tied up in citizenship, social values, and belonging (Cohen 2003).

There is a strong engineering and management ethos in Moskowitz's description of the environment of the home; for a certain class of post-war Americans, an ideal material world not only displayed their social position but also played a role in creating it. Objects and spaces were seen to be so powerful in affecting the lives of their users and inhabitants that citizens needed to be active in managing the materiality of their lives.

THE ARCHITECTURAL AND THE ONTOLOGICAL

Reports from official government agencies were not the only places where lay individuals were taught how to scientifically manage their homes and medicine cabinets (Apple 1995; Cowan 1983). In 1925, approximately a decade before the Consumer's Project report, *Popular Science Monthly* published an article titled 'First Aid For Your Family'. Written by Dr. John F. Anderson, former Director of the Hygienic Laboratory of the U.S. Public Service, the article focuses explicitly on both the design and the contents of medicine cabinets: 'The household medicine cabinet should be the best lighted part of the bathroom, and so placed that when the mirror-fronted door is open, a light shines full upon its contents. It should be painted and kept in spotless white, and its shelves should be of glass'. Instructions for supplying the cabinet were also provided (Anderson 1925).

Anderson incorporated explicit scare tactics into his appeal for proper medicine cabinet management. The subheadline to the article reads 'What you should keep in your medicine cabinet for every emergency – How to safeguard against mistakes', and Anderson warns of the possibility of mistaking a dangerous drug for a harmless one in an unorganised or poorly lit cabinet. Furthermore, he chastises readers against keeping items in the cabinet of which the family physician 'would not approve', emphasising that the medicine cabinet was no mere storage device. The article communicates the clear hierarchy of expertise that was embedded in the medicine cabinet. By labelling this collection of hygienic, health-related objects as explicitly medical, physicians and technology producers were able to claim authority over their deployment, which they then communicated to users. In response, as lay individuals began to incorporate their advice and tools into their intimate lives, they also adopted the impulse to properly (i.e. scientifically) manage their tools and their bodies.

Readers of Anderson's article may have recognised and enacted this impulse in a contest held by the same publication sixteen years later. In 1941, *Popular Science Monthly* held a contest for readers to design the ideal bathroom medicine cabinet. The contest was incredibly popular by the magazine's own standards: five prizes (one more than originally planned) and twenty-two honourable mentions were awarded, and the five winning medicine cabinets were featured in a full spread in the magazine. The article was accompanied by stylised representations as well as schematic design drawings of the winners, and it included descriptions and explicit encouragement for readers to attempt to build the cabinets for themselves. The magazine supplied a special award for a contest entrant who actually built their proposed cabinet (Anonymous 1941).

The features of the submitted cabinets give us a sense of how individuals were using their home medicine cabinets by showing us how they wished they could improve that use. For instance, the most highly desired innovations among contest participants were interior as well as exterior mirrors, followed by doors, shelves, and drawers that would maximise the usefulness of those mirrors. Designers also wanted more shelf space, more lighting, electrical outlets, and specialised holders and containers for devices like scissors, tweezers, and tissues. The winning entry also had additional 'his' and 'hers' shelves on either side of the main cabinet in order to eliminate gender conflict over space for items specifically designed for personal grooming. Runner-up medicine cabinets had even more specialised containment innovations: sterile drawers for first-aid supplies, shelves with different shapes for a multitude of bottles and jars, compartments designed especially for electric razors, etc. One design even included a special locked compartment for 'dangerous drugs', implicitly recognising that 'toilet items' and medical supplies belonged in the same physical and ontological space, and that in order to share this space effectively they had to be quite carefully managed.

Far from reading like a lifestyle magazine or a shopping guide, this report of this contest clearly portrays the medicine cabinet as a utilitarian object that its users wished to scientifically master. They showed a keen awareness for the values embedded in the object – clean lines, hygienic sterility, efficient organisation, and targeted clarity – that were in turn transferred to the tools within it and the bodies that those tools altered. According to the headline, the winning cabinet was 'as modern as tomorrow'; so, too, would be the people that it helped create.

CODA: ORGANISATION AND ERASURE

If the cultural narrative of the medicine cabinet has worked to obscure the work that patients do – and by doing so has excluded patients' work from crucial discussions about the structure and nature of health care – this chapter must ask one final question. If the ontological category of the medicine cabinet captures a certain kind of small, intimate technology of the body, what does the existence of this category imply about seemingly similar objects that do *not* belong in that box? This volume discusses at length the processes of making boxes, moving boxes, and putting things into boxes, but what we often overlook are the items – and therefore the identities – that are excluded from our categorisations and collections.

For her cultural history of menstruation, historian Lara Freidenfelds interviewed a number of women about their mid-twentieth-century menstrual practices (2009). These women recounted to her that during their youth, the commonly accepted place for storing menstrual products was not the bathroom, but the bedroom; such products were generally hidden under their beds, or sometimes tucked away in the corners of their closets. The bathroom medicine cabinet was considered to be far too public a place to store such intimate objects. This exclusion raises important questions about our cultural relationship with menstruation. Is it too dirty, too untoward for the medicine cabinet? Were (and are) the cycles and fluctuations of women's bodies too chaotic and messy for the hyper-rational, hyper-sanitised medicine cabinet? This relegation of menstrual technologies to the even more private (yet less culturally hygienic) space of the bedroom reveals the embarrassment that the women interviewed were meant to feel about their unruly bodies. Even in the domain of intimate health and body work of which women were the family stewards, each woman experienced her period alone.

In Freidenfelds' account, it was not until the emergence of another common bathroom storage innovation, the under-the-sink storage cabinet, that her interviewees felt comfortable storing menstrual products in the family bathroom (2009: 146–50). If we consider seriously what the medicine cabinet does as it orders, rationalises, and makes appropriate a very specific and ultimately limited kind of body work, we can see the ways that it contains, hides, tells stories about, and ultimately devalues that work and the bodies of those who perform it.

REFERENCES

Anderson, J. F., 'First Aid for Your Family', *Popular Science Monthly*, February 1925.
Anonymous, 'Prize-Winning Medicine Cabinet', *Popular Science Monthly*, May 1941.
Apple, R. D., 'Constructing Mothers: Scientific Motherhood in the Nineteenth and Twentieth Centuries', *Social History of Medicine*, 8. 2 (1 August 1995): 161–78.
Bynum, W. F., *Science and the Practice of Medicine in the Nineteenth Century* (Cambridge, UK: Cambridge University Press, 1994).

Cohen, L., *A Consumer's Republic: The Politics of Mass Consumption in Postwar America* (New York, NY: Knopf, 2003).

Cowan, R. S., *More Work for Mother: The Ironies of Household Technology from the Open Hearth to the Microwave* (New York, NY: Basic Books, 1983).

Freidenfelds, L., *The Modern Period: Menstruation in Twentieth-Century America* (Baltimore, MD: Johns Hopkins University Press, 2009).

Howell, J. D., *Technology in the Hospital: Transforming Patient Care in the Early Twentieth Century* (Baltimore, MD: Johns Hopkins University Press, 1996).

Hoy, S., *Chasing Dirt: The American Pursuit of Cleanliness* (New York, NY: Oxford University Press, 1996).

Johnson, R., 'Tabloid Brand Medicine Chests: Selling Health and Hygiene for the British Tropical Colonies', *Science as Culture*, 17.3 (2008): 249–68.

Kline, R., *Consumers in the Country: Technology and Social Change in Rural America* (Baltimore, MD: Johns Hopkins University Press, 2000).

Leach, William R., *Land of Desire: Merchants, Power, and the Rise of a New American Culture* (New York, NY: Vintage, 1994).

Melosh, B., *The Physician's Hand: Nurses and Nursing in the Twentieth Century* (Philadelphia, PA: Temple University Press, 1982).

Moskowitz, M., *Standard of Living: The Measure of the Middle Class in Modern America* (Baltimore, MD: Johns Hopkins University Press, 2008).

Ogle, M., *All the Modern Conveniences: American Household Plumbing, 1840–1890* (Baltimore, MD: Johns Hopkins University Press, 2000).

Palmer, R. L., *The Home Medicine Cabinet* (Washington, D.C.: Consumers' Project, U.S. Department of Labor, June 1936).

Porter, R., *The Greatest Benefit to Mankind: A Medical History of Humanity* (New York, NY: W. W. Norton & Company, 1999).

Rosenberg, C., *The Care of Strangers: The Rise of America's Hospital System* (Baltimore, MD: Johns Hopkins University Press, 1995).

Starr, P., *The Social Transformation of American Medicine: The Rise of a Sovereign Profession and the Making of a Vast Industry* (New York, NY: Basic Books, 1984).

Stevens, R., *In Sickness and in Wealth: American Hospitals in the Twentieth Century* (Baltimore, MD: Johns Hopkins University Press, 1999).

Thurber, J., 'Nine Needles', *The New Yorker*, 25 January 1936.

Vogel, M. J., and C. Rosenberg, eds, *The Therapeutic Revolution: Essays in the Social History of American Medicine* (Philadelphia, PA: University of Pennsylvania Press, 1979).

Warner, J. H., *The Therapeutic Perspective: Medical Practice, Knowledge, and Identity in America, 1820–1885* (Princeton, NJ: Princeton University Press, 1997).

FIG. 18.1 The Green Minna in front of a police station (source: Lindenberg 1891/92: 457)

18

THE GREEN MINNA: TRANSPORTING POLICE DETAINEES IN IMPERIAL BERLIN

Eric J. Engstrom

Designation: Green Minna (*Grüne Minna*; alternate designations: *Grüne Minne, Grüner Anton, Grüner Heinrich, Grüner Wagen, Arrestanten-Wagen, Criminalequipage*). **Physical characteristics**: *Body*: enclosed, wooden, windowless carriage, with a forward driver's perch (dickey box), dual lanterns, ventilation pipe with cap, half-louvered rear door, and two-step foot plate: *Interior Fitting*: all-round benching with two wooden, cell-like, bolted compartments next to the rear door; *Undercarriage*: four-wheel, half-axle coachwork with brake mechanism, shortened drawbar and flexible whippletree for enhanced manoeuvrability; *Length, Width, Height*: unknown; *Weight*: 1300 kg; *Colour*: dark green. **Crew**: 1 wagoner, 1 patrol officer, 2 draft horses; Support Personnel: 1 constable (mounted division), 1 head ostler (mounted division), 1 police officer (scribe); Equipment: harness, driving whip, hammer-key, transportation tickets (*Transportscheine*); Portage Capacity: 16–18 detainees, plus crew. **Operational range** (migration): 21 km/day. **Deployment** (distribution/habitat): At 0200, 0800, 1200, and 2000 hours on routes in four transport-districts (*Fahrbezirke*) throughout the city of Berlin, Germany. **Length of service** (status): 1866 – ????; extinct, no known surviving specimens.

Keywords: prisoner transport, policing, crime fighting, central booking, jailing, police, Berlin, Imperial Germany, urban governance, public relations

INTRODUCTION

CURIOUS ONLOOKERS WAITING OUTSIDE A POLICE STATION; RUBBER NECKS straining for a glimpse; a crowd parting to make way; a dark portal about to disgorge its contents. A picture of daily lives suspended in anticipation. But in anticipation of exactly what?

The sidewalk spectacle of fellow citizen-detainees in the clutches of Prussian law enforcement was a common sight on the streets of Imperial Berlin. Or at least it was common enough to warrant depiction in one of Germany's most popular and respectable illustrated weeklies, *Die Gartenlaube*. The image was published in 1892 as part of a serial article on crime and the criminal justice system in Berlin by the roving reporter Paul Lindenberg, whose popular vignettes of city-life in Berlin in the 1880s and '90s attracted a large readership (Lindenberg 1891/92: 457).[1] Lindenberg's image of an enclosed, green, horse-drawn wagon (Green Minna) parked in front of a police station captures one fleeting moment, repeated on countless occasions, in a much larger and ongoing public drama of crime.[2] In its many and daily enactments, this drama was usually played out in sequence, beginning with the discovery and investigation of a crime, proceeding to the criminal's arrest, and culminating in trial, sentencing, and punishment. Public onlookers were participants at various stages of this drama, be it directly as actual witnesses or indirectly as readers of reports like Lindenberg's.

The Green Minna had a supporting role to play in this drama. In order to understand that role, its historical meaning, and more generally the work it did in shaping the behaviour, perceptions, and imaginations of Berlin's street-side onlookers and its reading public, this article examines the use and place of these wagons in a larger habitat or economy of prisoner transportation schemes.

OPERATION AND CHOREOGRAPHY

In the late nineteenth century, the Green Minna was used to transport arrestees to and from police headquarters. The wagon transported its human cargo centripetally from district police stations to the central police station, and from there centrifugally to (or between) the court jail in Moabit, local prisons, the work house, and the Charité hospital. Up until 1866, the police had transported their detainees almost exclusively by foot. But that method had been plagued by escapes. The new wagons were ostensibly designed to prevent detainees from taking flight.

Initially, the wagons were operated by the police reserve and a team of horses supplied by private transport companies (Schmidt 1898: 112–14). In order to streamline operations and reduce costs,[3] the central police assumed responsibility for the wagons in 1880, and after 1889 all operations were consolidated in the central police's mounted division. The fleet of green wagons grew from two in 1866 to seven by 1890. A further eighth wagon was used to transport equipment and also, in emergencies like fires or riots, policemen. All told, in 1890 there were thirteen policemen, nine wagoners, and fourteen horses assigned to the transport detail, which carried between five and ten thousand detainees per month.

In equipping wagon and crew, police officials exploited resources that were readily available.[4] The draw-bar and wheels were standardised to fit existing stock. The wagoners' uniforms were patched together from pieces of the old, 'hand-me-down uniforms' of patrol officers and night watchmen'.[5] Similarly, the draft horses were recruited from old and retired ('*pflastermüden*') police horses; only in emergency cases were regular, 'active-duty' police horses used to draw the Green Minna.

Inside the wagon, the transportees were accompanied by one or two patrol officers. These officers were normally equipped with a sabre, but the close quarters within the wagon made its use impractical. And so, after 1890 the patrol officers were outfitted with a hybrid 'hammer-key'. As the name suggests, this much-feared piece of equipment was a combination key and hammer that could be used not just to subdue transportees, but also to quickly alert the coachman in the wagon's dickey box in case of emergency (Schmidt 1898: 114–115).

Police officials took care to document the different kinds of prisoners and detainees who were being transported, often on behalf of other institutions. Rules set down in 1884 distinguished four different types of transportees: 1) detainees who were in the custody of Berlin's courts, 2) convicted prisoners being moved between different prisons in Berlin, as well as to and from the Charité hospital, 3) prisoners under the jurisdiction of the military, or communities and police forces in other parts of Germany, and 4) all other kinds of police detainees.[6] Depending on the circumstances, wagon-runs could contain several of these different types of transportees.[7]

Throughout the day, the green wagons set out across Berlin on their circuits to pick up and disseminate their human cargo. These runs usually ended with the wagons returning to the main police station, where their dishevelled, soon-to-be-booked arrestees were discharged into the station's rear courtyard (**FIGURE 18.2**). One report of the detainees' disemboxment paints a picture of exotic criminal diversity that spanned a spectrum from prostitutes to ageing alcoholics, from homeless vagabonds and beggars to the mentally ill, from youthful troublemakers to transvestites (Lindenberg 1891/92: 457–58).

The disemboxment of the arrestees at police headquarters was a well-choreographed affair. Upon arrival for booking in the rear courtyard of the central police station, a bell would summon a constable and a squad of twelve police officers. The officers lined up next to the wagon's rear door, which was then unlocked (Lindenberg 1891/92: 457). The accompanying patrol officers would then shout out the number of prisoners in the wagon before handing their paperwork over to the constable. First the non-violent arrestees disembarked.

FIG. 18.2 Unloading the Green Minna in the courtyard of the Central Police Station (source: Lindenberg 1891/92: 457)

Then the violent criminals detained in the wagon's wooden compartments were removed and taken under heavy guard directly to the criminal division, where police officials confiscated their hats, knives, papers, and money. Whereas in transit no provision was made to segregate the sexes, upon disembarkment at the central police station gender selection ensued immediately. As part of this selection process, it was the fate of cross-dressing men to be designated as male. And to assist frail passengers and women (usually prostitutes) as they entered and/or exited the wagon, the foot plate had not just one, but two steps.

Disemboxment at other venues was rather less well choreographed and not without its own specific hazards. For example, at the Charité hospital prisoners brought for medical treatment sometimes escaped on their way to the hospital wards.[8] And after one convict died in transit, hospital administrators complained that the Green Minna was often overcrowded and should not be used to transport severely ill prisoners, especially in the wagon's cramped internal cells designed for dangerous felons.[9] Additional hazards arose from interactions with hospital personnel. When the police complained about delays in processing the sick detainees, Charité officials voiced moral concerns to justify their not deploying enough nursing staff. They suggested that only a bare minimum of staff members be used to receive the arriving detainees in order to avoid 'lewd exchanges with the sick and slutty prostitutes'.[10]

HABITATS AND ECONOMIES OF EMBOXMENT

No doubt the Green Minna helped prevent escapes. But its use also achieved much more than that. In order to gain a better sense of its significance – and more generally of what emboxed transport accomplished – it's helpful to situate the Green Minna in a larger urban habitat or economy of boxes and transport schemes. Some of these boxes were stationary, like jail cells or stalls for police horses. But others, like the Green Minna, were on the move. They were stopping and starting again, being loaded and unloaded, crossing paths, passing landmarks, negotiating traffic, traversing intersections and bridges, plying and sometimes deviating from their well-trodden circuits, all the while attracting the gaze of onlookers and evoking their reflections about crime and policing in Germany's foremost metropolis. Consider therefore the following examples, which illustrate some of the problems and environmental dynamics associated with different means of transportation.

Emboxed Transit: The Krankenkorb

Berlin's workhouse was one important receptacle used by the police to house the city's vagrant masses. Alongside beggars, prostitutes, and drunkards, the workhouse sometimes also served as a shelter of last resort for the impoverished and itinerant sick or mentally ill. When inmates of the workhouse were identified as needing hospital care, they were often transported to the local Charité hospital in an 'enclosed patient basket (*geschlossener Krankenkorb*)',[11] carried by fellow workhouse inmates.

The workhouse and the police had been using baskets to transport accident victims and the indigent sick at least since the 1820s.[12] But it was only in 1851 that a city-wide system of basket-transport was put into effect.[13] The origins of that system lay neither in the frequent cholera epidemics that ravished the city, nor in the mushrooming numbers of industrial accidents, but rather in the affliction that befell an official in the Finance Ministry, who was forced to wait for hours before a basket arrived.[14] Baskets were stationed throughout the city in each of Berlin's ten medical districts, often at fire stations.[15] At each location, three baskets were available, one each for smallpox and cholera victims, and a third for other illnesses or accident victims. Each basket contained a straw sack and pillow, a blanket, and a sheet. The police were responsible for ensuring the baskets' proper storage, their ready accessibility day and night, and the recruitment of porters from the immediate neighborhood. In transit, the baskets and their human cargo were always accompanied by a patrol officer who guarded against abuse and ensured that both the baskets and their equipment were returned intact and not stolen.[16]

Berlin's network of baskets proved to be rather cumbersome. Jurisdictional disputes over access and control, fluctuating contractual arrangements for the baskets' storage, and the difficulty of recruiting dependable working-class porters all conspired to thwart the development of an efficient system of basket transport. The basket's total envelopment of its cargo also caused problems: it was difficult to communicate with the transportees or to assess their condition, and at times their injuries were aggravated by the irregular, jolting gait of the porters.[17]

Furthermore, in the process of transporting inmates between the workhouse and the hospital there sometimes transpired 'disturbing events' that the Charité's doctors were powerless to prevent.[18] Especially disconcerting was the fact that even patients from the educated classes might be transported by basket. Baskets were also considered inappropriate for robust and non-agitated inmates. As a result of these concerns, the chief psychiatrist at the Charité successfully petitioned local welfare officials to ensure greater flexibility when it came time to embox transportees. Henceforth, upon discharging workhouse inmates from the hospital, the expertise of Charité doctors would be marshalled to determine what kind of box was best suited for the return trip to the workhouse: no box at all (transport by foot), an open box (transport by carriage), or a closed box (transport by basket). The basket, it seems, was still an acceptable means of transporting inmates, just not for the educated, robust, or placid ones.

Nevertheless, by the 1870s the *Krankenkorb* was gradually going out of fashion. The police had begun deploying their fleet of green wagons in 1866. Welfare administrators started shifting from the use of baskets to horse-drawn ambulances.[19] The Charité hospital discontinued its use of baskets altogether, and by the early 1890s local factories had long since stopped making them.[20]

In spite of the basket's demise, emboxed transport of the sick and the insane did not disappear. Indeed, the rules governing the transportation of mentally ill prisoners saw it explicitly reinforced, albeit only in large cities. A decree of the Prussian Ministry of the Interior in early 1905 mandated that the transportation of these inmates to and from prison be undertaken 'always in closed wagons'.[21] And as Berlin's frenetic growth forced the expansion of its emergency infrastructure, the local first aid society set up a telephone hotline: when mentally ill citizens needed to be transported to hospital, officials could order wagons through a hotline (Amt III, Nr. 2417 or 2424) or at any district police station.[22]

Open-Boxed Transit: The Draft Wagon

Unlike the police, Berlin's prisons and courts had no green wagons.[23] Nevertheless, at times they too needed to ferry convicted criminals serving time in local prisons, or defendants awaiting trial, either to a hospital or to judicial detention facilities. In 1865 the head of the Stadtvoigtei prison was asked to test a new cart that had served reliably in the recent Austro-Prussian invasion of the Dutchy of Schleswig. But for the purposes of transporting prisoners in Berlin, the cart was found wanting. It provided little protection from the elements and could neither adequately restrain 'unruly, raving individuals' nor prevent their transit from eliciting 'commotion in the streets'.[24]

Prior to 1890, the courts had relied on the open-wagon taxi services of private entrepreneurs – an arrangement that gave rise to numerous complaints.[25] The chief district attorney and the prison warden in Ploetzensee deplored coachmen who did nothing to prevent transportees from meeting with family, friends, and prostitutes. Sometimes the coachmen would accompany inmates into their homes or especially – and profitably – to local bars and pubs that they themselves owned. If the inmates returned from their court appearances at all, they were often drunk, loud-mouthed, and cantankerous. Occasionally they even arrived at the prison gates accompanied by a band of 'inebriated, hooting, and cursing men and women'.[26]

In order to resolve this problem, the taxi companies had suggested using enclosed wagons. But the chief district attorney had other ideas. According to him, at the root of the problem lay the coachmen's 'utter lack of authority' and 'moral unreliability'.[27] Because they weren't public employees and wore no uniform, they held neither power nor authority over inmates, let alone the public. In order to fill this disciplinary void, the district attorney therefore recommended using state employees. But which ones? Prison guards, although they could command the respect of the inmates, enjoyed no such standing in the eyes of the public and were therefore 'powerless to intervene against attempts by the public to interact with inmates'. Instead, the district attorney suggested using policemen: 'The policeman enjoys the necessary respect of both inmates and the general public [... and he is officially authorised] to intervene in the event of protests, riots and similar disturbances of public order'.

But Berlin's chief of police, Baron Ludwig von Richthofen, begged to differ.[28] Von Richthofen generally concurred with the district attorney's complaints, but he disagreed that policemen could better manage to keep the public away from inmates in transit.[29] Many of the prisoners' friends and associates, who were usually aware of the trial date, actively sought to prevent the police from performing their duties. It was precisely because of these confrontations that the police had resorted – whenever possible – to using the Green Minna to transport their arrestees. In rare instances, however, the police also used it to transport prisoners to and from the courts; but they did so only when courts deemed inmates to be dangerous felons, too volatile to be conveyed in private transporters. In such irregular cases, the police used the wagon that already serviced the prisons, or else deployed a separate one. But these trips could deliver inmates to the courts only by late morning, too late for most court proceedings. Furthermore, the vagaries of courtroom procedure made scheduling the return trip to prison especially difficult. Accommodating court scheduling therefore required special wagon-runs that severely disrupted the police's transportation schedules and their deployment of personnel. And in order to rectify these problems, additional resources would have to be mobilised. Given such difficulties, von Richthofen believed that not the police, but instead court officials, or preferably prison guards, should be put in charge of transporting inmates.

In addition to von Richthofen, the president of Prussia's supreme court, Friedrich Drenkmann, also let his views on this issue be known.[30] Drenkmann argued that it was impractical, indeed inadmissible, to delay and/or consolidate court cases on specific days in order to ensure more efficient transportation. And even if the trials could be consolidated, still more personnel would be needed to accompany the inmates to different chambers in the courthouse.

To resolve the problem, officials decided to explore the use of prison guards to transport inmates.[31] And although early efforts to recruit guards were unsuccessful, ultimately officials prevailed and lauded the new method a success.[32] The guards themselves, however, complained bitterly about their increased work load, because several of their number were always busy transporting inmates.[33]

Non-Boxed Transit: The Shackled March

But the use of prison guards or policemen – virtually all of whom were former Prussian military officers – did more than simply tax scarce personnel resources.

It also put the urban sensibilities of Berlin's streetwalking public to the test, because inmates who were vagabonds or who posed no danger to the public were, as a general rule, transported by foot (Wulff 1890: 205–06). On the streets of Germany's burgeoning capital, this too became a public spectacle. So for example, whenever scheduling difficulties made it impossible to transport prostitutes by wagon, and forced the police to march them through the streets under armed guard, 'disagreeable' encounters were bound to arise.[34] In 1888, and not for the first time, a prisoner had been shot by guards while in transit to the city's military police station, causing women to faint and 'harmless passers-by' to be traumatised. And more frequently, military prisoners in transit were accompanied by crowds of 'shouting and hooting' residents. This kind of 'embarrassing spectacle' moved city officials to call on the Prussian military to abstain from transporting prisoners by foot and resort instead to the use of green wagons.[35]

Nowhere were these concerns more acute than in the Moabit neighbourhood, home both to the city's largest prison near Ploetzensee and its main courthouse. The close proximity of these two institutions meant that local residents were frequent witnesses to inmates being marched through the streets from prison to the court and back again. In 1891 a local newspaper reported the sight of a small, young man, hands cuffed behind his back, accompanied by a 'warrior-like' prison guard with a bayonet, and followed by a band of between fifty and sixty school children.[36] Workers on their lunch-hour couldn't but shake their heads in dismay at the sight of this bizarre spectacle. The report went on to suggest that had the prisoner been transported by the green wagon, the public – and especially children – could have been spared this unsightly street scene.

The local Moabit neighbourhood organisation was even more concerned. In a letter to the Ministry of Justice, the association complained about the practice of marching inmates, shackled in pairs, through their community.[37] The association was concerned not just about the security threat posed by the band of followers, but also about the 'depressing' sight it presented to passive bystanders. Most importantly, however, the association worried about the corrupting moral influence that such spectacles had on children. In the interest of the local community, the association therefore called for officials to abstain from transporting inmates by foot, and instead rely on the police's green wagons.

On the face of it, Prussian officials paid little heed to such complaints.[38] In fact, they rejected outright the suggestion that witnessing inmates in chains was fraught with dangerous moral implications. They also believed that private transport companies, frustrated by their loss of business, were agitating against the new approach. Nevertheless, the criminal court soon acquired its own (used) 'cell-wagon' (*Zellenwagen*) and equipped it with a crew comprising a wagoner and one prison guard.[39] And in many cases, court officials even explicitly rejected any use of the Green Minna, arguing that it was necessary to segregate court detainees from prison convicts and police arrestees.[40]

The complaints of the Moabit neighbourhood association bear witness to the moral sensibilities and public dynamics that enveloped the use of the Green Minna in Imperial Berlin. The green wagon was a manifestation of urban sensibilities in the German capital. It was the expression of a kind of unspoken collusion between the police, with their concerns for security and public order, and the city's burghers, who desired a streetscape that not only spared them the bleak spectacle of their incarcerated fellow citizens being marched to and fro, but that also spared their children the moral hazard of witnessing one of their own caught up in the Prussian criminal justice system.

FIG. 18.3 In need of a box (source: Lindenberg 1891/92: 456)

CONCLUSION

What do these examples tell us about the Green Minna as a form of emboxed transportation? What exactly did the deployment of the enclosed green wagons achieve? From the perspective of law enforcement, they contributed to a diversification of transportation resources: they facilitated a finer calibration of a transportation system that already incorporated specific provisions for illness, social standing, and infirmity. They also helped to allay long-standing concerns about the fraternisation of detainees with other members of the public. As such, they reinforced the larger aim of disrupting any and all contact and communication between presumptive criminals – an aim that had long been a priority of nineteenth-century crime prevention and punishment (Rössler 1896: 18). More importantly, however, green wagons helped to limit the potentially damaging public spectacle of police authority being undermined, and resistance to this authority being openly flaunted. At no time since the revolutions of 1848 had that authority been so embattled as in the early 1890s, after anti-socialist legislation had lapsed and the number of mass demonstrations, boycotts, and strikes was peaking (Evans 1988).[41] Finally, green wagons could also help to assuage public objections to other, more conventional means of transportation: their enclosed, box-like qualities rendered invisible not just the coercive executive actions involved in daily practices of detainment, but also the very visibility of the 'unsightly' detainees themselves. As such, the green wagons were one of many executive tools designed to enhance urban governance in Imperial Berlin. They helped to ensure that the nodal points of public security remained well-connected, and that the wheels of the criminal justice system turned more efficiently.

As tools of Prussian governance, green wagons operated in the public domain. Even though their contents were obscured from the gaze of onlookers, the wagons themselves became – as their various designations indicate – a symbol of executive power and a magnet of public discourse and reflection about crime and justice. Among onlookers, watching the door close on the human cargo and the wagon depart on its journey through the streets of Berlin had the potential – depending on specific circumstances – to evoke any number of responses, from satisfaction that justice was being served and public order upheld, to simple indifference, or to outrage over the incarceration of innocent citizens (Paul n.d.: 19). Furthermore, as witnesses to the drama of detainees in transit, these onlookers occupied a space alongside executive and juridical power formations; a space with its own kind of adjudicative logic, lodged adjacent to the actions of Berlin's police force and courtroom procedures. It was a space inhabited by moral sentiments, by notions of justice and retribution, by affective states of fear, empathy, and satisfaction, by imaginary landscapes of people's own vulnerabilities and transgressions. The Green Minna helped to shrink this public space and render it less contentious. The wagon's deployment served to pre-empt moral discourse, to vacate deliberations of justice, to dampen affective public responses, and to occlude otherwise visible signs of state power in action. The Green Minna was as much about the modulation of public attitudes and perceptions as it was about effective carceral practices.

NOTES

1 A revised version of the article was later published without the image in Lindenberg 1893.

2 Thus Victor Turner, as cited in Müller 2005: 153–54. The Green Minna was but one of many different designations for the wagon (Lindenberg 1893: 23; Paul 2017). On the public drama of crime associated with the Green Minna, compare also 'Die Grüne Minna,' *Vorwärts*, Nr. 255, 3. Beilage, 22 August 1905.

3 Against the backdrop of Berlin's exploding population in the late nineteenth century, the costs of transporting detainees quickly became a bone of contention. Long and drawn-out legal disputes between the police and the city's welfare agency were taken all the way to Prussia's Supreme Administrative Court. On the court's decision and the subsequent contractual arrangement between the police and the city, see *Verwaltung der offenen Armenhilfe* 1905: 336–51, 360–66.

4 Police Headquarters to Ministry of Justice Accounting Office, 5 November 1894, Bl. 129, Geheimes Staatsarchiv Preußischer Kulturbesitz (henceforth GStAPK), I HA Rep. 84a, Nr. 58287.

5 Ibid.

6 Rules on the Allocation of Transportation in the Prisoner-Wagon, Police Headquarters, 25 February 1884, Bl. 5, Archiv der Humboldt-Universität zu Berlin (henceforth UAHUB), Charité Directorate, Nr. 1048.

7 See for example Police Headquarters to Charité Directorate, 23 February 1900, Bl. 177, UAHUB, Charité Directorate, Nr. 1048.

8 Interrogation protocol of the transporter Carl Dümke, 31 January 1878, Bl. 130–31, UAHUB, Charité Directorate, Nr. 1158.

9 Charité Directorate to Police Headquarters, 7 June 1872, Bl. 205, UAHUB, Charité Directorate, Nr. 1047.

10 Marginalia on Police Headquarters to Charité Directorate, 19 January 1872, Bl. 186, UAHUB, Charité Directorate, Nr. 1047.

11 Carl Westphal to Charité Directorate, 19 November 1872, Bl. 180, UAHUB, Charité Directorate, Nr. 1191.

12 Police Headquarters to Workhouse Curatory, 8 October 1837, Bl. 39, Landesarchiv Berlin (henceforth LAB), A Pr Br Rep 030, Nr. 2938.

13 Report on the joint consultation about transportation of the sick and accident victims, 30 June 1851, Bl. 109–10, LAB, A Pr Br Rep 030, Nr. 2938.

14 Promemoria to Director Horn, 12 March 1851, Bl. 102, LAB, A Pr Br Rep 030, Nr. 2938.

15 Berlin Welfare Authority Instruction, No. 115, 12 November 1851, *Monatsblatt der Armendirektion zu Berlin* 19 (1851): 173–74.

16 Police Instruction of 10 October 1852, Bl. 46, LAB, A Pr Br Rep 030, Nr. 2939.

17 Medical Transport Institute and Ambulance Factory F. M. Kopp to Charité Directorate, 20 April 1892, Bl. 255–57, UAHUB, Charité Directorate, Nr. 62.

18 Carl Westphal to Charité Directorate, 19 November 1872, Bl. 180, and Berlin Welfare Authority to Charité Directorate, 7 December 1872, Bl. 181, both UAHUB, Charité Directorate, Nr. 1191.

19 Berlin Welfare Authority to Police Headquarters, 20 November 1871, Bl. 319, LAB, A Pr Br Rep 030, Nr. 2939.

20 See Charité Directorate to City Council of Rummelsburg, 27 April 1892, Bl. 252–53 and E. Lück Ambulance Company to Charité Directorate, 17 April 1892, Bl. 254, both in UAHUB, Charité Directorate, Nr. 62.

21 Decree of the Ministry of the Interior, 23 January 1905, *Verordnungsblatt für die Strafanstalts-Verwaltung* 1905: 2. See also Trömmer 1898: 719 and Ministry of the Interior to Frankfurt/Oder District President, 29 September 1907, Brandenburgisches Landeshauptarchiv (henceforth BLHA), Rep 3B I Pol 1842.

22 'Transportierung Geisteskranker in Berlin', *Psychiatrisch-Neurologische Wochenschrift* 1904/5: 207.

23 On the general rules governing the transportation of prison inmates in Prussia, and specifically the use of wagons, see Wulff 1890: 202–35, especially 204.

24 Stadtvoigtei Directorate to Police Headquarters, 22 November 1865, Bl. 261–62, LAB, A Pr Br Rep 030, Nr 2939.

25 Chief District Attorney to Ministry of Justice, 31 October 1889, Bl. 1–11, GStAPK, I HA Rep. 84a, Nr. 58286.

26 Ibid. In the mid-1880s, these difficulties had already prompted the chief district attorney to issue a police order that imposed a fine on anyone fraternising with prisoners in transit. But the order failed to resolve the problem and was later even deemed unlawful by the courts, and rescinded. See Potsdam District President to District Council, 11 January 1887 and 22 February 1900, BLHA, Rep 31A Potsdam 1645 and 1646 respectively.

27 On the local notoriety of coachmen and their poor standing in the eyes of Berlin's police, see Lindenberger 1995: 134, 151–52. On rules governing the conduct of coachmen, see for example *Polizei-Verordnung*.

28 Chief of Police to Ministry of the Interior, 16 January 1890, Bl. 16–19, GStAPK, I HA Rep. 84a, Nr. 58286.

29 On the day-to-day running battles and resistance faced by police on the streets of Berlin, see Lindenberger 1995: 72–82, 107–72.

30 Royal Prussian Supreme Court to Ministry of Justice, 3 February 1891, Bl. 46–49, GStAPK, I HA Rep. 84a, Nr. 58286.

31 A decree of the Ministry of the Interior issued on 26 March 1890 stipulated the use of prison guards. See the notice of the Ministry of Justice Denkschrift, 20 September 1890, Bl. 26–32, GStAPK, I HA Rep. 84a, Nr. 58286.

32 See Chief District Attorney to Ministry of Justice, 9 July 1890, Bl. 20 and Royal Prussian Supreme Court to Ministry of Justice, 6 July 1891, GStAPK, I HA Rep. 84a, Nr. 58286.

33 See the anonymous letter dated 2 August 1892, Bl. 74–75, GStAPK, I HA Rep. 84a, Nr. 58287.

34 Police Headquarters to Charité Directorate, 30 October 1868, Bl. 59, UAHUB, Charité Directorate, Nr. 1128. See also *Zweiter Verwaltungs-Bericht* 1892: 8.

35 *Stenographische Berichte über die öffentlichen Sitzungen der Stadtverordnetenversammlung der Stadt Berlin*, 19 April 1888, 164–65.

36 *Berliner Lokal-Anzeiger*, Nr. 181, 6. Beiblatt, 19 April 1891.

37 Bezirksverein Moabit to Ministry of Justice, 8 June 1891, Bl. 54–55, GStAPK, I HA Rep. 84a, Nr. 58286. Up until 1902, the police had not decided about whether or not to shackle transportees. But thereafter, specific rules gave prison and court officials a say in this decision and took into account the political rights, personality, and social standing of the inmate. See the decree of the Ministry of the Interior, 5 May 1894, *Verordnungsblatt für die Strafanstalts-Verwaltung* 1896 [1894]: 6, and the joint decree of the Ministries of the Interior and Justice, 4 December 1902, *Verordnungsblatt für die Strafanstalts-Verwaltung* 1902: 171–72.

38 Royal Prussian Supreme Court to Ministry of Justice, 6 July 1891, GStAPK, I HA Rep. 84a, Nr. 58286.

39 Royal Prussian Supreme Court to Ministry of Justice, 11 September 1892, Bl.

85–92 and 27 February 1893, Bl. 107–13, GStAPK, I HA Rep. 84a, Nr. 58286. In nearby Potsdam, the local court and police had acquired their own Green Minna in 1906. See *Vorwärts*, Nr. 15, Beilage Vorort, 19 January 1906.

40 Royal Prussian Chief Prosecutor to Charité Directorate, 3 January 1895, Bl. 154, as well as to district prosecutors and prison directors, 14 December 1908, Bl. 284, UAHUB, Charité Directorate, Nr. 1048.

41 A better, city-run ambulance service to replace the more heavy-handed and militarised system used by Prussian agencies became a central demand of working-class protests in the early 1890s. See Beddies 2010.

REFERENCES

Beddies, T., et al., 'Kinder, Streik und neue Räume (1890–1918)', in J. Blecker, ed., *Charité: Geschichte(n) eines Krankenhauses* (Berlin: Akademie Verlage, 2010), pp. 126–46.

Evans, R. J., ed., *The German Underworld: Deviants and Outcasts in German History* (London: Routledge, 1988).

Lindenberg, P., 'Polizei und Verbrechertum der Reichshauptstadt', *Die Gartenlaube* (1891/92): 256–59, 456–59, 704–08, 812–16, 378–81. *Berliner Polizei und Verbrechertum* (Leipzig: Reclam, 1893).

Lindenberger, T., *Straßenpolitik: zur Sozialgeschichte der öffentlichen Ordnung in Berlin 1900 bis 1914* (Bonn: Dietz Nachf., 1995).

Müller, P., *Auf der Suche nach dem Täter: Die öffentliche Dramatisierung von Verbrechen im Berlin des Kaiserreichs* (Frankfurt a. M.: Campus, 2005).

Paul, G. 'Der Grüne Heinrich,' in G. Paul, ed., *Berliner Kriminalstudien* (Berlin: Janke, n.d.), pp. 16–24.

Paul, S., 'Die "Grüne Minna": Was ist eine "Grüne Minna" und woher kommt der Name?', <http://www.polizeihistorischesammlung-paul.de/wissenswertes/Minna/die_gruene_minna.htm> [accessed 22 January 2017].

Polizei-Verordnung für das Droschken-Fuhrwesen (Potsdam: Krammer'sche Buchdruckerei, 1885).

Rößler, A., *Sammlung der Polizei-Verordnungen und polizeilichen Vorschriften für den Regierungsbezirk Potsdam* (Berlin: Hayn's Erben, 1896).

Schmidt, P., *Die ersten 50 Jahre der Königlichen Schutzmannschaft zu Berlin: Eine Geschichte des Korps für dessen Angehörige und Freunde* (Berlin: Mittler, 1898).

Trömmer, E., 'Polizeipsychiatrie in Dresden,' *Berliner Klinische Wochenschrift* 35 (1898): 719–20.

Verwaltung der offenen Armenhilfe. Berliner Gemeinderecht, vol. 8 (Berlin: Loewenthal, 1905).

Wilewka, M., *Die Grüne Minna: Gefangenentransportfahrzeuge der Justiz aus Deutschland* (Norderstedt: Books on Demand, 2009).

Wulff, C., *Die Gefängnisse der Justizverwaltung in Preußen, ihre Einrichtung und Verwaltung* (Hamburg: Verlagsanstalt und Druckerei Actien-Gesellschaft, 1890).

Zweiter Verwaltungs-Bericht des Königlichen Polizei-Präsidiums von Berlin für die Jahre 1881–1890 (Berlin: Moeser, 1892).

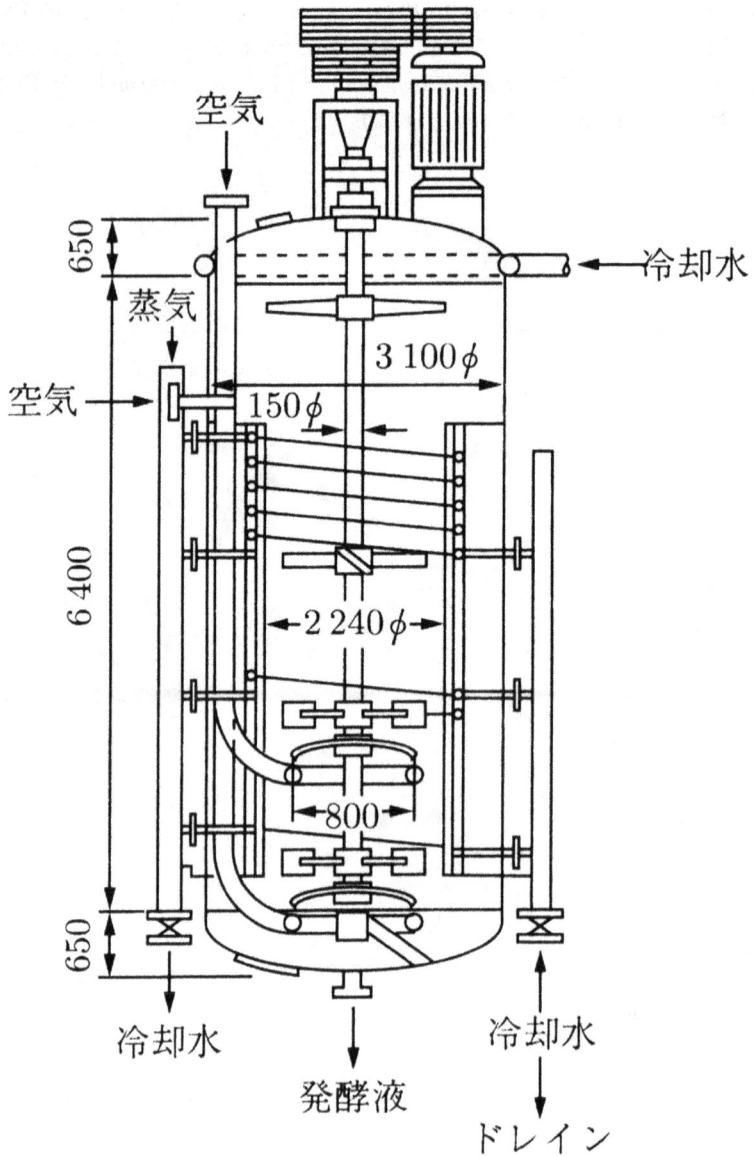

FIG. 19.1 50kl stirred aerated fermenter (source: Yoshida 2001: 491)

19

SCALING UP FROM THE BENCH: FERMENTATION TANK

Victoria Lee

Name: fermentation tank. Other names: fermenter, reactor, bioreactor. **Family**: chemical industry. **Size and shape**: the common types of tank can range in size, containing up to hundreds of kilolitres. Cylindrical. **Habitat**: outdoors or indoors at factory sites in the food and pharmaceutical industries. **Distribution in Japan**: nationwide. **Life cycle**: begins with bench research and the construction of a smaller pilot tank, followed by the industrial-scale fermentation tank. Able to make a variety of products once in operation. **Human connections**: produces food and drink for human consumption, including beer, vinegar, liquors, and yeasts. Also makes non-food products, including solvents, enzymes, biofuels, organic acids, antibiotics, and recombinant protein products. **Ecosystem connections**: culture media rely significantly on raw materials that are available locally and in abundance. Microbial strains are maintained locally but have widely varying origins. Waste products (such as yeasts) may be put to other uses.

Keywords: fermenting (hakkō), culturing (baiyō), growing (hatsuiku), converting (tenkan), producing (seisan), controlling and regulating (chōsetsu), maintaining (hoji), distributing (bunpu), operating (sōsa), consuming (shōhi), scaling up (suke-eruappu), industrialising (kōgyōka)

A FERMENTATION TANK IS MOST COMMONLY REPRESENTED IN A SCHEMATIC manner, as in the diagram in **FIGURE 19.1**. Fermentation tanks are physical objects that are made of hard materials such as steel. When in a tank's presence, it is hard to miss. It is often much larger than people or buildings, and as the focal point of a production process it dominates spaces, whether it stands outdoors in the sun within a factory site, or under the glow of indoor laboratory lamps. Yet the details concerning how any one tank became a physical reality have commercial value and need to be safeguarded. Publications that give information on these tanks in the public domain tend to emphasise the general and not the specific. Few photographs of fermentation tanks are widely available, since such images are carefully regulated by the producers, which are frequently corporations. A universal diagram, therefore, is more representative than a photograph. Mirroring the way in which tanks separate, protect, and conceal their interior contents from their surroundings, specific facts on individual tanks are also isolated, protected, and concealed from the outside technical community.

The diagram in **FIGURE 19.1** shows a fifty-kilolitre fermenter. A large-scale fermentation tank is a piece of industrial technology that cheaply mass-produces cells or goods from cells (for example, yeasts for bread and beer, alcohol, enzymes for detergents). It is a controlled space of conversion. The fermentation tank holds a culture medium that was created through a process of trial and error as the optimal, cost-efficient chemical environment to grow a particular microbial strain with available raw materials. The microbial strain was selected as the cell that has the ability to yield high amounts of a specific product in a short time. Together these make up the fermentation broth, which the tank isolates and insulates from the outside environment, keeping the inner environment artificially sterile and at a fixed temperature in order to maximise cell performance and, therefore, product yield. Inside some fermentation tanks, cells may perform an anaerobic fermentation process, and thus may not require an air supply, but in the tank depicted here, the process is aerobic and the cells need air to accomplish the reaction.

Sterilised air passes to the cells through the pipes depicted by the uppermost downward-pointing arrow as well as the rightward-pointing arrow on the left, which bring the air inside the tank. An agitator, which we can see attached to the vertical axis of the tank, stirs the fluid and breaks the air into bubbles that travel to the cells dispersed throughout the culture medium inside the tank. In order to keep the tank walls sterile, steam passes through the pipe that the leftmost downward-pointing arrow designates. An insulating jacket of cooled water – which we see flowing into the pipes shown by the leftward-pointing arrow on the top right and the upward-pointing arrow on the bottom right, and into drains on either side at the bottom of the tank – surrounds the tank and regulates its temperature. Collection of the fermentation broth takes place through the central pipe shown at the bottom of the tank. From the broth, the desired product will be extracted and refined elsewhere in the plant.

Before an existing industrial-scale fermentation tank can manufacture a new commercial product, such as a chemical, engineers must first 'scale up' the techniques used and preliminary data obtained when scientists culture strains and make chemicals at the laboratory bench. Only by a process of scale-up can engineers apply bench-scale techniques and data to industrial-level production. Scale-up takes place step by step, typically from shake flask to jar fermenter, to pilot plant, and to industrial tank. Much as the inputs and outputs of the tank contents must be measured and controlled, requiring supervision and surveillance at a distance, so the circulation of knowledge about fermentation and scale-up processes is also restricted. The components of a process must be designed in a way that does not violate existing patents. Many details of fermentation processes are commercial secrets or published only in patents. Similarly, details of scale-up methods are confidential information.

The type of tank about which there is the most information available to the public is the one depicted in the diagram in **FIGURE 19.1**: the stirred tank for aerobic fermentation. This type of tank first appeared in the late 1930s for yeast production, and scientists and engineers around the world researched the tank intensively in the immediate post-World War II period for mass-producing penicillin (made by a fungus). Since the end of the war, the stirred aerobic tank has predominated in the pharmaceutical industries, because the same tank can be used to produce any kind of antibiotic as well as many other cell metabolites made in aerobic conditions. We have numerous accounts of penicillin's history, even though its manufacturing processes were also patented (the drug itself was not patented, for humanitarian reasons). Here I focus especially on Japanese accounts, and this essay is based on translations from Japanese papers. Penicillin histories help sketch out a brief pedigree of fermentation tanks and, more broadly, the ways in which fermentation tanks compelled scientists to reconcile bench results with real-world engineering problems.

TANK PEDIGREE

Across the world, people have used non-sterile or 'open' tanks in diverse brewing industries for many centuries. In the late nineteenth century, scientists developed techniques to isolate, preserve, and define individual microbial strains, which relied on culturing the strains 'purely' – propagating a single strain in an otherwise sterile environment. Scientists argued that beer brewers could lower the risk of spoilage, and industrial alcohol manufacturers could raise yields, by sealing off the environment and using pure cultures, creating 'closed' fermentation tanks. These new microbiological concepts and techniques affected fermentation technologies in many places, including in Japan. There are different kinds of fermentation and, accordingly, different kinds of tank. Industry specialists divide fermentative production into three kinds: anaerobic fermentation (does not require air), aerobic fermentation (requires air), and photosynthesis (requires light). In that order, closed tanks for the three kinds of fermentation developed one after the other.

Brewers and yeast manufacturers built some of the earliest industrial fermentation tanks in the late nineteenth century. These anaerobic processes are part of what scientists call the 'older' kinds of fermentation industry. Nineteenth-century Carlsberg flasks for propagating pure cultures of yeast had a capacity of ten to twenty litres. Another 1885 tank for culturing yeasts had a capacity of three hundred to four hundred litres (Tanaka 2000). These were copper with a tin lining on the inside. 'Newer' anaerobic fermentation industries include acetone-butanol fermentation, for which fermentation tanks appeared during World War I, and glycerol fermentation. Fermentation tanks produced these substances for the heavy chemical and military-related industries, as well as for fuel. In the aerobic fermentation industries, which are 'new', fermentation tanks developed in the period between World War I and World War II. These made organic acids, from citric acid to lactic acid, for the food and pharmaceutical industries.

Penicillin tanks, which American scientists first developed during World

War II, differed from all of these previous tanks in being especially difficult to engineer. Penicillin fermentation (an aerobic process) demanded several new conditions that previous processes had not. The degree to which contamination affected yield was greater than before, since earlier fermentation processes had involved acidic cultures, anaerobic cultures, or cultures relying on a special substrate, and were less likely to halt or spoil when outside microbes entered the culture. In order to produce large enough quantities of penicillin for general use, it was not enough to grow the microbes on the surface of the culture medium, though this design more easily solved the problem of air supply since microbes on a liquid surface would simply be in contact with the surrounding air. For penicillin production, the microbes had to be thoroughly distributed inside the culture medium, a process known as submerged or deep fermentation. This meant building a tank that would pipe air into the culture fluid and then disperse it by mechanical stirring in order for the air to reach the cells. Moreover, incoming air and all of the components needed to be kept free of contamination. This necessity for a high degree of sterility, and the complexity of the mechanism required to supply air and stir the medium, made penicillin-tank engineering unprecedentedly difficult for the fermentation industries, even though scientists had developed closed tanks since the late nineteenth century.

For example, acetone-butanol fermentation, as mentioned above, was an anaerobic process. Chaim Weizmann's group designed the tank to be made of iron, with a capacity of tens of kilolitres (Tanaka 2000). The central body of the tank was shaped like a cylinder. The top and bottom components were of half-spherical shape and performed the function of pressurised-steam sterilisation of the tank to prevent contamination. Unlike for penicillin, there was no need to stir the culture broth to distribute fermentation products and speed the process, because the gas that the cells released during the fermentation process elicited mixing.

Before penicillin, aerobic fermentation was carried out largely by surface rather than submerged culture. Gluconic acid manufacture was one of the earliest aerobic industrial processes to use a closed tank system. In 1929, Orville E. May et al. used a tank made of aluminium that was shaped like a shallow circular dish. With a diameter of 109 centimetres and a height of five centimetres, it could hold forty-five litres of culture fluid (Tanaka 2000). Scientists would inoculate (introduce a microbial strain into a medium) the mould used for production onto the culture medium and then allow sterilised air to pass over the surface.

When submerged culture tanks for aerobic fermentation first appeared, they did not require stirring. Compared to surface culture, submerged culture was designed to make more efficient use of space. In 1938, Edward A. Gastrock et al. did this by constructing a rotating fermentation tank, and successfully employed the tank in gluconic acid production. The main tank of 1600 litres, as well as a small-scale inoculation tank of fifty litres (in order to culture the microbial strain used for inoculation), were cylindrical and made of aluminium. The cylinder was horizontal like a drum, and continuously rotated on a horizontal axis. The tank rotated eight to fourteen times per minute, while sterilised air passed at a fixed pressure and rate through the tank. As the culture fluid reached the top of the tank, it would fall, and the movement of the fluid created a large area of contact between the culture liquid and the oxygen supply. The spinning tank design reduced the fermentation time vis-à-vis surface culture by ten times and raised the resulting product's concentration. Later, Percy Wells et al. used a similar rotary tank to ferment sorbose (Tanaka 2000). However, while the rotary drum design was an improvement on surface-culture designs with regard to space, the culture-fluid volume was still limited to less than a third of the tank volume in order to ensure effective contact between the fluid and the air supply (**FIGURES 19.2A, 19.2B, 19.2C**).

Creating a tank for aerobic fermentation with stirring addressed the problem of economy of space. In 1937, George T. de Becze and Alfred J. Liebmann employed an unusual stirred tank in three different yeast factories in central Europe. This iron-bodied tank was an upright cylinder. It had an outer layer that acted like an insulating jacket, where water of a fixed temperature would flow and regulate the temperature within the tank. An agitator was installed inside the tank in order to stir the culture fluid, to create contact between the fluid and air. The air was injected into the tank through pipes that had numerous pores, a process known as air sparging. A board placed on the inner wall of the tank acted to further disperse the air and mix the fluid. Because the culture fluid had a tendency to foam under these conditions, later stirred tanks brought anti-foaming agent into the fluid through an added supply pipe. This tank reduced the amount of compressed air needed to one fifth of the previous amount, and

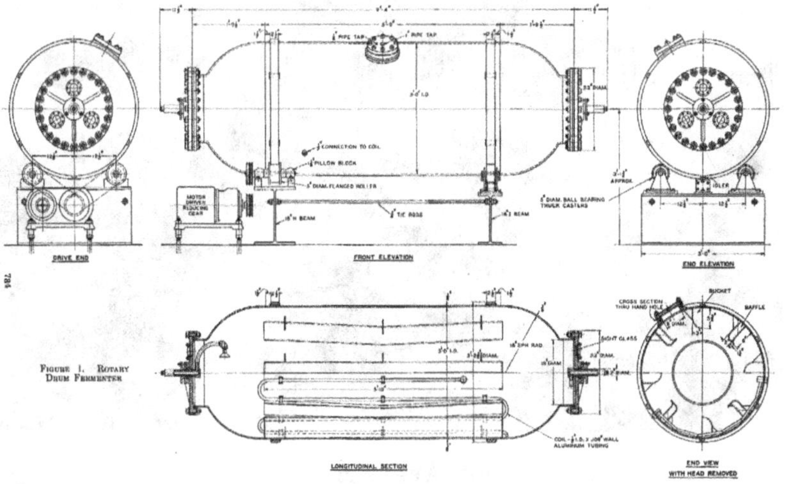

FIG. 19.2A Rotary drum fermenter (source: Gastrock 1938: 784)

LABORATORY-SCALE FERMENTATION APPARATUS

FIG. 19.2B Source: Gastrock 1938: 788

LARGE-SCALE FERMENTATION APPARATUS

FIG. 19.2C Source: Gastrock 1938: 789

now two thirds of the tank could be filled with the culture medium, further speeding the fermentation process and raising the product concentration, since the microbial strains were distributed throughout the liquid. Submerged culture was also much more efficient than surface culture because the air bubbles allowed rapid supply of enzymes as well as rapid removal of waste gases. That said, the energy costs for this process were still high, since steam had to be made for temperature regulation and compressed air (**FIGURES 19.3A, 19.3B, 19.3C, 19.3D**).

The photograph shows an aerating system of the perforated tube type for a huge propagating tub, where compressed yeast is produced by aeration in a European factory.

FIG. 19.3A Source: de Becze and Liebmann 1944: 882

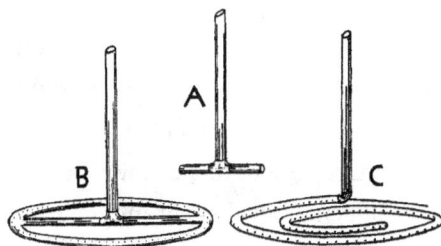

Figure 1.   Early Forms of Perforated Tube Systems
A.   Inverted T
B.   Perforated ring
C.   Spiral sparger

FIG. 19.3B Source: de Becze and Liebmann 1944: 885

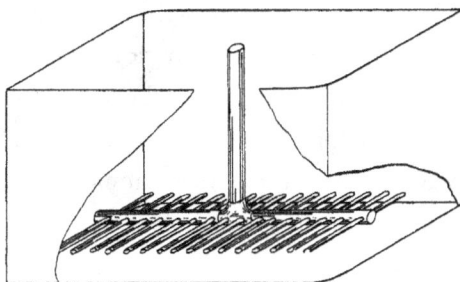

Figure 2.   Network of Perforated Tubes

FIG. 19.3C Source: de Becze and Liebmann 1944: 885

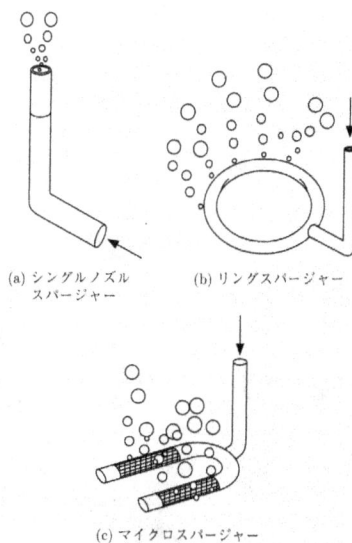

(a) シングルノズル
スパージャー

(b) リングスパージャー

(c) マイクロスパージャー

FIG. 19.3D Different kinds of spargers: a) single nozzle sparger, b) ring sparger, and c) micro sparger (source: Sakuma 2001: 488)

In the case of penicillin production, the technological bottleneck was not the problem of discovering a microbial strain that could produce penicillin, nor was it especially difficult to achieve bench-scale and small-scale penicillin production by surface culture. The bottleneck was being able to manufacture large enough quantities of penicillin cheaply enough to enable the drug to be used clinically among the general population, which scientists achieved only by using a stirred aerobic tank similar to the tank that de Becze and Liebmann used for yeast culture. In 1943, the penicillin tank had a capacity of fifty-four kilolitres. By 1955, penicillin tanks were about a hundred and twenty-five kilolitres in size, and by then the tanks were also beginning to make other antibiotics (Tanaka 2000). Eventually, the standard geometry of the tank settled at a cylinder with a depth of two to three times the width. The basic design of the stirred tank has changed little since then, although there have been innovations to the design of the agitator wing, for example, to better supply enzymes for yeast culturing or for high-viscosity culture fluids (which are common with fungal cultures) in order to distribute the shear exerted on the cells more evenly within the entire tank (**FIGURE 19.4**).

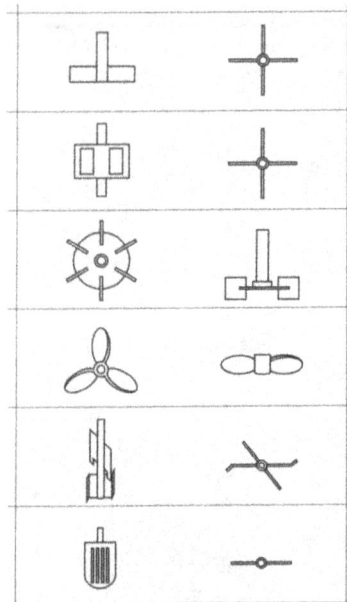

FIG. 19.4 Agitator wing designs (source: Sakuma 2001: 487)

SCALING UP

An industrial fermentation process begins with microbiological ideas and microbiologists' work at the laboratory bench to culture the relevant strain and produce the desired chemical. For any fermentation process, therefore, the tank executing that process often takes the original form of a shake flask with a capacity of several millilitres to several litres. By a procedure of scale-up, the tank changes form from the shake flask to a jar fermenter (up to tens of litres), and leaving the bench involves a further scale-up from the jar fermenter to a pilot plant (up to several kilolitres), and finally from the pilot plant to a large-scale tank for industrial use (up to hundreds of kilolitres) (**FIGURES 19.5 A–D**).

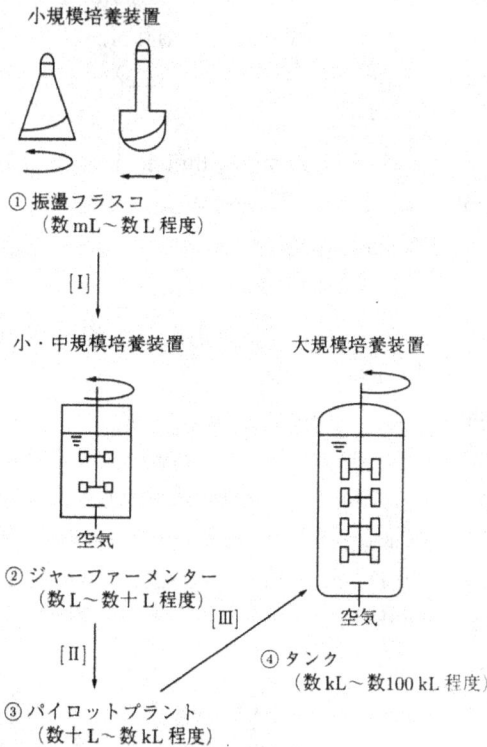

小規模培養装置

① 振盪フラスコ
（数 mL〜数 L 程度）

[I]

小・中規模培養装置　　　　　大規模培養装置

空気

② ジャーファーメンター
（数 L〜数十 L 程度）

[III]

空気

[II]

④ タンク
（数 kL〜数100 kL 程度）

③ パイロットプラント
（数十 L〜数 kL 程度）

FIG. 19.5 Scaling up: (1) shake flasks (small-scale), (2) jar fermenter (small to medium-scale), (3) pilot plant (medium-scale), (4) tank (large-scale) (source: Takanaka 2001: 498)

A quantitative index is used to compare the environments and ensure that the production amount and production speed do not change as the culture environment increases in scale. In aerobic fermentation there are many indices one can use to measure changes: physical indices, such as the consumed power per unit fluid, or the Reynolds number of the fluid, or the average diameter of the air bubbles; or more physiological indices, such as the hydrodynamic stress exerted on the cells by the mixing, which can be measured by the flow of leaked biological materials from inside the cells. Engineers tend to select the parameters that are seen to be rate-limiting. For scale-up in penicillin production, common parameters used were the power consumed per unit of culture fluid, or oxygen transfer. Because scale-up details are commercial secrets, there is little available information about how this is done. But for penicillin, it is known that in 1954, Ernst Chain used a ten-litre jar fermenter in the laboratory, and ninety-litre and three hundred-litre pilot tanks in the industrial plant (Tanaka 2000).

Scaling up is a very difficult process, where engineers prepare for failure as much as for success. It can be especially difficult when using fungal cultures that generate viscous, non-Newtonian fluids, since in such cases it is more challenging to find a suitable parameter. When scaling up from the shake flask to the jar fermenter, the air supply method changes: in the former, outside air passes through a cotton plug into the culture environment, while the latter uses a sparger and agitator. This means that the air transfer to and from the cells, as well as the physical stress on the cells, changes. If either of these is a rate-limiting factor in the fermentation process, scale-up becomes difficult. The industrial tank is much larger than the pilot tank. It can be several storeys high (five to ten metres), such that instead of the homogenous environment in the pilot tank, there are gradients of gas concentration and pressure in the industrial tank. Scientists have developed laboratory equipment specifically for helping to research these elements of scale-up, such as a variable-pressure small-scale tank.

In the case of penicillin, industrialising the mould-based fermentation process therefore required chemical engineering expertise, beyond the microbiology and biochemistry that guided early bench-scale work. In Japan, the chemical engineer who was appointed by the Allied occupation government to lead pilot-tank construction in state-sponsored penicillin research, Ōyama Yoshitoshi, later complained that the Japanese microbiologists and biochemists showed less concern for mechanical issues than did the American microbiologist who was sent to Japan as a consultant on penicillin production.[1] The Japanese submerged culture project began with a four hundred-litre pilot tank that eventually became a two-tonne tank. As is often the case for industrial processes, it was difficult for the researchers to get hold of engineering data.

The chemical engineers conceptualised the problems involved differently than the microbiologists and biochemists. To prevent contamination, micro-biologists were accustomed to using cotton plugs and heating with gas fires. Extrapolating from such experiences, the microbiologists advised the chemical engineers that they should weld a cover onto the large-scale fermentation tank, and that they should apply a phenol seal wherever a flange was used in the culture tank. To the engineers, however, these suggestions seemed utterly misguided, and Ōyama later recounted feeling frustrated that the microbiologists could not clearly explain how much air flow was needed, or what the stirring power should be, or even what the purpose of stirring was (Ōyama 1969). Scientists knew that older alcohol and fermentation industries did use cotton plugs to filter out bacteria from the air supply, but what thickness should the plug be, for what rate of air transfer? Because there was no data available, the chemical engineers had to undertake their own research into these issues, and accordingly carried out studies on the air resistance as it passed through cotton, the mechanism of filtration of the bacteria, and so on.

The design of the tank itself was a cylinder made of mild steel, with an agitator inside to divide and disperse the air bubbles, and an opening for the air supply. It was a temperature-regulated environment maintained constantly at 24 ± 1 degree Celsius. To achieve this, in the smaller pilot tanks there was a second layer of wall, and in the industrial tank there was a built-in coil, through which water of the set temperature would be passed. The air needed to be sup-plied to the tank in a completely sterile condition. Thus, the air passed through a compressor and then through a raw cotton or glass fibre filtration machine before entering the tank, which was itself maintained at a slightly elevated pres-sure to discourage air from entering from the outside. An anti-foaming agent was added. The tank had an opening for inoculating the tank with microbial strains, an exit mouth where the culture fluid and air could be collected, and an observation window; all such parts that had contact with the outside air needed to be sterilised with steam.

Particular engineering challenges included the heterogeneity of the culture fluid within the multi-storey tank. There was the issue of how to get the air to behave as desired, and how to get the agitator to stir it effectively so that the bubbles were distributed throughout the culture fluid and had as much contact as possible with the cells. There was the question of how to prevent foaming. There was the problem of how to keep the tank operating at a fixed temperature for long durations. There were all the various things that needed to be accounted for to stop outside microbes from entering the tank. All these problems had to be overcome before penicillin could be cheaply mass-produced in Japan. In the immediate post-war years, hundreds of scientists and technicians at the bench and in industrial plants, in clinics and in companies, universities and other research institutes collaborated to make penicillin production work. Tank engineering was one key component of the endeavour.

Once a fermentation tank exists, it is in the company's interests to keep the tank moving. A tank that sits idle is wasted. But each product has a life cycle after which it loses its market value. Antibiotics, the products that drove the fermentation tank boom, have an especially short life cycle due to antibiotic resistance. Other commercial products might become unprofitable or obsolete, or be driven out by new competition or regulation. Once a fermentation tank exists, researchers are compelled to think about a new product constantly.

A fermentation tank demands people for its survival. It needs people who can maintain and characterise microbes, who know which kinds of microbes and which kinds of products are likely to become interesting and profitable in the near future, who can screen microbes for an effective strain, who can develop culture media that are cheap and easily available in abundance, and who can work to deal with customer complaints. Much of this is bench-scale expertise. Then it needs people with the chemical engineering expertise to scale the process up to mass production and industrialise it, and to monitor and operate and maintain and repair the tank. It needs people who can develop an effective method for refining the chemical product, which relies on a supply of specific chemicals as well as specialised machines. Refinement is a separate process from tank construction, but it is a part of the fermentation process that similarly needs to be carefully engineered while keeping it a commercial secret. Moreover, the tank needs people who will work to develop uses for the by-products, and who will find economical ways to dispose of the waste.

As a box, a fermentation tank requires specialised scientific input in order to bring the tank and its associated fermentation processes into existence. The tank continues to demand the same kinds of scientific work, not only for maintenance and repairs, but each time the tank is called to make a new product to be brought to market. The fermentation tank determines what types of products can be made with it. When different kinds of products are introduced whose manufacturing processes do not quite fit the tank design (as in the case of penicillin fermentation) the design of the tank must be adjusted. The existence of the box is enabling – since it allows microbiologists to envision large-scale manufacture for a range of products that require similar fermentation processes – but also constraining – since when products are developed at the laboratory bench using different processes, the industrial tank environment must be altered for successful scale-up. This very tension between enabling and constraining compels innovation both at the bench and in the factory.

NOTES

1   Ōyama speculated that this may have been because it was less common in Japan than in the US at the time for people to drive (and, therefore, operate and maintain), cars (Ōyama 1969:62).

REFERENCES

de Becze, G., and A. J. Liebmann, 'Aeration in the Production of Compressed Yeast', *Industrial & Engineering Chemistry*, 36.10 (1944): 882–90.

Gastrock, E. A. et al., 'Gluconic Acid Production on Pilot-Plant Scale: Effect of Variables on Production by Submerged Mold Growths', *Industrial & Engineering Chemistry*, 30.7 (1938): 782–89.

Iijima T., *Nihon no kagaku gijutsu—Kigyōshi ni miru sono kōzō* (Chemical Technology in Japan—Structure from the Perspective of Business History) (Tokyo: Kōgyō chōsakai, 1981).

Ōyama Y., 'Kagaku kōgaku no riteihyō—Kaken to penishirin puranto' (Milestones in Chemical Engineering—Kaken and the Penicillin Plant), *Shizen*, 24.6 (1969): 60–67.

Sakuma H., 'Hakkōsō' (Fermenter), in Baioindasutorii kyōkai hakkō to taisha kenkyūkai, ed., *Hakkō handobukku* (Fermentation Handbook) (Tokyo: Kyoritsu shuppan, 2001), pp. 485–90.

Tanaka H., 'Hakkōsō, baiyō sōchi' (Fermenters and Bioreactors), *Seibutsu kōgakushi (Tokubetsu gō: Hakkō kōgaku 20 seiki no ayumi—Baiotekunorojii no genryū o tadoru)* (Special Issue: History of Fermentation Engineering in the 20th Century—Following the Origins of Biotechnology) (December 2000): 24–32.

——, 'Hakkō seisan no sukeeruappu' (Scale-Up for Fermentative Production), in Baioindasutorii kyōkai hakkō to taisha kenkyūkai, ed., *Hakkō handobukku* (Fermentation Handbook) (Tokyo: Kyoritsu shuppan, 2001), pp. 498–99.

Uchida S., 'Penishirin to kagaku kōgaku' (Penicillin and Chemical Engineering), *Kagaku kikai*, 12.1 (1948): 9–15.

Yoshida T., 'Hakkō sōchi' (Reactors for Fermentation), in Baioindasutorii kyōkai hakkō to taisha kenkyūkai, ed., *Hakkō handobukku* (Fermentation Handbook) (Tokyo: Kyoritsu shuppan, 2001), pp. 491–95.

FIG. 20.1 元末明初的黑漆书箱 Black shellac lacquer book-box from the late Yuan/early Ming Dynasty. Usually placed on a scholar's desk for the storage of letters or notes. Lid and body were melded together. The box lid is decorated with a deer pattern, and the sides with plum blossoms (source: private collection)

20

DEEP TIME HISTORY: THE LURE OF THE BLACK BOX

Dagmar Schäfer

Name: black box. **Specific**: late Yuan to Early Ming Dynastic book box, virtual box. **Other names**: green box (*qingxiang* 青箱), book box (*shujia* 書盒). **Size and shape**: ca. 32 cm W x 32 H x 42 L. **Colour**: black, lacquered. **Behaviour**: deflecting, entrusting, obscuring, facilitating, encasing. **Habitat**: now in a collector's household; originally it sat on desks and tables or on shelves, or travelled with scholars on mules, in carriages or boats. Now an object of the mind. **Distribution**: widespread in China during the Song (960–1279), Ming (1368–1645) and Qing (1645–1912); ubiquitous in twentieth-century households. Omnipotent in a scientist's mind. **Migration**: from the territory's north to south, east to west; minds to minds. **Status**: lid closed, exterior largely intact, but battered. With variable interiors. **Variations**: the deep-time history of the box shows that it spread worldwide as a useful device in knowledge production and as a performative thinking tool. The black boxes take different shapes, from the thingness of the box shown here to a modelling device and to methodological and metaphorical use across all scientific and artistic domains.

Keywords: ordering, hiding, unveiling, encasing, liberating, reducing complexity

After passing the civil service exam, I could never waste books and enjoyed visiting people and asking around. Hence my experience unconsciously multiplied. Time and again, I encountered issues to consider and decide, actions were accomplished and products magnificent. I recorded my thoughts as warnings and advice for later. Though loaded with trivialities and unorderly, I publish them here entitled 'Miscellaneous Jottings from the Black Box.'

Qing Xiang zaji 青箱雜記
('Miscellaneous Jottings from the Black Box')
preface dated 1087 by Wu Chuhou 吳處厚 (*jinshi* 1055)

IN THE MERITOCRACY OF THE SONG (960–1279), WHEN TALENTED COM-moners such as Wu Chuhou could attain high rank by honing their literary skills, black boxes populated most scholarly desks. Made of a fast-growing leafless wood (*qing* 青 a dark blue-green), black boxes were utilitarian objects with no decoration whatsoever. Scholars put into these boxes their private correspondence, their poetry or, like Wu Chuhou, their rambling thoughts (**FIGURE 20.1**). Out of these boxes came this era's knowledge and ideals.

A major quality of the box was the colour black. The plain exterior protected and disguised the mechanics of this era's most venerated skills: reading and writing texts. Though later on, black boxes would encase different services and ideas, the quotation from the Song ancestor well exemplifies the qualities that make up the allure of the black box: dealing with and managing the known and unknown. A protective utilitarian purpose goes hand in hand with the capacity to hide in plain sight. The human imagination stored inside can be accessed, though most people are entirely content with knowing only the surface and acting upon the results. Black boxes exemplify and embody changing compositions and epistemologies.

In this essay I suggest that black boxes have a history reaching far back into the past. It is this history on which their reputation is built, a history in which three functions of the black box are consistently addressed: (1) to hide knowledge, (2) to reduce knowledge complexity by directing attention to the in- and outputs, (3) to contain knowledge worth unveiling. These three are the idealised pure forms, whereas in fact various combinations populate the historical world and human minds. This is the oscillating nature of black boxes. In such a multiplying view, we can see various caesurae taking place, either because the box's contents or the reception of the box's contents changed.

Historians of science tend to focus mostly on the nineteenth century, when the human imagination in the box increasingly manifested in technologies rather than texts. With this alteration, black boxes such as radios and computers moved increasingly into the public view. Scholars then also gave the black box new contours, using it as an analytical tool. Scientists and historians in particular became increasingly attracted to the box's ambiguous effects. The action of closing the box liberated the actor by making the interior invisible and ignorable, but this created the risk of being trapped in a reductionist approach. Those who opened the box and looked inside might learn and know, and yet the action of opening the box disenchanted the magic inside.

TYPE 1. THE MYSTERY OF BOXED-UP THOUGHTS: HIDING KNOWLEDGE

a) as in words and texts (…)

Black boxes are utilitarian means, useful for storage and transportation of whatever the owners find worthwhile. During the long period when black boxes were mainly associated with the encasing of words and texts, secrecy became the boxes' major trait.

This secrecy is epitomised by the closed lid. In the area that we now call China, philosophical schools such as the *fangshi* 方士 lore (ca. third century BC) boxed scriptures that, for them, represented condensed *yuanqi* 元氣 (original *qi*) and that, existing prior to the world, would connect the adept to the origins of the world (Pregadio 2008: 24). Only those who understood achieved access to the boxed-up text.

Such an approach was not a prerogative of the Chinese alone. In the Black Box Inquiry of 1680 in England, it was rumoured, for example, that

> Sir Gilbert Girrard[1] had a black Box, in which the Marriage of the King with
> the Duke's Mother was fully proved and made out; and the fear of the Duke

of York's succession was so fix'd in Mens Minds, that the Story of the Black Box was generally divulged, and for ought I know believed by those who were fearful of the Duke of York's succession. (Coke 1697: 544)

The documents in the box evinced who was heir to the throne. The lid kept in place a content that required containment.

Closing hence empowered the box. Like the box of the Chinese *fangshi* lore, the power of the Jewish prayer boxes, *Tefillin*, take the form of words, letters. Orthodox Jewish men attach the little black boxes to their head and arm for weekday morning prayers. In the year 1908 the theologist and philologist O. Neufchotz de Jassy connected this Jewish custom back to the

worshipers of the Hindu Shadai, of Shiva, [who] put on their left arm a little receptable or a ring [...]. On two sides of this receptacle the letter *sheen,* representing the word *Shadai* is embossed. It is presumable that this little box, called *baith,* "the house", contained originally the same priapic emblems replaced later by the Talmudists with a few texts taken from the Bible. (Neufchotz de Jassy 1908: 128)

The Jewish prayer box, like the Chinese black box, held transformative textual powers in place.

With shifting approaches to texts, the Jews and Chinese both came to perceive the black box differently. Wu Chuhou represents a scholarly and social group (later identified as Neo-Confucians) who used black boxes mainly as repositories to collect information and food for thought in response to a political system in which literary education had become key. Wu Chuhou's *qingxiang* emphasises the box as a container for the instruments that the scholar then manipulated and controlled to trigger intellectual, scientific, technological, religious, and socio-political change.

A common trait of the pre-modern black box full of words was that the power of transformation lay with the scholar who would open and close the lid to awaken minds. Zhu Xi 朱熹 (1130–1200), a leading figure of the School of Principle (*lixue* 理學), who rose to prominence in the later era of the Ming (1368–1645), followed Wu when he contended that, 'if one has become completely familiar with the text and also has thought about it carefully, the mind and the principle will spontaneously become one, and one will never forget' (Zhu 1986: 170).

b) as in wires and cables

Black boxes as tools that transform by imagination go back into human deep time. Historians of science tend to focus mostly on the nineteenth century, when the human imagination in the box increasingly manifested in technologies rather than texts. In contrast to their deep time predecessors, 'modern' black boxes of the nineteenth century such as radios and computers transform the contents that pass through them quite materially. In modernity too, though scholars gave the black boxes new contours, using them increasingly as analytical tools.

Black boxes contained predominantly textual material for a long time, but by the nineteenth century they increasingly enclosed other kinds of materialisations/creations of the human mind: cog-wheels, wires, needles, or gears. Unlike their ancient ancestors, these black boxes themselves became agents of change. Running on electricity or other fuels, quintessential historical black-boxed machines such as the radio or telephone covertly morphed words into other forms, transporting them as signals and codes over great distances.

Such was also the power of the electric telegraph, the invention of which is attributed to Sir William Fothergill Cooke (1806–79). In 1843, Charles Wheatstone (1802–75) popularised a bridge circuit that, encased by a black box, was made fit for use by telephone engineers (**FIGURE 20.2**) (Morus 1998).[2] Guglielmo Marconi (1874–1937) (**FIGURE 20.3**) sheathed conductors and Hertzian waves with a flat black box, and created wireless telegraphy:

> Marconi's inventions, modifications, and improvements fit into a small box,
> at that time dubbed Marconi's "secret box" or "black-box". (Hong 2001: 23)

Historical accounts of Marconi's black box testify that mystery remained quintessential to black box mythology. It now addressed, however, an encased processing machine. How could these heaps of cables and a spark of electricity transmit speech and music over distances otherwise impossible to overcome:

FIG. 20.2 'Circuits in a Box'. The 'Wheatstone bridge' is the name for a simple circuit that can be used to calibrate measuring instruments by use of a long resistive slide wire. The circuit was invented by Hunter Charles, to whom Charles Wheatstone (1802–75) gave full credit when he encased the bridge circuit in the arrangement of four resistors, a battery, and a galvanometer for his needle telegraph (photo by Thomas B. Greenslade, Jr, Gambier, Ohio USA)

FIG. 20.3 'Transfer between Boxes'. Guiglieno Marconi (1874–1937) pictured between the spark-gap transmitter on the right and the coherer receiver on the left. Together he and Karl Ferdinand Braun were awarded the Nobel prize in physics in 1909 (source: Google-hosted LIFE Photo Archive)

> There was a little black box on a table, a fascinating mystery, which had come
> with him from Newark. Inside it he could create a spark which baffled the
> scientists and which we know now to have been wireless. (Shiers 1977: 52)

Distinctively different to the pre-modern black box, the modern box's mystique
had a technical and scientific rationale that was de-mystifiable and advanced.[3]
Another difference was that people now assigned the powers of transformation
to the innards of the black box and no longer to what was placed inside or taken
out. As a consequence of this, approaches to knowing also changed. Knowledge
no longer meant to be in charge of opening and closing the box, or utilising the
contents to make transformations take place. Instead, knowledge now meant
understanding the system's composites, or why and how inputs and innards
created the repeatedly observable and hence universally valid effects.

TYPE 2. THE WORKING MACHINE AND THE BOX-EFFECT: REDUCING KNOWLEDGE — CLOSING THE LID

The amazement that accompanied nineteenth-century black-boxed machines
addressed the human ingenuity that made the machine work towards a specific
effect. In Marconi's case the simplicity of the mechanical setup still generated awe:

> When Marconi "opened" this black-box by publicizing his first patent in
> 1897, people were amazed and intrigued by its simplicity. The solutions
> appeared so simple and so obvious that many began to wonder why no one
> else had come up with them. (Hong 2001: 23)

Clearly though, as cameras, 'the telephone, the television, the radio and in recent
years the computer and the facsimile machine' (Rosenberg 1994: 204) increasingly became ubiquitous, the black box functioned as a shield to protect users
from contact with the electric circuits as much as from the growing complexity
the box kept wrapped up inside.

Historian Elizabeth Cavicchi identifies the lived experience of the 'working' machine in the nineteenth and twentieth centuries as a major impetus for
the conceptual development of the black box in the following decades: 'once

an instrument operates with minimal fuss, these same properties recede into the background. It becomes a black box whose users need not understand the thing knowledge by which it runs' (Cavicchi 2005: 244).

Historians Robert W. Smith and Joseph N. Tatarewicz show how the twentieth-century claim that the black box encased what had become 'a well-established fact' made it prone to become a conceptual tool in research organisation. In the planning process of the NASA space telescope, in which various people and dozens of groups, committees, and industrial organisations throughout the United States were involved, researchers utilised the black box metaphor to distinguish the 'unproblematic object' from that very object that they wanted to analyse and understand (Smith and Tatarewicz 1994: 102). To compartmentalise tasks, each expert community black-boxed the other's knowledge as reliable and true; as the planning developed, provisional black boxes could be opened and their content changed.

Such conceptual black-boxing was utilitarian, in the sense that the black box encased issues in order to be able to set them aside. Setting aside was allowed because the interior was a generally accepted fact, a truth. The ambiguous role of encasing and setting aside in all these instances was the very source of the box's function as a liberating thinking device. For this liberating effect to work, as Bruno Latour emphasises, the lid of the box had to remain closed. A closed lid ensured that scientists were able to use and users able to consume without asking why, focusing entirely on the

> "working" of what was encased inside: A black box opens momentarily, and will soon be closed again, becoming completely invisible in the main sequence of action. (Latour 1999: 191)

Clearly, as Latour and Trevor Pinch have observed, scientists and engineers also wrapped up known processes to be able to mobilise their facilities, their in- and outputs, but otherwise focused on the revelation of bigger, more pressing or, simply, different concerns. Latour and Pinch both stress black-boxing as a means of dealing with complexity. Pinch points out that the box also often blackened the intricate assembly of potentially disparate elements that are made to act as one (Pinch 1992).

Such was the positivist approach. The closed box, however, with its long history of a tightly shut lid, met with a good deal of suspicion in this new era too. After all, the shield clearly separated the savant from the ignoramus who could not look inside and thus *had* to believe. Critics pointed out that people were left in the dark about how solutions were derived, when, instead of unravelling complexity, simple short-cuts came into use: 'the black box effect is looming, and so the risks of a "prince-pleasing" use of the black box', cautioned Asensio and Roca (2002: 233), referring to models that, targeting distinctive goals, are based mainly on input-output values and nothing more. Black-boxing could fall victim to ideology too, in that increasingly people also boxed up the complexity of knowledge-in-action that was otherwise not easy to explain. This form of black boxing created a knowledge category, namely the 'tacitness' of knowledge flows.

Such were the intentionally reductionist approaches to a 'black box effect' that scientists regularly encountered in their research, because they were unable to unlock the box.

Black boxes, as the very epitome of a functioning machine that produced reliable effects – similar to the pre-modern treasure trove – thus remained accessible to only a few. While people also increasingly claimed that the box contained scientifically explicable principles and truths, and no longer blind belief without rationale, this reductionism also had the potential to end in a puff of magic smoke, or fairy dust. Along these lines, the 1946 *Science News*, for instance, jibed that the lie detector did not require any content: 'an empty black box, if it looks mysterious, would serve the same purpose – and has been used for it' (*Science News Letter* 30 March 1946). The form alone had come to inspire enough trust all by itself, effectuating a guise that spurred people on to unveil the truth.

TYPE 3. 'WORKINGS' BEHIND THE CLOSED LID: UNVEILING KNOWLEDGE

What worked as a distraction for some, or raised suspicion in others, attracted still others like bees to a honeypot. Metaphorical references in twentieth-century science discourse elaborated on black boxes' working effects as a way to learn about microbes or DNA-stems. Historian M. J. Behe, for instance, claims that for Darwin the cell was a 'working' black box that he strove to unlock (Behe 1996).

The practising physician Philip M. Rosoff finds that genetic researchers regularly implement a black box effect when they attempt to relate changes in biochemical and physiological phenomena:

> something was done which could be described with a great deal of detail and specificity, then many things happened about which they could only speculate, … and then the cell divided. (Rosoff 2010: 209)

Upon direct attack, quite literally the 'lid' of the cell firmly closes and contracts like a mussel that has been hit. Whenever this happens the innards remain opaque.

Before the era of X-rays, microelectrodes, CAT and other imaging techniques, animals and the human brain were studied as transducers that could only be understood by reference to what went in and what came out. B. F. Skinner, for instance, assumed in his model of behavioural science that

> There is no doubt of the existence of sense organs, nerves, and *brain*, or of their participation in behavior. The organism is neither empty nor inscrutable; let the *black box* be opened. The body has always seemed to offer an attractive escape [...]. (Skinner 1969: 280)

In this metaphorical use, all one could do with a black box was to examine the relationships between various forms of input and their respective outputs. Skinner put people into an operant conditioning box to open the black boxes that he was interested in: how to enhance social justice and human well-being. In his experimental analysis of human behaviour, as discussed in *Walden Two*, Skinner explored, experimentally, how individuals could be induced to behave best as far as the group is concerned:

> We had already worked out a code of conduct – subject, of course, to experimental modification. The code would keep things running smoothly

if everybody lived up to it. Our job was to see that everybody did. Now, you can't get people to follow a useful code by making them into so many jacks-in-the box. You can't foresee all future circumstances, and you can't specify adequate future conduct. You don't know what will be required. Instead you have to set up certain behavioral processes which will lead the individual to design his own "good" conduct when the time comes. We call that sort of thing "self-control". But don't be misled, the control always rests in the last analysis in the hands of society. (Skinner 2005: 95–96)

In Skinner's box, humans and animals were reduced to sheer outputs and effects.

The desire to enlighten blackened spots hence occasionally blacked out the innards entirely. This effect, however, also spurred the development of new techniques of observation. Scientists, curious to be offered at least a glimpse of what was inside the body-black-box, increasingly used medical imaging technologies. Magnetic resonance and image-generating radiation conquered cognitive science (Nersessian 1995). The brain was often imagined to function like a machine: brains were wired organisms, emitting electrical signals, functioning algorithmically by design.

The associations now invoked by the black box were such that the nature of the operation inside the box was mainly what these relationships revealed. Black-boxing hence became a strategy in epidemiological research, later described as risk-factor epidemiology.

In the hope of unraveling causes of diseases, associations are sought between disease and various "exposures." "Black box" is an untested postulate linking the exposure and the disease in a causal sequence. [...] The causal mechanism remains unknown ("black"), but its existence is implied ("box"). (Skrabanek 1994: 553)

'Most important findings' were made this way.

While imaging – and thus the sights that technologies made visible inside the firmly closed box – held the doubts of the life sciences at bay, physics mobilised the black box with the closed lid with no unveiling in mind. Mario Bunge, Argentine physicist and philosopher of science, for instance, asserted that,

A black box is a fiction representing a set of concrete systems into which stimuli S impinge and out of which reactions R emerge. The constitution and structure of the box are altogether irrelevant to the approach under consideration, which is purely external or phenomenological. In other words, only the behavior of the system will be accounted for. (Bunge 1963: 346)

Bunge's use of the concept of the black box was inspired by the physicist James Clerk Maxwell's *Gedankenexperiment* (thought experiment) of how to explain that molecules do not move capriciously or irregularly, but instead according to a process of sorting. To explain the natural cause of such motion that happened in a realm too miniscule to observe, William Thompson Baron Kelvin (1824–1907) invoked the idea of a small demon who, with sophistication and care, sorted hot and cold molecules inside the box (**FIGURE 20.4**):[4]

Clerk Maxwell's demon is a creature of imagination having certain perfectly well-defined powers of action, purely mechanical in their character, invented to help us to understand the "Dissipation of Energy" in nature. He is a being with no preternatural qualities [...]. Endowed ideally with arms and hands and fingers – two hands and ten fingers suffice – he can do as much for atoms as a pianoforte player can do for the keys of the piano – just a little more, he can push or pull each atom *in any direction*. (Kelvin 1891: 144–45)

FIG. 20.4 'Boxed-up Ghosts'. Maxwell illustrated with a demon how the second law of thermodynamics could be violated. The demon was the gatekeeper.

In the sciences, then, black boxes were an object of enquiry, an epistemic thing (Rheinberger 1997), and at the same time a technique and an analytical tool. As a tool and technique, the black box circumscribed and encased the given problem, and thus enabled an approximation of what can at one point be fully known. In this sense the black box also quintessentially represents the scientific values of modern times: curiosity, an explorative mind, objectivity, and empirically induced theory combined with practical approach.

OSCILLATING BOXES

This last example, however, also shows that the very nature of the black box makes it useful as a performative tool in which types of function are combined. The black box types identified above hardly ever appear in a pure form. Its changeable nature makes it attractive not only for the scientist but also for the artist – for instance, the black box in which theatre takes place (**FIGURE 20.5**).

In the theatrical world the black box holds all aspects of its ancient allure as a utilitarian and mystical space. For artists of the 1960s who turned abandoned warehouses into their studios, the black box was appealing because it was cheap to maintain and had few technical requirements apart from some simple lighting. The absence of colour on the walls, together with the lack of a set or backdrop, focused attention directly onto the performer; a darkened auditorium, susceptible to multiple configurations, enabled theatrical artists to shape relationships between the audience and stage in various ways.

At the same time, the very object (black box) turns its verbal form (blackboxing) into a tool for performing thought. The theatrical box is a liberated space, with the fourth wall – the lid – open to the imagination of the human mind, and with three blackened walls that challenge its audience to be enlightened and see. Relationships are framed on stage and thus encased, and yet simultaneously they are openly delivered and displayed.

THE CONCEPT AND THE BOX: PRACTICES UNVEILED

Historians of science and technology are studying the black boxes that were created, identified, unravelled and used, or left untouched. They look at the

FIG. 20.5 'Scenes in "the Black"'. An unadorned black box in the theatre world gives the imagination free rein. Black box theatres are also popular spaces of experimentation. The theatre itself often has a square shape, emphasising the box effect (photo: 'The Davenport Theatre – black box', by August Laska, augustlaska.com)

creators, users, consumers, and observers of what was black-boxed and, if we follow Richard Whitley's lead, they then also black-box the historical sciences themselves by studying the inputs and outputs (but not science itself): 'sociologists of science are preoccupied with the producers in a way that takes little account of what is being produced, [...] Ideas are taken as given [...]' (Whitley 1970: 61).

Whitley, by employing the black box, acknowledges its major role as a manager of knowledge, a tool that regulates access and distinguishes those who open the lid – and understand the principles and have the know-how – from those who mainly act upon what goes in and comes out. The utilitarian shell is thus the dividing line between the haves and the have-nots of knowledge.

Criticising Merton and his followers, Whitley sees the sociology of science not only as keeping barriers intentionally in place, but also adding another black box by dividing scientific ideas from their enactment. Research hence concentrates on the effects, while Whitley wants historians to concentrate on the very processes by which scientific knowledge is developed and evaluated in different spatio-temporal locations.

In his later papers Whitley then calls for an analysis of the relation between organisational structures and the cognitive structures of the sciences. This indicates that the box's shell has a working function and is no longer a dividing line. Knowledge is not separated, but boxed, to grasp why and how interaction takes place when things move from the inside out.

Since ancient times, the black box has gained contours, but while its character has developed and expanded, it has remained quintessentially the same: a useful device and performative thinking tool. In the twenty-first century, black boxes have multiplied, populating the globe and the human mind. Nearly everything can be put into a black box, even vacuum space. Black boxes can also take many complicated forms, from the bookcase to micro-space.

In the deep time view the black box is an object of the sublime, an agent of fearful somethings that are greater than ourselves. Its imaginative power transcends and yet somehow affirms humanity and its lure is the versatility that contours and frames content, even as these contours are made to fade into the background. Of central significance is the lid that, with its potential to be opened and closed, makes the black box attractive for use in the arts and sciences, as well as in human daily life. Defining in- and outside, the black box shows what matters and the relational ties of the things that matter.

NOTES

1   Girrard (1587–1670) was an English politician and the first Baronet of Harrow on the Hill (Burke and Burke 1838: 217).

2   The circuit was invented by Samuel Hunter Christie (1784–1865) in 1833.

3   This notion is often implicit in the idea of magic, as discussed by William A. Stahl (1995).

4   James Maxwell speaks of a *Gedankenexperiment* in a letter to Peter G. Tait. William Thompson Baron Kelvin then calls Maxwell's trigger for the sorting of cold and hot molecules a demon in Kelvin 1891: 144–47. For the original theory see Maxwell 1908.

REFERENCES

Asensio, J., and O. Roca, 'Evaluation of Transport Infrastructure Projects beyond Cost-Benefit Analysis. An Application to Barcelona's 4th Ring Road', *International Journal of Transport Economics/Rivista internazionale di economia dei trasporti*, 29.2 (2002): 231–33.

Behe, M. J., *Darwin's Black Box: The Biochemical Challenge to Evolution* (New York/London: Free Press, 1996).

Bunge, M., 'A General Black Box Theory', *Philosophy of Science*, 30.4 (1963): 346–58.

Burke, J., and J. B. Burke, *A Genealogical and Heraldic History of the Extinct and Dormant Baronetcies of England* (London: Scott, Webster, and Geary, 1838).

Cavicchi, E., 'Thing Knowledge: A Philosophy of Scientific Instruments', *Technology and Culture*, 46.1 (2005): 243–45.

Coke, R., *A Detection of the Court and State of England during the Four Last Reigns and the Inter-regnum Consisting of Private Memoirs, &c., with Observations and Reflections, and an Appendix, Discovering the Present State of the Nation: Wherein are Many Secrets Never Before Made Publick: As also, a More Impartiall Account of the Civil Wars in England, than Has yet Been Given: in Two Volumes* (London, 1697).

Hong, S., *Wireless: From Marconi's Black-Box to the Audion* (Cambridge: MIT Press, 2001).

Kelvin, W. T., *Popular Lectures and Addresses*, vol. 1: Constitution of matter, 2nd edn (London and New York: Macmillan and Co., 1891).

Latour, B., *Pandoras Hope: Essays on the Reality of Science Studies* (Cambridge: Harvard University Press, 1999).

Maxwell, J. C., et al., *Theory of Heat 1871* (London/New York: Longmans Green, 1908).

Morus, I. R., *Frankenstein's Children: Electricity, Exhibition and Experiment in Early-Nineteenth-Century London* (Princeton: Princeton University Press, 1998).

Nersessian, N. J., 'Opening the Black Box: Cognitive Science and History of Science', *Osiris*, 10 (1995): 194–211.

Neufchotz de Jassy, O., 'The Mythological Hebrew Terms Explained by the Sanskrit', *The Monist*, 18.1 (1908): 126–42.

Pinch, T. J., 'Opening Black Boxes: Science, Technology and Society', *Social Studies of Science*, 22.3 (1992): 487–510.

Pregadio, F., *The Encyclopedia of Taoism*, 2 vols. (London: Routledge, 2008).

Rheinberger, H.-J., *Toward a History of Epistemic Things: Synthesizing Proteins in the Test Tube* (Stanford, CA: Stanford University Press, 1997).

Rosenberg, N., *Exploring the Black Box: Technology, Economics and History* (Cambridge: Cambridge University Press, 1994).

Rosoff, P. M., 'In Search of the Mommy Gene: Truth and Consequences in Behavioral Genetics', *Science, Technology, & Human Values*, 35.2 (2010): 200–43.

Science News, 'Lie Detector Doesn't', in *Science News Letter* 49.13 (30 March 1946).

Shiers, G., *The Electric Telegraph: An Historical Anthology* (New York: Arno Press, 1977).

Skinner, B. F., *Contingencies of Reinforcement: A Theoretical Analysis* (New York: Appleton-Century-Crofts, 1969).

——, *Walden Two* (Indianapolis: Hackett Publishing, 1976, reprint 2005).

Skrabanek, P., 'The Emptiness of the Black Box', *Epidemiology*, 5.5 (1994): 553–55.

Smith, R. W., and J. N. Tatarewicz, 'Counting on Invention: Devices and Black Boxes in Very Big Science', *Osiris*, 9 [Instruments] (1994): 101–23.

Stahl, W. A., 'Venerating the Black Box: Magic in Media Discourse on Technology', *Science, Technology, & Human Values*, 20.2 (Spring 1995): 234–58.

Whitley, R., 'Black Boxism and the Sociology of Science', *Sociological Review*, 18/S1 (1970): 61–92.

Zhu Xi (1130–1200), *Zhuzi yulei* 朱子語類 (Classified Conversations of Master Zhu), vol. 1, *juan 10* (Beijing: Zhonghua Shuju, 1986), 1:10:170.

VI

TEXT

21

Panels and Frames

Toward a New Relationship Between Text and Image in Academic Writing

Pit Arens and Martina Schlünder

Content: story (pictures, texts, events, thoughts). **Species:** text box, picture box, third box (hybrid box). **Other Names:** speech balloons, panels, frames. **Family:** storytelling boxes. **Size and Shape:** various. **Habitat:** comic stips, grapic novels, visual essays, zines. **Origin/First observed:** popular media. **Distribution:** worldwide. **Behaviour:** viral. **Migration:** spotted with increasing frequency bleeding in the accademosphere, certain disciplines are more receptive. **Status:** ubquitous.

Keywords: storytelling, containing, sequencing, separating, fragmenting, associating, connecting, building, hybridising

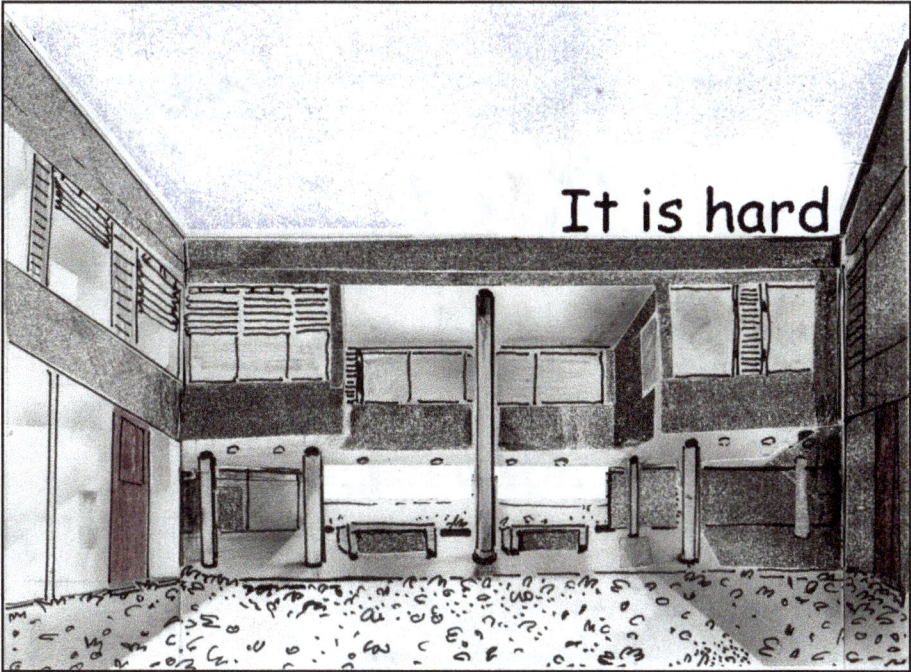

It is hard

to recognise the rules, hierarchies and orders inside the box of academic writing. Everything seems so naturally in place. **When writing academic papers, one does not usually problematise its familiar forms. Questioning starts when one gets to the margins.** Then you realise that

academic writing takes place in a box whose walls are made of many unasked questions.

...... for the between / instance relation text

and pictures

in historiography.

Inside the box, images are used as

illustrations

for an argument, as evidence that

has to be spelled out and written down. Or

images appear as 'enigmatic' pictures

...have to described explained / be and in the

text.

Visual material is dominated by text. It can't

stand for itself.

It is too ambiguous

– not clear enough academic / -cut for an argument.

happens

when your sources suddenly start pushing you

against the walls of

the box? your comes / When material clear

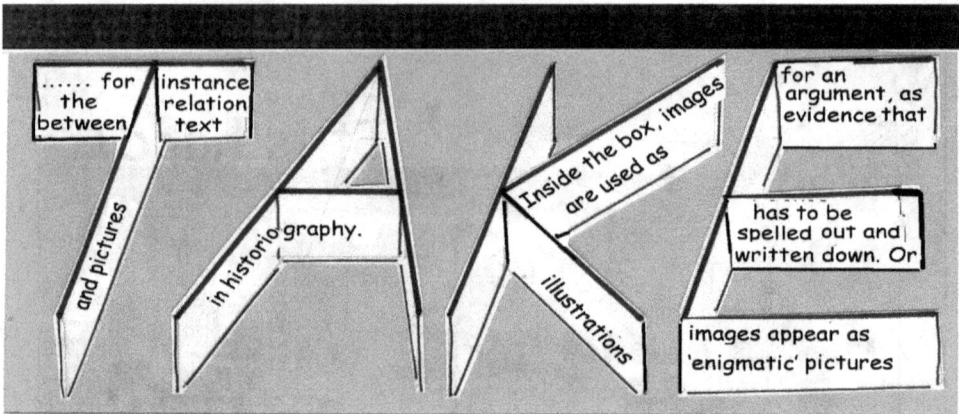

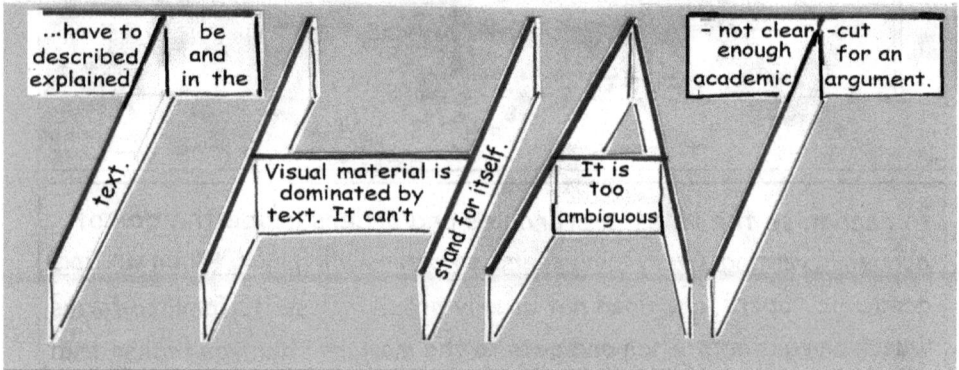

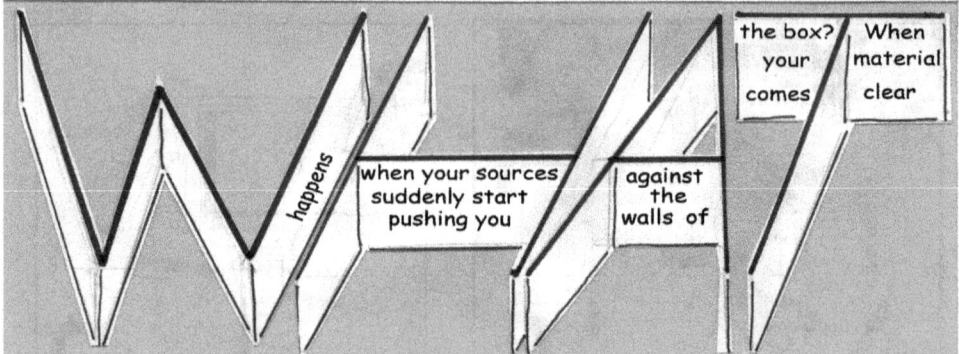

and argues visually that there is much more in images than that tiny portion of unambiguous text is able to squeeze from pictures?[1]

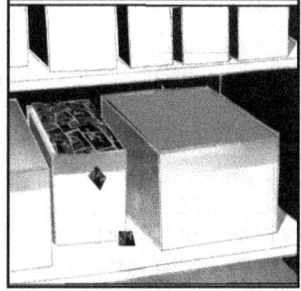

In a research project on the history of orthopedic surgery in Switzerland after World War II and the emergence of osteosynthesis — operative fracture care with metal implants like plates and screws — we came across the experimental animals (sheep) of these surgeons and their experimental stable; a high-tech facility at a research institute in the Swiss Alps. While taking pictures to document the status quo, we also tried to find documents on the history of the stable and its inhabitants. We started to track down the history of "bone sheep", (as we called them) since the material these new lab animals delivered was bones instead of wool or meat. [2]

Finding archival material turned out to be extraordinarily difficult until we gained access to the 'picture library' of the research institute. A real avalanche of different kinds of images burst out: historical slides from the mid 1960s when the surgeons became sheep breeders and sheep holders on their own, the development of the stables, and also the images that were co-produced by sheep: X-rays, macro and micro histological pictures, tables, drawings for academic papers....

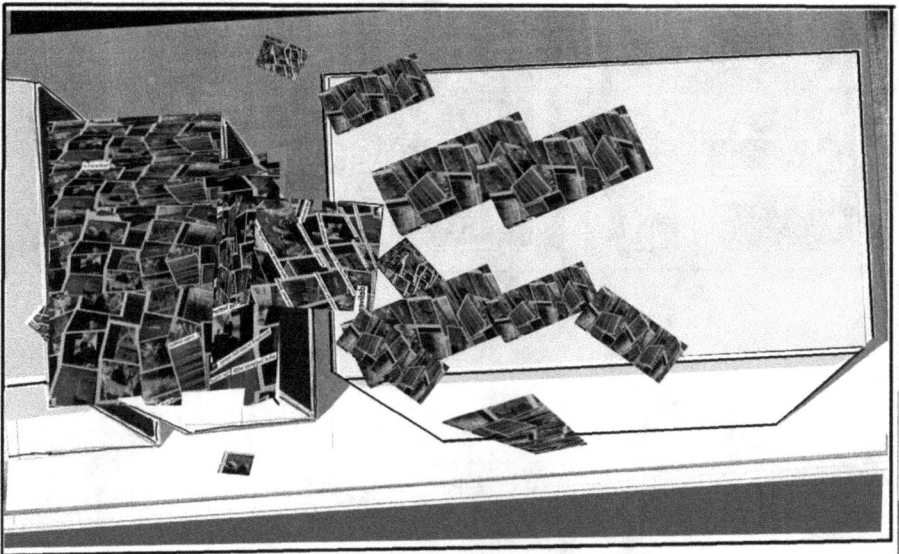

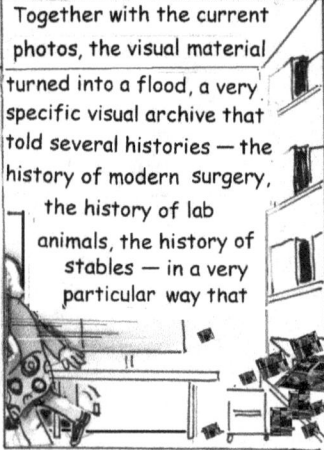

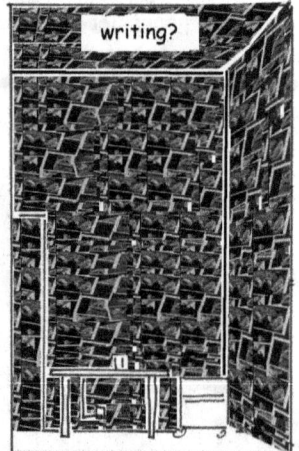

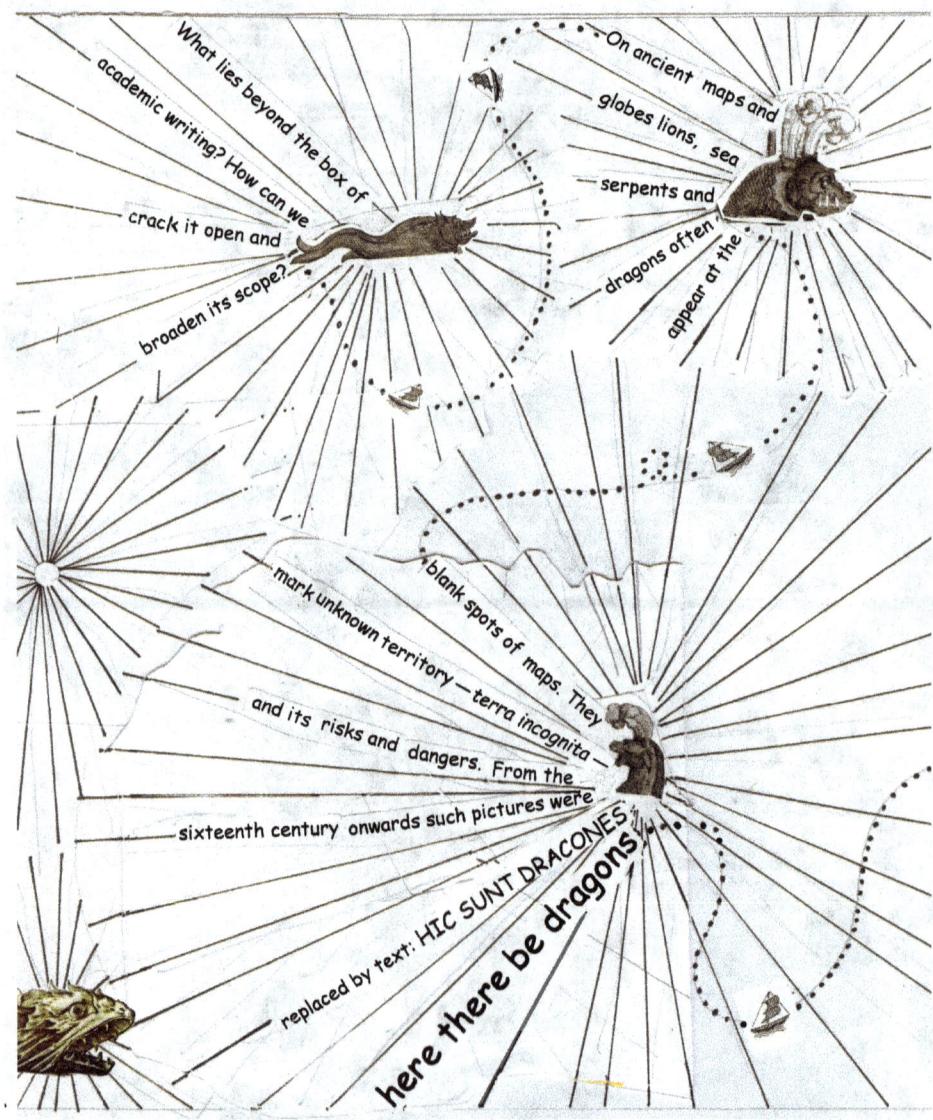

What lies beyond the box of academic writing? How can we crack it open and broaden its scope?

On ancient maps and globes lions, sea serpents and dragons often appear at the blank spots of maps. They mark unknown territory — terra incognita — and its risks and dangers. From the sixteenth century onwards such pictures were replaced by text: HIC SUNT DRACONES

here there be dragons

We have to sail into the terra incognita of academic writing if we want to change the relation between image and text.

In his cartography of academic essays Sean Sturm (2012) differentiates between expository and exploratory essays.[3] The traditional academic expository essay displays knowledge and works like an epistemic round trip. Its trajectory is well known and is completely tautological: it always ends where it has begun. The exploratory essay, however, works like a trip into *terra incognita* where the risks of unpleasant encounters loom — or the excitement of new knowledge! In short, it leads straight into the blank spots where the dragons are — or in our case:

HIC SUNT OVES – here be sheep!

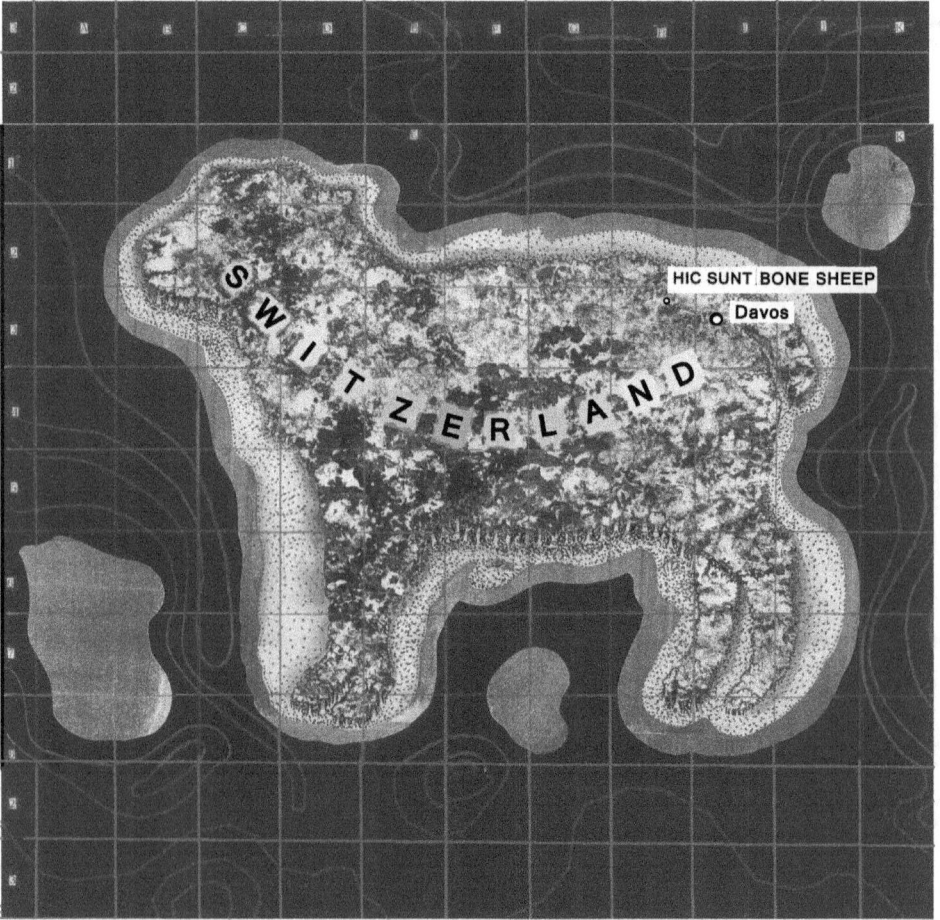

What does a visual trip into *the terra incognita* of sheep look like? In our journey into the dangers of the unknown, we took inspiration from both the exploratory essay and from the art of comic strips and graphic novels. Comics are the genre most open for mixing words and images. Though the visual part is predom inant, text is not subordi nated to pictures; on the cont rary, in comics both are mixed in most artful ways McCloud 2006: 128—140). They can also give insights into subjective and emotional aspects. Mostly drawn, they also integrate other kinds of visual material like paintings and photographs (Guibert, Levévre, and Lemercier 2009).

wörter, wörter, wörter, wörter, wörter, wörter,
wörter, wörter, wörter, wörter, wörter, wörter, wörter,
wörter, wörter, wörter, wörter, wörter, wörter, wörter,
wörter, wörter, wörter, wörter, wörter, wörter, wörter,
wörter, wörter, wörter, wörter, wörter, wörter, wörter, wörter,
wörter, wörter, wörter, wörter, wörter, wörter, wörter, wörter, wörter, wörter,
wörter, wörter, wörter, wörter, wörter,

We modified both genres. To the exploratory academic essay we added pictures. In contrast to comics and their focus on storytelling we set dialogues aside. Our story is strictly based on empirical material that was

researched in archives and through ethnographies. The story is centered on sheep-encounters, which also resulted in a narrative that is — similar to academic papers — not based on dialogues. We also inserted several personal experiences in cases that were so important redirected course research that they the of the Like all

academic papers we analyzed and generalized our data, though we preferred heuristic analysis to the more systematic one that is the preferred style of expository essays. Generalizations were not restricted to text and words, and we strove to make visual arguments and generalizations.

We are now zooming through several techniques that we used to illuminate the nexus between the medium of visual

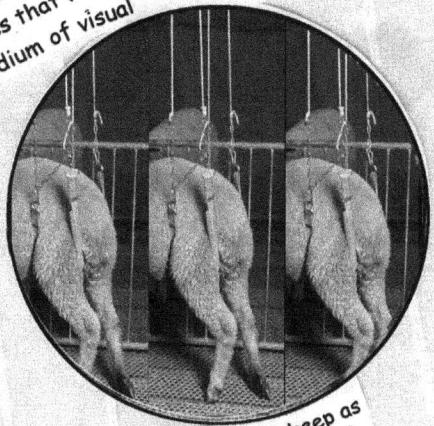

essays, the boxes practice, and our topic: the emergence of bone sheep as lab animals in orthopaedic surgery (Schlünder, Arens and Gerhardt 2014).

We especially look into the way events are sequenced, the space in-between panel boxes, the relation between

text (box) and image box, and how scaling, perspective and generalization are intertwined. But first we will give an overview of containment devices in (visual) storytelling.

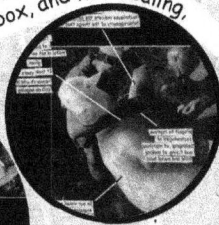

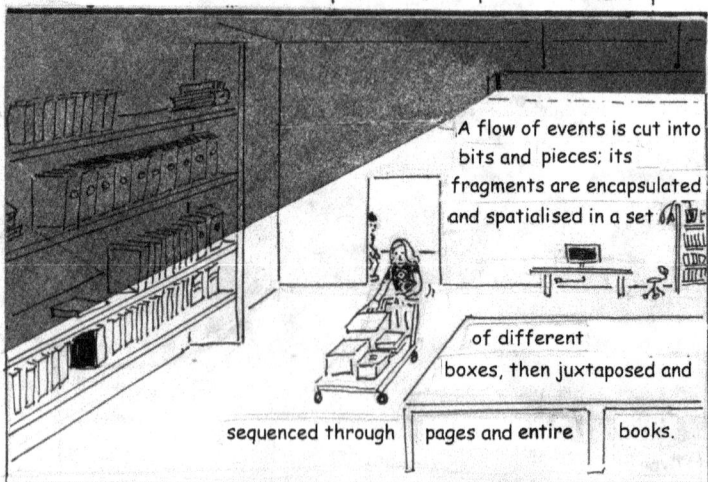

The boxes work in different ways. They contain text and pictures that can be part of a dialogue, of inner contemplations, of outcries, or just sound.

They convey action, time and emotions by their form, and the types of lettering, lining, composition and perspective.

By cutting a flow of action and storing the fragments in different species of containers, a story emerges. (4) The way of cutting — how specific moments of the flow of action are "frozen" and displayed in layers of sequenced boxes (panels) — sets the timing and rhythm of the story.

The visual material that we used for our essay captures this important strand of modern surgery:

the push to increased standardisation and regulation, to efficiency, time management and greater division of labour. During the twentieth century orthopaedic surgery

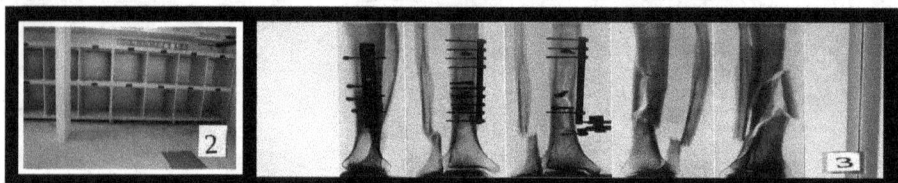

absorbed the principles of Taylorism, the scientific management of labour, the rationalisation

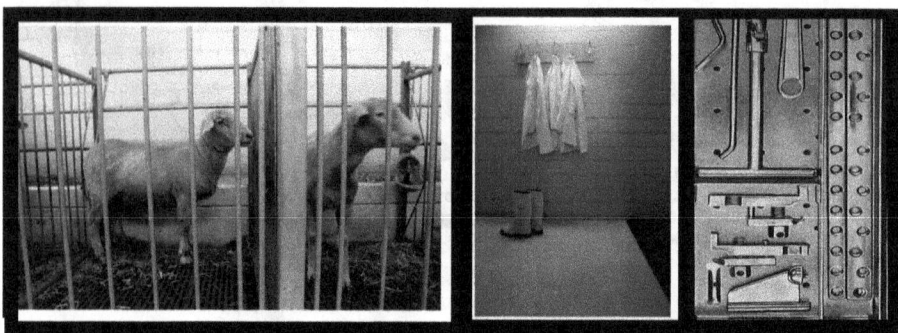

of workflows, and the adaption of practices and norms of the assembly line (Schlich 2009).

The principles of modularity, of dis-mantling and re-assembling, of synchronising, standardising and matching are omnipresent in the organisation of the workflow as well as in the material

culture, for instance in the plates, and screws, but also in the pens, with their compartmentalisation,

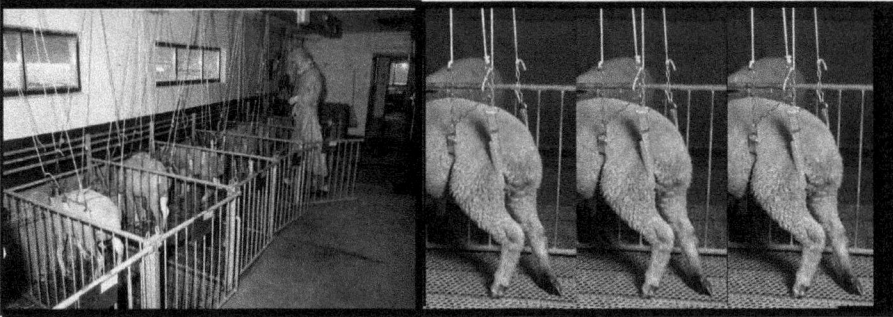

their grates, their fodder racks and suspension systems that help to reduce the pain of operated

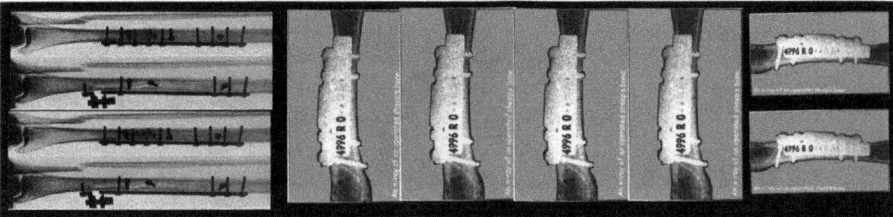

sheep. Thus, these practices can be found in the very heart of surgery — in the operating room — but also in its extended environment, the wards and in our case the stable and its stockrooms.

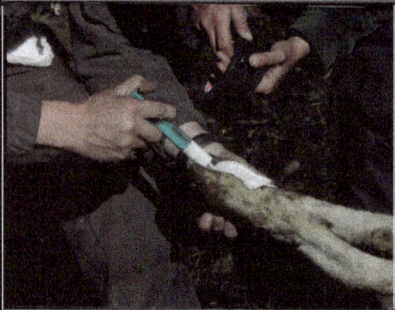

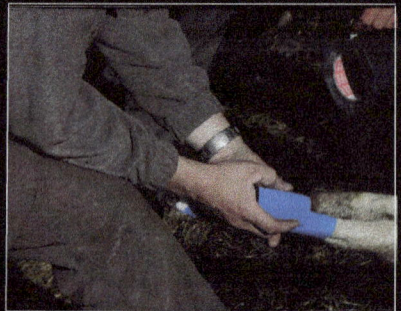

There is a correspondence between cutting and stitching in surgery, its assembly techniques, and the mix and split technique in comics and film editing which one can also find in literature and especially in exploratory essays. All these genres tell their stories in fragments.

Putting ▮ these pieces ▮ in boxes,
and ▮ afterwards ▮ into a
sequence, ▮ results in ▮ the production
of gaps ▮ between ▮ panels.
Readers ▮ have to ▮ fill in what
happens ▮ in the ▮ empty space
between ▮ the boxes. ▮ A silent,
'secret' ▮ contract ▮ between author
and ▮ audience ▮ is needed to
tell ▮ the story. ▮ This contract relies

on the principle of 'closure' (McCloud 1993: 60—69). By filling in the invisible action between two boxes the reader's imagination works like a third box that 'takes two separate images and trans-forms them into a single idea'(McCloud 1993:66). Audience and author must share similar ex:-

periences ▮ since closure ▮ is performed
by experience ▮ and imagination. ▮ Readers thus
are more active ▮ and entangled with the ▮ process of making a
story than ▮ the traditional ▮ academic scholar
who — ▮ as a reader ▮ usually consumes
the knowledge ▮ that is presented ▮ in the paper.[5]
In exploratory ▮ essays the reader ▮ is involved in the
emergence ▮ of knowledge, its ▮ possibilities and
uncertainties.

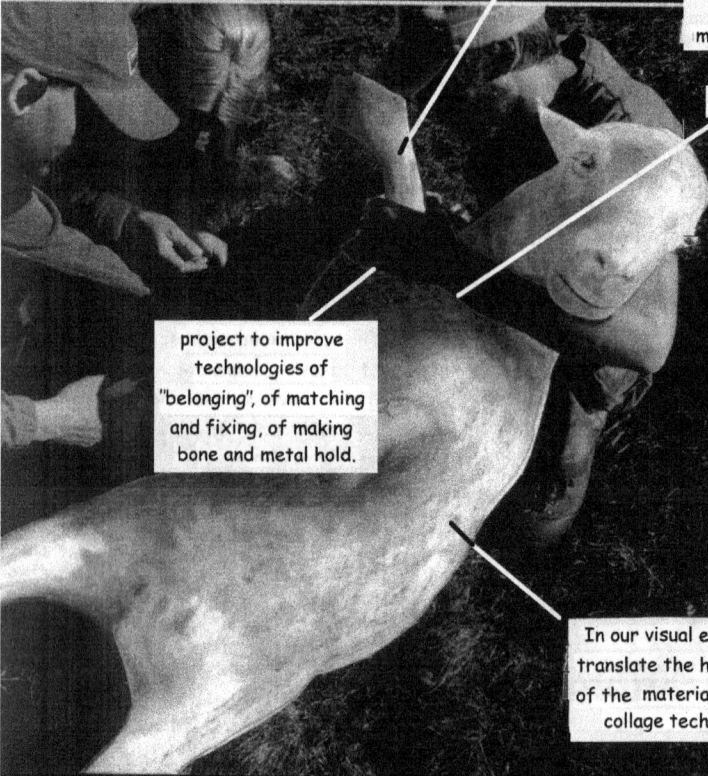

In contrast to most comics, our essay co-mixes historical visual material — photos, X-rays, graphs — and combines it with text and pictures from a visual ethnography of bone sheep and their stable. We do so since we think this hybridisation is a characteristic trait of the story the article tells, of our research tools — and our research field more generally — where diverse ways of knowing come together, where bone and metal are associated in a new way.[6]

Like all academic texts, our visual essay is not only a personal story. It also implies generalisations, though they mostly occur through visual arguments. In our visual essay on 'Bone Sheep,' we tried to understand how sheepness is produced and how to capture it visually. (7) On the farm, sheep live as a flock. This is what keeps them alive, what gives rhythm to their days. Even the stable at the farm is taking part in the production of this specific flock sheepness. One

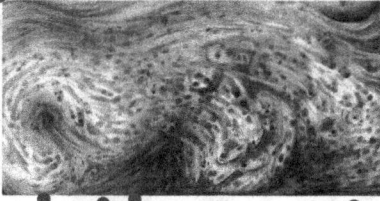

side of the stable is open and there are no compartments so that sheep have enough space to move as a flock. You can experience this yourself when you try to enter the flock and a white mass of bodies starts spinning around you; you feel in the eye of a tornado that carefully avoids making contact with you.

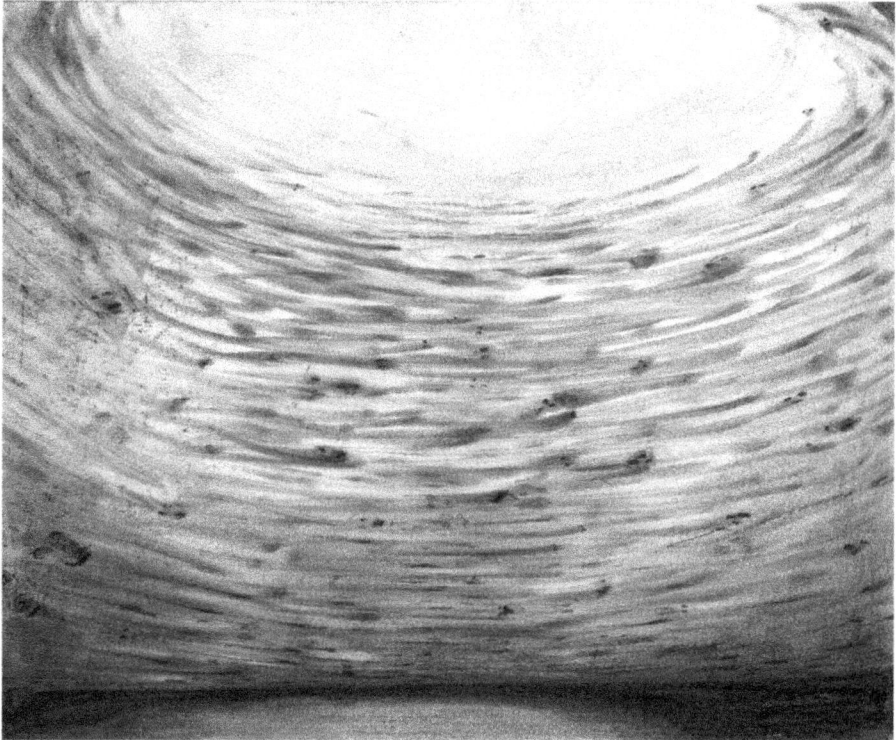

Sheep are de-flocked in the stable at the research institute. They become individual lab animals. In the logic of research, this is necessary for the production of reliable facts. Only later, having generated data, the individual sheep disappears again into a flock of aggregated data. Another form of sheepness emerges in the lab stable.

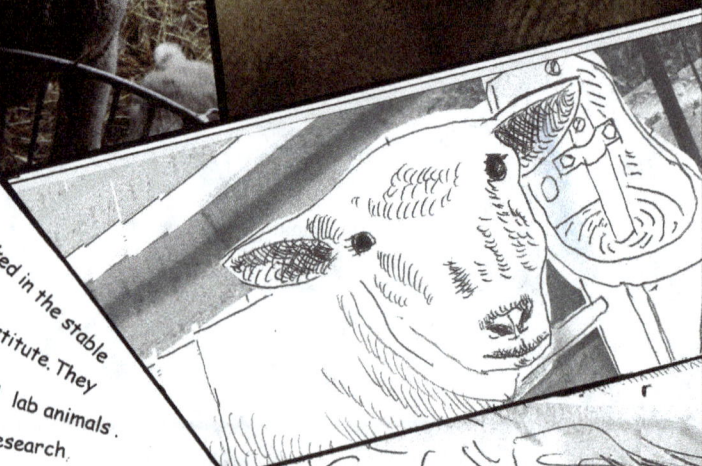

While producing data, sheep

are almost not moving. They

stand, and look, and eat,

and stand, and

look...

Cartooning is a way of
generalising and it brings the
sheepness of the lab stable
to the fore. In comics, it is
a form of turning a very
realistic image, for instance
a photo, into a more iconic one
with considerably less detail, a
drawing. It strips an image down to
its essential meaning
(McCloud 1993: 30). Though it
consists of fewer details,
it is not so much a process of elimination
as it is a process of
intensification.[8]

experimenting with image and text generated a list of questions, fragments causality and

experimenting with image and text generates a lot of questions, triggers curiosity, and sets free new dynamics.

what new forms

of relationship

...sible

between

wor ds

and images

are

possible?

Appendix

For this tableau we took our inspiration from studying miniatures
in medieval illuminated manuscripts. The first
letter of a text was usually enlarged and filled
with geometrical or zoomorphic elements. We

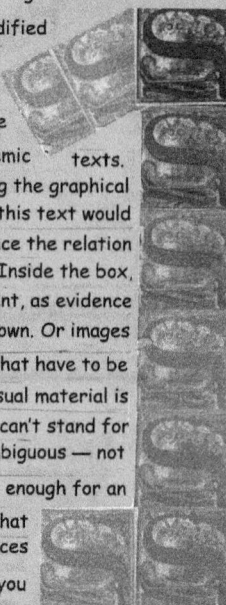

modified   this into the direction of
further   letters — letters
inhabiting   bigger ones in order to
emphasise the   importance of writing over
image in academic   texts.   But we also looked for a
form for highlighting the graphical   and visual elements of writing.
In a traditional paper this text would   read:
'Take for instance the relation   between text and pictures in
historiography. Inside the box,   images are used as illustrations
for an argument, as evidence   that has to be spelled out
and written down. Or images   appear as "enigmatic"
pictures that have to be   described and explained
in the text. Visual material is   dominated by text.
It can't stand for   itself. It is too
ambiguous — not   clear-cut
enough for an   academic argument.
What   happens when
your sources   suddenly
start pushing you   against the walls

of the box? When your material comes clear and argues visually that
there is much more in images than that tiny portion of
unambiguous text is able to squeeze from pictures?'

The method of osteosynthesis was developed by a group of Swiss surgeons who named themselves AO (Arbeits gemeinschaft Osteo synthese fragen) which translates to "working group on problems of osteo synthesis". For the history of the AO see Schlich 2002; for the history of the veterinary branch of the AO, the AO- Vet see Auer et al. 2013 ; for the history of 'Bone Sheep' see our visual essay Schlünder et al. 2014.

The "dragon" and "sheep" maps on this page and the previous and the following ones are inspired by psychogeographical experiences during field work in Switzerland. For psychogeography see McDonough 2002; we started with psychogeographical excursions in 2000 during a project on Ludwik Fleck`s life and work ‹http://www.ludwik-fleck-kreis.org/index.php›. Beyond the English-speaking part of the world, the expository essay is often not called an essay. The label "essay" is reserved for Sturm`s second type, the exploratory essay (Bude 1989). Michel Montaigne (1533—1592) is usually credited with the development of this genre. In German literature of the the twentieth century it was Robert Musil (1930/1995) who developed the format into a concept ("Essayismus") and an experimental style of writing to reflect the effects of modernism. Ludwik Fleck (1896—1961) differentiates in his epistemology (1979/1935) between two types of experiments that come very close to Sturm's order.

Experiments in life science are often (at the start of an new experimental system) irreproducible, uncertain, incomplete, and unique (this would be Sturm's exploratory essay). Fleck considers these kinds of experiments to have enormous heuristic value: 'When experiments become certain, precise and reproducible at any time, they are no longer neccesary for research purposes proper but function only for demonstration [...]' (Fleck 1979/1935: 85). Exploratory essays and experimental practices are closely related.

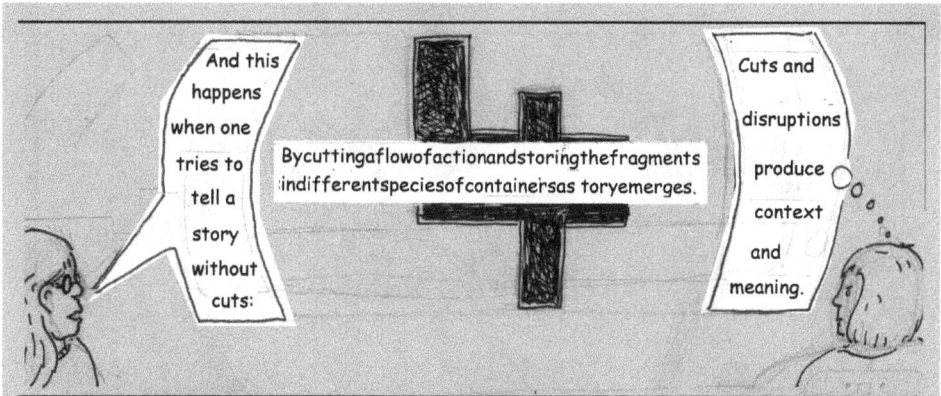

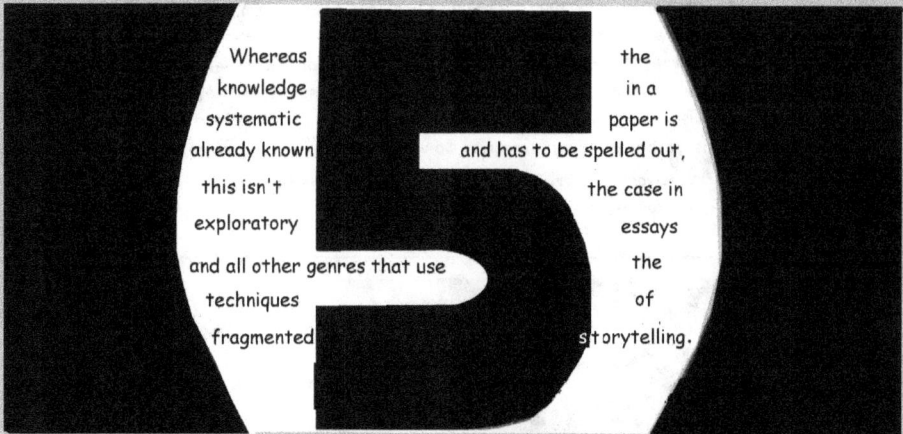

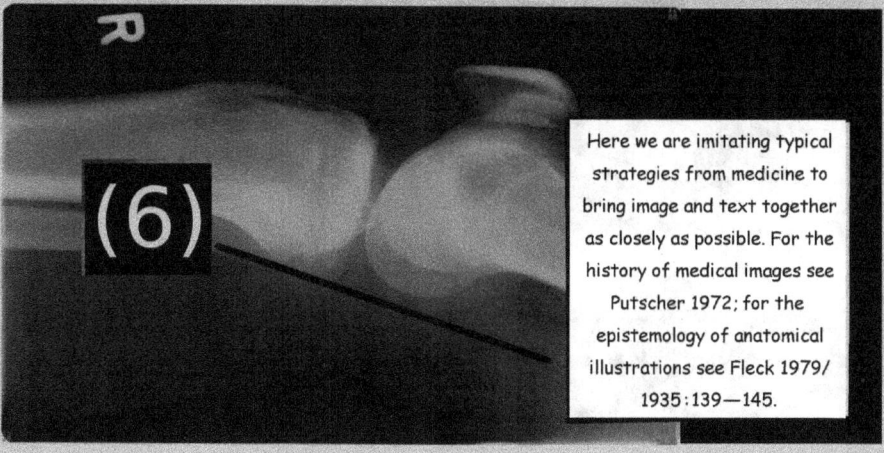

(**7**)

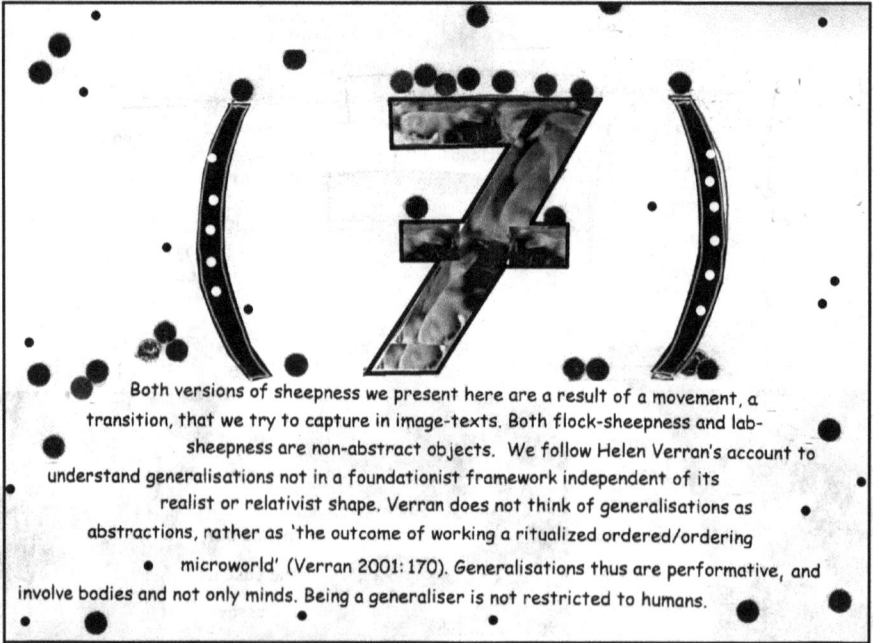

Both versions of sheepness we present here are a result of a movement, a transition, that we try to capture in image-texts. Both flock-sheepness and lab-sheepness are non-abstract objects. We follow Helen Verran's account to understand generalisations not in a foundationist framework independent of its realist or relativist shape. Verran does not think of generalisations as abstractions, rather as 'the outcome of working a ritualized ordered/ordering microworld' (Verran 2001: 170). Generalisations thus are performative, and involve bodies and not only minds. Being a generaliser is not restricted to humans.

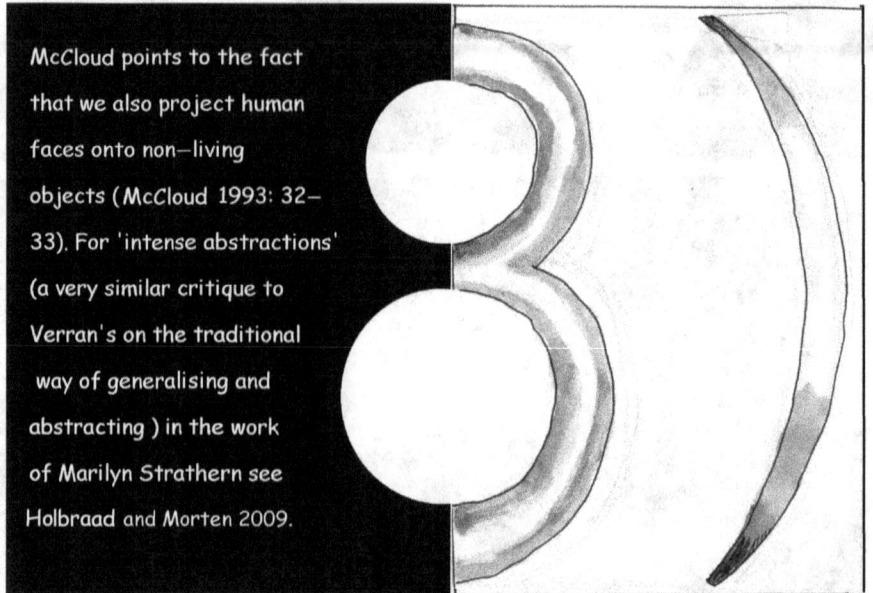

McCloud points to the fact that we also project human faces onto non—living objects (McCloud 1993: 32–33). For 'intense abstractions' (a very similar critique to Verran's on the traditional way of generalising and abstracting) in the work of Marilyn Strathern see Holbraad and Morten 2009.

References

Auer, Jörg, Pohler Ortrun, Schlünder, Martina, Kása, Ferenc, Kása, Gerhild, von Salis, Björn, Fackelman, Gustav, *History of AOVET—The First 40 Years* (Davos: AO Foundation, 2013).

Bude, Heinz, 'Der Essay als Form der Darstellung sozialwissenschaftlicher Erkenntnisse', *Kölner Zeitschrift für Soziologie und Sozialpsychologie* 41/3 (1989): 526–539.

Eisner, Will, *Comics and Sequential Art. Principles and Practice of the World's Most Popular Art Form* (Tamarac: Poorhouse Press, 1985).

Fleck, Ludwik, *Genesis and Development of a Scientific Fact* (Chicago: University of Chicago Press, 1979, first published in German 1935).

Guibert, Emmanuel, Lefèvre, Didier, Lemercier, Frederic, *The Photographer* (New York: First Second Books, 2009).

Holbraad, Martin, Pedersen, Morten Axel, 'Planet M: The Instense Abstractions of Marilyn Strathern', *Anthropological Theory* 9 (2009): 371–394.

McCloud, Scott, *Understanding Comics*: *The Invisible Art* (New York: Harper Collins, 1993).

McDonough, Tom (ed.), *Guy Debord and the Situationist International: Texts and Documents* (Cambridge, MA: MIT Press, 2002).

Musil, Robert, *The Man Without Qualities*, Vol 1 (London: Basingstoke, 1995, first published in German 1930).

Putscher, Marielene, *Geschichte der medizinischen Abbildung II. Von 1600 bis zur Gegenwart* (München: Heinz Moos Verlag, 1972).

Schlich, Thomas, Surgery, Science, and Industry: A Revolution in Fracture Care 1950s—1990s (Houndsmill: Palgrave, 2002).

Schlich, Thomas, 'The Perfect Machine': Lorenz Böhler's Rationalized Fracture Treatment in World War I', *Isis* 100 (2009): 758–791.

Schlünder, Martina, Arens, Pit, Gerhardt, Axel, 'Becoming Bone Sheep', *Configurations*, 22 (2014): 263–292.

Sturm, Sean, 'Terra (in)cognita: Mapping Academic Writing', *TEXT* 16/2 (2012) <http://www.textjournal.com.au/oct12/sturm.htm>.

Verran, Helen, *Science and an African Logic* (Chicago: University of Chicago Press, 2001).

FIG. 22.1 *Haberling Sicherheitsbehälter* at the Max Planck Institute for the History of Science: a locked container that securely stores documents prior to their being shredded (photo by Sarah Blacker)

FIG. 22.2 Paper shredder at the Max Planck Institute for the History of Science, with a view of the interior box collecting shredded remnants (photo by Martina Schlünder)

22

ANALOGUE PRIVACY: THE PAPER SHREDDER AS A TECHNOLOGY FOR KNOWLEDGE DESTRUCTION

Sarah Blacker

Box name: the paper shredder. Other names: Aktenvernichter (German, meaning 'file annihilator'). **Size and shape**: size and shape vary by geographic location and family type. Larger models bred for institutional settings can grow up to 760 x 580 x 1540 mm (see **FIGURE 22.2**). Smaller shredders, typically found in closets of apartment-dwelling humans, can measure only 296 x 161 x 297 mm (see **FIGURE 22.3**). **Appearance**: metallic, cold, and sometimes dusty. The metallic box is enlivened – its shredding function superseding its boxness and capacity for storage – when the electrical cord attached to the box is joined with an electrical outlet. **Behaviour**: regular, machinic, robotic, predictable. Incapable of discrimination. Equal opportunity destroyer. Except in the case of the so-called 'paper jam', which indicates the shredder's capacity for resistance, for overriding its commands, and saving rather than destroying. Could pose a fire hazard if overfilled, thus potentially enacting a form of meta-destruction of its own habitat. **Habitat**: in hidden places – corners, closets, and beneath desks – unless its use becomes the primary focus (at moments of urgently-required dismantling, erasing, moving, cleaning), in which case the shredder migrates to spaces of increased visibility and prominence. **Migration/ Distribution**: often found in hallways or in closets, the shredder shies away from excessive visibility. The shredder frequently stands next to its distant cousin, the paper recycling box, which stores and redistributes printed material, but, unlike the voracious shredder, does not destroy it. **Status**: population growth remains robust despite the 'digital revolution' that was framed as a threat to the population's survival in the early 2000s.

Keywords: fragmenting, concealing, secret-keeping, history-erasing, voracious, protective, incriminating, unappeasable, insatiable, compulsive, desirous, waste-producing, destructive, defiant

FIG. 22.3 Hama paper shredder (designed for home use; photo by Sarah Blacker)

To shred: 'to cut or hack in pieces' (OED).
Shredder: 'a machine for reducing documents to small unreadable fragments' (OED).
Fragment: 'A detached, isolated, or incomplete part; a part remaining or still preserved when the whole is lost or destroyed' (OED).

THE PAPER SHREDDER COULD ALSO BE CALLED A FRAGMENTATION MACHINE. Within the enclosure of its boxness, the shredder fragments the components of knowledge to the point at which they are no longer legible, no longer circulable, and no longer able to serve as evidence. By producing detachment, isolation, and incompleteness within a body of knowledge, the shredding box reverses the wheels of knowledge production. No longer marching onwards and upwards, knowledge production grinds to a halt as the shredder shifts the direction of production into reverse. The point is no longer accumulation, but the backwards motion of undoing what has already been done, unsaying what has been said, and preventing this knowledge from producing the transformative (and potentially damaging) effects that are expected to follow from its circulation.

Does its form as a box play a deterministic role in shaping the paper shredder's politics? While the shredding box's metal teeth render all that passes through them irreversibly illegible, the politics that this function enacts are not mono-dimensional or easily categorisable. Though paper passes through the shredder in one direction only (see **FIGURE 22.4**), and with a single epistemological result – destruction – the disappearance enacted can serve wildly different interests. The twin purposes of the paper shredder – to preserve security/privacy and to effect an imagined total form of destruction; to keep, store, save, but also to eliminate – are in fact deeply intertwined. Security can be preserved through the destruction of circulable materials. Security is threatened when circulable materials fall into the wrong hands. The shredder ensures that circulable materials never fall into the wrong hands. But in producing this security, the shredder also introduces the possibility that the printed materials will never fall into any

FIG. 22.4 The paper shredder's metal 'teeth', spinning shaft, and paper fragments produced. Friesens Corporation, Altona, Manitoba, Canada, 2011 (photo by Rosemarie and Pat Keough; reprinted with permission from Rosemarie and Pat Keough)

hands at all – including those of the historian and the archive waiting to preserve the knowledge that would otherwise pass into oblivion.[1]

What does it mean for knowledge[2] to pass into oblivion? For historians, the absence of archival documents is the stuff of nightmares – without them, how can the roots of today's norms, institutions, and ways of knowing be understood? Oblivion comes from the Latin *oblivio*, meaning 'forgetfulness, state of being forgotten, amnesty' (OED). Why do we need to ensure access to amnesty or the act of being pardoned as we participate in the production of knowledge? Why do we need to leave open the possibility of forgetfulness? What sorts of roles are played by infrastructures of forgetting (Bowker 2005)? We often think of work around knowledge as a linear, cumulative, and fundamentally *productive* activity, and a fundamental good in this very productivity, regardless of its lack of moral compass. But knowledge production is always risky. We need methods through which mis-steps can be erased, and, often, methods by which whole bodies of knowledge can disappear in the context of a change in political regime, when such knowledge becomes the enemy of power.

The effectiveness of the paper shredder in destroying knowledge tells us a great deal about the character of the knowledge that can be destroyed. Quality 1: a sense of wholeness (such that fragmentation can be the enemy of knowledge). Quality 2: legibility. Quality 3: corruptibility (the speed and ease with which a document can be altered threatens its robustness as a form of knowledge. While the social and political stabilisation of knowledge enacted by paper technology has always been inconsistent and uneven, digital documents have been understood as essentially volatile and unduly prone to corruption. One of the reasons that the digital is understood as volatile is that digital documents are seen as having skipped over processes of editing and of printing, both of which slow down the production of documents and lend a quality of evidenceness through the sense that the document has been 'checked' by multiple sets of eyes, with the result that corruption is less likely to reach the printed page). Quality 4: capacity to be circulated (previously: paper-ness, and now: digitality). The paper shredder, of course, is an analogue technology. Its closest relative in the digital era is the Right to Be Forgotten legislation (see the chapter on Dropbox and the impossibility of digital forgetting by Shih-Pei Chen, in this volume). Concerns surrounding the security of data in the online context have not yet eclipsed those of paper security. The shredder has not become obsolete in the digital era; shredding technology persists in both visual and auditory forms in today's computer programs, allowing for the virtual 'shredding' of documents. Many computer programs mimic the sounds made by paper shredding machines when the computer user deletes a document, and the visual icon denoting the computer's 'trash can' renders this destructive computer function visually legible to the computer user, who is assumed to be familiar with the paper shredder from non-virtual experience of using it.

The inventor of the paper shredder is acknowledged as Abbot Augustus Low, of Horseshoe, New York, who was granted a patent for his 'waste-paper receptacle' in 1909 (see **FIGURE 22.5**). In his patent application, Low describes his machine as one that provides 'improved means for disposing of waste paper' (1909: 1). By 'improved means', Low is referring to the machine's destructive tendencies. Low emphasises the ambivalent value of paper documents, noting that what we think of as the 'safe-keeping' of printed materials might not best take place in a filing cabinet, but instead in a box designed to make these documents – and all traces of their existence – disappear. He notes that the 'waste-paper receptacle' will be used 'in offices and other places where not only the collection and storage of waste paper is desirable, but also its cancellation or mutilation in such a manner as to render it unavailable or unintelligible for re-use or for information' (Low 1909: 1). Low's box, then, was designed to put dangerous documents to rest once and for all; in limiting printed materials' circulability and readability, authors and collectives were seeking to avoid accountability for the social and political fallout of these materials. The enthusiasm and energy imbuing the text of Low's patent application departs significantly from the cold, rational language usually used to describe storage methods in this period. The prospect of destruction can indeed produce levity! Low's description of the mechanism through which paper is fragmented within the box characterises paper as a sort of menace that must be contained, its powers curtailed. He writes: 'The invention consists primarily of a receptacle having a cutting or cancelling device interposed between it and a receiving hopper, whereby the papers are disintegrated and rendered useless as such before they enter the body of the receptacle' (Low 1909: 1). Low goes on to describe the risks one incurs if one does not make the practice of paper shredding as regular as other self-maintenance practices. He warns that printed materials can be appropriated by criminals and used to commit fraud, and, further, that 'the presence of papers scattered around promiscuously' in one's home or office increases the risk of fire (Low 1909: 1–2). These risks can be managed by the regular use of Low's 'waste-paper receptacle', whose name does not yet betray its destructive tendencies, instead suggesting a benign and protective function akin to that of a filing cabinet.

Unaware of Low's invention, the shopkeeper and member of the anti-Nazi resistance movement, Adolf Ehinger, invented the paper shredder again in Germany, in 1936 (Woestendiek 2002). As part of his political efforts, Ehinger printed texts supporting the resistance movement and decrying the actions of the Nazis. The activity of printing such materials for circulation was undoubtedly risky; for Ehinger, the development of a device that could destroy such materials became necessary when one of his neighbours found one of the printed anti-Nazi documents and threatened to file a report with the Nazi authorities documenting

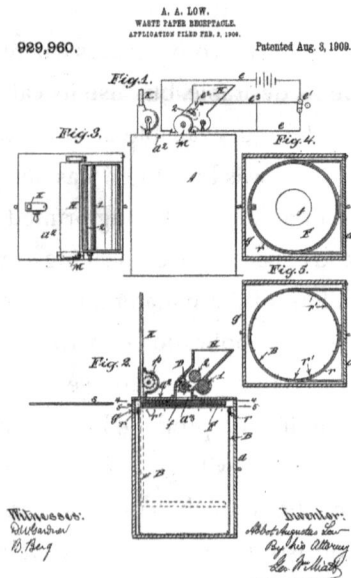

FIG. 22.5 Abbot Augustus Low's illustrations of his 'waste-paper receptacle' invention for his 1909 patent application (reprinted from Abbot Augustus Low's 'Waste-paper receptacle' patent application, filed at the United States Patent Office on 2 February 1909. US patent number 929960[3])

Ehinger's activities (Woestendiek 2002). The first paper shredder produced by Ehinger was operated by a hand crank and modelled after the pasta maker, an object that was ubiquitous in European kitchens during that period. This device allowed Ehinger to continue his resistance activities without fear of retaliation, for theoretically the shredder would allow all traces of the anti-Nazi material to be destroyed before they could 'fall into the wrong hands'.

Ehinger applied for a patent for his (now-motorised) shredder in the United States in October 1970. For the patent to be granted, Ehinger needed to successfully argue for the ways in which his 'document shredder' offered innovations not found in Low's previously patented shredder (see **FIGURE 22.6**). Ehinger's patent application, then, describes how his shredder is an improved model in that it circumvents the need for the paper shredder to be 'closely supervised' to prevent the machine 'from continuing operation even if the space provided for accommodating the shredded materials is filled to overflowing' (1970: 3). The risk incurred by the possibility of the shredding continuing after an overflow is

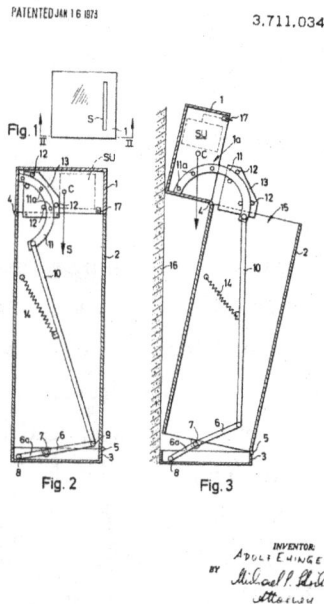

FIG. 22.6 Adolf Ehinger's 'diagrammatic top-plan view of a shredder' (image reprinted from Adolf Ehinger's 'Shredder for documents and the like' patent application, filed at the United States Patent Office on 26 October 26 1970. US patent number 84061[4])

that the employee supervising the shredding would need to make contact with 'the actual shredding unit off the main housing' (and its metal teeth!) in order to empty the receptacle. This contact could, of course, result in bodily harm to 'personnel who might inadvertently move a limb into the reach of the shredding unit in attempting to replace the cover portion' (Ehinger 1970: 3).

Acknowledging, then, that the paper shredder has become a ubiquitous object in workplaces even before his 'new and improved' model emerges onto the market, Ehinger describes the function of the shredder as a fundamental altering of the materials that pass through it, such that the shredded materials are no longer recognisable, thus forever protecting their original content. He writes that papers that go through the shredder are 'reduced to portions of such size as to make it impossible to piece them together and to reassemble the original document whose contents are intended to be kept secret' (Ehinger 1970: 3). The concept of secrecy – and the lengths we will go to maintain it – is crucial to the design of the shredder. The English noun 'secret' is derived from the Latin *secernere*, meaning 'to separate or divide off' (OED). The secret is kept through infinite division into smaller and smaller pieces, such that the documents' content becomes illegible, thus ensuring that no one after the person carrying out the shredding is privy to its content. The Oxford English Dictionary defines the noun 'secret' as 'that which is kept from knowledge or observation; hidden, concealed' (OED). It is this sense of withholding that is crucial here. The secret enacts a withholding that prevents the content of the secret from spilling into the public realm. Most intriguingly, this definition suggests that the secret does not function as a form of knowledge. In this sense, knowledge is by definition that which is *public*. What are the consequences, then, for private knowledge, knowledge to which access is curtailed through political repression or other forms through which circulation is limited? With the act of shredding, do documents lose not only their legibility but also their knowledgeness – that is, their status as an object containing and potentially circulating knowledge? This concept of knowledge also raises questions concerning ways in which knowledge is cloaked or disguised for safe circulation – i.e., by being encoded.

As Ehinger's daughter-in-law, Renate Ehinger, recounts concerning Ehinger's decision to invent a shredder: 'he thought, when you can't write what you want to write, it was time to do something' (Ehinger as quoted in Woestendiek 2002).

As Ehinger's case reveals, in contexts where free expression is denied, it is not only knowledge and the circulation of that knowledge that is threatened, but also the very act of writing. The act of committing words, ideas, thoughts, and politics to paper, whether by hand or through the use of a printing press of some kind, is itself threatened because of the risk posed by the afterlife of the printed paper. This directs our attention to the agency of the paper itself: once printed papers take their course in the world, the author must relinquish all control over the hands into which these papers will fall. This is a resurfacing of Roland Barthes' death of the author, but with an incriminating twist.

The connotations of the German word for paper shredder, *Aktenvernichter* (literally 'file annihilator' or 'record annihilator'), reflect the historical conditions under which the shredding technology arose in Germany: those of political repression. In the context of repressive governments (and for activists, in every context), the ability to destroy 'paper trails' that could lead to incrimination is crucial (and again, in the digital era, the impossibility of destroying digital paper trails presents a whole new set of problems). The German *Aktenvernichter*'s focus on the evidenceness of the materials being shredded explicitly highlights the shredder's capacity to destroy evidence that could lead to repression. The shredder itself, though, lacks a political orientation, and shreds materials at the same speed whether its 'on' button is pressed by someone on the Right or on the Left. Fragmentation can protect, or it can incriminate (in cases where the availability of paper evidence can result in vindication). The focus of the German word *Aktenvernichter* on the particular *type* of paper most likely to be shredded – the 'file' or 'record' – also gives a different connotation than the general 'paper' described by the English term. The German term emphasises that materials requiring shredding aren't just any old papers. These are papers containing knowledge of enough value to someone that they might incur risk; these are papers *worth* shredding. The term 'document' implies a paper upon which knowledge has been *inscribed*. 'Document' gives a connotation of permanence. The shredder takes the knowledge in-formation and directs it towards a process of de-formation. In this sense, the paper shredder technology draws attention to the perpetual contingency and impermanence of information as that which is constantly in flux, rather than a static and complete entity. While the document is designed to exist as a long-term record of a set of relations, the shredder is mobilised as an antidote to the sort of harm that could arise from these recorded relations falling into the wrong hands.

Most shredders have a 'reverse' button, located just next to the 'on/off'-button. When the 'reverse' button is pressed, though, the shredded materials are not reintegrated into a legible whole. It's too late for that. Instead, the reverse function is designed to alleviate the inevitable 'paper jam' produced by excessive shredding. Indeed, an important characteristic of the practice of paper shredding is the tendency for printed materials – and the knowledge contained therein – to be destroyed *en masse*. Such mass destruction of documents is an energy- and labour-intensive process that produces paper waste on a large scale. As shown in **FIGURE 22.7**, shredded paper fragments can be gathered together and fed into a 'compactor' machine that then produces 'paper bales' from the shredded material. Named after their agricultural relative, the hay bale – a technology that was developed to harness and preserve the surplus green matter grown during the productive months of summer – the paper bale is also designed to harness the productive capacity of the material that emerges as a by-product of paper shredding. Weighing between 1100 and 1500 pounds each, paper bales stand as a unit of potentiality that is often recycled into newly printable paper, or other products such as roof shingles (Keough 2011).

One notable example of a large-scale effort to reconstruct a body of knowledge that had been destroyed through shredding is the citizen-led initiative to prevent the complete loss of the records of governance under the GDR Ministry for State Security (Stasi) in Germany between 1950 and 1990. In 1989, amid growing social unrest and pressure, the GDR government ordered employees in its Ministry for State Security to systematically destroy all government files through the use of paper shredders. However, the shredders assigned to carry out this colossal task proved inadequate; they were not able to shred quickly enough. As a result, Stasi employees were ordered to supplement the shredders' destruction with their own manual shredding. In the end, the majority of the 600 million paper fragments produced by the Stasi document annihilation project were shredded by hand (Menzel 2014). When the public became aware of the Stasi's attempt to destroy this evidence, German citizens stepped in and prevented the total destruction of this archive by occupying Stasi offices and demanding a halt to the shredding. The citizens' group seized 16,250 large

FIG. 22.7 Ron Hildebrand sweeping shredded paper fragments into a 'compactor' to produce 'paper bales'. Friesens Corporation, Altona, Manitoba, Canada, 2011 (photo by Rosemarie and Pat Keough; reprinted with permission from Rosemarie and Pat Keough)

bags of paper fragments that the Stasi had planned to reduce to paper pulp, or to burn, following which any attempt to reconstruct these documents would have been impossible (*Spiegel* 2007; unnamed author). This seizure prompted the reunified German state to fund a long-term project dedicated to the reconstruction of destroyed Stasi documents. However, due to the sheer scale of the project, it was soon decided that manual reconstruction techniques would need to be replaced by a technological solution that would speed up the process of reconstructing destroyed evidence. It has been estimated that if human hands were to proceed alone with the reconstruction project, the task of rendering the fragments into coherent and readable documents would take between 600 and 800 years (*Spiegel* 2007).

The German federal government has dedicated more than 30 million Euros to the development of a technology that would carry out the reconstruction of these paper fragments without the need for human intervention in the process of document analysis. Researchers at the Fraunhofer Institute for Production

Systems and Design Technology in Berlin have been working to develop a machine for the automated analysis of annihilated documents, dubbed the 'Stasi-Schnipselmaschine' (the Stasi Snippet Machine), since 2000 (Nikolay and Schneider 2007). The 'Stasi-Schnipselmaschine' consists of a computer program that uses algorithms to recognise and sort the paper fragments through the use of scanners, thereby reuniting fragments with like fragments that had originally produced meaning together within the form of a single page (Nickolay and Schneider 2007). The program is designed to recognise and reconstruct shredded fragments (see **FIGURE 22.8**) and manually-torn fragments (see **FIGURE 22.9**). While the reconstruction project remains incomplete, the development of this reconstruction technology will likely soon be exported for use by other national reconstruction projects, including those taking place in the Czech Republic, Poland, Chile, Argentina, and Guatemala (Menzel 2014). The relative success of the government initiative to restore shredded documents points to the incomplete and reversible nature of the destruction carried out by paper shredders.

The stakes of the success of shredding are high; destruction must be total. For this reason, the frequency with which shredders become 'jammed', and

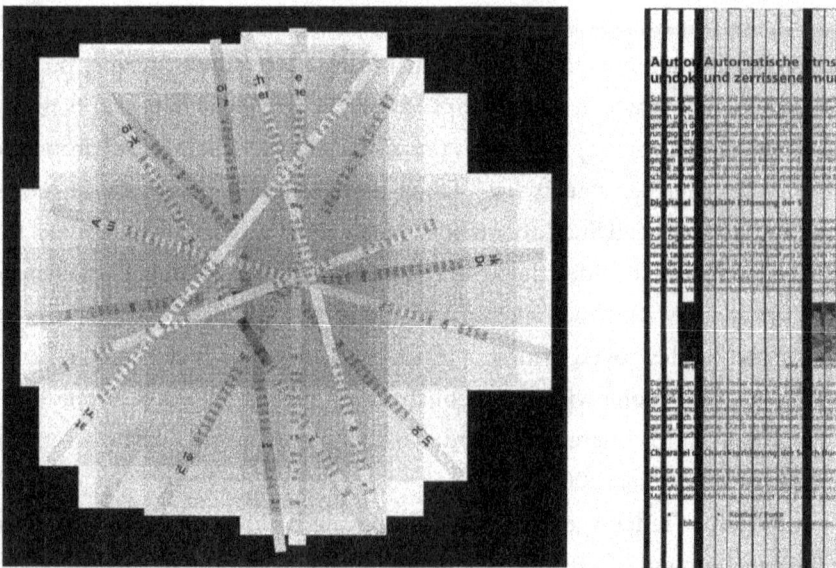

FIG. 22.8 Shredded paper fragments in the process of being reconstructed by the 'Stasi-Schnipselmaschine' (image reprinted from Nicoklay and Scheider 2007: 26)

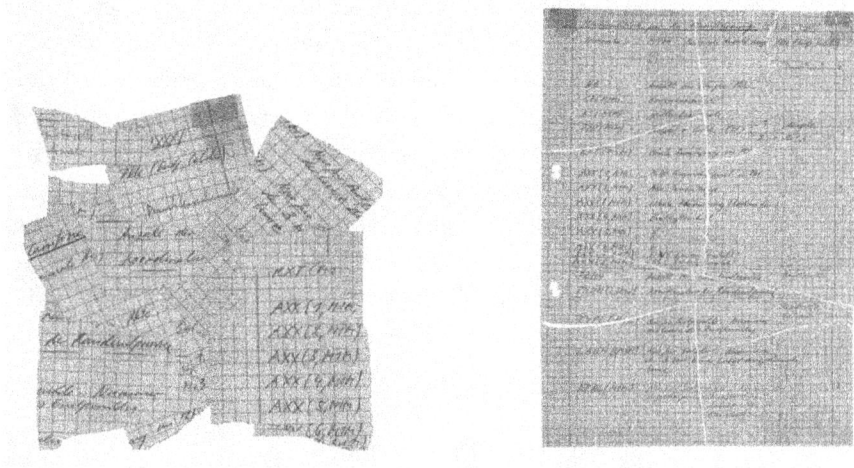

FIG. 22.9 Larger, hand-torn paper fragments in the process of being reconstructed by the 'Stasi-Schnipselmaschine' (image reprinted from Nickolay and Schneider 2007: 22)

the flow-through of paper materials suddenly halted, presents a significant problem for those who aspire to limit access to and traceability of a body of knowledge through shredding. To make matters worse, the shredder's 'reverse' button doesn't always solve the problem, by undoing the 'jam' and allowing the destruction to proceed as desired. The shredder doesn't always heed the call of 'reverse'; instead, the 'paper jam' speaks the shredder's desire to leave some instances of destruction incomplete. Perhaps both Low and Ehinger anticipated the need to undo processes of knowledge de-formation, leading to the design of a technology that would preserve at least partially legible traces as openings for reconstruction.

NOTES

1 It is important to note here that the destruction of knowledge through the technology of paper shredding stands as just one example of the many practices and processes of erasure that render the archive a site more accurately characterised by its exclusions and its absences than by that which it manages to protect.

2 Prior to the digital era, printed papers enjoyed a special status as a form of circulable – and thus both particularly valuable and particularly dangerous – knowledge. Paper was understood as a medium for the stabilisation of knowledge; the particular form of inscriptions on paper loaned a quality of robust evidenceness to a set of ideas inscribed on a document. Paper technology could, temporarily at least, and with great consequence, bring any particular form of knowledge – though always in flux – to a halt. It is in this form of temporal stasis that the paper document does its work as a form of evidence. And it was for this reason that a method by which it would be possible to destroy the document-as-proof was so urgently needed.

3 Available at: https://patentimages.storage.googleapis. com/03/9a/4e/1fc4360578ddd0/US929960.pdf

4 Available at: https://patentimages.storage.googleapis. com/43/6b/6f/88b00cbf9478a1/US3711034.pdf

REFERENCES

Bowker, G. C., *Memory Practices in the Sciences* (Cambridge, MA: MIT Press, 2005).

Ehinger, A., 'Shredder for documents and the like', patent application filed at the United States Patent Office on 26 October 1970, US patent number 84061.

Keough, R., and P. Keough, 'Destroyed Materials for Recycling', 27 January 2011, <http://www.keough-art.com/tome_passion_blog/tome_passion_blog_4.php> [accessed 29 October 2018].

Low, A. A., 'Waste-paper receptacle', patent application filed at the United States Patent Office on 2 February 1909, US patent number 929960.

Menzel, B., 'Das fetzt', *Zeit Online*, 27 November 2014, <http://www.zeit.de/2014/49/geschredderte-stasi-akten-maschine/komplettansicht> [accessed 29 October 2018].

Nickolay, B., and J. Schneider, 'Automatische virtuelle Rekonstruktion "vorvernichteter" Stasi-Unterlagen: Machbarkeit, Systemlösung, Potenziale', in J. Weberling and G. Spitzer, eds, *Virtuelle Rekonstruktion "vorvernichteter" Stasi-Unterlagen: Technologische Machbarkeit und Finanzierbarkeit – Folgerungen für Wissenschaft, Kriminaltechnik und Publizistik* (Berlin: Berliner Landesbeauftragten für die Unterlagen des Staatssicherheitsdienstes der ehemaligen DDR, 2007), pp. 11–28.

Woestendiek, J., 'The Compleat History of Shredding', *The Baltimore Sun*, 10 February 2002, <http://articles.baltimoresun.com/2002–02–10/entertainment/0202110302_1_paper-shredders-papyrus-thereof> [accessed 29 October 2018].

[Unnamed author], 'Geschredderte Akten: Computer puzzelt Stasi-Schnipsel zusammen', *Spiegel Online*, 9 May 2007, <http://www.spiegel.de/wissenschaft/mensch/geschredderte-akten-computer-puzzelt-stasi-schnipsel-zusammen-a-481984.html> [accessed 29 October 2018].

VII

ICE

FIG. 23.1 Freezer tanks at -160°C. Biobank sample storage for a study on nutrition and health in Denmark (photograph: Susanne Bauer, 2008)

23

BIOBANK BOXES: TECHNOLOGIES OF POPULATION

Susanne Bauer

Appearance: frosty, cold, opaque, white fog, from mundane to highly secured. **Colour**: outside: metallic silver with blue lid; inside: white, foggy. **Habitat**: basements, labs, corridors in research centres or hospitals, specialised facilities. **Behaviour**: still and frozen when in repository, fluid and mobile when retrieved. **Size**: diverse, fitting into each other like Russian dolls: small vials (grouped horizontally) in larger boxes, in household-sized freezers or industrial-sized storage tanks and specialised buildings. **Migration**: immobilised by temperature, embedded in data network; when defrozen, mutable and migrating between labs, circulating and in-forming publics, publications and policies.

Keywords: containing, storing, freezing, defreezing, mobilising, circulating, moving across scales

A MUNDANE BASEMENT CORRIDOR OF AN OFFICE BUILDING, WITH VARI-
ous ducts on concrete walls. A fireproof door and an alarm system; a security
badge is needed; everyone entering the room is documented by time and
name of employee and name of visitor. Inside the basement room there are
two rows of metallic storage tanks with blue lids. It is quiet except for the
low humming of some remote machinery. My guide, a researcher from the
biochemistry lab, puts on a long glove before she opens the lid. Nothing
is visible inside except the white fog from liquid nitrogen boiling off. She
reaches in and brings up an icy metal scaffold – named 'elevator' – holding
quadratic boxes. The plastic boxes are filled with yet smaller containers – vials
holding the frozen sample material, sometimes attached to straws inside,
which can be taken out when the material is needed. Each box on the front
side of the scaffold and each vial is labelled with an ID number, barcode
and project name.

Zooming in on the material organisation of these cold containers reveals
ever more boxes in boxes in boxes, like Russian matryoshkas. Boxes make up
and organise the materials and methods of research, in this case a large-scale
epidemiological study in ten countries: the 'European Investigation on Nutrition
and Cancer', which has collected specimens and data from more than half a
million participants. Citizens recruited for population-based studies gave the
blood samples that are now stored in these epidemiological biobanks. The
biobank described here belongs to the 'EPIC' study of the early 1990s – its
acronym was the pitch to launch a comprehensive European resource for research
on nutrition and chronic disease, and a research infrastructure for 'genomic
epidemiology'. Since the 1990s genomics has transformed both biomedical
and public health research practices and given rise to new research methods
in preventive medicine. Biobanks work by reconfiguring and infrastructuring
even questions as mundane as whether eating vegetables is good for you. These
collections of boxed materials are invested with modernist promises of scientific
novelty and hopes for medical cures, as well as fears about all-encompassing
biosurveillance and corporate exploitation of personal data. But how do these
biobanks work? What other infrastructures and calculative techniques do they
combine with? And what will these promissory boxes and the affects that surround them turn into?

My visit to the basement took place in the context of a research project I conducted at Medical Museion, University of Copenhagen. Exploring Copenhagen as a city of biomedicine took me to the National Hospital, to the Danish Cancer Society, to the clinical biochemistry unit at Herlev Hospital, and back to the former Surgeon's Academy – now the Medical Museion – where my office was located. I was able to sample some of the plastic vials and storage systems used in biobanking, take them back to the museum and juxtapose them with other pieces of medical apparatus. As a curator of recent biomedicine, I became interested in the materiality and artefacts, including the digital ones, of what practitioners referred to as 'bio-curation'. I was struck by how some samples were stored mundanely in household freezers, while at the same time being refashioned as a promissory resource. Since the 1990s, and especially in the Nordic countries, establishing biobank repositories has been part of the busy activity of creating research infrastructures for genomics, loaded with promises of medical progress and future health (Fortun 2008). When zooming in on the practices and infrastructures of biomedicine, old and new, one finds box techniques at their very core. My curatorial interest focused on those infrastructural devices for containment and mobilisation as a point of departure to rethinking the work of ordering that takes place in and with biobanks. How do these specific boxes classify, order, categorise, store away, im/mobilise? And, regarding the *banking* in biobanks, how do biobank boxings enact, accumulate, manage, and interfere with the value of their content?

FREEZING BOXES, HALTING TIME

Biobanking is about collecting and boxing biological materials by slowing down life processes using temperatures at which metabolism and decomposition come to a halt. The word 'biobank' is an umbrella term for a variety of collections; its taxonomies differentiate between kinds of biobanks using categories such as purpose, size, kinds of samples, retrospective or prospective collection, fixed or unlimited period of storage, types of data, security levels, and site of storage (Dove et al. 2012). Different from some of the local biobanks of epidemiological studies, in the UK, Sweden, Norway, and Canada generic 'national biobanks' for genomics research have been established in recent decades, and substantial amounts of funding have been put into their logistics and governance. *Nature* featured the massive endeavour of the UK Biobank bluntly, reporting that 'in the past few years, more than a half a million people in the United Kingdom have collectively peed into cups, spat into tubes and had needles stuck in their arms' (Baker 2012). Scientists and research funders alike seem to have been gripped by a collective fever to gather and store DNA and render the population as a frozen repository.

Large-scale funding has been acquired in a promissory rush for anticipated benefits, with spin-offs to develop biobank technologies from freezers to software and recruitment logistics. The need to convince participants and obtain their consent then transforms the project into a logistics task, necessitating strategies to reach the numbers envisaged in the design. Once set up, the repositories continue to enrol funders, health scientists, health policy-makers, and publics. The collective hopes and promises surrounding these intensified box activities seem largely uncontested in Scandinavian societies, where large publics have embraced the quest for intensified biomedical science for better futures and better health. In terms of the modes of knowledge, 'evidence-based approaches' using epidemiological techniques all across the research fields of public health, from biomarker studies to health policy evaluations, appealed to scientists and policy-makers alike. The redefinition of modern epidemiology as the 'study of the occurrence and distribution of health-related states or events in specified populations' (Porta 2008) resonates with how public health has been reconfigured as managerial 'outcome research'. Understood as the basic discipline of health research, epidemiological research practices enrol and formalise disease as disease-in-a-population, an entity that can be modelled as an outcome of any set of potential explanatory factors. These risk factors can range from DNA variation to air pollution, from lifestyle to socioeconomic status; multivariate modelling can analyse any variable distilled from inscription devices, testing it as a potential risk factor. These sets of study designs and analytics biometrics hold together epidemiology as a discipline and at the same time are highly mobile. Taken up by biomedicine, they have informed the movement of evidence-based medicine, and reshaped resource allocation for public health, health promotion and health services research.

Epidemiological studies, whether prospective or retrospective, have in common that they work with specific temporal alignments. They work as futuring devices and materialise a mode of 'living anticipation', an infrastructural model of preparedness (Adams et al. 2009). Sketching the hopes and resources invested in biobanking for epidemiology, the *Nature* article (quoted above) concludes that 'Samples will grow more valuable as data accumulate. In ten years, an estimated 9,000 of the original donors will have developed Alzheimer's disease, 10,000 will have breast cancer and 28,000 will have died from heart disease' (Baker 2012: 145). In this way, samples are expected to acquire value with the disease experience of their donors. Technically, so the hopes go, biomarkers of exposure, susceptibility, and disease – the classic triad of epidemiological inquiry – will be identified in those very samples. Epidemiology, now being scaled down into biobanks, has become a molecular endeavour in frozen population boxes, realigned with disease experience data traced over time. How are we to understand these re-visions and extractive practices at molecular levels, and what happens when they are scaled up from molecules to inform healthcare in society?

In an attempt to maximise the scientific value of the repository, the Danish part of the 'EPIC study' includes much more than just blood samples; it even stores fat tissue and toenail clippings as material that can later be analysed for chemical pollutants. However, the value usually attributed to the collection resides not in the different material as such, but in its completeness and statistical representativeness. For instance, UK Biobank refrained from collecting tissue biopsies in order to avoid participants dropping out when asked to undergo such invasive procedures. Instead UK Biobank preferred large case numbers; prioritising large numbers over sample variety is in line with the rules of scientific proof that rank statistical validity highest. This sample size optimising and its related trade-offs shapes the biobanks as infrastructures, and in doing so also shapes the kinds of research that they afford in the future. Decisions over sample collecting gamble on method at the expense of closing down and locking in certain options. Moving from vision to actual material collections, biobanks and databases literally infra-structure the conditions of possibility of future knowledge. I argue, however, that since science is constitutively open to change, present hypotheses and analytic techniques may no longer pertain once the envisaged case numbers have been achieved and the frozen samples retrieved. The tension between the stillness of 'frozen time' in the collection and the ever incomplete 'latest apparatus' of measurement constitutes the speculative economies and dynamics on which scientific endeavours, mediated by boxes, have come to surf.

Things can go wrong in the biobank boxes, too. If samples defreeze uncontrolledly upon blackout or technical failure, the samples are lost. Also, some biomarkers have been shown to be unstable after the freezing and defreezing process (Baker 2012). Even with minor temperature fluctuation, enzyme activity can change biomarker levels. The largest and most high-tech biobanks for long-term storage keep samples at temperatures as low as -196°C and are connected to emergency power systems at the hospital with redundant power back-up. The effort and resources put into establishing national biobanks might indicate that they are seen as being 'too big to fail'. More recently, in addition to biobank governance standards and ethics protocols, new biobanks have begun to include 'legacy planning' as well as inventories of all 'freeze–thaw events' (Matzke et al. 2016). These are means of preparedness for any failure that might occur, and they even factor in the potential future need to close down the biobank and redistribute the samples. Medical research, like museums, faces debates over the conditions of collecting and pressure for some mode of restitution of samples, to other repositories or to their owners, especially when related to colonial medicine and anthropology. For future biomedical research, scientists have suggested building on the ideas of 'open science' and 'wiki-governance' as a model for the regulation of repositories of biological materials, as has already happened in the case of scientific data platforms (Dove et al. 2012). Epidemiologists have long rejected bottom-up and participatory approaches on the grounds of their epistemologies that are committed to 'ruling out bias' at all costs. Yet it is worth asking the question what kind of publics are constituted by epidemiological research, and what biobank and epidemiological studies would look like if they followed less top-down principles. Whether and how the change from their risk governance to wiki approaches will shift controversies over evidence and precautions to new publics may depend on more than just rhetoric. Interestingly, many epistemic challenges to these practices seem to come from digital technology itself – the status of which is highly contested within (digital) epidemiology – as big data analytics may modify established techniques of knowledge-making.

INTO THE BOX, OUT OF THE BOX

Collecting and storing fluids is laborious, and the flows into and out of boxes differ between biobanks. Some of the large-scale biobanks use robotics technologies, yet there are a lot of minor and older collections with storage in laboratory spaces or freezers on corridors and in basements. The habitats of the freezers (**FIGURE 23.2**) are corridors of a clinical biochemistry department in a hospital. Visiting the adjacent busy clinical biochemistry labs offers a glimpse into the cumbersome steps and cycles of collecting, retrieving, and processing samples during the bio-curation process. Before samples enter the freezer box, they undergo a preparation process. They pass centrifuges that separate out different parts of the blood sample, the buffy coat – the DNA-containing part – serum, plasma, and blood cells. Different from the fully automated biobanks that are

FIG. 23.2 Biobank tanks in their habitat (photograph: Susanne Bauer 2008)

displayed in industry advertisements like high-tech cathedrals, the storage temperature in these hospital boxes is in the range of household freezers: -20°C or even just +4°C to store DNA before sequencing (Baker 2012). The duration of their storage depends on the research aspirations associated with them. In studies that run over many decades, special advisory boards take the decisions about which purpose justifies actual usage – and wastage – of samples.

The time it may take for frozen samples to move out of containment again, especially in long-term storage units, depends on risk-benefit considerations, protocols, and board decisions. Once it has been decided that samples are to be used, researchers or robots draw up the elevators with samples, identify the labels on the box, and pull out the horizontal plastic boxes and vials or straws holding the specimen. Human data labour combines tracing and linking materials and data, and generating new inscriptions with stored samples. Once they have been released from the logistics of freezers, and having become liquids again, specimens move up level by level and box by box. The unfrozen samples enter the wet lab, where they are channelled into different kinds of measurement apparatus. Some of these are automated – many look like inkjet printers or copy machines, others use 'gene chips' as surfaces that work as testing and inscription devices to generate expression signals. The passage through a measurement apparatus, and a series of transformations, reassemble these signals in terms of biological markers of exposure and disease – a new version of the classic epidemiological triad of 'environment, susceptibility and disease'. This reassembling takes place during the passage of data through various boxes and chains of translation, in which molecular signals become part of a population-alised measure of exposure, susceptibility, or disease – the latter as anticipated events bound to an uncertain future.

To acquire relevance for public health, biomarker concentrations and other inscriptions produced in the wet lab need to be mobilised. How exactly does this take place? It involves another box, this time a calculative box tool that transforms the inscriptions into determinants and potential risk factors, and aligns them with 'disease-in-the-population'. The box-machine that enacts this mobilisation is the 2x2 table, a quadratic box with four compartments (**FIGURE 23.3**). This is a different kind of box – and a rather powerful one. In epidemiological research, this calculative box is the receptacle for numbers; these count numbers of participants in the exposed and non-exposed groups (rows) and diseased versus non-diseased (columns). In this simplest version for binary variables, the contingency table features four boxes that order and denote the number of individuals in a study population. Using this matrix, researchers process the numbers and compute results in terms of aggregate measures of disease and measures of effects, such as relative risks, odds ratios, and absolute risks. Epidemiologists are trained to work with this box; it is a formal tool of quantification and a matrix for linking exposure and disease. The fourfold table also works as leverage to move variables between scales (from the molecular to the social), bringing frozen samples and data in action. The trick of the trade is to transform any situation, issue, or research question into the format of a 2x2 table. Study designs are geared to precisely this; the table provides the calculative technique to lift up the numbers generated by measurement devices including questionnaires. In short, samples are retrieved from storage logistics, channelled through measurement devices, and transformed into inscriptions that then pass through the leverage of the calculative box.

		DISEASE	
		Yes	No
EXPOSURE	Yes	a	b
	No	c	d

FIG. 23.3 Epidemiological box-apparatus: the 2 × 2 contingency table.

When tracing the material genealogies of calculative devices, it is found that a host of boxes for populations-in-aggregate have populated epidemiological practices. Before biobanks of frozen populations there were different aggregates, including the urn in statistics and the 'container model' or, as it has also been called, the 'bathtub model' (**FIGURE 23.4**). In this textbook image of 'population reservoirs', fluid mechanics are evoked to communicate epidemiologic thinking to student audiences. The use of hydraulics as a model is not exclusive to epidemiology; in fact, hydraulic models have been used as teaching devices in economics. The Philipps machine, developed in Britain in the late 1940s, was a hydraulic model used to teach macroeconomics (Morgan and Bouman 2004). In epidemiology, the container model works to promote an understanding of

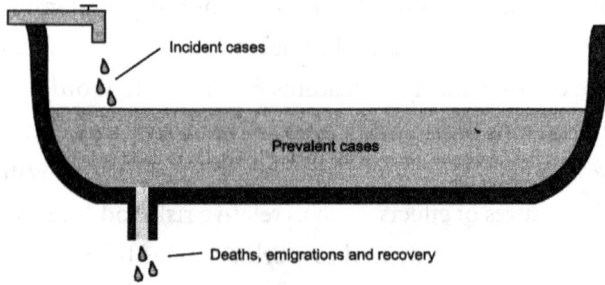

Fig. 7.6 Incidence, prevalence, and the bath model of disease (Adapted from a figure provided by Howel, see Permissions).

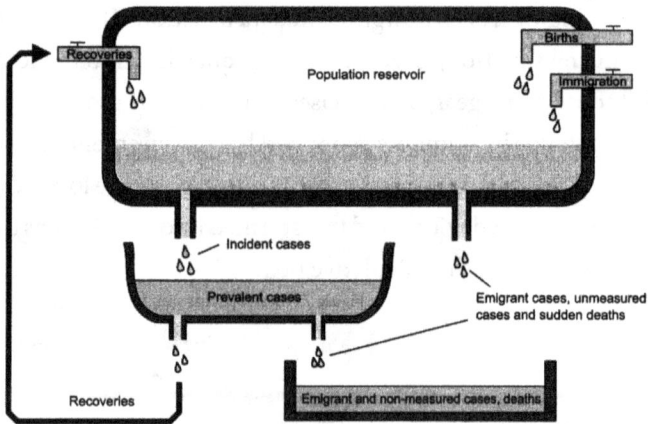

Fig. 7.7 Incidence, prevalence in a natural population: the population reservoir.

FIG. 23.4 A hydraulic model of population. The 'container model' or 'bathtub model' (source: Bhopal 2002)

metrics for health in much the same way as the Philipps machine promoted macroeconomics. The model enacts and habituates to the logic of flow and overflow of a liquid population (health) that is amenable to containment. The hydraulic model evokes analogies between epidemiological measures of disease frequency and the physical forces – such as gravity – that act on and in the fluid container. The 'population aggregate' is constituted as an object with measurable characteristics – with 'mortality output' and 'birth input' streams, and specific prevalence and incidence rates, producing a statistical state of health and disease. More than a metaphor, this virtual model conveys a mechanic of population with pertinent characteristics and behaviour – it makes an entity that *'possesses'* its own rates of disease. The dynamic model of flow and containment lends itself not only to monitoring but also to engineering through prevention measures. Evoking fluid mechanics and a hydraulic model of population (**FIGURE 23.4**) enacts the control of input and output as 'logical choice'. Thinking in terms of a hydraulic model prompts, for instance, technical modification of influx – including metrics such as birth or immigration rates – creating a need for responses to 'pressures' and 'bottlenecks'. These tools infra-structure the population thinking in demography and epidemiology, co-producing scientific modes of thinking that make appear logical or neutral policies that act on, optimise, and control populations. In this sense, the model being used is performative.

BOXES AS LEVERAGE. CONTAINING AND MOBILISING 'POPULATION'

Box-tools, like the 2x2 table, work as leverages that mobilise and transpose data into measurable and comparable aggregates. As a consequence, any claim about what is good for health can be channelled into the calculative machine of hypothesis testing that tests the assumption of a causal relation between exposure and disease; this operation results in an estimate of the association between exposure and disease, and a probabilistic test statistic that confirms statistical significance or else attributes the finding to chance. For the use of these calculative devices, it does not matter whether the treated variable is a particular exposure or disease or biomarker, or an economic outcome. These calculative boxes transport methods across domains and scales: no longer confined to risk factor epidemiology, these boxes take part in relating population health to the economic sphere. They enact epidemiology as 'outcome research' and as a generalised risk calculation and future-making device. There is hardly any limit to the mobility of these devices; in systematic reviews and meta-analyses epidemiologists even use the very same apparatus to compute an overall risk estimate from the 'population of results' from all available studies that meet certain criteria. This population of risk estimate is then formalised in exactly the same way – with the 2x2 table-box – as individuals are treated in an epidemiological study. The double use and scale-mobility of 'population' in epidemiology takes off from the scales for which it was developed, adding to and taking in from infrastructures of social sciences and economics.

Following the boxes further upscale takes one to the next box that surrounds the biobank freezers and their contents: the architectural box. That larger box – Herlev hospital – houses clinical staff, patients, researchers, samples, and data generated in clinical trials and epidemiological observation, thereby assembling and infra-structuring people, devices, and knowledge in space and time. Planned in the 1960s, Herlev hospital's spectacular architecture seems to have much in common with the box principles also found in the biobank (**FIGURES 23.5A, 23.5B**).[1] The building, designed by architects Gehrdt Bornebusch, Max Brüel and Jørgen Selchau, is known as the highest in the country and referred to as Denmark's 'largest piece of art'. Patients' rooms are located toward the windows, while labs, technical equipment, and services are at the centre and in the adjacent low building. The hospital has been praised, not only for the spectacular view it affords, but also for the interest its architecture holds for patients and staff, among whom stories of ghost floors and hidden tunnels have accompanied praise of its functionality and transparency. This modernist building seems to already belong to the future of a past, but one that can be actualised. In an 'explosion of colours' a bright alphanumeric grid is used in its interior as a navigation aid; it is quite striking how these

FIGS. 23.5A, 23.5B Left: Hospital box. Herlev Hospital, opened 1976; Right: Biobank elevators, inside Herlev Hospital (photographs: Susanne Bauer, 2008).

colours correspond with those in the logistics of twenty-first-century test tubes. Both are designed to help navigation and orientation within the abundance of rooms and vials.

In *The Birth of the Clinic* Foucault describes how new classifications of disease brought about certain spatial organisations and the hospitals of modern medicine (Foucault 1973). So, what are the effects of the bio-medical innovations, new numbers, biomarkers, and boxes, and how do they reorganise the clinic? Input and output flows, patient populations, flows of data, capital, and patients are managed side by side with the same calculative devices. Measuring performance indicators, estimating excess, and optimising are part of hospital management, and produce specific biopolitics. Both disciplines measure performance indicators and practise optimising healthcare systems and costs based on these metrics. While epidemiology has been termed the basic science of public health, I argue that logistics has become the basic science of twenty-first-century business operations and organisation. The logistics of scientific knowledge genera-tion include trading and optimising knowledge about risks and benefits against 'numbers needed to treat' or 'numbers needed to harm' – this is an epistemological necessity that can implicate collateral damage in every-day healthcare settings. The architecture of the late 1960s, which aimed to provide light, colour, openness, hope, and views of a brighter medicine in the hospital, seems like a science-fiction future belonging to an already distant past. While colourful interiors and wayfinding aids convey bright-ness and clear form, the regimes of economic governance and hospital operation streamline the management of the 'hospital population' towards efficiency. Albeit often with different goals in mind, public health research-ers and economists evaluate interventions with the same formalisations of aggregates and population. This mode of evaluating in terms of population metrics has reached social policies beyond health, including programmes in social work and poverty reduction. Not last, population reasoning in terms of fluid mechanics often brings about rhetorics of 'containment'. This is where notions of 'flood' and 'overflow' gain credibility and are evoked to justify health budget cuts or the closing of borders toward those joining the population. Indeed, techniques of boxing populations in aggregates are susceptible to politics of containment, for instance in health (costs) management in austerity Europe, as well as in recent rhetorics and policies of border enforcement.

Boxes and box technologies shape more than scientific knowledge production; they mediate and mobilize across scale. Biobank practices can lead to different journeys and effects in biomedicine – recombining and the production of novelty, storing away in deep future and falling into oblivion or becoming just waste in a more or less distant future. Upon arrival at the museum, biobank boxes enter yet different kinds of boxes, they might get wrapped in acid free paper or turn into curatorial puzzles about the long-term preservations of plastics. Rather than being package and storage medium as within the biobank, in the curatorial hands they enter the exhibition and then the collection, becoming the object of long-term preservation themselves. And this time it is the boxes and not the samples that are the object of curatorial care – no longer as bio-curating but now redefined as 'heritage'. In some instances, the boxes themselves might be thrown out as no longer relevant or preserved as infrastructural reminiscence – while becoming heritage they challenge collection and conservation policies. Both types of collections – biobanks and museums – are box-intensive and at times even face similar challenges in terms of changing valuations and issues of accountability, ownership and curatorial care. However, different from the natural history collections in early modern science, their paths seldom cross. It is open what becomes of and what comes after biobanks, how long the pertaining research systems will be active, and when and where they end – whether as waste and ruins of the old infrastructures, aged hypes, oblivion, or recast as heritage in shiny new boxes.

NOTES

1 For a presentation of the hospital architecture, see: https://www.herlevhospital.dk/om-hospitalet/Organisation/Sider/Arkitektur-og-udsmykning.aspx [accessed 10 November 2019].

REFERENCES

Adams, V., M. Murphy, and A. Clarke, 'Anticipation. Technoscience, Life, Affect, Temporality', *Subjectivity* 28 (2009): 246–265.

Baker, M., 'Building Better Biobanks', *Nature* 486 (7 June 2012), 141–46.

Bauer, S., 'From Administrative Infrastructure to Biomedical Resource: Danish Population Registries, the "Scandinavian Laboratory", and the "Epidemiologist's Dream"', *Science in Context* 27 (2014): 187–213.

——, M. Fleming, and J. E. Olsén, 'Im Zwischenraum von Labor und Museum: Eine Ausstellung zur Biomedizin', in A. te Heesen and M. Vöhringer, eds, *Wissenschaft im Museum – Ausstellung im Labor* (Berlin: Kulturverlag Kadmos, 2014), pp. 174–95.

Bhopal, R. S., *Concepts of Epidemiology* (Oxford: Oxford University Press, 2002).

Bowker, G. C., and S. L. Star, *Sorting Things Out. Classification and Its Consequences* (Cambridge, MA: MIT Press, 1999).

Dove, E. S., Y. Joly, and B. M. Knoppers, 'Power to the People: A Wiki-Governance Model for Biobanks', *Genome Biology* 13 (2012), 158.

Fortun, M., *Promising Genomics. Iceland and deCODE Genetics in a World of Speculation* (Berkeley, CA: University of California Press, 2008).

Foucault, M., *The Birth of the Clinic* (New York: Pantheon, 1973).

Matzke, L. A., B. Fombonne, P. H. Watson, and H. M. Moore, 'Fundamental Considerations for Biobank Legacy Planning', *Biopreservation and Biobanking*, 14 (2016), 99–106.

Morgan, M. S., and M. Boumans, 'Secrets Hidden by Two-Dimensionality: The Economy as a Hydraulic Machine', in S. de Chadaevian and Nick Hopwood, eds, *Models. The Third Dimension of Science* (Stanford CA: Stanford University Press, 2004), pp. 369–401.

Porta, M., ed., *A Dictionary of Epidemiology*, 5th edn (Oxford: Oxford University Press, 2008).

FIG. 24.1 The Dropbox icon (image credit: Google Data Center. Google and the Google logo are registered trademarks of Google Inc., used with permission)

24

THE MAGIC OF DROPBOX, ITS VIRTUALITY AND MATERIALITY

Shih-Pei Chen

Box: Dropbox.[1] **Habitat**: Dropbox lives only on computing devices. You can find Dropbox in the following habitats: on operating systems like Mac, Windows, and Linux; on mobile devices like iPhone/iPad, Android, Blackberry, and Kindle Fire; or in browsers like Firefox, Safari, and Chrome. One thing to note: no matter what habitat Dropbox lives in, it cannot live without Internet connection; Internet is the indispensable element that every habitat must have for Dropbox to work. **Appearance**: Dropbox's branding icon is a squared cardboard box with the top open, suggesting that Dropbox is just like a cardboard box where you can 'drop' your readings, writings, photos, music, or other computer files, and then carry the whole box with you – virtually. **Colour**: Dropbox icons, despite their variations, always come with their 'official colours' strictly defined by the company. In most cases, for example when displayed on websites, on desktops, or on mobile devices, Dropbox icons are blue. This is officially called 'Dropbox Blue' (colour code #007ee5). In some other situations, you will find the icons displayed in 'Cool Grey', especially when there is insufficient displaying space.[2] **Size and shape**: on the *outside* (the icon), Dropbox icons are squared images with sizes ranging from 16 x 16 pixels to 1024 x 1024 pixels, depending on the habitat.[3] However, on the *inside*, Dropbox begins at 2-Gigabytes and can grow up to 500 Gigabytes (as of 2015), depending on how deep the owner's pocket is. Unlike the other (physical) boxes discussed in this book, the in- and out-dimensions of the Dropboxes don't match, and they even don't correlate. In this aspect, Dropbox is like the TARDIS, **T**ime **A**nd **R**elative **D**imension **I**n **S**pace, the time machine and spaceship appearing in Doctor Who,[4] which often stuns its visitors by being 'bigger on the inside than it is on the outside'. This phenomenon is a direct result of the 'virtuality' of Dropbox, TARDIS, and the like. **Behaviour**:

Dropbox holds one's digital files and makes the files accessible from multiple computing devices.

Keywords: storing, carrying, transferring, sharing, backup, everywhere, virtual, boxness, cloudiness, hiding, distributed, redundancy

WHEN HERMIONE GRANGER PULLED OUT A PAIR OF JEANS, A SWEATSHIRT, and the silvery Invisible Cloak from her small, purple, beaded handbag, not only Ron Weasley and Harry Potter, but, I believe, all the readers and viewers were astonished by how such a small bag could hold items that were in total bigger than itself.[5] This is a typical scene that represents *magic*, which doesn't only appear in the 'Harry Potter' books and movie series, but also in fairy tales like 'Mary Poppins" (her purse is tiny, but appears to hold a huge quantity of items like clothes and lamps)[6] in Sci-Fi works like Doctor Who (the time machine and spaceship TARDIS is bigger on the inside than it is on the outside), and in other genres of creation. The scene works as magical since it conflicts with our physical common sense of how objects should behave – a container's outer dimensions should correspond with its inner dimensions, and thus it should be incapable of holding items bigger than itself. In other words, such scenes represent magic because they conflict with what we think we know about *materiality*.

Even though in real life scientists haven't gone that far and really found a way to produce Hermione's handbag or any other kind of container that can hold items bigger than itself, today we already have something closer to this goal. Thanks to the rapid development of computer hardware over the last five decades, our hand-sized mobile phones can now hold thousands of photos on them. And even a 5-cm-long USB stick can hold more or less the same quantity of photos, music, documents, and other types of digital files. This is also magical, considering that such a quantity of files, if they were not digital, not virtual, would take quite a big *physical* space to store. The trick here is the form of digital files – composed of 0s and 1s, represented by electronic pulses, magnetic transitions or other forms of energy, and stored in corresponding physical media. Such ways of storing information provide a high conversion ratio between amount of information and space for storage, meaning we are able to store huge amounts of digital/virtual information in physically small devices – boxes for digital files.

Despite the fact that digital files are virtual, they must still reside in *some* physical boxes – CDs, USB sticks, hard drives, or mobile phones. The compact storage these boxes offer is probably against common sense and seems magical, but it has a physical limit – by destroying the hosting medium, one can destroy a huge quantity of files for eternity. On the other hand, Dropbox, a special box for storing digital files, overturns this fundamental limitation of digital boxes by providing cloud storage and thus introducing a new level of *virtuality* of digital files which is not limited by physical devices. Although Dropbox is not the only and was not the first cloud service in the world, it is indeed the pioneer which brought this idea to the general public and let people embrace it – without even being aware of the technology behind it.

WHAT IS DROPBOX AND HOW DOES IT WORK?

Ever since Dropbox was officially launched in 2008, it has gained wide popularity for providing a safe and easy-to-use solution to store and transfer one's digital files on and via the Internet. At the period of its development computers were already popular in workspaces and at home, and many people had long been comfortable with working, reading, writing, and entertaining on computers. Great quantities of digital documents and files were created by non-professional computer users every day. Naturally, people also needed to move files from one computer to another, to bring home work, to share files with their colleagues, friends, and families, and to back up files to keep precious files safe.

One way of transferring digital files is to put them into a storage device and carry the device around. However, carrying devices around isn't always desirable or easy to do, due to the increasing size of files and the potentially long physical distance of transfer. Faced with these limitations, people began thinking about transferring files virtually – over the Internet. Although cloud storage hadn't been proposed at that time – there was no Google Docs, no Microsoft SkyDrive, and of course no Dropbox – there had been solutions to the problem of how to transfer files virtually. *File Transfer Protocol (FTP)* allowed people to transfer files between a local computer and a remote FTP server and was very popular for backing up and sharing files. But it required the user to have the knowledge and ability to set up such a solution and to have access to such a server. *Source Control Systems* were popular already at that time among programmers for having a remote secure backup for their work-in-progress codes with revision history – a feature that kept track of the modification history for each file and allowed the user to go back in time to a certain version. *Box*, a secure backup service which also adopted the 'box' as its iconography, already provided businesses with a secure way to back up files from office computers on remote servers. Despite all these technologies, when Dropbox hit the stage of TechCrunch,[7] it was a revelation to the market. Why did Dropbox stand out from all the other similar solutions?

To understand this, let's look at the image that Dropbox conveys to the public. It is mainly done with the brand name itself and the simple Dropbox icon, as shown at the beginning of this article. The icon is simply a blue cardboard box, symbolising a personal container for holding one's digital files (emphasised by the colour blue) that can be carried by the owner of the box.[8] One can simply 'drop' documents, photos, and memories into this box, and start carrying it around. In this way, Dropbox conveys the concepts of *easy storage* and *transferring* files at the same time.

Dropbox works like this: you first apply for an account to acquire a 'persona' Dropbox – a virtual box that resides on your computers and mobile phones – and then you have the ability to drop files into it. You can use a browser to access your personal box and begin to put files into it by uploading files. In this case, your personal box is on Dropbox's website. If you are on a desktop with Windows, MacOS, or Linux operating systems, Dropbox can create a 'local materiality', a local copy, of your personal box on your desktop for you, by automatically downloading all the files in your personal box to your local computer. In this case, you can drag and drop files from your computer to your local box easily. And when you do so, Dropbox automatically transfers the new or updated files to your remote personal box, the 'real' box. The next time you check your personal box through a web browser from any computer, your personal box is up to date with all the latest changes. You can even open the files in your local box to read or to work on while they are still *in* the box.

Now, how do you carry your Dropbox around, along with all the files you've dropped there? For example, when you want to take your work documents home from the office? Here is the first amazing thing about this box: you do not really need to carry your Dropbox with you at all. If this were necessary, then Dropbox would be no different to a USB drive, where you also dump all the files you want to carry, but really do have to carry the USB drive. How does this box work, then? Why does it not need to be carried?

The reason is that your Dropbox has many entrances (access points), but these are just portals that lead you to the same remote place – your personal box, the 'real' one, no matter where it is physically. You can deploy as many portals on as many computers or mobile devices as you want. For example, you can create a new portal at any time on any device by opening a browser to access your personal Dropbox, even from a computer that you have never used before. With these many portals, you can drop files to your personal Dropbox through your office computer, leave the office, go home, and acquire the same files through your home computer. You can even open your Dropbox from your mobile phone and read a previously uploaded ebook on your way home. As long as a device is connected to the Internet, you can access all the files in your personal box from almost everywhere, without really carrying them around. With Dropbox, you don't need to *carry* anything, because your box is virtual, because it's already *everywhere*.

So, the Dropbox icon is simply a portal, a symbolic entrance to your personal box. There is in fact no 'real' box right behind the icon. The *materiality* of your personal box is somewhere else – not on your local desktop or mobile phone, even though you have an exact copy of your Dropbox files there; it is not even on Dropbox's website, even though you can access all your files from there. This is also why Dropbox is bigger on the inside than it is on the outside: the icons, representing the entrances, are just portals; they are never the 'real' box. In other words, the linkages between the entrances and the real box are also virtual. So, where is the 'real' box? What is the physical existence, the materiality of your personal box?

Before we get into that, let's first explore the physical existence, the materiality, of *any* digital file.

RETHINKING THE VIRTUALITY OF DIGITAL FILES, AND OF DROPBOX

We tend to think that digital files are virtual. We are told that they are composed of binary digits – 0s and 1s – but most of us never really see the 0s and 1s when staring at our computers. It feels like the 0s and 1s are just metaphors and they don't exist in the physical world. But this is incorrect. Digital files *really are* composed of 0s and 1s in the form of electronic pulses, magnetic transitions, or other transitions, and the digits always need to be materialised on physical mediums like CDs, hard drives, and USB drives, depending on which type of physical energy is used for the storage device. In other words, digital files always need to reside on physical mediums in order to exist. This implies that when one destroys the physical media where a group of digital files reside, one also destroys those digital files. After all, digital files are *never* virtual. They always need to reside on some physical material, and, from that perspective, are in fact very real.

Dropbox is no exception to this rule, in that every personal Dropbox and the files inside must reside on some physical device. But where is the physical existence of one's personal Dropbox located, if not on one's desktop, mobile phone, nor on Dropbox's website, since all of these are all just portals and local copies?

In fact, probably no one can say where the physical existence of your personal Dropbox is located, not even the Dropbox engineers, since they don't know exactly where your files are stored at this very moment. The thing is, your real box might be divided into many pieces, and each of them is stored in a different physical device. Also, your box and each of its pieces may be stored many times in different physical devices – this is called 'redundancy' – and the devices are likely to be in different locations – 'distribution'. Redundancy and distribution are supposed to make sure your files are always available, accessible, safe, and secure, even when one physical copy is temporarily down or damaged due to hardware or network failure. Now you understand that all the above makes tracking the physical existence of your personal Dropbox complicated.

The technology behind the above-mentioned mechanism is called 'cloud storage', which Dropbox adopts for storing its enormous quantity of precious user files.[9] By adopting cloud storage, users' files are always available, accessible, safe, and secure within Dropbox. As Dropbox users, as long as we can always access our personal boxes, we don't really need to know on which physical devices our files are based.

By using cloud storage, Dropbox is able to create a virtual personal box where you can store and transfer your files without carrying any physical devices. By using cloud storage, Dropbox successfully hides the materiality of boxes and becomes purely virtual – one doesn't even know where the physical body of one's box is, and it doesn't matter. Cloudiness is the key to the Dropbox concept: one can simply drop files through one portal, and retrieve the files from another, without carrying any physical devices in between. The portals and the real box are detached, and the real box can be anywhere.

Cloudiness also sets Dropbox apart from other services that store and transfer files virtually through the Internet. For FTP and Source Control Systems, one still has to set up a physically existent server. Then, the issue appears: what if the server breaks down? The materiality of such solutions would then be destroyed, and so would the digital files on the servers. By adopting cloud storage, Dropbox avoids this materiality issue, since cloud storage is designed to guarantee secure and reliable file access by creating multiple copies of each file and storing files on different physical devices in different locations to prevent any kind of access failure.

THE MATERIALITY BEHIND THE CLOUD: DATA CENTRES

'Then, the cloud must have materiality. What is it like?', you might ask next. Indeed, no digital file can escape the law of physics, and it must reside on some physical device. So does the Cloud.

These days, software companies that own masses of customer data don't manage the storage on their own anymore. They seek help from 'hosting companies' like Amazon and Google, which provide cloud storage and guarantee availability and accessibility of files at any time in easy-to-manage ways. The idea is that cloud storage provides one big logical store for companies like Dropbox to keep their management simple, while the physical reality is that the data are distributed in many storage devices spread across different geographical locations. The benefit is that cloud stores are highly fault tolerant – meaning the service won't go down even when there are hardware or network failures, and they are also highly durable through redundancy and the duplication of the data stored on them. These distributed and redundant yet almost unimaginably numerous user data are stored in the many data centres built by those hosting companies.

What does a data centre look like? **FIGURE 24.2** shows us a normal setting for data centres. They are huge matrices of tens of thousands of computers; computers put on compact racks and connected to each other with wires. Computers there are reduced to only the machinery for computation and storage – unnecessary peripherals like monitors, mouse, and keyboards are all removed. The idea is to make thousands of machines act as one – logically. Data centres need an effective and low-cost power supply in order to keep the tens of thousands of computers running. They also need efficient cooling systems in order to reduce the significant amount of heat produced by those machines every minute. Hardware – hard drives, cables, etc. – in data centres are exhausted quickly, since the whole data centre is constantly running and responding to requests for file access, and thus the hardware needs to be changed frequently in order to keep the cloud storage service reliable.

Data centres are often located in isolated locations in big standalone warehouses and are hidden away from people. They require high-standard security

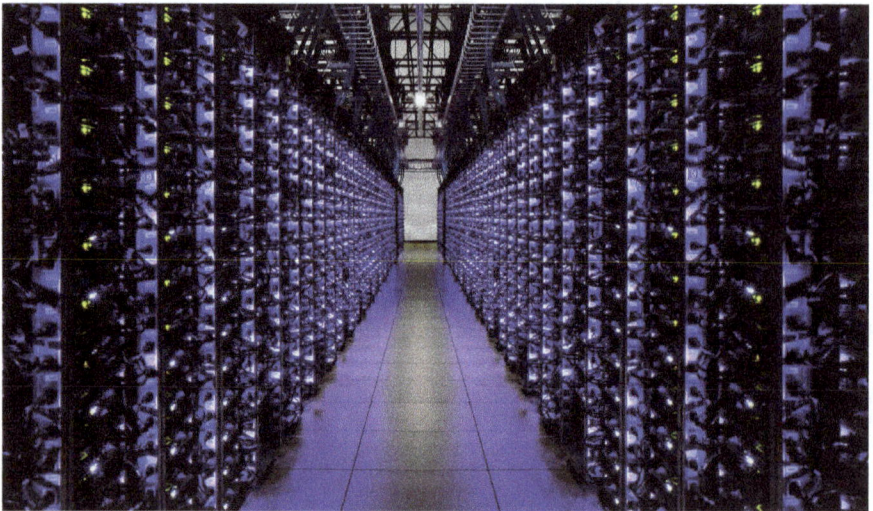

FIG. 24.2 What a data centre looks like (image credit: Google Data Center. Google and the Google logo are registered trademarks of Google Inc., used with permission)

to keep their hardware and service secure from man-made damage. Thus, data centres are often mysterious. Luckily, Google is generous enough to show us its data centres on its website,[10] where we can also see the interior of one of its data centres – how the machines are placed together and connected, how the cooling systems (normally great quantities of water) are designed, and how much the data centres are like big boxes of machines that keep people out.

THE COST OF VIRTUAL MATERIALITY

Cloud storage and data centres contribute to the most important part of Dropbox's magical virtuality, making Dropbox seem purely virtual without revealing the materiality behind it, which sets Dropbox apart from its competitors. But one must not forget that the easy-to-grasp concept of Dropbox, conveyed by its brand name and icon, is the key to its success, since it makes digital file transfer such an easy task that even school pupils have no difficulties understanding and using it.

Then again, cloudiness and the hidden materiality *behind* that virtuality produce their own costs. Data centres are designed to provide reliable and secure services, and thus they need to be built in safe places unsusceptible to natural disasters. These places are also highly secured sites, similar to military areas. Data centres consume a lot of energy, and thus they need to be built in regions or countries where energy supply is sufficient and electricity costs are low. Running a data centre is a very high-tech business that requires huge investments in technology, hardware, and facilities. The cost behind data centres, cloud storage, and services that rely on cloud storage, is very high. Being aware of these costs might trouble the picture of the 'magic' simplicity that Dropbox constantly evokes. But for us as users, it is crucial to open the 'blue box' and take a careful look into it.

NOTES

1   This article is not affiliated with or otherwise sponsored by Dropbox, Inc.

2   Dropbox, 'Our logo', <https://www.dropbox.com/branding> [accessed 29 February 2016].

3   See Visualpharm, 'Choosing the Right Size and Format for Icons', <http://www.visualpharm.com/articles/icon_sizes.html> [accessed 29 February 2016].

4 Doctor Who is a British science fiction television series and is the longest-running Sci-Fi TV series ever screened on earth.

5 Hermione Granger, Ron Weasley, and Harry Potter are the three main characters in the children's fiction series 'Harry Potter', a story written by British author J. K. Rowling about a fantasy world of wizards. In the story, Miss Granger is known for her smartness. The story was adapted into a movie series.

6 'Mary Poppins' is a series of children's books by Pamela L. Travers and was adapted into film in 1964. The story is about a magical nanny who visits dysfunctional families and improves their lives by using magic and other means to take care of their children.

7 TechCrunch is an annual conference where technology startups launch their products and services in front of media and potential investors.

8 According to an analysis done by 99designs based on over 1,000 tech company logos, blue is the most chosen staple colour. The design company explains the reason: 'In a fast-changing industry with many new players, reliability is key.' See 99designs, 'The Logo Colors of Technology', <https://en.99designs.de/logo-design/psychology-of-color/technology> [accessed 1 November 2018].

9 Note that Dropbox doesn't build its own cloud storage for users' files. On the contrary, it rents Amazon's S3 (Simple Storage Service), a cloud storage service launched in 2006, for storing its mass amount of user files.

10 See Google, 'Datacenters', <http://www.google.com/about/datacenters/> [accessed 2 March 2016].

REFERENCES

Dropbox, 'Our logo', <https://www.dropbox.com/branding> [accessed 29 February 2016].

Google, 'Datacenters', <http://www.google.com/about/datacenters/> [accessed 2 March 2016].

Rowling, J. K., *Harry Potter*, 7 vols (London: Bloomsbury Publishing, 1997–2007).

Travers, P. L., *Marry Poppins*, 8 vols (London: HarperCollins, 1934–1988).

Visualpharm, 'Choosing the Right Size and Format for Icons', <http://www.visualpharm.com/articles/icon_sizes.html> [accessed 29 February 2016].

VIII

ANXIETY

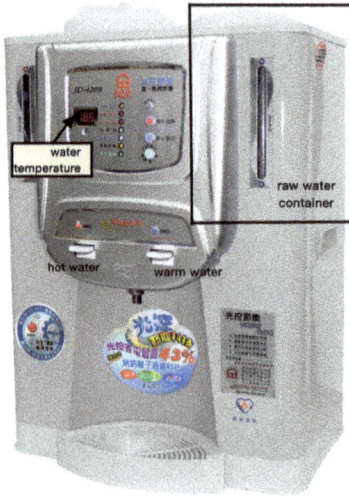

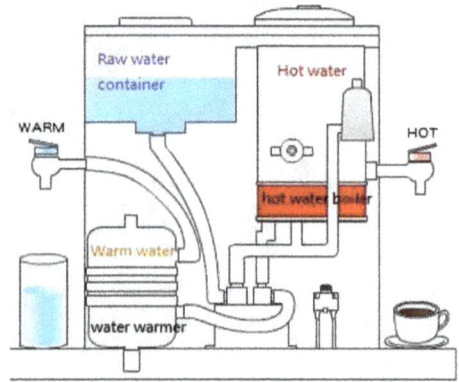

FIGS. 25.1, 25.1B Mirror perspective. Pictures and details of water dispensers (reproduced by kind permission of JINKON corporation, 2011)

2 5

DOMESTIC RESERVOIRS: MANAGING DRINKING WATER IN TAIWANESE HOUSEHOLDS

Yi-Ping Cheng

Size: 400 x 300 x 580 mm. **Total capacity:** 10.2 litres (includes 5.5 litres of 'raw' water, 3 litres of freshly boiled water, and 1.7 litres of tepid water). **Net Weight:** 7.4 kilogrammes. **Shape:** approximately a rectangular parallelepiped. **Colour:** silver white. **Functions:** drinking water filter, boiler, and warmer. **Locations:** It is generally located in the kitchen or dining room in Taiwan's households. Because of its size, it needs to be placed on a stable cabinet or on a table. **Other types: there are other kinds** of drinking water reservoirs in Taiwan's households: The picture shown in this paper is one of the typical drinking water reservoirs in Taiwan's households. There are several types of drinking water containers appropriated in Taiwan's domestic area, such as thermal kettles, boiling water pots, and so on. In order to clarify the intertwined water usage practice, I amplify this drinking water reservoir to make sense of how Taiwanese households purify and prepare their daily drinking water.

Keywords: purifying, preparing, transforming, containing, appropriating

ANXIETY OVER DAILY DRINKING WATER

> Water is experienced and embodied both physically and culturally. The
> meanings encoded in it are not imposed from a distance, but emerge from an
> intimate interaction involving ingestion and expulsion, contact and immersion.
> (Strang 2004: 4)

WATER IS VITAL NOT ONLY FOR FOOD PREPARATION BUT ALSO FOR FLUSHING
the toilet; cleaning clothes, dishes, and ourselves; and of course for drinking.
Within these different usages of water, I mainly focus on how Taiwanese manage
their drinking water in their households. The main purpose of studying drinking
water at home is not only that it represents a most ordinary part of domestic life
that we usually take for granted, but also because it shows co-ordinated systems of
material and immaterial culture in Taiwan. The ways of preparing drinking water
at home reveal the forms of people's physical and mental activities. The material
appliances for refining 'raw' water into drinking water, their uses, knowledge of
their function, and reasons to make it drinkable, are co-ordinated as an ordinary
domestic routine. Further, knowledge about how to manage the drinking water
at home also correlates with standards and criteria in wider society. Whether the
context is hygiene, health considerations, tastes, or seasonal alternations, ways
of managing drinking water embody the embedded culture context.

Because of the limited information about the uses of domestic tap water,
people are anxious about the quality of the water, its odour and taste, the
chemicals it contains, and even some diseases related to water. In general,
domestic water users have only a limited ability to evaluate the quality of the
water which runs through their domestic space. There is great anxiety over
hygiene standards when deciding which water resources are reliable, especially
concerning drinking water that will be absorbed into the human body. This
anxiety forces people to manage their drinking water in various ways. In Gray's
research (1994), when people worry about the quality of their drinking water,
they may boil their tap water or install alternative systems to purify it (filter
systems, activated carbon, reverse osmosis, ion exchange, disinfection, and so
on). Knowing how to manage the quality of drinking water correlates to maintaining a certain quality of life (Strang 2004), or even correlates to having cultural
'good taste' (Wilk 2006).

DRINKING WATER IN TAIWAN'S HOUSEHOLDS

Why do Taiwanese households worry about their domestic drinking water? Taiwan is a country which consists of many islands, and the main island is located in the northern subtropical area. Thus, the weather in Taiwan is warm and humid between May and September, typically between 27 and 35 degrees Celsius. The orientation of the main island is north to south, while the convergence of the Eurasian plate and Philippine Sea plate in Taiwan results in the orientation of the mountains in Taiwan also being north to south. This in turn causes the general direction of the rivers to have an east-to-west orientation, with the result that they are short and turbulent. In addition, as a result of the geographic location of Taiwan, the rainfall is intensive in summer, coming generally from typhoons and convective rain. Because of the uneven rainfall area and the marked seasonal variations, Taiwan has a flood problem in summer and water shortages in winter. Hence there are more than a hundred river reservoirs in Taiwan in order to provide even water distribution throughout the year. Further, due to the uneven rainfall patterns, the rain generally falls in summer as sudden downpours; thus, the water stored in summer is turbid and mixed with sand, which prolongs settlement time and the production of clear water. The soil conditions in Taiwan are also a factor in the quality of the water: in some areas the soil consists of limestone which easily leaches carbonate, calcium, and magnesium ions; in other areas, it consists of sandstone, which leads to serious problems of deposits and turbidity; all this causes experts to worry about the water quality in Taiwan.

The water resources in Taiwan are run by a single governmental organisation: the Taiwan Water Corporation (TWC). According to a report from the TWC,[1] the tap water in Taiwan is potable. However, because of the water storage infrastructure (it is stored in underground water tanks or in water towers) and an old pipeline system (which is affected by rust), the tap water may become polluted before it reaches homes. Therefore, on the official webpage of the TWC, a list of reliable companies for cleaning and disinfecting water tanks and/or towers, and stainless-steel pipes, is provided. In addition, the TWC provides a water quality testing service, at the customer's own cost, to ensure that people's drinking water quality is satisfactory. According to the drinking water regulations in

Taiwan,[2] since 2006 (at least from 2006), the tap water supplied by the TWC, and some other (community-installed) public water suppliers, should meet the criteria of the drinking water standard. Theoretically the tap water in Taiwan can be drunk directly from the tap.

Because of continuing anxiety over the quality of drinking water, however, Taiwanese people use many water appliances to purify their domestic drinking water. Owing to the complex nature of these appliances, and the various different hygiene standards, conventions, and preferences for drinking water, I portray the material paths of drinking water via their different temperature states to unfold the ways in which drinking water is managed in Taiwan's households (**FIGURE 25.2**).

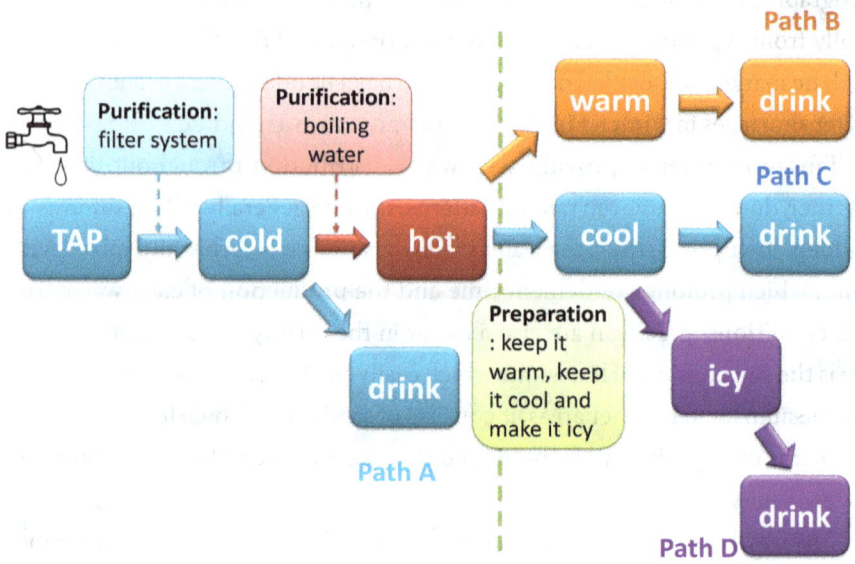

FIG. 25.2 Flow chart: material paths of drinking water in Taiwanese households

According to my small-scale empirical study in Taiwan, there are four material paths taken by drinking water. The purpose of grouping these paths of drinking water is to try to achieve a systematic comprehension of the enormous variety of treatments and preparations for drinking water in Taiwanese households. In order to achieve a clear understanding of how the Taiwanese typically manage their domestic drinking water, I mainly discuss path B in this chapter. The point in this path is not only that people purify their water by boiling it, but also that they prefer to keep their drinking water in a warm state. In this path, people adopt the second treatment for purifying their drinking water: boiling, compared to path A. One of my informants tells the reasons why they boil their drinking water:

> INTERVIEWER: So, you will not drink water directly after filtering it with a Brita?
> MING: That is not drinkable water!
> INTERVIEWER: Why!?
> MING: That is still "raw"/ [tap] water!
> (Informant: a person living on their own in a small flat)

CO-ORDINATED WATER FLOWS AND STORAGE SYSTEMS AT HOME

I use flows of drinking water as a metaphor to describe not only the fluidity of water but also the consumption of drinking water as a continuous process. Rather than tied to considering it as the moment of paying the water bill, the consumption of drinking water can be understood as a restless domestic water cycle, which consists of inflows, domestic circulation, and outflows. At each stage, the consumption of drinking water relates to a raft of material things and various social norms and conventions. It is clear that how water flows into the house affects the ways of using and storing water. Today, water is a fluid flow; it runs in and out through pipes, rather than being a 'living' flow from a stream or river. This means that turning the tap on is equal to turning the water flow on, and to turn the tap off means to stop the water flow. The house itself can thus be seen as a big container for water storage, which is fed through a network of pipes. The water pipes and water tanks at home are part of the supply chain of water which ensures that people can use water all the time without worrying about peak demand for water. In this sense, water is more or less stored (Shove and Chappells 2001: 53). In other words, water pipes and tanks, water appliances and containers play similar roles of regulating the demand for water.

In order to understand these co-ordinated household drinking water flows and storage methods, I emphasise two aspects involved in this practice:

materiality and material paths; convention and competence. Before I examine these elements, I shall elaborate this co-ordinated practice. The concept of practice can be traced to Ludwig Wittgenstein and Martin Heidegger. Theodore Schatzki's reinterpretation (1996) resituates Wittgenstein's idea of intelligibility and understanding from inside the human mind into a flow of praxis. Schatzki sees intelligibility and understanding of practice as something which is both social ordered and individual. He explains that a practice is a dispersed nexus of doings and sayings in a temporal and spatial complex. Further, for him, the concept of practice is a means for theorists to overcome the dilemma of structure and action (Schatzki, Knorr-Cetina, and von Savigny 2001). Anthony Giddens's *The Constitution of Society* also discusses practice in relation to the issue between agency and structure; he states that 'the day-to-day activity of social actors draws upon and reproduces structural features of wider social systems' (1984: 24). In other words, the flow of routinised social life depends on many forms of practical knowledge, being guided by social structural features, social rules, and resources.

Andreas Reckwitz suggests that practice is 'to regard agents as carriers of routinized, oversubjective complexes of bodily movements, of forms of interpreting, knowing how and wanting and of the usage of things' (2002: 259). He defines a practice as 'a routinized type of behaviour which consists of several elements, interconnected to one [an]other: forms of bodily activities, forms of mental activities, "things" and their use, a background knowledge in the form of understanding, know-how, states of emotion and motivational knowledge' (Reckwitz 2002: 249). In his terms, practice theory concerns not only the 'hardware' of material things, but also the 'software' of an individual's competence, emotion, and motivation. And the most important thing is how the hardware and software connect and interact with each other and make the practice with widely shared knowledge. Alan Warde goes further, asserting that practices are not only related to the integration and reproduction of the diverse elements of social existence – such as minds, texts, conversations, bodily movements, things, practical knowledge, and so on – but also require their competent practitioners to 'avail themselves of the requisite services, possess and command the capability to manipulate the appropriate tools, and devote a suitable level of attention to [...] conduct [them]' (2005: 145). More broadly still, for Schatzki, social life is a 'human coexistence, inherently transpir[ing] as part of nexuses of practices and material arrangements' (2010: 129). In addition, he constructs an ontology which considers that social phenomena consist in nexuses of practice(-materiality) arrangements. Practice in this context means an organised spatial-temporal manifold of human activity; material arrangements indicate a range of interconnected material entities. He then brings both social and material nature together, to evince that we exist in a complex of nexuses of practice and material arrangements (Schatzki 2010: 129). In Schatzki's latest account, it seems that he makes sense of social phenomena or social life through a temporal-spatial network and an entity comprising practice and material arrangements.

In sum, practice theory concerns routinised behaviours, competence, making do, bodily movements, mind, and even the proper level of devotion and attention to doing. Additionally, tools, objects, things, and materiality are also important to construct a practice. That is to say, using, holding, and keeping domestic things are part of the ongoing domestic practice in our daily lives. An enormous variety of material items and containers, and many cultural conventions, values of things, behaviours of using and storing, relevant competence and mind status are all included in routinised practice.

Therefore, in order to have a better sense of how drinking water is stored and how it circulates through the home, I focus on both the materiality and the relevant immateriality – the conventions and competence – which drive the movements of drinking water or make sense of how it is organised and stored. In the following sections, I discuss several concepts – materiality and material paths, conventions and competence – which are involved in the co-ordinated drinking water flows and storage facilities in Taiwan's households.

Materiality and Material Paths

What is materiality? Tilley et al. state that, owing to material objects being perceived as dead matter and having utilitarian significance, they can easily be considered as tools, technological substrates of life, or passive markers of social status and ethnic difference (2006: 2). They find that materiality could refer to very heterogeneous and ambiguous meanings which are entangled and rooted in several metaphors and cultural connections (Tilley et al. 2006:

3). Further, they examine the term 'things', which is used to refer to material-ity. Due to things usually being related to material possessions and to physical and economic goods, they have 'material *benefits* for persons. The object and the objectivity of things supposedly stand opposed to the subject and the subjectivity of persons' (Tilley et al. 2006: 3). Tilley et al. contend that one of the main features of studying material culture is that it reveals 'the dialectical and recursive relationship between persons and things: that persons make and use things and that the things make persons. Subjects and objects are indelibly linked' (Tilley et al. 2006: 4). Following this theoretical context, what the typi-cal material object is appears in this path of 'warm' drinking water in Taiwanese households, which connects the objectivity of things and the subjectivity of household users. This object is the water dispenser (**FIGURE 25.1**). In order to have an adequate understanding of how this type of water dispenser works in Taiwan's households I list several details of this material object. After reviewing the details of the water dispenser typically used in Taiwan's domestic space, we might be able to image how domestic water flows into, is stored in, and flows out of the water container.

Arjun Appadurai (1986) and Igor Kopytoff (1986) suggest making sense of materiality in two ways. One is through the 'cultural biography' of things, which focuses on the short-term path of things as they pass through different hands, contexts, and uses. The other is the social history of things, which concerns the long-term path of things in relation to a particular kind or class of object. This path reflects historical shifts and large-scale dynamic transformations. Attending to the social history of things allows us to appreciate their flow over a longer period of time and in a broad social context, but this social history of things depends for its detail on the relatively short-term, specific, and intimate trajectories of forms, meanings and structures. Equally, many small shifts in the cultural biography of things may influence changes in the social history of things (Appadurai 1986: 36).

Following the drinking water flow through a water dispenser, its cultural biography starts with the dispenser being refilled with tap water (or bottled mineral water); then the 'raw' water in the dispenser will be boiled and kept warm at a specific temperature; and finally the water will be ready to drink. As for the storage aspect of a water dispenser, according to the typical water reservoir shown in the beginning, it contains two compartments, one stores freshly boiled water and another stores warm water. In other words, a water dispenser is a boiler for raw water; after water is boiled it becomes the reservoir for more than two temperatures of drinking water. Water flows into the reservoirs of water dispensers regularly, and the dispenser transforms the state of drinking water as well as storing it, no matter which state it is in (**FIGURE 25.3**).

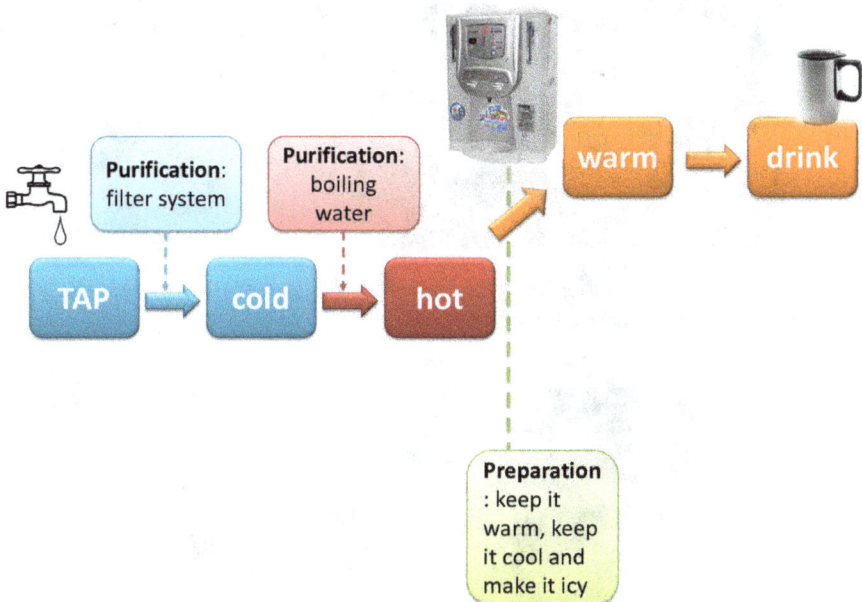

FIG. 25.3 Flow chart: material path and appliances of 'warm' drinking water in Taiwanese households

Because my research informants in this path preferred to have their drinking water in a warm state all the time, they mainly used water appliances that have a thermal function. In my interviews, there are four cases that mainly use a water dispenser to prepare their daily drinking water. For example, in Jio's house, her family uses filtered tap water and a water dispenser at the same time. The water dispenser also keeps their drinking water in a warm state all the time. In Jio's house they even use a flask for their daily drinking water – even in the summer (**FIGURES 25.4A, 25.4B**).

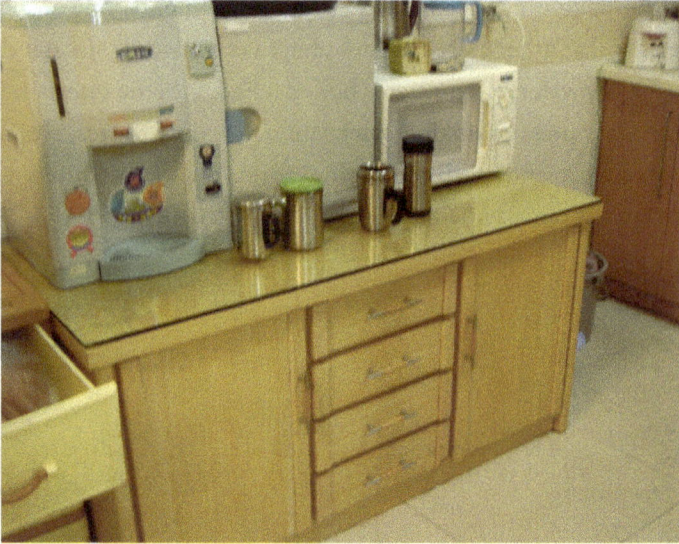

FIG. 25.4A Jio's water dispenser (there are four flasks in front of it, for the four adults in her family; photograph by Cheng Yi-Ping)

FIG. 25.4B Wu's water dispenser (photograph by Cheng Yi-Ping)

Conventions and Competence

Following the discussion above, what kind of cultural conventions and relevant competence is involved in this co-ordinated social practice of preparing domestic drinking water? There are two foci here: the first is the ways of purifying drinking water, and the second is the preference for warm drinking water.

Firstly, the purifying treatment of boiling water shows that people distrust tap water and reveals the hygiene conventions and traditions that affect even filtered, drinkable tap water. How are these normative conventions for drinking water formed? I want to argue that the knowledge to judge the hygiene standards of drinking water is formed unobtrusively and imperceptibly. It is not only based on scientific criteria but is also affected by cultural shifts over time in society. Before the tap water system was widely installed in Taiwan, people were used to boiling their water for drinking. This experience and convention of purifying drinking water then passed from one generation to the next. According to one of my informants, even though he belongs to the younger generation, he learned his hygiene standards and purification procedures for drinking water from his parents, and he still believes that this boiling procedure is 'necessary'. Even though he has tried to change this procedure, the conventional norms for drinking water make him comply.

> Jay: My filter system meets the criteria of drinking water, and I did try to drink water directly from tap for two weeks. But, you know, elderly people (his mother and elder cousins) still think that boiled water is better [than water directly from the tap]. They ask me to boil water after they found me drinking it directly from tap.
>
> (Informant: a person living on their own in a large flat)

Even where water-purification technology is up-to-date, then, Taiwanese households still appropriate the old habit of boiling water to manage the quality of their daily drinking water. Thus, we could consider that the social history of drinking water has not diverged from its original purifying treatment – 'boiling', even though individuals have alternative options.

Secondly, the preference for drinking warm water all the time correlates with cultivated cultural knowledge. Why does drinking warm water all the time indicate a healthier drinking habit? According to a Chinese medical approach, the human body takes more energy to consume cold (icy) drinks. In order to keep the body's energy and circulation in a warm state, it is better to serve drinks warm (or at room temperature) all the time, even in the hot summer. This kind of health notion is inherited from a cultural background and is practised in daily life. Therefore, people tend to drink water that is warm or at least at room temperature. In addition, people use various water appliances to make sure their flow and storage of drinking water suit their specific preferences.

Further, warm water is not only regarded as healthier than cold water, it is also convenient for making other drinks. Wu and Jio both mention that a water dispenser is convenient for preparing instant drinks and hot drinks for children and for themselves.

> Wu: We do not have time, brewing some instant coffee or tea is easier.
>
> (Informant: a couple living in a small flat)

> Jio: You know, my granddaughter needs warm water to make instant milk, and I need some instant tea (points to water dispenser and cabinets which have some tea bags).
>
> (Informant: a family lives in a large house)

Considering the effects of convention and competence on the social history of drinking water in Taiwan's households, we could conclude that the old habit of boiling water persists in the social history of drinking water in Taiwan, not diverging from its path as a purifying treatment. Also, we could say that inherited Chinese medical beliefs and the convenience of warm water make the social history of drinking water stay close to its purification through boiling path.

CONCLUSION

As a consequence of its topography and uneven rainfall patterns, water is generally turbid in Taiwan. However, the hygiene standards of tap water in Taiwan meet the required drinking water standards, according to the report from the Taiwan Water Corporation. The Corporation has also produced many publications advocating the proper ways to use water, how to protect it from secondary pollution, and how to clean water tanks. However, the behaviour of the Taiwanese people reveals that they ignore the published standards (and information); people have their own hygiene standards and their own ways to purify water. Based on their and their predecessors' experiences with water use before there was a mains water supply and domestic taps, people still tend to boil water to ensure that it is purer than the raw form. This kind of purifying treatment is cultivated as an inheritance passed on by previous generations. Like the preference for having warm water all the time, this kind of preparatory treatment is rooted in a cultural system and is practised in people's daily lives. In other words, the ways of preparing drinking water, cultivated over time, are rooted in cultural understanding, and are practised in accordance with the relationship between purification and preparation treatments.

According to different drinking water preferences, people use a raft of appliances to prepare their drinking water. I emphasise that these water appliances' materiality not only contributes to storing water, but also to purifying, preparing, and transforming drinking water. In other words, reservoirs of drinking water are not just containers; reservoirs help to form and transform various states of drinking water. Reservoirs represent the appropriation of material things, which relates to the continuous flow and consumption of drinking water, especially for storage considerations.

The flow and storage of drinking water in the domestic area demonstrates how water consumption at home is a continuous process of using and storing, rather than simply being the moment of paying the water bill. Water consumption is a co-ordinated routine which involves knowledge and conventional norms, and hygienic standards for drinking water, various preferences correlating to seasonal alternations, and a range of water appliances.

NOTES

1   http://www.water.gov.tw/eng/04water/wat_a_list.asp
2   http://law.moj.gov.tw/Eng/LawClass/LawHistory.aspx?PCode=O0040010

REFERENCES

Appadurai, A., ed., *The Social Life of Things, Commodities in Cultural Perspective* (Cambridge/New York: Cambridge University Press, 1986).

Giddens, A., *The Constitution of Society* (Cambridge: Polity Press, 1984).

Gray, N. F., *Drinking Water Quality* (Cambridge: Cambridge University Press, 1994).

JINKON Corporation, 'Eco-light control', Jinkon, 2011, <http://www.jinkon.com.tw/index.php?fn=prodent&no=428&no1%20=989&no%20 2=29117&no3=11&no5=E#> [accessed 26 January 2017].

Kopytoff, I., 'The Cultural Biography of Things: Commoditization as Process', in A. Appadurai, ed., *The Social Life of Things, Commodities in Cultural Perspective* (Cambridge/New York: Cambridge University Press, 1986), pp. 64–91.

Ministry of Justice, 'Drinking Water Management Act', Laws & Regulations Database of The Republic of China, 2017, <http://law.moj.gov.tw/Eng/LawClass/LawHistory.aspx?PCode=O0040010> [accessed 26 January 2017].

Reckwitz, A., 'Toward a Theory of Social Practices: A Development in Culturalist Theorizing', *European Journal of Social Theory*, 5.2 (2002): 243–63.

Schatzki, T., *Social Practices: A Wittgensteinian Approach to Human Activity and the Social* (Cambridge: Cambridge University Press, 1996).

——, 'Materiality and Social Life', *Nature and Culture*, 5.2 (2010): 123–49.

Schatzki, T., K. Knorr-Cetina, and E. von Savigny, eds, *The Practice Turn in Contemporary Theory* (London/New York: Routledge, 2001).

Shove, E., and H. Chappells, 'Ordinary Consumption and Extraordinary Relationships: Utilities and their Users', in J. Gronow, and A. Warde, eds, *Ordinary Consumption* (London/NewYork: Routledge, 2001), pp. 45–59.

Strang, V., *The Meaning of Water* (Oxford: Berg, 2004).

Tilley C., W. Keane, S. Küchler, M. Rowlands, and P. Spyer, eds, *Handbook of Material Culture* (London: Sage, 2006).

Warde, A., 'Consumption and Theories of Practice', *Journal of Consumer Culture*, 5.2 (2005): 131–53

Wilk, R., 'Bottled Water: The Pure Commodity in the Age of Branding', *Journal of Consumer Culture*, 6.3 (2006): 303–25.

FIG. 26.1 General civilian anti-gas respirator carrying case with British civilian gas mask (copyright Imperial War Museum, London (EQU 2706))

26

KEEP CALM AND CARRY ONE: THE CIVILIAN GAS MASK CASE AND ITS CONTAINMENT OF BRITISH EMOTIONS

Mats Fridlund

Box: general civilian anti-gas respirator carrying case. **Size and shape**: 17 cm x 13 cm x 11 cm rectangular cardboard box with two flaps under main lid and a string strap filled with a gas mask of small, medium or large size. **Colour**: brown. **Behaviour**: containing, protecting, swinging from shoulders or on hangers in homes or workplaces, rarely opened, never activated but always present. **Habitat**: throughout the United Kingdom. **Distribution**: spotted in big British cities and especially in London; some 50 million during its active phase. **Migration**: during the Second World War many travelled from public places to private homes and into dark closets. **Status**: currently more or less extinct except for some remaining specimens in museums, at flea markets, and on eBay.

Keywords: comforting, protecting, carrying, threatening, mobilising, signalling, awakening, frightening, waiting, simulating, practising, training

BY 4 SEPTEMBER 1939, THE DAY AFTER THE OUTBREAK OF THE SECOND
World War, millions of brown boxes had already transformed London. 'That
Monday morning, everywhere you went people were carrying their masks. It
was almost like an army with those brown cardboard boxes over their arms'
(Haining 1989). At the war's outset three out of four Londoners were estimated to be carrying one, and the public box-carrying was encouraged by
example, with members of the government and the Royal Family 'liberally
photographed carrying these' (Haining 1989: 60; Mass-Observation 1940:
111). A few weeks later a woman was given 'a full realization of the effect of
the war' upon arriving at Waterloo Station and seeing 'sober, respectable busi-
nessmen walking about solemnly with cardboard boxes strung around their
necks'. According to the government-contracted social research organisation
Mass-Observation (M-O), the 'masses' were to be 'helped to feel that if this
was a new kind of war, it was their war too. The gas mask was, for a time, the
best of any propaganda to uplift civilian morale. It gave the led a feeling of
equality with their leaders, a participation between the YOU and the US, the
civilian and the soldier. Everybody was armed. For a time' (Garfield 2005: 40;
Mass-Observation 1940: 111).

British civilians had been armed with gas-mask-loaded cardboard boxes
due to a widespread fear of a future war that could end civilisation through
aerial gas bombings. To discipline citizens' fear, the government had in 1936
announced that 'a simple but effective form of respirator for use by the civil
population' was in the works, and that this gas mask should be provided freely
if the need should arise. This was a new government obligation 'since in no
previous war had a Government had to contemplate the possible death or
injury of so large a proportion of the civil population, by one weapon' (Titmuss
1950: 21; O'Brien 1955: 70, 77). In January 1937, British cinema audiences
had been shown news reels proclaiming that the government's first gas mask
factory in Blackburn would be turning out half a million gas masks a week
(Aldgate 1979: 143–144, 152). The civilian gas mask thus became an iconic
materiality of wartime fear, and the most widely distributed everyday commodity for helping citizens cope with the future air war (Fritzsche 1992: 214–15;
Fritzsche 1993: 698).

FIG. 26.2 Civilians walking on the streets of London with gas mask cases after the outbreak of the Second World War (photo by Reg Speller/Hulton Archive/Getty Images)

FORGOTTEN FEELINGS OUT OF THE BOX

The gas mask's wider introduction came with the Munich crisis in 1938 when the British Prime Minister Neville Chamberlain visited Hitler three times to resolve the threatening Sudeten issue, which was solved in Germany's favour. Many British citizens got 'their first visible, personal proof of the threat which overhung them' when, during Chamberlain's second visit on 24 September, the Home Office asked local authorities to start distributing respirators to the public (O'Brien 1955: 157). Recollections of the gas mask case's sudden emergence in September 1938 make clear that it was not just an inanimate thing or a silent symbol of a possible war. The mundane case and its masked content were entangled with complex feelings of fear of death and hopes for survival, and inculcated immediate and new sensations and emotions. War – to one person at least – from

427

being a remote possibility, became almost overnight an immediate danger.
I can remember at my boarding school, where the wireless was banned
and interest in politics discouraged, how suddenly one evening, soon after
the start of the Christmas term, the lights began to dim in a trial black-out,
and how, when they were raised again, the staff hurried in with armfuls of
small cardboard boxes and one by one we were outfitted with a gas mask.
This was what brought home to most people the real meaning of the crisis.
(Longmate 1971: 2)

Similar close encounters with the small cardboard boxes generated new, previously unknown and visceral emotions. One woman described how the boxes
even produced a numbing physical fear:

as I looked through the lounge doors, I saw a sight which frightened me.
The whole family and all the guests were standing in the lounge, on the table
there were a lot of square boxes marked "Small" "Medium" and "Large". Each
contained a gas mask. A man was fitting my mother, he asked her to breathe
and he held a piece of paper against the end of the hideous contraption. Is
it really as bad as all that? [...] After I had my mask fitted I returned with
you [her fiancé] to our sitting room. You kissed me but I felt too frightened
to notice. (IWML, Hurford-Veazey)

But it is too easy and not correct to state that the cardboard boxes just made
people 'realise' or 'awoke' them to the actual threat of a coming war. It is true
that the fear and sensations of future war the cardboard cases created shared
aspects and affects of the actual war that materialised, but it was also something
radically different. Although that which was feared – indiscriminate gas attacks
upon the British civilian population – was not realised, the fear was very real; it
was imagined, embodied and experienced, contained inside people's bodies and
minds despite not materialising outside. The Second World War both wasn't
and was the gas mask cases' war. It wasn't, as the war saw no gas bombings, and
yet it also was, because the possibility of gas attacks was kept alive throughout
the war in the form of mental visions, public practices, visceral sensations, and
material things stowed away in minds, representations, bodies, and closets.

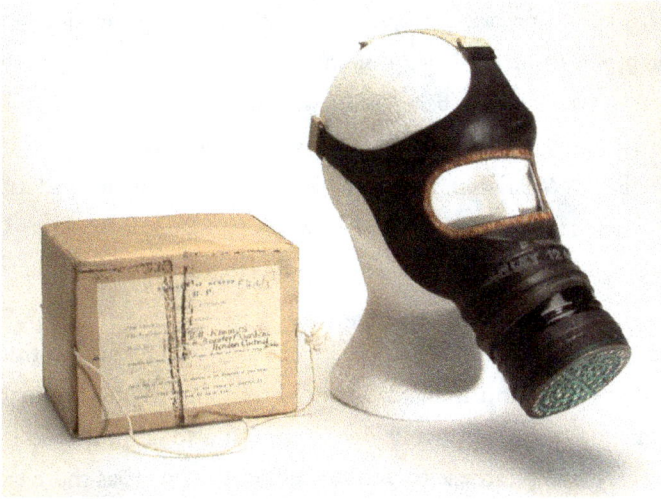

FIG. 26.3 The British civilian gas mask and officially issued cardboard gas mask case, with cord for carrying (courtesy of Islington Education Library Service)

What follows is a history of the 'subject politics of technology,' focusing more on material things' 'experiential effects on human subjects rather than the symbolic discursive meanings of technological objects' (Fridlund 2011: 392). This history seeks to recover a forgotten and fear-filled past by unpacking the tensions between fear of death and hopes for survival contained in the mundane cardboard boxes.

ALWAYS CARRY ONE

Immediately after the Munich crisis had ended in Germany's favour, the government booklet *The Protection of Your Home Against Air Raids* was delivered to every British home, to prepare the people of Britain for what to do if this country were ever at war'. The booklet contained an official description of the contents of the thirty-five million cardboard boxes that had been issued: the ordinary citizen's mask. It was 'designed for you by Government experts', came in three sizes and consisted 'of a rubber facepiece with a transparent window, and a container which holds the gas filters', of which one 'consists of specially prepared charcoal, and the other of pads of specially prepared material'. The mask, if properly put on, protects the eyes, nose, mouth and lungs; and it ensures a supply of *pure* air for breathing, by means of filters which are able to absorb any gas known to be capable of being used in war. The facepiece, the edges of which fit closely round the face, prevents any air from getting inside the respirator except that which passes through the filters. It is held in position by adjustable straps behind the head. Once these straps have been properly adjusted, the respirator, if needed, can be put on instantly (Home Office 1938: 7).

The booklet prefigured the future war by exhorting its readers to think things through, to prepare, and then to 'see how to apply them [the instructions contained in the booklet] to your own home'. It also admonished the public to 'always carry a respirator with you throughout the war', as there would be a

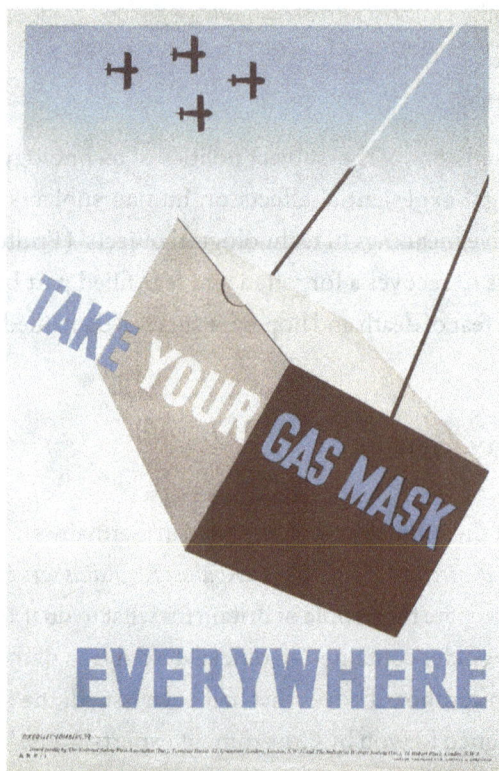

FIG. 26.4 Carry one everywhere. Poster by Thomas Eckersley and Eric Lombers, 1939. (Reproduced by kind permission of the Royal Society for the Prevention of Accidents and Imperial War Museum, London (Art. IWM PST 13860))

'limited number' of public refuges for 'those caught in the streets' (Home Office 1938: 28). Less than a year later, the war was no longer in the future.

On 1 September 1939 Germany attacked Poland. The British government immediately issued an ultimatum for German withdrawal, and began readying and issuing some fifty million civilian gas masks (O'Brien 1955: 231). The Londoner Valerie Reid's diary (IWML, Reid) makes visible the emotional effects connected to this. On that same day, she had been visiting various offices in a vain attempt to sign up for volunteer work:

> Outside in the hot street the sun shines. Now what? A gas mask. I had better go and get one. Lisson Grove they had said. […] It was not easy to find your way about the big supply station. Ambulances and lorries encumbered the yard. Men in the uniform of decontamination squads were busy under the open sheds. "TO GAS MASKS" read the clumsily printed notice with an arrow pointing up an iron fire escape staircase. "TO GAS MASKS" said another scrawled in blue pencil on an open door. "TO GAS MASKS" […] but here the crowd made further indications unnecessary. By this time I was both hungry and thirsty. Slowly, so slowly we moved forward. A large room at last arranged like a concert hall with chairs in rows down the middle and round the sides. On a small raised platform at the end two men in shirt sleeves were working doggedly persistently. They both looked dead tired, their movements automatic and careful as if they had no energy to spare for any false move. I looked at them to the waiting crowds. Here surely was work, the something I could do. No longer tired and in spite of scowls I pushed my way to the front. "Do you want any help?" I asked the man in the pink shirt. He was adjusting a head strap and without looking up his reply came, "My god, yes. This is how you do it".

Two days later, immediately before the war's outbreak, Reid returned to issue masks and cases under the supervision of 'Cap':

> We were short of cases and an order came through forbidding us to issue any more except with masks. A very old woman came in and talked to Cap after a minute or two. He beckoned to me. "Here, deal with this will you,"

and turned away to talk with a group of storekeepers. The old woman had come a long way. She and her husband wanted cases; they felt there was more protection with a case. Her rheumy eyes were anxious and tearful. "But I can't come again tomorrow. It's the fares dearie. My old man 'e's that upset with it all and him not able to get about like [...]. Besides they're better in a case, safer like [...]." Cap looked across as I handed her the precious cases, his left eyelid dropped imperceptibly as he turned his shoulder to this breach of official regulations.

When the British ultimatum generated no response, Chamberlain, at 11.15 am on 3 September declared in a short radio announcement that 'this country is at war with Germany'. Thirteen minutes later, the first air-raid siren went off in London. Although a false alarm, its responses demonstrate the existing gas fear. Many Londoners were conditioned by their previous indirect experience of gas war. One woman reported that her grandfather,

a badly gassed veteran of the first world war, said "this is it, we're in for it this time and we're not ready". The siren sounded the first air raid of the war and we thought that Grandad was right. ... We sat around and then suddenly Grandma said "Where are your gas masks?" In our hurry to leave home we had completely forgotten about our little cardboard boxes. With visions of our being gassed Grandma hastily produced large pads of wet flannel that we were to hold over our nose and mouth. We then departed from Islington very quickly to get away from vulnerable London and motored through Oxford Street heading west with our wet pads at the ready waiting for the first gas warning. With great relief we heard the "All Clear". We never went without our cardboard boxes for a very long time after that. (IWML, BBC Radio, Payne)

DOMESTICATION AND NATURALISATION

The fear of coming gas attacks was soon domesticated. Already on 13 September a London woman wrote that the 'little cardboard boxes which contain our gasmasks are slowly losing their "sameness" as the most fantastic and colourful covers are appearing everywhere. It doesn't take a woman long to ornament even that nasty little necessity!' (IWML, Hall). Many brown cardboard cases were replaced by colourful commercial variants in cloth, leather, or metal, and in 1940 it was reported that the most popular 'female carrying colours' for containers were brown, white, cream, and green (Mass Observation 1940: 114, 117). As the war continued, many volunteer women felt that 'anything that smacked of frivolity and femininity' after a long day in uniform became 'morale boosting'. The morale of some was raised by 'Elizabeth Arden's velvet-covered gas mask cases which had their little silk-lined pocket for cosmetics on top'. Furthermore, many old and new domesticated cases didn't actually contain masks anymore, but instead lunch sandwiches, make-up, and other personal belongings (Courcey 2005: 123).

FIGS. 26.5A, 26.5B Gendering the fear of gas. The *Illustrated London News* 7 October 1939 issue showing the 'chic' ladies fashion in gas mask cases, together with an advertising leaflet directed at male carriers for the 3.S ('simple – safe – sanitary') gas mask container (sources: Fig. 26.5a, *Illustrated London News* (1939); Fig. 26.5b, Mass Observation Archive)

The practice of carrying gas mask boxes changed fast. A London park-keeper noted on 6 October: 'Crowds of shoppers at Woolwich. Life is normal again. Many people do not carry their gas masks. Some, I am sure, imagine that this is all they will know of war, and have become bold again' (Mass Observation 1940: 117). In some cases, people were even chided for carrying masks. A Glasgow office worker reported that 'the office girl, has had many raggings in the past because of her attachment to her gas-mask, with the result that she has been ridiculed into leaving it behind in the office when she goes out for a message. She asked me (a confirmed gas-mask carrier) whether or not she should take it, and I said I would in her place' (Garfield 2005: 61). By November, many British apparently saw one of the 'main inconveniences of war-time on the home front' as 'having to carry gasmasks everywhere, especially in crowds', this being, at any rate, one of the 'most often' heard 'grouses'. One exemplary quote: 'Will the day ever come when we can go without these?' (MOA, SxMOA1/3/37).

By Spring 1940, gas mask carrying was so rare that M-O, which counted conspicuous carriage of gas mask boxes as an indicator of civilian morale, and reported on it to the government, started to measure adherence to protocol in actual cases instead of percentages. The gas mask's disappearance was described as one 'important outward symbol of "unity" that has gone by the board. One factor in this dwindling is the dwindling of fear'. M-O warned that 'the immediate

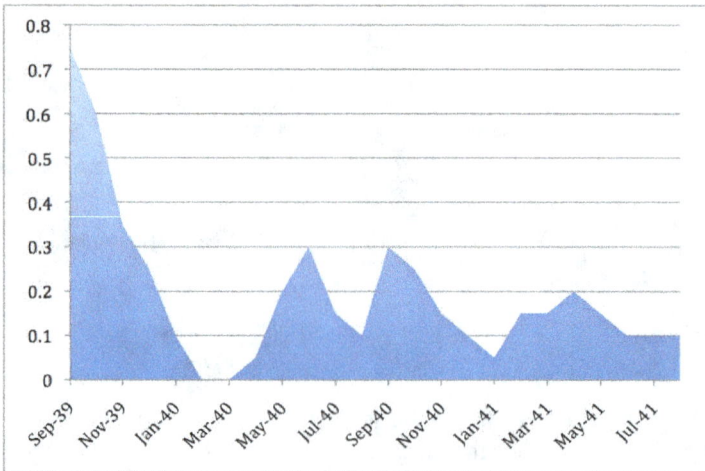

FIG. 26.6 Gas mask box counts in London by Mass Observation (data from Field Report 1666, Mass Observation Archive)

attack that was foreseen did not occur, but there is no telling when it may occur. When that time comes, it will be more difficult to attain 100% mask-carrying than if the percentage had been kept at a steadily high level by suitable stimulation' (Mass-Observation 1940: 116–117). However, the gas threat was still a reality to many. The day before the start of the Blitz, a couple wrote to American friends that although their masks were unused, 'we must be prepared, and not just think they never will be wanted' (IWML, Shean).

COMPLICATING CASE STUDIES

The gas mask began to appear again when the war entered a new phase with the German invasion of Denmark and Norway in April 1940 (O'Brien 1955: 366). M-O noted another spike with the invasion of Holland and Belgium in May, and another when the Blitz began in September (MOA, SxMOA1/2/55/2/L/3).

By 1941 Mass Observation's initial notion that gas mask carrying had a positive association to general morale had changed. There was a 'definite' association, but it was 'complicated' (MOA, SxMOA1/1/6/5/21). Now carriers were read as indicating fear, and abstainers as indicating fearlessness. Carrying tended 'to be associated with anxiety' and 'to go up in times of crisis, even though there is no immediate home threat' (MOA, SxMOA1/1/6/9/13). Admittedly there were also those like Dr P. E. Vernon, Director of Psychology at Glasgow University, whose research indicated that gas mask carrying mainly 'goes with support for the Government and optimistic opinions', and primarily depended 'on being a good citizen and doing what the government says without criticism' (MOA, SxMOA1/1/6/6/18; SxMOA1/1/6/11/1). However, several indicators showed the problems with using gas mask cases as an indicator of morale. One was that a number of people who did not carry masks appeared 'to possess 2 and even 3 gas masks which they keep at home and office, to save carrying up and down' (MOA, SxMOA1/2/55/1/B/3). Furthermore, it was also evident that there was '*no evidence at all*' that mask carrying correlated with gas expectations, as those who did not believe that gas would be used 'carry their masks as much as the others' (emphasis in the original). This produced the somewhat puzzling result that in addition to those generally worried about gas, many of those carrying masks had no confidence in the masks or no expectations that gas would be used. It appears as if the de facto situation was more about emotions than anything else. It seems 'possible that those who regularly carry their masks may tend to do so without particular logical reference to the actual value of the gasmask as a method of protection against gas – i.e., they use it as a sort of psychological weapon' (MOA, SxMOA1/2/55/2/C/1).

During the spring of 1941, government gas mask propaganda intensified. In March the Minister of Home Security gave a radio talk telling people to carry their gas masks regularly, and this was followed in April by the production of the leaflet *What to Do about Gas,* estimated to have been seen by some sixty percent of Londoners, and which was apparently responsible for a temporary increase in gas-mask carrying (MOA, SxMOA1/1/6/5/2). The threat and fear of gas was still alive. M-O, which had interviewed Londoners about their attitudes to gas, concluded a 'general trend' 'for more people to expect gas than not to expect it', with almost half believing that gas was going to be used. More than ten percent 'had little faith' in the efficiency of their masks, with one respondent believing the mask's value to be 'psychological only, it would prevent panic and people would die quieter, which is all that interests the Government' (MOA, SxMOA1/2/55/1/B/3).

PACKING UP AND UNPACKING

Gas-mask use waned in 1941 when Germany opened up a second front in the Soviet Union in June and the USA entered the war in December (Bell 2009: 158). Following the invasion of the Soviet Union, mask carrying went down to about 10 percent, which led to a new Ministry of Home Security campaign with 400,000 posters encouraging gas-mask use. It had little effect. People asked about it approved, although some saw it as 'silly sensation-mongering' and others as 'not startling enough'. The main problem was seen as an excessive saturation of 'gas propaganda', as a result of which most people had already 'mainly made up their minds or reached boredom point about gas'; furthermore many who believed that gas would come still did 'not believe in their gas-mask'. In addition, there was the 'deeper' problem that many people did 'not want to think about gas at all'. Nevertheless, the campaign was still seen as valuable because, in the long-term, it 'undoubtedly keeps gas as an idea alive in the public mind, and keeps people more conscious of their gas-mask, even if they do not carry it' (MOA, SxMOA1/1/6/7/31; MOA, SxMOA1/1/6/8/6).

After the summer the bombings receded but the fear remained. The domestication of the gas threat in 1942 took somewhat of a turn towards entertainment and spectacle with the arrangement of local 'Poison Gas Weeks'. One of these, held in Richmond on 15–20 June 1942, featured shop windows 'literally plastered with yellow notices' warning that there 'will be surprise poison gas attacks' and that there 'will have to be A FIRST TIME. Carry your gas mask!!'. Wall posters screamed: 'POISON GAS WEEK. FACE IT WITH YOUR MASK' and 'IT'S IN THE AIR POISON GAS WEEK'. A slogan competition had been won by an anonymous submission, 'Gas? Mask it!', with second prize to a 9-year-old girl: '"PRIVATE" Gas Mask your own "HOME GUARD"'. An observer was told by the Week's publicity manager that 'In the event of a Tear Gas Raid, people are expected to move freely and to continue with their shopping – if this occurs then Richmond will have created a precedent'. All shop keepers participated by carrying notices, and the handbag and leather shop had a special window display of mask cases. The following day at 11.20 the 'rattles went off' following the release of tear gas bombs. What followed was, according to the observer, 'a most amazing sight. Out came gas-masks from their cases – everyone acted with promptitude, clearness of mind as if the public had previously been drilled into their part. Some people continued with their shopping; others waited expectantly, ready for anything to happen'. He even saw a lorry with a gas-masked driver and was told by the Chief Warden to go and see 'the queue outside the Greengrocers waiting to be served with new potatoes – all wearing their gas masks' (MOA, SxMOA1/2/55/1/A/16).

The government continued to focus on possible gas attacks until the end of the war. In May 1942 Churchill had warned that if Germany used gas against the Soviet Union, Britain would use its 'growing air superiority to carry gas warfare on the largest possible scale far and wide against military objectives in Germany'. This was followed three months later by a government announcement that it was no longer considered necessary to carry gas masks in London and other 'danger areas' (Longmate 1971: 76; O'Brien 1955:

436–37). This was supposedly due to the need to save rubber and to reduce the masks' wear and tear. Following this statement M-O concluded that due to 'this or another reason, gas-mask carrying, already very low, has almost become non-existent' (MOA, SxMOA1/1/7/9/1, SxMOA1/1/7/9/1). The government, however, emphasized 'with all the force at their command' that they did not 'consider the gas threat as gone, and people were asked to keep their masks at hand in their homes. For many the gas mask remained close by throughout the war. Like the sixty-three-year-old school-mistress, who in the first week of peace in 1945 said she wished, 'we could be told what to do with our gasmasks. I'm tired of seeing them hanging in the hall' (MOA, SxMOA1/1/10/6/9).

The uncertainty and the gas mask boxes had remained throughout the war. When the pioneering social policy researcher, Richard Titmuss, looked back on the war in 1950, he pointed out that 'each spring the threat of invasion returned, and even when victory seemed only a matter of months away there was still the possibility of desperate attempts at invasion, of gas attacks and of secret weapons still more destructive. Behind each test successfully passed there lurked the danger of greater ordeals. In retrospect, these fears and the precautions they demanded are easily overlooked' (Titmuss 1950: 443).

The fears and precautions of the civilian gas mask boxes have been overlooked, undervalued, or forgotten by researchers until now. But the time to use them has come. The time to open and unpack them, to understand and experience the forgotten fears, high hopes, and terrifying things they contained.

REFERENCES

Aldgate, A., *Cinema and History: British Newsreels and the Spanish Civil War* (London: Scolar Press, 1979).

Bell, A., 'Landscapes of Fear: Wartime London, 1939–1945', *Journal of British Studies*, 48 (2009): 153–75.

Courcey, A. D., *Debs at War: How Wartime Changed Their Lives, 1939–1945* (London: Weidenfeld & Nicolson, 2005).

Fridlund, M., 'Buckets, Bollards and Bombs: Towards Subject Histories of Technologies and Terrors', *History and Technology*, 27 (2011): 391–416.

Fritzsche, P., *A Nation of Fliers: German Aviation and the Popular Imagination* (Cambridge: Harvard University Press, 1992).

——, 'Machine Dreams: Airmindedness and the Reinvention of Germany', *American Historical Review*, 98 (1993): 685–709.

Garfield, S., *We Are at War: The Diaries of Five Ordinary People in Extraordinary Times* (London: Ebury Press 2005).

Haining, P., *The Day War Broke Out: 3 September 1939* (London: WH Allen, 1989).

Home Office, *The Protection of Your Home Against Air Raids* (London: HMSO, 1938).

Longmate, N., *How We Lived Then: A History of Everyday Life During the Second World War* (London: Hutchinson of London, 1971).

Mass-Observation, *War Begins at Home* (London: Chatto & Windus, 1940).

O'Brien, T. H., *Civil Defence* (London: HMSO, 1955).

Titmuss, R. M., *Problems of Social Policy* (London: HMSO, 1950).

ARCHIVAL MATERIAL

University of Sussex Library, The Mass Observation Archive (MOA), Brighton

SxMOA1/3/37: Directive: November 1939, Diarist (DR) 2002, DR2265

SxMOA1/1/5/5/50: Field Report (FR) 146 'Gas mask carrying', 28.5.40

SxMOA1/1/6/5/2: FR681 'Report on Gas Mask Leaflet', 30.4.41

SxMOA1/1/6/5/21: FR701 GASMASK CARRYING 16.5.41.

SxMOA1/2/55/2/C/1: FR705 Gas mask Carrying

SxMOA1/1/6/6/18: FR739 QUESTIONNAIRE ON PSYCHOLOGICAL WAR WORK AND ON AIR RAIDS, July 1941;

SxMOA1/1/6/7/31: FR800 'Report on Gasmask Posters', 21.7.41;

SxMOA1/1/6/8/6: FR814 'Supplementary Report on Effectiveness of Gasmask Posters', 5.8.41.

SxMOA1/1/6/9/13: FR869 SALVAGING HISTORY

SxMOA1/1/6/11/1: FR938–9 BULLETIN AND DIRECTIVE, 6 June 1941.

SxMOA1/1/7/9/1: FR1401 MORALE IN AUGUST 1942, July 1942.

SxMOA1/1/10/6/9: FR2263 VICTORY IN EUROPE, 1945.

SxMOA1/2/55/1/A/16, Handwritten special report; 'Richmond Gas Week'. Index of events and handwritten interviews, observations etc. 18.6.42 (LB)

SxMOA1/2/55/1/B/2, Typed questionnaire as above; Kilburn 29.3.41

SxMOA1/2/55/1/B/3 Typed and handwritten questionnaire replies, approx. 50 replies 29.3.41

SxMOA1/2/55/2/L/3: Typed note on gas mask carrying 26.5.40 M-O

Imperial War Museum London (IWML), London

PP/MCR/199, Joan Hurford-Veazey, *Love and War; An Autobiographical study of the years 1939–1945: Covering the Second Great War,* September 15, 1938

Misc.: BBC Radio, 67/278/1–2 (1), Folder 'Sunday 16th July. Waterlings', A[nthony]. W. Payne 111188 (461) in Islington

Miss M. J. Shean, vol. 3, Con Shelf, 090740

Miss V. Reid microfilm PP/MCR/88, V.W. Reid, *Cameos of 1939–40* Diary

V Hall Con Shelf DS/MISC/88 & 84/35/1A

FIG. 27.1 A homeless man sleeps inside a cardboard box on Ermou street in central Athens in the early hours of Sunday, 28 June 2015 (source: Associate Press/Daniel Ochoa de Olza)

27

CARDBOARD BOX: THE POLITICS OF MATERIALITY

Maria Rentetzi

Material: cardboard paper, that is, heavy-duty paper consisting either of a single thick sheet of paper or multiple corrugated and non-corrugated layers. **Size and shape**: it is produced in a variety of sizes and shapes. **Origin**: we first come across its modern broad commercial appearance in the early nineteenth century in the US. **Habitat**: it often appears sleek and decorated in store windows; loaded with all kinds of objects in attics, storerooms, and warehouses; orderly arranged in archival depositories; flattened and crumbled on pavements; greasy and worn out in storefronts. **Behaviour**: attractive and seductive when performing its original function; protective when it appears as a home of the homeless person; political when appearing in newspapers and TV news. **Migration**: from packaging industries, window stores, and commercial warehouses to pavements and the open urban environment.

Keywords: seducing, persuading, commercialising, modernising, storing, packaging, protecting, shipping, housing, ordering/disordering, displacing, huddling

I HAVE A STRANGE INTEREST IN ALL BOXES. I USED TO COLLECT TIN AND paper boxes, most of the time empty ones, just because I enjoyed the graphics on their exterior. An odd habit. A close friend of mine was courageous enough to suggest that Freudian theory might hold the answer. In his general introduction to psychoanalysis, Freud discusses the symbolic interpretations of dream elements. The great majority of symbols in the dream, he argued, are sex symbols. Boxes find a prominent place there. 'The female genital is symbolically represented by all those objects which share its peculiarity of enclosing a space capable of being filled by something – viz., by *pits, caves,* and *hollows,* by *pitchers* and *bottles,* by *boxes* and *trunks, jars, cases, pockets,* etc.' (Freud 1920). I was not sure what to make of this and so I pushed it under the carpet for a long time – that is, until boxes began turning up in my scientific work (Rentetzi 2011) and, more persistently, in my daily life. I always thought of boxes as objects that enclose other objects. But my recent daily experience proves that boxes have also been extensively used for enclosing human beings. I'll begin with this.

I live in Athens, Greece, and I love walking on Ermou Street, a once-bustling pedestrian destination with an impressive history and some of the best coffee shops in the world. A symbol of the city's modernisation, it was designed in 1834 by Stamatios Kleanthis and the court architect Eduard Schaubert. It served as the base of an isosceles triangle with its peak at the Royal Palace – today's Greek Parliament – and has been a symbolic geometric apex of power since then. Ermou Street was named after Hermes, the Olympian god and patron of commerce, and served from the early days as the city's upscale shopping heaven.

The idea of modernity that Bavarian King Otto and his royal court tried to impose on Greece, although at odds with the locals, sought to politically incorporate the country into modern Europe. Architects and city planners were called upon to do part of this job. The report by Emmanuel Manitakis, a general in charge of public works in Greece, on the progress of Athens' reconstruction in 1866 is indicative of this intent. The report refers to Athens's 'large and well-aligned streets, beautiful houses built according to Italian taste, the oldest of which dates to 1834, numerous public structures and its population which, in its manner of dressing, living, and thinking, is to such a degree similar with the great family of civilized nations of Europe' (quoted in Bastea 2010: 30).

Indeed, throughout the nineteenth century, Ermou Street, with its 360 shops selling goods such as hats, shoes, stationery and jewellery, embodied the notion of modernity that Manitakis had in mind. A destination for the royal family and the upper class, Ermou remained so even during the inter-war period, monopolising women's fashion and hosting some of the most extravagant artists of the period. Among them was Nelly, the well-known Greek photographer, who set up her studio in Ermou Street in 1924. Interestingly, the street never lost its flavour and flair for exclusive shoppers. In 1997 it was turned into a pedestrian thoroughfare, becoming the city's most expensive commercial street and a colourful cultural destination. Along with New York's Fifth Avenue, Paris's Champs-Élysées, and Milan's Via Montenapoleone, it appeared in the list of the ten most expensive streets in the world. Yet in 2009, because of the financial crisis that hit the country, Ermou began losing its glamour. Recent statistics show that two in ten of the street's ground level stores are vacant.

Today I take fewer walks in the area, but not because I no longer enjoy shopping. I never did anyway. Rather, I caught myself feeling sad as I watched the transformation of the cardboard box from a symbol of commercial prosperity to an icon of financial depression.

After Greece's first bailout in 2010, unemployment rocketed from 9.5% in 2009 to 17.7% in 2011, and finally to 25.2 % in 2015 (The World Bank; Eurostat). As I write this, Greece has the highest unemployment rate of all EU Member States. A massive wave of layoffs that started right after 2009 led many to unemployment and soon to homelessness. In addition, Greece's social infrastructure collapsed from the impact of the most brutal austerity measures that a European country has seen since World War I. When limited and meagre unemployment benefits expire, people are left with no income and no right to health insurance. Until the crisis started, homelessness was relatively unusual in a country of strong family ties. In 2009 there were just over 7,000 homeless people in Athens. Today, there are more than 20,000, among them even middle-class people who lost their jobs and were unable to pay rent.

As Marianella Kloka, advocacy officer of PRAKSIS, which works with Doctors without Borders, reported

I could never imagine there would be so many homeless people in the center of Athens. There used to be a very small number of people who lived in the streets all their lives. Now I see young people in the streets, I see people my age, around 40. They are on the street begging or sleeping. (World Socialist Website 2015)

Greek and international newspapers report on how the new homeless find shelter during warm summer nights and cold, rainy ones in makeshift homes. Photographers such as the Spaniard Daniel Ochoa de Olza from the Associated Press, or the Greek Yannis Behrakis from Reuters, have extensively documented what has become part of our everyday lives: people huddled on flattened cardboard boxes or sleeping inside them, as others sleep wrapped up in blankets in entrances and in arcades all over the city centre. Despite its historical and glamorous past, Ermou Street was among the first to be populated by the homeless and their cardboard boxes. Indeed, these cardboard boxes now characterise a particular urban aesthetic of homelessness.

THE HISTORY OF THE CARDBOARD BOX

The cardboard box goes largely unappreciated. We usually associate it with changing locations and residences. We use it for shipping products, storing our books, packaging our food and an endless number of commodities, preserving our personal mementos, archiving our research projects, holding children's toys in order to keep their rooms tidy. Often, we break up the boxes that arrive home as packaging. We flatten them, convinced as we are by the recycling industry that this is a way to reduce our environmental footprint. And indeed, the environmental burden is not trivial. For example, in the United States, one of the most industrialised countries, over 90% of goods are packaged and shipped in cardboard. Statistics inform us that in the United States and Canada there are approximately 1500 corrugated packing plants and over 400 million tons of cardboard are produced worldwide. The demand for cardboard as packaging material has turned the cardboard box into the single largest waste product in the developing world. It has been estimated that over 24 million tons of cardboard are discarded each year.

A symbol of industrialisation and commercialisation, the cardboard box also reflects recent changes in the geopolitics of power. Since 2009, China has taken the lead in cardboard manufacturing, with the United States trailing by some margin. In 2009 China produced a little over 86 million metric tons of paper and cardboard, and the United States almost 72 million tons. Yet by 2013 had China reached 105 million tons compared to the United States's 74 million. These numbers reflect China's rapid growth and its attempt to build the most extensive global commercial market.

Cardboard boxes have always been associated with the rise of consumerism and the need to both protect and promote new consumables and thus new desires. The story goes that the first commercial cardboard box package design was created in England in 1817 to hold a German game called 'the Besieging Game', inspired by armed forces and war (Groth 2006: 7).[1] Paper and cardboard remained luxuries until the end of the century when Albert Jones of New York filed a patent in 1871 for the 'improvement in paper for packing'. He proposed to turn corrugated paper into packing boxes instead of wrapping for vials or bottles. According to the patent,

> The object of this invention is to provide means for securely packing vials and bottles with a single thickness of the packing material between the surface of the article packed; and it consists in paper, card-board, or other suitable material, which is corrugated, crimped, or bossed, so as to present an elastic surface by reason of such corrugated, crimped, or bossed surface, as will be hereinafter more fully described (Jones 1871).

The objective was to protect the content of the box and prevent the delicate glass products from breaking. In these early days, box making was an intensive labour craft that was carried out by hand and catered mainly to hat and shoe factories. However, the most efficient cardboard box was created by the American lithographer Robert Gair a few years later. American printers were among the earliest paper-based packaging makers. Gair saw potential in the use of paper packaging for marketing household items, but the invention of the actual cardboard box was serendipitous. Gair, who was already in the paper bag business, had set up his first paper factory in 1864 in New York, and soon mechanised his

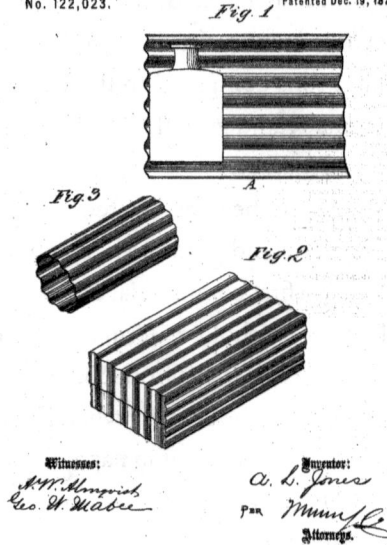

(108.)

A. L. JONES.

Improvement in Paper for Packing.

No. 122,023.

Fig. 1

Patented Dec. 19, 1871.

Fig. 3

Fig. 2

A

Witnesses:

Inventor:

a. L. Jones

per Munn

Attorneys.

FIG. 27.2 Albert Jones's patent for the improvement in paper for packing, 1871 (source: United States Patent and Trademark Office, patent number 122023)

production. In 1879, one of his workers accidentally cut through 20,000 paper seed bags by setting up a type ruler too high. This has been described as the event that inspired Gair to develop an efficient mechanised method to produce folding cardboard boxes by printing, cutting, and creasing cardboard in one go (Twede et al. 2015). The major advantage of his invention was that boxes could be stored flat and easily transported – the first ready-to-assemble folding boxes. With this modification Gair was able to cut 750 sheets an hour on one press, something that had previously taken a day. Gradually he introduced the direct printing of cartons, facilitating both branding and advertising.

By 1900 all kinds of products were already being shipped in corrugated paper boxes. Soon, Gair built up a paper and packaging empire. His first clients were mainly tea, tobacco, and cosmetics companies. His big break, though, came when Nabisco, the National US Biscuit Company, decided to pre-box the Uneeda Biscuit, placing a two million-unit order in 1898. To respond to such high demand, Gair built two six-story brick factories in Brooklyn, and in 1909 he commissioned the construction of one of the earliest industrial buildings in reinforced concrete. As he bragged in one of the company's advertisements,

> From its housing in the little loft in down-town Manhattan, our business has expanded to occupy a large group of modern steel and concrete buildings on the Brooklyn waterfront. We have recently further enlarged our facilities by the acquisition of the three paper mills... These plants, located on tide-water, offer in combination with our Brooklyn factory unusual resources to meet the needs of our clients. (Robert Gair Company 1920: 7)

But while Gair was building his paper empire, working conditions in many paper box factories were below par. Already by 1910, during the thirteenth US census, New York dominated the country's fancy- and paper box manufacture with 315 establishments and close to 13,000 workers. In industries that produced folding boxes, such as Gair's, the majority of tasks were performed by a large die-cutting and creasing machine, which cut and creased the entire box form in one piece. In many cases, trade names, design, and descriptions were printed on the pasteboard prior to cutting and creasing. Women, mostly young girls, worked in the printing department, lifting the uncut sheets and feeding them into the press. A report published in 1915 by the Commonwealth of the State of Massachusetts on the wages of women in the paper box industry revealed the occupational risks of working in these factories. More than 43% of those injured were women, the majority under thirty years old. Similar reports on the New York paper box industry for 1913 and 1914 showed that women were paid 40% less than their male colleagues. With little education, and under social pressure to leave work after marriage, women were destined to earn less for more work (Vitaliano 2009; The Commonwealth of the State of Massachusetts, Minimum Wage Commission 1915).[2]

An extended review produced by the Department of Labor for the State of New York in 1928 was revealing of the gender differences in the paper box industry, even during the interwar years. Men represented a third and women two-thirds of all the workers in the industry. While fewer in number, however, men were employed in better and more well-paid positions. They were exclusively employed in box shipping and transportation, and in the mechanised cutting department, as highly-skilled machinists who repaired, set up, and maintained the machines. Women were largely employed in finishing and manual work. Work conditions were poor and had already led to a major strike in 1927, an event that triggered the report. In short, physical working conditions, plant hours, rates, and salaries were particularly controversial issues. Among the outstanding facts mentioned in the report were cleanliness and sanitary arrangements: 'Workrooms were dirty and there was inexhaustible neglect in regards to sanitary arrangements. Cellars were often used as cutting rooms, exposing workers to cold and dampness in the spring and fall and to excessive heat from the boilers in winter' (Hamilton 1928: 8).

Gender differences in the industrial production of goods weren't and aren't news, but they have been an intimate part of the commercialisation of the modern world and the triumph of capitalism. The gender profile of the paper industry did not really change even after World War II. By 1940, the Paper Box Manufacturers Association ran 865 shops, most of which were located in the north-eastern part of the country. It is telling that the industry employed 40,000 workers, of whom 75% were women. In several New York shops, the few men and native-born American women who were employed did the skilled work, while immigrant women, mainly from Italy, posted labels or stuffed finished boxes.

FROM SYMBOL OF COMMERCIAL PROSPERITY TO ICON OF FINANCIAL DEPRESSION

'Changing the buying habits of a nation: How the individual package has grown from an experiment to an essential in modern business' was the telling title of a text and image advertisement that the Robert Gair Company placed in *The Sun and New York Herald* in 1920. With the growth of consumerism came the rise of packaging, which in turn changed consumer habits. There is nothing intrinsically surprising about this development. After all, packaging economies provide a context for understanding such a correlation. Until the end of the nineteenth century, to manufacturers and retailers in the US, packaging meant tying up a parcel with wrapping paper and string. Merchandise was sold in bulk in makeshift packages and then transported home. As merchandise changed in the early twentieth century, however, so did the packaging of commodities. Using a container to convey the product to the end consumer reduced handling and transportation costs. Packaging reinforced by publicity and advertising induced consumers to pay a higher price for goods and served to identify a product by its brand name, and thus facilitate sales. Gair's invention gave manufacturers the opportunity to take control of the market. Products were pre-packaged in the factory and not in the store, and thus direct advertisement became possible in magazines and newspapers. The cardboard box was elevated to a symbol of the American commercial boom.

In general, this was the time when new materials such as glazed paper, aluminium foil, glass containers, and folding cartons influenced the ways products were marketed. Political factors, such as the eighteenth amendment that prohibited the consumption of alcohol and came into effect in 1920, led to novel uses of glass beyond the manufacture of liquor containers (which was no longer a profitable option). As the economic depression eased, and the world of business and technological improvements boosted, the use of colour and the shaping of materials offering a wider range of choices in package design.

In the midst of the Great Depression, folding carton manufacturers established the first packaging association in 1929, known later as the Folding Paper Box Association in America (FPBAA). In 1933, thirteen folding cartoon manufacturers set up the first Code of Fair Competition regulating work in the paper box industry. Yet women were still paid five cents per hour, when the Code suggested a minimum wage of forty cents (Paperboard Packaging Council).

By the mid-1930s, the packaging industry had grown stronger as it became clear that container-design clearly affected merchandising. At that point, package manufacturers were in control of the market. In 1936, five years after the first Packaging Conference in New York, Irwin Wolf, the vice president of the American Management Association, proclaimed that packaging was 'a vital factor' required to move stocks and that packaging had undergone 'revolutionary changes' in development within the past five years (Wolf 1936: vii). Kellogg's is a good example here. In a full-page advertisement in *LIFE* on 12 December 1938, the company urged its customers to collect the package-tops of Kellogg's *Rice Krispies*, a 'real-rice cereal'. The company's customers dutifully collected twenty such package tops and mailed them with $1.40 to receive framed, full-colour copies of six illustrations featuring characters such as Humpty Dumpty and Pumpkin Easter. The packages themselves had become traded goods, and market research into consumers' preferences fuelled the packaging industry. As package designer Egmont Arens later argued, 'mass production and changing ways of living have elevated [package] design to a merchandise science' (Arens 1952, 153).

As the American economy stabilised in the 1950s and 1960s, and technology advanced, the cardboard box packaging industries tried to streamline production. The aim was to use statistics, marketing information, and management tools in order to improve their business. Their lavish annual meetings were living proof of the booming packaging industry (**FIGURE 27.3**).

Ironically, as the cardboard box was elevated to the status of a symbol of America's economic success, commercialisation, and industrialisation, it also

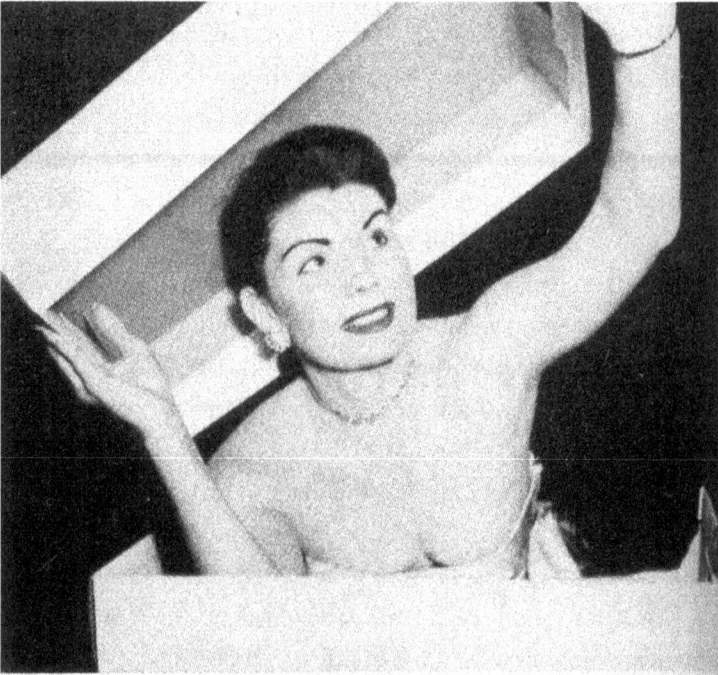

FIG. 27.3 American singer Wyoma Winters was named Miss Folding Paper Box 1952 at the annual Folding Paper Box Association of America (source: aperboard Packaging Council)

signalled the increase in the numbers and the visibility of homeless people in urban areas. Closely connected to, but at the same time a counterpoint of, the country's economic transformation, the cardboard box served as a shelter and precious possession of the American homeless person (**FIGURE 27.4**).

Throughout the twentieth century urban homelessness had a particular aesthetic, one that to social researcher Myrto Tsilimpounidi 'seems to reinforce the imbrication of market forces within its very conditions; with homeless men and women often purloining shopping trolleys from super markets in which they wheel their belongings.' Instead of carrying purchased goods from supermarkets to apartments, these trolleys hold the 'vestiges of home, becoming piled high with fresh cardboard boxes and throwaway items' (Tsilimpounidi 2015). In most cases, the homeless person's home is a cardboard box, a makeshift shelter on the pavement, in front of the shop windows of major pedestrian shopping areas. Paradoxically, the cardboard box – the waste of our commercial world – is recycled in such a way as to make visible the disorder in our societies, the faults of capitalism.

FIG. 27.4 An elderly homeless African-American woman pushes a pram with a large cardboard box on top (source: Scurlock Studio Records, ca. 1905–1994, Archives Center, National Museum of American History)

I look again at Daniel Ochoa de Olza's picture of the homeless man sleeping in front of a chain store on Ermou street. My friend's suggestion begins to make sense. I walk down Ermou Street less often because the house of the homeless – the crumpled cardboard box – is a womb-like enclosure that upsets my sense of security and eats away at my trust in order. It reveals the fragility of our social world and the fluidity of its boundaries. I might be next. This is why I/we should probably go back and resume our walks on Ermou Street, piecing together a new order, a new kind of humanism that eliminates the cardboard box from sidewalks and reveals the inhuman politics of materiality.

NOTES

I An example of this game can be found in Victoria and Albert Museum in England, see <http://collections.vam.ac.uk/item/O25924/the-game-of-besieging-das-board-game-unknown/>

2 See also The Commonwealth of the State of Massachusetts, Minimum Wage Commission 1915.

REFERENCES

Arens, E., '25 Years of Progress in Package Design', *Modern Packaging* (March 1952): 152–59.

Bastea, E., 'Athens', in E. G. Makas and T. D. Conley, eds, *Capital Cities in the Aftermath of Empires* (New York: Routledge, 2010), pp. 29–44.

Eurostat, 'Unemployment statistics', in *Eurostat Statistics Explained*, <http://ec.europa.eu/eurostat/statistics-explained/index.php/Unemployment_statistics>.

Freud, S., *An Introduction to Psychoanalysis* (New York: Boni and Liveright, 1920), <http://www.bartleby.com/283/10.html>.

Groth, C., *Exploring Package Design* (Clifton Park, NY: Thomson Delmar Learning, 2006)

Hamilton, J., 'The Paper Box Industry in New York City', Department of Labor, *Special Bulletin*, 154 (1928): 8.

Jones, A., 'Improvement in Paper for Packing', U.S. 122023 A Patent, 1871.

Paperboard Packaging Council, 'PPC: Over 80 Years of Excellence', <http://paperbox.org/About-PPC/PPC-History>

Rentetzi, M., 'Packaging Radium, Selling Science: Boxes, Bottles and Other Mundane Things in the World of Science', *Annals of Science*, 68., 3 (2011), 375–99.

Robert Gair Company, 'Changing the Buying Habits of a Nation', *The Sun and New York Herald*, Thursday, 15 April 1920.

The Commonwealth of the State of Massachusetts, Minimum Wage Commission, 'Wages of Women in the Paper Box Industry', Bulletin 8 (September 1915).

The World Bank, 'Unemployment, total', in *The World Bank Database*, <http://data.worldbank.org/indicator/SL.UEM.TOTL.ZS?order=wbapi_data_value_2011%20wbapi_data_value%20wbapi_data_value-first&sort=desc>

Tsilimpounidi, M., 'Topographies of Illicit Markets: Trolleys, Rickshaws and Yiusurums', in M. Zaroulia and P. Hager, eds, *Performances of Capitalism, Crisis and Resistance Inside/Outside Europe* (Basingstoke, UK: Palgrave MacMillan, 2015), pp. 56–76.

Twede, D., et al., *Cartons, Crates and Corrugated Board. Handbook of Paper and Wood Packaging Technology*, 2nd edn (Lancaster, PA: DEStech Publications, Inc., 2015).

Vitaliano, D., 'Gender Wage Differences and Human Capital in the Early Twentieth Century: The Case of the Paper Box Industry in New York', in *Review of Economics of the Household*, 7 (2009), pp. 179–88.

Wolf, I., 'Foreword', in James Rice, ed., *Packaging, Packing and Shipping* (New York: American Management Association, 1936), pp. vii–viii.

World Socialist Website, 'I could never imagine so many homeless people in Athens', *World Socialist Web Site*, 9 March 2015, <http://www.wsws.org/en/articles/2015/03/09/gree-m09.html>

IX

COUNT

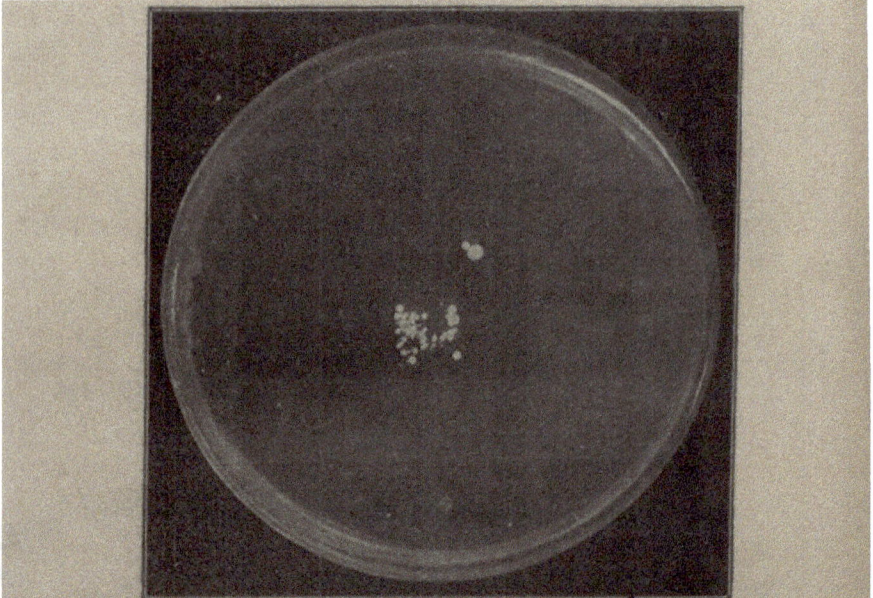

Emil Walter phot.

Abb. 25c. Ein Kuß als Keimüberträger.

Wo die sterile Gelatineschicht in der Petrischale durch die küssenden Lippen berührt worden ist, haben sich reichlich Bakterienkolonien entwickelt. Mindestens soviele Keime, als wir auf der Platte Kolonien zählen, sind durch den Kuß von den Lippen auf die Platte übertragen worden.

FIG. 28.1 Petri dish (photo by Emil Walter, 1919. Kosmos)

28

PETRI DISH (BOÎTE DE PETRI, PETRISCHALE)

Mathias Grote

Size and shape: two circular dishes in the shape of a shallow cylinder; c. 10 cm in diameter and 1–1.5 cm in height, differing slightly in size to fit into each other. **Colour**: transparent, made from either glass or, since the 1950s, thermoplastic materials such as polystyrene. **Usage**: container or culturing device for various organisms. The smaller cylinder holds solid culture media, liquids, or organisms; the larger one, with its slightly craned rim, functions as a cover. Closed dish creates artificial, sterile environments for the growth or maintenance of diverse organisms (e.g. microbes, plants, cell cultures); also used as a container for chemical reactions with a large surface-to-volume ratio. **Origin**: devised in 1887 by Richard Julius Petri, medical bacteriologist and member of Robert Koch's team. **Distribution**: found in biological and chemical laboratories worldwide, from routine bacteriological diagnostics to reproductive medicine, biotechnologies or research in the molecular life sciences. **Status**: omnipresent, mundane disposable of the life sciences laboratory that has become proverbial as the site of an experiment, or for the artificial reproduction of organisms.

Keywords: enclosing, isolating, containing, creating a milieu, culturing, storing

THE TRACE OF A KISS IN A BOX

'*WO DIE STERILE GELATINESCHICHT IN DER PETRISCHALE DURCH DIE KÜSSENDEN Lippen berührt worden ist, haben sich reichlich Bakterienkolonien entwickelt'* [Ample bacterial colonies have formed where the sterile gelatine layer within the Petri dish has been touched by the kissing lips] (Oettli 1919: 64). This microbial trace of a kiss – in the form of whitish spots, certainly less indelible than its memory – informs an early twentieth-century reader that germs are everywhere. They fall down from the air like snowflakes, as *Versuche mit lebenden Bakterien* [*Trials with Living Bacteria*] puts it, this being a small book which appeared in the German popular science series *KOSMOS* (**FIGURE 28.1**).

The Petri dish is an article as mundane yet as indispensable to biological laboratories as a plate is to a kitchen. When catching the trace of a kiss, its function to the authors of *Versuche mit lebenden Bakterien* was obvious: the dish provided a protected, sterile environment for the growth of a microbial sample. Without such a box, it would have been hard to detect any specific bugs within the plethora of microbes populating every part of our biosphere; the traces left by the lips would have rapidly been contaminated or outgrown. The imprint of the kiss as depicted in this amateur manual rendered the box itself somewhat elusive. Against a dark background, we can only discern the Petri dish's circular halo from above. This refers to another of the dish's char-acteristics: its transparency allows rapid inspection of the organisms with a microscope or even with the naked eye, in this way making possible precise manipulations.

The Petri dish has become an archetypal box of the twentieth-century experimental life sciences. Whether made of glass or plastic, the Petri dish, the test tube, and the Eppendorf cup exemplify the concept of '*in vitro*' in the life sciences. Organisms, or their bits and pieces (cells, biochemical substances) are enclosed in controlled environments (media, buffers) for culture or examina-tion (Rheinberger 2009; on glassware and 'laboratory ecology', see Espahangizi 2015). Petri dishes continue to serve as containers for the growth, display, manipulation, and storage not only of bugs (from bacteria to insects), but also of our bodies' components, such as cultured cells.

A BOX TO PURIFY AND RE-PRODUCE MICROBES

The twin glass dishes fitting loosely into one another were presented somewhat modestly by their eponym, Julius Richard Petri, as '*Eine kleine Modification des Koch'schen Plattenverfahrens*' [A small modification of Koch's plate technique] (Petri 1887). No longer than a page, Petri's contribution was nevertheless well placed in bacteriology's heroic age, and the device rapidly became adopted. A few years before, Robert Koch, who had just demonstrated anthrax infection, had also introduced solid media for culturing bacteria. Among these were gelatine and agar-agar – reportedly on the advice of a staff member's wife, who knew the substance as a gelling agent for food preparation (Collard 1976). The liquid media that microbiologists such as Louis Pasteur had used before, e.g. heat-sterilised broth or other types of infusions, constantly mixed the microbes grown therein. This rendered it impossible to determine which cell had developed from which, that is, to obtain 'colonies', solid masses of bacteria such as those planted by the kissing lips.

Koch devised solid culture plates by pouring broth mixed with a gelling agent onto a glass surface. This almost ludicrously simple innovation allowed him to make a powerful argument in a controversy raging in late nineteenth-century bacteriology between the so-called monomorphists (Koch himself, and his former mentor, Ferdinand Julius Cohn), who assumed that stable bacterial species existed, and the opposing pleomorphists, who argued that the microbial realm manifested a continuity of life forms that changed in cell shape and physiological effects through life cycles and in reaction to varying environments (Gradmann 2005). Once a microbial sample – isolated, for example, from an infected animal – was growing immobilised on the surface of Koch's plates, '*Reinkulturen*' [pure cultures] could be obtained. Such colonies, spots similar to those in our image, were understood as clonal lines, stemming theoretically from a single cell that had divided billions of times. These cell materials could then be transferred to different environments, such as an animal's body or a different plate, allowing observers to monitor the stability of traits such as cell shape, colour, appearance, causation of disease symptoms, and so on.

Koch accused the pleomorphists of lumping different bacteria together, and advised researchers to follow the principles he saw operative in botany and zoology, namely to distinguish all forms of bacteria differing in traits, as long as their identity or close relatedness had not been demonstrated (Koch 1881). The culture plate, which actually allowed researchers to physically separate and discern microbes by growing pure lines in the laboratory, was a tool for this splitting of microbial diversity. Moreover, the plate and the linked ideal of pure culturing allowed the monomorphists to turn the controversy over the existence of stable bacterial species akin to those of plants and animals into a matter of good versus bad technique. Pleomorphists appeared simply as those using the wrong tools, and towards the end of the nineteenth century, bacteriology rapidly adapted monomorphism. The debate was never really closed however – some decades later, bacterial variability, their interactions with the environment and ideas of 'life cycles' rose to prominence again in pathology and beyond (Amsterdamska 1991, Méthot 2015). Ludwik Fleck, in the interwar time a microbiologist, deliberated about the issue at length, wondering why bacteriology had for a while hardly seen phenomena of variability. In his 1935 monograph, he thus took the 'rigid thought style' of the 'classic Pasteur-Koch era' as a prime example for his epistemological argument (Fleck 1980: 122; my translation).

The solid culture plate was only one part of the ensemble needed to take a kiss into the laboratory. The other part was the container of this plate. Early users of Koch's plate method had faced technical problems when pouring the agar onto glass plates, which had to be evenly labelled with the help of a large apparatus. Moreover, the plates needed to be kept free from contamination by airborne microbes, present even in the cleanest and most disciplined bacteriological laboratory. This was achieved by storing them under large bell jars, which one would need to lift in order to manipulate plates or cultures (Collard 1976). Enter Petri: the later director of a tuberculosis sanatorium (described by one of his staff members as a 'stalwart, priggish Prussian schoolmaster', Plesch 1951: 40 f.) suggested pouring the inoculated liquid gelatine directly into a small, sterilised glass dish: 'Geschieht dies, indem man die überfallende Schale nur wenig lüftet und unter ihrem Schutze das [...] Gelatineröhrchen ausgiesst, so hat man nur äußerst selten Verunreinigungen durch Luftkeime zu gewärtigen.' [If this is done by lifting the top dish only slightly and pouring out the gelatine-containing test tube under its cover, one has to face contamination by airborne germs only extremely rarely] (Petri 1887: 279; on Petri, see Plesch 1951: 40 f.). Petri's dishes rapidly became a staple of the bacteriological laboratory, as they facilitated the adoption of Koch's plate method. The dishes' small size made for greater ease of handling in the lab, and they could also be stacked upside down in an incubator, which prevented condensation forming on the plate. The cultures could also be easily inspected through the flat lid (see Collard 1976). A 1915 catalogue of the Berlin instrument-making company *F. & M. Lautenschläger*, a purveyor to bacteriological and chemical laboratories as well as medical facilities, offered 100 '*Doppelschale[n] nach Petri, Modell des Instituts für Infektionskrankheiten, Berlin*' [double dishes according to Petri, model of the Institute of Infectious Diseases, Berlin] at a price of 32.50 Marks. This was the suggested number to equip a medium-sized lab (F. & M. Lautenschläger 1915: 486, 687).

Picture the Petri dish in an investigator's hand: thumb and index slightly lift its cover, the other hand carefully effuses a test tube's content into the lower dish, before the cover is lowered again to close the dish. This key routine of microbiological lab work has been described and depicted over and over again in various textbooks and manuals during the past century.[1] Yet words and images can only do so much. Every student, from medics to biotech, from Bangalore to Cambridge, has to learn the handwork to handle microbes aseptically by imitation in practical courses. It is almost a ritual of microbiology to master holding plugs and test tubes in one hand while fiddling around with a Petri dish in the other, all items close to a Bunsen burner flame. And for good reason: being able to transfer microbes in a sterile manner from one box into another (i.e. by pouring out a test tube into a dish, or by streaking a sample onto a culture plate's surface) is a prerequisite to properly carry out any microbiological experimentation. If a lab worker does not master these routines under all conditions (such as ill-fitting lab coats, ambient temperature of 35°C, blaring radio, or colleagues calling for lunch), doubt can be cast on any result of culturing, since – as the kiss told us – germs are everywhere. For a technician or a doctoral student, it is not uncommon to carry out these plating routines dozens of times every day. Many of the early breakthroughs in molecular genetics were based on not much more than a few strains of bacteria and phage cultured on plates in Petri dishes. French molecular biologist François Jacob vividly remembered the sound of breaking glass mixed with the warm and sweet smell of agar and rising rage against himself for having impatiently thrown over a pile of dishes that may have harboured a long looked-for mutant colony (Jacob 1987, 315).

If one does not want to kiss the agar in a Petri dish, a number of other simple tools are needed to transfer microbes under sterile conditions. Among these are certainly a Bunsen burner (to rapidly disinfect utensils by heating them), cotton or rubber plugs to seal test tubes, and a glass or platinum wire spatula to transfer the microbial materials. Most of these inevitable little helpers – one may speak of 'microbiology's dishes and cutlery', or of its experimental infrastructure – were devised in the heroic age of Koch and Pasteur. Just like the Petri dish, they are still operative in today's labs, and they have changed surprisingly little over more than a hundred years. The *longue durée* use of omnipresent laboratory tools such as these is a peculiar example of continuity in science, which deserves more profound historical scrutiny. An answer to why these tools became so widely used, and why they have remained relatively unchanged, has to address details pertaining to design, practicality, or social factors; moreover, alternative approaches and technologies would need to be studied.[2]

Even when plastic Petri dishes were introduced in the 1950s, this did not significantly change their simple but essential function. Certainly, the 'disposable culturing device' made laboratory life easier; plastic dishes were less prone to slide when wet, or to shatter when falling of a table (with potentially disastrous consequences); hence they were also more easily transported, e.g. by mail, and they could be made to comprise different compartments (Fisk 1959). Moreover, contamination by fungi or viruses through insufficiently cleaned glassware did not occur with a disposable. This latter point, and the different adhesive properties of plastic surfaces, were particularly important for cultures of animal or plant cells, as these often grew attached to the dish, bathed in a liquid medium – which brings us to the Petri dish beyond microbiology.

BETWEEN TUMOURS AND METAPHORS — THE PETRI DISH IN THE MOLECULAR LIFE SCIENCES AND BEYOND

In the twentieth century, cell and developmental biology adopted the Petri dish, among other devices and routines from microbiology, for culturing cells and tissues of higher organisms. Thereby, bodies of animals and humans became amenable to manipulations similar to those described above, and pure mass reproduction of, for example, cancer cells in artificial environments could be achieved. Petri dishes, in combination with other culture plates, flasks, and so on, allowed researchers to expose, study, transfer, and store parts and processes of organisms that had hitherto been hidden in their insides (on cell culture, see Landecker 2007). Moreover, in the second half of the twentieth century, the Petri dish became an important device for screening routines, such as in the 'Ames test', which allows the detection of potentially carcinogenic chemicals by incubating them with microbes on a culture plate and looking for mutant colonies (Creager 2014). The early biotech age even saw the construction of a robot to screen large numbers of Petri dishes automatically, and nowadays a number of specially adapted dishes, such as microplates, are on the market (on the screening robot, see Vettel 2006). The classical Petri dish however, its design fitting so well into a human hand, remains a staple of quotidian work. In combination with an arsenal of other tools and skills to put life into boxes, it has therefore become an emblem for artificial reproduction in the laboratory.

At least since the 1980s, the term 'Petri dish' has become a trope in literature and the press. One may suspect that this resulted from the 1970s/80s discourse on clones, i.e. identical copies of animals or humans created by scientists. This discourse reflected developments in both genetic engineering and organismic cloning, that is, the transfer of nuclei from somatic cells into enucleated frog egg cells, which resulted in genetically identical animals – a procedure that became widely publicised again in the 1990s with the cloned sheep, Dolly. Cloning in the lab rapidly cross-fertilised with fiction and movies then as now, not only taking up older imaginations (think of the bottled babies in Aldous Huxley's *Brave New World*) but also giving the figure of the clone a time-specific guise regarding questions of personal identity or character (Brandt 2009). Importantly, human *in vitro* fertilisation as practised routinely since the 1980s seems to actually have relied on Petri dishes as the site for bringing isolated egg and sperm cells together (Ebner and Dietrich 2013). While newspapers baptised Louise Brown and her followers according to the various pieces of glassware in which 'they' may have floated in their morula stages ('test tube', 'retort' or 'Petri dish babies' have all been mentioned), Petri's dish became used to refer to more than just living beings (re)-made.[3] Even more so than the test tube, the Petri dish turned into a metaphor for 'a place, environment, etc. in which rapid growth or development can take place', as the *Oxford English Dictionary* has it (Oxford English Dictionary 2005). Thus, when *The New York Times* asserted in a 1984 piece on contemporary dance that '[t]he Lower East Side has traditionally been a source, a petri dish of New York culture', this certainly did not refer to reproducing the identical in an artificial environment behind glass walls, but to a site of sprawling, experimental life (Gautier 1984: 20).

THE TEEMING MICROWORLD AND THE DIALECTICS OF BOXING LIFE

Back to the kisses' imprint in a Petri dish. This experiment suggested to the amateur microbiologists of 1919 that they were surrounded, and in fact inhabited, by a plethora of whirling, invisible creatures. A sterile Petri dish revealed that not only disease, rot, and decay, but also soil, 'fresh' food, and the air they breathed, not to mention their own hands and mouths, were teeming with bacterial life. In fact, the amateur manual seems much more relaxed about microbial presences than one might expect, bearing in mind the 'microbe hunting' ideal of early medical bacteriology (Anderson 2004, Sarasin 2007). Certainly, the instructions urge hygiene and care when handling microbes, suggesting for example that experimenters who detect spirochaetes in their mouths should brush their teeth more frequently. However, the manual's author – the Swiss high school teacher, amateur botanist, and temperance activist Max Oettli – seems to have been positively fascinated by what he called his '*Versuchspflanzen*' (experimental plants), that is, the '*Spaltpilze*' (fission fungi, modern bacteria) and the '*Sproßpilze*' (shoot fungi, modern yeasts; on Oettli, see Spöring 2014).[4] Oettli elaborated on the usefulness of microbes in food production – elderflower lemonade and *Sauerkraut* were on the menu – and he evoked the awe that luminous bacteria obtained from marine fish would create in youngsters and the '*Naturfreund*' (nature lover) generally.

With his fairly sympathetic attitude to the copiousness and wonder of what teems in and among us, and what small creatures can do, Oettli appears unexpectedly contemporary. Recent scientific and popular discourse abounds with similar tropes about 'friendly microbes' – when diseases are not considered infection events *per se* or when microbial communities are described as global players in biogeochemistry and climate, as helpers of our own metabolism, or as biotechnological all-rounders for the ecological production of biofuels, synthetics, and so forth (O'Malley 2014). And 'biohackers' – perhaps the most recent avatar of Oettli's *Naturfreunde* – still delight in inoculating their Petri dishes with chunks of mackerel from the fishmonger next door, to marvel at bioluminescent *Vibrio fischeri*.

The ways in which the modern life sciences enquire into microbial diversity are obviously quite different from those available a century ago. Today, metagenomic technologies allow scientists to probe the diversity and interconnectedness of the microbial world without putting samples and cells into Petri dishes. This is achieved by preparing the DNA of the entire microbial community, for example, in a sample of seawater or from a cow's rumina. This DNA is then digested into short strands, which are sequenced and assembled *in silico* to the genomes of organisms assumed in the sample, many of which have never been successfully cultured (O'Malley 2014). By contrast, Oettli and microbiologists in general until the 1990s, first needed to culture the microbes behind glass walls, until colonies became amenable to inspection and manipulations with an investigator's hands and eyes.

This dichotomy of pure culture versus culture-independent microbiology catches only part of the picture and deserves a more extended analysis. Microbial ecologists such as Sergei Winogradsky, for example, repeatedly criticised pure culturing throughout the twentieth century, and came forward with other methods of studying diversity, such as enrichment cultures – for which other containers were developed (on Winogradsky, see Ackert 2013). Moreover, even our days of high-throughput DNA sequencing cannot abstain from culturing: the question of the organism behind the genome remains pertinent when it comes to classification or (obviously) to using microbes.

Petri's sterile, transparent, double glass dish, an epitome of pure, controlled life, has nevertheless been arguably the most important tool since the late nineteenth century for making sense of the microcosm by isolating and purifying microbes. Even though the limitations of studying pure cultures in the artificial environment provided by a glass box had been long discussed, it only recently became possible to transcend these limitations on a broad scale. Moreover, while metagenomic DNA sequencing suggests to us nowadays that the microcosm is much more abundant, sprawling, and diverse than assumed in the age of pure culturing, this should not be seen as the last word on the problems of diversity, variability, and specificity within and beyond the lab. Nowadays, a trial person would probably not be asked to kiss a culture plate but instead a cotton bud, which would then be transferred into a plastic Eppendorf cup for DNA preparation. The tools and the specific ramifications of working with microbes may have changed, then, but what has not changed is the need to enclose the diverse microworld in the controlled environment of a box to produce traces (be they cultures or DNA sequences) of what teems in and among us.

NOTES

1 Kreuder-Sonnen (2012) analyses how a similar skill (transfer of bacteria between test tubes) was transferred from Koch's laboratory to Poland in the late nineteenth century – in this case by a meticulous description of the necessary hand movements, illustrated by drawings. In the twentieth century, manuals continued to display series of photographs taken 'at the bench'.
2 See Grote 2018. On what the *'longue durée'* could mean for contemporary history of science, see Grote 2015.
3 Numerous such mentions can be found e.g. in *The Guardian* or *The New York Times*, with absolute numbers of the term Petri dish rising in the 1980s and 1990s.
4 Today's fungi and bacteria were considered part of the plant kingdom until at least the mid-twentieth century.

REFERENCES

Ackert, L., *Sergei Vinogradskii and the Cycle of Life: From the Thermodynamics of Life to Ecological Microbiology, 1850–1950* (Amsterdam: Springer, 2013).

Amsterdamska, O., 'Stabilizing Instability: The Controversy over Cyclogenic Theories of Bacterial Variation during the Interwar Period', *Journal of the History of Biology* 24 (1991): 191–222.

Anderson, W., 'Natural Histories of Infectious Disease: Ecological Vision in Twentieth-Century Biomedical Science', *Osiris* 19 (2004): 39–61.

Brandt, C., '"In his image" Klonexperimente zwischen Biowissenschaft und Science-fiction', in Birgit Griesecke et al., eds, *Kulturgeschichte des Menschenversuchs im 20. Jahrhundert* (Frankfurt: Suhrkamp, 2009), pp. 373–93.

Collard, P., *The Development of Microbiology* (Cambridge: Cambridge University Press, 1976).

Creager, A. N. H., 'The Political Life of Mutagens. A History of the Ames Test', in Soraya Boudia and Natalie Jas, eds, *Powerless Science?: Science and Politics in a Toxic World*, vol. 2 (New York: Berghahn Books, 2014), pp. 46–64.

Ebner, T., and K. Diedrich, 'In-vitro-Fertilisation und intrazytoplasmatische Spermieninjektion', in K Diedrich, M. Ludwig, and G. Griesinger, *Reproduktionsmedizin* (Berlin: Springer, 2013), pp. 215–24.

Espahangizi, K., 'From Topos to Oikos: The Standardization of Glass Containers as Epistemic Boundaries in Modern Laboratory Research (1850–1900)', *Science in Context* 28 (2015): 397–425.

Fisk, R. T., 'Disposable culturing device', US Patent 2,874,091; 17 February 1959.

Fleck, L., *Entstehung und Entwicklung einer wissenschaftlichen Tatsache* (Frankfurt a. M.: Suhrkamp, 1980 [1935]).

Gautier, R., 'Reinventing Dance at the Grass Roots', *The New York Times*, 3 February 1984, p. 20.

Gradmann, C., *Krankheit im Labor. Robert Koch und die medizinische Bakteriologie* (Göttingen: Wallstein, 2005).

Grote, M., 'What Could the 'longue durée' Mean for the History of Modern Sciences?', *Working Paper Fondation Maison des Sciences de l'Homme*, FMSH-WP-2015–98 (2015), <https://halshs.archives-ouvertes.fr/halshs-01171257>.

Grote M., 'Petri dish versus Winogradsky column: a longue durée perspective on purity and diversity in microbiology, 1880s–1980s', *History and Philosophy of the Life Sciences* 40 (2018), 11.

Jacob, F., *La statue intérieure* (Paris: Seuil, 1987).

Koch, R., 'Zur Untersuchung von pathogenen Mikroorganismen' [1881], in Julius Schwalbe, ed., *Gesammelte Werke von Robert Koch*, vol. 1 (Leipzig, 1912), pp. 112–63.

Kreuder-Sonnen, K., 'Wie die Mikroben nach Warschau kamen', *NTM Zeitschrift für Geschichte der Wissenschaften, Technik und Medizin* 20 (2012): 157–80.

Landecker, H., *Culturing life: How cells Became Technologies* (Cambridge, MA: Harvard University Press, 2007).

Lautenschläger, F. & M., ed., *Komplette Einrichtung von bakteriologischen, serologischen und chemischen Laboratorien und Untersuchungsanstalten, Operationssälen, Krankenhäusern, Sektionssälen usw.* [product catalogue] (Berlin, 1915).

Méthot, P.-O., 'Bacterial Transformation and the Origins of Epidemics in the Interwar

Period: 'The Epidemiological Significance of Fred Griffith's "Transforming Experiment"', *Journal of the History of Biology* 49 (2016), 311–358.

Oettli, M., *Versuche mit lebenden Bakterien. Eine Anleitung zum selbständigen Arbeiten mit Bakterien und anderen Kleinpilzen für den naturwissenschaftlichen Arbeitsunterricht und den Naturfreund* (Stuttgart: Franckh'sche Verlagshandlung, 1919).

O'Malley, M., *Philosophy of microbiology* (Cambridge: Cambridge University Press, 2014)

Oxford English Dictionary, 'Petri dish', OED 3rd ed. (2005), <http://www.oed.com/view/Entry/141888?redirectedFrom=Petri+dish&> [accessed 08 Nov 2019].

Petri, J. R., 'Eine kleine Modification des Kochschen Plattenverfahrens', *Centralblatt für Bacteriologie und Parasitenkunde* 1 (1887): 279–80.

Plesch, J., *Ein Arzt erzählt sein Leben* (München: Paul List Verlag, 1951).

Rheinberger, H.-J., 'Experimentalsysteme, In-vitro-Kulturen, Modellorganismen', in Birgit Griesecke et al., eds., *Kulturgeschichte des Menschenversuchs im 20. Jahrhundert* (Frankfurt a. M.: Suhrkamp, 2009), pp. 394–404.

Sarasin, P., et al., ed., *Bakteriologie und Moderne: Studien zur Biopolitik des Unsichtbaren 1870–1920* (Frankfurt a. M.: Suhrkamp, 2007).

Spöring, F., '"Du mußt Apostel der Wahrheit warden": Auguste Forel und der sozialhygienische Antialkohol-Diskurs, 1886 – 1931', in Judith Große, Francesco Spöring and Tschurenev, J., *Biopolitik und Sittlichkeitsreform: Kampagnen gegen Alkohol, Drogen und Prostitution 1880–1950* (Frankfurt: Campus Verlag, 2014), pp. 111–44.

Vettel, E. J., *Biotech: The Countercultural Origins of an Industry* (Philadelphia: University of Pennsylvania Press, 2006).

FIG. 29.1 Prussian census box as used for the 1871 census, reconstructed to size by Norbert Massuthe, Berlin (2016) (photo: Laura Selle 2017). The larger box contained 75 kilograms of enumeration material (10,000 counting cards), the smaller one 37.5 kilograms (5,000 cards)

29

PRUSSIAN CENSUS BOX: MOVING AND FREEZING DATA

Christine von Oertzen

Size and shape: comes in two sizes (and some variations thereof), custom made. Big: 51 x 69 x 27.5 cm, small: 51 x 34.5 x 27.5 cm. **Material**: plain wood, untreated. **Weight**: big: ca. 75 kg (full), small: ca. 37.5 kg (full). **Accessories**: label with state emblem, a number, and name of enumeration district. **Behaviour**: heavy when full. Lid completely detachable, must be firmly closed with eight screws before transport. When opened and closed repeatedly, additional nails must be deployed to prevent unintentional opening. **Habitat**: first winter (from December to January): some local administration office in Prussia; rest of life span: Berlin, fixed assigned spot in unheated basement or attic of Prussian Census Bureau, or in shed on adjacent premises; from there, circulating within Berlin between the bureau and some 2000 private households. **Distribution**: ca. 3,000 (2,500 big, 500 small) in 1871, multiplying over the following decades to peak around 1895 with 27,760 in total; occurrence declining between 1914 and 1918. Extinct by 1925. During migration period, spread over Prussia's provinces and enumeration districts, with a higher concentration in urban and industrial areas. After migration, entirely bound to Berlin. **Migration**: at beginning of life span, when new. Usually leaves Berlin after production and filling with enumeration material, travels to predetermined locations within Prussia by means of train and/or horse carriage (later by truck). Outbound migration period: late November; inbound migration: late January of following year. **Life span**: produced ca. every three years. Lives for ca. two years, thereafter dismantled and recycled. **Content**: four (big box) resp. two (small box) stacks of 2,500 enumeration cards (330 x 240 cm, weight 7.5 gm) for census taking. **Cost**: 3.11 Reichsmark (on average, excluding recycling fee).

Keywords: portioning, circulating, shipping, handling, protecting (keeping clean and dry), signifying, performing, controlling, ordering, archiving, governing, obstructing, disappearing

TO MY KNOWLEDGE, NOT ONE OF THE ORIGINAL PRUSSIAN CENSUS BOXES has survived. They were not meant to endure, but what we do possess is information about their measurements, material, and above all context: what census boxes were for and how they were used. Made of untreated wood, the boxes were first and foremost simple, sturdy, and cheap. They were produced on a mass scale for a strict date: 3,000 (2,500 big ones and 500 small ones) of them had to be ready for a huge delivery that would not tolerate delays. Boxes of this kind must have looked like the ones depicted here (**FIGURE 29.1**), reconstructed with accurate dimensions by a Berlin carpenter: slim boards cut to size for bottom, top, front, back, and sides. With neither time nor funds for any costly extras, the boxes were likely to be nailed or screwed together, with slats not just holding together each segment, but also providing stability for the entire structure. Eight screws kept the top shut. Reopening and closing the box was a procedure that could not be indefinitely repeated.

So, what makes these ordinary objects special? Notwithstanding their simplicity, these boxes played a crucial part in what was a new and exciting endeavour. Almost everywhere in Europe, census and population statistics had expanded into complex operations by the second half of the nineteenth century, driven by efforts to render them 'scientific', i.e. to turn them into verifiable, 'objective' descriptions of the population (Porter 1995; Desrosières 2002). International statistical congresses hosted in different European cities after 1853 intensified methodological exchange and created state-of-the-art standards. Initially slow to adapt this new trend, by the end of the 1860s Prussia's statisticians had radically transformed their methods and practices of census taking. At the heart of this fundamental shift towards modern data processing lay a new paper tool: the so-called individual counting card. This was a simple sheet, 210 mm in length and 120 mm in width, designed to record all enumeration data of one person. Counting cards had replaced enumeration lists in Prussian census-taking by 1871. In contrast to the bulky lists, the cards were light and movable. These data carriers were also praised for their ability to greatly enhance statistical complexity. Prussian statisticians were proud to emphasise that the counting card allowed them to compile tables displaying a richness in combination of variables that no other nation in the world was able to achieve (von Oertzen 2017).

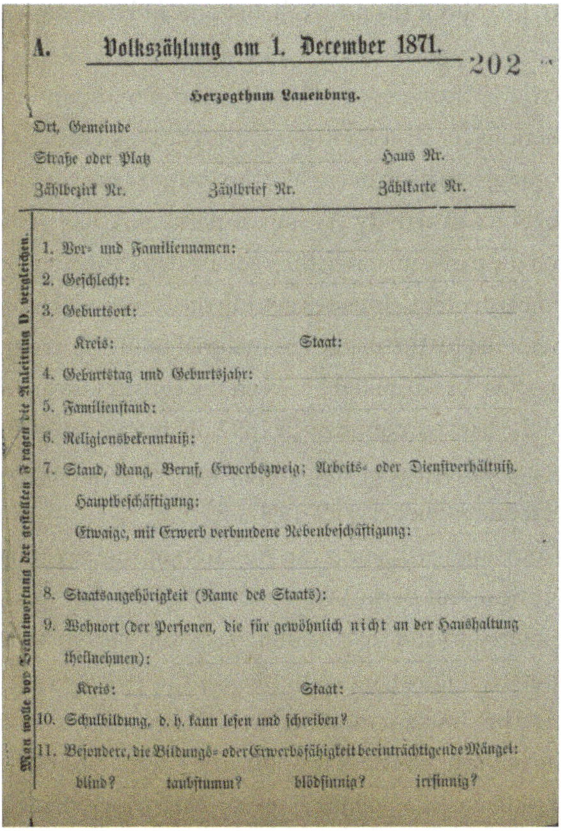

A. Volkszählung am 1. December 1871. 202

Herzogthum Lauenburg.

Ort, Gemeinde

Straße oder Platz Haus Nr.

Zählbezirk Nr. Zählbrief Nr. Zählkarte Nr.

1. Vor- und Familiennamen:
2. Geschlecht:
3. Geburtsort:
   Kreis: Staat:
4. Geburtstag und Geburtsjahr:
5. Familienstand:
6. Religionsbekenntniß:
7. Stand, Rang, Beruf, Erwerbszweig; Arbeits- oder Dienstverhältniß.
   Hauptbeschäftigung:
   Etwaige, mit Erwerb verbundene Nebenbeschäftigung:
8. Staatsangehörigkeit (Name des Staats):
9. Wohnort (der Personen, die für gewöhnlich nicht an der Haushaltung theilnehmen):
   Kreis: Staat:
10. Schulbildung, d. h. kann lesen und schreiben?
11. Besondere, die Bildungs- oder Erwerbsfähigkeit beeinträchtigende Mängel:
    blind? taubstumm? blödsinnig? irrsinnig?

Man wolle vor Beantwortung der gestellten Fragen die Anleitung D. vergleichen.

FIG. 29.2 Prussian Counting Card, 210x210 mm (1871) (source: Prussian Secret State Archives (Geheimes Staatsarchiv Preußischer Kulturbesitz), Berlin)

Although each counting card weighed a mere 7.5 grams, taken together, the almost 50 million cards produced for the 1871 census amounted to 375 tons of material. The daunting mass of loose paper slips needed to be moved to all the Prussian enumeration districts and then be circulated within Berlin, where the centralised processing of the data was to take place. This is where the census boxes came into play: custom-made to hold between two and four stacks of 2,500 counting cards, the boxes allowed the enumeration material to be apportioned into manageable units. Five thousand cards packed into a small box provided enumeration material for more sparsely populated rural districts, whereas the big boxes filled with 10,000 cards accommodated larger, urban, and industrial areas. Filled with the papery load, each box weighed 37.5 kilograms or 75 kilograms, just about the limit of what one and two workers respectively could lift and carry (Engel 1873).

The production of the boxes, and the printing of the counting cards, control lists, and instructions for enumerators set Prussia's data machinery in motion. Once all the material had been delivered, the Prussian census bureau was transformed into a beehive of activity. As census clerks and their assistants checked and apportioned the paper material, the packing department teemed with packers, porters, and carpenter helpmates getting the boxes ready for their journey, a task often hampered by the masses of material piling up around them. Only after a telephone line was installed between the census bureau, the printer, the box factory, and the haulage company in 1892 did the work flow more smoothly without delays 'caused by the bothersome congestion of empty boxes and the lingering of filled ones' (Blenck 1897, 197–8).

While transporting was their main function at the beginning of their life span when heading out of Berlin, the boxes were never just vessels for hauling enumeration material to and fro. Coming back into the city two months later, after the enumeration effort was completed, the boxes assumed additional importance. They became a wandering archive, keeping the state of their content stable while being in constant motion. The enumeration effort had turned the boxes' load from packs of identical pre-printed paper forms into thousands of distinct and irreplaceable carriers of original census information. All of the census data were inscribed on individual counting cards. The looseness of the gathered data was considered crucial for the abstraction process, but at the same time, all depended on the order in which the cards were kept. The boxes ensured such order: they protected the cards from being separated, and thus preserved their context.

When the 3,000 boxes – with 375,000 kilograms' worth of millions of filled-in counting cards and various control lists from all the Prussian enumeration districts – reappeared at the census bureau's headquarters in early 1872, each one of them was placed in a fixed pre-assigned space, ranging from the basement or attic of the main building to a shed on the adjacent premises. The three-storey domicile of the census bureau, completed in 1869, was not designed for storing and moving such massive amounts of enumeration material (Blenck 1897). Handling the colossal masses of data entirely in-house proved daunting, with boxes piling up in every corner. Storing, tracking, retrieving, opening, and clos-ing the cases, and handling the millions of cards required much more space and time than previously assumed, mounting to a point that the planned abstrac-tion procedure had to be altered. Rather than exhaust the material category by category in many successive rounds of sorting, compilers were advised to not move each box more than three times. This meant that the compilation work had to be completed in three comprehensive counts, each including the abstraction of numerous criteria in one fell swoop (Engel 1 December 1872. GStA, HA I, Rep. 77, Tit. 77, Nr. 132).

The census bureau hired an extra three hundred workers to check the incoming data and handle the counting and sorting of the cards. That said, it is important to note that most of the work was not done on the bureau's premises, but instead distributed for homework. The scope and steadiness of outsourcing to the private homes of the bureau's workers and their wives and female kin suggests that homework expanded to accommodate the abstraction process: much space and many faithful helpers were needed to process the data (von Oertzen 2019). Keeping the boxes with the paper cards in constant motion between the bureau and different homes proved an efficient way to handle the volumes of material.

Homework emerged as a key component in the processing of Prussian census data over the following decades, growing in volume considerably each year. For the 1890 census, the main bulk of abstracting census records was performed by up to two hundred and sixty-four women, toiling at piece-rate from home (Blenck 1892: 256). A peak was reached in 1895, when the census bureau employed 1,000 wage-workers and about 3,000, mostly female, home workers to compile the commerce, trade, and agricultural statistics of that year, the most comprehensive statistical investigation the agency had ever under-taken. Between October 1895 and May 1896, no fewer than 27,760 of the big 75-kilogram boxes were shipped to the homes of workers and collected each time one of the three counts was completed. 2,137,600 kg of statistical material was circulated during this time, with counting cards strewn all over Berlin and its outskirts. During this process, 362,284,360 numbers were abstracted from the cards and written by (many different) hand(s) in half a million table forms, which, spread out side by side, would have covered 53,000 square meters. All this was achieved by circulating thousands of boxes across the vast city (Blenck 1897: 302).

The sheer mass of the material, then, required the boxes to migrate beyond the census bureau, but it was their movability that rendered such a system possible. A close look at the workflow exposes a further function of the boxes: they enabled the sequencing and control of the circular abstraction process. The census data were processed in the following way: first, each box was carried from its fixed storage location in the census bureau to a clerk's desk, where it was opened and checked for completeness. Re-sealed safely, and accompanied by table forms and meticulous instructions explaining the sorting plan, the box was then dispatched to a home. There it was re-opened and unpacked. The cards were sorted into piles according to prescribed criteria, counted, and the resulting numbers noted in the respective table forms. Kept in its new order, each pile of cards was wrapped in paper, labeled in a specific manner, and put back into the box. Re-sealed and secured with the lid-screws, the box returned to the census office for control. In this fashion, each box was sent back and forth up to three times between the bureau and individual dwellings (additional nails had to ensure the lids would not fall off) (Blenck 1892: 214). During this process, each counting card was subjected to three comprehensive rounds of sorting and counting in order to establish the numbers and combinations of variables for the complex Prussian statistics, which soon gained international recognition. What reads like a complex, if relatively straightforward, method of circulation turned out to be a good deal messier in practice. Because at-home workers were compelled to pay the bureau's transport costs, many chose to pick up and bring back their boxes themselves; also, different portions of material were delivered to each household, depending on the capacities of the respective workers. The expansive machinery of manual census abstraction turned Berlin's city space into a fine-meshed net of actors, destinations, and routes, transforming the dispatching of material into a choreography preciously few of the bureau's workers mastered (von Oertzen 2017).

While the boxes circulated within Berlin on different routes, the cards in them could only move in one direction. Each new round of sorting built upon the piles assembled in the previous turn. There was no way to restore the cards' original order, and hence no reason to keep them for re-use. When the last round of sorting was completed, the cards in the boxes were, indeed, exhausted like a pile of waste, and the data on them wilted. What 'counted' were the tables fixed in publications. Circulation had come to an end. Bereaved of their movement, the boxes found themselves merely in the way. And soon, along with the census records they carried, they were discarded, demolished, and recycled.

REFERENCES

Blenck, E., 'Die Volkszählung vom 1. December 1890 in Preussen und deren endgültige Ergebnisse', in *Zeitschrift des königlich preussischen statistischen Bureaus*, 32 (1892): 177–264.

——, 'Das Königlich preussische statistische Bureau während der Jahre 1885–1896' in *Zeitschrift des königlich preussischen statistischen Bureaus*, 37 (1897): 191–198.

Desrosières, A., *The Politics of Large Numbers. A History of Statistical Reasoning* (Cambridge: Harvard University Press, 2002).

Engel, E. 'Die Verwaltung des königlich preussischen statistischen Bureaus im Jahre 1873' in *Zeitschrift des königlich preussischen statistischen Bureaus*, 13 (1873): 345–64.

von Oertzen, C., 'Hidden Helpers: Gender, Skill, and the Politics of Workforce Management for Census Compilation in Late Nineteenth-Century Prussia', in J. Bangham and J. Kaplan, eds, *(In)visible Labor: Knowledge Production in the Human Sciences* (Berlin: Max Planck Institute for the History of Science preprint series, 474, 2015).

——, 'Machineries of Data Power: Manual versus Mechanical Census Compilation in Nineteenth-Century Europe', in *Osiris* (2017).

——, 'Keeping Prussia's House in Order: Census Cards, Housewifery, and the State's Census Compilation', in C. Bittel, E. Leong, C. von Oertzen, eds., *Working and Knowing With Paper: Towards a Gendered History of Knowledge* (Pittsburgh: University of Pittsburgh Press 2019).

Porter, T., *Trust in Numbers. The Pursuit of Objectivity in Science and Public Life* (Princeton: Princeton University Press, 1995).

FIG. 30.1 The photograph shows an open glass DT-60 personnel dosimeter used in the 1950s and 1960s. It was placed in a circular plastic container that opened only with a special tool to protect sensitive radiation data (source: ORAU, Health Physics Historical Instrumentation Museum Collection)

30

BLACK-BOXING KNOWLEDGE: GLASS DOSIMETERS AND GOVERNMENTAL CONTROL

Maria Rentetzi

Material: plastic case that opens only with a special tool; the sensitive material is encased within, in a single ½ inch x ½ inch radiophotoluminescent glass block. **Shape**: circular. **Size**: the case is 3.8 cm in diameter and close to 1 cm thick. **Colour**: black. **Weight**: slightly above 56 grams. **Dose range**: up to 600 R. **Minimum detectable dose**: 10 R. **Accuracy**: ± 20%. **Price**: $1 in 1958. **Origin**: designed to monitor US Navy personnel. **Habitat**: hung from human necks.

Keywords: black-boxing knowledge, monitoring, controlling, measuring, governing

SINCE THE MID-1950S, THE PROTECTION OF WORKERS IN THE NUCLEAR industry, and public health concerns about exposure to ionising radiation, have been key research topics but also major sources of controversy. The hazards from radiation released by nuclear power plants, and the increasing use of radiation technologies in cancer treatments, have sparked governmental concerns and public anxiety. Research on the production of reliable instruments that could monitor accidental exposure to radiation has been stepped up. Civilian and military personnel in the US Army and Navy have been especially monitored since they were among the first to be occupationally exposed to various forms of radiation. Glass dosimeters of the DT-60 type were the first instruments offered to military personnel for personal radiation monitoring.

Dosimeters are measurement devices that detect invisible radiation based on the various phenomena – i.e., ionisation, scintillation, and luminescence – that are produced when radiation interacts with matter. Dosimeters are classified as either active or passive, depending on their use. Active dosimeters are used for recording data immediately, and include scintillation counters, semi-conductor detectors, and gas filled counters. Passive dosimeters are used mainly for monitoring radiation levels for people working in environments with radiation. The most usual types of passive dosimeters are film badges, thermoluminescence dosimeters known as TLDs, optical stimulated luminescence dosimeters, and radio-photoluminescence glass dosimeters (RPGD). The DT-60 belongs to the last category of passive dosimeters, and these devices were extensively used by the US military throughout the 1950s and 1960s.

In 1952, James Schulman and Robert Ginther from the US Navy Research Laboratory filed a patent for a glass dosimeter for high-energy radiation. As they stated:

> an object of the invention is the provision of a dosimeter utilizing a detecting element composed of a glass sensitive to high energy radiation and in such geometrical form as to enhance the readability of response of the detecting element by eye or by a photoelectric device… the detector element is of a suitable substantially transparent radiophotoluminescent material, such as silver activated phosphate glass in the form of a rod capable of being worn by personnel subjected to high energy radiation.[1]

The term photoluminescence was introduced during the interwar period by Karl Prizbram and his research team at the Institute for Radium Research in Vienna (Rentetzi 2007). But it was not until the 1950s, and through Schulman's work, that the phenomenon was used as a basis for a radiation dosimetry system. Schulman studied chemistry at MIT and worked extensively in industry during the war. In 1946 he joined the US Naval Research Laboratory and initiated research in luminescence phenomena. He argued that dosage measurements could be made with the use of a silver-activated phosphate glass, employing a simple fluorophotometer (Schulman et al. 1951). Based on this early patent and several later modifications, the DT-60 dosimeter in its earliest application included a silver-activated phosphate glass in the form of a block (1.6 x 1.6 x 0.5 cm). After exposure to x or gamma radiation, the glass emitted luminescent light. The whole block was enclosed in a black plastic locket that opened like a box, but only with special equipment. The reason was to protect sensitive data from misuse, but what misuse was meant had not been explained.

Along with the DT-60 dosimeter, the navy also introduced the Radiac Computer-Indicator CP-95A/PD, a portable reader that computed and indicated the total amount of radiation to which the dosimeter had been exposed. The dosimeter had to be opened and placed in the reader's special holder. A lever on the reader was pulled upwards to rotate the dosimeter into the unit and finally position it in front of a photomultiplier tube that amplified the initial electron emission. The output was then applied to an indicating circuit to obtain the final reading. The DT-60 and its reader were the first mass-produced dosimetry system based on the photoluminescence phenomenon. It is telling that the US Navy commissioned the production of over four million glass dosimeters for use as 'accident' dosimeters to monitor its personnel (Schulman, James H. et al. 1953: 52).

A recent Radiation Protection Health Manual, published in 2001, refers to the DT-60 as a battlefield dosimeter[2] that was assigned to all navy, army, and air force personnel (**FIGURE 30.2**). Yet, as the Air Force Safety Center admitted in 2014, in the 1960s 'many nuclear-capable units issued DT-60 accident dosimeters to their workers as a precaution for an unlikely occurrence of an accidentally high radiation exposure, from perhaps a nuclear criticality'. The dosimeters, nonetheless, 'would have been insensitive to the relatively low

FIG. 30.2 A set of ten original DT-60 dosimeters packaged with instructions and specifications. The box is dated 1951, and the dosimeters were manufactured by the Polaroid Corporation. They are sold as 'a Cold-War beauty', which 'shows you just how fried you are after a radiation exposure' (source: Omaha's Surplus 2016)

exposures received by nuclear weapons maintenance and other technicians that worked in these facilities'. In short, the minimum sensitivity of these dosimeters, approximately 10 Roentgen, was twice the current annual exposure limit for occupationally-exposed workers.[3] So those who wore it simply did not have access to the data that the instrument accumulated; the box was protectively closed but still able to be opened with special equipment. In addition, it was insensitive to low radiation doses.

In the 1960s, increased public concern about nuclear fallout turned the dosimeters into a part of popular culture. As Paul Frame from ORAU Health Physics Historical Instrumentation Museum Collection reports, in October 1961 the Associated Press published a picture of a woman holding a DT-60. The caption reads 'Nuclear Neckwear. Linda Bromley of New Rochelle, N.Y., holds in her left hand a personal radiation detector whose maker says could be the next thing in ladies' neckwear should the threat of nuclear fallout increase. The lead shield plastic-covered detector, called a dosimeter, is the size of a half dollar and weighs one and a half ounces'. The DT-60 became the standard dosimeter throughout the 1950s and early 1960s, until thermoluminescent dosimeters took over.[4]

GLASS DOSIMETERS ONCE AGAIN IN THE SPOTLIGHT

After the nuclear plant in Fukushima Daichii was hit by a tsunami in March 2011, three out of six nuclear reactors experienced meltdown followed by high radioactive releases. The accident was rated 7, the highest possible level on the International Nuclear and Radiological Event Scale (INES). In the following month, over 150,000 people were evacuated from their homes – forced, actually, to move several times, given the frequent change of official instructions. In August 2011, and while decontamination efforts were still underway, some children, with their families, returned to affected areas to attend school.

> Perhaps the starkest reminders that all was not right were the dosimeters encased in plastic sleeves that were dangling from their [children's] necks', wrote a report of *The Asahi Shimbun*, one of the country's national newspapers. 'Students call the tool "glass badges"'. (The Asahi Shimbun 2011)

At the time of the Fukushima accident there were three major types of radio-photoluminescence glass dosimeter on the market. Among them was the GD-450, and it was this that was used for monitoring the radiation exposure of children in the Fukushima Prefecture (Huang and Hsu 2011). This type of glass dosimeter, along with the automatic reader known as FGD-650, had actually

FIG. 30.3 Children in Fukushima with their radiation dosimeters called 'glass badges'. The regional government requires children and pregnant women to wear them as a way 'to calm the anxiety of the children and their guardians' after the Fukushima nuclear disaster (source: Nagano 2017 [2012])

been introduced in Japan in 2001. They were marketed by the Chiyoda Technol Corporation, a Japanese company specialising in radiation monitoring since 1958 (**FIGURE 30.3**), and were advertised as the most popular personal monitor in Japan. They were developed for large-scale monitoring service, providing the possibility to record both the ID code of the radiophotoluminescent glass and the ID code of the person wearing it.

In order to process the big data produced by the use of its dosimeters, the Chiyoda Technol Corporation constructed a new centre, known as the Radiation Monitoring Center, in Oarai, Ibaraki, Japan, in 2000. The centre was able to process 2,700,000 glass dosimeters per month. More specifically, the glass dosimetry system (GD-450 together with its reading system FDG-650) was capable of processing 2000 dosimeters in less than seven hours, with a readout time of twelve seconds per dosimeter. Not surprisingly, in 2007 the Institut de Radioprotection et de Sûreté Nucléaire (IRSN) in France bought Chiyoda's dosimetric system and replaced the photographic film-based monitoring of about 150.000 radiation workers (Chiyoda Technol Corporation; Bhatt and Kulkarni 2013: 9).

Immediately after the accident, the Fukushima Prefecture, in cooperation with the Chiyoda Technol Corporation, launched a programme for measuring the radiation exposure levels of children, provoking harsh criticism from bloggers and activists for the kind of experiment and the purposes that it served.[5] Dosimeters were not designed to give warning of when radiation exceeded the permissible levels, and they did not measure internal exposure by inhaling radioactive dirt and consuming contaminated food. At specific times, the company would collect the badges, download the data and, after a statistical analysis, report the results to local authorities and municipalities.

A short report published by the United Nations Office for Disaster Risk Reduction cites a similar policy. 'On October 2011, So-so area launched a voluntary external radiation exposure screening program using Glass dosimetre (Glass Badge GD-450, Chiyoda Technology Co.). The participants were instructed to bring it all the time for three months and yearly dose were calculated' (UNISDR 2015). In response to the question 'did it make a difference?', the report concludes that these studies show that the air dose rate for the 'so-so area' was decreased. Based on this knowledge, the local government concluded 'there is no fear of external radiation exposure in So-so area'.

In 2013, and despite government promises and residents' persistent requests for decontamination, central government officials from the Miyakoji district of Tamura, Fukushima Prefecture, came up with a different suggestion. Having failed to reach its original radiation decontamination target, the government proposed that evacuees return to their homes and assume responsibility for their own safety. During a meeting with evacuees on 23 June 2013, a Cabinet Office official presented a new type of dosimeter, the 'glass badge', that allowed residents to check radiation exposure levels themselves. 'The residents called for continued clean-up efforts, but government officials offered them dosimeters instead', revealed Miki Aoki of *The Asahi Shimbun* (Aoki 2013). On 5 September 2015 the Japanese government lifted for the first time the evacuation order for the north-eastern town of Naraha, allowing 7400 residents to return to their homes after the site had been decontaminated. But fifty-three per cent of the evacuees were not ready to return, and since April 2015 – the trial period before the government's final decision – only 100 out of 2600 households returned to the town. Once again '[r]esidents have been given personal dosimeters to check their own radiation levels. To accommodate their concerns, the town is also running 24-hour monitoring at a water filtration plant, testing tap water for radioactive materials' reported *The World Post* (The Associated Press 2015)· And once again dosimeters were actually transforming public concerns over radiation safety into issues of personal responsibility.

Today, Chiyoda, together with IRSN, promotes one of the most advanced glass dosimeters, recommended for dosimetric monitoring of workers in many sectors of activity, including industrial, medical, dental, and research. The dosimeter is advertised for its ergonomic design and the fact that it ensures compliance with health and safety practices. Small and portable, it is designed to detect x, gamma, and beta rays. It is worn either on a strap around the neck or pinned to work clothes. It is 61.5 mm long and 28.9 mm wide, and very slim and light (12 g). It carries a series of numbers – designating badge number, distribution unit code, and period of wear – and allows the identification of the person that wears it and the site where it is used. In contrast to its predecessor, the DT-60 with its box like container, the new glass dosimeter is fixed, lighter, compact, and ergonomic. The box-case that contains it is sealed. Yet what remains the same is the fact that these dosimeters do not provide immediate readings. Users are not aware of the levels of radiation they are exposed to. Dosimeters, as was the case in the 1950s and 1960s, are collected and read in the absence of those who actually wear them.

What are dosimeters, then? Regardless of whether their box-like case is sealed or not, dosimeters such as the above are not just measurement devices, simple portable instruments, and part of the laboratory's material culture. They are also first and foremost black-boxed regulatory devices, constitutive of concepts of public health, safety, and the permissible level of radiation exposure. They become involved in public debates about radiation safety to the extent that they become instruments of government or military politics. In extreme cases, dosimeters are used to manipulate limits to radiation exposure. In a summary of reports on a range of issues arising from the Fukushima disaster by *Nuclear Monitor*, it was reported that,

> Last July, a subcontracting company admitted that an executive told 14 workers to cover their radiation dosimeters in an effort to give false readings. Workers were told that if they did not comply, they would rapidly exceed the one-year legal limit of 50 mSv and they would have to stop working. (World Information Service on Energy 2013: 9; Menezes 2012)

Clearly, dosimeters have never been 'purely scientific', but instead a matter of social and political importance. By putting dosimeters in boxes and making them portable, right after World War II, the US Navy sought to win the confidence of its personnel and the public's support for putting nuclear energy to military uses. By offering dosimeters to the Fukushima evacuees, the Japanese government hoped to transfer the responsibility of radiation safety to those who wore them. However, now and then, readings of radiation exposure doses were not immediately available to the users. After all, the black-boxing of knowledge on radiation safety that has been produced by today's radiation dosimeters is definitely a means of achieving political and economic goals.

Acknowledgements: This project has been supported by the Austrian Science Fund: project number M 1727 - G16. I would like to thank Spiros Petrounakos for his insightful comments. To Paul Frame I owe special thanks for his generosity and his support for my work. I would also like to thank Charlie and Brad Williams from Omaha's Surplus for allowing me to use their photographic material, and the Chiyoda Technol Corporation for providing information.

NOTES

1 Schulman, James H. et al., 'Dosimeter for high energy radiation', US Patent 2787714 filed on 28 November 1952.
2 U.S. Bureau of Medicine and Surgery 2001: par. 6.9, p. 40.
3 Appeal from the Department of Veterans Affairs Regional Office in Columbia, South Carolina, 3 March 2015, <http://www.va.gov/vetapp15/Files2/1510226.txt>.
4 The most informative source on the DT-60 dosimeter and its reader is Paul Frame's descriptions in the ORAU Health Physics Historical Instrumentation Museum Collection, see <http://www.orau.org/ptp/collection/radiac/DT60.htm> and <http://www.orau.org/ptp/collection/radiac/CP95APD.htm>.
5 See for example <http://ex-skf.blogspot.co.at/2011/06/radiation-in-japan-experiment-just-got.html> and <http://www.fukuleaks.org/web/?p=7216>.

REFERENCES

Aoki, M., 'Government Offers Dosimeters – Not Decontamination – for Fukushima Evacuees', in *The Asahi Shimbun*, 29 June 2013, <http://ajw.asahi.com/article/0311disaster/fukushima/AJ201306290074>.

Bhatt, B. C., and M. S. Kulkarni, 'Worldwide Status of Personnel Monitoring using Thermoluminescent (TL), Optically Stimulated Luminescent (OSL) and Radiophotoluminescent (RPL) Dosimeters', *International Journal of Luminescence and Applications*, 3. 1 (2013), 6–10.

Chiyoda Technol Corporation, 'Our History', in Chiyoda Technol Corporation, <http://www.c-technol.co.jp/eng/e-about/e-history>.

Huang, D. Y. C., and S-M Hsu, 'The Radio-Photoluminescence Glass Dosimeter (RPLGD)', in Hala, G-M., *Advances in Cancer Therapy* (InTech, 2011), pp. 553–68, <http://cdn.intechopen.com/pdfs-wm/23935.pdf>.

Menezes, S., 'Fukushima Workers Told to Lie about Radiation Exposure', in *Australian Broadcasting Corporation*, 21 July 2012, <http://www.abc.net.au/news/2012-07-21/fukushima-workers-told-to-lie-about-radiation-exposure/4146056>.

Nagano, T., 'The Occupation and Glass Badges', 2017 [2012], <https://nuclear-news.net/2017/12/23/the-occupation-and-glass-badges/>.

Omaha's Surplus, 'Radiac Detector', 2016, <http://www.omahas.com/radiac-detector#.VsN5DoQemRs>.

Rentetzi, M., *Trafficking Materials and Gendered Experimental Practices: Radium Research in Early Twentieth Century Vienna* (New York: Columbia University Press, 2007).

Schulman, J. H., et al., 'Dosimetry of X-Rays and Gamma-Rays by Radiophotoluminescence', *Journal of Applied Physics*, 22. 12 (1951), 1479–87.

Schulman, J. H., et al., 'Radiophotoluminescence Dosimetry Systems of the U.S. Navy', *Nucleonics*, 11. 10 (1953): 52–54.

The Asahi Shimbun, ' "Glass Badges" Remind Fukushima Students of Radiation Risks', in *The Asahi Shimbun*, 25 August 2011, <http://ajw.asahi.com/article/0311disaster/fukushima/AJ201108257640>.

The Associated Press, 'Japan Ends Evacuation Order for Town Hit By Fukushima Nuclear Disaster', in *The World Post*, 5 September 2015, <http://www.huffingtonpost.com/entry/japan-ends-evacuation-order-fukushima_us_55eaea9fe4b093be51bbaa4a>.

UNISDR Scientific and Technical Advisory Group, 'Eliminating residents' concerns after the nuclear disaster in Fukushima', in UNISDR The United Nations Office for Disaster Risk Reduction, *Case Studies*, 2015, <http://www.preventionweb.net/files/workspace/7935_ochifukishima.pdf>.

US Bureau of Medicine and Surgery – Department of the Navy, 'Radiation Protection Health Manual', August 2001, <http://fas.org/irp/doddir/milmed/rhpm.pdf>.

World Information Service on Energy, 'In Brief', in *Nuclear Monitor*, 758 (15 March 2013), 8–10, <http://www.wiseinternational.org/sites/default/files/images/NM758-Fukushima.pdf>.

x

MIRROR

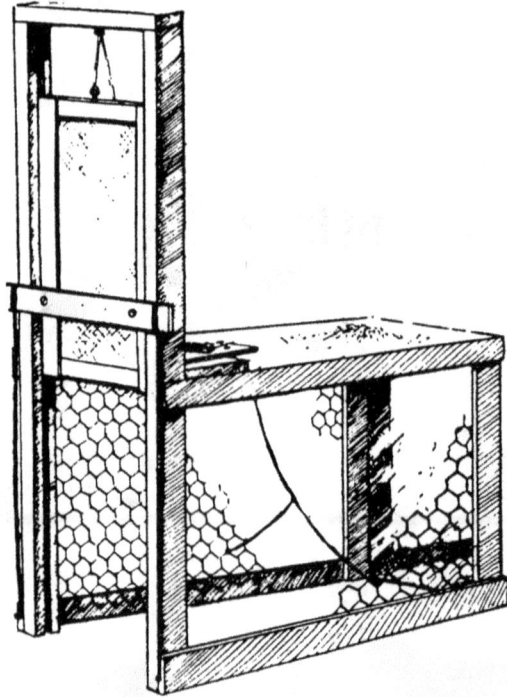

FIG. 31.1 'Mirror trap set, showing trigger mechanism, mirror, and rubber bands, fastened to bottom of door' (source: Figure 1a in J. F. S. Bendell and C. David Fowle 1950: 481)

3 1

THE MIRROR TRAP

Etienne S. Benson

Box: the mirror trap. **Size**: 28 inches long, 14 inches wide, 18 inches high. **First observed**: Pennsylvania, 1947. **Distribution**: North American forests, often found on or near the drumming logs of ruffed grouse. **Behaviour**: sudden, automatic, sometimes violent. **Sexual dimorphism**: none (asexual: a box), but made for males. **Common uses**: trapping birds, exercising coercive care, affirming human exceptionalism. **Possible risks**: serious injury, profound misrecognition. **Status**: rare but not endangered. **Sometimes mistaken for**: a rival, oneself.

Keywords: captivating, caring, confining, injuring, preserving, managing, recognising, misrecognising

THE MIRROR TRAP WAS INVENTED IN THE SPRING OF 1947 BY GLENN L. Bowers and Ward D. Tanner, two graduate assistants working for the Pennsylvania Cooperative Wildlife Research Unit (Bowers and Tanner 1947, 1948). Its design is simple but ingenious.

The trap itself is fairly ordinary: a box of wood and wire mesh measuring 28 inches long, 14 inches wide, and 18 inches high, with a spring-loaded sliding door at one end that is triggered by a treadle on the floor of the trap. It is the bait that is unusual. One of the inner sides of the box is fitted with an 8-by-10-inch mirror. That's it. No alluring scents, no tempting morsels, no beguiling camouflage.

For at least one particular target, however, the mirror is enough. That target is the ruffed grouse, a species distantly related to the chicken that can be found in early successional forests across North America (Dessecker and McAuley 2001). The ingenuity of the trap lies in its simplicity, which in turn depends on a single penetrating insight into the grouse's capabilities and vulnerabilities.

In the mating season a male ruffed grouse will attack other males who venture too close to the fallen log, rock, or other site he has selected for his 'drumming' display. (The sound is actually made by the rapid beating of the bird's wings). Unable to recognise the image reflected in the mirror as his own, the grouse rushes toward his imagined competitor, triggering the trap's release mechanism and sealing himself inside the box. In the grandiloquent terms of the press release issued by the Unit once the success of the trap had become clear in the spring of 1947: 'The King Succumbs to his Own Image' (Pennsylvania Cooperative Wildlife Research Unit 1947a). At a time when grouse were scarce in the state of Pennsylvania, the new design seems to have dramatically facilitated their capture (Bowers 1947).

I have been unable to find any detailed account of the trap's genesis. Did Bowers and Tanner know of the ancient Roman belief that a tigress pursuing her stolen cubs could be distracted by a mirror, which she would misrecognise as the very offspring she was trying to rescue (Toynbee 1996: 72–81)? Were they familiar with the *miroir aux alouettes*, a spinning block of wood embedded with small mirrors that was used to snare larks and other songbirds in early modern Europe? (The device seems to have attracted birds by its shiny, water-like surfaces rather than by reflections of their own images (see Arentsen and Fenech 2004)). Were they simply struck by inspiration after spending long hours in the field watching the antics of amorous birds from afar? However it came about, the box they built embodied a refined understanding of the grouse's world.

All successful traps require some such understanding. The target must walk, fly, swim, or slither into the trap of his or her own volition; this is what distinguishes a trap from a weapon. And so the trapper must know something of the target's habits, desires, and capabilities, so that they can be used against him. Like a hunter, he must imagine himself into the animal's life, perhaps even see himself as animal (Willerslev 2007); unlike the hunter, he must embody this knowledge in an apparatus that will operate in his absence (Kassung 2012). A collection of all the traps ever made would be a treasure-trove of such knowledge in material form, a kind of map of animal worldviews in reverse. It would be a very incomplete map, since the hardest part of trapping is often knowing when, where, and how to place the trap, but it would be a wonder nonetheless.

Much of this fantastical collection would consist of devices that kill or maim: the leghold traps, the deadfalls, the snares, the spiked pits, and the drowning sets (see Spencer 2007), as well as those miniature modern horrors, the glue boards, 'responsible for more suffering than virtually any other wildlife control product on the market' (Humane Society of the United States 2012). But a good portion would consist of live traps, of which the mirror trap is a specialised variety.

The live trap requires an even more intimate knowledge of the animal than the death trap. Not only must it be designed in such a way as to take advantage of the animal's blind spots, but it must also allow the animal to survive within the trap until the trapper arrives, which may take hours or even days. It thus combines a ruthless exploitation of the animal's vulnerabilities with a limited but genuine concern for his survival. The slamming shut of the trip-wired door is the moment that divides the two.

Even when an intent to injure is absent, there is a violence inherent to such traps. One of the first grouse caught in Tanner and Bowers' trap died before the trap was inspected, probably as a result of wounds sustained in his frantic attempt to escape (Bowers 1948: 4). Another 'succumbed' after being removed from the trap and photographed (Pennsylvania Cooperative Wildlife Research Unit 1947b: 14). Many others were severely injured within the trap, despite a lining of soft netting having been installed on the inside of the top panel to cushion their collisions. Scalping was particularly common, if rarely fatal. Later refinements further reduced but never eliminated the possibility of injury (Bendell and Fowle 1950; Dorney and Mattison 1956; Chambers and English 1958; Gullion 1965). Getting the bird into the box was difficult; keeping him alive and well once inside was even harder.

There are many reasons for wanting to trap an animal alive. One is to ensure, before killing him, that he is actually the kind of animal one wants to kill. Another is to bring him into captivity – that is, to move him from the box in which he was caught to the cage, paddock, tank, or enclosure in which he will live out the rest of his life, short or long as it may be. Neither of these was Tanner and Bowers' goal. Instead they used the trap to hold the grouse in place, just for a moment, so that they could weigh, sample, band, mark, photograph, and release him. Grouse biologists today continue to use versions of the mirror trap for similar purposes (e.g., Zimmerman and Gutiérrez 2007).

The figure of the live trap encapsulates some of the basic axioms of twentieth-century wildlife management, a field that emerged in the wake of failures to preserve wild animals simply by placing prohibitions on killing them (Dunlap 1988; Reiger 2001; Newton 2006). Setting limits on the animal's freedom, the trap materialises a belief in a limited biological world, hemmed in by human activity, which only the reasoned application of science and technology can redeem. In this context, rather than being a tool of exploitation, the trap becomes a means of conservation, however coercive. Paradoxically, it comes to stand for freedom, for it is only because of the knowledge produced through trapping that grouse can continue to pursue their lives and interests in a landscape dominated by humans.

Or rather, one should perhaps say, in a landscape dominated by 'man', since the gendered aspects of live-trapping are difficult to ignore. For most of the history of live-trapping of oft-hunted 'game' birds such as grouse, the field has been dominated by male biologists, hunters, and conservationists. Care is often associated with the feminine, but perhaps this is only because attention to care has tended to focus on its most maternal and nurturing aspects (e.g., Gilligan 1982; see Gardiner 2002). When a male wildlife biologist seeks to manage a 'king' among birds — the very same king whom he and his fellow hunters may later seek to kill — care wears another face.

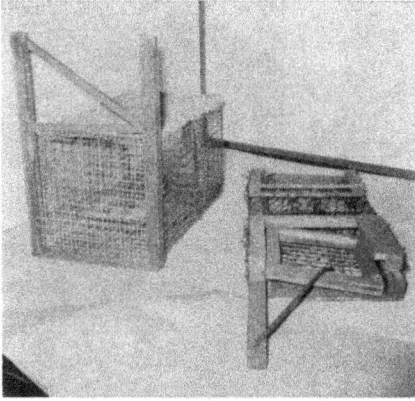

FIG. 1. Original mirror trap at left and modified trap in collapsed position.

FIG. 2. Original mirror trap at left with modified version erected. Both in set position.

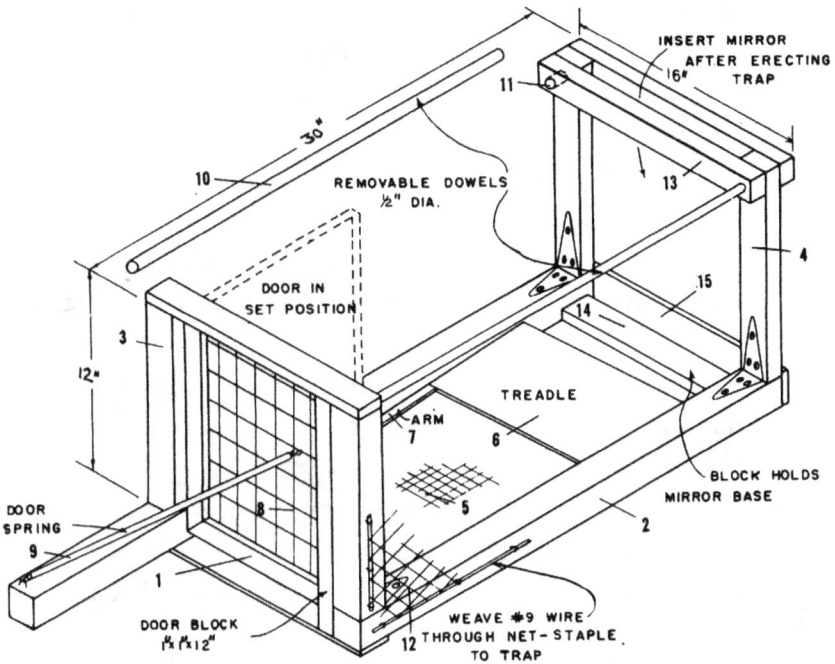

FIG. 3. Construction diagram of modified mirror trap. The numbers are explained in the text.

FIG. 31.2 A modified design of the mirror trap that could be collapsed for easy transportation in the field (source: figures 1–3 in Chambers and English (1958, 200–2))

Such patriarchal care can be empathetic but coercive, other-oriented but ego-affirming; it can foster individual flourishing even as it reinforces power, custom, and law.

Such forms of coercive care are not pretty – perhaps not even good, in some absolute sense – but they are not necessarily any less genuine for that. For the grouse, which is counted among the most valued game birds of North America, patriarchal care in the twentieth century was linked to a vision of authentic contact with the land through hunting that could only be preserved in the modern world through the use of science and technology (Reiger 2001; see Holsman 2000).

This vision of coercive care and conservation-for-and-through-killing is mirrored, in miniature, in the positioning of biologist and grouse in relation to the mirror trap. To understand the grouse as essentially unable to recognise himself in the mirror is to draw a line between those beings – humans, 'man' – who are self-consciously capable of taking responsibility for earthly life, and those who are unconscious victims of forces beyond their comprehension. Each trapped grouse is then living proof of the line's reality. The grouse's very inability to recognise himself establishes the ethical ground for human intervention – just as, more broadly, a vision of nonhuman animals as unconscious machines (Stam and Kalmanovitch 1998; Crist 1999) helps undergird some of the more hubristic visions of the Anthropocene, the geological age when 'man's' impact on the Earth rivals the great forces of 'Nature' (Crutzen 2002; Crist 2013; Hamilton 2013). In such visions, coercive care appears as an ethical obligation for those who stand on one side of an ontological divide toward those who stand on the other.

At first glance, the mirror trap, consciously built to exploit the grouse's tendency to mistake himself, might seem like material corroboration of the validity of this view. But divisions like these, so clear from a distance, often dissolve on close inspection.

First it must be noted that the ideal grouse as depicted in the early media coverage of the mirror trap, a 'passionate male' who 'leaps jealously across the trigger-door' to attack his supposed rival, is just that, an ideal (Associated Press 1947). In practice the mirror trap is most effective at catching very aggressive males and those in areas of high competition, as the great grouse biologist Gordon W. Gullion noted. Timid or wary males may ignore the mirror completely; some become frightened rather than provoked. These more wary birds – one is tempted to call them more intelligent – can sometimes be captured once with the mirror trap, but rarely twice. Such birds, Gullion observed, 'tend to survive longer than other males' (Gullion 1965: 112).

The mirror trap is thus doubly selective, trapping not only males rather than females but also the most aggressive rather than the least aggressive males. To see the trap as reflecting something essential about male grouse, or about grouse-ish masculinity, is to make a mistake even more fundamental than the grouse's misrecognition of himself in the mirror. The mirror trap becomes a norm in the shape of a box, trapping only males who meet certain mid-twentieth-century expectations about what a male should be. Males who fail to meet those expectations – those who think twice before attacking – slip out of view (Despret 2004; Law and Lien 2012).

If all traps embody an intimate knowledge of an animal's habits, capabilities, and vulnerabilities, all traps embody such misrecognitions, too. The ruffed grouse in the abstract cannot be trapped; only a particular grouse can be trapped, the precise nature of whose divergence from the ideal cannot be known in advance. Traps are thus predictions, even self-fulfilling prophecies, and the knowledge they embody produces its subject as much as it reflects it.

Beyond the specific selectivities of the mirror trap, the automatism inherent to all traps is a prophecy of this sort, pre-emptively framing the human-animal encounter in such a way that the trapped animal must necessarily be the kind of being who can be taken unawares by a mechanism. A kind of 'latent Umwelt' becomes manifest, one in which the relation between human and animal is mechanised and objectified (Kassung 2012: 207). In this way a line is drawn between those who are free to respond and those who are doomed to react (Derrida 2002). It is only the latter who end up in the trap, available to be made into objects of science. To ask whether or not grouse really are unconscious animal-machines is to miss the point; the trap itself is a technological means of bringing forth just this reality and not another (see Cussins 1996; Mol 2002; Barad 2007).

At first glance, then, the mirror trap might seem to offer material proof of the existence of a dividing line between self-conscious humanity and the vast unconscious immanence of nature, but on closer inspection the line begins to fracture and blur. Some male grouse, confronted by a mirror image of their bodies, leap to the attack and are trapped. Others, more timid, wary, perceptive, or perhaps even intelligent, keep their distance or flee. Still others proceed unperturbed with their drumming and strutting, for all the world as if a large box with a mirror inside it had not just been placed near the centre of their universe. A small proportion of male grouse seem to never drum at all (Gullion 1981). In one of Gordon Gullion's early studies with the mirror trap, even the reactions of those who were successfully trapped could only be described as 'highly variable' (Gullion 1965: 114). For researchers attentive to the limits of traps and the variability of life, it is clear that no grand generalisations can be made.

If the mirror trap is based on a fundamental misrecognition of the grouse, it is also based on a misrecognition of recognition itself. In the second half of the twentieth century some animal-behaviour scientists began to argue that the ability to recognise oneself in a mirror could serve as an experimental test of self-awareness, even of the existence of a self. That chimpanzees passed this test, it was claimed, provided evidence of 'self-concept in a subhuman form'; that macaques flunked it provided evidence of a clear line dividing humans and great apes from the rest of the animal world (Gallup 1970: 87). Although this line has since been made more sinuous by the discovery of mirror self-recognition in dolphins (Reiss and Marino 2001) and elephants (Plotnik et al. 2006), it is still used to reinforce the border between humanity and the other animals.

Whatever the validity of such experiments may be, there is nothing simple or self-evident about the idea that one can see oneself in the image reflected in a mirror. The problem is not that the outer surface always belies the more authentic inner depths, but that that inner self is itself fragmented, socially distributed, and non-identical from moment to moment (Lacan 2006). To recognise oneself in a mirror is undoubtedly to prove that one has a concept of self, but it is also to admit that one has been seduced – despite abundant experiential evidence to the contrary – by an illusion of wholeness, autonomy, and self-similarity. It is to be lured by the eye into a trap of one's own making.

The experimental situations in which mirror self-recognition is tested are just such traps, into which certain animals called scientists invite other animals to fall.

Those who do fall are counted as conscious kin. Those who do not are consigned to unconscious animality, to that part of the living world that is, in the words of Georges Bataille, 'in the world like water in water' (Bataille 1989: 19; see Tyler 2005). Both grouse and grouse researchers misrecognise themselves, then, if in different ways. Which is the more fundamental error: to mistakenly think one is confronted by another, or to mistakenly think one is confronted by oneself?

Thus, the image of the grouse that is reflected in the mirror trap becomes both partial and multiple, as do the images of all those animals whose vulnerabilities, capabilities, and habits have been exploited by myriad ingeniously designed traps over the millennia. We construct a world of traps that depend on others being unable to recognise themselves just as we do, and then we take their failure to do so as a sign of our superiority and our right, and perhaps even our responsibility, to keep constructing. Our treasure-trove of animal worlds in reverse is revealed to be an embodied collection of misrecognitions – effective, certainly, but hardly the veridical map of otherness it first seemed to be. Certain trappable individuals become objects of knowledge-making, while others live out their lives 'on the margins of what is knowable to the human' (Law and Lien 2012: 373). The box is filled with those who fit in it, while the rest remain outside.

REFERENCES

Arentsen, H. F., and N. Fenech, *Lark Mirrors: Folk Art from the Past* (Malta: [s.n.], 2004).

Associated Press, 'Simple Mirror Trap Developed to Catch Wild Grouse Alive', *The Southeast Missourian*, 18 December 1947.

Barad, K. M., *Meeting the Universe Halfway: Quantum Physics and the Entanglement of Matter and Meaning* (Durham: Duke University Press, 2007).

Bataille, G., *Theory of Religion*, trans. by Robert Hurley (New York: Zone, 1989).

Bendell, J. F. S., and C. D. Fowle, 'Some Methods for Trapping and Marking Ruffed Grouse', *Journal of Wildlife Management*, 14 (1950): 480–82.

Bowers, G. L., 'Progress Report on a Population Study of the Ruffed Grouse (Bonasa u. umbellus) in Pennsylvania at the Low of the Cycle', *Quarterly Report of the Pennsylvania Cooperative Wildlife Research Unit*, 10, Apr-May-June (1947), separately paginated, 9pp.

——, 'Roughed Grouse Study', *Quarterly Report of the Pennsylvania Cooperative Wildlife Research Unit*, 11, Apr-May-June (1948): 2–6.

Chambers, R. E., and P. F. English, 'Modifications of Ruffed Grouse Traps', *Journal of Wildlife Management*, 22 (1958): 200–02.

Crist, E., *Images of Animals: Anthropomorphism and Animal Mind* (Philadelphia: Temple University Press, 1999).

——, 'On the Poverty of Our Nomenclature', *Environmental Humanities*, 3 (2013): 129–47.

Crutzen, P., 'Geology of Mankind', *Nature* 415 (3 January 2002): 23.

Cussins, C., 'Ontological Choreography: Agency Through Objectification in Infertility Clinics', *Social Studies of Science*, 26 (1996): 575–610.

Derrida, J., 'The Animal That Therefore I Am (More to Follow)', trans. by David Wills, *Critical Inquiry*, 28 (2002): 369–418.

Despret, V., 'The Body We Care For: Figures of Anthropo-Zoo-Genesis', *Body and Society*, 10 (2004): 111–34.

Dessecker, D. R., and D. G. McAuley, 'Importance of Early Successional Habitat to Ruffed Grouse and American Woodcock', *Wildlife Society Bulletin*, 29 (2001): 456–65.

Dorney, R. S., and H. M. Mattison, 'Trapping Techniques for Ruffed Grouse', *Journal of Wildlife Management*, 20 (1956): 47–50.

Dunlap, T. R., *Saving America's Wildlife* (Princeton, NJ: Princeton University Press, 1988).

Gallup, G. G., Jr., 'Chimpanzees: Self-Recognition', *Science* 167. 3914 (2 January 1970): 86–7.

Gardiner, J. K., ed., *Masculinity Studies and Feminist Theory: New Directions* (New York: Columbia University Press, 2002).

Gilligan, C., *In a Different Voice: Psychological Theory and Women's Development* (Cambridge, MA: Harvard University Press, 1982).

Gullion, G. W., 'Improvements in Methods for Trapping and Marking Ruffed Grouse', *Journal of Wildlife Management*, 29 (1965): 109–16.

——, 'Non-Drumming Males in a Ruffed Grouse Population', *Wilson Bulletin* 93 (1981): 372–82.

Hamilton, C., *Earthmasters: The Dawn of the Age of Climate Engineering* (New Haven: Yale University Press, 2013).

Holsman, R. H., 'Goodwill Hunting? Exploring the Role of Hunters as Ecosystem Stewards', *Wildlife Society Bulletin*, 28 (2000): 808–16.

Humane Society of the United States, 'Glue Boards: Cheap, Cruel, and Indiscriminate', 29 March 2012, <http://www.humanesociety.org/animals/resources/facts/glue_boards.html> [accessed 13 June 2015].

Kassung, C., 'Animal Machines. Eine Falle ist kein Ge-Stell', in T. Conradi, G. Ecker, N. O. Eke and F. Muhle, eds, *Schemata und Praktiken* (Munich: Wilhelm Fink, 2012), pp. 191–211.

Lacan, J., 'The Mirror Stage as Formative of the *I* Function as Revealed in Psychoanalytic Experience', in *Écrits*, trans. by Bruce Fink (W.W. Norton & Co., 2006), pp. 75–81.

Law, J., and M. E. Lien, 'Slippery: Field Notes in Empirical Ontology', *Social Studies of Science*, 43 (2012): 363–78.

Mol, A., *The Body Multiple: Ontology in Medical Practice* (Durham, NC: Duke University Press, 2002).

Newton, J. L., *Aldo Leopold's Odyssey* (Washington: Island Press/Shearwater Books, 2006).

Pennsylvania Cooperative Wildlife Research Unit, 'The King Succumbs to his Own Image', *Quarterly Report of the Pennsylvania Cooperative Wildlife Research Unit*, 10. July-Aug-Sept (1947a): 1–2.

Pennsylvania Cooperative Wildlife Research Unit, 'Ruffed Grouse Study', *Quarterly Report of the Pennsylvania Cooperative Wildlife Research Unit*, 10. Oct-Nov-Dec (1947b): 13–14.

Plotnik, J. M., F. B. M. de Waal, and D. Reiss, 'Self-Recognition in an Asian Elephant', *Proceedings of the National Academy of Sciences of the United States of America*, 103 (2006): 17053–57.

Reiger, J. F., *American Sportsmen and the Origins of Conservation*, 3rd edn (Corvallis: Oregon State University Press, 2001).

Reiss, D., and L. Marino, 'Mirror Self-Recognition in the Bottlenose Dolphin: A Case of Cognitive Convergence', *Proceedings of the National Academy of Sciences of the United States of America*, 98 (2001): 5937–42.

Spencer, J., *Guide to Trapping* (Mechanicsburg, PA: Stackpole Books, 2007).

Stam, H. J., and T. Kalmanovitch, 'E. L. Thorndike and the Origins of Animal Psychology: On the Nature of the Animal in Psychology', *American Psychologist*, 53 (1998): 1135–44.

Tanner, W. D., and G. L. Bowers, 'A Method for Trapping Male Ruffed Grouse', *Quarterly Report of the Pennsylvania Cooperative Wildlife Research Unit*, 10. Oct-Nov-Dec (1947): 15–16.

——, 'A Method for Trapping Male Ruffed Grouse', *Journal of Wildlife Management*, 12 (1948): 330–31.

Toynbee, J. M.C., *Animals in Roman Life and Art* (Baltimore: Johns Hopkins University Press, 1996 [1973]).

Tyler, T. 'Like Water in Water', *Journal for Cultural Research*, 9 (2005): 265–79.

Willerslev, R., *Soul Hunters: Hunting, Animism, and Personhood among the Siberian Yukaghirs* (Berkeley: University of California Press, 2007).

Zimmerman, G. S., and R. J. Gutiérrez, 'The Influence of Ecological Factors on Detecting Drumming Ruffed Grouse', *Journal of Wildlife Management*, 71 (2007): 1765–72.

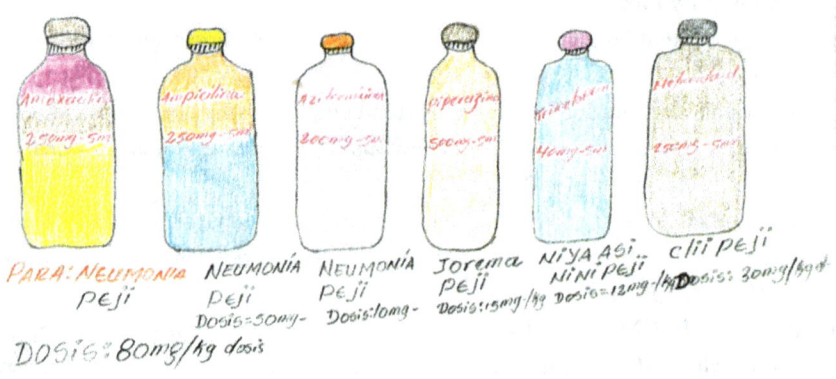

FIG. 32.1 Drawing of a variety of medicine bottles, made by a Yanomami health agent (Wisilio García) during a training course. Note that each bottle is depicted with a cap, the name of the medicine contained, and its concentration. Underneath each bottle the health agent has added the illnesses for which the medicines are to be used, and the recommended dosages (photo by Johanna Gonçalves Martín, 2010)

32

SHIFTING MEDICAL BOTTLES: IN BETWEEN MEDICAL AND INDIGENOUS WORLDS

Johanna Gonçalves Martín

	FIRST LIFE: MEDICAL USE	SECOND LIFE: GIVEN TO PATIENTS
NAMES RECEIVED	Medicinal jar, medicinal bottle	*Horokoto, toutamou kesi,* or various Spanish neologisms, such as *pote*
COSMOLOGY	Naturalistic (by Venezuelan doctors, mostly biomedically trained)	Animistic (by Yanomami people living in Venezuela)
MODE OF USE	Related to its biomedical properties: preserving, storing, transporting, dosing, dispensing, accounting	Related to its animistic properties: creating discontinuities, enveloping, healing, holding powerful transformational substances
PERCEIVED ORIGIN	Pharmaceutical factories inside and outside Venezuela	Somewhere in the land of the outsiders
CONTENTS	Different pharmaceutical medicines	After medicines are emptied, many other substances produced by the Yanomami
COLOUR	Variable: white, transparent, amber	May be further blackened by smoke or tainted by the products held inside
HABITAT	Deposits, boxes for transportation, pharmacies, consultation rooms	In houses, usually hanging from the roof beams
SIZE	Usually fits in a hand	(Unchanged)
SHAPE	Usually cylindrical, with a bottleneck and a screw-on or popping cap	(Unchanged)
ACCESSORIES	Labels, security seals, measuring cups, boxes, leaflets	Strings are sometimes tied to the rims in order to hang them

Keywords: preserving, separating, holding, measuring, dosing, transporting, healing, encapsulating, covering, protecting, encompassing, wrapping, packaging, separating, containing, enveloping

A SEEMINGLY SIMPLE EXCHANGE HABITUALLY TAKES PLACE IN THE HEALTH posts in the Upper Orinoco, Venezuela, where many Yanomami live. Yanomami people come to a health post when ill and receive from doctors a variety of medicines in different presentations. Some of these are directly applied at the health post, being injected, nebulised for inhalation, or given as a single dose of medicine to be ingested right away. But very often, Yanomami patients receive a small bottle with liquid medicine, or a box containing blisters with many pills, and they are instructed to take them at home at specific times and in specific doses. An extensive amount of anthropological work has paid attention to the exchange of these medicines. Adapting the concept of 'social lives' (Appadurai 1988) to medicines, researchers have examined how medicines shift along 'regimes of value' as they go from being part of scientific research, to market commodities or healing technologies distributed to health centres and pharmacies, until they are finally prescribed to patients who will ingest them in order to experience some bodily effect usually associated with healing (van der Geest et al. 2003). These are important points in thinking about medicine as a thing, and in uncovering its multiplicity across societies. However, another constitutive element of medicines has remained relatively unaddressed, namely, its artefacts of containment. What happens when pots, boxes, and blisters travel across societies?

Pharmaceuticals never come on their own but need something to contain them. They come in bottles or jars made of plastic or glass, in metal or plastic blisters, glass ampules and vials, plastic infusion bags, or other more complex forms such as the pumps for inhaled medicines. But these containers have remained invisible due to a prevailing Western notion that they are inert – and they are actually supposed to be inert in order to 'just contain'. But if medicines shift, become other substances throughout their 'careers' in between worlds, and have other effects, can we imagine that the containment accomplished by boxes, jars, pots, and vials may also shift and involve other kinds of operations? I will focus on the medicinal bottle for a simple reason. While blisters and pumps are discarded after use, medicine jars usually have a second life in the Upper Orinoco. They may be re-used for containing all sorts of things, both by the doctors and by the Yanomami. And in their use by the Yanomami, they reveal a different concept of what exactly is contained, what the container is, and what kind of operation containment is.

The lifetime of these medicines and their containers does not seem immediately cyclical: they begin in research and are then industrially produced and packed for distribution to pharmacies and health posts, where health professionals hand them out in specific dosages to people with different afflictions. Then they are consumed, but their containers are never returned for recycling, for example. In the Amazon, empty containers end up in improvised landfills where doctors bury their rubbish (where they begin a long and unlikely process of decomposition that may last many centuries). Alternatively, they take a spiral leap and are used as another kind of container to hold something else. For doctors, crucial elements of their initial properties are lost in this kind of social recycling – they are no longer clean, no longer sealed. But it may be that for the Yanomami, properties of containment continue undisturbed.

I will begin by describing medicine bottles' lives among the worlds of doctors and pharmacists, when they contain medicines and protect them from the elements. Though there is a rich history of different kinds of medicinal bottles (Griffenhagen and Bogard 1999), a single dominant cosmology predominates: that of an increasingly technological Western medicine, in which better containers also follow. But in the daily practice of medicine, even the history of these objects recedes into the background. While an older doctor or nurse may reminisce about a time before plastic and sterile packaging – for example, about using reusable glass syringes, now unthinkable in the era of HIV – young doctors rarely waste time reflecting on the transformations of these containing techniques; most just assume that such techniques get better with technical and material improvements.

Doctors in training learn that these containers help preserve the biochemical properties of the medicine, and thus achieve a certain concentration in the body when ingested. The hermetic seals on the jar make sure that no air or water comes in that could alter the chemical composition of the pharmaceutical product. The amber or brown colour of the jar prevents the degradation of medicines sensitive to UV light. The hermetic seal also guarantees that the product inside is sterile, preventing not only chemical transformations but also contamination by a range of bacteria or fungi. To further ensure this, the materials from which the container is made have to be chemically inert, so as to not react with either the environment or the substances contained. In sum, medicinal bottles make sure that what the patient consumes has the expected quality and amount of substance, and therefore, that assumptions about its bioavailability (how much medicine is actually absorbed through different routes) and pharmacological effect can be made. These preserving and protecting properties become especially crucial in the moist and hot conditions of the rainforest where the Yanomami live, and during expeditions in which doctors take medicines in their backpacks through muddy paths or along rivers. Inside the health post, pharmacies allow for medicines to be arranged and preserved (**FIGURE 32.2**). But when doctors take medicines on fieldtrips, further precautions – and layers of envelopment – are needed. Many containers are still sensitive to the elements, and in addition to the frequent rainfall, when visiting the villages one commonly encounters rivers that need to be crossed. Therefore, medicinal containers are often further contained in plastic boxes or waterproof bags, some of them specially designed for carrying medicines (**FIGURES 32.3, 32.4**).

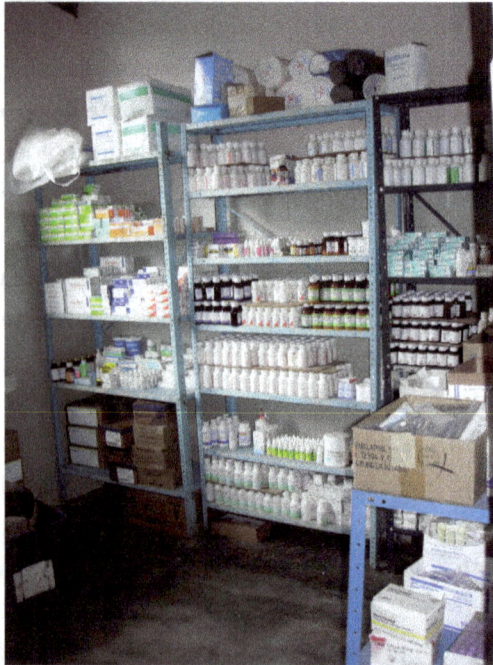

FIG. 32.2 Pharmacy of a health post containing an assortment of medicines and other medical equipment (photo by Johanna Gonçalves Martín in 2010)

FIG. 32.3 Doctor's case for carrying injectable medicines during a visit to the villages (photo by Johanna Gonçalves Martín in 2010)

FIG. 32.4 A Yanomami health agent looks for medicines carried to a village in a special backpack, and also within a Yanomami basket. Note that medicines are further contained within plastic bags (photo by Johanna Gonçalves Martín in 2010)

Another fundamental aspect of medicine bottles is that each jar has a label with the name and concentration of its pharmaceutical components, and a specific date of expiration which tells until when it should be used. Labelling bottles is also an old tradition. In contrast to older labels, nowadays all references to the curative properties of the medicines contained are omitted by law. Labels are relatively more sophisticated, with catchy commercial names, and colourful strokes and font styles which respond to shifting marketing aesthetics. However, these newer labels are much more sensitive to the elements and are often damaged or washed away when they get wet. When a medical jar loses its label, doctors discard the whole bottle, being unable to know which medicine was held within, and its expiration date. So apart from preserving and protecting, labels may also have properties of attracting and marketing. Most importantly, labels give medicinal bottles other important functions of naming and classifying the substances contained inside them and indicating their lifetime.

In some cases, the bottle itself may serve as a dosing or dispensing device. However, it should be clarified that there is no practice in Venezuela of dispensing prescription bottles – that is, bottles with a personalised amount of a medicine meant to last for a specific amount of time. Standard concentrations and amounts of medicines are packed in each bottle, blister, or vial, and the task of calculating how much will be needed falls to doctors. Doctors may instruct people to administer or take the contents of a bottle in a prescribed way (for example, one spoonful three times a day), and to come for a second one when the bottle is empty – the need for a second bottle sometimes drives follow-up consultations, just as in other systems prescriptions must be filled each month or so by doctors, to be collected at pharmacies by the patients. Knowing, as they do, how much of a bottle a child will need for a full course of antibiotics, means that doctors may use the bottle as an indicator of how well the treatment has been administered: during a follow up visit at the patient's house, the doctor may check how much medicine is left in the bottle, and calculate if it has been given too fast, or not at all. In these situations, the container becomes an object of evidence and of accountability from patients to doctors about whether they have 'complied' with – that is, ingested – the treatment.

On an administrative level, all forms of medicine containers, including medicine bottles, are part of an auditing system in which the health administration tracks how many containers are required and sent for each period of time, and uses this data to estimate how many medicines are actually distributed to a given number of people. Therefore, the total number of containers serves also as a proxy for measuring the health of a population, and doctors' prescribing practices.

In a rainforest region like the Upper Orinoco, where spoons – commonly used elsewhere to measure liquid medicines – are not widely available, different parts of the bottle, or the bottle itself, may additionally serve as dosing devices. The screw-on cap holds more or less the same volume as the bowl of a teaspoon and serves as a good substitute. Some bottles come with their own plastic measuring cup, with which more accurate measurements can be made. But because most Yanomami are not skilled in Western numeracy, doctors add marks to the cup for people to remember how much medicine should be given. It should be added that the notion of dosing is not foreign to the Yanomami; it is part of their own use of plants for healing or for magical purposes, and they are usually very aware of the effects of over- or under-dosing.

Finally, some medicines come in a small bottle that holds a single dose to be administered entirely at once, so that the bottle itself becomes the measuring device. The whole bottle can also serve as an artefact for measuring in a different sense than dosing, as when powdered medicines come with a notch or indication of the level of water that needs to be added, in order to be reconstituted at the right concentration of its active principle.

Now, what happens when a bottle of a certain medicine is given to the Yanomami? A few words about the Yanomami may help us understand the context of the exchange and subsequent transformations. The Yanomami are an indigenous people who live in a rainforest area between Venezuela and Brazil. In their perception, practice, and understanding of the world, humans, animals, plants, spirits, and even other elements such as rocks are animated. Diseases are never or only very rarely accidental: they result from the agency of other living beings who may use powerful transformative substances (called *hëri*) to affect a person, or from spirits who may attack the integrity of the body envelope that contains the vital inner principle or soul-like components of a person. They also result from failing to observe food prescriptions or activity prohibitions, which mostly aim to keep living beings – which in Amazonia are all endowed with agency – separate.

Health and disease are manifestations of interactions within an ecology of life, in which shamans have a privileged role in managing the forms that relations between different beings take.

Doctors are perceived as having an analogous power to shamans, given that they can also see inside a body, and their medicines are very effective in healing. The Yanomami also call doctors' medicines *hëri*, a semantic extension of the term which suggests that Yanomami people conceive medicines, too, as some kind of powerful transformative substance with bodily effects. As for the health system caring for the Yanomami in Venezuela, there are only seven health posts in an area as large as Ireland. For many Yanomami people, health posts are too far away to walk to them, especially when ill. But for the people who live in the vicinity of one of these health posts, they constitute important alternatives for treating disease. While shamans are still consulted first, health-post doctors are frequently part of a network of therapies the Yanomami may consult.

Adults come to the consultation on their own, or if they are too sick they are often accompanied by a relative. Mothers, or another female relative, are usually the ones to bring young children when ill. The most common diseases in children are infectious: diarrhoea, pneumonia, malaria, colds. Adults often complain of more chronic conditions such as abdominal pain and chronic coughs. These diseases very often call for antibiotics, fever reducers, or cough suppressants. While adults generally receive tablets, children often receive liquid medicines, so that medicinal bottles are more commonly given to mothers for their children. However, these are often subsequently shared between members of the household.

In the course of my anthropological work among them, the Yanomami often – and especially in the case of blisters – asked for an additional wrapping to contain the medicines: a piece of paper, or preferably some plastic, as this extra container would help keep the medicines dry until they arrived home. When none of these were available, it was common to see people take certain palm leaves – which they usually use for wrapping different kinds of things – in which to carry the blisters, syringes, or medicine jars given. They folded these medicines with remarkable meticulousness. When plastic bags were used, the Yanomami did not just drop the medicine inside the bag, as people in urban contexts in Venezuela might well do. They folded the medicines neatly inside the paper and then within the plastic bag, as they would also do with many other substances, such as food and *hëri* substances.

The care given to containing the medicines suggests that it is not a trivial task. One explanation may be that there is an intimate relation between a substance and its envelope. The envelope does more than just contain something: it also helps *constitute* that something. We find this relationship in other important forms of encompassing or enveloping care, and notably in practices of embodiment. For the Yanomami, as for all Amazonian people, the body is an important centre of perception and social action (Seeger et al. 1979). But this body is not conceived in a dualist way, divided between an inorganic or spiritual inner body and an outer organic skin. The skin is equally a 'spiritual' component that as an outer cloak shapes the perspective and the agency of the person (Viveiros de Castro 1998). Many practices that change the envelope have also the property of changing the person within it, such as ornamenting, clothing, and massaging. Similarly, the medicine container, more than just limiting a medicine within a volume, may also help to make up the medicine itself.

Given the importance of the envelope, it is not surprising that the Yanomami usually refer to the container as the sign of an effective medicine. Throughout several decades of medical care, the Yanomami have engaged in their own reverse anthropology and empirical evaluation of doctors, coming to identify what works. They often show up at the health post with preset ideas about which medicine they want, based on past efficacy. The way they indicate which medicines are good may be a matter of the colour and taste of the tablets or liquids contained in the bottles, but the outer container is also significant. Just as in the case of doctors, for trained Yanomami health workers the names and numbers on the labels become important indicators of what the medicine inside is used for. The health workers often share these names with patients, and therefore many people arrive at the health post asking for a specific name of antibiotic, even though they cannot read the labels.

Finally, having been dispensed by the doctors or health care workers, the medicines and their containers set off towards their final destinations among patients. After the doctor has given the patient or mother the medicine, these are carried to the village with varying instructions on how much to take and how often to administer them (**FIGURE 32.5**). The Yanomami often string the jars or boxes from the poles of the thatched roof, near the fire (**FIGURE 32.6**). Not only is this the driest and safest place in the house, protected from the dogs and children at ground level, but it is also the common repository of other important objects, such as calabashes containing the mortuary remains of relatives, or a variety of other *hëri* substances collected by people and used for different afflictions (or as love and hunting magic). Receiving the constant smoke of the fire – smoke that is also used to preserve meat – they acquire a blackish tint that further erases the details of the labels.

What happens when the contents are emptied and nothing remains inside the bottle? Sometimes, if doctors are the ones to empty a bottle at the health post, they may use it to store other substances, such as the colouring reagents used in microscopy, or rubbing alcohol. Doctors may also use bottles to transport liquid soap or shampoo, or even as a good way of keeping matches dry. These other uses continue to enact a naturalistic ontology in which certain substances need to be kept separate from the environment or from other elements in order to preserve their physical and chemical state.

When Yanomami people themselves are the ones who empty the bottles, they are rarely returned to the doctors, but put to a new use. While some of these transformed uses still suggest a simple need for keeping something within a physical limit, the bottles may acquire other forms of containing agency among the Yanomami. In a context of reduced exchange with outsiders, and a relative scarcity of industrialised merchandise, any kind of pot is greatly valued, even if already used. For example, plastic, two-litre fizzy drink containers are especially coveted for carrying and storing water, and may be kept by people for several years, until they break. Doctors are asked to bring them back from their trips to the city (either filled or empty). But while we can perceive a very pragmatic need for using these large bottles for carrying and storing water, the various uses of smaller and seemingly less useful medicinal pots suggest that for the Yanomami these containers are not just about storing, carrying, or keeping some substance or thing separate from other elements.

The second lives the medicinal bottles take among the Yanomami suggest instead that these are sometimes devices of spiritual or animistic containment.

FIG. 32.5 Drawing of a mother holding a child, with a diversity of containers for diarrhoea medicine. From left to right there seem to be a metal pot with a syringe (to administer the fluid to the child), a gourd, and towards the bottom what seems to be a medicine bottle. Drawing made by Manuel Pérez, a Yanomami community health worker (photo by Johanna Gonçalves Martín in 2010)

FIG. 32.6 Area of the roof above the hearth where Yanomami people often hang important substances and objects such as mortuary calabashes, powerful *hëri* substances, tobacco leaves, and bags with medicines (photo by Johanna Gonçalves Martín in 2010)

While the Yanomami may use the pots to protect medicines from the elements, this protection is not conceived in chemical or physical ways. It may still be important to keep them dry or to prevent contact with other substances, but in an animistic world in which different kinds of beings may be infused with vital principle (Descola 2005; Santos Granero 2012), a series of wrapping or enveloping practices have to do with a similarly animistic separation of different forms of life-principle or substance.

Let us examine some practices that delineate the relations between substance and container in Amazonia. It is by looking into these other practices of folding that certain aesthetic forms in Yanomami practices of containment or envelopment begin to emerge. We see that packaging, enveloping, and containing are very ubiquitous practices. They are used traditionally for bringing back hunted or collected food – which in Amazonia may also have some invisible or soul-like qualities – and for cooking it on the embers of the hearth. Men and women collect and keep their *hëri* inside different kinds of palm leaves, though nowadays they also use plastic bags, or very frequently, old medicine bottles. These *hëri* – which are used for attracting or repelling a love partner, for attracting prey in hunting expeditions, for chasing away snakes and supernatural spirits which may cause disease, and also for making other people ill – would result in uncontrolled and probably dangerous transformations if left unbounded.

However, I want to turn now to another set of analogies – based on the body – in order to understand better this need for enveloping and for maintaining boundaries between beings among the Yanomami and other Amazonian people. I remarked above that the external envelope or skin – for the Yanomami, the *pei siki* – is an essential spiritual or animistic component of the body, one which provides a form, the 'cloak' that both contributes to and results in a certain particular understanding of what constitutes personhood. Bearing this in mind, we can turn to examine practices of illness and bodily reconstitution to which this envelope is central. It is important to remember here that in Amazonia a disease is often conceived as a breakdown of the envelope of a person, by which vital substances may leak from or pathogenic substances enter a person. Alternatively, the orifices of a body may behave improperly by allowing too much – diarrhoea, frequent urination, vomiting – or too little flow – not speaking, not eating, not seeing/recognising, not urinating.

Shamans, or other ordinary people with certain shamanic abilities, may subtract components of a person or insert pathogenic *hëri* to make a person ill. One example of the first case is when someone 'takes the footprint' a person has left in the forest (*pei mãyo tëai*). The stalking enemy collects the earth from a footprint with extreme care and wraps it inside palm leaves. Back home, he will either rub it with a pathogenic *hëri* or make a spirit-snake bite into it. At that same time, a snake in the forest will bite the person too. Unlike ordinary snakebites, this kind of bite progresses rapidly towards swelling, necrosis, and death. Important to note in this case is that the damage occurs by a series of transformations relating to the skin: a footprint that is left in the earth, a shamanic snake that bites onto this earth, and a real snake that simultaneously bites through the person's skin, causing serious skin symptoms which end in death.

Rather than an accessory organ (as in a common biomedical understanding of dermatological problems), the skin in Amazonia is a fundamental site of articulation of histories and transformative interactions (Yvinec 2014). Many authors have registered the significance of skin transformations (including clothing) in an ongoing process of interethnic encounters (Bonilla 2009, Erikson 1996). Compared to other, more stable, components of the person or self in Amazonia, the skin is on a temporal scale of rapid changes that may seriously threaten existence. This explains why, in contrast to a relative negligence by Western health professionals of the skin, for Amazonian people diseases of the skin or body orifices are intensely feared. While in Western medicine greater importance is given to what is contained by the skin, for Amazonian people the container (skin) is what allows the body itself to emerge.

A further insight from Fausto (2011) concerning multiple encompassing layers of the body also helps us to perceive the complexity of container-contained relationships in Amazonia. Fausto argues that the duality between a powerful invisible or spiritual interior substance, and a visible, physical exterior fails to grasp the recursive constitution of a person. His ethnographical artefacts are masks with interior and exterior designs, which are used on top of already ornamented bodies and faces. A mask does not simply hold a unique inner subjectivity, temporally transforming a human into a spirit or animal. It also combines with and relates to underlying or superimposed designs. Masks are just another layer in a multiple and composite subjectivity.

A final example from my ethnography among the Yanomami further evidences a temporally and spatially disjointed process of Amazonian formation of the self that happens by a composite envelopment or encompassment of layers. This example concerned a young Yanomami man who spent several weeks in the intensive care unit of a city hospital (Gonçalves Martín 2015). He was suffering from intense swelling and haemorrhages that were suggestive of the much-feared snakebites. During the time he was hospitalised, his uncle tried several treatments in an attempt to reconstitute the external 'skin' (*pei siki*) envelope of his nephew, and also to control the adverse environmental conditions in the hospital, the entire hospital being perceived as a dangerous healing container. He massaged his nephew's unresponsive limbs as a way of 'awakening the body'. He used blankets to keep him warm. However, what really revealed the importance of re-containing or remaking the body envelope during healing was the following event: one day I saw the uncle tightly tying up a package made out of leaves. When I asked what was held inside, he explained he had taken part of his nephew's vital principle (the *pei puhi*) and was sending it to the shamans back in his village for them to heal him. It was clear that the vital principle could be fragmented, split and sent elsewhere for shamans to work on the whole body. Why not just sent the vital principle on its own? Why use a package? It seems somehow that for certain things to exist or to have a form, an envelope is necessary.

I began with medical bottles that are used in recognisably medical ways in the Upper Orinoco by doctors, and then take on a second life as Yanomami people use them to store valuable or powerful substances such as *hëri*. I have suggested that in this second life, bottles may be much more than simple physical containers. The transformations implied by this change of use and understanding are often difficult to observe in practice. They involve operations that are sometimes outside of the range of possible observation, such as shifts between the potency of things enveloped in palm leaves or in plastic. However, the kinds of substances subsequently kept in these bottles, and the care with which they are prepared, do seem to support a theory in which the container exerts an important effect on the substance contained.

I have supported my ethnographically-based intuitions with further examples of healing containers among the Yanomami, and the way in which they function in an animistic mode of constitution through multiple and mutually encompassing layers. These layers include the skin in relation to the constitution of the body, but also other forms of envelopes such as hospitals, palm leaves, and baskets. I also touched on the importance of masks, but similar ideas are applicable to clothes or ornamentation. Examples abound, and I could have included other ubiquitous objects and practices among the Yanomami: calabashes for keeping the ashes of the dead; different kinds of tree bark that are either used as containers in ceremonial feasts, or are themselves burned or crushed to make powerful shamanic substances; baskets of different kinds which are selectively weaved either by women or by men, and in which the Yanomami transport their food and other belongings; pottery for cooking and storing certain foods – although these latter have virtually disappeared since the introduction of aluminium cooking points since the 1950s (Lizot 1984). Even the Yanomami's round houses may be seen as another kind of sophisticated and multi-layered container. Each of these objects demands very careful preparation. The materials that compose these containers, and the ritual restrictions that are brought into effect during their making, are as important as the substances or materials they will come to hold.

This attention to containers is not a unique characteristic of Yanomami practices: other Amazonian people, and Amerindian people more widely, dedicate special attention to the materials and the process of making different kinds of containers. In his masterful analysis of Amerindian myths, *The Jealous Potter* (1985), Claude Lévi-Strauss emphasises the existence of a special philosophy of containment in Amazonia. In this book he compares myths about the origin of pottery, the regulation of flow of certain substances through the orifices of the body, and certain dispositions such as jealousy and stinginess. Although the aims of his comparison are broader, these myths show how the making of pottery brings into relation shapeless matter (clay, also disordered vines), which must then be turned into discontinuous pots through very precise (and gendered) practices. Containers are not only inert objects of separation but are themselves powerful shapeless matter that needs to be made into powerful but discontinuous forms. Here emerges another important topic in Amazonian cosmologies: the significance of a primordial ancestral state of infinite similarity, which gives rise to a (human) time of finite difference and discontinuity

(Viveiros de Castro 2007). The containers – pots, bodies, masks, baskets – are above all creative devices of discontinuity.

Although the industrial production of medicinal bottles remains invisible to the Yanomami, their origin is still significant. The many objects brought by foreigners – their papers, their medicines, their machetes – are conceived by the Yanomami as loaded with real power coming from the outside. And the same understanding applies to containers. If such a significant ideology of containment is common among Amazonian people, these new, often plastic, containers must be seen as having a set of alternative properties. Their significance may lie precisely in their otherness: the medicines, the material, shapes and labels of these containers have been made by others, and therefore belong to a world of radical others, being thus able to enact other forms of healing or transformative power.

The medicinal bottle therefore resists taxonomical classification. In the dualism between the material and the spiritual which is common to Western naturalism, we may see the medicinal bottles and their labels as representing a medicine contained inside: a bottle and its label say something about the medicine's potency or effects, and it may allow us, for example, to identify a group of sufferers who use the same bottle. By paying attention to the enactment of these bottles, a series of agencies is further revealed: protecting, measuring, dosing, accounting. But when we shift our attention to the use of medical bottles by Yanomami people, we find that these objects no longer fit into our naturalistic taxonomy. Within an Amazonian animistic ontology – in which there is a continuity of souls, and differences in identity are given by bodies – medicinal bottles are a device of form. But what is essential to keep in mind is that the relations between the envelope and the body in Amazonia are much more complex than an exterior-interior relationship. We may even say that the envelope is in fact the body itself.

We are left with a medicine bottle that when given to the Yanomami shifts before our eyes, so to speak, becoming a different object capable of different operations. Our habitual methods of making meaning, of designing taxonomies, or thinking through things as analytics, constitute an obstacle in conceiving this shift. The alternative approach described by Henare et al. (2007) is to think through things as heuristics – that is, to assemble a description of things as practised by other people, which leads to theories that refuse to follow our dichotomist predispositions. Rather than a taxonomy, we would need some sort of ontological grid that could show these transforming objects. An ethnography – or praxiology – serves this. However, we must be cautious in that any grid may still present us with too many divisions between containers and the contained.

REFERENCES

Appadurai, A., *The Social Lives of Things. Commodities in Cultural Perspective* (Cambridge: Cambridge University Press, 1988).

Bonilla, O., 'The Skin of History: Paumari Perspectives on Conversion and Transformation', in A. Vilaça, and R. Wright, eds, *Native Christians: Modes and Effects of Christianity among Indigenous Peoples of the Americas* (Aldershot: Ashgate, 2009).

Descola, P., *Par-delà nature et cultur* (Paris: Éditions Gallimard, 2005).

Erikson, P., *La griffe des aïeux: Marquage du corps et démarquages ethniques chez les Matis d'Amazonie* (Leuven: Peeters Publishers, 1996).

Fausto, C., 'Le masque de l'animiste. Chimères et poupées russes en Amérique indigène', *Gradhiva*, 13 (2011): 48–67.

van der Geest, S., S. R. Whyte, and A. Hardon, *Social Lives of Medicines* (Cambridge: Cambridge University Press, 2003).

Gonçalves Martín, J., 'Healing in the Hospital: The Caring Sensorium and the Containment of Yanomami Bodies', *Tipití: Journal of the Society for the Anthropology of Lowland South America*, 13.2 (2015): 120–36.

Griffenhagen, G., and M. Bogard, *History of Drug Containers and Their Labels* (Madison, WI: American Institute of the History of Pharmacy, 1999).

Henare, A., M. Holbraad, and S. Wastell, *Thinking Through Things: Theorising Artifacts Ethnographically* (New York and London: Routledge, 2007).

Lévi-Strauss, C., *La potière jalouse* (Paris: Plon, 1985).

Lizot, J., *Les Yanomami centraux* (Paris: Éditions de l'École des hautes études en sciences sociales, 1984).

Mol, A., *The Body Multiple: Ontology in Medical Praxis* (Durham: Duke University Press, 2002).

Santos-Granero, F., 'Beinghood and People-Making in Native Amazonia: A Constructional Approach with a Perspectival Coda', *HAU: Journal of Ethnographic Theory*, 2.1 (2012): 181–211.

Seeger, A., R. da Matta, and E. Viveiros de Castro, 'A construção da pessoa nas sociedades indígenas brasileiras', in J. P. de Oliveira Filho, ed., *Sociedades indígenas e indigenismo no Brasil* (Rio de Janeiro: UFRJ Editora Marco Zero, 1979).

Viveiros de Castro, E., 'Cosmological Deixis and Amerindian Perspectivism', *Journal of the Royal Anthropological Institute*, 4 (1998): 469–88.

——, 'The Crystal Forest: Notes on the Ontology of Amazonian Spirits', *Inner Asia*, 9.2 (2007): 153–72.

Yvinec, C., 'Temporal Dimensions of Selfhood: Theories of Person among the Suruí of Rondônia (Brazilian Amazon)', *Journal of the Royal Anthropological Institute*, 20.1 (2014): 20–37.

FIG. 33.1 Box by Agfa, Germany. Photographic Archive, Benaki Museum, Athens, Greece

33

GUARDING THE MEMORY: PHOTOGRAPHIC GLASS PLATES NEGATIVES' BOXES

Mirka Palioura, Spyridoula Pyrpili, Myrto Vouleli

Box: cardboard packaging of photographic negatives/commercial containers of glass plates. **Size and shape**: 13 x 18 cm, rectangular. **Colour**: various. **Behaviour**: tensile. **Habitat**: photographic studios, archives. **Distribution**: Greece. **Migration**: from England, Germany, France, Italy, to Greece. **Status**: usually imported by many professional photographers. **Practices**: glass plates' first users (amateur and professional photographers), and the scientists (archaeologists, historians, archivists) who used and categorised them kept handwritten notes on the external surface of the box, on the labels.

Key words: encasing, preserving, protecting, recording, reconfiguring, informing

IT WAS A MOST FELICITOUS OCCASION THAT BROUGHT THE THREE OF US together a few years after our previous collaboration in the Byzantine & Christian Museum (BCM) in Athens, a conservator, an art historian, and a museologist. As former colleagues in the BCM's Photographic Collection we now share common and rather fond memories, especially of the 'magical' moment when we found in the museum's depository the collection of photographic glass plates negatives' boxes while working on the documentation and digitisation of the BCM's Photographic Archive. In the present paper we have had the opportunity to further develop an idea which emerged through our professional cooperation.

From all the photographic collection's material we were fascinated by the photographic glass plates negatives' boxes. We have had the opportunity to see and examine them closely, so we consider them as an unknown voice from the past to us, not only because they are rare and special objects, but also because they are objects in the service of photography.

Photography's value rests upon its visual content, or else upon the image created on its surface. It is, however, important to consider photographs, not as passive 'resources' without identity, but as material which meditates social relations between people and things; photographs are thus 'resourceful' objects which can give us the potential to interpret the dynamic relations between persons and objects. Photographs reveal traces of the line of their production in a specific historical frame, and traces of the persons who acquired, owned, stored, displayed, and collected them (Edwards 2009: 47–49).

Photography, to us, expresses exactly the need to commit something to memory, to leave an indelible mark on the mind of others that is actually 'encased' in photography. It is thus a 'magical' and universally accessible way of perpetuating the existence of experiences, faces, or events by means of a two-dimensional surface. Susan Sontag (1973) formulated this process rather aptly by suggesting that photographic images preserve a large part of our knowledge of the past and shape our notion of the present. The awareness of this process has always fascinated us, and that is why we were touched by the photographic glass plates negatives' boxes – rare, fragile, and meaningful – and decided to outline their micro-history.

In the early years of photography its content was captured on glass plate negatives, kept to this day inside cardboard boxes. It could be said that they are the subject of photography's 'archaeology'. From the last quarter of the nineteenth until the first half of the twentieth centuries, such boxes were used for the transportation and safekeeping of these sensitive negatives.

In 1880, the American industrialist George Eastman (1854–1932) managed to produce glass plates on a mass scale. Thereafter it was only a matter of time before photography would spread around the world and introduce a revolutionary new way of creating art, documenting reality, and preserving or shaping individual and collective memories.

For several decades, easily produced cardboard boxes were the *par excellence* commercial containers of glass plates. Cardboard was a practical and affordable material, but, as it turned out, it was also perfectly adapted to the purpose for which it was chosen. Paradoxically, despite its frail nature it has endured over time: so far, glass plates have been preserved more or less intact inside such boxes, which are still ubiquitous in museums and private collections.

It seems reasonable to assume that in the early years companies opted for this type of container because it was the least costly and most functional solution. Cardboard boxes were ideal in many ways: easy to produce and move, they facilitated the dissemination of photography and became carriers of both a product and a captured 'piece of memory'. This latter semantically loaded function was achieved only after the photosensitive plate was exposed to the reversed reflection of a fleeting visual reality. External light entering the camera obscura of the capturing device produced a memory fossil, chemically encoded on a glass surface.

During their production, glass plates were wrapped in paper and placed horizontally inside cardboard containers. This practice was common both in Greece and abroad. The original low-quality wrapping survives in most cases, but, contrary to its protective purpose, it often operated as a corrosive factor due to gradual polymerisation. The use of paper wrapping or paper envelopes having a high content of lignin (the part of wood without cellulose) resulted in the gradual oxidisation and deterioration of the glass plates' photosensitive surface and, by interacting with the current environmental conditions, in the glass substrate's chemical decay. These specific paper wrappings or envelopes, although they were not designed for long-term protection, were used by photographers to store the used glass plates in the cardboard boxes (Lavèdrine 2003).

Consequently, boxes become ever more brittle over the years; their corners and edges are now worn down, and they no longer offer adequate protection against adverse environmental conditions. Glues and adhesive substances, once used to piece the boxes together, are now oxidising; they acquire a brown hue and cause further discolouration of the glass plates. But despite their material, which in part catalyses chemical decay, these cardboard boxes have done a relatively good job of preserving their content.

Such containers are of specific interest to us, given our studies and research interests in material culture, not only because of the protection they offered to the photographic plates, but also as industrial products *per se*. Nowadays, they are mostly to be found in museum storage areas or private collections, and are normally preserved in good condition, regardless of their flimsy material.

It is quite possible that these boxes would not have survived if it were not for their function as glass plate containers. Normally, they do not attract attention, stored as they are in drawers, closets, or larger boxes away from public view (**FIGURE 33.1**). They have come down to us because museums and private collectors, although they are interested solely in their content and not in the boxes' intrinsic character, preserve this packaging on the grounds that it constitutes part of the history of the archival material it contains.

The awareness of Greek museums with respect to less sensational facets of material culture is increasing. The role of technology as a powerful driver of culture is no longer underestimated, and the industrial and commercial products of the past are studied and brought to the fore. Today the boxes are mostly deposited in public and private collections of photographic material (the Byzantine & Christian Museum, the Benaki Museum, the Hellenic Literary and Historical Archive, the Historical Archive of the National Bank, the Alkis Xanthakis Collection); they are concrete and compact testimonia as an annexe to the more important content tracing the development of photographic activity in Greece.

Many professional photographers and paper trade/photographic product trade companies imported photographic plates, especially glass ones, to Greece. Our first available information about them is an advertisement from (circa) 1900. The photographic products store of Dimitris Ntoulis (importer) in Athens sold papers and glass plates of the Imperial Company. Politis, French importer and commercial agent of photographic products, having his store in 37, Ermou st. in

1920–1930, sold glass plates and papers (of the Lumière Company). Agfa-Leitz Company's German importer and commercial agent, Venzlaff, cooperated with photographers in 1925. Georgios Kogetsof had a store of photographic products from 1922 to 1945, while Hauff's general importer of glass plates and papers, P. Manolidis, had his store of photographic products at 4 Aggelou Vlachou st. from 1930 to 1946. D. I. Kandreotis, importer, sold products of the GEVEART Company in 1946. Certainly one of the oldest import companies of photographic products in Greece was Pallis and Kotzias Company (1870–1930), which sold glass plates and photographic papers at its store in 8, Ermou St. The only company having its own store in Greece from 1920 to 1940 was Kodak, based at 18, Stadiou St. In 1964, the Kodak Company reopened its store in Alexandras avenue, not only for the sale of films and papers, but also for photo editing (Xanthakis 2015).

Despite frequent dispersal, damage, or destruction, a substantial number of these stores' photographic objects have survived. Unfortunately, they are more than often undated, and the same holds true for the vast majority of glass plate negatives.

Be that as it may, cardboard glass plate containers form part of our material culture and can be studied from different points of view. Such perspectives can originate from more nuanced theories that view material objects as physical traces of memory (Freud 1925: 207), or as vestiges of earlier epochs to be read as indices of past events (Jones 2007: 18). Therefore, they possess both a material and a representational character. They contributed to the dissemination of the photographic technique, and now form a largely untapped source of information, carrying bits of memory either on the surfaces of the glass plates contained therein or on the labels glued to their exterior surfaces. Finally, they envelope collective memory when it comes to the technical evolution of photography itself.

These cardboard containers are material traces of past actions. They physically 'encase' memory through their use and alteration (Jones 2007: 21). In this respect they are 'imbued' with informative-documentary value.

As objects and at the same time agents of semantic value, boxes convey meaning in multiple ways. They encapsulate traces of the past and provide a physical space for experiencing memory (Jones 2007); they do not store memory as much as protect it. If we accept that objects act as mnemonic aids, then how do these particular glass plate boxes become conveyors of memory? Do they perform their mnemonic function through materiality? In other words, how is it that glass plate boxes speak to us? How do they participate in the process of reconstructing the past material culture through their museum use? The above questions lead to the examination of the different elements and connotations carried on the photographic boxes (Burke 2001).

In contrast to the boxes' interiors, which engender emotions born from the variety of subjects depicted on – and the visual stimuli captured in – the negatives, their exteriors acquire a stable and repetitive form, pertinent to the information imparted. This tension, resulting from the bipolarity of the container and the contained, corresponds to the personal and impersonal character of the elements presented. It creates, as it were, both an external, but 'closed', or else, an impersonal and clearly delineated system, lacking in pronounced emotional connotations and, on the other hand, an internal and 'open', or else, a personal and emotional system. What is more, the difference between the two lies in the tangibility of the container and the 'visuality' of the contained, and corresponds nicely to the dichotomy of the sign, which is composed of the signifier and the signified.

Yet another point of departure between the container and the contained has to do with the presence of external 'textuality' and its absence from the boxes' interiors, where the subjects arrested on glass plate negatives are not textually but chemically encoded (relative to the constitution of the material [emulsion] covering the surface of the glass plate). This material embodiment enables the visual imprint of a theme. Of course, discrepancies do not cease at this level; in fact, they go even further, since labels served as visual records of the evolving aesthetic tendencies in the history of graphic design. On these small coloured surfaces various constituents of material culture can be studied and 'read'. These tiny elements carry the memory of a composite past through a slice of space and time, in such a way that a symbolic space is emanated where visuality meets physicality. They certify values produced to impose objects onto our consumerist culture (Burke 2001). Photographic boxes, even though they carry this varied information, have not been a subject for study and display in Greece till today.

The informative character of the boxes with regard to photographic techniques features prominently on the labels attached: Gelatino – Bromure d'

Argent (Jougla), Extra Rapid (Agfa), Ultra Rapid (Hauff), Anti Halo (Gevaert), Orthochrom (Schleussner), Isochrom (Agfa), and others.

The production company's country of origin occupies a secondary position on the labels (Ilford, Kodak, and Wellington came from England, Richard Jahr, R. Stock, Otto Perutz, Hauff, Gevaert hailed from Germany; Jougla, Lumière, and Grieshaber from France; Lastre Cappelli from Italy, and so on), and the emulsion lots are always distinctly marked to facilitate order placement (**FIGURE 33.2**).

Company trademarks and foundation dates were symmetrically arranged and appeared twice on both lateral label borders. The factory's picture featured prominently in the middle (**FIGURE 33.3**). Such illustrations alluded to a powerful and rather positivistic symbolism of industrial and technological progress (so characteristic of the late nineteenth and early twentieth-centuries' capitalist mentality), thus hinting at the product's quality. User instructions, glass plate dimensions, and all sorts of technical details filled the relatively small label with a multitude of information.

FIG. 33.2 Box by Lastre M. Cappelli, Italy. Alkis Xanthakis's Collection, Athens, Greece

FIG. 33.3 Box by J. Jougla, France. Alkis Xanthakis's Collection, Athens, Greece

FIG. 33.4 Box by Grieshaber Frères & Cie, France. Alkis Xanthakis's Collection, Athens, Greece

Although they perhaps fall short of being real works of art, these labels captivate the viewer's gaze by virtue of the complexity of their design, which often took the form of a visual arabesque expressed in terms of an almost simplistic or even pedantic *horror vacui*. Colours were uniformly stark, while decorative frames remained steadily evocative of the prevailing artistic trend of the time – with one example openly revealing its strong Art Nouveau influences. Each label was unique in terms of its aesthetic quality and language, which was consciously chosen by the manufacturing company (**FIGURE 33.4**). Yet another interesting aspect was the evocative reproduction of stereotypes – the way they are formed in the frame of the European collective imaginary – encountered on certain labels: intricate decorative elements and elegant fonts would prevail on French labels, whereas clear geometric lines and gothic fonts would set the tone on their German counterparts (**FIGURE 33.5**). As identity depends on the idea of memory and vice versa (Gillis 1994: 3–4), these elements are added in the representation or construction of the subjective rather than the objective European collective imaginary.

FIG. 33.5 Box by Richard Jahr, Germany. Alkis Xanthakis's Collection, Athens, Greece

References to awards and quality distinctions in international exhibitions – quasi visual documents – added to the informative and commercial nature of labels, acting as symbolic capital. Differentiations in their design indicate the changing status of manufacturing companies – quite telling in this respect is the change on Jougla's label after its merger with the Lumière company – and offer a whole new spectrum of pictorial interpretation possibilities.

As the history of an object is recorded by its wear and tear, historiographical layers as well as different levels of memory can be 'read' on these boxes. The fields for such 'readings' abound: glass plate negative images, box labels, hand written notes on the labels themselves or on small scraps of paper pasted on the containers – these often record subjects, persons, monuments, historical events, etc., captured on the plates. We notice therefore that memories residing on labels are often supplemented by the notes of photographers or editors, who kept a kind of 'diary' of the boxes' contents. On characteristic examples of the boxes we can see handwritten notes of the photographic material's user or researcher/archeologist/archivist, etc., who writes on the upper left side of the box the photographer's name, as well as the number of the stored photographs (**FIGURE 33.6**), while on another box it is noted that the photographs are related to the Ancient Olympia Museum (**FIGURE 33.7**).

These simple taxonomic descriptions 'ultimately shape histories, through the preserving contexts' (Edwards and Hart 2004: 49). Based on this ascertainment, our contribution to the attempt to form collective memory is related to our professional identities and positions in institutions that manage archival material, artworks, and material culture's vestiges more generally. Our scientific interests and elective affinities lead us to researching issues which add up to various versions of collective memory.

Memory provides a cognitive map that helps us understand ourselves and others (Eyerman 2004: 159–69). It involves both individual and collective identities. Cardboard photographic boxes envelope and protect a part of individual memory within, and a trace of collective human activity without. Their apparently passive nature (Edwards 2009: 47–56) narrates memory (Bal, Crewe and Spitzer 1999: viii), shapes our critical reflection, meets our tactile needs, and offers a wide range of different interpretative possibilities. It rests upon us to reclaim and exploit it.

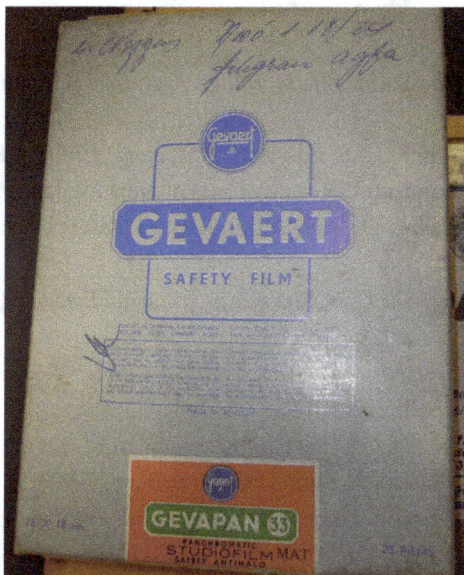

FIG. 33.6 Box by Gevaert, Belgium. Photographic Archive, Benaki Museum, Athens, Greece

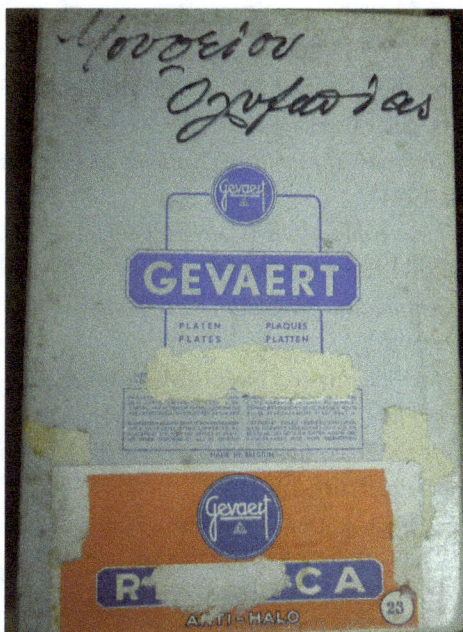

FIG. 33.7 Box by Gevaert, Belgium. Photographic Archive, Benaki Museum, Athens, Greece

REFERENCES

Appadurai, A., ed., *The Social Life of Things* (Cambridge: Cambridge University Press, 1986).

Bal, M., J. Crewe and L. Spitzer, eds, *Acts of Memory: Cultural Recall in the Present* (Hanover and London: University Press of New England, 1999).

Batchen, G., *Photography's Objects* (Albuquerque: University of New Mexico Art Museum, 1997).

Burke, P., *Eyewitnessing: The Uses of Images as Historical Evidence* (London: Reaktion Books, 2001).

Douglas, M., and Isherwood, B., *The World of Goods: Towards Anthropology of Consumption* (London: Allan Lane, 1978).

Edwards, E., 'Photographs as Objects of Memory' in M. Kwint, C. Breward, and J. Aynesley, eds, *Material Memories* (Oxford: Berg, 1999).

——, 'Photographs: Material Form and the Dynamic Archive', in *Photo Archives and the Photographic Memory of Art History*, Part II (Max-Planck-Institute, Florence-Italy, 29–31 October 2009), pp. 47–56.

Edwards, E., and J. Hart, eds, *Photographs Objects Histories: On the Materiality of Images* (London and New York: Routledge, 2004).

Eyerman, R., 'The Past in the Present, Culture and the Transmission of Memory', *Acta Sociologica*, 47.2 (June 2004): 159–69.

Freud, S., 'A Note upon the "Mystic Writing Pad"', in *General Psychological Theory* (Chapter XIII) (Collier Books, 1925).

Gillis, J., ed., *Commemorations: The Politics of National Identity* (Princeton: Princeton University Press, 1994).

Jones, A., *Memory and Material Culture* (Cambridge: University Press, 2007).

Kopytoff, I., 'The Cultural Biography of Objects', in A. Appadurai, ed., *The Social Life of Things: Commodities in Cultural Perspective* (Cambridge: Cambridge University Press, 1986).

Kwint, M., 'Introduction: The Physical Past', in M. Kwint, C. Breward, and J. Aynsley, ed., *Material Memories* (Oxford: Berg, 1999).

Lavèdrine, B., *A Guide to the Preventive Conservation of Photograph Collections*, second printing (J. Paul Getty Trust, 2003).

Parkin, D., 'Mementoes as Transitional Objects in Human Displacement', *Journal of Material Culture*, 4.3 (1999): 303–20.

Συλλογές Φωτογραφίας: από τις στρατηγικές στις πολιτικές, Διεθνές Συνέδριο, Μουσείο Φωτογραφίας Θεσσαλονίκης, Θεσσαλονίκη 12–14 December 2008 [*Photographic collection: Strategies to Politics*, International Conference, Museum of Photography Thessaloniki, Thessaloniki 12–14 December 2008].

Sontag, S., *On Photography* (New York: Farrar, Straus and Giroux, 1973).

Xanthakis, A., *Λεξικό Φωτογράφων (1839–1960) Έλληνες φωτογράφοι και ξένοι φωτογράφοι στην Ελλάδα, εμπλουτισμένη ψηφιακή έκδοση* (Οκτώβριος 2015), [*Dictionary of Photographers (1839–1960) Greek and Foreigner Photographers in Greece,* enriched digital version (October 2015)].

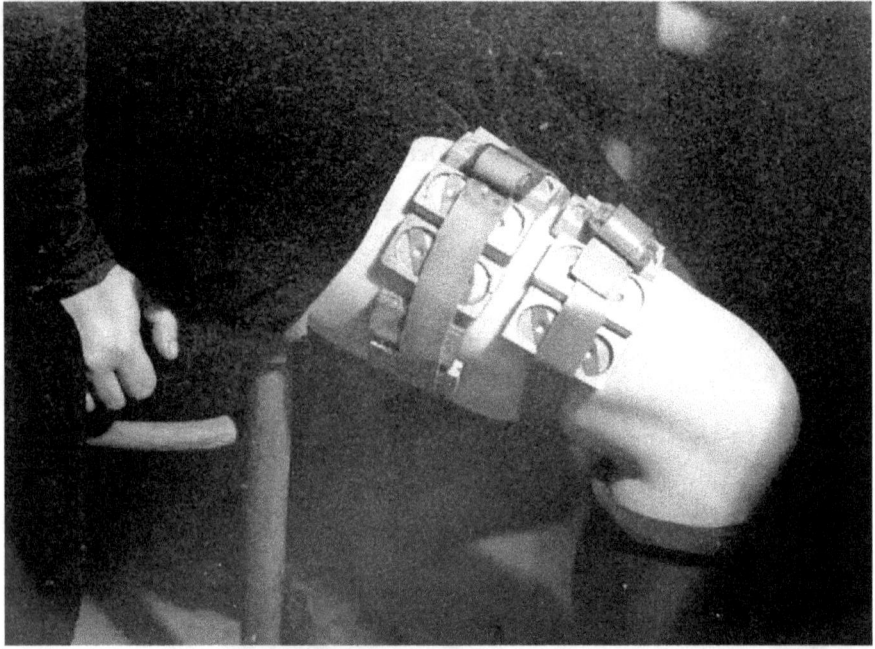

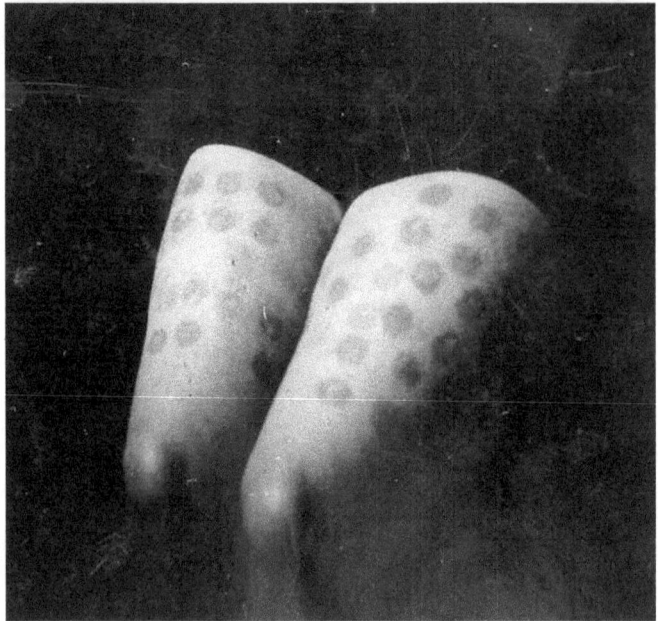

FIGS. 34.1A, 34.1B The box and the imprinting of its content: During and after feeding the lice (source: National Museum, Przemyśl, Poland)

34

LOUSY RESEARCH: THE HISTORY OF TYPHUS VACCINE PRODUCTION, 1915–1945

Martina Schlünder

Box: cages for breeding lice as experimental animals, with the goal of producing a vaccine against typhus. **Size and shape**: 3 cm x 5 cm x 1.5 cm rectangular box with a lid; the opposite side open, covered with a mesh fabric, also having a buckle for attaching straps. **Box species or specific variant:** larger or smaller boxes adjusted for specific purposes (i.e. breeding). **Principles/Behaviour:** Chinese boxes, similar to Matryoshka dolls, nested boxes, system of boxes. **Subtypes:** pill boxes, socks, glass cases. **Material:** plywood, plastics like Bakelite and Galalith, glass, felt, metal. **Colour**: brown, beige, silvery, transparent. **First sightings:** beginnings of First World War, around 1915. **Habitat**: human skin, strapped to the forearms or calves; microbiology labs. **Distribution**: during First World War and interwar period found in labs all over Europe, especially in Poland. **Migration**: during the Second World War they moved to research sites in concentration camps. **Status**: extinct, some specimens can be seen in museums (Przemyśl/Poland) or on the internet.

Keywords: confining, protecting, carrying, mobilising, caring, practising, killing

LOUSE IN A BOX

Profoundly exhausted, she leaned against the wall, her fingers still clenching the railing of the balcony. Then a new coughing fit shook her body. When it ebbed away she immediately checked the little boxes that were strapped with a rubber belt around her forearm. Everything seemed to be okay; the boxes were firmly secured and in place. She couldn't find any of the tiny creatures wandering along her arm or hand. Her coughing fit hadn't allowed any to escape. She wondered what it would be like to live without them. On any given day, for more than twenty-five years without pause, her body had been home to no fewer than five hundred lice. Of course, the individuals changed from time to time; once she succeeded in breeding a very successful strain up to the eleventh generation in the crook of her arm (Sikora 1944: 543, 551). When she was just starting out in her research, she had kept the creatures in little glass jackets that she hid in the pockets of her lab coat. To feed them, she had to put them one by one on a bridge made of thread across which they could climb out of the glass tube down to her skin to drink her blood. In this way, she was able to study them very closely. After a while, she thought she could distinguish a few individuals. She would use the tip of a pair of tweezers to nudge those that had fallen asleep, and let time slip away as the lice fed, often forgetting to enjoy her own meal (Sikora 1915: 524). Naturally, breeding hundreds of lice demanded continual sacrifices.

She started breeding lice in 1915, during the First World War, when she was working for Stanislaus von Prowazek (1875–1915) at Hamburg's Institute for Maritime and Tropical Diseases. Some years before, in 1909, Charles Nicolle (1866–1936) had identified body lice as the vector of epidemic typhus, and now the hunt for the pathogenic agent – hidden in the lice – was underway. But it seemed more difficult to identify and much more dangerous to get close to the microbe than in the golden age of Robert Koch's bacteriology. Howard Ricketts (1871–1910) had fallen prey to the microbe during his research in Mexico. Five years later, Prowazek caught typhus while studying an outbreak of the disease in a prisoner of war camp in Germany. It seemed wise to study lice (the container of the microbe) more carefully, since this had not been done before. After Prowazek's death, she, Hilda Sikora, had courageously plunged into her work, and had published one of the first monographs on the anatomy of the body louse *Pediculus vestimenti* (Sikora 1916).

To study lice in the lab it was necessary to know how to breed them so that new strains of healthy lice could be built. Developing containment and feeding techniques were the keys for the successful breeding of lice. Hilda developed a set of different boxes that were later named after her (**FIGURE 34.2**).

A 'Sikora-cage' was the prototype of a louse box that could be easily modified and adjusted to particular needs: the size of the strain, its morphology, and its purpose (either for use in experiment or later, for mass breeding for vaccine production). The frame of an average Sikora-box was made from either plywood, Bakelite or Galalith.[1] The chamber was closed on the top by a hinged lid. On the bottom it consisted of cloth mesh. The cages were small and flat, about three and a half centimetres long and half to one and a half centimetres high, each accommodating about one hundred lice. The flatter the boxes, the easier it was to secure them firmly in place by straps around the arm or the leg. A couple of holes were drilled into the lid for ventilation. All the holes had to be covered with mesh cloth that was glued to the frame with a specially formulated glue. Every precaution was taken to prevent lice from escaping.[2] The boxes could remain attached to the body of the researcher for days and

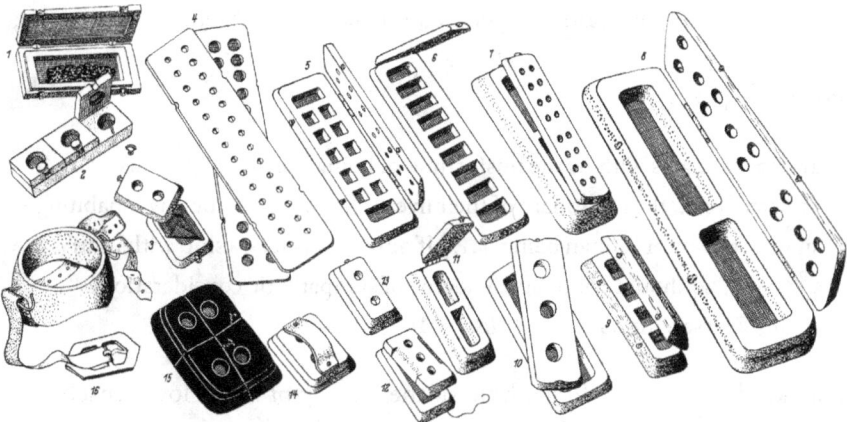

Abb. 1. *1* Läusekäfig nach *Weigl.* (Arch. Inst. Pasteur Tunis **1936**.) *2* Läusekäfig nach *Haase* (Bakelite oder Holz, ein zweites Modell enthält 24 kleine Abteilungen). *3* Kleiner Käfig (Galalith). *4* Käfig zur Aufzucht einzelner Larven (Puppe). *5* und *6* Käfig für Experimente (Galalith). *7* und *8* Zuchtkäfige zum ständigen Anschnallen (Sperrholz). *9* Käfig für Experimente (Sperrholz). *10* Zuchtkäfig für Brutschrankaufenthalt (Galalith). *11* Käfig für Experimente [Sperrholz *(Lautenschläger)*]. *12—14* Kleine Käfige (Galalith). *15* Zuchtkäfig (Kautschuk). *16* Kunstharzring für Freifütterung. Auf ¹/₅ verkleinert.

Die Gaze mußte im Verhältnis zu den Käfigen zu grob gezeichnet werden, der Verkleinerung halber.

FIG. 34.2 A set of Sikora boxes and its kin species (source: Sikora 1944: 542)

nights at a time, preferably in a position where they would not interfere with the performance of other lab activities while the lice sucked blood whenever they needed.

To maintain a steady flow of lice, boxes had to be constantly replaced, cleaned, and adjusted to meet the increasing demands and size of the young. As important as it was to seal the boxes to prevent lice from escaping, it was a similar priority to grant continual access to the skin for their nourishment. Thus the correct size of the apertures in the weave of the mesh cloth was an important issue of research. The width of the openings had to be exactly measured with a thread counter, a tool used in sieve making. Twenty-six holes per square centimetre was the smallest opening through which the lice could still feed, but only if the threads were half as wide as the holes (Sikora 1944: 545). Conveniently, these were the same parameters that prevented the smallest lice from escaping. Confinement and openness had to be balanced in the most delicate ways.

Hilda knew that her attitude toward her lice, her devotion to every single tiny individual louse, bewildered people in the institute. But she was unable to separate curiosity and research from care and love.[3] Now, though, she knew that her long experience of interspecies conviviality would have to come to an end. Over the preceding months, the allergic reactions had increased. The asthma attack that kept her on the balcony that night confirmed that she would have to part with her creatures. But who else could take care of them?[4]

LOUSE AS BOX

> The louse shares with us the misfortune of being prey to the typhus virus. If lice can dread, the nightmare of their lives is the fear of some day inhabiting an infected rat or human being. [...] If only for his fellowship with us in suffering, he should command a degree of sympathetic consideration.
> (Hans Zinsser, *Rats, Lice, and History* 1935: 168)

What kind of mesh could get hold of the history of lice? How densely must we weave the threads to grasp even tinier creatures? Are boxes of any help? In bacteriology it turned out to be so. Organisms can work like boxes in which smaller boxes are hidden, the hidden organism often more dangerous than its container. You can put lice in a box to study and nurture them. You can also treat lice as a box that you can fill up or empty. Of course, you first have to create a lot of empty boxes – healthy lice – which later can be filled with microbes (full boxes, sick lice). But often one can't control how boxes are nested, since in microbiology one is working with sets of living boxes, with an 'emboxed' (Engstrom, this volume) assemblage of living organisms. The historian can follow these arrangements and study how these interspecies ensembles were put together – or separated – in specific historical situations.

With the start of the First World War, bacteriology became lousy. Hilda was a unique female voice in a chorus of male scientists who were eagerly conversing with each other about the body louse, *Pediculus vestimenti*, the species that lives in the clothes of humans. At least twice a day these lice leave their hiding places in seams and under buttons to climb down to the skin to nourish themselves by sucking blood. In a vast array of scientific publications, microbiologists and doctors who were wartime enemies discussed passionately how to chase and catch lice, where to contain them, how to breed a strain, where to breed it, and how to feed the hatchlings. Papers abounded with technical details and bore witness to the emergent material culture of lice in bacteriological labs. Even though Hilda's love for lice might have been unique, she was not the only researcher who was hosting lice on her body. Most of her male colleagues' bodies also turned into incubators. They tried other kinds of containers too, like glass casings, metal pill boxes, boxes made of felt or cloth, and even stockings. Each method made lice into a box, turning them from a disease vector into an experimental animal, a technical 'apparatus' (da Rocha Lima and Sikora 1925: 770). The purpose of this 'apparatus' was to apprehend, isolate, and culture the pathologic agent of typhus that obviously lived in the louse box and was transmitted through it to humans.

Hidden within layers of enclosure like a Chinese box or a Russian doll, the microbe nested in the lice that were hiding in the clothes of humans. To breed healthy lice in the lab was thus a way to bring this dangerous 'emboxed' assemblage under control. To precisely follow the path of infection, healthy lice from the labs, nurtured on the typhus-free blood of the researchers, were brought to the typhus wards. Secure in Hilda's cages, the lice then sucked the infectious blood of the patients and were turned into typhus-infected lice that could be studied in the lab (**FIGURES 34.3A, 34.3B**).

Gesunde Läuse

Kranke, mit Rickettsia Prowazeki infizierte Läuse

FIGS. 34.3A, 34.3B Empty boxes (healthy lice) and full boxes (filled with Rickettsia prowazeki) (source: Emil von Behring Archiv, Philipps Universität Marburg, No. 2261,09–03 W II, Lade I I)

Even though everybody knew that the microbe lived in the louse, it was extraordinarily difficult to identify – and dangerous, too. After Prowazek's death, his Brazilian collaborator, bacteriologist Henrique da Rocha Lima (1879–1956), analysed the data Prowazek had collected, and continued with experiments in the lab. In 1916, he described the unknown microbe under scrutiny 'as somewhat smaller than the smallest bacteria' (da Rocha Lima 1916: 568). It was able to invade and propagate massively in the digestive tract of lice. Thus was typhus contracted by a contamination with lice faeces. Rocha Lima named the microbe in honour of its two most famous victims: 'Rickettsia prowazekii'. Though it had a name, the microbe remained a bacteriological enigma. Rocha Lima's evidence relied on histopathology; he wasn't able to cultivate the microbe on an artificial medium like solid gelatine. Thus his proof didn't follow the gold standard of the Koch postulates (Harden 1987). The microbes seemed to possess a bacterium-like morphology, but they were too small for typical bacteria. They were difficult to stain and impossible to culture outside living organisms. Microbiologists at that time had no idea how to find the right box, how to classify rickettsia: was it a virus, a new class of bacteria, the product of cell lysis, or simply a variant of another organism that turned into a pathologic agent under specific conditions?[5] The difficulty of classifying rickettsiae, and the impossibility of culturing them outside living organisms, was not only of purely theoretical importance, but was also a hindrance for treatment and especially for the problem of vaccine production.

DE-LOUSING: DISENTANGLING, CONTAINMENT, AND MOBILITY

He felt that something was utterly wrong but couldn't grasp what. Shouldn't people treat him – the king, the emperor even – more respectfully? Yesterday somebody put something on his head; had it been a crown, perhaps? He wasn't sure. Why was everyone so jealous? They obviously envied the fact that he was able to fly. Why else would he have been strapped to his bed? In Peter Englund's 2011 history of the First World War, he tells the story of Vincenzo d'Aquila, an American-Italian who came as a war volunteer to Italy and soon attracted epidemic typhus. In his visions he believed himself to be a king or a pregnant woman who could fly. Besides high fever, intense headaches, and a rash, patients undergo a stage of nervous excitement, with paranoia, delirium, and manic episodes. The word typhus – meaning hazy or smoky – points to these most striking symptoms. Englund gives a lively account of how typhus patients experienced their own illness, and how a ward with typhus patients might have looked. Patients often had to be strapped to their beds to protect the staff from being attacked, or to prevent the patients from harming themselves based on manic or delirious misperceptions of their surroundings and their bodies (Allen 2014: 22–23).

Epidemic typhus is the medical label of a disease that has been known under many names. 'Jail fever', 'famine- and war-typhus', or 'typhus ambulatorius' (ambulant typhus), all spell out the dire conditions under which the disease usually emerged. In contrast to traditional bacteriological accounts that understand infectious diseases to be uniquely defined by their pathogenic agents, it is worthwhile to consider typhus as arising from specific encounters that usually occur in the circumstance of war, famine, and living in barracks. The notion of 'ambulant typhus' highlights the fact that the mass movement of people, such as refugees, itinerant army troops, or a starving population wandering in search of food, are crucial ingredients for the emergence of typhus. The congestion of flows and the collapse of infrastructures trigger dangerous encounters between rickettsia, lice, and humans, and that finally produces typhus by making this deadly entanglement more likely to happen, and their mutual emboxment more stable.

This was especially true of the ferocious outbreak of epidemic typhus in Serbia during the first winter of the First World War. Within about six months, by the beginning of June 1915, more than 150,000 people had been killed.[6] Troops from the Austrian and Serbian armies, their wounded soldiers and prisoners of war, and a starving Serbian population of about 250,000 people moved through the country. When the winter set in, soldiers, casualties, refugees, and prisoners of war took shelter in improvised, badly equipped camps and hospitals. Roads in the territory were constantly congested, the railroad overcrowded, and the transport of the sick and wounded could not be guaranteed. The lack of adequate infrastructure, not only in terms of transportation but also in terms of accommodation, shelter, and public health more generally certainly promoted the outbreak of the typhus epidemic. The situation attracted considerable international attention. Sanitary commissions from France, the UK, and the US were sent to Serbia. Beyond their humanitarian mission, these commissions also had a scientific interest, since the Serbian outbreak was the first significant one since Charles Nicolle's discovery of lice as the vector of typhus.

The public health strategy of these commissions was aimed at disentangling lice (and thus rickettsiae) from humans. Since mobility lay at the heart of the spread, it was seen as a major task to control and contain railways and roads. People needed travel permits to use the train, the number of trains was reduced, and the unburdened railway infrastructure was used for the circulation of mobile disinfestation trains (**FIGURES 34.4A, 34.4B**).

Sanitary trains usually consisted of three freight cars. One was reserved for a boiler supplying steam, a second for disinfecting clothes and a third for showers and baths. The train stopped at specifically marked locations where huge tents were erected, beneath which the local population gathered, and several hundred at a time were asked to undress. Then their hair was cut and their clothes hung in the disinfection car while they were taking showers (Strong et al. 1920: 31–32). Sanitary trains were thus arranged as a sequence of boxes, each car containing one of a variety of methods for disentangling and separating the emboxed assemblage of microbe-lice-humans.

FIG. 1. STEAM BATHING AND DISINFESTING UNIT IN CHARGE OF DR. T. W. JACKSON

FIG. 1. LEAVING BATH

FIGS. 34.4A, 34.4B A sanitary train during the Serbian typhus epidemic of 1915, and men leaving the train after having been de-loused in the steam bath (source: Strong et al. 1920, Fig. 1 Plate XII, Fig. 1 Plate XIII)

RE-LOUSING: RE-ENTANGLING LICE EMBOXMENT

If the lice will not swallow the cocktail of Rickettsias,
the contagious fluid will be served to the pests by rectum.

Rudolf Weigl

In the labs, a different strategy prevailed: instead of disentangling humans-lice-
and microbes, the goal was to bring them as close together as possible, but in
very controlled and manipulated ways. Usually a vaccine is made of a microbe
in its weakened, dead, inactivated, or fragmented form. How to prepare a vaccine from a microbe that, so far, had not been isolated, let alone cultured? Since
there was no known way of growing rickettsia on an artificial medium, a living
form had to be found in which to culture the microbe. It was Rudolf Weigl, an
Austrian-Polish biologist from Lwów, who came up with a way to manipulate the
emboxment of 'humans-lice-microbes', and transform their deadly entanglement
into a vaccine- producing assemblage. The most important step in the direction
of a vaccine was Weigl's development of an intrarectal inoculation technique for
lice in 1919 (Weigl 1919: 372–75; Allen 2014: 19–20). This rendered possible
the injection of a suspension made of infected lice containing rickettsiae into
the rectums of healthy lice, thus turning them into a box that contained the
dangerous and precious microbe. In this way Weigl systematically cultivated
and built up stocks of the microbe. He no longer depended on the presence of
typhus *patients* whose blood had formerly been used to infect healthy lice for
the purposes of research.

Weigl took his time bringing the different steps of the vaccine to perfection.
From the 1930s onwards, he was constantly urged by the Polish government to
test his vaccine. Doing so would have meant upscaling the very cumbersome
procedures that differed substantially from standard industrialised forms of
vaccine production. Weigl succeeded in turning lice into vaccine producers
by transforming the normally deadly emboxment into a carefully designed
and controlled interspecies assembly line. He did so by navigating the passage
of the microbe through an ensemble of living boxes, sequencing the stages of
the passage and its temporalities. He reorganised his laboratory according to
a Fordist division of labour, and accelerated the vaccine production, making it
more secure and more efficient. The production started in so-called 'breeding

units' consisting of a supervisor and twelve to fifteen lice feeders. The breeding units produced healthy lice that were then transferred to the 'injection units' where specially trained 'injectors' inoculated lice manually with the infected rickettsia suspension. They were also responsible for feeding the injected (sick) lice on their blood. The injector units thus consisted of people who had survived a typhus infection and had consequently acquired immunity against rickettsia. Highly skilled and experienced injectors could inoculate 2000 lice per hour. After five days, the sick lice were brought to the 'dissector's station' where specially trained dissectors harvested the guts of the lice that contained the highest concentration of rickettsiae (**FIGURES 34.5A, 34.5B**).

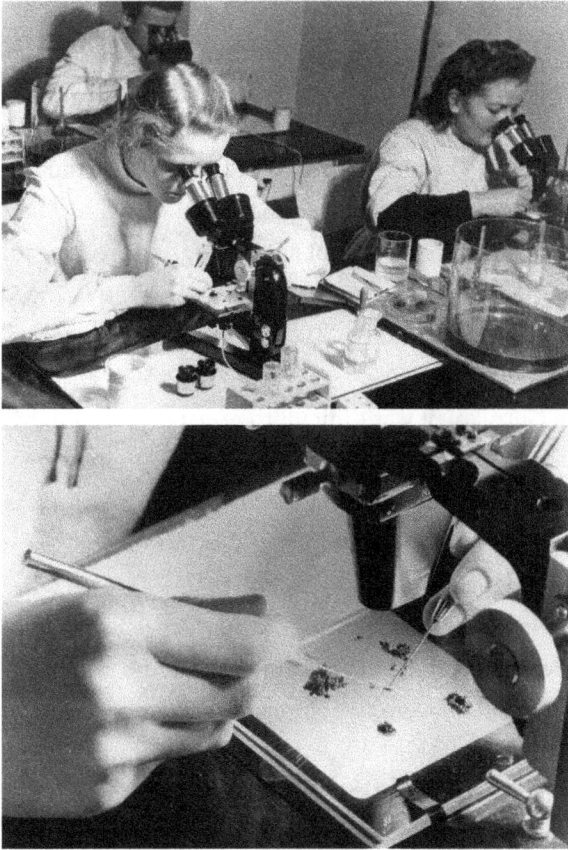

FIGS. 34.5A, 34.5B Dissecting lice, emptying the box. Dissecting units at the Behring Institute, Lwów (Fleckfieber-Forschungsstätte Lemberg) around 1942 (source: Emil von Behring Archiv, Philipps Universität Marburg, No. 2261,09–03 W II, Lade 11)

On average, a trained dissector could process three hundred lice per hour. A standard vaccination against typhus comprised three injections over three weeks, and contained the equivalent of the guts of ninety lice, and so one dissector could prepare vaccines for about thirty people a day. Even after the 'Fordist' reorganisation of his lab, production of the Weigl vaccine remained very difficult and cumbersome (Krynski et al. 1974; Szybalski 1999; Allen 2014: 67–72).

LOUSY RESEARCH — HIDING AND KILLING

'When you put on the lice cages [...] the first feeling is like a hot iron, as five hundred or one thousand of them pierce your skin. You don't want that to be repeated, so you try not to move the cages, because then the lice lose their place and have to bite again'. Wacław Szybalski (Allen 2014: 150) clearly remembers his first time as a lice feeder. Later, after the occupation of Lwów by Nazi Germany in June 1941, he would become supervisor of a breeding unit. Already, for the mass production of the vaccine during the 1930s, Weigl had had to hire about fifty louse feeders, since there was not enough staff to produce the quantities of lice that would meet the increasing demand. The scene changed dramatically with the occupation of Poland by Nazi Germany. Germany hadn't prioritised the study of epidemic typhus since the First World War, and as the disease was not endemic in Germany it was difficult to research. Now, in the middle of the next war, it became clear that Germany was not well equipped to protect its own soldiers. Epidemic typhus was back, and vaccine production was crucial to the war effort. The Weigl vaccine was known as the only reliable one, whereas other types were still under scrutiny (Weindling 2000: 345–52). Due to its intricate production method, and Weigl's notorious perfectionist reluctance to publish, the German occupiers couldn't easily appropriate the knowledge to make the vaccine themselves. They were therefore entirely dependent on his help. Weigl advised several newly established research and production sites that were set up by the Germans (e.g. the Behring Institute in Lwów), and he once again expanded the production scale at his institute (**FIGURE 34.6**).

Almost 3,000 lice feeders were provided with official identification documents proving that their holders were involved in strategically important German war efforts. Weigl's institute became an (almost) safe space for persecuted non-Jewish

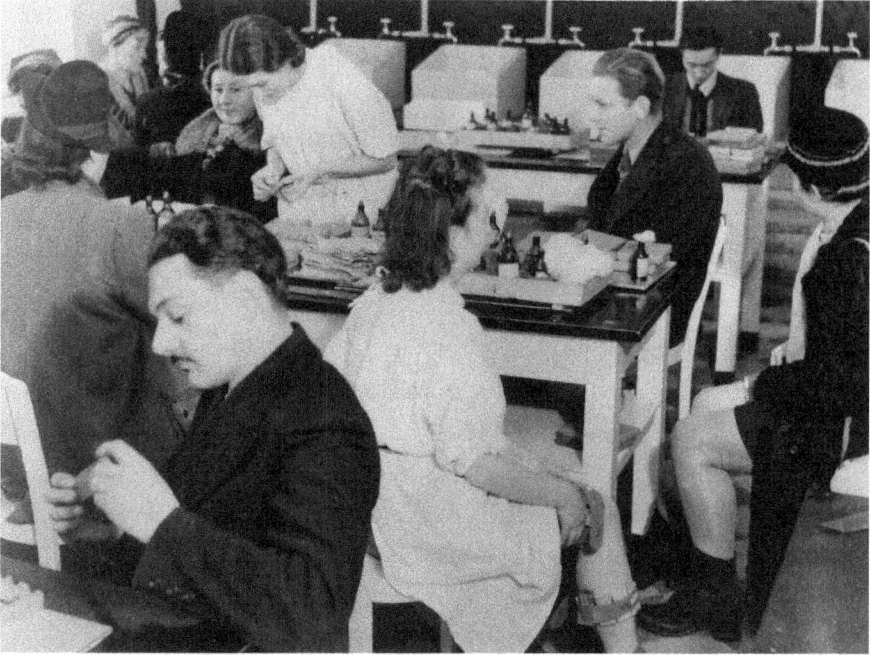

FIG. 34.6 Louse feeders at the Behring Institute, Lwów ca. 1942 (source: Emil von Behring Archiv, Philipps Universität Marburg, No. 2261,09–03 W II, Lade 11)

Poles in an otherwise nightmarish environment: 'Anyone who needed saving became a louse feeder', one of Weigl's assistants claimed after the war (Allen 2014: 136). His institute became a kind of safe haven, as German occupiers were frightened of lice and all things typhus related – things that had been created through their own policies of deportation, ghettoisation, and barracking.

The encounter and emboxment of rickettsiae, lice, and humans, usually results in epidemic typhus and ends with the deaths of lice and people. Weigl's manipulation of this living assemblage allowed researchers to control the passage of the microbe through the lice as through a living box. In the end, the lice alone died, thereby producing the ingredient for the most desired vaccine. But the complex interspecies ensemble could also be differently arranged yet again, as research carried out at Buchenwald concentration camp shows. This was where most of the different products of the attempted vaccination methods were tested. Besides a trial and a control group, so-called 'passage persons' were also infected with the microbe. Their only purpose was to serve as a reservoir, as a living box for rickettsia that needed living cells to grow (Weindling 2000: 354–55; Werther 2004: 117–18). Before they died, other 'passages' had to be infected. Thus these 'passages' took the position that the lice had occupied in Weigl's vaccine production line. It might be more precise to say that passage people were not a *container* for the microbe, but rather that in the laboratory setting they were treated like microbes, since the difference between container and content had vanished. A corresponding position in the living assemblage of humans-lice-microbes was assigned to the Jews. Nazi 'racial hygiene' didn't claim that they were dirty and filthy, thus attracting lice, thus spreading typhus. According to the de-humanising logics and logistics of the Holocaust, the Jews were, simply, lice. They were killed with the same technology – and 'the same routinised indifference' (Raffles 2007: 528). The boundary of a metaphor and the boundary between container and content – so crucial for Weigl's work – completely collapsed into the 'box' of the parasite (**FIGURE 34.7**).

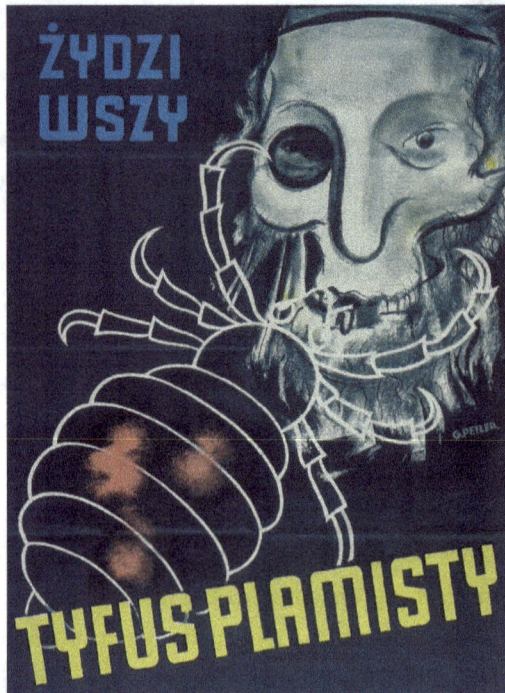

FIG. 34.7 Jews-Lice-Typhus, Nazi propaganda poster, 1941 (source: Bundesarchiv Berlin, Plak 003–039–001)

With the emergence of antibiotics after the Second World War passages through emboxed interspecies assemblages disappeared in the field of epidemic typhus. One burning question however remains: do anthropocentricism and dehumanisation entail each other? If yes, new questions arise: what kind of Enlightenment would get us out of this cul-de-sac?

ACKNOWLEDGEMENTS

This project has been supported by OPO Foundation Zurich and the Ludwik Fleck Center at Collegium Helveticum, Zurich, as part of a research project on Ludwik Fleck and the material culture of laboratories. I thank Oriana Walker for thoughtful discussions about lice and the careful editing. I would also like to thank Ulrike Enke (Emil von Behring Archiv Marburg) and Urte Brauckmann (Max Planck Institute for the History of Science library in Berlin) for helping me to access archival material, images, and image permissions.

NOTES

1   Bakelite and Galalith are both early synthetic plastics. Bakelite is best known through the iconic black telephones of the 1920s and 1930s, see e.g. <http://www.ericssonhistory.com/products/the-telephones/The-Bakelite-telephone-1931> [accessed 12 October 2016].

2   A meticulous instruction in how to construct the boxes can be found in da Rocha Lima and Sikora 1925: 773–78.

3   The ethical, epistemic, and political importance of care in research has been studied intensely over the last years in STS. See Despret 2004, Mol, Moser, and Pols 2010, Puig de la Bellacasa 2011, Martin, Myers, Viseu 2015, and especially Schrader 2015 for a similar case about the study of insects (leaf bugs after Chernobyl).

4   Allen summarises the comments of Hilda's colleagues towards her attitude to lice as an 'attentiveness that tottered perversely on the border of love' (Allen 2014: 63–64). On Hilda Sikora (1889–1974), who never trained as an academic scientist and was hired initially as an illustrator, see Lindenmann 2005 and Hulverscheidt 2013.

5   The classification of rickettsiae remained unclear until the 1960s (Harden 1987: 295). Nowadays they are included among bacteria since they maintain a metabolism independent of their host, but at the same time they are – similar to viruses – strictly intracellular parasites and cannot be cultivated on artificial media. In 1938, Herald Cox developed a method of growing rickettsiae in egg yolk sacs that was later used for the development of the Cox vaccine against typhus (Harden 1987: 295). An overview of all the attempts to produce a vaccine, most of them unsuccessful, is given in Weindling 2000: 435–36.

6 For comparison, the 2014–2016 outbreak of Ebola in West Africa resulted in a loss of ca. 11,325 lives over two years (see <https://www.cdc.gov/vhf/ebola/outbreaks/2014-west-africa/case-counts.html> [accessed 7 September 2016]). The WHO believes that a large percentage (up to 70%) of cases and deaths were not reported.

REFERENCES

Allen, A., *The Fantastic Laboratory of Dr. Weigl: How Two Brave Scientists Battled Typhus and Sabotaged the Nazis* (New York/London: W.W. Norton & Company, 2014).

Despret, V., 'The Body We Care for: Figures of Anthro-zoo-genesis', *Body & Society*, 10.2–3 (2004): 111–34.

Englund, P., *The Sorrow and the Beauty: An Intimate History of the First World War* (London: Profile Books, 2011).

Harden, V., 'Koch's Postulates and the Etiology of Rickettsial Diseases', *Journal of the History of Medicine and Allied Sciences* 42 (1987): 277–95.

Hulverscheidt, M., 'Hilda Sikora – Die Unsichtbare', *Flugmedizin Tropenmedizin Reisemedizin*, 20.5 (2013): 213–17.

Krynski, S., E. Becla, and M. Machel, 'Weigl's Method of Intrarectal Inoculation of Lice in Production of Typhus Vaccine and Experimental Works with *Rickettsia prowazeki*', 1974, <http://www.lwow.home.pl/Weigl/krynski/teoria.html> [accessed 12 August 2014].

Lindenmann, J., 'Women Scientists in Typhus Research during the First Half of the Twentieth Century', *Gesnerus*, 62 (2005): 257–72.

Martin, A., N. Myers, and A. Viseu, 'The Politics of Care in Technoscience', *Social Studies of Science*, 45.5 (2015): 625–41.

Mol, A., I. Moser, and J. Pols, eds, *Care in Practice: On Tinkering in Clinics, Homes, and Farms* (Bielefeld: transcript, 2010).

Murphy, M., 'Unsettling Care: Troubling Transnational Itineraries of Care in Feminist Health Practices', *Social Studies of Science*, 45.5 (2015): 717–37.

Puig de la Bellacasa, M., 'Matters of Care in Technoscience: Assembling Neglected Things', *Social Studies of Science*, 41.1 (2011): 85–106.

Raffles, H., 'Jews, Lice, and History', *Public Culture*, 19.3 (2007): 521–66.

da Rocha Lima, H., 'Zur Aetiologie des Fleckfiebers', *Berliner Klinische Wochenschrift*, 53 (1916): 567–72.

da Rocha Lima, H., and H. Sikora, 'Methoden zur Untersuchung von Läusen als Infektionsträger', in Emil Abderhalden, ed., *Handbuch der biologischen Arbeitsmethoden*, XII/1 (Berlin: Urban & Schwarzenberg, 1925), pp. 769–814.

Schrader, A., 'Abyssal Intimacies and the Temporalities of Care: How (Not) to Care about Deformed Leaf Bugs in the Aftermath of Chernobyl', *Social Studies of Science*, 45.5 (2015): 665–90.

Sikora, H., 'Beiträge zur Biologie von Pediculus vestimenti', *Zentralblatt für Bakteriologie, Parasitenkunde und Infektionskrankheiten*, 76 (1915): 523–37.

——, *Beiträge zur Anatomie, Physiologie und Biologie der Kleiderlaus (Pediculus vestimenti Nitzsch)* (Leipzig: Johannes Barth, 1916).

——, 'Meine Erfahrungen bei der Läusezucht', *Zeitschrift für Hygiene und Infektionskrankheiten*, 125.5 (1944): 541–52.

Strong, R., et al., *Typhus Fever with a Specific Reference to the Serbian Epidemic* (Cambridge, MA: Harvard University Press, 1920).

Szybalski, W, 'Maintenance of Human-Fed Live Lice in the Laboratory and Production of Weigl's Exanthematous Typhus Vaccine', 1999, <http://www.lwow.home.pl/tyfus.html> [accessed 12 August 2014].

Weigl, R., 'Untersuchungen und Experimente an Fleckfieberläusen', *Beiträge zur Klinik der Infektionskrankheiten und zur Immunitätsforschung*, 8 (1919): 353–76.

Weindling, P., *Epidemics and Genocide in Eastern Europe 1890–1945* (Oxford: Oxford University Press, 2000).

Werther, T., *Fleckfieberforschung im Deutschen Reich 1914.1945. Untersuchungen zur Beziehung zwischen Wissenschaft, Industrie und Politik unter besonderer Berücksichtigung der IG Farben*. PhD Thesis. Marburg University, 2004.

Zinsser, H., *Rats, Lice, and History* (Boston: Little, Brown, and Company, 1935).

XI

TOOL

FIG. 35.1 This example of a tool chest, often referred to as a Highboy Tool Chest, is of a type commonly found in professional and amateur garages and workspaces. This particular eighteen-drawer steel chest was constructed in the 1990s by Snap-On and was in use until 2015. The chest consists of two pieces, with the lower portion resting on casters for mobility. While the chest has been retired, remnants of the previous owner's personal items can be seen in the top of the chest (photo by Don Duprez)

FIG. 35.2 The chest in this photo represents a wheeled, steel chest with a wooden top that was designed to be used either on its own – in which case it would be termed a 'Lowboy' – or as a lower portion to a two-chest 'Highboy' set. This particular chest was constructed during the early 2000s by Snap-On as a special commemorative racing edition (photo by Don Duprez)

35

THE MECHANIC'S TOOLBOX AND TOOL CHEST: A NEXUS OF THE PERSONAL AND THE SOCIAL

Don Duprez

Purpose: the storage, protection, and organisation of general and specific tools to meet the needs of the specialist, master craftsman, or casual user. The boxes often contain hammers, wrenches, screwdrivers, picks, files, punches, various pliers and nippers, saws and other cutting instruments, plugs, pullers, compressors, and marking and measuring tools (Sennett 2008: 199–209). **Construction**: while contemporary boxes and chests are generally constructed of metal or wood, they can also be formed from polymer or composite shells, or may be composed of several different materials. **Appearance**: the colours and decorations are as varied as the people who own and work out of them. Over the years each box or chest develops its own patina of grease, stains, smudges, dents, and scrapes, adding to the character of the box and making the boxes readily identifiable to their owners. Owing to this, a toolbox as an object is something that can generate deeply formed attachments in a person. **Size and mobility**: toolboxes and chests are to be found in all manner of shapes and sizes, while generally being of a square or rectangular design with a hinged lid. Toolboxes and chests can contain a battery of drawers and tiered trays, accessible from the front or from the opened top. Toolboxes tend to be highly portable, whereas tool chests tend to be large, stacked structures presenting challenges to portability. Within shop spaces, the terms tool chest and toolbox are often used interchangeably. **Habitat**: these boxes can often be found within garages, repair shops, homes, mobile facilities, and in vehicles. While there are communal toolboxes, the overwhelming majority are privately owned and maintained. **Cost**: The cost can be as little as US$20 or as great as $25,000 for a chest fully outfitted with additional cabinets and accessories (Snap-On

Tools 2015 [<store.snapon.com>]). **Distribution and use**: these boxes are still widespread and in common use.

Keywords: organising, collecting, protecting, storing, transporting, identifying, fixing, building, creating, surviving, behaving, reflecting, projecting, dreaming, personalising, maintaining livelihood

EXPLORING TOOLBOXES AND TOOL CHESTS

AS A MASTER MECHANIC, MY FATHER HAS TURNED WRENCHES FOR OVER fifty years. While a child in the 1970s and 1980s, and for much of my early adult life, I spent an incredible amount of time in my father's shop, learning to repair engines and fabricate needed parts, while constantly organising and fetching tools that resided in a massive red tool chest. Many of my earliest memories of my father are of him standing at his tool chest, producing instrument after instrument, on occasion releasing a slew of colourful language as he rummaged for a misplaced piece. When I was tall enough, I found that within the chest there resided a copious number of drawers, cabinets, nooks, cubbies, and trays. Here, every tool and component had its place.

Toolboxes and tool chests are meant to be used, often under harsh conditions where they are subjected to heat, dirt, and chemicals. They are a mainstay of auto mechanics and are understood to be a fundamental fixture in the shop and a central part of the workday. Nearly every morning my father and his employees would gather at their respective chests and go over the day's tasks, gathering their thoughts while preparing the tools they expected to use. Throughout the day they would return to their chests to gather, clean, and take different tools, and at times, to eat their lunches. At night the tools scattered about the workspace would find their way to the waiting benches to be cleaned, polished, and placed carefully in their respective nests to be ready for the next day's tasks. Just as the day begins at the chest, so it ends with the last tool put away and its drawer clicking into place.

When I could see into the top of the chest while standing on stacked blocks of wood, I found that I had become drawn into the workflow whenever I was near the work areas. Along with getting supplies of oil and rags, and sanding oil spills, I was asked more and more often to ferry tools from the chest to the waiting hands of my father sticking out from beneath the cars. After some time I became responsible for returning to the bench tools that I had either used or had collected from around the workspace. I would wipe them down and then watch my father place them in the chest. Eventually I was entrusted to return tools to their proper space within the chest. Through a process of trial and error and reprimand, I learned my way through the different drawers and trays and became familiar with the quirks of the different sections, the dents and scrapes, the smells of grease and oil in certain drawers, and the overall logic and purpose of the chest's organisation. Principal tools, such as the collections of metric and imperial spanners, were easily accessible in the middle set of drawers. These middle drawers were bracketed by screwdrivers and pry bars located just above the spanners and hammers below. Fine tools and specialty items lay in the smaller drawers closest to the top of the chest, while pneumatic tools and larger, heavier items filled out the lowest sections, thereby providing stability. Depending on the job at hand, one could start with aggressive tools from the lower section of the chest, or for finer work, more delicate tools from the very top. In either case a person is able to work through the chest as they choose to access and use their tools independently or in conjunction with one another.

In addition to matters of function and workflow, toolboxes and tool chests can certainly be addressed by their physical characteristics and aesthetics. Tolpin's (1998) work approaches these subjects from the perspective of the end user and presents the reader with a wide array of styles and forms of antique and contemporary toolboxes and chests. Christopher Schwarz has written extensively on these topics concerning tool chests for the joiner and cabinetmaker (2011 and 2015). Additionally, notable woodworker Paul Sellers has addressed the topic of historical and contemporary toolbox aesthetics and function through promotional YouTube videos (2014) and through his online site (2015). Within these studies, it can also be seen that tool boxes and chests range from the simple and unadorned, such as a shop-made joiner's wooden tool chest, to the elegant and extravagant, such as the nineteenth-century woodworking tool chest of

Duncan Phyfe, or the tool cabinet of H. O. Studley (Tolpin 1998: 16, 76–78). In consideration of these points, one may see that for some people their toolbox is both a source of self-expression and a castle that safeguards their tools and livelihood, while others may see the box simply as a means of transport and storage, and as an organisation solution.

What follows is intended to expand upon the idea of the toolbox as a physical container and system of tool organisation. Here, the toolbox can be further examined or understood as an expression or extension of the individual craftsperson. Moreover, toolboxes and their status and representation reveal a nexus of moral and ethical understanding and behaviour about how individuals are expected to conduct themselves as professionals, and how they interact with one another.

THE TOOLBOX AND THE SELF

In addition to my own hands-on experiences, the years of working with my father permitted me an opportunity to observe and explore different toolboxes and chests as I found myself in the shops of those of my father's friends and relatives who were also tradesmen. They included mechanics, machinists, fabricators, welders, joiners, carpenters, and cabinetmakers. While there are certainly women who fill these roles and use toolboxes, the vast majority of those I have observed over the years have been men. My limited observations of women working with toolboxes revealed to me that men and women interact with the boxes and chests, and ascribe value to their chests and tools, in a similar manner. By value I mean to suggest that individuals develop deep-seated personal attachment, or affect, to their tools and to their toolboxes and chests. I experienced a similar degree of affect when learning my way through my father's tool chest and becoming accustomed to its nuanced details. The chest became something familiar to me and it became a trusted point of organisation in the shop and in my work experiences. From an even more personal standpoint, the character of the chest stood as a reminder of my father's years of experience and his identity as a professional mechanic.

To this last point, when addressing matters of value and attachment, the boxes and chests can be understood as being an extension of the owner, reflecting their personalities through personal aesthetics and perspectives. Russell

Belk's (1988) work offers an analysis of objects which suggests that possessions are critical to the formation and sense of self. Belk asserts that possessions can serve as a means of establishing, developing, and stabilising one's identity. This is further developed in Tian and Belk's article, 'Extended Self and Possessions in the Workplace' (2005), which explores the notion that objects can serve as narratives of the self. In their examination of workplace possessions, personal items from home are seen to assist in a person's understanding of themselves in the workplace. Through this construction and stabilisation of self, people are better able to manage the boundaries of their personal and work lives (Tian and Belk 2005: 299–304). Aaron Ahuvia has critiqued Belk's notion of the core self and the extended self by suggesting that analysis of person-object relations should also account for strong and weak relations to items and possessions. Ahuvia has further argued that by accounting for these variations, examinations of the extended self will be able to provide a better understanding of how people demarcate, compromise, and synthesise identity solutions through objects (2005: 181).

In the case of many auto mechanics, it is not uncommon to find the lids of their tool chests plastered with product decals, humorous and at times crass messages or comic strips, and idealised images of favourite cars, events, places, or people, real or imagined. By these adornments, the top of the toolbox is transformed into a colourful stage of personal expression. In my father's case, the top of the chest held several pictures of his key racing victories and important moments at the racetrack spanning decades. In addition to the photos and small plaques of racing events, good luck charms, such as a tiny pink haired troll doll that had been strapped to the roll cage of a past racing car, and smaller work-related promotional items, were tucked into the different compartments in the top. These items speak to the ideas of Belk and Tian in that they impart an image of the person's attitudes, intent, hopes, passions, and desires: in essence, a balanced representation of their work lives and their lives outside the shop. What they choose to place here is a part of how they see themselves and how they may want to see themselves, while adding to the presentation of themselves to others.

In reference to Ahuvia's points, the lid of the boxes or chests offer only so much space on which to display things, and it can be argued that items selected for display in such a visible spot hold strong social or professional meaning for the person. In opposition to this, product decals can hold significantly weaker meaning. This is not to say that they are without merit, as these decals and badges display brand loyalties or reflect ideas of quality products from the viewpoint of the mechanic, but they may not hold the same degree of meaning or significance to the chest owner as personal objects.

While the owner influences the presentation, persona, or character of the chest, so the chest influences an understanding of the self within the owner. Returning to Belk (1988), people seek identity through items and objects in order to project who they understand themselves to be and how they wish to be understood by others. In the case of mechanics, the chest becomes an essential item in representing the self as a mechanic and becomes a part of what a person's idea of being a mechanic is, just as a uniform or tools denote the mechanic's professionalism and knowledge.

These points of relationship between an individual and their tools, chests, and the formation of identity are reinforced through Christopher Schwarz's (2011) examination of a traditional joiner's chest. Here, Schwarz suggests that the acquisition, organisation, and care of tools create an opportunity for a person to develop and master the essential skills that will serve to empower themselves through craft. By extension, the chest is associated with the owner's independence, their self-empowerment, and a decoupling of the self from a culture of mass production, all characteristics Schwarz sees as essential to his vision and definition of the anarchist craftsman.

This process of connection and involvement in the relationship of the craftsman and the chest is also marked by the dynamic license to express their ideas and be creative in their work. In this sense, the toolbox is laden with potentialities of what can be imagined, constructed, and brought to fruition. In all of this, the toolbox stands as an intersection of a person's past, their future, their experiences, expressions, their abilities and potential, their dreams and aspirations, freedom, and the personal derivations of what constitutes professionalism and visions of practising their respective crafts.

In consideration of these perspectives, approaching toolboxes and tool chests from beyond the physical qualities of the box has permitted an opportunity to observe these objects as a nexus of the personal and the social. As an extension of the self, the toolbox assists in defining and shaping images of how one perceives the self and how that self is perceived by others. It also represents a merging of boundaries between private lives and the social through the things people choose to display. Furthermore, these points are tied to a projection of what a tradesman or craftsman is supposed to be and what they are able to do.

THE TOOLBOX AS A POINT OF ETHICAL CONDUCT

Along the top of my father's chest, among the different racing associations, product decals, and pictures of his own racing cars, was one large bumper sticker that for decades displayed a caricature of a mechanic with the statement, 'Don't Ask to Borrow My Tools, *Its How I Make My Living!*'. This is a statement that I often saw repeated on the tops of tool chests of my father's friends and associates. In one shop, a sign on the lid simply stated, 'NO, you may not borrow my tools!'. When I asked my father about these statements, he explained that they were meant to be seen by customers and potentially by other mechanics too. He went on to tell me that everyone in the shops has stories of tools being borrowed and not returned, or outright stolen. And while the sharing of tools does go on between individuals, it was best to mitigate or simply avoid any troublesome situations or conflicts by not consistently loaning tools.

As the bumper sticker on my father's chest suggests, tools are the means by which mechanics are able to accomplish their tasks and are then able to provide for themselves and their families. Missing tools represent a potential loss of income by limiting what tasks they can address. Moreover, tools are usually collected over the course of a person's career and represent significant time and financial investments. Along with immediate out-of-pocket expenses, the acquisition and replacement of tools can result in the tradesman incurring significant debt to tool vendors. During my last visit to my father's shop in 2014, the course of one discussion with a few mechanics revealed that one of their co-workers had amassed a $40,000 debt to the tool vendor. Another man was known to sell his tool chest every year and purchase a new one, at times going into debt, in order to constantly upgrade. For many, the idea of replacing their toolbox every year borders on the absurd. However, it could be argued that the purchase of a new chest may also speak to the man's personal understanding of a professional and modern image of the mechanic, and of the self as a mechanic. While the chests and tools are an integral part of the self and public images of the self, these degrees of financial debt also generate additional forms of affect in that the tools must be used to pay for themselves while meeting the owner's professional goals.

Within these different situations, emphases, perspectives, and investments, the importance of their tools and the tool chests as carefully protected loci of a worker's livelihood further reveals degrees of affect and expectations of ethical conduct. These expectations of ethical conduct can be understood to emanate from social conventions and interactions, and through personal experiences and perspectives. In 'Between Reproduction and Freedom: Morality, Value, and Radical Cultural Change' (2007), Joel Robbins explores the ethical foundations and issues raised by James Laidlaw (2002) concerning individual moral freedom of choice as described by Kant, and the reproduction of social mores and norms posed by Durkheim. In the case of toolboxes, it can be argued that both positions are at play. The message regarding a request to borrow tools expresses an expectation others will acknowledge: the importance of the tools to their owner, and that they (the borrowers) will conduct themselves accordingly. As a shared sentiment, the message reveals social expectations of behaviour within the shop, where activity is governed by social and collective rules, principles, and guidelines (Keller and Dixon Keller 1996: 126). To violate this expectation raises questions of an individual's respect for other's property and matters of ownership.

From a personal perspective, each individual brings with them a self-formulated moral foundation drawn from life experience that informs their respective views of property, ownership, and behaviour. Here, moral codes are synthesised between the moral expectations of the social and the inner moral dialogue of the individual, further refining what can be understood through Foucault's term, a 'technology of the self' (1990). In turn, this synthesis then becomes observable through interactions and attitudes in the workplace. These points concerning tools, access and control, concerns of costs, and moral perspectives and expectations not only further establish the importance of the protection and maintenance of the tool chest but also suggest that we can perceive the toolbox or tool chest as a locus of ethical conduct.

While subjective, the practice of these ethics, and the chest as a point of contention, can be observed in matters of access to tools within the chest. While there are garages and shops that operate with an understanding of shared tool resources, the vast majority of mechanics own their own tools and chests. As noted earlier, there is a tendency to discourage people from asking to borrow tools, and to limit who can have access to the tools. Returning to my father's shop, there were rules concerning tool use for those who were allowed to access his tool chest. If a tool was borrowed, it was expected that when returning the tool, it would be left on the bench to the left of the chest or, if the chest was closed, on top of the chest. This was done so that the tool could be accounted for at the end of the day, and so the owner of the tool could return it to its proper place. Additionally, by accounting for the tool and returning the tool themselves, the owner knows exactly where the tool is, and doesn't accidentally purchase a replacement. In these situations, there is a system of trust in place. Those borrowing tools from the chest are aware of their responsibility to return items, while the owner trusts the person with access to the chest to account for their actions. If this relationship is violated and that trust is broken, the dynamics of the shop can change dramatically, leading in some cases to the breaking of professional and personal relationships.

The situation above is predicated upon access having been granted to the chest; however, in some cases tools are borrowed and returned without permission. Additionally, the theft of tools is a serious matter, although difficult to prove without clearly identifiable tradesmen's marks of ownership. Theft and loss greatly inhibit a worker's capabilities and generate missed opportunities while also potentially affecting the performance and production of an entire facility or programme. The few times that I have witnessed a person being confronted for taking a tool without permission, the wrongdoer was engaged in conversation in a manner which allowed everyone around to witness the confrontation. Not only did this directly address the issue, it also made everyone else in the shop aware that the person who had borrowed the tools was someone whose trust was in question, that they did not respect the boundaries of ownership, and that they did not respect the owner. Going beyond distrust, extreme situations can result in the offender becoming ostracised in the shop. Finally, if a tool is known to have been stolen, and not simply lost, a conversation can emerge for the purpose of making others aware of the situation and that they should be aware of where their own tools are and who has access to them.

Just as theft by someone in the shop is an issue, outside theft is also a major concern. In the early 1980s, a mechanic who worked in the same neighbourhood as my father had his shop broken into and his tool chest stolen. The next morning, he stopped by my father's shop after speaking with the police and asked us to watch out for anyone selling any tools bearing his machinist's mark. He was understandably distraught and, while insured, was worried about getting work done while he waited to replace everything. That weekend he went to a car boot sale at the local fairgrounds and was lucky enough to find someone selling the bulk of his tools. He contacted the authorities and his property was returned to him. While some things were missing, he was relieved that he was able to return to work to some degree. Much of this was discussed while he visited my father, and it was a topic my parents continued to talk about during the week. My father was happy to hear about the recovery, but he was concerned that people were breaking into shops in the area. He remarked that the thieves had taken his friend's way of making a living away from him, and that he was incredibly lucky to get back what he did. As a precaution, my father began to take a greater interest in the security of everything related to the shop, and his distrust of strangers wandering into the shop increased.

Looking at this situation, the theft of the chest is in clear conflict with the ethical underpinnings of the law. It also violates the ideas formed by the community as a whole and by individuals within the community regarding ownership and access to a person's property, and what the chest means to someone's livelihood. Within this view of their livelihood, the time invested in collecting the tools and the financial investment must also be accounted for. In addition to these points, the theft also speaks to the issues identified in this essay related to matters of identity. Just as a chest can serve as an extension of the self, the loss of a chest can issue challenges to the person's identity. The theft prohibited the man from fulfilling the occupational duties that marked him as a mechanic. Moreover, theft of the chest took away personal items and images in the chest that represented his past and future, further stripping away a part of the attached identity.

As an outcome of these perspectives, the toolbox and tool chest can be understood to be something much more than a means of tool storage. Through the personalisation of the toolbox and chest, an extension of the self emerges to reflect personalised images of what, in this case, mechanics should be and how they should be perceived, as well as reflections of the person's past and future aspirations. In addition to this, how individuals and groups interact and engage with one another is of particular importance when addressing access to tools and tool chests. In sum, looking beyond the physical, the objects become a sounding board of the self, while situated as a nexus of interaction and a means of reflecting on the moral and ethical foundations and expectations of the social and the personal.

REFERENCES

Ahuvia, A. C., 'Beyond the Extended Self: Loved Objects and Consumers' Identity Narratives', *Journal of Consumer Research*, 32 (2005): 171–84.

Belk, R. W., 'Possessions and the Extended Self', *Journal of Consumer Research*, 15 (1988): 139–68.

Foucault, M., *The Care of the Self: The History of Sexuality* (New York: Random House Books, 1990).

Keller, C., and J. D. Keller, 'Thinking and Acting with Iron', in S. Chaiklin and J. Lave, eds, *Understanding Practice: Perspectives on Activity and Context* (New York, NY: Cambridge University Press, 1996).

Laidlaw, J., 'For an Anthropology of Ethics and Freedom', *Journal of the Royal Anthropological Institute*, 8 (2002): 311–32.

Robbins, J., 'Between Reproduction and Freedom: Morality, Value, and Radical Cultural Change', *Ethos: Journal of the Society for Psychological Anthropology*, 72 (2007): 293–314.

Schwarz, C., *The Anarchist's Tool Chest* (Mitchell, KY: Lost Art Press, 2011).

——, 'The Chris Schwarz Blog', <http://www.popularwoodworking.com/woodworking-blogs/chris-schwarz-blog> [accessed 6 August 2015].

Sellers, P., 'The Joiner's Toolbox', 29 December 2014, <https://www.youtube.com/watch?v=kuUrY4y478w> [accessed 9 July 2015].

——, 'A Lifestyle Woodworker', <https://paulsellers.com> [accessed 1 August 2015].

Sennett, R., *The Craftsman* (New Haven and London: Yale University Press, 2008).

Snap-On Tools, 'Tool Storage', <https://store.snapon.com/Tool-Storage-C700030.aspx> [accessed 6 August 2015].

Tian, K., and R. W. Belk, 'Extended Self and Possessions in the Workplace', *Journal of Consumer Research*, 32 (2005): 297–310.

Tolpin, J., *The Toolbox Book* (Newtown, CT: The Taunton Press, 1998).

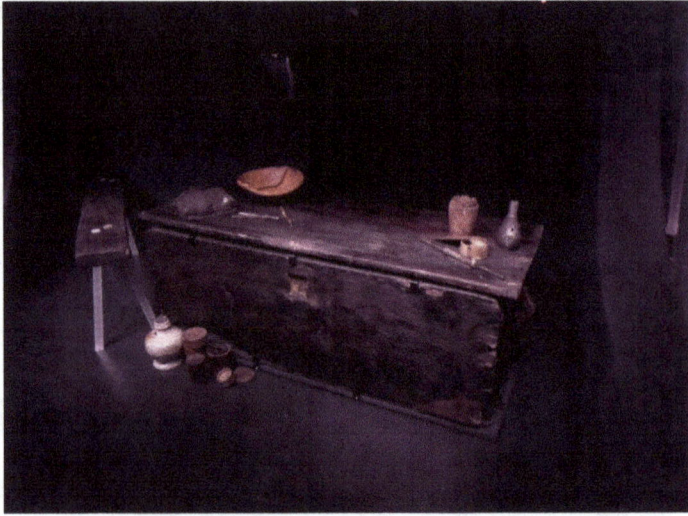

FIG. 36.1 The surgeon's chest from the surgeon's cabin in the Mary Rose, the Mary Rose Museum, Portsmouth

36

SURGEONS' CHESTS FROM THE MARY ROSE

Hanako Endo

Appearance: simple, rectangular parallelepiped, and made of approximately two centimetres of wooden boards, probably oak. **Size:** varies but mostly large, the average size of early modern chests might be 120 cm × 60 cm × 70 cm. **Habitat:** Mary Rose, the sixteenth century warship. **Origin:** used since ancient times, but for different purposes.

Keywords: excavating, revealing, containing, operating, voyaging

ON THE 31 MAY 2013, THE MARY ROSE MUSEUM, LOCATED JUST 400 METRES from the main entrance to Portsmouth Historic Dockyard, opened for the first time to the public. The Mary Rose is a carrack-type warship of the English Tudor navy of King Henry VIII, built in Portsmouth between 1509 and 1511. Its great size, and the huge number of weapons it carried, served as an expression of power and established it as an awe-inspiring status symbol in the sixteenth century. After being in service for thirty-four years, the ship sank in the Solent between the Isle of Wight and the mainland of England on the 19 July 1545. In 1971, the shipwreck was discovered. A team of over 500 volunteer divers explored the area, using dredgers, water jets, and airlifts. Ever since its rediscovery in 1971, the Mary Rose has been in the process of restoration, and it is currently in the final stages of conservation.

The Mary Rose Museum houses about 19,000 artefacts. In most cases, they were cleaned, documented, and photographed for further research. Remarkably, many of these artefacts were retrieved from the wooden chests which had held them in the sea for several centuries. The durability of the Early Modern chests undoubtedly protected them. Historically, the definition of boxes includes their lack of legs, and in this they are distinguished from chests, which may or may not have legs (Miyauchi 1991: 18–19). The majority of the chests found on the Mary Rose are without legs but have handles for carrying on both sides and the lid. These handles could also help to keep the lids firmly closed, and to keep the damp out.

Each chest was used as a container, but for different purposes in different parts of the ship. The artefacts in some of the chests are carpentry tools, such as mallet, drill handle, plane, and ruler, but there are also other items, such as a backgammon set, a book, three plates, a sundial, and a tankard. There are chests that contain animal bones: one chest includes the skeletons of a rat, a frog, and a dog; and in another chest, the bones of pigs and fish, stored in baskets, are found. As for musical instruments, two fiddles and a bow, three three-hole pipes and a tabor drum with a drumstick were discovered. Further, a set of navigation instruments, such as compasses, divider callipers, a stick used for charting, protractors, sounding leads, tide calculators, and a log reel – an instrument for calculating speed – were found in some of the chests. Chests were commonly used everywhere on the ship.

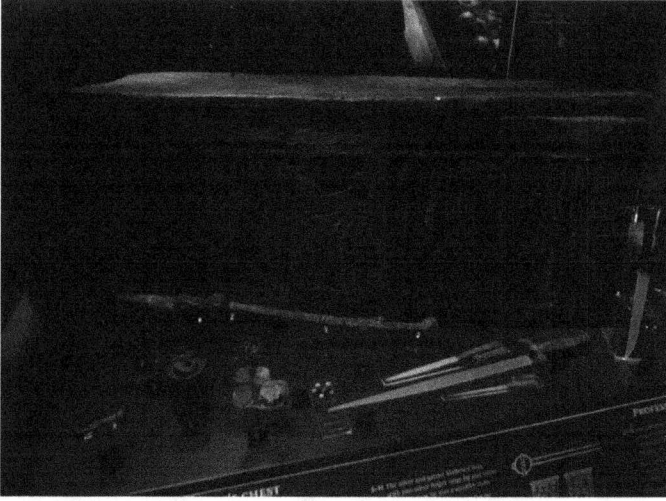

FIG. 36.2 Another surgeon's chest from the Mary Rose

Among the large number of cultural artefacts recovered from the Mary Rose are the surgical instruments from surgeons' chests (**FIGURE 36.2**). These give special insight into the medical history of sixteenth-century England. As revealed by the excavation, the surgeons – who were in charge of the health care and welfare of the crews, in addition to the medical practice on board – seem to have stayed in the cabin located on the main deck underneath the sterncastle of the Mary Rose. An intact wooden chest contained over sixty important objects relating to the surgeons' medical practice. They kept a copper syringe for wound irrigation and treatment of gonorrhoea, and even skilfully crafted feeding bottles for feeding incapacitated patients. Other objects related to barbers' duties were also found around the cabin, such as ear scoops, shaving bowls, and combs.

One of the surgeons' chests includes a complete set of surgical tools such as a surgeon's cap, a wooden dish, two wooden bowls, eight bandage rolls of a sticky resinous material, the wooden ointment canisters, ceramic medicine jars, a scalpel, a whetstone, a leather flask, wooden tankards, a bronze pan, a heavy bronze mortar, a spatula to mix and spread ointment, and a brush. Other chests, in addition, contain traditional surgical instruments such as syringes, lancets, and the trepanning instrument to drill into the skull. The tools found in surgeons' chests or cabins in the Mary Rose are the same tools as the ones general surgeons used in the Early Modern period. Such general tools used by surgeons would have included tongs, pincers, saws, scissors, scalpels, bowls for blood-letting, a wooden mallet, flasks of yellowed glass, a brass syringe, and so on (Siraisi 1990: 154).

The surgeons' chests in the Mary Rose show how and what surgeons treated on the ship. The chests and their contents are the concrete evidence of medical history. One of the most basic objects is a lancet. The presence of a lancet illustrates that surgeons performed the typical and traditional treatment of blood-letting, which was regarded as the most common primary medical treatment for many injuries and diseases. It was believed for many centuries that four humours – blood, phlegm, yellow bile, and black bile – constitute the human body, and that their imbalance makes people sick. It was therefore important for medical men to restore the balance of the four humours in order to bring about recovery from the disease. This was done by means of surgical venesection, which was the commonest task performed by the barber-surgeon in the Early Modern period (Siraisi 1990: 140). The biggest problem of venesection was that it could lead to the death of many patients, especially after the loss of blood through injury (Sloan 1996: 114).

As is also shown from the surgeons' chests, blood-letting was often accompanied by the administration of vomits (emetics), purges (purgatives) or clysters (enemas), in order to restore the balance of the humours, by reducing one humour identified as being in excess. Surgeons applied plants to perform emetics and purgatives, because plants were acknowledged as fairly safe, although tartar emetic (antimony potassium tartrate), a highly toxic inorganic compound, was prescribed by some physicians (Sloan 1996: 61). Enemas were administered just as they are nowadays, but in the Early Modern period, simple piston syringe clysters were used for bowel cleansing.

The syringes found in some of the chests from the Mary Rose are surprisingly similar to the syringes doctors still use today. The needles of these syringes are long and thin, but cylindrical. The biggest difference between the syringes from the Mary Rose and those used today lies in their use. In the Early Modern period, the syringe was used not to inject medicines under the skin, nor to inoculate against diseases, but rather to drain infected wounds of pus, or to apply alcohol to fresh wounds, cleaning them in order to avoid infection.

Another important surgical instrument, and a staple of surgeons' chests, is the saw. Surgeons would sometimes have a soldier's leg amputated at the infected joint. When a soldier with a wounded leg was carried in, the assistant would punch the soldier in order to render him unconscious, or more frequently, patients sniffed at opium-soaked sponges or drank alcohol before the operation (Barber 2013: 35). However, the pain of sawing was so horrible that, in the course of the operation, some died of physiological shock, loss of blood, or infection from the filthy environment – dirty saws, dirty floor, dirty clothes, and so on.

The Mary Rose surgeons' chests also include the mallet, which may have been used for performing small amputations on the arms and legs, and used with a chisel and block to remove damaged fingers and toes. The mallet is also thought to have been used to treat bone ulcers and for tooth removal. Scalpels were common surgical tools. Then, as now, they were frequently used for dissecting dead bodies rather than operating on live patients. Although opportunities to dissect a human body were limited, it was the privilege of military surgeons to see inside the body, by means of autopsies performed on corpses carried into the surgery.

The chests on the Mary Rose were not only used for storing surgical tools, but also for medicines. Generally, in the case of rich families, medicines such as herbs, chemicals, and ointments were kept in small bottles, and there were special boxes for those bottles. Chests for household medicine were therefore another type of medicine chest. The sixteenth-century Genoese medicine chest of Governor Vincenzo Giustiniani, for instance, is a beautiful chest that can hold 126 bottles and pots for drugs (Science & Society Picture Library 2015). The chest is made of leather-coated wood. A beautiful landscape is painted on the inside of the lid. The chest is a four-tiered set, and each tier can be slid sideways. Although there are many holes for glass bottles in the box, they are beautifully lined up, and in fact the box resembles a jewel case. This type of medicine chest was generally owned by rich people, who not only used them as medicine chests but also displayed them as furniture for their beautiful design.

Although beautiful bottles like those possessed by rich ladies were not found on the Mary Rose, the surgeon's cabin held three pale-green glass bottles. Bottles were commonly used everywhere in daily life, so it seems that they are not special to this ship from the perspective of medicine, although the bottles found on the Mary Rose would have been relatively expensive. The contents of these bottles have, of course, been lost, but it is likely that they would have contained either mercury or scented oils. The latter could have been used as aftershave for officers. Mercury was also regarded as one of the best medicines for the treatment of syphilis, one of the commonest diseases amongst ships' crews. Mercury is believed to have been injected by a syringe just like the one found on the Mary Rose.

Shipboard surgeons were generally employed by navies and the merchant marine. The number of surgeons' chests recovered from the Mary Rose indicates that its final voyage was going to be a long one. During the Middle Ages, travel had generally been for professional or military reasons, or for the purpose of pilgrimage. By the Elizabethan period, however, personal secular travel – tourism – had become a well-established activity (Singman 1995: 91). Therefore, the sixteenth century was the time when people started moving more than before. Chests were used not only on voyages, but also for personal use as travellers moved from one place to another. These were called 'travelling chests'. Generally, dishes, jewellery, or clothes were placed in such a chest. Sometimes chests were covered with leather in order to avoid their getting wet in the rain.

I have so far investigated the inventory of surgeons' chests on the Mary Rose; however, also deserving of attention are the chests themselves, which were designed to protect what was inside. The highly efficient Early Modern chests were useful for containing small sorted batches of items. In churches, chests were often used to keep important documents and items. This is because churches were rich enough to buy expensive chests. In order to make a big chest for churches, a big log was used, though logs had a tendency to crack as they dried. Therefore, hoop iron was often wound around the chest to prevent it cracking (Gloag 1977: 305).

Chests could also be seen in the private areas of manor houses and castles. In the chest were important household materials such as cloth, clothes, money, documents related to land, and other pecuniary contracts. For these reasons, the chests were often put in the upstairs rooms or basements which are connected with spiral staircases, rather than in the hall where many people passed in and out. In other words, chests were kept in the safest places (Mercer 1969: 38). The relationship between chests and money was frequently pointed out in the medieval and Renaissance periods. Merchants stored money in the boxes or chests. In Shakespeare's *The Merchant of Venice*, Jessica, a Jew's daughter, brings out the 'casket' when she elopes with a Christian man. It is revealed later by Shylock, her father, that the casket contained a diamond worth 'two thousand ducats' and 'other precious, precious jewels' (2001: 3.1.76–80). In fact, many illustrations from the period show that money and other treasures were kept in special boxes and chests.

Chests seem to have been used to store important possessions. They could frequently be seen in sixteenth-century houses and in many shops. Carpenters and farmers used chests for storing their implements, as they were nicely shaped and could be placed side by side along the walls of a room.

The closet, which is one of the secret areas in the house, stored many items directly related to everyday life. In sixteenth- and seventeenth-century kitchens, flour, dried fruits, bread, and cheese were often kept in an oaken chest called an ark. Especially in the manor houses, rich ladies had a tendency to prepare and keep seasonings and medicines in chests for the members of their households, but when those items filled too many chests, the chests were placed in the closet. The closet was the private and concealed area, and it was the best storage space in the house.

In Shakespeare's *Pericles*, the closet is mentioned as the place to keep medicine chests. Cerimon, a lord in Ephesus, helps a lady called Thaisa who was thought to have died aboard ship after a difficult birth. Thaisa was in critical condition when she arrived at Ephesus, but she was saved by Cerimon's careful treatment. Cerimon mentions the closet when Thaisa is carried into his house:

> Make a fire within;
> Fetch hither all my boxes in my closet.
> Death may usurp on nature many hours
> And yet the fire of life kindle again
> The o'erpressed spirits. I heard of an Egyptian
> That had nine hours lain, who was
> By good appliance recovered.
>
> (2004: 3.2.79–85)

Cerimon is not introduced as a doctor, but as a lord in Ephesus. However, his closet, like that of rich ladies in the Early Modern period, contained medicine boxes which were linked to Thaisa's recovery from a coma.

Medical people also kept books and receipt books in their chests, alongside their surgical tools and medicines. As there were no bookshelves, people kept books in chests, because books were costly and many books were passed down to their descendants as inherited property. As the printing industry was still under development, universities, churches, and abbeys kept their important books in chests locked with sturdy keys to maintain their condition. Some of the chests found in the library at the University of Oxford, for example, are too big to pass through the door, so that it is considered that they were made inside the room. This proves that books were treated with care, and their condition carefully preserved.

Although books relating to surgery, medicine, or herbs could be obtained from book shops, a more reliable means of transmission in the Early Modern period was family medicine books handed down from generation to generation. Fantastic records of medicine in response to minor daily disorders were written down by aristocratic mothers, in a book called a receipt book. Those books were passed down from mother to daughter as receptacles of knowledge about family medicine. In teaching, both family receipt books and published guides were used as instruction manuals (Whaley 2011: 154). Receipt books conveyed how to cook and otherwise prepare herbs and ointment for treatments.

Another Shakespeare character, Helena in *All's Well that Ends Well*, owns receipt books. Her books were passed down from her father, a famous doctor, Gerard de Narbon:

> The rather will I spare my praises towards him;
> Knowing him is enough. On's bed of death
> Many receipts he gave me; chiefly one,
> Which, as the dearest issue of his practice,
> And of his old experience th' only darling,
> He bade me store up as a triple eye,
> Safer than mine own two; more dear I have so,
> And hearing your high majesty is touch'd

With that malignant cause, wherein the honour
Of my dear father's gift stands chief in power,
I come to tender it and my appliance,
With all bound humbleness.

(1959: 2.1.102–113)

Helena succeeds admirably in curing the French King's fistula, which was regarded as an incurable disease by all the court physicians. This provides evidence that receipts contributed immensely to medicine.

Chests from the Mary Rose show that they were constructed in such a manner as to preserve the objects inside, and they convey the fantastic history of medicine in the Early Modern period through their contents. As the Early Modern chests were outstanding products of the time, they were used as containers for professional or important materials, as well as for items of daily use. Chests therefore played an important role in conveying the accumulated knowledge of time to future generations.

REFERENCES

Barber, N., *Renaissance Medicine* (London: Raintree, 2013).

Cooper, N., *Houses of the Gentry, 1480–1680* (New Haven and London: Yale University Press, 1999).

Elmer, P., and O. P. Grell, *Health, Disease and Society in Europe 1500–1800: A Source Book* (Manchester: Manchester University Press, 2004).

Gloag, J., *A Short Dictionary of Furniture* (London: George Allen and Unwin, 1977).

Knight, L., *Of Books and Botany in Early Modern England: Sixteenth-Century Plants and Print Culture* (Farnham: Ashgate, 2009).

Lindemann, M., *Medicine and Society in Early Modern Europe* (Cambridge: Cambridge University Press, 2010).

Markham, G., *The English Housewife*, ed. by M. R. Best (Montreal and Kingston: McGill-Queen's University Press, 1986).

Mary Rose Museum <http://www.maryrose.org/discover-our-collection/> [accessed 10 February 2015].

Mercer, E., *Furniture 700–1700* (London: Weidenfeld and Nicolson, 1969).

Miyauchi, S., *Boxes* (Tokyo: Hosei University Press, 1991).

Porter, R., *Disease, Medicine and Society in England, 1550–1860*, 2nd edn (Cambridge: Cambridge University Press, 1993).

Science & Society Picture Library <http://www.scienceandsociety.co.uk/results.asp?image=10288238&itemw=4&itemf=0002&itemstep=1&itemx=14> [accessed 10 February 2015].

Shakespeare, William, *All's Well that Ends Well*, ed. by G. K. Hunter (Walton-on-Thames: Thomas Nelson, 1959).

——, *The Merchant of Venice*, ed. by John Russel Brown (London: Thomson Learning, 2001).

——, *Pericles*, ed. by Suzanne Gossett (London: Thomson Learning, 2004).

Singman, J. L., *Daily Life in Elizabethan England* (Westport: Greenwood Press, 1995).

Siraisi, N. G., *Medieval and Early Renaissance Medicine: An Introduction to Knowledge and Practice* (Chicago: University of Chicago Press, 1990).

——, *History, Medicine, and the Traditions of Renaissance Learning* (Ann Arbor: University of Michigan Press, 2007).

Sloan, A. W., *English Medicine in the Seventeenth Century* (Durham: Durham Academic Press, 1996).

Taavitsainen, I., and P. Pahta, eds, *Medical Writing in Early Modern English* (Cambridge: Cambridge University Press, 2011).

Wear, A., *Knowledge & Practice in English Medicine, 1550–1680* (Cambridge: Cambridge University Press, 2000).

Whaley, L., *Women and the Practice of Medical Care in Early Modern Europe, 1400–1800* (New York: Palgrave, 2011).

FIG. 37.1 Open electrotherapy box

37

RUMINATIONS ON AN ELECTROTHERAPEUTIC BOX

Jan Eric Olsén

Size and shape: convenient. **Colour**: black. **Behaviour**: discarded. **Habitat**: homeless. **Distribution**: portable. **Migration**: second-hand market. **Status**: outmoded.

Keywords: transporting, protecting, powering, electrifying, ruminating

KAPUT OBJECT, CONFINED SENSE

THIS IS A BOX CONTAINING AN APPARATUS FOR ELECTROTHERAPEUTIC treatment. I found it in a flea market in Malmö where it was displayed openly so that passers-by could admire its glass electrodes, purple velvet lining, and electric generator. The combination of glass, velvet, and power supply was impossible to resist, even if the machinery did not work. One could tell that the different parts had not been replaced and that the box itself was an original part of the ensemble. Clothed in black embossed paper, with a small handle and two metal clasps, it has an air of discretion and intimacy about it. Obviously, it was made not to disclose its contents. No manufacturer's logo distracts from the uneven touch of its riffled surface. Then again, its handy shape and portable design bear evidence of its prior use: an electrotherapeutic kit for easy transport.

Long before the box ended up in a flea market, it was used to ease numerous kinds of pain that affected the bodies of early-twentieth-century persons. Regarded as a historical object, the box comes with a practice – or at least the remnants of a practice – that can be contextualised with the aid of documents. Had I encountered the box in a museum setting, signs would undoubtedly

FIG. 37.2 Closed electrotherapy box

had provided me with information concerning the medical use of electricity, how the instrument was applied to the body, and what kinds of ailments it was prescribed against. However, it would certainly not have been possible to touch the box. As Fiona Candlin has pointed out, the modern museum space is one that circumscribes the possibility of tactile engagement with the displayed objects (2010: 58). Occasionally, museums will give visitors the opportunity to touch and handle parts of their collections, but these items have been selected by the curators, and tactile engagement with the object in question will only occur under their supervision. If it was vision that first drew my attention to the box in the flea market, it was only by handling the box and its different parts that I first became aware of its original purpose. But touch is not only important as a means to make sense of historical objects. Deeper acquaintance with the box reveals that electrotherapy was a profoundly tactile application to the skin, muscles, and nerves. What follows here is a combination of historical enquiry and flea market curating, which is to say that I approach the box per se as an aficionado of things thrown in the dustbin of history rather than as a professional curator. But first of all, let us place our box in a historical context.

TYING TOGETHER HISTORICAL THREADS

The idea that electricity can be employed for medical reasons can be traced back at least to the eighteenth century, a period in which natural philosophers pondered over the affinity between a possible vital principle that distinguished the living organism from non-living entities and electricity. Empirically, the notion that the spark of life was somehow akin to electricity emerged through the comparison between distinct objects and phenomena such as the Leyden jar (a device to store static electricity), electric fishes such as the torpedo fish, the twitch of dead frogs' legs when stimulated by electricity, and eventually the voltaic pile.[1] An illustrative example of this interest in biological electricity was the study of a torpedo fish that the British colonel John Walsh carried out on the island of Ré, off La Rochelle, in 1772. In a letter to Benjamin Franklin, Walsh gave an account of the electric jolts that the fish emitted and described how the shock could be led through a chain of people whose hands were lowered in tubs of water (1774: 466). In a similar vein, naturalists such as Geoffroy Saint-Hilaire (1803: 398) and Alexander von Humboldt (1806: 6) also marvelled at the shock of the torpedo fish. Both of them drew extensive parallels between the electric nature of the fish and the discharge of physical devices like the Leyden jar and the voltaic pile. In this hybrid landscape of forces, fluids, organic material, and experimental devices we also encounter medical attempts to apply electricity as a treatment against various kinds of somatic disorders.[2]

If the scientific ideas behind our electrotherapeutic box originated in the eighteenth century, it was only during the following century that electrotherapy established itself as a medical cure. By that time, the belief that organic life emanated from a vital principle had become outdated. Instead, physicians who offered their patients electrotherapeutical treatment drew far-reaching parallels between the energy that resides in the human body and the mechanical forces that powered industrial machines such as the steam engine. According to Carolyn Thomas de la Peña, the rise of electrotherapy as a recognised medical practice coincided with the expansive electrification of modern society in the late nineteenth and early twentieth centuries, a period in which electric street lightning, animated signs, trams, and telephones rapidly transformed the habits of urban life, especially in the US (2003: 99). De la Peña describes how electrotherapy provided a medical counterpart to the electrical machines and devices that altered the townscape of modernity. Through analogical inference, the human body could be compared to a modern machine. Both depended on an intake of substances, nutrition, and fuel in order to convert energy into work. In line with this analogy, electrotherapy offered patients an up-to-date cure. If physical afflictions could be cured with electricity, this meant that the body responded in a positive way to the forces that maintained modern society (de la Pena 2003: 99).

A person who is difficult to overlook when talking about electrotherapy is the American physician George Beard. Together with his colleague Alphonso Rockwell, Beard set up the most renowned electrotherapeutical practice of the late nineteenth century, offering electric currents against various kinds of neural and muscular pains. But Beard was not only a practising physician. In a number of studies, he introduced electrotherapy to a wider public and grouped the symptoms that many of his patients suffered from under a common label: neurasthenia. Moreover, by linking neurasthenia to the rise of capitalist society with its competitive and stressful lifestyle, Beard helped define the image of nervousness as an illness that exclusively affected modern civilisations (1881: 6). A lack of nerve force being attributed to them, neurasthenic patients were prescribed electrotherapeutic treatment, which was considered to have an invigorating influence on body and mind.

Beard's practice and writings rendered electrotherapy a fashionable cure. By the 1890s, manufacturers of health-related goods were marketing electrotherapeutic batteries for domestic use. Packaged as a handy and portable technology that came with accompanying manuals, electrotherapeutic equipment was utilised by specialists, unlicensed practitioners, and patients alike (de la Pena 2003: 96). The ease with which battery-powered devices could be purchased, however, made it difficult to distinguish neural specialists from physicians who simply wanted to embellish their practices with the latest trends. In his comprehensive treatise, which he wrote together with Rockwell, Beard raised a warning finger against a too casual approach to electrotherapy: 'There is danger that now, as of old, the details of the applications will be entrusted too much to the patients themselves, or their friends or servants, or, what is but little better, to physicians who know nothing of electro-therapeutics as a science or as an art' (Beard and Rockwell 1875: 250).

INVESTIGATING THE BOX AT HOME

Home again after my visit to the flea market, I begin to investigate my box with much curiosity. It is heavier than I first thought – obviously the glass electrodes tricked me into believing that it would be lighter – although its handle enables a steadfast grip and smooth transportation. As we saw above, portable electrotherapeutic kits were available for personal use already in the late nineteenth century. Compared with earlier attempts to apply electricity to the ill body, these devices made the technology less dependent on a particular space or clinic. While we are on the subject of stationary techniques, I cannot help but think of the cumbersome equipment that illustrated George Adams's exposition on electric medicine from 1785 (FIGURE 37.3).

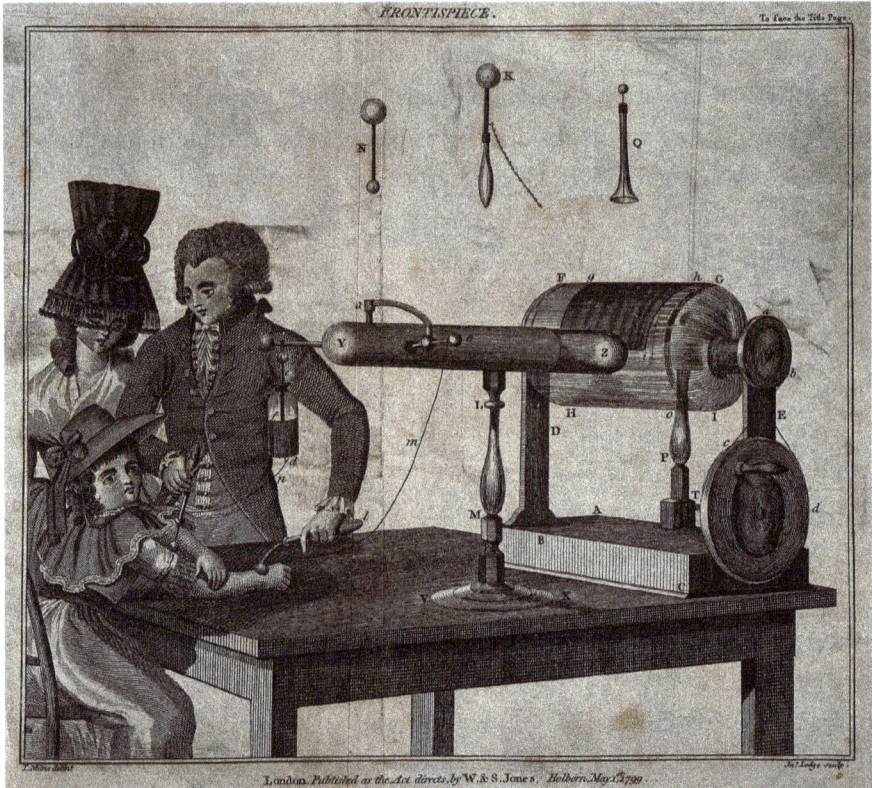

FIG. 37.3 George Adams's prototype; 1785 essay on electricity or a later edition

In the picture we see a doctor applying electric currents to a child seated at the edge of a huge electric apparatus. A hundred years later, and the much smaller apparatus could be moved with very little effort. (It was not only electrotherapy that became portable in this sense. The doctor's bag is another object that was intended for carrying, a strong symbol of medical practice in the patient's home). Portable or secured, the history of electrotherapy revolves around one and the same idea: that electricity, whether akin to a vital principle or simply congruous with nerve force, could relieve patients from their incessant pains. This is also something that my box clearly testifies to. It is no coincidence that the electric battery inside the box is labelled *Innerva*, a name that brings to mind the physiological principle of innervation and its explicit relation to the nervous system, its extension in the body and the connection between nervous stimulus and action. In a broader sense, a battery called *Innerva* also evokes the organic metaphors that were used to conceptualise a new scientific understanding of the body at the turn of the twentieth century.[3] But let us not read too much into the choice of label. Instead let us see what more information can be extracted from the material and tactile qualities of the box itself.

As mentioned above, the box is clothed in embossed black paper. Visually as well as tactually, it resembles saffiano leather. Clearly, the manufacturer wanted to give the box a refined impression without going to too much expense. After all, it was the electrical apparatus and the glass electrodes that were the key components. Therefore, in order to protect the therapeutic devices from damage, the inside of the box was covered with velvet and provided with clips that keep the frail glass pieces in place. This is definitely an important but inconspicuous part of the equipment, and one that emphasises the tactile approach of the electrotherapeutic technique: to press the heated glass electrodes against parts of the body that were sore, tense, and generally fatigued. If the aim of the treatment was to restore muscles and nerves, the means to do this was to reach the hidden organs via the skin. In this sense, electrotherapy was mainly a tactile therapy that stood in close relation to other tactile surface-to-depth techniques such as palpation, percussion, and massage. On closer inspection, this basic fact is an intrinsic feature of the box itself. From the riffled black cover to the soft velvet interior on which the cool glass devices rest, the box literally draws our attention to the texture of its material form. Not unlike jewellery, the glass electrodes lie on the bed of velvet, waiting to be electrically charged and applied to the skin of the patient. Their delicate and transparent appearance forms a strong contrast to the black and solid generator that is placed on the opposite side. It is an enthralling thought that, if the machine still worked, electricity would travel from the generator to the glass electrodes and diffuse the latter with heat. But as it is now the machine is *kaput*. The box contains an obsolete remedy that cannot be made to work, and the transparent electrodes and the opaque generator remain two pieces of technology that can no longer communicate with one another.

CONSULTING THE TRADE CATALOGUES

Tactile examination can yield valuable information concerning the nature of objects and their intended use. Yet when it comes to dating the box from the flea market, my knowledge of materials and the design of health-related devices was insufficient. For all I knew, the electrotherapeutic box could have been manufactured sometime between the late nineteenth century and the 1930s, an all too imprecise date. Therefore, in order to specify the historical period, I ordered a couple of trade catalogues – originally used as advertising brochures for electrotherapeutical kits – from the University Library of Lund and sifted through them in search of historical clues. Eventually, my archival efforts paid off as I found an image of what appeared to be an almost exact copy of my electrotherapeutical equipment, marketed as a 'high frequency generator "Texal Violette", the true quality apparatus' (Trade catalogue 1925). Printed in Östersund, Sweden, the catalogue provides a concise introduction to high frequency electricity and its putative effect on rheumatic disorders, sciatica, gout, insomnia, headaches, nervousness, and alopecia. Claims are also made for the beneficial effect of violet rays on sleep, viability, work capacity, appetite, and digestion, as well as their curative influence on the nervous system (Trade catalogue 1925: 8). High frequency electricity, unlike induction current, produced a barely palpable violet-coloured current that permeated the body down to the cell level. The catalogue also includes a price list of electrodes, accessories, and spare parts that were in stock.

A second catalogue, printed a few years earlier, emphasises the painless procedure of the violet rays. Compared to previous electrotherapeutical techniques that were more or less painful and unpleasant, high frequency electricity was announced as a testament to the scientific progress within the electro-medical field (Trade catalogue 1920: 2). This catalogue proudly states that the portable box has finally made electrotherapy available for everyone (Trade catalogue 1920: 18). Although they are not manuals in the true sense of the word, trade catalogues such as these suggest that the portable violet ray kits were intended for personal use. On closer inspection, the target group seems to have been women. At least one of the catalogues is illustrated with two pictures of women applying glass electrodes to their bodies. The gendered nature of health products such as the violet ray apparatus is also something that de la Peña discusses in her study. Whereas electrotherapeutical products intended for men alluded to the productive and societal aspects of electricity, articles targeted at women were instead marketed as beauty products that arrested bodily decay (de la Peña 2003: 125). To what extent Swedish products reiterated the gendered notions of the North American market cannot be answered within the framework of this present essay, but there is no reason to believe that things differed all that much in Sweden, even if the catalogues in question, apart from these two images, do not display stereotypical images of gender. What consultation of these catalogues does reveal, however, is that by the 1920s electrotherapy had established itself as a commodity meant for domestic use.

CLOSING REMARKS

Let us now try to define our electrotherapeutic box in more general terms. Regarded as a piece of medical equipment, it was launched at the decline of electrotherapy as a renowned cure, in the 1920s. Technologically standardised and culturally embedded in modern society, it describes the course of the phenomenon of electro-medicine, from a spectacular and experimental agent in the eighteenth century to a theoretically grounded and socially secured procedure in the twentieth century, no longer associated with painful shocks and jolts but recommended nevertheless against a plethora of ailments and maladies. This would be the historical classification. The box carries within it the promise of previous prototypes, countless attempts to channel electricity in an appropriate way, numerous devices applied to the body of the patient and, one might assume, the recurrent twitch when too strong a current was applied. But of course the box per se does not tell us all this, especially since it is out of order. In his writings on media materialism, Wolfgang Ernst distinguishes the cultural life span of a medium from its operational life span (2011: 240). Even if the cultural life span of an object has come to an end, this does not mean that the object has ceased to exist in a functional sense. Technically speaking, the electrotherapeutic box from the flea market could still have been working. Its cultural era has long since disappeared, but, except for its technical demise, its status as an object is unaltered. We can toy with the knob, run our fingers over the smooth velvet cover, take out the glass electrodes to admire their handicraft, and even try them against our skin. But in the end its mechanism, its electrically embedded *Eigenzeit* – to use Ernst's term – is dormant. By turning to historical documents, we can evoke the golden era of electrotherapy and place our box in its historical context, but taken for what it is, a broken box that I stumbled over in a flea market, its initial purpose has ceased to work.

Unable to experience the glow of violet rays as they pervade the glass electrodes, we are left with the box itself and its material evidence. A classification derived from its inert parts will once again underscore its portable design, its riffled and smooth texture, the tranquil isolation of the transparent glass devices and opaque generator as they remain out of contact from each other, and last but not least, its morphological structure in which the different glass electrodes, through their very form, indicate that this is a machine intended for the human body and its different folds: one electrode is shaped as a comb, another one is designed for the ears, a third one for the rectum, and so on. In the absence of its electrical function, we must turn to these immediate attributes in order to establish an overarching principle for this broken machine within a whole box. As mentioned above, electrotherapy can be described as a surface-to-depth technique that treats the body in a physical, tactile way. It does not deal with the body in a representative manner, but directs its entire energy towards the body as flesh. This non-representative tactic distinguishes electrotherapy from other medical surface-to-depth techniques such as x-rays, which redirect our focus from the flesh of the body to the image on the screen.

Electrotherapy is all about skin and flesh. It is an instrument or a medium that makes use of the skin to massage the flesh with electricity. Notwithstanding its electric function, it is essentially a tactile technique. As a matter of fact, had the box functioned properly, the sight of violet rays emerging in the void of the glass electrodes would most likely have affected my overall impression in favour of a more visually oriented account. But strictly speaking, what kind of touch is mediated through the electrotherapeutic technique, and where in the body does it make itself known? Aristotle once remarked that the sense of touch tends to evade us since it lacks a clear organ, in contrast to the other senses which reside in more defined parts of the body. Is the sense organ of touch situated in the flesh or is the flesh only a medium that mediates sensation to a primary internal organ (Aristotle 1907: 97)? Applied to the electrotherapeutic box, we could ask with Aristotle whether the main target for the current was muscles, nerves, cells, or even a more profound organ whose fluids permeated the flesh with life. Depending on where in history we choose to look, we will run up against different answers. Skin, flesh, or imponderable force, our box comes to a halt here.

NOTES

1   For a thorough account of the debates on animal electricity between Luigi Galvani and Alessandro Volta see Pera 1992.

2   See, for instance, the British optician and instrument maker George Adams's essay on electricity, which included a special section on electrotherapy; Adams 1785.

3   Two studies that unfold this topic vividly are Killen (2006) and Otis (2001).

REFERENCES

Adams, G., An Essay on Electricity. *Explaining the Theory and Practice of that Useful Science and the Mode of Applying it to Medical Purposes* (London, 1785).

Aristotle, *De Anima*, trans. by R. D. Hicks (Cambridge: Cambridge University Press, 1907).

Beard, G. M., and A. D. Rockwell, *A Practical Treatise on the Medical and Surgical Uses of Electricity* (London: H. K. Lewis, 1875).

Beard, G. M., *American Nervousness: Its Causes and Consequences, a Supplement to Nervous Exhaustion (Neurasthenia)* (New York: Putnam, 1881).

Candlin, F., *Art, Museums and Touch* (Manchester: Manchester University Press, 2010).

Ernst, W., 'Media Archaeography: Method and Machine versus History and Narrative of Media', in E. Huhtamo and J. Parikka, eds, *Media Archaeology. Approaches, Applications, and Implications* (Berkeley: University of California Press, 2011).

Geoffroy, E., 'Vergleichende Anatomie der electrischen Organe des Zitterrochens, Zitteraals und Zitterwelses', *Annalen der Physik*, 14 (1803).

von Humboldt, A., 'Versuche über die electrischen Fische', *Annalen der Physik*, 22 (1806).

Killen, A., *Berlin Electropolis: Shock, Nerves, and German Modernity* (Berkeley: University of California Press, 2006).

Otis, L., *Networking: Communicating with Bodies and Machines in the Nineteenth Century* (Ann Arbor: University of Michigan Press, 2001).

de la Peña, C. T., *The Body Electric: How Strange Machines Built the Modern American* (New York: New York University Press, 2003).

Pera, M., *The Ambiguous Frog: The Galvani-Volta Controversy on Animal Electricity* (Princeton: Princeton University Press, 1992).

Trade Catalogue, *Högfrekventelektriciteten och de violetta strålarna samt dess betydelse vid behandling av sjukdomar* (Stockholm: Lincoln Bloms Boktryckeri, 1920), no author.

Trade Catalogue, *Högfrekvenselektriciteten och de violetta strålarnas medicinska egenskaper (elekroterapi)* (Östersund: Affärstryckeriet, 1925), no author.

Walsh, J., 'Of the Electric Property of the Torpedo', *Philosophical Transactions of the Royal Society*, 63 (1773–1774).

FIG. 38.1 Reliquary with scenes from the martyrdom of St Thomas Becket, c.1173–1180; British; silver, partial gilt, niello, garnet cabochon; 5.5 × 7 × 4.7 cm (source: Metropolitan Museum of Art: Accession no. 17.190.520; gift of J. Pierpont Morgan, 1917; image provided by the Metropolitan Museum of Art courtesy of Open Access for Scholarly Content)

38

RELIQUARY: A BOX FOR A RELIC

Lucy Razzall

Origin: in religious cultures and practices since ancient times, especially Christianity, as containers for relics – body parts and other earthly remains from holy persons, saints, and martyrs. **Function**: to protect human remains considered sacred, for display and veneration, and to provide a focal point for individual and communal acts of devotion to the dead saint. **Appearance**: reliquaries can be made from many possible materials, including wood, marble, ivory, alabaster, stone, glass, and crystal. They are often richly decorated with precious metals, precious stones, and other materials which might point to their sanctity. They might have glass panels so that the relic can be viewed from outside, and they may be labelled or inscribed with the name of the person whose relics they purportedly contain. **Shape**: any box can become a reliquary, by virtue of containing a relic, but reliquaries are usually specially made. They might take the form of a simple box or a much more elaborate container in the shape of a locket, a body part, or a building. **Size:** very wide-ranging, from tiny boxes that might be held in one hand, or worn as a piece of jewellery, to huge shrines the size of a building. **Habitat**: holy places across the world, especially Catholic shrines, chapels, churches, cathedrals, which often become pilgrimage destinations, attracting visitors seeking physical or spiritual succour from the relics. **Interaction:** reliquaries are the focus of devotional activities to the dead saint and to God. They might be static or moved around in religious processions and ceremonies. Pilgrims to relics might touch or kiss the reliquary or pray in front of it. The reliquary might be within reach or kept at a distance. **Age**: reliquaries and relics survive from ancient times to the present day. Reliquaries challenge earthly temporalities, resisting material decay and enshrining the relic as part of the timeless glories of heaven.

Keywords: enshrining, sanctifying, framing, revealing, concealing, occluding, protecting, transporting

IN THE AUTUMN OF 2009, SOME REMAINS OF ST THÉRÈSE OF LISIEUX WERE brought to the UK for the first time, where they were taken on a tour of cathedrals, churches, convents, schools, hospitals, a university, a hospice, and a prison. St Thérèse, often referred to as 'the Little Flower of Jesus', was a nineteenth-century French Carmelite nun, who died from tuberculosis at the age of twenty-four. She was canonised in 1925 and has since become one of the most popular modern Catholic saints, honoured for the deep commitment to her Christian faith that she showed in the face of intense physical suffering. Her earthly remains undertake a perpetual journey around the world, travelling in an alabaster box. The alabaster box is locked inside a wooden casket elaborately decorated with gold and marble, which is in turn displayed in a large glass case.

Each of these concentrically-arranged receptacles signifies something about what is within. The innermost box entombs the bodily remains, whereas the next box, a wooden casket with an elaborate architectural structure, encloses them in a basilica-like form, a symbolic representation of the universal Church to which the saint brings blessings. The final layer, the glass case, is completely transparent (tarnished only by the ghostly marks left by pious hands and lips as they touch and kiss the case), allowing the inner container to be seen with clarity. The transparency of this outermost container suggests the ready access to the holy that the object provides, while at the same time separating off and protecting its sacred contents from the outside world.

These three containers are reliquaries: they exist to enclose their contents, which are considered holy relics. A relic is an object associated with a dead holy person; it is usually a bodily fragment, such as a piece of bone or flesh, or a tooth, hair, or fingernail. Other material remains, like garments, or personal belongings, can become relics too. The earthly traces of a dead person, however, do not assume relic status automatically. The transformation of material remains into holy relics worthy of veneration has to be brought about by the beliefs and practices that surround them, that is, by the particular social and cultural contexts in which they exist. Enclosure inside a reliquary is often a crucial part of this process of imbuing sacred status upon something otherwise very ordinary. A bare bone is anonymous, silent, and possibly even repellent, but when placed inside a reliquary it becomes a holy fragment, which is believed to have inherent supernatural, salvific, or magical power. A reliquary is therefore one of the most tangible and formal manifestations of the convictions that determine where the sacred can be found.

From as early as the third century AD, relics of Christ and the saints provided essential points of contact between earth and heaven, breaking down the barriers that separated the worlds of the living and the dead. As the Christian faith took over from antique pagan beliefs, the remains of holy men and women had the potential to become conduits of divine power, bringing spiritual succour and miracles to the faithful. By the early medieval period, relics were integral to religious practice: the consecration of a medieval church required holy remains to be installed inside it, usually in the altar (Brown 1981). The entire building was sanctified by the relic it contained, and so the church itself became a kind of macrocosmic reliquary. While the relic served as a bridge between the material and the spiritual, and concentrated the two together within the enclosed space of the reliquary, it also transcended the bounds of the reliquary to sanctify the whole building. The architectural structure of the church pointed outwards and upwards to heaven as well as inwards to what the building contained, acknowledging the ultimate source of the sacred but also inscribing sacred presence within itself.

In medieval Europe, relics were the focus of individual devotion as well as elaborate public liturgies, rituals, and ceremonies. Pilgrimage to places honouring significant relics was essential to the Christian life. While Jerusalem was the most important pilgrimage destination, the faithful were also drawn to many other locations associated with the relics of particular saints and martyrs, where they sought physical or spiritual relief or other divine favours. At these sites, the relic was usually located at the heart of various concentric layers – enclosed inside a richly jewelled reliquary, which might be protected by another container such as a chest, which in turn was contained in a sanctuary, shrine, or chapel, which was part of the larger architectural structure of a church or cathedral. At the end of a long journey, the pilgrim's gradual progression through these increasingly hidden spaces increased the momentousness of his or her eventual encounter with the relic (Turner and Turner 1978: 22–23).

The functions of the reliquary are many, and their theological and material significance are closely interwoven. The hundreds of examples extant in Catholic churches across continental Europe (especially in Italy and Spain), and in museum collections, reveal the ways in which these containers were required to 'protect, hide, temporarily reveal, draw attention to, explain, assert ownership of, or make more visually exciting their often desiccated contents' (Cannon 2005: 240). Only a few medieval English reliquaries survive today, but from written sources we can gain a sense of the richness of the treasures that embellished religious institutions across much of Europe until the Reformation. At Durham Cathedral, according to a late sixteenth-century description of the monastic foundation before its dissolution in 1538, the glorious shrine of the Anglo-Saxon bishop Cuthbert, one of England's northern patron saints, contained 'almeryes [boxes] of fine wenscote [wainscot, or superior oak imported from northern Europe], being uarnished and finelye painted and gilted finely ouer with little images uerye seemly and beautifull to behould, for the reliques belonginge to St Cuthbert to lye in' (Anon. 1903: 17).

While the reliquaries for St Cuthbert's remains were made from 'fine wenscote', a wide variety of other materials could be used in the construction of receptacles for relics, including bone, ivory, metal, glass, crystal, and marble. Many of these substances had scriptural associations with the heavenly realm, as in the description of the New Jerusalem in Revelation 21, and they also signalled the spiritual purity and divine value of the box's contents. As well as being 'uarnished and finelye painted and gilted', as above, reliquaries could also be encrusted with enamelled images, metalwork, and precious stones, and thus were some of the most valuable religious objects in monetary as well as spiritual terms.

In 2010, an exhibition at the British Museum, *Treasures of Heaven: Saints, Relics and Devotion in Medieval Europe*, brought together many different medieval relics and their reliquaries, a range which demonstrated the astonishing richness of the materials and the impressive technical skill involved in making these objects (for the exhibition catalogue see Bagnoli and Klein 2010). Many medieval reliquaries were simple, box-shaped receptacles, but they could also take the form of a locket or pendant, a Eucharistic monstrance, a folding diptych or triptych, or a container for multiple relics, each enclosed in its own tiny box-like compartment. They were also often elaborate architectural forms which emphasised their own identity as a shrine – a cathedral in miniature (Walker Bynum 1995: 202–03).

By the later Middle Ages, reliquaries increasingly exposed and explored materiality in complicated ways. The relationship between the container and its content could be more explicitly one of physical correspondence. This period saw the rise of a distinctive type of reliquary, sometimes called a 'speaking reliquary', which took the shape of a human body part, such as a head, arm, or foot, constructed to glorify the corporeal portion it purported to contain by reconstructing it in the finest possible materials, while still recognising its fragmentary nature (Hahn 1997: 20–31; Walker Bynum and Gerson 1997: 3–7).

Reliquaries could visually engage with the relationship between their own form and their contents in other striking ways. A twelfth-century casket containing some of Thomas Becket's blood, now in the Metropolitan Museum of Art (see illustration above), is inscribed with the words INTUS SANGUIS EST SANCTE TOME SANCTUS TOMAS ACCIDITUR ('within is the blood of St Thomas, St Thomas is killed'). The large imitation ruby on top of the box reinforces the reflexive dynamic between container and content, its glowing redness reminding the viewer visually of the precious substance hidden inside. Like this one, many reliquaries bear engraved text with the name of the saint whose remains they purportedly contain, and such inscriptions work as further enshrining and enclosing techniques. Another kind of reliquary, the 'ostensory', emphasises its displaying function, often featuring hosts of angels thrusting the relic towards the viewer (Schmidt 2007: 202–03). Other reliquaries feature glass panels through which the enclosed relics can be seen or at least partially glimpsed. These examples illustrate just a few of the many variations that can be played upon the reliquary's basic box form.

The reliquary, and other multiple layers surrounding the medieval relic, have an essential theological function, articulating the relic's identity as a material fragment of the sacred. The material features of the reliquary often say something about the dynamic between container and contained: a reliquary might frame, conceal, and reveal its contents all at once. This theological function is inextricably bound up with the other purposes of these containers. As a sealed box, the reliquary protects the relic from decay and damage by human touch or exposure to the elements, and both the relic and the reliquary may have to be further protected against theft or desecration.

The material layers enclosing the relic are thus implicated in the complicated issue of access to the holy. Medieval pilgrims embarked on their journey to a shrine with the hope that they would be able to gaze upon or possibly even make direct bodily contact with the relic it contained. While physical proximity to the relic was desirable, the relationship between the individual pilgrim and the relic was typically defined by a tension between closeness and distance, or a 'strategy of material occlusion' (Malo 2008: 88). The displaying of a relic was paradoxically often as much about emphatic enclosure and concealment, keeping the faithful at a distance, as it was about exposure. The reliquary sanctified and protected the relic, but also enabled access to the relic to be carefully controlled. This 'occlusion' of the relic was not only material, as the relic could also be surrounded by powerfully obfuscating social rituals, which reinforced the boundaries of access and control. Rather than direct contact with the relic, pilgrims may well have had to be satisfied with just a glimpse of the reliquary held aloft to a huge crowd during a procession.

When St Thérèse's reliquary was taken to a church in Taunton, Somerset, in 2009, journalists reported that 'people queued patiently to approach the relics, some kneeling on the floor beside the case, others resting their foreheads on it. One woman was tentative about touching the glass, as though it was a precious object; others rubbed the case with both hands as though it was warm like a radiator' (de Bertodano and Lamb 2009: 13). People were 'tentative' in their approach to this imposing object, but they desired physical contact, touching different parts of their bodies against it. Their caresses inspire a simile – it was as if the glass 'was warm like a radiator' – which offers an interpretation of the way in which the reliquary operates in relation to its contents. The glass case assumes a kind of porosity, suggested by its transparency, whereby the holiness of its contents is emitted invisibly, to be absorbed through the power of touch. Historically, the spiritual bounteousness of relics was sometimes manifested in even more tangible, physical ways, through generous outpourings of blood, water, oil, or scent. According to the thirteenth-century hagiographer Jacobus de Voragine, St Nicholas 'was buried in a marble tomb, and a fountain of oil began to flow from his head and a fountain of water from his feet. Even today a holy oil issues from his members and brings health to many' (1993: 25). There is a specific term, 'myroblyte', for a saint whose remains exude miracle-working liquids – in these cases, the porosity of the reliquary is part of its miraculous potential.

In the sixteenth century, the Protestant Reformation changed the religious landscape of Europe forever. During its most violent periods, many traditional receptacles for the sacred – including shrines, instruments of the Mass, contentious books, and reliquaries – were systematically destroyed across northern Europe. This literal desecration was matched by a rhetorical offensive against traditional ideologies and practices – including the veneration of relics – in an attempt to empty and expose as false the 'vessels' of Catholic doctrine. Some reliquaries, along with other confiscated items from church treasuries, were turned into secular objects, while others became fugitive objects, lovingly preserved by recusant Catholics in secret.

The reliquary not only offers the physical protection and transportation of a relic, but also works as a crucial boundary of belief. For those who believe in the inherent qualities of the relic as a sacred object, the reliquary enshrines the relic, setting it apart from the profane world. Yet critiques of relics written by sixteenth-century Protestants, including those by Jean Calvin in 1543, sought to shatter the reliquary in ideological terms – to destroy any notion that the reliquary could enclose a fragment of the sacred. Reformers saw the veneration of relics as idolatrous and superstitious, and their arguments reveal the ways in which they turned the material form of the reliquary to their own rhetorical ends. Such denouncements express suspicion of the reliquary as a dark, secretive box that contains merely rotting animal bones, while deceiving the faithful into believing that it contains the remains of a holy person – and furthermore, making the outrageous suggestion that these bones offer access to divine power.

The multiple enclosures in reliquaries and shrines were evidence, according to reformers, of the inherent falsehood of all relics, the darkness of the reliquary betraying the metaphorical darkness of unreformed religious doctrine and practices. For the Counter-Reformation, however, relics became more important than ever as tools of evangelism, and despite the polemical surge against them, many relics retained the status of mementoes or historical curiosities. Some relics irrevocably transformed their reliquaries, so that their presence was felt even when they were long gone: in the words of historian Alexandra Walsham, when 'the relics in question have been lost, destroyed, or confiscated, the containers themselves have a tendency to become surrogate foci of devotion and reverence' (2010: 12). The emptiness of the reliquary might speak to the faithful just as powerfully as the relic itself.

The reliquary may ultimately be seen as less precious than its contents, but it employs the splendour of earthly riches to signal what the inscrutable fragment it contains cannot say on its own. The relic is a metonym – a part of a body standing in for the whole body, and an earthly fragment standing in for the greater glory of the divine – but the reliquary itself is 'both a metaphor for its means of conveying meaning, and the instrument that makes this possible'. The relic-reliquary dynamic produces a 'complex effect whereby contained and containing are interchangeable, and the borders between them are indeterminate even as the containing act continues to articulate itself in the object's physical features' (Chaganti 2008: 15).

As boxes with multiple material possibilities, reliquaries engage intensely with their contents. The relic itself is inherently paradoxical, being fragmentary and yet also complete, a full manifestation of divine presence in a small scrap of profane material. While a relic is usually something very humble, the beauty of the reliquary that encloses it insists that it is something beyond earthly value. The reliquary may enable a dead saint to move across great distances, as opposed to being permanently immured at one site, and also to be present in several places simultaneously. The temporal aspect of the relic is crucial too; preserved inside the reliquary, the fragment of the saint is set in motion, potentially perpetually so, resisting decay and the sense of loss in a journey through time. In this material denial of putrefaction, the reliquary offers a more complicated picture of temporality, and plays a crucial role in establishing the relic as part of the timeless glory of heaven.

Relics are objects around which many important questions about devotion, cult, and art coalesce. Although the focus here has been on the Christian tradition, relics are also important in the Islamic and Buddhist faiths. They are often congruent with or closely related to other holy objects, such as images, statues, and tombs – and they can reveal much about religious and cultural beliefs surrounding the dead. The ever-popular devotion to St Thérèse of Lisieux is just one example of the enduring significance of relics for Catholic

Christians today, and her travelling reliquary vividly illustrates the transformative potential of all such holy boxes, to turn their profane contents into eternal sources of the sacred.

REFERENCES

Anon., *Rites of Durham, Being A Description or Brief Declaration of all the Ancient Monuments, Rites, & Customs Belonging or being within the Monastical Church of Durham before the Suppression* (Durham: Andrews & Co, 1903).

Bagnoli, M., and H. A. Klein, eds, *Treasures of Heaven: Saints, Relics and Devotion in Medieval Europe* (New Haven: Yale University Press, 2010).

de Bertodano, I., and C. Lamb, 'It's as if They Need Thérèse', *The Tablet*, 26 September 2009, pp. 13–14.

Brown, P., *The Cult of the Saints: Its Rise and Function in Latin Christianity* (Chicago: University of Chicago Press, 1981).

Cannon, J., 'Afterword', in S. J. Cornelison and S. B. Montgomery, eds, *Images, Relics, and Devotional Practices in Medieval and Renaissance Italy* (Tempe: Arizona State University Press, 2005).

Chaganti, S., *The Medieval Poetics of the Reliquary: Enshrinement, Inscription, Performance* (New York: Palgrave Macmillan, 2008).

Hahn, C., 'The Voices of the Saints: Speaking Reliquaries', *Gesta*, 36 (1997): 20–31.

Malo, R., 'The Pardoner's Relics (and Why They Matter the Most)', *The Chaucer Review*, 43 (2008): 82–102.

Schmidt, V., 'Curtains, *Revelation*, and Pictorial Reality in Late Medieval and Renaissance Italy', in K. M. Rudy, and B. Baert, eds, *Weaving, Veiling, and Dressing: Textiles and their Metaphors in the Late Middle Ages* (Turnhout: Brepols, 2007), pp. 191–214.

Turner, V., and E. Turner, *Image and Pilgrimage in Christian Culture* (New York: Columbia University Press, 1978).

de Voragine, J., *The Golden Legend: Readings on the Saints*, trans. by William Granger Ryan, 2 vols. (Princeton: Princeton University Press, 1993).

Walker Bynum, C., *The Resurrection of the Body in Western Christianity, 200–1336* (New York: Columbia University Press, 1995).

Walker Bynum, C., and P. Gerson, 'Body-Part Reliquaries and Body Parts in the Middle Ages', *Gesta*, 36 (1997): 3–7.

Walsham, A., 'Introduction: Relics and Remains', *Past and Present*, Supplement 5 (2010): 9–36.

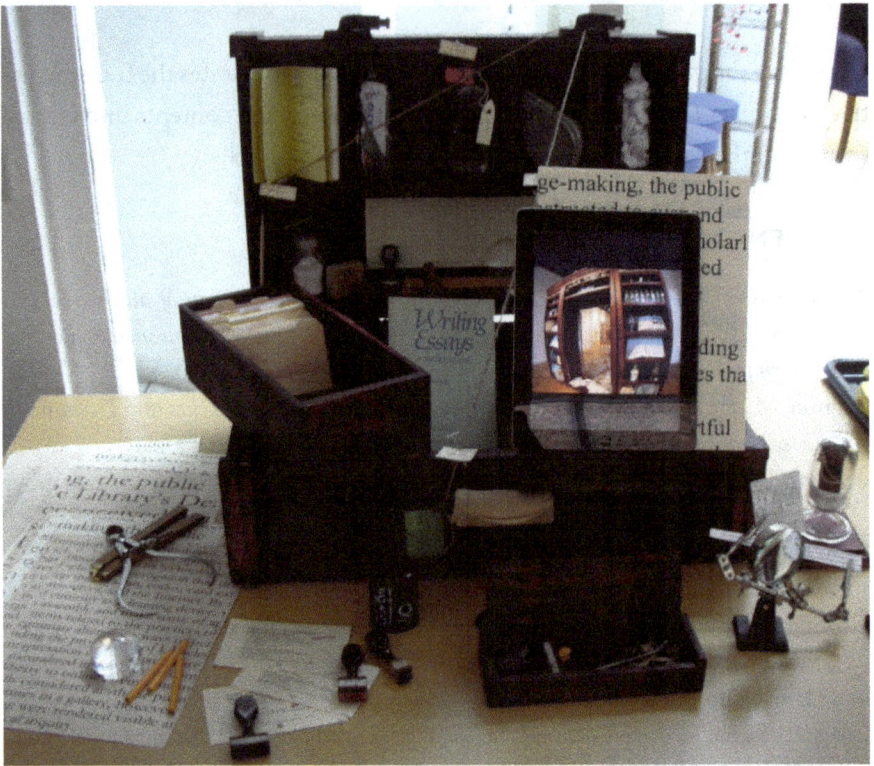

FIG. 39.1 Research Box, on display

FIG. 39.2 Research Box, in closed form

39

THE RESEARCH BOX

Bonnie Mak and Julia Pollack

TAXONOMY

LEVEL	DESCRIPTION
Kingdom	Objects
Phylum	Rectangular Objects
Class	Objects called Boxes
Order	Portable Boxes
Family	Boxes that Open
Genus	Wooden boxes
Species	Research Box

Keywords: information infrastructure, knowledge production, performance, publication

DESCRIPTIVE 'METADATA'

Box: research box.

Function: to make infrastructures of knowledge visible and viable for study.

Conservation Status: endangered. Very restricted range and limited population size make this species extremely vulnerable. To date, only one specimen has been positively identified.

Description: rectangular in its closed position, with protrusions of handle, clasps, hinges, and ornamented corner details. Approximately the size and shape of a small suitcase. When performing, the box adopts an open, sprawling habit (**FIGURE 39.1**).

Colour: reddish-brown and mottled with light streaks. Metallic pieces are dark brown and bronze (**FIGURE 39.2**).

Behaviour: Prefers human companionship (**FIGURE 39.3**). Puts on a display in academic and community venues. This performance, also known as an exhibition, involves the extrusion of the box's interior parts. Incorporated into the display are objects related to scholarly research, in an arrangement intended to make visible the practices and infrastructures of knowledge. Performances can be many minutes long, and frequently prompt a dialogue with human interlocutors.

FIG. 39.3 Research Box prefers human companionship

When on display, the research box opens in the manner of a clamshell; its lid stands at a ninety-degree angle to the rest of the body. The inside of the lid is subdivided into compartments that house glass bottles, measuring devices, and other paraphernalia associated with the practices of research (**FIGURE 39.4**). During performances, a metallic arm from inside the box will extend upward and outward, with an easel-like appendage at its terminus that is used to showcase items such as books, images, and iPads. Sheltered inside the box is a smaller, free-standing box that is rectangular in shape, with no lid. This smaller box detaches from the research box and becomes a card catalogue that itemises the contents of the display.

By generating a safe space for expressions of surprise, awe, curiosity, and discovery in its immediate environment, the research box guards against hostile reactions. The box thus employs charm to attract interlocutors and divert potential predators. The research box is also able to camouflage itself, and does so with regularity. When pressed, it takes on the language of a particular milieu, and adapts its display accordingly. The flexibility of its performance helps the box appeal to the widest possible audience.

One of the most remarkable features of the research box is its ability to bestow material dimensions upon the processes of thinking and research. In so doing, the box makes visible the infrastructures of knowledge production, which in turn recommends them for scrutiny. For example, the contents of the research box sometimes include bottles of angry tears from a frustrated researcher and sweat from the brow of a librarian. In other performances, different embodiments of scholarly practice may be featured. Individuated in this way, the processes of academic activity are able to be seen and studied. The research box not only makes the infrastructures of knowledge perceptible, but also legitimates them as objects of investigation.

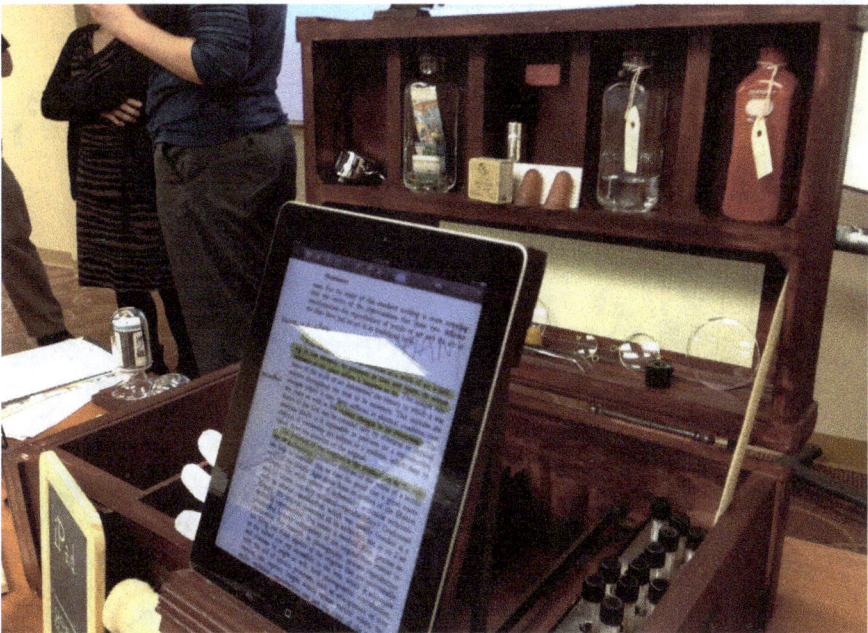

FIG. 39.4 Research Box, detail of performance

Sound: The research box is usually silent. However, it may make a clicking or rattling noise if especially agitated.

Habitat: Urban environments, usually academic. Considers rooms inside man-made buildings suitable for habitation. Roosts mainly on table-tops that are often near sources of natural light. Requires regular conversation and interaction with humans to thrive.

Distribution: Makes its home near its birthplace at the western edge of a major research university in the American Midwest.

Migration: Irregular flight pattern, dependent on opportunities and enticements for display.

Field Marks: Although its skeletal system is highly adapted for travel, the body of this unique specimen betrays signs of the hardships of age (**FIGURE 39.5**). Damage has been detected on both the exterior and interior of the box.

FIG. 39.5 Research Box, field marks

The vulnerability of this specimen has been recognised by officials in Athens, who have affixed a large red label that reads 'fragile'. Captured, marked with a green tag, and released by Athens International Airport (AIA) Security, Station O, Zone N, on 24 July 2012, at 10:19 am. Recaptured by the same authorities on 2 August 2012, at 6:33 am, tagged at Station O, Zone Z.

The box has been marked with a label of ownership by the State of Illinois of the United States of America.

FIELD NOTES

1) Kavala

The first significant sighting of the research box occurred on 24 July 2012. The box was spotted on a rooftop of a hotel in Kavala, in north-eastern Greece, overlooking the city's port (**FIGURE 39.6**). Two days later, the research box was observed on display at the Municipal Tobacco Warehouse, at an event that

FIG. 39.6 Research Box, in Kavala

brought together boxes from across the globe (**FIGURE 39.7**). The functions of the research box were compared with those of other boxes, including boxes for children's games, tobacco, musical instruments, and medicine, as well as artistic interpretations of boxes.

In its performance in Kavala, the research box exhibited alternative ways to measure the labours of scholarship in the humanities. Such work includes the search for relevant resources in the library; the curatorial support that negotiates access to those materials; and the subsequent and arduous process of writing, re-writing, revising, and editing. For instance, the sweat of a librarian was bottled for display, and presented next to a copy of the 1959 edition of Melvil Dewey's *Dewey Decimal Classification*, a library classification scheme, devised in the late nineteenth century, that correlates the subjects of books with a system of decimal numbers. The performance of these items in the research box attempted to make material the often-invisible practices related to the production of knowledge.

FIG. 39.7 Research Box, on display in the Kavala Municipal Tobacco Warehouse

The infrastructures around knowledge have been carefully cultivated by librarians through time, and it is through such work that scholars now encounter, engage with, and comprehend both primary and secondary sources. These disciplinary systems, moreover, are not static, and change in response to institutional, societal, and other pressures. The malleability of such infrastructures was highlighted in the research box in its adaptable card catalogue. The index card for the particular edition of Dewey proposed that although the book was once assigned the number 025.4, indicating that it should be understood as concerning 'subject control' or classification, it could be given a different number. Indeed, by assigning the book a new number based on its contribution to the exhibition, the research box endowed the 1959 edition of the *Dewey Decimal Classification* with another significance: it should now be considered as having to do with 'Museums, Including educational functions, collecting and preparation of materials for exhibit'. With this example, the research box made visible the ways that the provision and interpretation of information can shift over time. The practices by which information is classified are thus implicated in meaning-making and participate in the broader architectures that organise knowledge.

2) Copenhagen

Three months later, the research box was spotted on 14 October 2012, in the vicinity of the Chicago O'Hare International Airport. It was then tracked northeast to Copenhagen, where it was seen on display at the Copenhagen Business School (**FIGURE 39.8**). Its performance appears to have been prompted by a colloquium about how the approaches of art and design might be used in social studies of science and technology. During the event in Copenhagen, found objects were used to build 'enquiry machines', or devices that would aid the study of science and scientific practice (**FIGURE 39.9**). In response to these activities, the research box transformed itself into a kind of enquiry machine for the exploration of humanistic research (**FIGURES 39.10, 39.11**). By using sculpture to make palpable the processes of scholarly work – for example, with its bottles of tears and sweat – the research box modelled how art and performance might be deployed to critically examine the activities related to the production of knowledge.

FIG. 39.8 Research Box, at the Copenhagen Business School

FIG. 39.9 Human interlocutors at the Copenhagen Business School, building enquiry machines; meanwhile, Research Box reconfigures itself as an enquiry machine

FIG. 39.10 Enquiry machines in Copenhagen

FIG. 39.11 Research Box, transformed into enquiry machine

Although the research box is generally concerned with work in the humanities, it proposed a way to analyse corresponding practices in the sciences. The research box adopted scientific equipment and vocabulary to re-cast the book, the card catalogue, the database, and the labours of the librarian as objects of investigation. For instance, the performance involved a set of culture tubes, pieces of laboratory glassware that are frequently used for handling live organisms. But instead of preserving samples of blood and other fluids, the culture tubes in the research box contained lines of prose. By assembling a specimen collection of vague ideas, passing thoughts, and unspoken words, the box offered a novel reading of both humanistic and scientific research. The labour of scholarship in the humanities was thus presented for scientific scrutiny; at the same time, the box implied that scientific practice itself could be examined by interrogating why and which particular bodies had been selected for study. In this performance, the research box challenged the constitution of that which is called 'data' – that is, what might be uncritically considered specimens – across the disciplines and explored how assumptions about evidence continue to organise our systems of understanding.

3) Washington, D.C.

On 14 December 2012, the research box was spotted at the Folger Shakespeare Library in Washington, D.C., performing to an audience of book historians, librarians, and literary scholars. This particular exhibition of the research box framed the printed book as a writing technology. The box helped its interlocutors perceive modern books as objects of study by comparing the printed codex with the technologies of medieval manuscripts and their digitisations. More than developing a simple genealogy, however, the box shed light on the labour of making books and transmitting ideas. The circumstances in which books are manufactured and circulated exert influence upon how they are received – a mass-produced paperback conveys a different message from a hand-tooled volume; a book in a research library communicates differently from its counterpart in a museum. Social, cultural, and technical conditions related to the production and dissemination of books, whether a thirteenth-century manuscript or twenty-first-century digitisation, were therefore made material by the box, to lay bare their effects on meaning-making.

Because the audience was already familiar with how a printed book might be produced, the performance of the research box focused on the practices related to the digitisation of books. The audience was invited to use a portable scanner to digitise texts and images (**FIGURE 39.12**). The resulting digital files were saved to a laptop, and then – given a viable Internet connection – uploaded to a cloud server, whereupon they were retrieved back to be viewed on the iPad that sat on the easel-like appendage of the research box. By physically explicating the non-trivial task of digitisation, the box urged its interlocutors to take into account the expenditures of time, energy, and resources in service of the manufacture, dissemination, and preservation of digital information. Just as the production of a manuscript or printed book requires the investment of labour and resources, so too do their digitisations. Moreover, the particular labour and resources, different in each case, crucially shape the end-product.

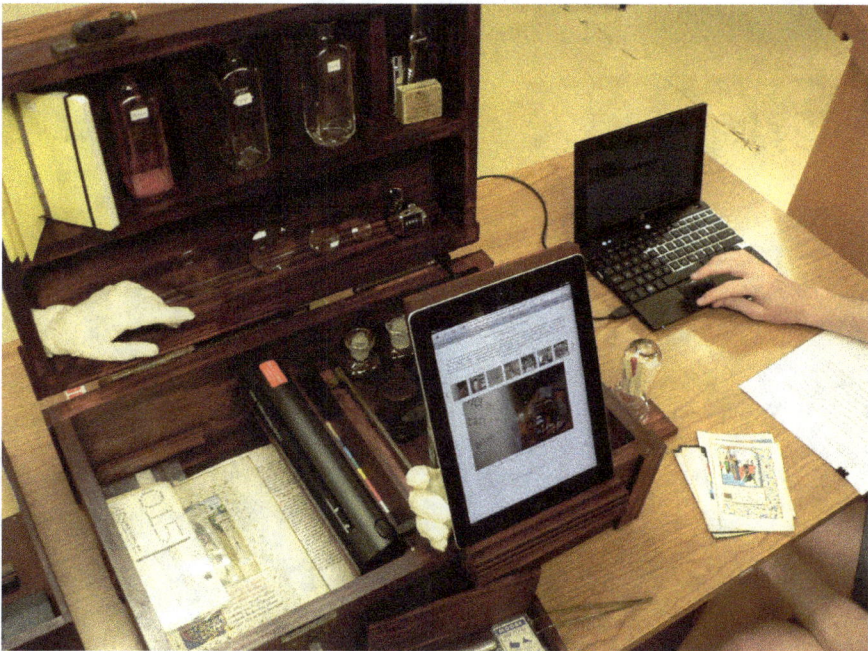

FIG. 39.12 Research Box, performing the digitisation of a text

The box demonstrated how difficult it was to grasp with accuracy the dimensions, weight, and sensations of a particular codex when mediated through computational technologies. By exhibiting pages that had been printed from a digitisation – in a surprisingly varied range of size, form, and quality – the research box provided an embodied argument about the relationship between a book and its so-called digital surrogate (**FIGURE 39.13**). In so doing, the performance called into question the frequent perception of such resources as interchangeable. By foregrounding the practices that underpin materials (both analogue and digital), the box contended that scholarship relying on books or digitisations as evidence must also reckon with the social and cultural conditions of their production. Such resources not only enable the transmission of ideas, but also serve to control and constrain it, and thereby influence the process of knowledge-making.

4) Champaign, Illinois

The research box performed for a group of computer professionals on 17 April 2013, in a basement of a building on the campus of the University of Illinois.

FIG. 39.13 Research Box, drawing attention to the varying sizes of digitised texts and images

In this exhibition, an iPad – a device quite unremarkable to the audience – was arranged with other technologies of communication, including wax tablets, medieval manuscripts, and printed books. Defying the received narrative around digital technologies that proclaims that they are new and ahistorical, the research box suggested how the iPad might be located in a longer trajectory of writing technologies. Wax tablets, for instance, share a striking resemblance to the iPad. These tablets were used from antiquity to the nineteenth century for ephemera such as school exercises, letters, notes, and other documentation of transient importance. The iPad is notably employed for similar purposes that include sending brief e-mails, following social media, and watching videos. The juxtaposition of the wax tablet and the iPad underscored the relationship between their form and function; despite the millennia that separate them, the respective technologies suggest how they are meant to be used. The research box made the iPad central to its performance so that the audience might come to regard the device as an object of study and begin to imagine the ways that digital technologies can actively direct the provision and transmission of information.

In the performance, the iPad displayed one of the many apps developed for the annotation of e-texts. However, the box intimated that the honing of such programs might profit from an examination of the rich history of commentary, and, in particular, the complicated systems of interlinear and marginal glosses that flourished through the twelfth century. Confronted with earlier forms of writing technologies, interlocutors were asked to think carefully about the perceived newness of the iPad, and how this perceived newness forecloses our ability to build upon – and take advantage of – well-established strategies for visualising information and communicating ideas.

Because this performance was designed for computer experts, its emphasis was slightly different from that of the previous exhibition at the Folger Shakespeare Library. Whereas the display in Washington located the book as a kind of technology, produced as a digitisation is produced, the central focus of the performance in Illinois was to make visible and to historicise digital technologies. The iPad was used to promote a critical exchange about how modern technologies might operate to configure information and its reception. That is, the infrastructures related to the manufacture and maintenance of computational devices, networks, and cloud computing, among others, also wield significant dominion over the ways that knowledge is transmitted and produced today; it is increasingly through these apparatuses and their protocols that information is generated, disseminated, and received. Only by investigating technologies and their infrastructures may we develop a more nuanced understanding of knowledge practices in the twenty-first century.

5) London

The box was seen on display on 14 June 2013, at the Centre for Creative Collaboration, an initiative of the University of London (**FIGURE 39.1**). The performance of the research box in London occurred during a conference about inventive modes of transmitting knowledge.

The performance made a spectacle of the practices and processes of different methods of publication. The time and labour of writing and revising an article were materialised in an exhibition of the 3000 words and four images that had to be excised for the final copy. The efforts and insights of the peer review process were likewise made physical for examination as lines of prose, bottled in culture tubes. Also available for scrutiny in the specimen collection were the costs and networks involved in the circulation of ideas. The performance invoked various means of transportation and telecommunication: aircraft, postal services, computers, and the Internet. Such costs were embodied as taxi receipts from Kavala; postage paid to Post Danmark, the Danish postal service; and invoices from airlines for excessive baggage related to the travels of the research box in its attempt to circulate knowledge. Furthermore, the box made reference to the paywalls, journal databases, and publishing contracts that restrict access to peer-reviewed articles. In this way, the performance highlighted the various pressures that shape the dissemination of ideas, whether in sculpture or prose, whether in printed or digital form.

The research box in London thus charted the infrastructures related to publication, its performance revealing the constraints of both traditional and inventive modes of transmitting knowledge. Moreover, the box illustrated how academic publishing is increasingly subject to the agenda of private multi-national corporations. The exhibition thus sought to animate a debate about the conditions of publication, a topic of considerable interest to scholars whose productivity is assessed according to their publishing record. As the research box contends, the evolving infrastructures of academic publication regulate the dissemination of scholarship, of course, but more importantly they may soon also alter how research is to be conceived and conducted in the public sector.

6) Champaign, Illinois

Probably because of its advancing age and increasing frailty, the research box appears to be hesitant to stray far from its regular habitat in the American Midwest. The last confirmed sighting of the box occurred on 6 May 2014, where it was observed as part of a celebration of books published by scholars in the humanities. The event was held at the Illinois Program for Research in the Humanities, on the campus of the University of Illinois (**FIGURE 39.14**). The performance was designed to fuel a discussion about the prevailing metrics of scholarly assessment and what kinds of publication may be registered as products of the humanities.

Responding to the occasion, the research box included a book publication in its performance, but additionally staged the processes and practices involved in that scholarly endeavour. Showcased were early drafts of the book, *How the*

FIG. 39.14 Research Box, performing as a publication in the humanities

Page Matters; the e-mail conversations between the author and copy-editor; the book and page layouts created by a graphic designer that were ultimately rejected by the publisher; and the hardcover and paperback versions of the book that were published in 2011 and 2012 respectively. Furthermore, the research box made visible the processes of peer review by including the three rounds of reports that spanned two years, the judgement of the manuscript committee of the press, and the author's responses to these appraisals. In this way, the research box attempted to bring to light some of the different hands and kinds of labour that contributed to the publication of *How the Page Matters*. The performance was a way to problematise authorship and authorial intention. Namely, to what extent may a book be said to have been written by an author or to represent an author's intention when its production is enmeshed in the varying agenda of peer reviewers, editors, designers, publicists, and the academic press? Furthermore, given this complicated history of manufacture that draws upon the expertise of many parties, what does it mean that the single-authored book continues to be recognised as the standard for research productivity in the humanities? The research box also raised questions about what should constitute a scholarly contribution in the humanities, and whether such contributions are accurately acknowledged and measured by current methods of evaluation.

The production and transmission of knowledge have always been entangled in the familiar infrastructures of classificatory schemes and institutional man-dates, but now must also be considered in light of information networks that are subject to foreign policy and the private interests of multi-national corporations. Although these infrastructures may be difficult to perceive, they play a critical role in how we engage with all informational resources – whether archival materials, early printed books, or digital video. In order to grapple with the practices of knowledge-making in the twenty-first century, it is also necessary to understand the conditions in which such activities take place. The research box materialises some of these circumstances through an array of sculptures and performances. By bestowing physical dimension upon the infrastructures of information, the box is able to propose the apparatus of knowledge-making as a legitimate object of study. The biological imperative of the research box, then, is not focused on reproduction, but on inspiring human interlocutors to interrogate the ways that knowledge has been and continues to be produced and transmitted.

Since its last performance in May 2014, there have been no reported sightings of the research box. Rumours of its retirement or death continue to circulate, but these accounts remain speculative in nature.

APPENDIX: CONFIRMED SIGHTINGS OF THE RESEARCH BOX

LOCATION: Graduate School of Library and Information Science, now known as the School of Information Sciences; Champaign, Illinois.
DATE: 18 July 2012
EVENT: *Boxing Up the Cabinet: A Preview*

LOCATION: Kavala Municipal Tobacco Museum; Kavala, Greece.
DATE: 26–29 July 2012
EVENT: *Knowledge in a Box: How Mundane Things Shape Knowledge Production*

LOCATION: Copenhagen Business School; Copenhagen, Denmark.
DATE: 17 October 2012
EVENT: *Experiments in (and out of) the Studio: Art and Design Methods for Science and Technology Studies,* a European Association for the Study of Science & Technology (EASST) Workshop

LOCATION: Folger Shakespeare Library; Washington, D.C.
DATE: 14 December 2012
EVENT: *Teaching Book History Workshop*

LOCATION: University of Illinois; Champaign, Illinois.
DATE: 17 April 2013
EVENT: *Teaching with Technology Brown Bag Series, Campus Information Technologies and Educational Services*

LOCATION: Centre for Creative Collaboration; London, UK.
DATE: 14 June 2013
EVENT: *Inventive Enactments of the Social: Transmissions and Entanglements*

LOCATION: Illinois Program for Research in the Humanities; Urbana, Illinois.

DATE: 6 May 2014

EVENT: *Awards Reception, Illinois Program for Research in the Humanities, University of Illinois*

MATTERING PRESS TITLES

Boxes: A Field Guide
EDITED BY SUSANNE BAUER, MARTINA SCHLÜNDER AND MARIA RENTETZI

An Anthropology of Common Ground
Awkward Encounters in Heritage Work
NATHALIA SOFIE BRICHET

Ghost-Managed Medicine
Big Pharma's Invisible Hands
SERGIO SISMONDO

Inventing the Social
EDITED BY NOORTJE MARRES, MICHAEL GUGGENHEIM, ALEX WILKIE

Energy Babble
ANDY BOUCHER, BILL GAVER, TOBIE KERRIDGE, MIKE MICHAEL, LILIANA OVALLE, MATTHEW PLUMMER-FERNANDEZ AND ALEX WILKIE

The Ethnographic Case
EDITED BY EMILY YATES-DOERR AND CHRISTINE LABUSKI

On Curiosity
The Art of Market Seduction
FRANCK COCHOY

Practising Comparison
Logics, Relations, Collaborations
EDITED BY JOE DEVILLE, MICHAEL GUGGENHEIM AND ZUZANA HRDLIČKOVÁ

Modes of Knowing
Resources from the Baroque
EDITED BY JOHN LAW AND EVELYN RUPPERT

Imagining Classrooms
Stories of Children, Teaching and Ethnography
VICKI MACKNIGHT